PASTOR CHARLES CHINIQUY.

FIFTY YEARS
IN THE
CHURCH OF ROME

The life story of Pastor
Chiniquy, who was for
twenty-five years a priest in
the Roman Catholic Church

by
Charles Chiniquy

BAKER BOOK HOUSE
Grand Rapids 6, Michigan

Library of Congress Catalog Card Number: 58-11377

Reprinted 1958, by
BAKER BOOK HOUSE

First Printing, May 1958
Second Printing, April 1960
Third Printing, March 1961
Fourth Printing, March 1962
Fifth Printing, October 1963
Sixth Printing, March 1965
Seventh Printing, January 1967
Eighth Printing, July 1968

Standard Book Number: 8010-2308-4
Ninth Printing, November 1970

Reprinted from the
1886 edition printed
in London by the
Protestant Literature
Depository

Printed in the United States of America

DEDICATION.

Venerable Ministers of the Gospel! Rome is the great danger ahead for the Church of Christ, and you do not understand it enough.

The atmosphere of light, honesty, truth, and holiness in which you are born, and which you have breathed since your infancy, makes it almost impossible for you to realize the dark mysteries of idolatry, immorality, degrading slavery, hatred of the Word of God, concealed behind the walls of that Modern Babylon. You are too honest to suspect them ; and your precious time is too much taken by the sacred duties of your ministry, to study the long labyrinth of argumentations which form the bulk of the greater number of controversial books. Besides that, the majority of the books of controversy against Rome are of such a dry character that, though many begin to read them, very few have the courage to go to the end. The consequence is an ignorance of Romanism which becomes more and more deplorable and fatal every day.

It is that ignorance which paves the way to the triumph of Rome, in a near future, if there is not a complete change in your views on that subject.

It is that ignorance which paralyses the arm of the Church of Christ, and makes the glorious word " Protestant " senseless, almost a dead and ridiculous word. For who does really protest against Rome to-day ? where are those who sound the trumpet of alarm ?

When Rome is striking you to the heart by cursing your schools and wrenching the Bible from the hands of your children ; when she is not only battering your doors, but scaling your walls and storming your citadels, how few dare to go to the breach and repulse the audacious and sacrilegious foe ?

Why so ? Because modern Protestants have not only forgotten what Rome was, what she is, and what she will for ever be ; the most irreconcilable and powerful enemy of the Gospel of Christ ; but they consider her almost as a branch of the church whose corner stone is Christ.

Faithful ministers of the Gospel ! I present you this book that you may know that the monster Church of Rome, who shed the blood of your forefathers is still at work to-day, at your very door, to enchain your people to the feet of her idols. Read it, and, for the first time, you will see the inside life of Popery with the exactness of photography. From the supreme art with which the mind of the young and timid child is fettered, enchained, and paralysed, to the unspeakable degradation of the priest under the iron heel of the bishop, everything will be revealed to you as it has never been before.

The superstitions, the ridiculous and humiliating practices, the secret and mental agonies of the monks, the nuns and the priests, will be shown to you

as they were never shown before. In this book, the sophisms and errors of
Romanism are discussed and refuted with a clearness, simplicity, and evidence, which my twenty-five years of priesthood only could teach me. It is
not in boasting that I say this. There can be no boasting in me for having
been so many years an abject slave of the Pope. The book I offer you is an
arsenal filled with the best weapons you ever had to fight, and, with the help
of God, to conquer the foe.

The learned and zealous champion of Protestantism in Great Britain,
Rev. Dr. Badenoch, who has revised the manuscript, wrote to a friend : " I
do not think there is a Protestant work more thrilling in interest and more
important at the present time. It is not only full of incidents, but also of
arguments on the side of truth with all classes of Romanists, from the
bishops to the parish priest. I know of no work which gives so graphically
the springs of Roman Catholic life, and, at the same time, meets the plausible objections to Protestantism in Roman Catholic circles. I wish, with
all my heart, that this work would be published in Great Britain."

The venerable, learned, and so well known Rev. Dr. Kemp, Principal of
the Young Ladies' College, of Ottawa, Canada, only a few days before his
premature death, wrote : " Mr. Chiniquy has submitted every chapter of his
'Fifty Years in the Church of Rome' to me : I have read it with care and
with the deepest interest ; and I commend it to the public favour in the
highest terms. It is the only book I know that gives anything like a full
and authentic account of the inner workings of Popery on this continent,
and so effectively unmasks its pretence to sanctity. Besides the most interesting biographical incidents, it contains incisive refutations of the most
plausible assumptions and deadly errors of the Romish Church. It is well
fitted to awaken Protestants to the insidious designs of the arch-enemy of
their faith and liberties, and to arouse them to a decisive opposition. It is
written in a kindly and Christian spirit, does not indulge in denunciations,
and, while speaking in truth, it does so in love. Its style is lively and its
English good, with only a delicate flavour of the author's native French."

TO THE BISHOPS, PRIESTS, AND PEOPLE OF ROME

this book is also dedicated.

In the name of your immortal souls, I ask you, Roman Catholics, to read
this book.

By the mercy of God, you will find, in its pages, how you are cruelly
deceived by your vain and lying traditions.

You will see that it is not through your ceremonies, masses, confessions,
purgatory, indulgences, fastings, etc., you are saved. You have nothing to
do but to believe, repent, and love.

Salvation is a gift ! Eternal life is a gift ! Forgiveness of sin is a gift !
Christ is a gift !

Read this book, presented by the most devoted of your friends, and, by
the mercy of God, you will see the errors of your ways—you will look to
the GIFT—you will accept it—and in its possession you will feel rich and
happy for time and eternity.

CONTENTS.

x

CONTENTS.

FIFTY YEARS

IN THE

CHURCH OF ROME.

CHAPTER I.

My father, Charles Chiniquy, born in Quebec, had studied in the Theological Seminary of that city, to prepare himself for the priesthood. But a few days before making his vows, having been the witness of a great iniquity in the high quarters of the church, he changed his mind, studied law, and became a notary.

Married to Reine Perrault, daughter of Mitchel Perrault, in 1803 he settled at first in Kamoraska, where I was born on the 30th July, 1809.

About four or five years later my parents emigrated to Murray Bay. That place was then in its infancy, and no school had yet been established. My mother was, therefore, my first teacher.

Before leaving the Seminary of Quebec my father had received from one of the Superiors, as a token of his esteem, a beautiful French and Latin Bible. That Bible was the first book, after the A B C, in which I was taught to read. My mother selected the chapters which she considered the most interesting for me; and I read them every day with the greatest attention and pleasure. I was even so much pleased with several chapters, that I read them over and over again till I knew them by heart.

When eight or nine years of age, I had learned by heart the history of the creation and fall of man ; the deluge ; the sacrifice of Isaac ; the history of Moses; the plagues of Egypt ; the sublime hymn of Moses after crossing the Red Sea ; the history of Samson; the most interesting events of the life of David; several Psalms; all the speeches and parables of Christ; and the whole history of the sufferings and death of our Saviour as narrated by John.

I had two brothers, Louis and Achille; the first about four, the

1

second about eight years younger than myself. When they were sleeping or playing together, how many delicious hours I have spent by my mother's side, in reading to her the sublime pages of the divine book.

Sometimes she interrupted me to see if I understood what I read ; and when my answers made her sure that I understood it, she used to kiss me and press me on her bosom as an expression of her joy.

One day, while I was reading the history of the sufferings of the Saviour, my young heart was so much impressed that I could hardly enunciate the words, and my voice trembled. My mother, perceiving my emotion, tried to say something on the love of Jesus for us, but she could not utter a word—her voice was suffocated by her sobs. She leaned her head on my forehead, and I felt two streams of tears falling from her eyes on my cheeks. I could not contain myself any longer. I wept also ; and my tears were mixed with hers. The holy book fell from my hands, and I threw myself into my dear mother's arms.

No human words can express what was felt in her soul and in mine in that most blessed hour ! No ! I will never forget that solemn hour, when my mother's heart was perfectly blended with mine at the feet of our dying Saviour. There was a real perfume from heaven in those my mother's tears which were flowing on me. It seemed then, as it does seem to me to-day, that there was a celestial harmony in the sound of her voice and in her sobs. Though more than half a century has passed since that solemn hour when Jesus, for the first time, revealed to me something of His suffering and of His love, my heart leaps with joy every time I think of it.

We were some distance from the church, and the roads, in the rainy days, were very bad. On the Sabbath days the neighbouring farmers, unable to go to church, were accustomed to gather at our house in the evening. Then my parents used to put me up on a large table in the midst of the assembly, and I delivered to those good people the most beautiful parts of the Old and New Testaments. The breathless attention, the applause of our guests, and—may I tell it—often the tears of joy which my mother tried in vain to conceal, supported my strength and gave me the courage I wanted, to speak when so young before so many people. When my parents saw that I was growing tired, my mother, who had a fine voice, sang some of the beautiful French hymns with which her memory was filled.

Several times, when the fine weather allowed me to go to church with my parents, the farmers would take me into their *caleches* (buggies) at the door of the temple, and request me to give them some chapter of the Gospel. With a most perfect attention they listened to the voice of the child, whom the Good Master had chosen to give them the bread which comes from heaven. More than once, I remember, that when the bell called us to the church, they expressed their regret that they could not hear more.

On one of the beautiful spring days of 1818 my father was writing in his office, and my mother was working with her needle, singing one of her favourite hymns, and I was at the door, playing and talking to a fine robin which I had so perfectly trained that he followed me wherever I went. All of a sudden I saw the priest coming near the gate. The sight of him sent a thrill of uneasiness through my whole frame. It was his first visit to our home.

The priest was a person below the common stature, and had an unpleasant appearance—his shoulders were large and he was very corpulent; his hair was long and uncombed, and his double chin seemed to groan under the weight of his flabby cheeks.

I hastily ran to the door and whispered to my parents, "M. le curé arrive ("Mr. Curate is coming"). The last sound was hardly out of my lips when the Rev. Mr. Courtois was at the door, and my father, shaking hands with him, gave him a welcome.

That priest was born in France, where he had a narrow escape, having been condemned to death under the bloody administration of Robespierre. He had found a refuge, with many other French priests, in England, whence he came to Quebec, and the bishop of that place had given him the charge of the parish of Murray Bay.

His conversation was animated and interesting for the first quarter of an hour. It was a real pleasure to hear him. But of a sudden his countenance changed as if a dark cloud had come over his mind, and he stopped talking. My parents had kept themselves on a respectful reserve with the priest. They seemed to have no other mind than to listen to him. The silence which followed was exceedingly unpleasant for all the parties. It looked like the heavy hour which precedes a storm. At length the priest, addressing my father, said, "Mr. Chiniquy, is it true that you and your child read the Bible?"

"Yes, sir," was the quick reply, "my little boy and I read the Bible, and what is still better, he has learned by heart a great number of its most interesting chapters. If you will allow it, Mr. Curate, he will give you some of them."

"I did not come for that purpose," abruptly replied the priest; "but do you not know that you are forbidden by the holy Council of Trent to read the Bible in French."

"It makes very little difference to me whether I read the Bible in French, Greek, or Latin," answered my father, "for I understand these languages equally well."

"But are you ignorant of the fact that you cannot allow your child to read the Bible?" replied the priest.

"My wife directs her own child in the reading of the Bible, and I cannot see that we commit any sin by continuing to do in future what we have done till now in that matter."

"Mr. Chiniquy," rejoined the priest, "you have gone through a whole course of theology; you know the duties of a curate; you know it is my painful duty to come here, get the Bible from you and burn it."

My grandfather was a fearless Spanish sailor (our original name was Etchiniquia), and there was too much Spanish blood and pride in my father to hear such a sentence with patience in his own house. Quick as lightning he was on his feet. I pressed myself, trembling, near my mother, who trembled also.

At first I feared lest some very unfortunate and violent scene should occur; for my father's anger in that moment was really terrible.

But there was another thing which affected me. I feared lest the priest should lay his hands on my dear Bible, which was just before him on the table; for it was mine, as it had been given me the last year as a Christmas gift.

Fortunately, my father had subdued himself after the first moment of his anger. He was pacing the room with a double-quick step; his lips were pale and trembling, and he was muttering between his teeth words which were unintelligible to any one of us.

The priest was closely watching all my father's movements; his hands were convulsively pressing his heavy cane, and his face was giving the sure evidence of a too well-grounded terror. It was clear that the ambassador of Rome did not find himself infallibly sure of his position on the ground he had so foolishly chosen to take; since his last words he had remained as silent as a tomb.

At last, after having paced the room for a considerable time, my father suddenly stopped before the priest, and said, "Sir, is that all you have to say here."

"Yes, sir," said the trembling priest.

"Well, sir," added my father, "you know the door by which you entered my house: please take the same door and go away quickly."

The priest went out immediately. I felt an inexpressible joy when I saw that my Bible was safe. I ran to my father's neck, kissed and thanked him for his victory. And to pay him, in my childish way, I jumped upon the large table and recited, in my best style, the fight between David and Goliath. Of course, in my mind, my father was David and the priest of Rome was the giant whom the little stone from the brook had stricken down.

Thou knowest, O God, that it is to that Bible, read on my mother's knees, I owe, by thy infinite mercy, the knowledge of the truth to-day; that Bible had sent, to my young heart and intelligence, rays of light which all the sophisms and dark errors of Rome could never completely extinguish.

CHAPTER II.

IN the month of June, 1818, my parents sent me to an excellent school at St. Thomas. One of my mother's sisters resided there, who was the wife of an industrious miller called Stephen Eschenbach. They had no children, and they received me as their own son.

The beautiful village of St. Thomas had already, at that time, a considerable population. The two fine rivers which unite their rapid waters in its very midst before they fall into the magnificent basin from which they flow into the St. Lawrence, supplied the water-power for several mills and factories.

There was in the village a considerable trade in grain, flour and lumber. The fisheries were very profitable, and the game was abundant. Life was really pleasant and easy.

The families Tachez, Cazeault, Fournier, Dubord, Frechette, Tetu, Dupuis, Couillard, Duberges, which were among the most ancient and notable of Canada, were at the head of the intellectual and material movements of the place, and they were a real honour to the French Canadian name.

I met there with one of my ancestors on my mother's side whose name was F. Amour des Plaines. He was an old and brave soldier, and would sometimes show us the numerous wounds he had received in the battles in which he had fought for his country. Though nearly eighty years old, he sang to us the songs of the good old times with all the vivacity of a young man.

The school of Mr. Allen Jones, to which I had been sent, was worthy of its wide-spread reputation. I had never known any teacher who deserved more, or who enjoyed in a higher degree the respect and confidence of his pupils.

He was born in England, and belonged to one of the most respectable families there. He had received the best education which England could give to her sons. After having gone through a perfect course of study at home, he had gone to Paris, where he had also completed an academical course. He was perfectly master of the French and English languages. And it was not without good reasons that he was surrounded by a great number of scholars from every corner of Canada. The children of the best families of St. Thomas were, with me, attending the school of Mr. Jones. But as he was a Protestant, the priest was much opposed to him, and every effort was made by that priest to induce my relatives to take me away from that school and send me to the one under his care.

The name of the priest was Loranger. He had a swarthy countenance, and in person was lean and tall. His preaching had no attraction, and he was far from being popular among the intelligent part of the people of St. Thomas.

Dr. Tachez, whose high capacity afterwards brought him to the head of the Canadian Government, was the leading man of St. Thomas. Being united by the bonds of a sincere friendship with his nephew, L. Cazeault, who was afterwards placed at the head of the University of Laval, in Quebec, I had more opportunities of going to the house of Mr. Tachez, where my young friend was boarding.

In those days Dr. Tachez had no need of the influence of the priests, and he frequently gave vent to his supreme contempt for them. Once a week there was a meeting in his house of the principal citizens of St. Thomas, where the highest questions of history and religion were freely and warmly discussed; but the premises as well as the conclusions of these discussions were invariably adverse to the priests and religion of Rome, and too often to every form of Christianity.

Though these meetings had not entirely the character or exclusiveness of secret societies, they were secret to a great extent. My friend Cazeault was punctual in telling me the days and hours of the meetings, and I used to go with him to an adjoining room, from which we could hear everything without being suspected. From what I heard and saw in these meetings I most certainly would have been ruined, had not the Word of God, with which my mother had filled my young mind and heart, been my shield and strength. I was often struck with terror and filled with disgust at what I heard in those meetings. But what a strange and deplorable thing! My conscience was condemning me every time I listened to these impious discussions, while there was a strong craving in me to hear them that I could not resist.

There was then in St. Thomas a personage who was unique in his character. He never mixed with the society of the village, but was, nevertheless, the object of much respectful attention and inquiry from every one. He was one of the former monks of Canada, known under the name of Capucin or Recollets, whom the conquest of Canada by Great Britain had forced to leave their monastery. He was a clockmaker, and lived honourably by his trade. His little white house, in the very midst of the village, was the perfection of neatness.

Brother Mark, as he was called, was a remarkably well-built man; high stature, large and splendid shoulders, and the most beautiful hands I ever saw. His long black robe, tied around his waist by a white sash, was remarkable for its cleanliness. His life was really a solitary one, always alone with his sister, who kept his house.

Every day that the weather was propitious, Brother Mark spent a couple of hours in fishing, and I myself was exceedingly fond of that exercise, I used to meet him often along the banks of the beautiful rivers of St. Thomas.

His presence was always a good omen to me; for he was more expert than I in finding the best places for fishing. As soon as he found a place where the fish were abundant, he would make signs to me, or call me at the top of his voice, that I might share in his good luck. I appreciated his delicate attention to me, and repaid him with the marks of a sincere gratitude. The good monk had entirely conquered my young heart, and I cherished a sincere regard for him. He often invited me to his solitary but neat little home, and I never visited him without receiving some proofs of a sincere kindness. His good sister rivalled him in overwhelming me with such marks of attention and love as I could only expect from a dear mother.

There was a mixture of timidity and dignity in the manners of Brother Mark which I have found in no one else. He was fond of children; and nothing could be more graceful than his smile every time that he could see that I appreciated his kindness, and that I gave him any proof of my gratitude. But that smile, and any other expression of joy, were very transient. On a sudden he would change, and it was obvious that a mysterious cloud was passing over his heart.

The pope had released the monks of the monastery to which he belonged, from their vows of poverty and obedience. The consequence was that they could become independent, and even rich by their own industry. It was in their power to rise to a respectable position in the world by their honourable efforts. The pope had given them the permission they wanted, that they might earn an honest living. But what a strange and incredible folly to ask the permission of a pope to be allowed to live honourably on the fruits of one's own industry!

These poor monks, having been released from their vows of obedience, were no longer the slaves of a man; but were now permitted to go to heaven on the sole condition that they would obey the laws of God and the laws of their country! But into what a frightful abyss of degradation men must have fallen, to believe that they required a licence from Rome for such a purpose. This is, nevertheless, the simple and naked truth. That excess of folly, and that supreme impiety and degradation are among the fundamental dogmas of Rome. The infallible pope assures the world that there is no possible salvation for any one who does not sincerely believe what he teaches in this matter.

But the pope who had so graciously relieved the Canadian monks from their vows of obedience and poverty, had been inflexible in reference to their vows of celibacy. From this there was no relief.

The honest desires of the good monk to live according to the laws of God, with a wife whom heaven might have given him, had become an impossibility—the pope vetoed it.

The unfortunate monk was bound to believe that he would be for ever damned if he dared to accept as a gospel truth the Word of God which says :—

"Propter fornicationem autem, unusquisque uxorem suam habeat, unaquaque virum suum habeat. (Vulgate Bible of Rome.) Nevertheless to avoid fornication let every man have his own wife, and let every woman have her own husband" (1 Cor. vii. 2.) That shining light which the world contains and which gives life to man, was entirely shut out from Brother Mark. He was not allowed to know that God himself had said, "It is not good that man should be alone, I will make him an help-meet for him" (Gen. ii. 18.) Brother Mark was endowed with such a loving heart! He could not be known without being loved; and he must have suffered much in that celibacy which his faith in the pope had imposed upon him.

Far away from the regions of light, truth and life, that soul, tied to the feet of the implacable modern Divinity, which the Romanists worship under the name of Sovereign Pontiff, was trying in vain to annihilate and destroy the instincts and affections which God himself had implanted in him.

One day, as I was amusing myself, with a few other young friends, near the house of Brother Mark, suddenly we saw something covered with blood thrown from the window, and falling at a short distance from us. At the same instant we heard loud cries, evidently coming from the monk's house: "O my God! Have mercy upon me! Save me! I am lost!"

The sister of Brother Mark rushed out of doors and cried to some men who were passing by : "Come to our help! My poor brother is dying! For God's sake make haste, he is losing all his blood!"

I ran to the door, but the lady shut it abruptly and turned me out, saying, "We do not want children here."

I had a sincere affection for the good brother. He had invariably been so kind to me! I insisted, and respectfully requested to be allowed to enter. Though young and weak, it seemed that my friendly feelings towards the suffering brother would add to my strength, and enable me to be of some service. But my request was sternly rejected, and I had to go back to the street, among the crowd which was fast gathering. The singular mystery in which they were trying to wrap the poor monk, filled me with trouble and anxiety.

But that trouble was soon changed into an unspeakable confusion when I heard the convulsive laughing of the low people, and the shameful jokes of the crowd, after the doctor had told the nature of the wound which was causing the unfortunate man to bleed almost to death. I was struck with such horror that I fled away; I did not want to know any more of that tragedy. I had already known too much!

Poor Brother Mark had ceased to be a man—he had become an eunuch!

O cruel and godless church of Rome! How many souls hast thou deceived and tortured! How many hearts hast thou broken with that celibacy which Satan alone could invent ! This unfortunate victim of a most degrading religion, did not, however, die from his rash action : he soon recovered his usual health.

Having, meanwhile, ceased to visit him; some months later I was fishing along the river in a very solitary place. The fish were abundant and I was completely absorbed in catching them, when, on a sudden, I felt on my shoulder the gentle pressure of a hand. It was Brother Mark's.

I thought I would faint through the opposite sentiments of surprise, of pain and joy, which at the same time crossed my mind.

With an affectionate and trembling voice he said to me, "My dear child, why do you not any more come to see me ? "

I did not dare to look at him after he had addressed me these words. I liked him on account of his acts of kindness to me. But the fatal hour when, in the street before the door, I had suffered so much on his account—that fatal hour was on my heart as a mountain which I could not put away—I could not answer him.

He then asked me again with the tone of a criminal who sues for mercy : " Why is it, my dear child, that you do not come any longer to see me ? you know that I love you."

"Dear Brother Mark," I answered, "I will never forget your kindness to me. I will for ever be grateful to you ! I wish that it would be in my power to continue, as formerly, to go and see you. But I cannot, and you ought to know the reason why I cannot."

I had pronounced these words with downcast eyes. I was a child, with the timidity and happy ignorance of a child. But the action of that unfortunate man had struck me with such a horror that I could not entertain the idea of visiting him any more.

He spent two or three minutes without saying a word, and without moving. But I heard his sobs and his cries, and his cries were those of despair and anguish, the like of which I have never heard since.

I could not contain myself any longer, I was suffocating with suppressed emotion, and I would have fallen insensible to the ground if two streams of tears had not burst from my eyes. Those tears did me good—they did him good also—they told him that I was still his friend.

He took me in his arms and pressed me to his bosom—his tears were mixed with mine. But I could not speak—the emotions of my heart were too much for my age. I sat on a damp and cold stone in order not to faint. He fell on his knees by my side.

Ah! if I were a painter I would make a most striking tableau of that scene. His eyes, swollen and red with weeping, were raised to heaven, his hand lifted up in the attitude of supplication : he was crying out with an accent which seemed as though it would break my heart—

"Mon Dieu! Mon Dieu! que je suis malheureux!"

My God! My God! what a wretched man am I!

*   *   *   *   *   *   *   *   *   *

The twenty-five years that I have been a priest of Rome, have revealed to me the fact that the cries of desolation I heard that day, were but the echo of the cries of desolation which go out from almost every nunnery, every parsonage and every house where human beings are bound by the ties of Romish Celibacy.

God knows that I am a faithful witness of what my eyes have seen and my ears have heard, when I say to the multitudes which the Church of Rome has bewitched with her enchantments: Wherever there are nuns, monks and priests who live in forced violation of the ways which God has appointed for man to walk in, there are torrents of tears, there are desolated hearts, there are cries of anguish and despair which say in the words of brother Mark :

"Oh! que je suis malheureux!"

Oh! how miserable and wretched I am!

CHAPTER III.

No words can express to those who have never had any experience in the matter, the consternation, anxiety and shame of a poor Romish child, when he hears, for the first time, his priest saying from the pulpit, in a grave and solemn tone, "This week, you will send your children to confession. Make them understand that this action is one of the most important of their lives, and that for every one of them, it will decide their eternal happiness or misery. Fathers and mothers, if, through your fault, or his own, your child is guilty of a bad confession —if he conceals his sins and commences lying to the priest, who holds the place of God Himself, this sin is often irreparable. The devil will take possession of his heart: he will become accustomed to lie to his father confessor, or rather to Jesus Christ, of whom he is a representative. His life will be a series of sacrileges; his death and eternity those of the reprobate. Teach him, therefore, to examine thoroughly his actions, words and thoughts, in order to confess without disguise."

I was in the church of St. Thomas when these words fell upon me like a thunderbolt.

I had often heard my mother say, when at home and my aunt

since I had come to St. Thomas, that upon the first confession depended my eternal happiness or misery. That week was, therefore, to decide about my eternity.

Pale and dismayed, I left the church, and returned to the house of my relatives. I took my place at the table, but could not eat, so much was I troubled. I went to my room for the purpose of commencing my examination of conscience and to recall all my sinful actions, words, and thoughts. Although I was scarcely over ten years of age, this task was really overwhelming for me. I knelt down to pray to the Virgin Mary for help; but I was so much taken up with the fear of forgetting something, and of making a bad confession, that I muttered my prayers without the least attention to what I said. It became still worse when I commenced counting my sins. My memory became confused, my head grew dizzy; my heart beat with a rapidity which exhausted me, and my brow was covered with perspiration. After a considerable length of time spent in those painful efforts, I felt bordering on despair, from the fear that it was impossible for me to remember everything. The night following was almost a sleepless one; and when sleep did come, it could scarcely be called a sleep, but a suffocating delirium. In a frightful dream, I felt as if I had been cast into hell, for not having confessed all my sins to the priest. In the morning, I awoke, fatigued and prostrated by the phantoms of that terrible night. In similar troubles of mind were passed the three days which preceded my first confession. I had constantly before me the countenance of that stern priest who had never smiled upon me. He was present in my thoughts during the day, and in my dreams during the night, as the minister of an angry God, justly irritated against me on account of my sins. Forgiveness had indeed been promised to me, on condition of a good confession; but my place had also been shown to me in hell, if my confession was not as near perfection as possible. Now, my troubled conscience told me that there were ninety-nine chances against one, that my confession would be bad, whether by my own fault I forgot some sins, or I was without that contrition of which I had heard so much, but the nature and effects of which were a perfect chaos in my mind.

Thus it was that the cruel and perfidious Church of Rome took away from my young heart the good and merciful Jesus, whose love and compassion had caused me to shed tears of joy when I was beside my mother. The Saviour whom that church made me to worship, through fear, was not the Saviour who called little children unto Him, to bless them and take them in His arms. Her impious hands were soon to torture and defile my childish heart, and place me at the feet of a pale and severe looking man—worthy representative of a pitiless God. I was made to tremble with terror at the footstool of an implacable divinity, while the gospel asked from me only tears of love and joy, shed at the feet of the incomparable Friend of sinners.

At length came the day of confession; or rather of judgment and condemnation. I presented myself to the priest.

Mr. Loranger was no longer priest of St. Thomas. He had been succeeded by Mr. Beaubien, who did not favour our school any more than his predecessor. He had even taken upon himself to preach a sermon against the heretical school, by which we had been excessively wounded. His want of love for us, however, I must say, was fully reciprocated.

Mr. Beaubien had, then, the defect of lisping and stammering. This we often turned into ridicule, and one of my favourite amusements was to imitate him, which brought bursts of laughter from us all.

It had been necessary for me to examine myself upon the number of times I had mocked him. This circumstance was not calculated to make my confession easier, or more agreeable.

At last the dreaded moment came. I knelt at the side of my confessor. My whole frame trembled. I repeated the prayer preparatory to confession, scarcely knowing what I said, so much was I troubled by fear.

By the instructions which had been given us before confession, we had been made to believe that the priest was the true representative—yea, almost the personification of Jesus Christ. The consequence was, that I believed my greatest sin had been that of mocking the priest. Having always been told that it was best to confess the greatest sin first, I commenced thus: "Father, I accuse myself of having mocked a priest."

Scarcely had I uttered these words, "mocked a priest," when this pretended representative of the humble Saviour, turning towards me, and looking in my face in order to know me better, asked abruptly, "What priest did you mock, my boy?" I would rather have chosen to cut out my tongue than to tell him to his face who it was. I therefore kept silent for a while. But my silence made him very nervous and almost angry. With a haughty tone of voice he said, "What priest did you take the liberty of thus mocking?"

I saw that I had to answer. Happily his haughtiness had made me firmer and bolder. I said, "Sir, you are the priest whom I mocked."

"But how many times did you take upon you to mock me, my boy?"

"I tried to find out," I answered, "but I never could."

"You must tell me how many times; for to mock one's own priest is a great sin."

"It is impossible for me to give you the number of times," answered I.

" Well, my child, I will help your memory by asking you questions. Tell me the truth. Do you think you have mocked me ten times ? "

" A great many times more, sir."

" Fifty times ? "

" Many more still."

" A hundred times ? "

" Say five hundred times, and perhaps more," answered I.

" Why, my boy, do you spend all your time in mocking me ? "

" Not all ; but unfortunately I do it very often."

" Well may you say *unfortunately* ; for so to mock your priest, who holds the place of our Lord Jesus Christ, is a great misfortune, and a great sin for you. But tell me, my little boy, what reason have you for mocking me thus ? "

In my examinations of conscience I had not foreseen that I should be obliged to give the reasons for mocking the priest; and I was really thunderstruck by his questions. I dared not answer, and I remained for a long time dumb, from the shame that overpowered me. But with a harassing perseverance the priest insisted upon my telling why I had mocked him; telling me that I should be damned if I did not tell the whole truth. So I decided to speak, and said, " I mocked you for several things."

" What made you first mock me ? " continued the priest.

" I laughed at you because you lisped. Among the pupils of our school, it often happens that we imitate your preaching to excite laughter."

" Have you often done that ? "

" Almost every day, especially in our holidays, and since you preached against us."

" For what other reasons did you laugh at me, my little boy ? "

For a long time I was silent. Every time I opened my mouth to speak courage failed me. However, the priest continuing to urge me, I said at last, " It is rumoured in town that you love girls; that you visit the Misses Richards every evening, and this often makes us laugh."

The poor priest was evidently overwhelmed by my answer, and ceased questioning me on this subject. Changing the conversation, he said :

" What are your other sins ? "

I began to confess them in the order in which they came to my memory. But the feeling of shame which overpowered me in repeating all my sins to this man was a thousand times greater than that of having offended God. In reality this feeling of human shame which absorbed my thought—nay, my whole being—left no room for any religious feeling at all.

When I had confessed all the sins I could remember, the priest began to ask me the strangest questions on matters about which my pen must be silent. I replied, "Father, I do not understand what you ask me."

"I question you on the sixth commandment (seventh in the Bible). Confess all. You will go to hell, if through your fault you omit anything."

Thereupon he dragged my thoughts to regions which, thank God, had hitherto been unknown to me.

I answered him : "I do not understand you," or "I have never done these things."

Then, skilfully shifting to some secondary matter, he would soon slyly and cunningly come back to his favourite subject, namely, sins of licentiousness.

His questions were so unclean that I blushed, and felt sick with disgust and shame. More than once I had been, to my regret, in the company of bad boys ; but not one of them had offended my moral nature so much as this priest had done. Not one of them had ever approached the shadow of the things from which that man tore the veil, and which he placed before the eye of my soul. In vain did I tell him that I was not guilty of such things ; that I did not even understand what he asked me ; he would not let me off. Like the vulture bent upon tearing the poor bird that falls into his claws, that cruel priest seemed determined to defile and ruin my heart.

At last he asked me a question in a form of expression so bad that I was really pained. I felt as if I had received a shock from an electric battery ; a feeling of horror made me shudder. I was so filled with indignation that speaking loud enough to be heard by many, I told him : "Sir, I am very wicked ; I have seen, heard and done many things which I regret ; but I never was guilty of what you mention to me. My ears have never heard anything so wicked as what they have heard from your lips. Please do not ask me any more of those questions ; do not teach me any more evil than I already know."

The remainder of my confession was short. The firmness of my voice had evidently frightened the priest, and made him blush. He stopped short and began to give me some good advice, which might have been useful to me if the deep wounds which his questions had inflicted upon my soul had not so absorbed my thoughts as to prevent me from giving attention to what he said.

He gave me a short penance and dismissed me.

I left the confessional irritated and confused. From the shame of what I had just heard from the mouth of that priest I dared not lift my eyes from the ground. I went into a retired corner of the church to do my penance ; that is, to recite the prayers he had indicated to me. I remained for a long time in church. I had need of a calm after the terrible trial through which I had just passed. But vainly sought I for rest. The shameful questions which had been asked me, the new world of iniquity into which I had been introduced, the impure phantoms by which my childish heart had been defiled, confused and troubled my mind so strangely that I had began to weep bitterly.

Why those tears? Why that desolation? Wept I over my sins? Alas! I confess it with shame, my sins did not call forth these tears. And yet how many sins had I already committed, for which Jesus shed His precious blood. But I confess my sins were not the cause of my desolation. I was rather thinking of my mother, who had taken such good care of me, and who had so well succeeded in keeping away from my thoughts those impure forms of sin, the thoughts of which had just now defiled my heart. I said to myself, " Ah! if my mother had heard those questions; if she could see the evil thoughts which overwhelm me at this moment—if she knew to what school she sent me when she advised me in her last letter to go to confession, how her tears would mingle with mine!" It seemed to me that my mother would love me no more—that she would see written upon my brow the pollution with which that priest had profaned my soul.

Perhaps the feeling of pride was what made me weep. Or perhaps I wept because of a remnant of that feeling of original dignity whose traces had still been left in me. I felt so downcast by the disappointment of being removed farther from the Saviour by that confessional which had promised to bring me nearer to Him. God only knows what was the depth of my sorrow at feeling myself more defiled and more guilty after than before my confession.

I left the church only when forced to do so by the shades of night, and came to my uncle's house with that feeling of uneasiness caused by the consciousness of having done a bad action, and by the fear of being discovered.

Though this uncle, as well as most of the principal citizens of the village of St. Thomas, had the name of being a Roman Catholic, he yet did not believe a word of the doctrines of the Roman Church. He laughed at the priests, their masses, their purgatory, and especially their confession. He did not conceal that, when young, he had been scandalized by the words and actions of a priest in the confessional. He spoke to me jestingly. This increased my trouble and my grief. " Now," said he, " you will be a good boy. But if you have heard as many new things as I did the first time I went to confess, you are a very learned boy; " and he burst into laughter.

I blushed and remained silent. My aunt, who was a devoted

Roman Catholic, said to me, "Your heart is relieved, is it not, since you confessed all your sins?" I gave her an evasive answer, but I could not conceal the sadness that overcame me. I thought I was the only one from whom the priest had asked those polluting questions. But great was my surprise, on the following day, when going to school I learned that my fellow pupils had not been happier than I had been. The only difference was, that instead of being grieved, they laughed at it. "Did the priest ask you such and such questions?" they would demand, laughing boisterously. I refused to reply, and said, "Are you not ashamed to speak of these things?"

"Ah! ah! how very scrupulous you are," continued they. "If it is not a sin for the priest to speak to us on these matters, how can it be a sin for us?" I stopped, confounded, not knowing what to say.

I soon perceived that even the young schoolgirls had not been less polluted and scandalized by the questions of the priest than the boys. Although keeping at a distance, such as to prevent us from hearing all they said, I could understand enough to convince me that they had been asked about the same questions. Some of them appeared indignant, while others laughed heartily.

I should be misunderstood were it supposed that I mean to convey the idea that this priest was more to blame than others, or that he did more than fulfil the duties of his ministry in asking these questions. Such, however, was my opinion at the time, and I detested that man with all my heart until I knew better. I had been unjust towards him, for this priest had only done his duty. He was only obeying the pope and his theologians. His being a priest of Rome was, therefore, less his crime than his misfortune. He was, as I have been myself, bound hand and foot at the feet of the greatest enemy that the holiness and truth of God have ever had on earth—the pope.

The misfortune of Mr. Beaubien, like that of all the priests of Rome, was that of having bound himself by terrible oaths not to think for himself, or to use the light of his own reason.

Many Roman Catholics, even many Protestants, refuse to believe this. It is, notwithstanding, a sad truth. The priest of Rome is an automaton—a machine which acts, thinks and speaks in matters of morals and of faith, only according to the order and the will of the pope and of his theologians.

Had Mr. Beaubien been left to himself, he was naturally too much of a gentleman to ask such questions. But no doubt he had read Liguori, Dens, Debreyne, authors approved by the pope, and he was obliged to take darkness for light, and vice for virtue.

CHAPTER IV.

SHORTLY after the trial of auricular confession, my young friend, Louis Cazeault, accosted me on a beautiful morning and said, "Do you know what happened last night?"

"No," I answered. "What was the wonder?"

"You know that our priest spends almost all his evenings at Mr. Richards' house. Everybody thinks that he goes there for the sake of the two daughters. Well, in order to cure him of that disease, my uncle, Dr. Tache, and six others, masked, whipped him without mercy as he was coming back at eleven o'clock at night. It is already known by everyone in the village, and they split their sides with laughing."

My first feeling on hearing that news was one of joy. Ever since my first confession I felt angry every time I thought of that priest. His questions had so wounded me that I could not forgive him. I had enough self-control, however, to conceal my pleasure, and I answered my friend :

"You are telling me a wicked story; I can't believe a word of it."

"Well," said young Cazeault, "come at eight o'clock this evening to my uncle's. A secret meeting is to take place then. No doubt they will speak of the pill given to the priest last night. We shall place ourselves in our little room as usual and shall hear everything, our presence not being suspected. You may be sure that it will be interesting."

"I will go," I answered, "but I do not believe a word of that story."

I went to school at the usual hour. Most of the pupils had preceded me. Divided into groups of eight or ten, they were engaged in a most lively conversation. Bursts of convulsive laughter were heard from every corner. I could very well see that something uncommon had taken place in the village.

I approached several of these groups, and all received me with the question :

"Do you know that the priest was whipped last night as he was coming from the Misses Richards'?"

"That is a story invented for fun," said I. "You were not there to see him, were you? You therefore know nothing about it; for if anybody had whipped the priest he would not surely boast of it."

"But we heard his screams," answered many voices.

"What! was he then screaming out?" I asked.

"He shouted out at the top of his voice, 'Help, help! Murder!'"

2

"But you were surely mistaken about the voice," said I. "It was not the priest who shouted, it was somebody else. I could never believe that anybody would whip a priest in such a crowded village."

"But," said several, "we ran to his help and we recognized the priest's voice. He is the only one who lisps in the village."

"And we saw him with our own eyes," said several.

The school bell put an end to this conversation. As soon as school was out I returned to the house of my relatives, not wishing to learn any more about this matter. Although I did not like this priest, yet I was much mortified by some remarks which the older pupils made about him.

But it was difficult not to hear any more. On my arrival home I found my uncle and aunt engaged in a very warm debate on the subject. My uncle wished to conceal the fact that he was among those who had whipped him. But he gave the details so precisely, he was so merry over the adventure, that it was easy to see that he had a hand in the plot. My aunt was indignant, and used the most energetic expressions to show her disapprobation.

That bitter debate annoyed me so that I did not stay long to hear it all. I withdrew to my study.

During the remainder of the day I changed my resolution man[y] times about my going to the secret meeting in the evening. At [one] moment I would decide firmly not to go. My conscience told me th[at] as usual, things would be uttered which it was not good for me to hea[r]. I had refused to go to the two last meetings, and a silent voice, as i[t] were, told me I had done well. Then a moment after I was tormented by the desire to know precisely what had taken place the evening before. The flagellation of a priest in the midst of a large village was a fact too worthy of note to fail to excite the curiosity of a child. Besides, my aversion to the priest, though I concealed it as well as I could, made me wish to know whether everything was true on the subject of the chastisement. But in the struggle between good and evil which took place in my mind during that day, the evil was finally to triumph. A quarter of an hour before the meeting my friend came to me and said :

"Make haste, the members of the association are coming."

At this call all my good resolutions vanished. I hushed the voice of my conscience, and a few minutes later I was placed in an angle of that little room, where for more than two hours I learned so many strange and scandalous things about the lives of the priests of Canada.

Dr. Tache presided. He opened the meeting in a low tone of voice. At the beginning of his discourse I had some difficulty to understand what he said. He spoke as one who feared to be overheard when disclosing a secret to a friend. But after a few preliminary sentences he forgot the rule of prudence which he had imposed upon himself, and spoke with energy and power.

Mr. Etienne Tache was naturally eloquent. He seemed to speak on no question except under the influence of the deepest conviction of its truth. His speech was passionate, and the tone of his voice clear and agreeable. His short and cutting sentences did not reach the ear only : they penetrated even the secret folds of the soul. He spoke in substance as follows :

" Gentlemen,—I am happy to see you here more numerously than ever. The grave events of last night have, no doubt, decided many of you to attend debates which some began to forsake, but the importance of which, it seems to me, increases day by day.

" The question debated in our last meeting—' The Priests '—is one of life and death, not only for our young and beautiful Canada, but in a moral point of view it is a question of life and death for our families, and for every one of us in particular.

" There is, I know, only one opinion among us on the subject of priests ; and I am glad that this opinion is not only that of all educated men in Canada, but also of learned France—nay, of the whole world. The reign of the priest is the reign of ignorance, of corruption, and of the most barefaced immorality, under the mask of the most refined hypocrisy. The reign of the priest is the death of our schools ; it is the degradation of our wives, the prostitution of our daughters ; it is the reign of tyranny—the loss of liberty.

" We have only one good school, I will not say in St. Thomas, but in all our county. This school in our midst is a great honour to our village. Now see the energy with which all the priests who come here work for the closing of that school. They use every means to destroy that focus of light which we have started with so much difficulty, and which we support by so many sacrifices.

" With the priest of Rome our children do not belong to us : he is their master. Let me explain. The priest honours us with the belief that the bodies, the flesh and bones of our children, are ours, and that our duty in consequence is to clothe and feed them. But the nobler and more sacred part, namely, the intellect, the heart, the soul, the priest claims as his own patrimony, his own property. The priest has the audacity to tell us that to him alone it belongs to enlighten those intelligences, to form those hearts, to fashion those souls as it may best suit him. He has the impudence to tell us that we are too silly or perverse to know our duties in this respect. We have not the right of choosing our school teachers. We have not the right to send a single ray of light into those intellects, or to give to those souls who hunger and thirst after truth a single crumb of that food prepared with so much wisdom and success by enlightened men of all ages.

" By the confessional the priests poison the springs of life in our children. They initiate them into such mysteries of iniquity as would terrify old galley slaves. By their questions they reveal to them secrets of a corruption such as carries its germs of death into the very marrow of their bones, and that from the earliest years of their infancy. Before I was fifteen years old I had learned more real blackguardism from the mouth of my confessor than I have learned ever since, in my studies and in my life as a physician for twenty years.

" A few days ago I questioned my little nephew, Louis Cazeault, upon what he had learned in his confession. He answered me ingenuously, and repeated things to me which I would be ashamed to utter in your presence, and which you, fathers of families, could not listen to without blushing And just think, that not only of little boys are those questions asked, but also of our dear little girls. Are we not the most degraded of men if we do not set ourselves to work in order to break the iron yoke under which the priest keeps our dear country, and by means of which he keeps us, with our wives and children, at his feet like vile slaves.

" While speaking to you of the deleterious effects of the confessional upon our children, shall I forget its effects upon our wives and upon ourselves? Need I tell you that, for most women, the confessional is a rendezvous of coquetry and of love? Do you not feel as I do myself, that by means of the confessional the priest is more the master of the hearts of our wives than ourselves? Is not the priest the private and public confidant of our wives? Do not our wives go invariably to the feet of the priest, opening to him what is most sacred and intimate in the secrets of our lives as husbands and as fathers? The husband belongs no more to his wife as her guide through the dark and difficult paths of life: it is the priest! We are no more their friends and natural advisers. Their anxieties and their cares they do not confide to us. They do not expect from us the remedies for the miseries of this life. Towards the priest they turn their thoughts and desires. He has their entire and exclusive confidence. In a word, it is the priest who is the real husband of our wives! It is he who has the possession of their respect and of their hearts to a degree to which no one of us need ever aspire !

" Were the priest an angel, were he not made of flesh and bones just as we are, were not his organization absolutely the same as our own, then might we be indifferent to what might take place between him and our wives, whom he has at his feet, in his hands—even more, in his heart. But what does my experience tell me, not only as a physician, but also as a citizen of St. Thomas ? What does yours tell you ? Our experience tells us that the priest, instead of being stronger, is weaker than we generally are with respect to women.

His sham vows of perfect chastity, far from rendering him more invulnerable to the arrows of Cupid, expose him to be made more easily the victim of that god, so small in form, but so dreadful a giant by the irresistible power of his weapons and the extent of his conquests.

"As a matter of fact, of the last four priests who came to St. Thomas, have not three seduced many of the wives and daughters of our most respectable families ? And what security have we that the priest who is now with us does not walk in the same path ? Is not the whole parish filled with indignation at the long nightly visits made by him to two girls whose dissolute morals are a secret to nobody ? And when the priest does not respect himself, would we not be silly in continuing to give him that respect of which he himself knows he is unworthy ?

"At our last meeting the opinions were divided at the beginning of the discussion. Many thought it would be well to speak to the bishop about the scandal caused by those nightly visits. But the majority judged that such steps would be useless, since the bishop would do one of two things, namely, he would either pay no attention to our just complaints, as has often been the case, or he would remove this priest, filling his place with one who would do no better. That majority, which became a unanimity, acceded to my thought of taking justice into our own hands. The priest is our servant. We pay him a large tithe. We have therefore claims upon him. He has abused us, and does so every day by his public neglect of the most elementary laws of morality. In visiting every night that house whose degradation is known to everybody, he gives to youth an example of perversity the effects of which no one can estimate.

"It had been unanimously decided that he should be whipped. Without my telling you by whom it was done, you may be assured that Mr. Beaubien's flagellation of last night will never be forgotten by him !

"Heaven grant that this brotherly correction be a lesson to teach all the priests of Canada that their golden reign is over, that the eyes of the people are opened, and that their domination is drawing to an end ! "

This discourse was listened to with deep silence, and Dr. Tache saw by the applause that followed that his speech had been the expression of every one.

Next followed a gentleman named Dubord, who in substance spoke as follows :

"Mr. President,—I was not among those who gave the priest the expression of public feeling with the energetic tongue of the whip. I wish I had been, however; I would heartily have co-operated in giving that lesson to the priests of Canada. Let me give my reason.

" My daughter who is twelve years old, went to confession as did the others a few weeks ago. It was against my will. I know by my own experience that of all actions confession is the most degrading in a person's life. I can imagine nothing so well calculated to destroy for ever one's self-respect as the modern invention of the confessional. Now, what is a person without self-respect—especially a woman? Without this all is lost to her for ever.

" In the confessional everything is corruption of the lowest grade.

" In the confessional, a girl's thoughts are polluted, her tongue is polluted, her heart is polluted—yes, and for ever polluted! Do I need to tell you this? You know it as well as I do. Though you are now all too intelligent to degrade yourselves at the feet of a priest, though it is long since you have been guilty of that meanness, not one of you have forgotten the lessons of corruption received, when young, in the confessional. Those lessons were engraved on your memory, your thoughts, your heart, and your souls like the scar left by the red-hot iron upon the brow of the slave, to remain a perpetual witness of his shame and servitude. The confessional is a place where one gets accustomed to hear, and repeat without a scruple, things which would cause even a prostitute to blush!

" Why are Roman Catholic nations inferior to nations belonging to Protestantism? Only in the confessional can the solution of that problem be found. And why are Roman Catholic nations degraded in proportion to their submission to the priest? It is because the oftener the individuals composing those nations go to confession, the more rapidly they sink in the scale of intelligence and morality. A terrible example of this I had in my own house.

" As I said a moment ago, I was against my daughter going to confession ; but her poor mother, who is under the control of the priest, earnestly wanted her to go. Not to have a disagreeable scene in my house, I had to yield to the tears of my wife.

" On the day following that of her confession they believed I was absent; but I was in my office, with the door sufficiently open to allow me to hear what was said. My wife and daughter had the following conversation :

" ' What makes you so thoughtful and sad, my dear Lucy, since you went to confession? It seems to me you should feel happier since you had the privilege of confessing your sins.'

" Lucy made no answer.

" After a silence of two or three minutes her mother said :

" ' Why do you weep, dear child? Are you ill?'

" Still no answer from the child.

" You may well suppose that I was all attention. I had my

suspicions about the dreadful ordeal which had taken place. My heart throbbed with uneasiness and anger.

"After a short time my wife spoke to her child with sufficient firmness to force her to answer. In a trembling voice and half suppressed with sobs my dear little daughter answered :

"'Ah! mamma, if you knew what the priest asked me, and what he said to me in the confessional, you would be as sad as I am.'

"'But what did he say to you ? He is a holy man. You surely did not understand him if you think he said anything to pain you.'

"'Dear mother,' as she threw herself into her mother's arms, 'do not ask me to confess what the priest said! He told to me things so shameful that I cannot repeat them. But that which pains me most is the impossibility of banishing from my thoughts the hateful things which he has taught me. His impure words are like the leeches put upon the chest of my friend Louise—they could not be removed without tearing the flesh. What must have been his opinion of me to ask such questions ! '

"My child said no more, and began to sob again.

"After a short silence my wife rejoined :

"'I'll go the priest. I'll tell him to beware how he speaks in the confessional. I have noticed myself that he goes too far with his questions. I, however thought that he was more prudent with children. After the lesson that I'll give him, be sure that you will have only to tell your sins, and that you will be no more troubled by his endless questions. I ask of you, however, never to speak of this to anybody, especially never let your poor father know anything about it; for he has little enough religion already, and this would leave him without any at all.'

"I could contain myself no longer. I rose and abruptly entered the parlour. My daughter threw herself, weeping, into my arms. My wife screamed with terror, and almost fell into a swoon. I said to my child :

"If you love me, put your hand on my heart and promise me that you'll never go to confession again. Fear God, my child; walk in His presence, for His eye seeth you everywhere. Remember that day and night He is ready to forgive us. Never place yourself again at the feet of a priest to be defiled and degraded by him !

"This my daughter promised me.

"When my wife had recovered from her surprise I said to her :

"Madam, for a long time the priest has been everything, and your husband nothing to you. There is a hidden and terrible power that governs your thoughts and affections as it governs your deeds—it is the power of the priest. This you have often denied ; but providence has decided to-day that this power should be for ever broken for you and for me. I want to be the ruler in my own house; and from this moment the power of the priest over you must cease, unless you prefer to leave my house for ever. The priest has reigned here too long! But now that I know he has stained and defiled the soul of my daughter, his empire must fall! Whenever you go and take your heart and secrets to the feet of the priest, be so kind as not to come back to the same house with me."

Three other discourses followed that of Mr. Dubord, all of which were pregnant with details and facts going to prove that the confessional was the principal cause of the deplorable demoralisation of St. Thomas.

If, in addition to all that, I could have mentioned before that association what I already knew of the corrupting influences of that institution given to the world by centuries of darkness, certainly the determination of its members to make use of every means to abolish the usage would have been strengthened.

CHAPTER V.

THE day following that of the meeting at which Mr. Tache had given his reasons for boasting that he had whipped the priest, I wrote to my mother : "For God's sake, come for me; I can stay here no longer. If you knew what my eyes have seen and my ears have heard for some time past, you would not delay your coming a single day."

Indeed, such was the impression left upon me by that flagellation, and by the speeches which I had heard, that had it not been for the crossing of the St. Lawrence, I would have started for Murray Bay on the day after the secret meeting at which I had heard things that so terribly frightened me. How I regretted the happy and peaceful days spent with my mother in reading the beautiful chapters of the Bible, so well chosen by her to instruct and interest me! What a difference there was between our conversations after these readings, and the conversations I heard at St. Thomas!

Happily my parents' desire to see me again was as great as mine to go back to them. So that a few weeks later my mother came for me. She pressed me to her heart, and brought me back to the arms of my father.

I arrived at home on the 17th of July, 1821, and spent the afternoon and evening till late by my father's side. With what pleasure did he see me working difficult problems in algebra, and even in geometry! for under my teacher, Mr. Jones, I had really made rapid progress in those branches. More than once I noticed tears of joy in my father's eyes when, taking my slate, he saw that my calculations were correct. He also examined me in grammar. "What an admirable teacher this Mr. Jones must be," he would say, "to have advanced a child so much in the short space of fourteen months!"

How sweet to me, but how short, were those hours of happiness passed between my good mother and my father! We had family worship. I read the fifteenth chapter of Luke, the return of the prodigal son. My mother then sang a hymn of joy and gratitude, and I went to bed with my heart full of happiness to take the sweetest sleep of my life. But, O God! what an awful awakening Thou hadst prepared for me!

About four o'clock in the morning heartrending screams fell upon my ear. I recognized my mother's voice.

"What is the matter, dear mother?"

"Oh, my dear child, you have no more a father! He is dead!"

In saying these words she lost consciousness and fell on the floor!

While a friend who had passed the night with us gave her proper care, I hastened to my father's bed. I pressed him to my heart, I kissed him, I covered him with my tears, I moved his head, I pressed his hands, I tried to lift him up on his pillow: I could not believe that he was dead! It seemed to me that even if dead he would come back to life—that God could not thus take my father away from me at the very moment when I had come back to him after so long an absence! I knelt to pray to God for the life of my father. But my tears and cries were useless. He was dead! He was already cold as ice!

Two days after he was buried. My mother was so overwhelmed with grief that she could not follow the funeral procession. I remained with her as her only earthly support. Poor mother! How many tears thou hast shed! What sobs came from thine afflicted heart in those days of supreme grief!

Though I was then very young, I could understand the greatness of our loss, and I mingled my tears with those of my mother.

What pen can portray what takes place in the heart of a woman when God takes suddenly her husband away in the prime of his life, and leaves her alone, plunged in misery, with three small children, two of whom are even too young to know their loss! How long are the hours of the day for the poor widow who is left alone, and without means, among strangers! How painful the sleepless night to the heart which has lost everything! How empty a house is left by the eternal absence of him who was its master, support, and father! Every object in the house and every step she takes remind her of her loss and sinks the sword deeper which pierces her heart. Oh, how bitter are the tears which flow from her eyes when her youngest child, who as yet does not understand the mystery of death, throws himself into her arms and says: "Mamma, where is papa? Why does he not come back? I am lonely!"

My poor mother passed through those heartrending trials. I heard her sobs during the long hours of the day, and also during the longer hours of the night. Many times I have seen her fall upon her knees to implore God to be merciful to her and to her three unhappy orphans. I could do nothing then to comfort her, but love her, pray and weep with her!

Only a few days had elapsed after the burial of my father when I saw Mr. Courtois, the parish priest, coming to our house (he who had tried to take away our Bible from us). He had the reputation of being rich, and as we were poor and unhappy since my father's death, my first thought was that he had come to comfort and to help us. I could see that my mother had the same hopes. She welcomed him as an angel from heaven. The least gleam of hope is so sweet to one who is unhappy!

From his very first words, however, I could see that our hopes were not to be realized. He tried to be sympathetic, and even said something about the confidence that we should have in God, especially in times of trial; but his words were cold and dry.

Turning to me, he said:

"Do you continue to read the Bible, my little boy?"

"Yes, sir," answered I, with a voice trembling with anxiety, for I feared that he would make another effort to take away that treasure, and I had no longer a father to defend it.

Then, addressing my mother, he said:

"Madam, I told you that it was not right for you or your child to read that book."

My mother cast down her eyes, and answered only by the tears which ran down her cheeks.

That question was followed by a long silence, and the priest then continued:

"Madam, there is something due for the prayers which have been sung, and the services which you requested to be offered for the repose of your husband's soul. I will be very much obliged to you if you pay me that little debt."

"Mr. Courtois," answered my mother, "my husband left me nothing but debts. I have only the work of my own hands to procure a living for my three children, the eldest of whom is before you. For these little orphans' sake, if not for mine, do not take from us the little that is left."

"But, madam, you do not reflect. Your husband died suddenly and without any preparation; he is therefore in the flames of purgatory. If you want him to be delivered, you must necessarily unite your personal sacrifices to the prayers of the Church and the masses which we offer."

" As I said, my husband has left me absolutely without means, and it is impossible for me to give you any money," replied my mother.

" But, madam, your husband was for a long time the only notary of Mal Bay. He surely must have made much money. I can scarcely think that he has left you without any means to help him now that his desolation and sufferings are far greater than yours."

" My husband did indeed coin much money, but he spent still more. Thanks to God, we have not been in want while he lived. But lately he got this house built, and what is still due on it makes me fear that I will lose it. He also bought a piece of land not long ago, only half of which is paid and I will, therefore, probably not be able to keep it. Hence I may soon, with my poor orphans, be deprived of everything that is left us. In the meantime I hope, sir, that you are not a man to take away from us our last piece of bread."

" But, madam, the masses offered for the rest of your husband's soul must be paid for," answered the priest.

My mother covered her face with her handkerchief and wept.

As for me, I did not mingle my tears with hers this time. My feelings were not those of grief, but of anger and unspeakable horror. My eyes were fixed on the face of that man who tortured my mother's heart. I looked with tearless eyes upon the man who added to my mother's anguish, and made her weep more bitterly than ever. My hands were clenched, as if ready to strike. All my muscles trembled ; my teeth chattered as if from intense cold. My greatest sorrow was my weakness in the presence of that big man, and my not being able to send him away from our house, and driving him far away from my mother.

I felt inclined to say to him : " Are you not ashamed, you who are so rich, to come and take away the last piece of bread from our mouths ? " But my physical and moral strength were not sufficient to accomplish the task before me, and I was filled with regret and disappointment.

After a long silence, my mother raised her eyes, reddened with tears, towards the priest and said :

" Sir, you see that cow in the meadow, not far from our house ? Her milk and the butter made from it form the principal part of my children's food. I hope you will not take her away from us. If, however, such a sacrifice must be made to deliver my poor husband's soul from purgatory, take her as payment of the masses to be offered to extinguish those devouring flames."

The priest instantly arose, saying, " Very well, madam," and went out.

Our eyes anxiously followed him ; but instead of walking towards the little gate which was in front of the house, he directed his steps towards the meadow, and drove the cow before him in the direction of his home.

At that sight I screamed with despair : " Oh, my mother! he is taking our cow away ! What will become of us ? "

Lord Nairn had given us that splendid cow when it was three months old. Her mother had been brought from Scotland, and belonged to one of the best breeds of that country. I fed her with my own hands, and had often shared my bread with her. I loved her as a child always loves an animal which he has brought up himself. She seemed to understand and love me also. From whatever distance she could see me, she would run to me to receive my caresses, and whatever else I might have to give her. My mother herself milked her ; and her rich milk was such delicious and substantial food for us.

My mother also cried out with grief as she saw the priest taking away the only means which heaven had left her to feed her children.

Throwing myself into her arms, I asked her : " Why have you given away our cow ? What will become of us ? We shall surely die of hunger ? "

" Dear child," she answered. " I did not think the priest would be so cruel as to take away the last resource which God had left us. Ah! if I had believed him to be so unmerciful I would never have spoken to him as I did. As you say, my dear child, what will become of us ? But have you not often read to me in your Bible that God is the Father of the widow and the orphan? We shall pray to that God who is willing to be your father and mine : He will listen to us, and see our tears. Let us kneel down and ask of Him to be merciful to us, and to give us back the support of which the priest has deprived us."

We both knelt down. She took my right hand with her left, and, lifting the other hand towards heaven, she offered a prayer to the God of mercies for her poor children such as I have never since heard. Her words were often choked by her sobs. But when she could not speak with her voice, she spoke with her burning eyes raised to heaven, and with her hand uplifted. I also prayed to God with her, and repeated her words, which were broken by my sobs.

When her prayer was ended she remained for a long time pale and trembling. Cold sweat was flowing on her face, and she fell on the floor. I thought she was going to die. I ran for cold water, which I gave her, saying : " Dear mother ! Oh, do not leave me alone upon earth ! " After drinking a few drops she felt better, and taking my hand, she put it to her trembling lips; then drawing me near her, and pressing me to her bosom, she said: " Dear child, if ever you become a priest, *I ask of you never to be so hard-hearted towards poor widows as are the priests of to-day.*" When she said these words, I felt her burning tears falling upon my cheek.

The memory of these tears has never left me. I felt them constantly during the twenty-five years I spent in preaching the inconceivable superstitions of Rome.

I was not better, naturally, than many of the other priests. I believed, as they did, the impious fables of purgatory; and as well as they (I confess it to my shame), if I refused to take, or if I gave back the money of the poor, I accepted the money which the rich gave me for the masses I said to extinguish the flames of that fabulous place. But the remembrance of my mother's words and tears has kept me from being so cruel and unmerciful towards the poor widows as Romish priests are, for the most part, obliged to be.

When my heart, depraved by the false and impious doctrines of Rome, was tempted to take money from widows and orphans, *under pretence of my long prayers*, I then heard the voice of my mother, from the depth of her sepulchre, saying : " My dear child, do not be cruel towards poor widows and orphans, as are the priests of to-day." If, during the days of my priesthood at Quebec, at Beauport, and Kam-arouska, I have given almost all that I had to feed and clothe the poor, especially the widows and orphans, it was not owing to my being better than others, but it was because my mother had spoken to me with words never to be forgotten. The Lord, I believe, had put into my mother's mouth those words, so simple but so full of eloquence and beauty, as one of His great mercies towards me. Those tears the hand of Rome has never been able to wipe off: those words of my mother the sophisms of Popery could not make me forget.

How long, O Lord, shall that insolent enemy of the gospel, the Church of Rome, be permitted to fatten herself upon the tears of the widow and of the orphan by means of that cruel and impious invention of paganism—purgatory ? Wilt Thou not be merciful unto so many nations which are still the victims of that great imposture ? Oh, do remove the veil which covers the eyes of the priests and people of Rome, as Thou hast removed it from mine ! Make them to understand that their hopes of purification must not rest on these fabulous fires, but only on the blood of the Lamb shed on Calvary to save the world.

CHAPTER VI.

GOD had heard the poor widow's prayer. A few days after the priest had taken our cow she received a letter from each of her two sisters, Genevieve and Catherine.

The former, who was married to Etienne Eschenbach, of St. Thomas, told her to sell all she had and come, with her children, to live with her.

"We have no family," she said, "and God has given us the good things of this life in abundance. We shall be happy to share them with you and your children."

The latter, married in Kamouraska to the Hon. Amable Dionne wrote : " We have learned the sad news of your husband's death. We have lately lost our only son. We wish to fill the vacant place with Charles, your eldest. Send him to us. We shall bring him up as our own child, and before long he will be your support. In the meantime, sell by auction all you have, and go to St. Thomas with your two younger children. There Genevieve and myself will supply your wants."

In a few days all our furniture was sold. Unfortunately, though I had carefully concealed my cherished Bible, it disappeared. I could never discover what became of it. Had mother herself, frightened by the threats of the priest, relinquished that treasure? or had some of our relatives, believing it to be their duty, destroyed it? I do not know. I deeply felt that loss, which was then irreparable to me.

On the following day, in the midst of bitter tears and sobs, I bade farewell to my poor mother and young brothers. They went to St. Thomas on board a schooner, and I crossed in a sloop to Kamouraska.

My uncle and aunt Dionne welcomed me with every mark of the most sincere affection. Having soon made known to them that I wished to become a priest, I begun to study Latin under the direction of Rev. Mr. Morin, vicar of Kamouraska. That priest was esteemed to be a learned man. He was about forty or fifty years old, and had been priest of a parish in the district of Montreal. But, as is the case with the majority of priests, his vows of celibacy had not proved a sufficient guarantee against the charms of one of his beautiful parishioners. This had caused a great scandal. He consequently lost his position, and the bishop had sent him to Kamouraska, where his past conduct was not so generally known. He was very good to me, and I soon loved him with sincere affection.

One day, about the beginning of the year 1822, he called me aside and said

, "Mr. Varin (the parish priest) is in the habit of giving a great festival on his birthday. Now, the principal citizens of the village wish on that occasion to present him with a bouquet. I am appointed to write an address, and to choose some one to deliver it before the priest. You are the one whom I have chosen. What do you think of it?"

"But I am very young," I replied.

"Your youth will only give more interest to what we wish to say and do," said the priest.

"Well, I have no objection to do so, provided the piece be not too long, and that I have it sufficiently soon to learn it well."

It was already prepared. The time of delivering it soon came. The best society of Kamouraska, composed of about fifteen gentlemen and as many ladies, were assembled in the beautiful parlours of the parsonage. Mr. Varin was in their midst. Suddenly Squire Paschal Tache, the seigneur of the parish, and his lady entered the room, holding me by each hand, and placed me in the midst of the guests. My head was crowned with flowers, for I was to represent the angel of the parish, whom the people had chosen to give to their pastor the expression of public admiration and gratitude. When the address was finished, I presented to the priest the beautiful bouquet of symbolical flowers prepared by the ladies for the occasion.

Mr. Varin was a small but well-built man. His thin lips were ever ready to smile graciously. The remarkable whiteness of his skin was still heightened by the red colour of his cheeks. Intelligence and goodness beamed from his expressive black eyes. Nothing could be more amiable and gracious than his conversation during the first quarter of an hour passed in his company. He was passionately fond of these little fetes, and the charm of his manners could not be surpassed as the host of the evening.

He was moved to tears before hearing half of the address, and the eyes of many were moistened when the pastor, with a voice trembling and full of emotion, expressed his joy and gratitude at being so highly appreciated by his parishioners.

As soon as the happy pastor had expressed his thanks, the ladies sang two or three beautiful songs. The door of the dining-room was then opened, and we could see a long table laden with the most delicious meats and wines that Canada could offer.

I had never before been present at a priest's dinner. The honourable position given me at that little fete permitted me to see it in all its details, and nothing could equal the curiosity with which I sought to hear and see all that was said and done by the joyous guests.

Besides Mr. Varin and his vicar, there were three other priests, who were artistically placed in the midst of the most beautiful ladies of the company. The ladies, after honouring us with their presence for an hour or so, left the table and retired to the drawing-room. Scarcely had the last lady disappeared when Mr. Varin rose and said:

"Gentlemen, let us drink to the health of these amiable ladies, whose presence has thrown so many charms over the first part of our little fete."

Following the example of Mr. Varin each guest filled and emptied his long wine glass in honour of the ladies.

Squire Tache then proposed "The health of the most venerable and beloved priest of Canada, the Rev. Mr. Varin." Again the glasses were filled and emptied, except mine; for I had been placed at the side of my uncle Dionne, who, sternly looking at me as soon as I had emptied my first glass, said: "If you drink another I will send you from the table. A little boy like you should not drink, but only touch the glass with his lips."

It would have been difficult to count the healths which were drank after the ladies had left us. After each health a song or a story was called for, several of which were followed by applause, shouts of joy, and convulsive laughter.

When my turn to propose a health came, I wished to be excused, but they would not exempt me. So I had to say about whose health I was most interested. I rose, and turning to Mr. Varin, I said, "Let us drink to the health of our Holy Father, the Pope."

Nobody had yet thought of our Holy Father the Pope, and the name, mentioned under such circumstances by a child, appeared so droll to the priests and their merry guests that they burst into laughter, stamped their feet, and shouted "Bravo! bravo! To the health of the Pope!" Everyone stood up, and at the invitation of Mr. Varin, the glasses were filled and emptied as usual.

So many healths could not be drunk without their natural effect—intoxication. The first that was overcome was a priest, Noel by name. He was a tall man, and a great drinker. I had noticed more than once, that instead of taking his wine glass he drank from a large tumbler. The first symptoms of his intoxication, instead of drawing sympathy from his friends, only increased their noisy bursts of laughter. He endeavoured to take a bottle to fill his glass, but his hand shook, and the bottle, falling on the floor, was broken to pieces. Wishing to keep up his merriment he began to sing a Bacchic song, but could not finish. He dropped his head on the table, quite over-come, and trying to rise, he fell heavily upon his chair. While all this took place the other priests and all the guests looked at him, laughing loudly. At last, making a desperate effort, he rose, but after taking two or three steps, fell headlong on the floor. His two neighbours went to help him, but they were not in a condition to help him. Twice they rolled with him under the table. At length another, less affected by the fumes of wine, took him by the feet and dragged him into an adjoining room, where they left him.

This first scene seemed strange enough to me, for I had never before seen a priest intoxicated. But what astonished me most was the laughter of the other priests over that spectacle. Another scene, however, soon followed, which made me sadder. My young companion and friend, Achilles Tache, had not been warned, as I had, only to touch the wine with his lips. More than once he had emptied his glass. He also rolled upon the floor before the eyes of his father, who was too full of wine to help him. He cried aloud, " I am choking ! " I tried to lift him up, but was not strong enough. I ran for his mother. She came, accompanied by another lady, but the vicar had carried him into another room, where he fell asleep after having thrown off the wine he had taken.

Poor Achilles! he was learning, in the house of his own priest, to take the first step of that life of debauchery and drunkenness which twelve or fifteen years later was to rob him of his manor, take from him his wife and children, and to make him fall a victim to the bloody hand of a murderer upon the solitary shores of Kamouraska!

This first and sad experience which I made of the real and intimate life of the Roman Catholic priest was so deeply engraved on my memory that I still remember with shame the bacchic song which that priest Morin had taught me, and which I sang on that occasion. It commenced with these Latin words :—

> Ego, in arte Bacchi,
> Multum profeci :
> Decies pintum vini
> Hodie bibi.

I also remember one sung by Mr. Varin. Here it is :—

> Savez-vous pourquoi, mes amis, (*bis*)
> Nous sommes tous si rejouis ? (*bis*)
> Amis n'endoutez pas,
> C'est qu'un repas
> N'est bon.
> Qu' appreté sans façon,
> Mangeons à la gamelle.
> Vive le son, vive le son,
> Mangeons à la gamelle,
> Vive le son du flacon !

When the priests and their friends had sung, laughed, and drank for more than an hour, Mr. Varin rose and said, " The ladies must not be left alone all the evening. Will not our joy and happiness be doubled if they are pleased to share them with us."

3

This proposition was received with applause, and we passed into the drawing-room, where the ladies awaited us.

Several pieces of music, well executed, gave new life to this part of the entertainment.   This resource, however, was soon exhausted. Besides, some of the ladies could well see that their husbands were half drunk, and they felt ashamed.   Madam Tache could not conceal the grief she felt, caused by what had happened to her dear Achilles. Had she some presentiment, as many persons have, of the tears which she was to shed one day on his account ? Was the vision of a mutilated and bloody corpse—the corpse of her own drunken son fallen dead, under the blow of an assassin's dagger, before her eyes ?

Mr. Varin feared nothing more than an interruption in those hours of lively pleasure, of which his life was full, and which took place in his parsonage.

"Well, well, ladies and gentlemen, let us entertain no dark thoughts on this evening, the happiest of my life. Let us play blind man's buff."

"Let us play blind man's buff!" was repeated by everybody.

On hearing this noise, the gentlemen who were half asleep by the fumes of wine seemed to awaken as if from a long dream.   Young gentlemen clapped their hands ; ladies, young and old, congratulated one another on the happy idea.

"But whose eyes shall be covered first ? " asked the priest.

"Yours, Mr. Varin," cried all the ladies.   " We look to you for the good example, and we shall follow it."

" The power and unanimity of the jury by which I am condemned cannot be resisted.   I feel that there is no appeal.   I must submit."

Immediately one of the ladies placed her nicely-perfumed handkerchief over the eyes of her priest, took him by the hand, led him to an angle of the room, and having pushed him gently with her delicate hand, said, "Mr. Blindman! Let everyone flee ! Woe to him who is caught ! "

There is nothing more curious and comical than to see a man walk when he is under the influence of wine, especially if he wishes nobody to notice it.   How stiff and straight he keeps his legs ! How varied and complicated, in order to keep his equilibrium, are his motions to right and left ! Such was the position of priest Varin.   He was not *very* drunk.   Though he had taken a large quantity of wine he did not fall.   He carried with wonderful courage the weight with which he was laden.   The wine which he had drank would have intoxicated three ordinary men ; but such was his capacity for drinking that he could still walk without falling.   However, his condition was sadly betrayed by each step he took and by each word he spoke.   Nothing, therefore, was more comical than the first steps of the poor priest in his efforts to lay hold of somebody in order to pass his band to him.

He would take one forward and two backward steps, and would then stagger to the right and to the left. Everybody laughed to tears. One after another they would all either pinch him or touch him gently on his hand, arm, or shoulder, and, passing rapidly off, would exclaim, "Run away!" The priest went to the right and then to the left, threw his arms suddenly now here and then there. His legs evidently bent under their burden; he panted, perspired, coughed, and everyone began to fear that the trial might be carried too far, and beyond propriety. But suddenly, by a happy turn he caught the arm of a lady who in teasing him had come too near. In vain the lady tries to escape. She struggles, turns round, but the priest's hand holds her firmly.

While holding his victim with his right hand he wishes to touch her head with his left, in order to know and name the pretty bird he had caught. But at that moment his legs gave way. He falls, and drags with him his beautiful parishioner. She turns upon him in order to escape, but he soon turns on her in order to hold her better.

All this, though the affair of a moment, was long enough to cause the ladies to blush and cover their faces. Never in all my life did I see anything so shameful as that scene. This ended the game.

Everyone felt ashamed. I make a mistake when I say *everyone,* because the men were almost all too intoxicated to blush. The priests also were either too drunk or too much accustomed to see such scenes to be ashamed.

On the following day every one of those priests celebrated mass, and ate what they called the body and blood, the soul and divinity of Jesus Christ, just as if they had spent the previous evening in prayer and meditation on the laws of God! Mr. Varin was the arch-priest of the important part of the diocese of Quebec from La Riviere Ouelle to Gaspe.

Thus, O perfidious Church of Rome, thou deceivest the nations who follow thee, and ruinest even the priests whom thou makest thy slaves.

CHAPTER VII.

NOTHING can exceed the care with which Roman Catholic priests prepare children for their first communion. Two and three months are set apart every year for that purpose. All that time the children between ten and twelve years of age are obliged to go to Church almost every day, not only to learn by heart their catechism, but to hear the explanations of all its teachings.

The priest who instructed us was the Rev. Mr. Morin, whom I

have already mentioned. He was exceedingly kind to children, and we respected and loved him sincerely. His instructions to us were somewhat long ; but we liked to hear him, for he always had some new and interesting stories to give us.

The catechism taught as a preparation for our first communion was the foundation of the idolatries and superstitions which the Church of Rome gives as the religion of Christ. It is by means of that catechetical instruction that she obtains for the Pope and his representatives that profound respect, I might say adoration, which is the secret of her power and influence. With this catechism Rome corrupts the most sacred truths of the Gospel. It is there that Jesus is removed from the hearts for which He paid so great a price, and that Mary is put in His place. But the great iniquity of substituting Mary for Jesus is so skilfully concealed, it is given with colours so poetic and beautiful, and so well adapted to captivate human nature, that it is almost impossible for a poor child to escape the snare.

One day the priest said to me, " Stand up, my child, in order to answer the many important questions which I have to ask you."

I stood up.

" My child," he said, " when you had been guilty of some fault at home—who was the first to punish you—your father or your mother ? "

After a few moments of hesitation I answered, " My father."

" You have answered correctly, my child," said the priest. " As a matter of fact, the father is almost always more impatient with his children, and more ready to punish them, than the mother."

" Now, my child, tell us who punished you most severely—your father or your mother ? "

" My father," I said, without hesitation.

" Still true, my child. The superior goodness of a kind mother is perceived even in the act of correction. Her blows are lighter than those of the father. Further, when you had deserved to be chastised, did not one sometimes come between you and your father's rod, taking it away from him and pacifying him ? "

" Yes," I said ; " mother did that very often, and saved me from severe punishment more than once."

" That is so, my child, not only for you, but for all your companions here. Have not your good mothers, my children, often saved you from your father's corrections even when you deserved it ? Answer me."

" Yes, sir," they all answered.

" One question more. When your father was coming to whip

you, did you not throw yourself into the arms of some one to escape?"

"Yes, sir; when guilty of something, more than once, I threw myself into my mother's arms as soon as I saw my father coming to whip me. She begged pardon for me, and pleaded so well that I often escaped punishment."

"You have answered well," said the priest. Then turning to the children, he continued :

"You have a Father and a Mother in heaven, dear children. Your Father is Jesus, and your Mother is Mary. Do not forget that a mother's heart is always more tender and more prone to mercy than that of a father.

"Often you offend your Father by your sins; you make Him angry against you. What takes place in heaven then? Your Father n heaven takes His rod to punish you. He threatens to crush you down with His roaring thunder; He opens the gates of hell to cast you into it, and you would have been damned long ago had it not been for the loving Mother whom you have in heaven, who has disarmed your angry and irritated Father. When Jesus would punish you as you deserve, the good Virgin Mary hastens to Him and pacifies Him. She places herself between Him and you, and prevents Him from smiting you. She speaks in your favour, she asks for your pardon and she obtains it.

"Also, as young Chiniquy has told you, he often threw himself into the arms of his mother to escape punishment She took his part, and pleaded so well that his father yielded and put away the rod. Thus, my children, when your conscience tells you that you are guilty, that Jesus is angry against you and that you have good reason to fear hell, hasten to Mary! Throw yourselves into the arms of that good mother; have recourse to her sovereign power over Jesus, and be assured that you will be saved through her!"

It is thus that the Pope and the priests of Rome have entirely disfigured and changed the holy religion of the Gospel! In the Church of Rome it is not Jesus, but Mary, who represents the infinite love and mercy of God for the sinner. The sinner is not advised or directed to place his hope in Jesus, but in Mary, for his escape from deserved chastisement! It is not Jesus, but Mary, who saves the sinner! Jesus is always bent on punishing sinners; Mary is always merciful to them !

The Church of Rome has thus fallen into idolatry : she rather trusts in Mary than in Jesus. She constantly invites sinners to turn their thoughts, their hopes, their affections, not to Jesus, but to Mary!

By means of that impious doctrine Rome deceives the intellects, seduces the hearts, and destroys the souls of the young for ever.

Under the pretext of honouring the Virgin Mary, she insults her by outraging and misrepresenting her adorable Son.

Rome has brought back the idolatry of old paganism under a new name. She has replaced upon her altars the Jupiter Tonans of the Greeks and Romans, only she places upon his shoulders the mantle and she writes on the forehead of her idol the name of Jesus, in order the better to deceive the world!

CHAPTER VIII.

FOR the Roman Catholic child, how beautiful and yet how sad is the day of his first communion! How many joys and anxieties by turn rise in his soul when for the first time he is about to eat what he has been taught to believe to be his God! How many efforts has he to make, in order to destroy the manifest teachings of his own rational faculties! I confess with deep regret that I had almost destroyed my reason, in order to prepare myself for my first communion. Yes, I was almost exhausted when the day came that I had to eat what the priest had assured us was the true body, the true blood, soul and divinity of Jesus Christ. I was about to eat Him, not in a symbolical or commemorative, but in a literal way. I was to eat His flesh, His bones, His hands, His feet, His head, His whole body! I had to believe this or be cast for ever into hell, while, all the time, my eyes, my hands, my mouth, my tongue, my reason told me that what I was eating was only bread!

Has there ever been, or will there ever be, a priest or a layman to believe what the Church of Rome teaches on this dreadful mystery of the Real Presence? Shall I say that I believed in the real presence of Jesus Christ in the communion? I believed in it as all those who are good Roman Catholics believe. I believed as a perfect idiot or a corpse believes. Whatever is essential to a reasonable act of faith had been destroyed in me on that point, as it is destroyed in every priest and layman in the Church of Rome. My reason as well as my external senses had been, as much as possible, sacrificed at the feet of that terrible modern god, the Pope! I had been guilty of the incredibly foolish act, of which all good Roman Catholics are guilty—I had said to my intellectual faculties, and to all my senses, "Hush, you are liars! I had believed to this day that you had been given to me by God in order to enable me to walk in the dark paths of life, but, behold! the holy Pope teaches me that you are only instruments of the devil to deceive me!"

What is a man who resigns his intellectual liberty, and who cares not to believe in the testimony of his senses? Is he not acting the

part of one who has no gift or power of intelligence ? A good Roman
Catholic must reach that point! That was my own condition on
the day of my first communion.

When Jesus said, " If I had not come and spoken unto them they
had not had sin ; but now they have no cloke for their sin. . . . . If I
had not done among them the works which none other man did, they had
not had sin ; but now have they both seen and hated both Me and
My Father " (John xv. 22, 24). He showed that the sin of the Jews
consisted in not having believed in what their eyes had seen and their
ears had heard. But behold, the Pope says to Roman Catholics that
they must not believe in what their hands undoubtedly handle and
their eyes most clearly see ! The Pope sets aside the testimony most
approved by Jesus. The very witnesses invoked by the Son of God
are ignominiously turned out of court by the Pope as false
witnesses !

As the moment of taking the communion drew near, two feelings
were at war in my mind, each struggling for victory. I rejoiced in
the thought that I would soon have full possession of Jesus Christ,
but at the same time I was troubled and humbled by the absurdity
which I had to believe before receiving that sacrament. Though
scarcely twelve years old, I had sufficiently accustomed myself to
reflect on the profound darkness which covered that dogma. I had
been also greatly in the habit of trusting my eyes, and I thought that
I could easily distinguish between a small piece of bread and a full-
grown man !

Besides, I extremely abhorred the idea of eating human flesh and
drinking human blood, even when they assured me that they were the
flesh and blood of Jesus Christ Himself. But what troubled me most
was the idea of that God, who was represented to me as being so
great, so glorious, so holy, being eaten by me like a piece of common
bread ! Terrible then was the struggle in my young heart, where joy
and dread, trust and fear, faith and unbelief by turns had the upper
hand.

While that secret struggle, known only to God and to myself, was
going on, I had often to wipe off the cold perspiration which came on
my brow. With all the strength of my soul I prayed to God and the
Holy Virgin to be merciful unto me, to help, and give me sufficient
strength and light to pass over these hours of anguish.

The Church of Rome is evidently the most skilful human machine
the world has ever seen. Those who guide her in the dark paths
which she follows are often men of deep thought. They understand
how difficult it would be to get calm, honest and thinking minds
to receive that monstrous dogma of the real corporal presence of Jesus
Christ in the communion. They well foresaw the struggle which

would take place even in the minds of children at the supreme
moment when they would have to sacrifice their reason on the altar
of Rome. In order to prevent those struggles, always so dangerous
to the Church, nothing has been neglected to distract the mind and
draw the attention to other subjects than that of the communion
itself.

First, at the request of the parish priest, helped by the vanity of the
parents themselves, the children are dressed as elegantly as possible.
The young communicant is clothed in every way best calculated to
flatter his own vanity also. The church building is pompously
decorated. The charms of choice vocal and instrumental music form a
part of the fête. The most odorous incense burns around the altar and
ascends in a sweet-smelling cloud towards heaven. The whole parish
is invited, and people come from every direction to enjoy a most
beautiful spectacle. Priests from the neighbouring churches are
called, in order to add to the solemnity of the day. The officiating
priest is dressed in the most costly attire. This is the day on which
silver and gold altar-cloths are displayed before the eyes of the
wondering spectators. Often a lighted wax taper is placed in the
hand of each young communicant, which itself would be sufficient
to draw his whole attention ; for a single false motion would be
sufficient to set fire to the clothes of his neighbour, or his own, a
misfortune which has happened more than once in my presence.

Now, in the midst of that new and wonderful spectacle—of singing
Latin Psalms, not a word of which he understands ; in view of gold
and silver ornaments, which glitter everywhere before his dazzled
eyes ; busy with the holding of the lighted taper, which keeps him
constantly in fear of being burned alive—can the young communicant
think for a moment of what he is about to do ?

Poor child ! his mind, ears, eyes, nostrils are so much taken up
with those new, striking and wonderful things that, while his
imagination is wandering from one object to another, the moment of
communion arrives, without leaving him time to think of what he is
about to do ! He opens his mouth, and the priest puts upon his
tongue a flat thin cake of unleavened bread, which either firmly sticks
to his palate or otherwise melts in his mouth, soon to go down into his
stomach just like the food he takes three times a day !

The first feeling of the child, then, is that of surprise at the
thought that the Creator of heaven and earth, the upholder of the
universe, the Saviour of the world, could so easily pass down his
throat !

Now, follow those children to their homes after that great and
monstrous comedy. See their gait ! Listen to their conversation
and their bursts of laughter ! Study their manners, their coming in,

their going out, their glances of satisfaction on their fine clothes, and the vanity which they manifest in return for the congratulations they receive on their fine dresses. Notice the lightness of their actions and conversation immediately after their communion, and tell me if you find anything indicating that they believed in the terrible dogma they have been taught.

No, they have not believed in it, neither will they ever do so with the firmness of faith which is accompanied by intelligence. The poor child thinks he believes, and he sincerely tries to do so. He believes in it as much as it is possible to believe in a most monstrous and ridiculous story, opposed to the simplest notions of truth and common sense. He believes as Roman Catholics believe. He believes as an idiot believes ! !

That first communion has made of him, for the rest of his life, a real machine in the hands of the Pope. It is the first but most powerful link of that long chain of slavery which the priest and the Church pass around his neck. The Pope holds the end of that chain, and with it he will make his victim go right or left at his pleasure, in the same way that we govern the lower animals. If those children have made a good first communion they will be submissive to the Pope, according to the energetic word of Loyola. They will be in the hands of the Supreme Pontiff of Rome just what the stick is in the hands of the traveller—they will have no will, no thought of their own !

And if God does not work a miracle to bring them out from that bondage which is a thousand times worse than the Egyptian, they will remain in that state during the rest of their lives.

My soul has known the weight of those chains. It has felt the ignominy of that slavery ! But the great Conqueror of souls has cast down a merciful eye upon me. He has broken my chains, and with His holy Word He has made me free.

May His name be for ever blessed

CHAPTER IX.

I FINISHED, at the College of Nicolet, in the month of August, 1829, my classical course of study which I had begun in 1822. I could easily have learned in three or four years what was taught in these seven years.

It took us three years to study the Latin grammar, when twelve months would have sufficed for all we learned of it. It is true that during that time we were taught some of the rudiments of the French grammar, with the elements of arithmetic and geography. But all this was so superficial, that our teachers often seemed more desirous to pass away our time than to enlarge our understandings.

I can say the same thing of the *Belles Lettres* and of rhetoric, which we studied two years. A year of earnest study would have sufficed to learn what was taught us during these twenty-four months. As for the two years devoted to the study of logic, and of the subjects classed under the name of philosophy, it would not have been too long a time if those questions of philosophy had been honestly given us. But the student in the college of the Church of Rome is condemned to the torments of Tantalus. He has, indeed, the refreshing waters of Science put to his lips, but he is constantly prevented from tasting them. To enlarge and seriously cultivate the intelligence in a Roman Catholic college is a thing absolutely out of the question. More than that, all the efforts of the principals in their colleges and convents tend to prove to the pupil that his intelligence is his greatest and most dangerous enemy—that it is like an untamable animal, which must constantly be kept in chains. Every day the scholar is told that his reason was not given him that he might be guided by it, but only that he may know the hand of the man by whom he must be guided. And that hand is none other than the Pope's. All the resources of language, all the most ingenious sophisms, all the passages of both the Fathers and the Holy Scriptures bearing on this question are arranged and perverted with inconceivable art to demonstrate to the pupil that his reason has no power to teach him anything else than that it must be subjected to the Supreme Pontiff of Rome, who is the only foundation of truth and light given by God to guide the intelligence and to enlighten and save the world.

Rome, in her colleges and convents, brings up, or raises up, the youth from their earliest years ; but to what height does she permit the young man or woman to be raised ? Never higher than the feet of the Pope !! As soon as his intelligence, guided by the Jesuit, has ascended to the feet of the Pope, it must remain there, prostrate itself and fall asleep.

The Pope! That is the great object towards which all the intelligence of the Roman Catholics must be converged. It is the sun of the world, the foundation and the only support of Christian knowledge and civilisation.

What a privilege it is to be lazy, stupid, and sluggish in a college of Rome ! How soon such an one gets to the summit of science, and becomes master of all knowledge. One needs only to kiss the feet of the Pope, and fall into a perfect slumber there ! The Pope thinks for him ! It is he (the Pope) who will tell him what he can and should think, and what he can and should believe!

I had arrived at that degree of perfection at the end of my studies, and J. B. Barthe, Esq., M.P.P., being editor of one of the principal papers of Montreal in 1844, could write in his paper when my "Manual of Temperance" was published: "Mr. Chiniquy has crowned his apostleship of temperance by that work, with that ardent and holy ambition of character of which he gave us so many tokens in his collegiate life, where we have been so many years the witness of his piety, when he was the model of his fellow-students, who had called him the Louis de Gonzague of Nicolet."

These words of the Montreal Member of Parliament mean only that, wishing to be saved as St. Louis de Gonzague, I had blindly tied myself to the feet of my superiors. I had, as much as possible, extinguished all the enlightenments of my own mind to follow the reason and the will of my superiors. These compliments mean that I was walking like a blind man whom his guide holds by the hand.

Though my intelligence often revolted against the fables with which I was nurtured, I yet forced myself to accept them as gospel truths; and though I often rebelled against the ridiculous sophisms which were babbled to me as the only principles of truth and Christian philosophy, yet as often did I impose silence on my reason, and force it to submit to the falsehoods which I was obliged to take for God's truth! But, as I have just confessed it, notwithstanding my goodwill to submit to my superiors, there were times of terrible struggle in my soul, when all the powers of my mind seemed to revolt against the degrading fetters which I was forced to forge for myself.

I shall never forget the day when, in the following terms, I expressed to my Professor of Philosophy, the Rev. Charles Harper, doubts which I had conceived concerning the absolute necessity of the inferior to submit his reason to his superior. "When I shall have completely bound myself to obey my superior, if he abuses his authority over me to deceive me by false doctrines, or if he commands me to do things which I consider wrong and dishonest, shall I not be lost if I obey him?"

He answered: "You will never have to give an account to God for the actions that you do by the order of your legitimate superiors. If they were to deceive you, being themselves deceived, *they alone* would be responsible for the error which you would have committed. Your sin would not be imputed to you as long as you follow the golden rule which is the base of all Christian philosophy and perfection— humility and obedience!"

Little satisfied with that answer, when the lesson was over I expressed my reluctance to accept such principles to several of my fellow-students. Among them was Joseph Turcot, who died some years ago when, I think, he was Minister of Public Works in Canada.

He answered me : " The more I study what they call their principles of Christian philosophy and logic, the more I think that they intend to make *asses of every one of us !* "

On the following day I opened my heart to the venerable man who was our principal—the Rev. Mr. Leprohon. I used to venerate him as a saint and to love him as a father. I frankly told him that I felt very reluctant in submitting myself to the crude principles which seemed to lead us into the most abject slavery, the slavery of our reason and intelligence. I wrote down his answer, which I give here :

" My dear Chiniquy, how did Adam and Eve lose themselves in the Garden of Eden, and how did they bring upon us all the deluge of evils by which we are overwhelmed ? Is it not because they raised their miserable reason above that of God ? They had the promise of eternal life if they had submitted their reason to that of their Supreme Master. They were lost on account of their rebelling against the authority, the reason of God. Thus it is to-day. All the evils, the errors, the crimes by which the world is overflooded come from the same revolt of the human will and reason against the will and reason of God. God reigns yet over a part of the world, the world of the elect, through the Pope, who controls the teachings of our infallible and holy Church. In submitting ourselves to God, who speaks to us through the Pope, we are saved. We walk in the paths of truth and holiness. But we would err, and infallibly perish, as soon as we put our reason above that of our superior, the Pope, speaking to us in person, or through some of our superiors who have received from him the authority to guide us."

" But," said I, " if my reason tells me that the Pope, or some of those other superiors who are put by him over me, are mistaken, and that they command me something wrong, would I not be guilty before God if I obey them ? "

" You suppose a thing utterly impossible," answered Mr. Leprohon, " for the Pope and the bishops who are united to him have the promise of never failing in the faith. They cannot lead you into any errors, nor command you anything against the law of God. But supposing for a moment that they would commit any error, and that they would compel you to believe or do something contrary to the teachings of the Gospel, God would not ask of you any account of an error committed when you are obeying your legitimate superior."

I had to content myself with that answer, which I put down word for word in my note-book. But in spite of my respectful silence, the Rev. Mr. Leprohon saw that I was yet uneasy and sad. In order to convince me of the orthodoxy of his doctrines, he instantly put into my hands the two works of De Maistre,—" Le Pape " and " Les

Soirees de St. Petersburgh,"—where I found the same doctrines supported. My superior was honest in his convictions. He sincerely believed in the sound philosophy and Christianity of his principles, for he had found them in these books approved by the "infallible Popes."

I will mention another occurrence to show the inconceivable intellectual degradation to which we had been dragged at the end of seven years of collegiate studies. About the year 1829 the curate of St. Anne de la Parade wrote to our principal, Rev. Mr. Leprohon, to ask the assistance of the prayers of all the students of the College of Nicolet in order to obtain the discontinuance of the following calamity : " For more than three weeks one of the most respectable farmers was in danger of losing all his horses from the effects of a sorcery ! From morning to night, and during most of the night, repeated blows of whips and sticks were heard falling upon these poor horses, which were trembling, foaming and struggling ! We can see nothing ! The hand of the wizard remains invisible. Pray for us, that we may discover the monster, and that he may be punished as he deserves."

Such were the contents of the priest's letter ; and as my superior sincerely believed in that fable I also believed it, as well as all the students of the college who had a *true piety*. On that shore of abject and degrading superstitions I had to land after sailing seven years in the bark called a college of the Church of Rome !

The intellectual part of the studies in a college of Rome, and it is the same in a convent, is therefore entirely worthless. Worse than that, the intelligence is dwarfed under the chains by which it is bound. If the intelligence does sometimes advance, it is in spite of the fetters placed upon it ; it is only like some few noble ships which, through the extraordinary skill of their pilots, go ahead against wind and tide.

I know that the priests of Rome can show a certain number of intelligent men in every branch of science who have studied in their colleges. But these remarkable men had from the beginning secretly broken for themselves the chains with which their superiors had tried to bind them. For peace' sake they had outwardly followed the rules of the house, but they had secretly trampled under the feet of their noble souls the ignoble fetters which had been prepared for their understanding. True children of God and light, they had found the secret of remaining free even when in the dark cells of a dungeon !

Give me the names of the remarkable and intelligent men who have studied in a college of Rome, and have become real lights in the firmament of science, and I will prove that nine-tenths of them have been persecuted, excommunicated, tortured, some even put to death for having dared to think for themselves.

Galileo was a Roman Catholic, and he is surely one of the greatest men whom science claims as her most gifted sons. But was he not sent to a dungeon ? Was he not publicly flogged by the hands of the executioner ? Had he not to ask pardon from God and man for having dared to think differently from the Pope about the motion of the earth around the sun !

Copernicus was surely one of the greatest lights of his time, but was he not censured and excommunicated for his admirable scientific discoveries ?

France does not know any greater genius among her most gifted sons than Pascal. He was a Catholic. But he lived and died excommunicated.

The Church of Rome boasts of Bossuet, the Bishop of Meaux, as one of the greatest men she ever had. Yes; but has not Veuillot, the editor of the *Univers*, who knows his man well, confessed and declared before the whole world that Bossuet was a disguised Protestant ?

Where can we find a more amiable or learned writer than Montalembert, who has so faithfully and bravely fought the battle of the Church of Rome in France during more than a quarter of a century ? But has he not publicly declared on his death-bed that that Church was an apostate and idolatrous Church from the day that she proclaimed the dogma of the Infallibility of the Pope ? Has he not virtually died an excommunicated man for having said with his last breath that the Pope was nothing else than a false god ?

Those pupils of Roman Catholic colleges of whom sometimes the priests so imprudently boast, have gone out from the hands of their Jesuit teachers to proclaim their supreme contempt for the Roman Catholic priesthood and Papacy. They have been near enough to the priest to know him. They have seen with their own eyes that the priest of Rome is the most dangerous, the most implacable enemy or intelligence, progress and liberty; and if their arm be not paralyzed by cowardice, selfishness, or hypocrisy, those pupils of the colleges of Rome will be the first to denounce the priesthood of Rome and demolish her citadels.

Voltaire studied in a Roman Catholic college, and it was probably when at their school he nerved himself for the terrible battle he has fought against Rome. That Church will never recover from the blow which Voltaire has struck at her in France.

Cavour, in Italy, had studied in a Roman Catholic college also, and under that very roof it is more than probable that his noble intelligence had sworn to break the ignominious fetters with which

Rome had enslaved his fair country. The most eloquent of the orators of Spain, Castelar, studied in a Roman Catholic college; but hear with what eloquence he denounces the tyranny, hypocrisy, selfishness and ignorance of the priests.

Papineau studied under the priests of Rome in their college at Montreal. From his earliest years that Eagle of Canada could see and know the priests of Rome as they are; he has weighed them in the balance; he has measured them; he has fathomed the dark recesses of their anti-social principles; he has felt his shoulders wounded and bleeding under the ignominious chains with which they dragged our dear Canada in the mire for nearly two centuries. Papineau was a pupil of the priests; and I have heard several priests boasting of that as a glorious thing. But the echoes of Canada are still repeating the thundering words with which Papineau denounced the priests as the most deadly enemies of the education and liberty of Canada! He was one of the first men of Canada to understand that there was no progress, no liberty possible for our beloved country so long as the priests would have the education of our people in their hands. The whole life of Papineau was a struggle to wrest Canada from their grasp. Everyone knows how he constantly branded them, without pity, during his life, and the whole world has been the witness of the supreme contempt with which he has refused their services, and turned them out at the solemn hour of his death!

When, in 1792, France wanted to be free, she understood that the priests of Rome were the greatest enemies of her liberties. She turned them out from her soil or hung them to her gibbets. If to-day that noble country of our ancestors is stumbling and struggling in her tears and her blood—if she has fallen at the feet of her enemies—if her valiant arm has been paralyzed, her sword broken, and her strong heart saddened above measure, is it not because she had most imprudently put herself again under the yoke of Rome?

Canada's children will continue to flee from the country of their birth so long as the priest of Rome holds the influence which is blasting everything that falls within his grasp, on this continent as well as in Europe; and the United States will soon see their most sacred institutions fall, one after the other, if the Americans continue to send their sons and daughters to the Jesuit colleges and nunneries.

When, in the warmest days of summer, you see a large swamp of stagnant and putrid water, you are sure that deadly miasma will spread around, that diseases of the most malignant character, poverty, sufferings of every kind, and death will soon devastate the unfortunate country; so, when you see Roman Catholic colleges and

nunneries raising their haughty steeples over some commanding hills
or in the midst of some beautiful valleys, you may confidently expect
that the self-respect and the manly virtues of the people will soon
disappear—intelligence, progress, prosperity will soon wane away, to
be replaced by superstition, idleness, drunkenness, Sabbath-breaking,
ignorance, poverty and degradation of every kind. The colleges and nunneries are the high citadels from which the Pope darts his surest missiles
against the rights and liberties of nations. The colleges and nunneries
are the arsenals where the most deadly weapons are night and day
prepared to fight and destroy the soldiers of liberty all over the world.

The colleges and nunneries of the priests are the secret places
where the enemies of progress, equality and liberty are holding their
councils and fomenting that great conspiracy the object of which is
to enslave the world at the feet of the Pope.

The colleges and nunneries of Rome are the schools where the
rising generations are taught that it is an impiety to follow the
dictates of their own conscience, hear the voice of their intelligence,
read the Word of God, and worship their Creator according to the
rules laid down in the Gospel.

It is in the colleges and nunneries of Rome that men learn that
they are created to obey the Pope in everything—that the Bible must
be burnt, and that liberty must be destroyed at any cost all over the
world.

CHAPTER X.

In order to understand what kind of moral education students in
Roman Catholic colleges receive, one must only be told that from the
beginning to the end they are surrounded by an atmosphere in which
nothing but Paganism is breathed. The models of eloquence which
we learned by heart were almost exclusively taken from Pagan
literature. In the same manner Pagan models of wisdom, of honour,
of chastity were offered to our admiration. Our minds were constantly fixed on the masterpieces which Paganism has left. The doors of
our understanding were left open only to receive the rays of light which
Paganism has shed on the world. Homer, Socrates, Lycurgus, Virgil,
Horace, Cicero, Tacitus, Cæsar, Xenophon, Demosthenes, Alexander,
Lucretia, Regulus, Brutus, Jupiter, Venus, Minerva, Mars, Diana,
etc., etc., crowded each other in our thoughts, to occupy them and be
their models, examples and masters for ever.

It may be said that the same Pagan writers, orators and heroes are
studied, read and admired in Protestant colleges. But there the
infallible antidote, the Bible, is given to the students. Just as nothing
remains of the darkness of night after the splendid morning sun has

arisen on the horizon, so nothing of the fallacies, superstitions and sophisms of Paganism can trouble or obscure the mind on which that light from heaven, the Word of God, comes every day with its millions of shining rays. How insignificant is the Poetry of Homer when compared with the sublime songs of Moses! How pale is the eloquence of Demosthenes, Cicero, Virgil, etc., when read after Job, David or Solomon! How quickly crumble down the theories which those haughty heathens of old wanted to raise over the intelligence of men when the thundering voice from Sinai is heard; when the incomparable songs of David, Solomon, Isaiah or Jeremiah are ravishing the soul which is listening to their celestial strains! It is a fact that Pagan eloquence and philosophy can be but very tasteless to men accustomed to be fed with the bread which comes down from heaven, whose souls are filled with the eloquence of God, and whose intelligence is fed with the philosophy of heaven.

But, alas! for me and my fellow-students in the college of Rome! No sun ever appeared on the horizon to dispel the night in which our intelligence was wrapped. The dark clouds with which Paganism had surrounded us were suffocating us, and no breath from heaven was allowed to come and dispel them. Moses with his incomparable legislation, David and Solomon with their divine poems, Job with his celestial philosophy, Jeremiah, Isaiah and Daniel with their sublime songs, Jesus Christ Himself with His soul-saving Gospel, as well as His apostles Peter, John, Jude, James and Paul—these were all put in the Index! They had not the liberty to speak to us, and we were forbidden, absolutely forbidden, to read and hear them!

It is true that the Church of Rome, as an offset to that, gave us her principles, precepts, fables and legends that we might be attached to her, and that she might remain the mistress of our hearts. But these doctrines, practices, principles and fables seemed to us so evidently borrowed from Paganism—they were so cold, so naked, so stripped of all true poetry, that if the Paganism of the ancients was not left absolute master of our affections, it still claimed a large part of our souls. To create in us a love for the Church of Rome our superiors depended greatly on the works of Chateaubriand. The "Genie du Christianisme" was the book of books to dispel all our doubts, and attach us to the Pope's religion. But this author, whose style is sometimes really beautiful, destroyed, by the weakness of his logic, the Christianity which he wanted to build up. We could easily see that Chateaubriand was not sincere, and his exaggerations were to many of us a sure indication that he did not believe in what he said. The works of De Maistre, the most important history-falsificator of France, were also put into our hands as a sure guide in philosophical and historical studies. The "Memoirs du Conte Valmont," with some authors of

4

the same stamp, were much relied upon by our superiors to prove to us that the dogmas, precepts and practices of the Roman Catholic religion were brought from heaven.

It was certainly our desire as well as our interest to believe them. But how our faith was shaken, and how we felt troubled when Livy, Tacitus, Cicero, Virgil, Homer, etc., gave us the evidence that the greater part of these things had their root and their origin in Paganism.

For instance, our superiors had convinced us that scapulars, medals, holy water, etc., would be of great service to us in battling with the most dangerous temptations, as well as in avoiding the most common dangers of life. Consequently, we all had scapulars and medals, which we kept with the greatest respect, and even kissed morning and evening with affection, as if they were powerful instruments of the mercy of God to us. How great, then, was our confusion and disappointment when we discovered in the Greek and Latin historians that those scapulars and medals and statuettes were nothing but a remnant of Paganism, and that the worshippers of Jupiter, Minerva, Diana and Venus believed themselves also free, as we did, from all calamity when they carried them in honour of these divinities! The further we advanced in the study of Pagan antiquity, the more we were forced to believe that our religion, instead of being born at the foot of Calvary, was only a pale and awkward imitation of Paganism. The modern Pontifex Maximus (the Pope of Rome), who, as we were assured, was the successor of St. Peter, the Vicar of Jesus Christ, resembled the "Pontifex Maximus" of the great republic and empire of Rome as much as two drops of water resemble each other. Had not our Pope preserved not only the name, but also the attributes, the pageantry, the pride, and even the garb of that high pagan priest? Was not the worship of the saints absolutely the same as the worship of the demigods of olden time? Was not our purgatory minutely described by Virgil? Were not our prayers to the Virgin and to the saints repeated, almost in the same words, by the worshippers who prostrated themselves before the images of their gods, just as we repeated them every day before the images which adorned our churches? Was not our holy water in use among the idolaters, and for the same purpose for which it was used among us?

We knew by history the year in which the magnificent temple consecrated *to all the gods,* bearing the name of Pantheon, had been built at Rome. We were acquainted with the names of several of the sculptors who had carved the statues of the gods in that heathen temple, at whose feet the idolaters bowed respectfully, and words cannot express the shame we felt on learning that the Roman Catholics of our day, under the very eyes and with the sanction of the Pope, still prostrated themselves before the SAME IDOLS, in the SAME TEMPLE, aud to obtain the SAME FAVOURS!

When we asked each other the question, " What is the difference between the religion of heathen Rome and that of the Rome of to-day ?" more than one student would answer : " The only difference is in the name. The idolatrous temples are the same : the idols have not left their places. To-day, as formerly, the same incense burns in their honour ? Nations are still prostrated at their feet to give them the same homage and to ask of them the same favours; but instead of calling this statue Jupiter, we call it Peter; and instead of calling that one Minerva or Venus, it is called St. Mary. It is the old idolatry coming to us under Christian names."

I earnestly desired to be an honest and sincere Roman Catholic. These impressions and thoughts distracted me greatly, inasmuch as I could find nothing in reason to diminish their force. Unfortunately many of the books placed in our hands by our superiors to confirm our faith, form our moral character, and sustain our piety and our confidence in the dogmas of the Church of Rome, had a frightful resemblance to the histories I had read of the gods and goddesses. The miracles attributed to the Virgin Mary often appeared to be only a reproduction of the tricks and deceits by which the priests of Jupiter, Venus, Minerva, etc., used to obtain their ends and grant the requests of their worshippers. Some of those miracles of the Virgin Mary equalled, if they did not surpass, in absurdity and immorality what mythology taught us among the most hideous accounts of the heathen gods and goddesses.

I could cite hundreds of such miracles which shocked my faith and caused me to blush in secret at the conclusion to which I was forced to come, in comparing the worship of ancient and modern Rome. I will only quote three of these modern miracles, which are found in one of the books the best approved by the Pope, entitled "The Glories of Mary."

First miracle. The great favour bestowed by the Holy Virgin upon a nun named Beatrix, of the Convent of Frontebraldo, show how merciful she is to sinners. This fact is related by Cesanus, and by Father Rho. This unfortunate nun, having been possessed by a criminal passion for a young man, determined to leave her convent and elope with him. She was the doorkeeper of the convent, and having placed the keys of the monastery at the feet of a statue of the Holy Virgin she boldly went out, and then led a life of prostitution during fifteen years in a far off place.

" One day, accidentally meeting the purveyor of her convent, and thinking she would not be recognized by him, she asked him news of Sister Beatrix.

" ' I know her well,' answered this man; ' she is a holy nun, and is mistress of the novices.'

" At these words Beatrix was confused; but to understand what it meant she changed her clothing, and going to the convent, enquired after Sister Beatrix.

" The Holy Virgin instantly appeared to her in the form of the statue at whose feet she had placed the keys at her departure. The Divine Mother spoke to her in this wise : ' Know, Beatrix, that in order to preserve your honour I have taken your place and done your duty since you have left your convent. My daughter, return to God and be penitent, for my Son is still waiting for you. Try, by the holiness of your life, to preserve the good reputation which I have earned you.' Having thus spoken, the Holy Virgin disappeared. Beatrix re-entered the monastery, donned her religious dress, and, grateful for the mercies of Mary, she led the life of a saint." (" Glories of Mary," chap. vi., sec. 2.)

Second miracle. Rev. Father Rierenberg relates that there existed in a city called Aragona a beautiful and noble girl by the name of Alexandra, whom two young men loved passionately. One day, maddened by the jealousy each one had of the other, they fought together, and both were killed. Their parents were so infuriated at the young girl, the author of these calamities, that they killed her, cut her head off, and threw her into a well. A few days after St. Dominic, passing by the place, was inspired to approach the well and to cry out, "Alexandra, come here!" The head of the deceased immediately placed itself upon the edge of the well, and entreated St. Dominic to hear its confession. Having heard it, the Saint gave her the communion in the presence of a great multitude of people, and then he commanded her to tell them why she had received so great a favour.

She answered that, though she was in a state of mortal sin when she was decapitated, yet as she had a habit of reciting the holy rosary, the Virgin had preserved her life.

The head, full of life, remained on the edge of the well two days before the eyes of a great many people, and then the soul went to purgatory. But fifteen days after this the soul of Alexandra appeared to St. Dominic, bright and beautiful as a star, and told him that one of the surest means of removing souls from purgatory was the recitation of the rosary in their favour. (" Glories of Mary," chap. viii., sec. 2.)

Third miracle. " A servant of Mary one day went into one of her churches to pray, without telling her husband of it. Owing to a terrible storm she was prevented from returning home that night. Harassed by the fear that her husband would be angry, she implored Mary's help. But on returning home she found her husband full of kindness. After asking her husband a few questions on the subject she discovered that during that very night the Divine Mother had taken her form and features and had taken her place in all the affairs of the household! She informed her husband of the great miracle, and they both became very much devoted to the Holy Virgin." ("Glories of Mary," Examples of Protection, 40.)

Persons who have never studied in a Roman Catholic college will hardly believe that such fables were told us as an appeal for us to become Christians. But, God knows, I tell the truth. Is it not a profanation of a holy word to say that Christianity is the religion taught the students in Rome's colleges?

After reading the monstrous metamorphoses of the gods of Olympus, the student feels a profound pity for the nations who have lived so long in the darkness of Paganism. He cannot understand how so many millions of men were, for such a long time, deceived by such crude fables. With joy his thoughts are turned to the God of Calvary, there to receive light and life. He feels, as it were, a burning desire to nourish himself with the words of life, fallen from the lips of the "great victim." But here comes the priest of the college, who places himself between the student and Christ, and instead of allowing him to be nourished with the Bread of Life he offers him fables, husks with which to appease his hunger. Instead of allowing him to slake his thirst from the waters which flow from the fountains of eternal life, he offers him a corrupt beverage!

God alone knows what I have suffered during my studies to find myself absolutely deprived of the privilege of eating this bread of life —His Holy Word!

During the last years of my studies my superiors often confided to me the charge of the library. Once it happened that, as the students were taking a holiday, I remained alone in the college, and shutting myself up in the library I began to examine all the books. I was not a little surprised to discover that the books which were the most proper to instruct us stood on the catalogue of the library marked among the forbidden books. I felt an inexpressible shame on seeing with my own eyes that none but the most indifferent books were placed in our hands—that we were permitted to read authors of the third rank only (if this expression is suitable to such whose only merit consisted in flattering the Popes, and in concealing or excusing their crimes). Several students more advanced than myself, had already made the observation to me, but I did not believe them. Self-love gave me the hope that I was as well educated as one could be at my age. Until then I had spurned the idea that, with the rest of the students, I was the victim of an incredible system of moral and intellectual blindness.

Among the forbidden books of the college I found a splendid

Bible, It seemed to be of the same edition as the one whose perusal had made the hours pass away so pleasantly when I was at home with my mother. I seized it with the transports of a miser finding a lost treasure. I lifted it to my lips, and kissed it respectfully. I pressed it against my heart, as one embraces a friend from whom he has long been separated. This Bible brought back to my memory the most delightful hours of my life. I read in its divine pages till the scholars returned.

The next day Rev. Mr. Leprohon, our director, called me to his room during the recreation, and said : " You seem to be troubled, and very sad to-day. I noticed that you remained alone while the other scholars were enjoying themselves so well. Have you any cause of grief ? or are you sick ?"

I could not sufficiently express my love and respect for this venerable man. He was at the same time my friend and benefactor. For four years he and Rev. Mr. Brassard had been paying my board ; for, owing to a misunderstanding between myself and my uncle Dionne, he had ceased to maintain me at college, By reading the Bible the previous day I had disobeyed my benefactor, Mr. Leprohon ; for when he entrusted me with the care of the library he made me promise not to read the books in the forbidden catalogue.

It was painful to me to sadden him by acknowledging that I had broken my word of honour, but it pained me far more to deceive him by concealing the truth. I therefore answered him : " You are right in supposing that I am uneasy and sad. I confess there is one thing which perplexes me greatly among the rules that govern us. I never dared to speak to you about it : but as you wish to know the cause of my sadness, I will tell you. You have placed in our hands, not only to read, but to learn by heart, books which are, as you know, partly inspired by hell, and you forbid us to read the only book whose every word is sent from heaven ! You permit us to read books dictated by the spirit of darkness and sin, and you make it a crime for us to read the only book written under the dictation of the Spirit of light and holiness. This conduct on your part, and on the part of all the superiors of the college, disturbs and scandalizes me ! Shall I tell you, your dread of the Bible shakes my faith, and causes me to fear that we are going astray in our Church."

Mr. Leprohon answered me : " I have been the director of this college for more than twenty years, and I have never heard from the lips of any of the students such remarks and complaints as you are making to me to-day. Have you no fear of being the victim of a deception of the devil, in meddling with a question so strange and so new for a scholar whose only aim should be to obey his superiors ?"

" It may be " said I, " that I am the first to speak to you in this manner, for it is very probable that I am the only student in this college who has read the Holy Bible in his youthful days. I have already told you there was a Bible in my father's house, which disappeared only after his death, though I never could know what became of it. I can assure you that the perusal of that admirable book has done me a good that is still felt. It is, therefore, because I know by a personal experience that there is no book in the world so good, and so proper to read, that I am extremely grieved, and even scandalised, by the dread you have of it. I acknowledge to you I spent the afternoon of yesterday in the library reading the Bible. I found things in it which made me weep for joy and happiness—things that did more good to my soul and heart than all you have given me to read for six years. And I am so sad to-day because you approve of me when I read the words of the devil, and condemn me when I read the Word of God."

My superior answered : " Since you have read the Bible, you must know that there are things in it on matters of such a delicate nature that it is improper for a young man, and more so for a young lady, to read them."

" I understand," answered I ; " but these delicate matters, of which you do not want God to speak a word to us, you know very well that Satan speaks to us about them day and night. Now, when Satan speaks about and attracts our thoughts towards an evil and criminal thing, it is always in order that we may like it and be lost. But when the God of purity speaks to us of evil things (of which it is pretty much impossible for men to be ignorant), He does it that we may hate and abhor them, and He gives us grace to avoid them. Well, then, since you cannot prevent the devil from whispering to us things so delicate and dangerous to seduce us, how dare you hinder God from speaking of the same things to shield us from their allurements ? Besides, when my God desires to speak to me Himself on any question whatever, where is your right to obstruct His word on its way to my heart ? "

Though Mr. Leprohon's intelligence was as much wrapped up in the darkness of the Church of Rome as it could be, his heart had remained honest and true ; and while I respected and loved him as my father, though differing from him in opinion, I knew he loved me as if I had been his own child. He was thunderstruck by my answer. He turned pale, and I saw tears about to flow from his eyes. He sighed deeply, and looked at me some time reflectingly, without answering. At last he said : " My dear Chiniquy, your answer and your arguments have a force that frightens me, and if I had no other but my own personal ideas to disprove them, I acknowledge I do not know how I would do it. But I have something better than my own weak thoughts. I have the thoughts of the Church, and of our Holy father the Pope. *They forbid us to put the Bible in the hands of our students.* This should suffice to put an end to your troubles. To obey his legitimate superiors in all things and everywhere is the rule a Christian scholar like you should follow; and if you have broken it yesterday, I hope it will be the last time that the child whom I love better than myself will cause me such pain."

On saying this he threw his arms around me, clasped me to his heart, and bathed my face with tears. I wept also. Yes, I wept abundantly.

But God knoweth, that though the regret of having grieved my benefactor and father caused me to shed tears at that moment, yet I wept much more on perceiving that I would no more be permitted to read His Holy Word.

If, therefore, I am asked what moral and religious education we received at college, I will ask in return, What religious education can we receive in an institution where seven years are spent without once being permitted to read the Gospel of God? The gods of the heathen spoke to us daily by their apostles and disciples—Homer, Virgil, Pindar, Horace! and the God of the Christians had not permission to say a single word to us in that college!

Our religion, therefore, could be nothing but Paganism disguised under a Christian name. Christianity in a college or convent of Rome is such a strange mixture of heathenism and superstition, both ridiculous and childish, and of shocking fables, that the majority of those who have not entirely smothered the voice of reason cannot accept it. A few do, as I did, all in their power, and succeed to a certain extent, in believing only what the superior tell them to believe. They close their eyes and permit themselves to be led exactly as if they were blind, and a friendly hand were offering to guide them. But the greater number of students in Roman Catholic colleges cannot accept the bastard Christianity which Rome presents to them. Of course, during the studies they follow its rules, for the sake of peace; but they have hardly left college before they proceed to join and increase the ranks of the army of sceptics and infidels which overruns France, Spain, Italy and Canada—which overruns, in fact, all the countries where Rome has the education of the people in her hands.

I must say, though with a sad heart, that moral and religious education in Roman Catholic colleges is worse than void, for from them has been excluded the only true standard of morals and religion, —THE WORD OF GOD!

CHAPTER XI.

WE read in the history of Paganism that parents were often, in those dark ages, slaying their children upon the altars of their gods, to appease their wrath or obtain their favours. But we now see a stranger thing. It is that of Christian parents forcing their children into the temples and to the very feet of the idols of Rome, under the fallacious notion of having them educated ! While the Pagan parent destroyed only the temporal life of his child, the Christian parent, for the most part, destroys his eternal life. The Pagan was consistent : he believed in the almighty power and holiness of his gods ; he sincerely THOUGHT that they ruled the world, and that they blessed both the victims and those who offered them. But where is the consistency of the Protestant who drags his child and offers him as a sacrifice on the altars of the Pope ! Does he believe in his holiness or in his supreme and infallible power of governing the intelligence ? Then why does he not go and throw himself at his feet and increase the number of his disciples ? The Protestants who are guilty of this great wrong are wont to say, as an excuse, that the superiors of colleges and convents have assured them that their religious convictions would be respected, and that nothing should be said or done to take away or even shake the religion of their children.

Our first parents were not more cruelly deceived by the seductive words of the serpent than the Protestants are this day by the deceitful promises of the priests and nuns of Rome.

I had been myself the witness of the promise given by our superior to a judge of the State of New York, when, a few days later that same superior, the Rev. Mr. Leprohon, said to me : " You know some English, and this young man knows French enough to enable you to understand each other. Try to become his friend and to bring him over to our holy religion. His father is a most influential man in the United States, and that, his only son, is the heir of an immense fortune. Great results for the future of the Church in the neighbouring republic might follow his conversion."

I replied : " Have you forgotten the promise you have made to his father, never to say or do anything to shake or take away the religion of that young man ?"

My superior smiled at my simplicity, and said : " When you shall have studied theology you will know that Protestantism is not a religion, but that it is the negation of religion. Protesting cannot be the basis of any doctrine. Thus, when I promised Judge Pike that the religious convictions of his child should be respected, and that I would not do anything to change his faith, I promised the easiest thing in the world, since I promised not to meddle with a thing *which has no existence.*"

Convinced, or rather blinded by the reasoning of my superior, which is the reasoning of every superior of a college or nunnery, I set myself to work from that moment to make a good Roman Catholic of that young friend; and I would probably have succeeded had not a serious illness forced him, a few months after, to go home, where he died.

Protestants who may read these lines will, perhaps, be indignant against the deceit and knavery of the superior of the college of Nicolet. But I will say to those Protestants, It is not on that man, but on yourselves, that you must pour your contempt. The Rev. Mr. Leprohon was honest. He acted conformably to principles which he thought good and legitimate, and for which he would have cheerfully given the last drop of his blood. He sincerely believed that your Protestantism is a mere negation of all religion, worthy of the contempt of every true Christian. It was not the priest of Rome who was contemptible, dishonest and a traitor to his principles, but it was the Protestant who was false to his Gospel and to his own conscience by having his child educated by the servants of the Pope. Moreover, can we not truthfully say that the Protestant who wishes to have his children bred and educated by a Jesuit or a nun *is a man of no religion?* and that nothing is more ridiculous than to hear such a man begging respect for his *religious principles!* A man's ardent desire to have his religious convictions respected is best known by his respecting them himself.

The Protestant who drags his children to the feet of the priests of Rome is either a disguised infidel or a hypocrite. It is simply ridiculous for such a man to speak of his religious convictions or beg respect for them. His very humble position at the feet of a Jesuit or a nun, begging respect for his faith, is a sure testimony that he has none to lose. If he had any he would not be there, an humble and abject suppliant. He would take care to be where there could be no danger to his dear child's immortal soul.

When I was in the Church of Rome, we often spoke of the necessity of making superhuman efforts to attract young Protestants into our colleges and nunneries, as the shortest and only means of ruling the world before long. And as the mother has in her hands, still more than the father, the destinies of the family and of the world, we were determined to sacrifice everything in order to build nunneries all over the land, where the young girls, the future mothers of our country, would be moulded in our hands and educated according to our views.

Nobody can deny that this is supreme wisdom. Who will not

admire the enormous sacrifices made by Romanists in order to surround the nunneries with so many attractions that it is difficult to refuse them preference above all other female scholastic establishments ? One feels so well in the shade of these magnificent trees during the hot days of summer ! It is so pleasant to live near this beautiful sheet of water, or the rapid current of that charming river, or to have constantly before one's eye the sublime spectacle of the sea ! What a sweet perfume the flowers of that parterre diffuse around that pretty and peaceful convent ! And, besides, who can withstand the almost angelic charms of the Lady Superior ! How it does one good to be in the midst of those holy nuns, whose modesty, affable appearance and lovely smile present such a beautiful spectacle, that one would think of being at heaven's gate rather than in a world of desolation and sin !

O foolish man ! Thou art always the same—ever ready to be seduced by glittering appearances—ever ready to suppress the voice of thy conscience at the first view of a seductive object !

One day I had embarked in the boat of a fisherman on the coast of one of those beautiful islands which the hand of God has placed at the mouth of the Gulf of St. Lawrence. In a few minutes the white sail, full-blown by the morning breeze, had carried us nearly a mile from the shore. There we dropped our anchor, and soon our lines, carried by the current, offered the deceitful bait to the fishes. But not one would come. One would have thought that the sprightly inhabitants of these limpid waters had acted in concert to despise us. In vain did we move our lines to and fro to attract the attention of the fishes ; not one would come ! We were tired. We lamented the prospect of losing our time, and of being laughed at by our friends on the shore who were waiting the result of our fishing to dine. Nearly one hour was spent in this manner, when the captain said, "Indeed, I will make the fishes come."

Opening a box, he took out handfuls of little pieces of finely-cut fishes and threw them broadcast on the water.

I was looking at him with curiosity, and I received with a feeling of unbelief the promise of seeing, in a few moments, more mackerel than I could pick up. These particles of fish, falling upon the water, scattered themselves in a thousand different ways. The rays of the sun, sporting among these numberless fragments, and thousands of scales, gave them a singular whiteness and brilliancy. They appeared like a thousand diamonds, full of movement and life, that sported and rolled themselves, running at each other, while rocking upon the waves.

As these innumerable little objects withdrew from us they looked like the milky way in the firmament. The rays of the sun continued to be reflected upon the scales of the fishes in the water, and to transform them into as many pearls, whose whiteness and splendour made an agreeable contrast with the deep green colour of the sea.

While looking at that spectacle, which was so new to me, I felt my line jerked out of my hands, and soon had the pleasure of seeing a magnificent mackerel lying at my feet. My companions were as fortunate as I was. The bait so generously thrown away had perfectly succeeded in bringing us not only hundreds, but thousands of fishes, and we caught as many of them as the boat could carry.

The Jesuits and the nuns are the Pope's cleverest fishermen, and the Protestants are the mackerel caught upon their baited hooks. Never fisherman knew better to prepare the perfidious bait than the nuns and Jesuits, and never were stupid fishes more easily caught than Protestants in general.

The priests of Rome themselves boast that more than half of the pupils of the nuns are the children of Protestants, and that seven-tenths of those Protestant children, sooner or later, become the firmest disciples and the true pillars of Popery in the United States. It is with that public and undeniable fact before them that the Jesuits have prophesied that before twenty-five years the Pope will rule that great republic; and if there is not a prompt change their prophecy will probably be accomplished.

"But," say many Protestants, "where can we get safer securities that the morals of our girls will be sheltered than in those convents? The faces of those good nuns, their angelic smiles, even their lips, from which seems to flow a perfume from heaven—are not these the unfailing signs that nothing will taint the hearts of our dear children when they are under the care of those holy nuns?"

Angelic smiles! Lips from which flow a perfume from heaven! Expressions of peace and holiness of the good nuns! Delusive allurements! Cruel deceptions! Mockery of comedy! Yes, *all* these angelic smiles, all these expressions of joy and happiness, are but allurements to deceive honest but too trusting men!

I believed myself for a long time that there was something true in all the display of peace and happiness which I saw reflected in the faces of a good number of nuns. But how soon my delusions passed away when I read with my own eyes, in a book of the *secret rules* of the convent, that one of their rules is *always*, especially in the presence of strangers, to have an appearance of joy and happiness, even when the soul is overwhelmed with grief and sorrow! The motives given to the nuns, for thus wearing a continual mask, is to secure the esteem and respect of the people, and to win more securely the young ladies to the convent!

All know the sad end of life of one of the most celebrated female comedians of the American Theatre. She had acted her part in the evening with a perfect success. She appeared so handsome, and so happy on the stage ! Her voice was such a perfect harmony; her singing was so merry and lively with mirth ! Two hours later she was a corpse ! She had poisoned herself on leaving the theatre ! For some time her heart was broken with grief which she could not bear.

Thus it is with the nun in her cell ! forced to play a sacrilegious comedy to deceive the world and to bring new recruits to the monastery. And the Protestants, the disciples of the Gospel, the children of light, suffer themselves to be deceived by this impious comedy.

The poor nun's heart is often full of sorrow, and her soul is drowned in a sea of desolation ; but she is obliged, under oath, always to appear gay ! Unfortunate victim of the most cruel deception that has ever been invented, that poor daughter of Eve, deprived of all the happiness that heaven has given, tortured night and day by honest aspirations which she is told are unpardonable sins, she has not only to suppress in herself the few buds of happiness which God has left in her soul ; but, what is more cruel, she is forced to appear happy in anguish of shame and of deception.

Ah ! if the Protestants could know, as I do, how much the hearts of those nuns bleed, how much those poor victims of the Pope feel themselves wounded to death, how almost every one of them die at an early age, broken-hearted, instead of speaking of their happiness and holiness, they would weep at their profound misery. Instead of helping Satan to build up and maintain those sad dungeons by giving both their gold and their children, they would let them crumble into dust, and thus check the torrents of silent though bitter tears which those cells hide from our view.

I was travelling in 1851 over the vast prairies of Illinois in search of a spot which would suit us the best for the colony which I was about to found. One day my companions and myself found ourselves so wearied by the heat that we resolved to wait for the cool night in the shade of a few trees around a brook. The night was calm ; there were no clouds in the sky, and the moon was beautiful. Like the sailor upon the sea, we had nothing but our compass to regulate our course on those beautiful and vast prairies. But the pen cannot express the emotions I felt while looking at that beautiful sky and those magnificent deserts opened to our view.

We often came to sloughs which we thought deeper than they really were, and of which we would keep the side for fear of drowning our horses. Many a time did I get down from the carriage and stop to contemplate the wonders which those ponds presented to our view.

All the splendours of the sky seemed brought down in those pure and limpid waters. The moon and the stars seemed to have left their places in the firmament to bathe themselves in those delightful lakelets. All the purest, the most beautiful things of the heavens seemed to come down to hide themselves in those tranquil waters as if in search of more peace and purity.

A few days later I was retracing my steps. It was day-time; and, following the same route, I was longing to get to my charming little lakes. But during the interval the heat had been great, the sun very hot, and my beautiful sheets of water had been dried up. My dear little lakes were nowhere to be seen.

And what did I find instead? Innumerable reptiles, with the most hideous forms and filthy colours! No brilliant stars, no clear moon were there any more to charm my eyes. There was nothing left but thousands of little toads and snakes, at the sight of which I was filled with disgust and horror!

Protestants! when upon life's way you are tempted to admire the smiling lips and unstained faces of the Pope's nuns, please think of those charming lakes which I saw in the prairies of Illinois, and remember the innumerable reptiles and toads that swarm at the bottom of those deceitful waters.

When, by the light of Divine truth, Protestants see behind these perfect mockeries by which the nun conceals with so much care the hideous misery which devours her heart, they will understand the folly of having permitted themselves to be so easily deceived by appearances. Then they will bitterly weep for having sacrificed to that modern Paganism the future welfare of their children, of their families, and of their country!

"But," says one, "the education is so cheap in the nunnery." I answer, "The education in convents, were it twice cheaper than it is now, would still cost twice more than it is worth. It is in this circumstance that we can repeat and apply the old proverb, 'Cheap things are always too highly paid for.'"

In the first place, the intellectual education in the nunnery is completely null. The great object of the Pope and the nuns is to captivate and destroy the intelligence.

The moral education is also of no account; for what kind of morality can a young girl receive from a nun who believes that she can live as she pleases as long as she likes it—that nothing evil can come of her, neither in this life nor in the next, provided only she is devout to the Virgin Mary?

Let Protestants read the "Glories of Mary," by St. Liguori, a book which is in the hands of every nun and every priest, and they will understand what kind of morality is practised and taught inside

the walls of the Church of Rome. Yes; let them read the history of
that lady who was so well represented at home by the Holy Virgin,
that her husband did not perceive that she had been absent, and
they will have some idea of what their children may learn in a
convent.

CHAPTER XII.

THE word EDUCATION is a beautiful word. It comes from the Latin
educare, which means to raise up, to take from the lowest degrees to
the highest spheres of knowledge. The object of education is, then, to
feed, expand, raise, enlighten, and strengthen the intelligence.

We hear the Roman Catholic priests making use of that beautiful
word education as often, if not oftener, than the Protestant. But that
word "education" has a very different meaning among the followers
of the Pope than among the disciples of the Gospel. And that
difference, which the Protestants ignore, is the cause of the strange
blunders they make every time they try to legislate on that question
here, as well as in England or in Canada.

The meaning of the word education among Protestants is as far
from the meaning of that same word among Roman Catholics as the
southern pole is from the northern pole. When a Protestant speaks of
education, that word is used and understood in its true sense. When
he sends his little boy to a Protestant school, he honestly desires that
he should be reared up in the spheres of knowledge as much as his
intelligence will allow. When that little boy is going to school, he
soon feels that he has been raised up to some extent, and he expe-
riences a sincere joy, a noble pride, for this new, though at first very
modest raising; but he naturally understands that this new and
modest upheaval is only a stone to step on and raise himself to a
higher degree of knowledge, and he quickly makes that second step
with an unspeakable pleasure. When the son of a Protestant has
acquired a little knowledge, he wants to acquire more. When he has
learned what *this* means, he wants to know what *that* means also.
Like the young eagle, he trims his wings for a higher flight, and turns
his head upward to go farther up in the atmosphere of knowledge. A
noble and mysterious ambition has suddenly seized his young soul.
Then he begins to feel something of that unquenchable thirst for
knowledge which God Himself has put in the breast of every child of
Adam, a thirst of knowledge, however, which will never be perfectly
realised except in heaven.

The object of education, then, is to enable man to fulfil that kingly
mission of ruling, subduing the world, under the eyes of his Creator.

Let us remember that it is not from himself, nor from any angel, but it is from God Himself that man has received that sublime mission. Yes, it is God Himself who has implanted in the bosom of humanity the knowledge and aspirations of those splendid destinies which can be attained only by " Education."

What a glorious impulse is this that seizes hold of the newly-awakened mind, and leads the young intelligence to rise higher and pierce the clouds that hide from his gaze the splendours of knowledge that lay concealed beyond the gloom of this nether sphere! That impulse is a noble ambition; it is that part of humanity that assimilates itself to the likeness of the great Creator; that impulse which education has for its mission to direct in its onward and upward march, is one of the most precious gifts of God to man. Once more, the glorious mission of education is to foster these thirstings after knowledge and lead man to accomplish his high destiny.

It ought to be a duty with both Roman Catholics and Protestants to assist the pupil in his flight toward the regions of science and learning. But is it so? No. When you, Protestants, send your children to school, you put no fetters to their intelligence; they rise with fluttering wings day after day. Though their flight at first is slow and timid, how happy they feel at every new aspect of their intellectual horizon! How their hearts beat with an unspeakable joy when they begin to hear voices of applause and encouragement from every side saying to them, " Higher, higher, higher!" When they shake their young wings to take a still higher flight, who can express their joy when they distinctly hear again the voices of a beloved mother, of a dear father, of a venerable pastor, cheering them and saying, " Well done! Higher yet, my child, higher!"

Raising themselves with more confidence on their wings, they then soar still higher, in the midst of the unanimous concert of the voices of their whole country encouraging them to the highest flight. It is then that the young man feels his intellectual strength tenfold multiplied. He lifts himself on his eagle wings, with a renewed confidence and power, and soars up still higher, with his heart beating with a noble and holy joy. For from the south and north, from the east and the west, the echoes bring to his ears the voices of the admiring multitudes—" Rise higher, higher yet!"

He has now reached what he thought, at first, to be the highest regions of thought and knowledge: but he hears again the same stimulating cries from below, encouraging him to a still higher flight toward the loftiest dominion of knowledge and philosophy, till he enters the regions where lies the source of all truth, and light, and life. For he has also heard the voice of his God speaking through His Son Jesus Christ, crying, " Come unto Me! Fear not! Come ur to

Me! I am the light, the way! Come to this *higher* region where the Father, with the Son and the Spirit, reign in endless light!"

Thus does the Protestant scholar, making use of his intelligence as the eagle of his wing, go on from weakness unto strength, from the timid flutter to the bold confident flight, from one degree to another still higher, from one region of knowledge to another still higher, till he loses himself in that ocean of light and truth and life which is God.

In the Protestant schools no fetters are put on the young eagle's wings; there is nothing to stop him in his progress, or paralyse his movements and upward flights. It is the contrary : he receives every kind of encouragement in his flight.

Thus it is that the only truly *great* nations in the world are Protestants! Thus it is the truly *powerful* nations in the world are Protestants! Thus it is that the *only free* nations in the world are Protestants! The Protestant nations are the only ones that acquit themselves like men in the arena of this world ; Protestant nations only march as giants at the head of the civilized world. Everywhere they are the advanced guard in the ranks of progress, science and liberty, leaving far behind the unfortunate nations whose hands are tied by the ignominious iron chains of Popery.

After we have seen the Protestant scholar raising himself, on his eagle wings, to the highest spheres of intelligence, happiness, and light, and marching unimpeded toward his splendid destinies, let us turn our eyes toward the Roman Catholic student, and let us consider and pity him in the supreme degradation to which he is subjected.

That young Roman Catholic scholar is born with the same bright intelligence as the Protestant one; he is endowed by his Creator with the same powers of mind as his Protestant neighbour; he has the same impulses, the same noble aspirations implanted by the hand of God in his breast. He is sent to school apparently, like the Protestant boy, to receive what is called "Education." He at first understands that word in its true sense; he goes to school in the hope of being *raised*, elevated as high as his intelligence and his personal efforts will allow. His heart beats with joy, when at once the first rays of light and knowledge come to him; he feels a holy, a noble pride at every new step he makes in his upward progress; he longs to learn more, he wants to rise higher; he also takes up his wings, like the young eagle, and soars up higher.

But here begin the disappointments and tribulations of the Roman Catholic student; for he is allowed to raise himself—yes, but when he has raised himself high enough to be on a level with the big toes of the Pope he hears piercing, angry, threatening cries coming from every side—" Stop! stop! Do not raise yourself higher than the toes of the Holy Pope! . . . . Kiss those holy toes, ... and stop

5

your upward flight! Remember that the Pope is the only source of science, knowledge, and truth! . . . . The knowledge of the Pope is the ultimate limit of learning and light to which humanity can attain. . . . . You are not allowed to know and believe what his Holiness does not know and believe. Stop! stop! Do not go an inch higher than the intellectual horizon of the Supreme Pontiff of Rome, in whom only is the plenitude of the true science which will save the world."

Some will perhaps answer me here : "Has not Rome produced great men in every department of science?" I answer, Yes; as I have once done before. Rome can show us a long list of names which shine among the brightest lights of the firmament of science and philosophy. She can show us her Copernices, her Galileos, her Pascals, her Bossuets, her Lamenais, etc., etc. But it is at their risk and peril that those giants of intelligence have raised themselves into the highest regions of philosophy and science. It is in spite of Rome that those eagles have soared up above the damp and obscure horizon where the Pope offers his big toes to be kissed and worshipped as the *ne plus ultra* of human intelligence; and they have invariably been punished for their boldness.

On the 22nd of June, 1663, Galileo was obliged to fall on his knees in order to escape the cruel death to which he was to be condemned by the order of the Pope ; and he signed with his own hand the following retractation : "I abjure, curse, and detest the error and heresy of the motion of the earth," etc., etc.

That learned man had to degrade himself by swearing a most egregious lie, namely, that the earth does not move around the sun. Thus it is that the wings of that giant eagle of Rome were clipped by the scissors of the Pope. That mighty intelligence was bruised, fettered, and, as much as it was possible to the Church of Rome, degraded, silenced, and killed. But God would not allow that such a giant intellect should be entirely strangled by the bloody hands of that implacable enemy of light and truth—the Pope. Sufficient strength and life had remained in Galileo to enable him to say, when rising up, "This will not prevent the earth from moving!"

The infallible decree of the infallible Pope, Urban VIII., against the motion of the earth is signed by the Cardinals Felia, Guido, Desiderio, Antonio, Bellingero, and Fabriccio. It says : "In the name and by the authority of Jesus Christ, the plenitude of which resides in His Vicar, the Pope, that the proposition that the earth is not the centre of the world, and that it moves with a diurnal motion is absurd, philosophically false, and erroneous in faith."

What a glorious thing for the Pope of Rome to be infallible! He infallibly knows that the earth does not move around the sun! And what a blessed thing for the Roman Catholics to be governed and taught by such an *infallible* being.　In consequence of that infallible decree, you will admire the following act of humble submission of two celebrated Jesuit astronomers, Lesueur and Jacquier: "Newton assumes in his third book the hypothesis of the earth moving around the sun.　The proposition of that author could not be explained, except through the same hypothesis: we have, therefore, been forced to act a character not our own.　*But we declare our entire submission to the decrees of the Supreme Pontiffs of Rome against the motion of the earth.*"　(Newton's "Principia," vol. iii., p. 450.)

Here you see two other learned Jesuits, who have written a very able work to prove that the earth moves around the sun; but, trembling at the thunders of the Vatican, which are roaring on their heads and threaten to kill them, they submit to the decrees of the Popes of Rome against the motion of the earth.　These two learned Jesuits tell a most contemptible and ridiculous lie to save themselves from the implacable wrath of that great light-extinguisher whose throne is in the city of the seven hills.

Had the Newtons, the Franklins, the Fultons, the Morses been Romanists, their names would have been lost in the obscurity which is the natural heritage of the abject slaves of the Popes.　Being told from their infancy that no one had any right to make use of his "private judgment," intelligence and conscience in the research of truth, they would have remained mute and motionless at the feet of the modern and terrible god of Rome, the Pope.　But they were Protestants!　In that great and glorious word "Protestant" is the secret of the marvellous discoveries with which they have changed the face of the world.　They were Protestants!　Yes, they had passed their young years in Protestant schools, where they had read a book which told them that they were created in the image of God, and that that great God had sent His eternal Son Jesus to make them free from the bondage of man.　They had read in that Protestant book (for the Bible is the most Protestant book in the world) that man had not only a conscience, but an intelligence to guide him; they had learned that that intelligence and conscience had no other master but God, no other guide but God, no other light but God.　On the walls of their Protestant schools the Son of God had written the marvellous words: "Come unto Me; I am the Light, the Way, the Life."

But when the Protestant nations are marching with such giant strides to the conquest of the world, why is it that the Roman Catholic nations not only remain stationary, but give evidence of a decadence which is, day after day, more and more appalling and remediless?　Go to their schools and give a moment of attention to the principles which are sown in the young intelligences of their unfortunate slaves, and you will have the key to that sad mystery.

What is not only the first, but the daily school lesson taught to the Roman Catholic ? Is it not that one of the greatest crimes which a man can commit is to follow his " private judgment ?" which means that he has eyes, but cannot see ; ears, but he cannot hear ; and intelligence, but he cannot make use of it in the research of truth and light and knowledge, without danger of being eternally damned. His superiors —which mean the priest and the Pope—must see for him, hear for him, and think for him. Yes, the Roman Catholic is constantly told in his school that the most unpardonable and damnable crime is to make use of his own intelligence and follow *his own private judgment* in the research of truth. He is constantly reminded that man's own private judgment is his greatest enemy. Hence all his intellectual and conscientious efforts must be brought to fight down, silence, kill his " private judgment." It is by the judgment of his superiors—the priest, the bishop and the pope—that he must be guided in everything.

Now, what is a man who cannot make use of his " private personal judgment ?" Is he not a slave, an idiot, an ass ? And what is a nation composed of men who do not make use of their private personal judgment in the research of truth and happiness, if not a nation of brutes, slaves and contemptible idiots ?

But as this will look like an exaggeration on my part, allow me to force the Church of Rome to come here and speak for herself. Please pay attention to what she has to say about the intellectual faculties of men. Here are the very words of the so-called Saint Ignatius Loyola, the founder of the Jesuit Society :—

" As for holy obedience, this virtue must be perfect in every point —in execution, in will, in intellect ; doing which is enjoined with all celerity, spiritual joy and perseverance ; persuading ourselves that everything is just, suppressing every repugnant thought and judgment of one's own in a certain obedience; and let every one persuade himself, that he who lives under obedience should be moved and directed, under Divine Providence, by his superior, JUST AS IF HE WERE A CORPSE (*perinde acsi cadaver esset*) which allows itself to be moved and led in every direction."

Some one will, perhaps, ask me what can be the object of the popes and the priests of Rome in degrading the Roman Catholics in such a strange way that they turn them into moral corpses ? What can be the use of those hundreds of millions of corpses ? Why not let them live? The answer is a very easy one. The great, the only object of the thoughts and workings of the Pope and the priests is to raise themselves above the rest of the world. They want to be high !

high! high above the heads not only of the common people, but of the kings and emperors of the world. They want to be not only as high, but higher than God. It is when speaking of the Pope that the Holy Ghost says : " He opposeth and exalteth himself above all that is called God, or that is worshipped ; so that he, as God, sitteth in the temple of God, shewing himself that he is God " (2 Thess. ii. 4). To attain their object, the priests have persuaded their millions and millions of slaves that they were mere corpses ; that they must have no will, no conscience, no intelligence of their own, just " as corpses which allow themselves to be moved and led in any way, without any resistance." When this has been once gained, they have made a pyramid of all those motionless, inert corpses which is so high, that though its feet are on the earth, its top goes to the skies, in the very abode of the old divinities of the Pagan world, and putting themselves and their popes at the top of that marvellous pyramid, the priests say to the rest of the world : " Who among you are as high as we are ? Who has ever been raised by God as a priest and a pope ? Where are the kings and the emperors whose thrones are as elevated as ours ? Are we not at the very top of humanity ?" Yes ! yes ! I answer to the priests of Rome, you are high, very high indeed ! No throne on earth has ever been so sublime, so exalted as yours. Since the days of the tower of Babel, the world has not seen such a huge fabric. Your throne is higher than anything we know. But it is a throne of corpses ! ! !

And if you want to know what other use is made of those millions and millions of corpses, I will tell it to you. There is no manure so rich as dead carcasses. Those millions of corpses serve to manure the gardens of the priests, the bishops and the popes, and make their cabbages grow. And what fine cabbages grow in the Pope's garden !

But that you may better understand the degrading tendencies of the principles which are as the fundamental stone of the moral and intellectual education of Rome, let me put before your eyes another extract of the Jesuit teachings, which I take again from the " Spiritual Exercises," as laid down by their founder, Ignatius Loyola : " That we may in all things attain the truth, that we may not err in anything, we ought ever to hold as a fixed principle that what I see white I believe to be black, if the superior authorities of the Church define it to be so."

You all know that it is the avowed desire of Rome to have public education in the hands of the Jesuits. She says everywhere that they are the best, the model teachers. Why so ? Because they more boldly and more successfully than any other of her teachers aim at the destruction of the intelligence and conscience of their pupils. Rome proclaims everywhere that the Jesuits are the most devoted, the most reliable of her teachers; and she is right, for when a man has been trained a sufficient time by them, he most perfectly becomes a moral corpse. His superiors can do what they please with him. When he knows that a thing is white as snow, he is ready to swear that it is black as ink if his superior tells him so. But some may be tempted to think that these degrading principles are exclusively taught by the Jesuits; that they are not the teachings of the Church, and that I do an injustice to the Roman Catholics when I give, as a general iniquity, what is the guilt of the Jesuits only. Listen to the words of that infallible Pope Gregory XVI., in his celebrated Encyclical of the 15th of August, 1832:—"If the holy Church so requires, let us sacrifice our own opinions, our knowledge, *our intelligence*, the splendid dreams of our imagination, and the most sublime attainments of the human understanding."

It is when considering those anti-social principles of Rome that Mr. Gladstone wrote, not long ago : "No more cunning plot was ever devised against the freedom, the happiness and the virtue of mankind than Romanism." ("Letter to Earl Aberdeen.") Now, Protestants, do you begin to see the difference of the object of education between a Protestant and a Roman Catholic school? Do you begin to understand that there is as great a distance between the word "Education" among you, and the meaning of the same word in the Church of Rome, than between the southern and the northern poles! By education you mean to raise man to the highest sphere of manhood. Rome means to lower him below the most stupid brutes. By education you mean to teach man that he is a free agent, that liberty within the limits of the laws of God and of his country is a gift secured to every one; you want to impress every man with the noble thought that it is better to die a free man than to live a slave. Rome wants to teach that there is only one man who is free, the Pope, and that all the rest are born to be his abject slaves in thought, will and action.

Now, that you may still more understand to what a bottomless abyss of human degradation and moral depravity these anti-Christian and anti-social principles of Rome lead her poor blind slaves, read what Liguori says in his book "The Nun Sanctified": "The principal and most efficacious means of practising obedience due to superiors, and of rendering it meritorious before God, is to consider that in obeying them we obey God Himself, and that by despising their commands we despise the authority of our Divine Master. When, thus, a religious receives a precept from her prelate, superior or confessor, she should immediately execute it, *not only to please them* but principally to please God, whose will is made known to her by their command. In obeying their command, in obeying their directions, she is more certainly obeying the will of God than if an angel came down from heaven to manifest His will to her. Bear this always in your mind, that the obedience which you practise to your superior is paid to God. If, then, you receive a command from one who holds the place of God, you should observe it with the same diligence as if it came from God Himself. Blessed Egidus used to say that it is more meritorious to obey man for the love of God than God Himself. It may be added that there is more certainty of doing the will of God by obedience to our superior than by obedience to Jesus Christ, should He appear in person and give His commands. St. Phillip de Neri used to say that religious shall be most certain of not having to render an account of the actions performed through obedience; for these the superiors only who commanded them shall be held accountable." The Lord said once to St. Catherine of Sienne, " Religious will not be obliged to render an account to *me* of what they do through obedience; for that I will demand an account from the superior. This doctrine is conformable to Sacred Scripture: ' Behold, says the Lord, as clay is in the potter's hand, so are you in My hands, O Israel!' (Jeremiah xviii. 6.) A religious man must be in the hands of the superiors to be moulded as they will. Shall the clay say to Him that fashioneth it, What art Thou making? The Potter ought to answer ' Be silent; it is not your business to inquire what I do, but to obey and to receive whatever form I please to give you.' "

I ask of you, American Protestants, what would become of your fair country if you were blind enough to allow the Church of Rome to teach the children of the United States? What kind of men and women can come out of such schools? What future of shame, degradation, and slavery you prepare for your country if Rome does succeed in forcing you to support such schools? What kind of women would come out from the schools of nuns who would teach them that the highest pitch of perfection in a woman is when she obeys her superior, the priest, *in everything he commands* her! that your daughter will never be called to give an account to God for the actions she will have done to please and obey her superior, the priest, the bishop, or the Pope? That the affairs of her conscience will be arranged between God and that superior, and that she will never be asked why she had done this or that, when it will be to gratify the pleasures of the superior and obey his command that she has done it. Again, what kind of men and citizens will come out from the schools of those Jesuits who believe and teach that a man has attained the perfection of manhood only when he is a perfect spiritual corpse before his superior; when he obeys the priest with the perfection of a *cadaver*, that has neither life nor will in itself.

CHAPTER XIII.

TALLEYRAND, one of the most celebrated Roman Catholic bishops of France, once said, "Language is the art of concealing one's thoughts." Never was there a truer expression, if it had reference to the awful deceptions practised by the Church of Rome under the pompous name of "Theological studies."

Theology is the study of the knowledge of the laws of God. Nothing, then, is more noble than the study of theology. How solemn were my thoughts and elevated my aspirations when, in 1829, under the guidance of the Rev. Messrs. Rimbault and Leprohon, I commenced my theological course of study at Nicolet, which I was to end in 1833!

I supposed that my books of theology were to bring me nearer to my God by the more perfect knowledge I would acquire, in their study, of His holy will and His sacred laws. My hope was that they would be to my heart what the burning coal, brought by the angel of the Lord, was to the lips of the prophet of old.

The principal theologians which we had in our hands were "Les Conferences d'Anger," Bailly, Dens, St. Thomas, but above all Liguori, who has since been canonised. Never did I open one without offering up a fervent prayer to God and to the Virgin Mary for the light and grace of which I would be in need for myself and for the people whose pastor I was to become.

But how shall I relate my surprise when I discovered that, in order to accept the principles of the theologians which my Church gave me for guides I had to put away all principles of truth, of justice, of honour and holiness! What long and painful efforts it cost me to extinguish, one by one, the lights of truth and of reason kindled by the hand of my merciful God in my intelligence. For to study theology in the Church of Rome signifies to learn to speak falsely, to deceive, to commit robbery, to perjure one's self! It means how to commit sins without shame, it means to plunge the soul into every kind of iniquity and turpitude without remorse!

I know that Roman Catholics will bravely and squarely deny what I now say. I am aware also that a great many Protestants, too easily deceived by the fine whitewashing of the exterior walls of Rome, will refuse to believe me. Nevertheless they may rest assured it is true, and my proof will be irrefutable. The truth may be denied by many, but my witnesses cannot be contradicted by any one. My witnesses are even infallible. They are none other than the Roman Catholic theologians themselves, approved by infallible Popes! These very men who corrupted my heart, perverted my intelligence and poisoned my soul, as they have done with each and every priest of their Church, will be my witnesses, my only witnesses. I will just now forcibly bring them before the world to testify against themselves!

Liguori, in his treatise on oaths, Question 4, asks if it is allowable to use ambiguity, or equivocal words, to deceive the judge when under oath, and at No. 151 he answers : " These things being established, it is a certain and a common opinion amongst all divines that for a just cause it is lawful to use equivocation in the propounded modes, and to confirm it (equivocation) with an oath. . . . Now a just cause is any honest end in order to preserve good things for the spirit, or useful things for the body." *

" The accused, or a witness not properly interrogated, can swear that he does not know a crime, which in reality he does know, by understanding that he does not know the crime, concerning which he can be legitimately enquired of, or that he does not know it so as to give evidence concerning it." †

When the crime is very secret and unknown to all, Liguori says the culprit or the witness must deny it under oath. " The same is true, if a witness on another ground is not bound to depose ; for instance, if the crime appear to himself to be free from blame. Or if he knew a crime which he is bound to keep secret, when no scandal may have gone abroad." ‡

" Make an exception in a trial where the crime is altogether concealed. For then he can, yea, the witness is bound to say that the accused did not commit the crime. And the same course the accused can adopt, if the proof be not complete, etc., because then the judge does not legitimately interrogate." §

Liguori asks himself, " Whether the accused legitimately interrogated, can deny a crime, even with an oath, if the confession of the crime would be attended with great disadvantage." The saint replies : —" Elbel, etc., denies that he can, and indeed more probably because the accused is then bound for the general good to undergo the loss.

* " His positis, certum est et commune apud omnes, quod ex justa causa licitum sit uti æquivocatione modis expositis, et eam juramento firmare.' (Mor. Theol. t. ii. cap. ii. de jur p. 316, n. 151. Mech. 1845.)

† " II. Reus, aut testis a judice non legitime interrogatus, potest jurare, se nescire crimen, quod revera scit ; subintelligendo, nescire crimen, de quo legitime possit inquiri, vel nescire ad deponendum." (Mor. Theol, tom ii. n. 153. Mech. 18.)

‡ " Idem, si testis ex alio capite, non teneatur deponere ; nempe si ipsi constet crimen caruisse culpa, ut Salm. tr. 17, c. 2, n. 159, et Elbel, n. 145. Vel si sciat crimen, sed sub secreto, cum nulla praecesserit infamia, ut Card. ibid. n. 151, ibid.

§ " Excipe in judicio, si crimen fuerit omnino occultum ; tunc enim potest, imo tenetur testis dicere reum non commisisse. Tamb. c. 4, § 2, n. 4, cum Card. et Pot. ut sup. Et idem potest reus, si non adest semiplena probatio, etc., Tamb. § 3, n. 2, cum communi ; quia tunc judex non legitime interrogat." (Mor. Theol. t. ii. n. 154, p. 320, ibid.)

But sufficiently probable Lugo, etc., with many others, say, that the accused, if in danger of death, or of prison, or of perpetual exile, the loss of all property, the danger of the galleys, and such like, can deny the crime even with an oath (at least without great sin) by understanding that he did not commit it so that he is bound to confess it,— only let there be a hope of avoiding the punishment." *

" He who hath sworn that he would keep a secret, does not sin against the oath by revealing that secret when he cannot conceal it without great loss to himself, or to another, because the promise of secrecy does not appear to bind, unless under this condition, if it does not injure me."

" He who hath sworn to a judge that he would speak what he knew, is not bound to reveal concealed things. The reason is manifest." †

Liguori asks whether a woman, accused of the crime of adultery, which she has really committed, may deny it under oath? He answers : " She is able to assert equivocally that she did not break the bond of matrimony, which truly remains. And if sacramentally she confessed adultery, she can answer, 'I am innocent of this crime,' because by confession it was taken away. So Card, who, however, here remarks that she cannot affirm it with an oath, because in asserting anything the probability of a deed suffices, but in swearing certainty is required. To this it is replied that in swearing moral certainty suffices, as we said above. Which moral certainty of the remission of sin can indeed be had, when any, morally well disposed, receives the sacrament of penance." ‡

---

* "Negat Elbel, n. 44, cum D. Th. d. art. 1 ad 2, et quidem probabilius, quia reus tenetur tunc pro communi bono damnum illud subire. Sed satis probabiliter Lugo de Just. d. 10, n. 15. Tamb. lib. 3, c. 4, § 3, n. 5, cum Sanch. Viva q. 7, art. 4, n. 2 ; Sporer de præc. c. 1, n. 13, item Elbel dict. num 144, Card. in Propt, Innoc. XI., diss. 19, n. 78, cum Nav. Less, Sa, et Fill, et aliis plurib. dicunt, posse reum, si sibi imminest poena mortis, vel carceris, aut exilii perpetui, amissionis omnium bonorum, triremium, et similis, negare crimen, etiam cum juramento (saltem sine peccato gravi) subintelligendo, se non commisisse, quatenus teneatur illud fateri, modo sit spes vitandi pœnam." (Mor. Theol. t. ii. n. 156, p. 321. Mech. 1845).

† " Qui. juravit se servaturum secretum, non peccat contra juramentum, illud detegendo, quando non potest illud celari absque gravi suo, vel alterius damno, quia ipsa promissio secreti non videtur obligare, nisi hac conditione, si non noceat."
" Qui juravit judici, se dicturum quæ novit, non tenetur revelare occulta. Ratio patet. Less. Bonac. Trull. loc. sit. (Mor. Theol. t. ii. p. 340, ibid.)

‡ " Quaeritur 2, an adultera possit negare adulterium viro, intelligens, ut illi revelet? Potest æquivoce asserere, se non fregisse matrimonium, quod vere persistit. Et si adulterium sacramentaliter confessa sit, potest respondere ' Innocens sum ab hoc crimine,' quia per confessionem est jam oblatum. Ita Card. diss. 19, n. 54, Qui tamen hic advertit, quod nequeat id affirmare cum juramento, quia ad asserendum aliquid sufficit probabilitas facti : sed ad jurandum requiritur certitudo. Sed respondetur, quod adjurandum sufficiat certitudo moralis, ut diximus supra, dub. 3, n. 147, cum Salm. c. 2, num. 44, Less. Sanch. Suar.

Liguori maintains that one may commit a minor crime in order to avoid a greater crime. He says : " Hence Sanchez teaches, etc., that it is lawful to persuade a man, determined to slay some one, that he should commit theft or fornication." *

" Whether is it lawful for a servant to open the door for a harlot ? Croix denies it, but more commonly Bus. etc., with others answer that it is lawful."

" Whether from fear of death, or of great loss, it may be lawful for a servant to stoop his shoulders, or to bring a ladder for his master ascending to commit fornication, to force open the door, and such like ? Viva, etc., deny it, and others, because, as they say, such actions are never lawful, inasmuch as they are intrinsically evil. But Busemb, etc., speak the contrary, whose opinion, approved of by reason, appears to me the more probable." †

" But the Salmanticenses say that a servant can, according to his own judgment, compensate himself for his labour, if he without doubt judge that he was deserving of a larger stipend. Which indeed appears sufficiently probable to me, and to other more modern learned men, if the servant, or any other hired person, be prudent, and capable of forming a correct judgment, and be certain concerning the justice of the compensation, all danger of mistake being removed."‡

" A poor man, absconding with goods for his support, can answer the judge that he has nothing. In like manner an heir who has concealed his goods without an inventory, if he is not bound to settle with his creditors from them, can say to a judge that he has not con-

Pal et communi. Quae certitudo moralis remissionis peccati potest quidem haberi, quando quis bene moraliter dispositus recepit poenitentiae sacramentum (Tom. ii. p. 322, ibid.)

* " Hinc docet id. Sanch. n. 19, cum Cajet. Sot. ˊCovar. Valent. parato aliquem occidere, licite posse suaderi, ut ab eo furetur, vel ut fornicetur." (Mor. Theol. t. ii. lib. iii. cap. ii. n. 57, p. 157.)

† " Quær. III. utrum liceat famulo ostium meretrici aperire ? Negat Croix lib. ii. n. 253. At communius affirmant cum Bus. Salm., d. cap. 8 n. 174, Laym. de Carit. c. 13, resp. 5, Tamb cum Sanch. Dian. Azor. Sa. Rodr., etc."

" Quær. IV. an ex metu mortis vel magni damni liceat famulo subjicere humeros, vel deferre scalam domino ascendenti ad fornicandum, vi aperire januam. et similia ? Negant Viva et Milanti in dict. prop. 51, P. Concina t. 2, pag. 280 Salm. n. 75. Croix lib. 2, num. 244, et alii, quia, ut dicunt, tales actiones nunquam licent, utpote intrinsece malæ. Sed contradicunt Busemb. infra n. 68. Sanch. dict. c. 7, 22, et Less. 1, 2, cap. 16, n. 59, quorum sententia spectata ratione mihi probabilior videtur." (Mor. Theol. t. ii. c. ii. n. 166, p. 182. Mech. 1845.)

‡ " Attamen Salm. de 4 præc. num. 137, dicunt famulum posse etiam ex proprio judicio sibi compensare suam operam, si ipse certe judicet se majus stipendium mereri. Quod sane videtur satis probabile mihi et aliis doctis recentioribus, si hic famulus, vel quicunque alius mercenarius sit vir prudens timoratus, et vere aptus ad recte judicandum ac certus sit de justitia compensationis, remoto omni hallucinationis periculo," (Mor. Theol. t. iii. p. 246, n. 524. Mech. 1845.)

cealed anything—in his own mind meaning those goods with which he is bound to satisfy his creditors."*

Liguori, in Dubium II., considers what may be the quantity of stolen property necessary to constitute mortal sin. He says:—

"There are various opinions concerning this matter. Navar too scrupulously has fixed the half of regalem, others with too great laxity have fixed ten aureos. Tol., etc., moderately have fixed two regales, although less might suffice, if it would be a serious loss."†

"Whether it be mortal sin to steal a small piece of a relic? There is no doubt but that in the district of Rome it is a mortal sin, since Clement VIII. and Paul V. have issued an excommunication against those who, the rectors of the churches being unwilling, steal some small relic: otherwise Croix probably says, etc., if any one should steal any small thing out of the district [of Rome], not deforming the relic itself nor diminishing its estimation; unless it may be some rare or remarkable relic, as for example, the holy cross, the hair of the Blessed Virgin, etc."‡

"If any one on an occasion should steal only a moderate sum either from one or more, not intending to acquire any notable sum, neither to injure his neighbour to a great extent by several thefts, he does not sin grievously, nor do these, taken together, constitute a mortal sin; however, after it may have amounted to a notable sum, by detaining it, he can commit mortal sin. But even this mortal sin may be avoided, if either then he be unable to restore, or have the intention of making restitution immediately, of those things which he then received."§

---

* "Indigens bonis absconditis ad sustentationem, potest judici respondere, se nihil habere. Salm. n. 140. Pariter hæres, qui sine inventario occultavit bona, si non teneatur ex illis satisfacere creditoribus, potest judici respondere, se nihil occultasse, subintelligens, de bonis, quibus satisfacere teneatur. Salm. loc. cit. et Ronc. c. 4, reg. 2 in Praxi." (Mor. Theol. t. ii. p. 321, n. 158. Mech. 1845.)

† "Variæ ea de re sunt sententiæ. Nav. nimis scrupulose statuit medium regalem, alii nimis laxe 10 aureos; moderatius, Tol, Med. Less., etc. duos regales, etsi minus sufficiat, si notabiliter noceat." (Mor. Theol. t. iii. p. 248, n. 526. Mech. 1845.)

‡ "Quæritur hic, an sit mortale furari parum reliquiæ sacræ? Nulli dubium, quin in districtu Romano sit mortale, cum Clemens VIII. et Paulus V. excommunicationem indixerint contra eos, qui, invitis rectoribus ecclesiarum, furantur reliquias etiam minimas: secus probabiliter ait Croix 1, 3, p. 1, n. 1603, cum Sanch. Castrop. Dian. et Badell. si quis furetur extra districtum aliquid minimum, ipsam reliquiam non deformans, neque minuens illius æstimationem, nisi sit aliqua reliqua insignis, aut rara, ut puta sanctæ Crucis, capillorum B. Mariæ Virg., etc." (Mor. Theol. t. iii. p. 256, n. 532. Mech. 1845.)

§ "Si quis ex occasione tantum furatur, sive uni, sive pluribus, modicum, non intendens notabile aliquid acquirere, nec proximo graviter nocere singulis furtis, non peccat graviter, neque ea simul sumta unum mortale constituunt, postquam tamen ad quantitatem notabilem pervenerit, eam detinendo, mortaliter peccare potest. Less d. 7, Sanch. lib. 7, c. 21. Bon. q. 8, p. 2 (Etsi nunquam advertat ad culpam gravem, ut Tamb. Croix, dicenda, n. 553. Verum et hoc mortale evitabit, si vel tunc restituere non possit, vel animum habeat paulo post restituendi ea saltem quæ tunc accepit. Gran. Dian. p. 3, t. 6, r. 25." (Mor. Theol. t. iii. p. 257, n. 533. Mech. 1845.)

"This opinion of Bus. is most probable, viz., if many persons steal small quantities, that none of them commit grievous sin, although they may be mutually aware of their conduct, unless they do it by concert: also Habert, etc., hold this view; and this, although each should steal at the same time. The reason is, because then no one person is the cause of injury, which, per accidens, happens by the others to the master."*

Liguori, speaking of children who steal from their parents, says:— "Salas, etc., say that a son does not commit grievous sin, who steals 20 or 30 aurei from a father possessing yearly 1500 aureos, and Lugo does not disprove of it. If the father be not tenacious, and the son have grown up and receive it for honest purposes. Less, etc., say that a son stealing two or three aureos from a rich father does not sin grievously; Bannez says that fifty aureos are required to constitute a grievous sin who steals from a rich father; but this opinion, Lug, etc., reject, unless perchance he is the son of a prince; in which case Holzm. consents." †

The theologians of Rome assure us that we may, and even that we must, conceal and disguise our faith.

"Notwithstanding, indeed although it is not lawful to lie, or to feign what is not, nevertheless it is lawful to dissemble what is, or to cover the truth with words, or other ambiguous and doubtful signs for a just cause, and when there is not a necessity of confessing. It is the common opinion." ‡

"Whence, if thus he may be able to deliver himself from a troublesome investigation, it is lawful (as Kon has it), for generally it is not true that he who is interrogated by public authority is publicly bound to profess the faith, unless when that is necessary, lest he may appear to those present to deny the faith." §

* "Probabilissima est hæc sententia Bus. scilicet, si plures modica furentur, neminem peccare graviter, etsi mutuo sciant grave damnum domino fieri, nisi ex communi consilio faciant; ita etiam tenent Habert, t. 4, c. 7, § 5, qu. 6   Lugo, d. 16, n. 55. Salm. de Rest., cap. 5, num. 28, cum Less. Sanch., etc. Et hoc, etiamsi singuli eodem tempore furentur; ut cum Bus. censet Less. cap. 12, n. 24 (contra Lugo). Ratio, quia tunc nemo est causa damni, quod, per accidens, ab aliis domino evenit." (Mor. Theol. t. iii. p. 259, n. 536. Mech. 1845).

† "Dicit Salas apud Croix 1, 3, p. 1, n. 1032, non esse grave furtum filii 20 vel 30 aureorum a patre, possidente annuos 1500 aureos, et non improbat Lugo d. 16, a. n. 76. Si pater non sit tenax, et filius adoleverit, et accipiat ad usus honestos. Less. Nov. et Fill. ap. Spor. de 7, præc. c. 5, num 57, dicunt non peccare graviter filium furantem 2 vel 3 aureos a patre divite. Bannez dicit ad furtum grave filii parentis prædivitis requiri saltem 50 aureos: sed hoc Lug et La Croix ll. cc rejiciunt, nisi forte esset filius principis, in quo consentit Holzm. num. 755." (Mor. Theol. t. iii. p. 262, n. 543. Mech. 1845.)

‡ "Interim vero, etsi licitum non est mentiri, seu simulare quod non est, licet tamen dissimulare quod est, sive tegere veritatem verbis, aliisve signis ambiguis et indifferentibus, ob justam causam, et cum non est necessitas fatendi. Est comm. S. Thom. Kon. dis. 15, dub. 2, n. 9, Laym. l. 2, t. 1, c. 11." (Mor. Theol. t. ii. lib. iii. cap. iii. p. 116, n. 12. Mech. 1845.)

§ "Unde, si sic possit molesta inquisitione liberari, licet, ut habet Kon. l.c.

" When you are not asked concerning the faith, not only is it lawful, but often more conducive to the glory of God and the utility of your neighbour to cover the faith than to confess it; for example, if concealed among heretics you may accomplish a greater amount of good; or if, from the confession of the faith more of evil would follow —for example, great trouble, death, the hostility of a tyrant, the peril of defection, if you should be tortured. Whence it is often rash to offer one's self willingly." *

The Pope has the right to release from all oaths.

" As for an oath made for a good and legitimate object, it seems that there should be no power capable of annulling it. However, when it is for the good of the public, a matter which comes under the immediate jurisdiction of the Pope, who has the supreme power over the Church, the Pope has full power to release from that oath." (St. Thomas, Quest. 89, art. 9, vol. iv.)

The Roman Catholics have not only the right, but it is their duty to kill heretics.

" Excommunicatus privatur omni civili communicatione fideliun, ita ut ipsi non possit cum aliis, et si non sit toleratus, etiam aliis cum ipso non possint communicare; idque in casibus hoc versu comprehensis, Os, orare, communio, mensa negatur."

Translated : " Any man excommunicated is deprived of all civil communication with the faithful, in such a way that if he is not tolerated they can have no communication with him, as it is in the following verse, 'It is forbidden to kiss him, pray with him, salute him, to eat or to do any business with him.' " (St. Liguori, vol. ix., page 62.)

" Quanquam heretici tolerandi non sunt ipso illorum demerito, usque tamen ad secundam correptionem expectandi sunt, ut ad sanam redeant ecclesiæ fidem; qui vero post secundam correptionem in suo errore obstinati permanent, non modo excommunicationis sententia, sed etiam sæcularibus principibus exterminandi tradendi sunt."

Translated : " Though heretics must not be tolerated because they deserve it, we must bear with them till, by a second admonition, they may be brought back to the faith of the Church. But those who,

---

Generatim enim verum non est, quod interrogatus ab auctoritate publica teneatur positive fidem profiteri, nisi quando id necessarium est, ne præsentibus videatur fidem negasse." (Mor. Theol. t ii. p. 117, n. 13. Mech. 1815.)

* " Cum non rogaris de fide, non solum licet, sed sæpe melius est ad Dei honorem, et utilitatem proximi, tegere fidem quam fateri; ut si latens inter haereticos plus boni facias; vel si ex confessione plus mali sequeretur, verbi gratia, turbatio, neces, exacerbatio tyranni, periculum defectionis, si torquereris. Unde temerarium plerumque est offerre se ultro." (Mor. Theol. t. ii. p. 817, n. 14. Mech. 1845.)

after a second admonition, remain obstinate in their errors must not
only be excommunicated, but they must be delivered to the secular
powers to be exterminated."

"Quanquam heretici revertentes, semper recipiendi sint ad pœnitentiam quoties cumque relapsi fuerint; non tamen semper sunt
recipiendi et restituendi ad bonorum hujus vitæ participationem
. . . recipiuntur ad pœnitentiam . . . non tamen ut liberentur
a sententia mortis."

Translated : "Though the heretics who repent must always be
accepted to penance, as often as they have fallen, they must not in
consequence of that always be permitted to enjoy the benefits of this
life. When they fall again they are admitted to repent. But the
sentence of death must not be removed." (St. Thomas, vol. iv.,
page 91.)

"Quum quis per sententiam denuntiatur propter apostasiam excommunicatus, ipso facto, ejus subditi a dominio et juramento
fidelitatis ejus liberati sunt."

"When a man is excommunicated for his apostasy, it follows from
that very fact that all those who are his subjects are released from the
oath of allegiance by which they were bound to obey him." (St.
Thomas, vol. iv., page 91.)

Every heretic and Protestant is condemned to death, and every
oath of allegiance to a government which is Protestant or heretic is
abrogated by the Council of Lateran, held in A.D. 1215. Here is the
solemn decree and sentence of death, which has never been repealed,
and which is still in force :

"We excommunicate and anathematize every heresy that exalts
itself against the holy, orthodox and Catholic faith, condemning all
heretics, by whatever name they may be known; for though their
faces differ, they are tied together by their tails. Such as are condemned are to be delivered over to the existing secular powers, to
receive due punishment. If laymen, their goods must be confiscated.
If priests, they shall be first degraded from their respective orders,
and their property applied to the use of the church in which they have
officiated. Secular powers of all ranks and degrees are to be warned,
induced, and, if necessary, compelled by ecclesiastical censure, to swear
that they will exert themselves to the utmost in the defence of the
faith, and extirpate all heretics denounced by the Church who shall
be found in their territories. And whenever any person shall assume
government, whether it be spiritual or temporal, he shall be bound to
abide by this decree.

"If any temporal lord, after being admonished and required by
the Church, shall neglect to clear his territory of heretical depravity,
the metropolitan and the bishops of the province shall unite in ex-

communicating him. Should he remain contumacious for a whole year, the fact shall be signified to the Supreme Pontiff, who will declare his vassals released from their allegiance from that time, and will bestow the territory on Catholics to be occupied by them, on the condition of exterminating the heretics and preserving the said territory in the faith.

"Catholics who shall assume the cross for the *extermination* of heretics shall enjoy the same indulgences and be protected by the same privileges as are granted to those who go to the help of the Holy Land. We decree, further, that all who may have dealings with heretics, and especially such as receive, defend, or encourage them, shall be excommunicated. He shall not be eligible to any public office. He shall not be admitted as a witness. He shall neither have the power to bequeath his property by will, nor to succeed to any inheritance. He shall not bring any action against any person, but anyone can bring an action against him. Should he be a judge, his decision shall have no force, nor shall any cause be brought before him. Should he be an advocate, he shall not be allowed to plead. Should he be a lawyer, no instruments made by him shall be held valid, but shall be condemned with their author."

But why let my memory and my thoughts linger any longer in these frightful paths, where murderers, liars, perjurers and thieves are assured by the theologians of the Church of Rome that they can lie, steal, murder and perjure themselves as much as they like, without offending God, provided they commit those crimes according to certain rules approved by the Pope for the good of the Church!

I should have to write several large volumes were I to quote all the Roman Catholic doctors and theologians who approve of lying, of perjury, of adultery, theft and murder, for the greatest glory of God and the good of the Roman Church! But I have quoted enough for those who have eyes to see and ears to hear.

With such principles, is it a wonder that all the Roman Catholic nations, without a single exception, have declined so rapidly?

The great Legislator of the World, the only Saviour of nations, has said : " Man shall not live by bread alone, but by every word that proceedeth out of the mouth of God."

A nation can be great and strong only according to the truths which form the basis of her faith and life. "Truth" is the only bread which God gives to the nations that they may prosper and live. Deceitfulness, duplicity, perjury, adultery, theft, murder, are the deadly poisons which kill the nations.

Then, the more the priests of Rome, with their theology, are venerated and believed by a people, the sooner that people will decay and fall. "The more priests the more crimes," a profound thinker has said; for then the more hands will be at work to pull down the only sure foundations of society.

How can any man be sure of the honesty of his wife as long as a hundred thousand priests tell her that she may commit any sin with her neighbour in order to prevent him from doing something worse? or when she is assured that, though guilty of adultery, she can swear that she is pure as an angel!

What will it avail to teach the best principles of honour, decency and holiness to a young girl, when she is bound to go many times a year to a bachelor priest, who is bound in conscience to give her the most infamous lessons of depravity under the pretext of helping her to confess all her sins?

How will the rights of justice be secured, and how can the judges and the juries protect the innocent and punish the guilty, so long as the witnesses are told by one hundred thousand priests that they can conceal the truth, give equivocal answers, and even perjure themselves under a thousand pretexts?

What government, either monarchical or republican, can be sure of a lease of existence? how can they make their people walk with a firm step in the ways of light, progress, and liberty, as long as there is a dark power over them which has the right, at every hour of the day or night, to break and dissolve all the most sacred oaths of allegiance?

Armed with his theology, the priest of Rome has become the most dangerous and determined enemy of truth, justice, and liberty. He is the most formidable obstacle to every good Government, as he is, without being aware of it, the greatest enemy of God and man.

CHAPTER XIV.

WERE I to write all the ingenious tricks, pious lies, shameful stories called miracles, and sacrilegious perversions of the Word of God made use of by superiors of seminaries and nunneries to entice poor victims into the trap of perpetual celibacy, I should have to write ten large volumes, instead of a short chapter.

Sometimes the trials and obligations of married life are so exaggerated that they may frighten the strongest heart. At other times the joys, peace and privileges of celibacy are depicted with such brilliant colours that they fill the coldest mind with enthusiasm.

The Pope takes his victim to the top of a high mountain, and there shows him all the honours, praise, wealth, peace and joys of this world, united to the most glorious throne of heaven, and then tells

6

him : "I will give you all those things if you fall at my feet, promise me an absolute submission, and swear never to marry in order to serve me better."

Who can refuse such glorious things ? But before entirely shutting their eyes, so that they may not see the bottomless abyss into which they are to fall, the unfortunate victims sometimes have forebodings and presentiments of the terrible miseries which are in store for them. The voice of their conscience, intelligence and common sense has not always been so fully silenced as the superior desired.

At the very time when the tempter is whispering his lying promises into their ears, their Heavenly Father is speaking to them of the ceaseless trials, the shameful falls, the tedious days, the dreary nights, and the cruel and insufferable burdens which are concealed behind the walls where the sweet yoke of the good Master is exchanged for the burdens of heartless men and women.

As formerly, the human victims crowned with flowers, when dragged to the foot of the altar of their false gods, often cried out with alarm and struggled to escape from the bloody knife of the heathen priest, so at the approach of the fatal hour at which the impious vow is to be made, the young victims often feel their hearts fainting and filled with terror. With pale cheeks, trembling lips and cold-dropping sweat they ask their superiors, " Is it possible that our merciful God requires of us such a sacrifice ? "

Oh ! how the merciless priest of Rome then becomes eloquent in depicting celibacy as the only way to heaven, or in showing the eternal fires of hell ready to receive cowards and traitors who, after having put their hand to the plough of celibacy, look back ! He speaks of the disappointment and sadness of so many dear friends, who expected better things of them. He points out to them their own shame when they will again be in a world which will have nothing for them but sneers for their want of perseverance and courage. He overwhelms them with a thousand pious lies about the miracles wrought by Christ in favour of his virgins and priests. He bewitches them by numerous texts of Scripture, which he brings as evident proof of the will of God in favour of their taking the vows of celibacy, though they have not the slightest reference to such vows.

The text of which the strangest abuses are made by the superiors to persuade the young people of both sexes to bind themselves by those shameful vows is Matthew xix. 12, 13 : " For there are eunuchs which were born from their mother's womb; and there are some eunuchs which were made eunuchs of men ; and there are eunuchs which have made themselves eunuchs for the kingdom of heaven's sake. He that is able to receive it, let him receive it."

Upon one occasion our superior made a very pressing appeal to our religious feelings from this text, to induce us to make the vow of celibacy and become priests. But the address, though delivered with a great deal of zeal, seemed to us deficient in logic.

The next day was a day of rest (*conge*). The students in theology who were preparing themselves for the priesthood, with me, talked seriously of the singular arguments of the last address. It seemed to them that the conclusions could not in any way be drawn from the selected text, and therefore determined to respectfully present their objections and their views, which were also mine, to the superior; and I was chosen to speak for them all.

At the next conference, after respectfully asking and obtaining permission to express our objections with our own frank and plain sentiments, I spoke about as follows :

"Dear and venerable sir : You told us that the following words of Christ, '*There be eunuchs which have made themselves eunuchs for the kingdom of heaven's sake,*'—show us evidently that we must make the vow of celibacy and make ourselves eunuchs if we want to become priests. Allow us to tell you respectfully, that it seems to us that the mind of our Saviour was very different from yours when He pronounced these words. In our humble opinion, the only object of the Son of God was to warn His disciples against one of the most damnable errors which were to endanger the very existence of nations. He was foretelling that there would be men so wicked and blind as to preach that the best way for men to go to heaven would be to make eunuchs of themselves. Allow us to draw your attention to the fact that in that speech Jesus Christ neither approves nor disapproves of the idea of gaining a throne in heaven by becoming eunuchs. He leaves us to our common sense and to some clearer parts of Scripture to see whether or not He approves of those who would make eunuchs of themselves to gain a crown in heaven. Must we not interpret this text as we interpret what Jesus said to His apostles, 'The time cometh that whosoever killeth you will think that he doeth God service' (John xvi. 1, 2).

Allow us to put these two texts face to face :

"'There are eunuchs which have made themselves eunuchs for the kingdom of heaven's sake' (Matt. xix. 12, 13).

"'The time cometh that whosoever killeth you will think that he doeth God service' (John xvi. 1, 2).

"Because our Saviour has said that there would be men who would think that they would please God (and of course gain a place in heaven) by killing His disciples, are we, therefore, allowed to conclude that it would be our duty to kill those who believe and follow Christ ? Surely not!

"Well, it seems to us that we are not to believe that the best way to go to heaven is to make ourselves eunuchs, because our Saviour said that some men had got that criminal and foolish notion into their mind!

" Christian nations have always looked with horror upon those who have voluntarily become eunuchs. Common sense, as well as the Word of God, condemns those who thus destroy in their own bodies that which God in His wisdom gave them for the wisest and holiest purposes. Would it not, therefore, be a crime which every civilised and Christian nation would punish, to preach publicly and with success to the people that one of the surest ways for a man to go to heaven would be to make himself an eunuch. How can we believe that our Saviour could ever sanction such a practice ?

" Moreover, if being eunuchs would make the way to heaven surer and more easy, would not God be unjust for depriving us of the privilege of being born eunuchs, and thus being made ripe fruits for heaven ?

" It seems to us that that text does not in any way require us to believe that an eunuch is nearer the kingdom of God than He who lives just according to the laws which God gave to man in the earthly paradise. If it was not good for man to be without his wife when he was so holy and strong as he was in the Garden of Eden, how can it be good now that he is so weak and sinful ?

" Our Saviour clearly shows that He finds no sanctifying power in the state of an eunuch, in His answer to the young man who asked Him, ' Good Master, what must I do that I may have eternal life ?" (Matt. xix. 16). Did the good Master answer him in the language we heard from you two days ago, namely, that the best way to have eternal life is to make yourself an eunuch—make a solemn vow never to marry ? No ; but He said, ' Keep the commandments !'

" Were the blessed Saviour to-day in your place, and I should ask him, ' What must I do to be saved,' and to show the way of God to my brethren ? would He not say to me, ' Keep the commandments ! ' But where is the commandment of God, in the Old or New Testament, to induce us to make such a vow as that of celibacy ? The promise of a place in heaven is not attached in any way to the vow of celibacy. Christ has not a word about that doctrine.

" Allow us to respectfully ask, if the views concerning the vows of celibacy entertained by Christ had been like yours, is it possible that He would have forgotten to mention them when He answered the solemn question of that young man ? Is it possible that He would not have said a single word about a thing which you have represented to us as being of such vital importance to those who sincerely desire to know what to do to be saved ? Is it not strange that the Church should attach such an importance to that vow of celibacy, when we look in vain for such an ordinance in both the Old and New Testaments? How can we understand the reasons or the importance of such a strict and, we dare say, unnatural obligation in our day, when we know very well that the holy apostles themselves were living with their wives, and that the Saviour had not a word of rebuke for them on that account?"

This free expression of our common views on the vows of celibacy evidently took our superior by surprise. He answered me, with an accent of indignation which he could not suppress: "Is that all you have to say?"

"It is not quite all we have to say," I answered; "but before we go further we would be much gratified to receive from you the light we want on the difficulties which I have just stated."

"You have spoken as a true heretic," replied Mr. Leprohon, with an unusual vivacity; "and were it not for the hope which I entertain that you have said these things to receive the light you want than to present and support the heretical side of such an important question, I would at once denounce you to the bishop. You speak of the Holy Scriptures just as a Protestant would do. You appeal to them as the only source of Christian truth and knowledge. Have you forgotten that we have the holy traditions to guide us, the authority of which is equal to that of the Scriptures?

"You are correct when you say that we do not find any direct proof in the Bible to enforce the vows of celibacy upon those who desire to consecrate themselves to the service of the Church. But if we do not find the obligation of that vow in the Bible, we find it in the holy traditions of the Church.

"It is an article of faith that the vow of celibacy is ordered by Jesus Christ, through His Church. The ordinances of the Church, which are nothing but the ordinances of the Son of God, are clear on that subject, and bind our consciences just as the commandments of God upon Mount Sinai; for Christ has said, those who do not hear the Church must be looked upon as heathen and publicans. There is no salvation to those who do not submit their reason to the teachings of the Church.

"You are not required to understand all the reasons for the vow of celibacy; but you are bound to believe in its *necessity* and *holiness*, as the Church has pronounced her verdict upon that question. It is not your business to argue about those matters; but your duty is to obey the Church, as dutiful children obey a kind mother.

"But who can have any doubt about the necessity of the vows of celibacy, when we remember that Christ had ordered His apostles to separate themselves from their wives?—a fact on which no doubt can remain after hearing St. Peter say to our Saviour, 'Behold, we have

forsaken all and followed Thee; what shall we have, therefore?'
(Matt. xix. 27). Is not the priest the true representative of Christ on
earth? In his ordination, is not the priest made the equal and in a
sense the superior of Christ? for when he celebrates Mass he commands Christ, and that very Son of God is bound to obey! It is not
in the power of Christ to resist the orders of the priest. He must
come down from heaven every time the priest orders Him. The
priest shuts Him up in the holy tabernacles or takes Him out of them,
according to his own will.

"By becoming priests of the New Testament you will be raised to
a dignity which is much above that of angels. From these sublime
privileges flows the obligation to the priest to raise himself to a degree
of holiness much above the level of the common people—a holiness
equal to that of the angels. Has not our Saviour, when speaking of
the angels, said ' *Neque nubent neque nubentur?* ' They marry not, nor
are given in marriage. Surely, since the priests are the messengers
and angels of God, on earth they must be clad with angelic holiness
and purity.

"Does not Paul say that the state of virginity is superior to that of
marriage? Does not that saying of the apostle show that the priest,
whose hands every day touch the divine body and blood of Christ,
must be chaste and pure, and must not be defiled by the duties of
married life? That vow of celibacy is like a holy chain, which keeps
us above the filth of this earth and ties us to heaven. Jesus Christ,
through His holy Church, commands that vow to His priests as the
most efficacious remedy against the inclinations of our corrupt nature.

"According to the holy Fathers, the vow of celibacy is like a
strong high tower, from the top of which we can fight our enemies,
and be perfectly safe from their darts and weapons.

"I will be happy to answer your other objections, if you have any
more," said Mr. Leprohon.

"We are much obliged to you for your answers," I replied, "and
we will avail ourselves of your kindness to present you with some
other observations.

"And, firstly, we thank you for having told us that we find
nothing in the Word of God to support the vows of celibacy, and that
it is only by the traditions of the Church that we can prove their
necessity and holiness. It was our impression that you desired us to
believe that the necessity of that vow was founded on the Holy
Scriptures. If you allow it, we will discuss the traditions another
time, and will confine ourselves to-day to the different texts to which
you referred in favour of celibacy.

"When Peter says, 'We have given up everything,' it seems to us
that he had no intention of saying that he had for ever given up his

wife by a vow. For St. Paul positively says, many years after, that Peter had his wife; that he was not only living with her in his own house, but was travelling with her when preaching the gospel. The words of Scripture are of such evidence on that subject that they can neither be obscured by any shrewd explanation nor by any tradition, however respectable it may appear.

"Though you know the words of Paul on that subject, you will allow us to read them: ' Have we not power to eat and drink? have we not power to lead about a sister, a wife, as well as other apostles and as the brethren of the Lord, and Cephas?' (1 Cor. ix. 4, 5). St. Peter saying 'We have forsaken everything' could not then mean that he had made a vow of celibacy, and that he would never live with his wife as a married man. Evidently the words of Peter mean only that Jesus had the first place in his heart—that everything else, even the dearest objects of his love, as father, mother, wife, were only secondary in his affections and thoughts.

"Your other text about the angels who do not marry, from which you infer the obligation and law of the vow of celibacy, does not seem to us to bear on that subject as much as you have told us. For, be kind enough to again read the text: 'Jesus answered and said to them, Ye do err, not knowing the Scriptures, nor the power of God. For in the resurrection they neither marry nor are given in marriage; but are as the angels of God in heaven' (Matt. xxii. 29, 30). You see that when our Saviour speaks of men who are like angels, and who do not marry, He takes care to observe that He speaks of the state of men *after the resurrection*. If the Church had the same rule for us that Christ mentioned for the angelic men to whom He refers, and would allow us to make a vow never to marry after the resurrection, we would not have the slightest objection to such a vow.

"You see that our Saviour speaks of a state of celibacy; but He does not intimate that that state is to begin on this side of the grave. Why does not our Church imitate and follow the teachings of our Saviour? Why does she enforce a state of celibacy before the resurrection, while Christ postpones the promulgation of this law till after that great day?

"Christ speaks of a perpetual celibacy only in heaven! On what authority, then, does our Church enforce that celibacy on this side of the grave, when we still carry our souls in earthly vessels?

"You tell us that the vow of celibacy is the best remedy against the inclinations of our corrupt nature; but do you not fear that your remedy makes war against the great one which God prepared in His wisdom? Do we not read in our own vulgate: 'Propter fornicationem autem unus quisque uxorem suam habeat, et unaquaque virum suum'? 'To avoid fornication let every man have his

own wife, and let every woman have her own husband' (2 Cor.
vii. 2).

"Is it not too strange, indeed, that God does tell us that the best
remedy He had prepared against the inclinations of our corrupt
nature is in the blessings of a holy marriage. 'Let every man have
his own wife, and every woman her own husband.' But now our
Church has found another remedy, which is more accordant to the
dignity of man and the holiness of God, and that remedy is the vow
of celibacy!"

The sound of my last words were still on my lips when our
venerable superior, unable any longer to conceal his indignation,
abruptly interrupted me, saying :

"I do exceedingly regret to have allowed you to go so far. This
is not a Christian and humble discussion between young Levites and
their superior, to receive from him the light they want. It is the
exposition and defence of the most heretical doctrines I have ever
heard. Are you not ashamed, when you try to make us prefer your
interpretation of the Holy Scriptures to that of the Church ? Is it to
you, or to His holy Church, that Christ promised the light of the
Holy Ghost ? Is it you who have to teach the Church, or the Church
who must teach you ? Is it you who will govern and guide the
Church, or the Church who will govern and guide you ?

"My dear Chiniquy, if there is not a great and prompt change in
you and in those whom you pretend to represent, I fear much for you
all. You show a spirit of infidelity and revolt which frightens me.
Just like Lucifer, you rebel against the Lord ! Do you not fear to
share the eternal pains of his rebellion ?

"Whence have you taken the false and heretical notions you
have, for instance, about the wives of the apostles ? Do you not
know that you are supporting a Protestant error, when you say that
the apostles were living with their wives in the usual way of married
people ? It is true that Paul says that the apostles had women with
them, and that they were even travelling with them. But the holy
traditions of the Church tell us that those women were holy virgins,
who were travelling with the apostles to serve and help them in
different ways. They were ministering to their different wants—
washing their underclothes, preparing their meals, just like the
housekeeper whom the priests have to-day. It is a Protestant impiety
to think and speak otherwise.

"But only a word more, and I am done. If you accept the
teaching of the Church, and submit yourselves as dutiful children to
that most holy Mother, she will raise you to the dignity of the
priesthood, a dignity much above kings and emperors in this world.
If you serve her with fidelity, she will secure to you the respect and

veneration of the whole world while you live, and procure you a crown of glory in heaven.

"But if you reject her doctrines, and persist in your rebellious views against one of the most holy dogmas; if you continue to listen to the voice of your own deceitful reason rather than to the voice of the Church, in the interpretation of the Holy Scriptures, you become heretics, apostates and Protestants; you will lead a dishonoured life in this world, and you will be lost for all eternity."

Our superior left us immediately after these fulminating words. Some of the theological students, after his exit, laughed heartily, and thanked me for having so bravely fought and gained so glorious a victory. Two of them, disgusted by the sophisms and logical absurdities of our superior, left the seminary a few days after. The rest, with me had not the moral courage to follow their example, but remained, stunned by the last words of our superior.

I went to my room and fell on my knees, with a torrent of tears falling from my eyes. I was really sorry for having wounded his feelings, but still more so for having dared for a moment to oppose my own feeble and fallible reason to the mighty and infallible intelligence of my Church!

At first it appeared to me that I was only combating, in a respectful way, against my old friend, Rev. Mr. Leprohon; but I had received it from his own lips that I had really fought against the Lord!

After spending a long and dark night of anguish and remorse, my first action, the next day, was to go to confession, and ask my confessor, with tears of regret, pardon for the sins I had committed and the scandal I had given.

Had I listened to the voices of my conscience, I certainly would have left the seminary that day; for they told me that I had confounded my superior and pulverized all his arguments. Reason and conscience told me that the vow of celibacy was a sin against logic, morality and God; that that vow could not be sustained by any argument from the Holy Scriptures, logic or common sense. But I was a most sincere Roman Catholic. I had therefore to fight a new battle against my conscience and intelligence, so as to subdue and silence them for ever! Many a time it was my hope, before this, to have succeeded in slaughtering them at the foot of the altar of my Church; but that day, far from being for ever silenced and buried, they had come out again with renewed force, to waken me from the terrible illusions in which I was living. Nevertheless, after a long and frightful battle, my hope was that they were perfectly subdued and buried under the feet of the holy Fathers, the learned theologians and the venerable popes, whose voice only I was determined now to follow. I felt a real calm after that struggle. It was evidently the silence of death, although my confessor told me it was the peace of God. More than ever I determined to have no knowledge, no thought, no will, no light, no desires, no science but that which my Church would give me through my superior. I was fallible, she was infallible! I was a sinner, she was the immaculate spouse of Jesus Christ! I was weak, she had more power than the great waters of the ocean! I was but an atom, she was covering the world with her glory! What, therefore, could I have to fear in humbling myself at her feet, to live of her life, to be strong of her strength, wise of her wisdom, holy with her holiness? Had not my superior repeatedly told me that no error, no sin would be imputed to me as long as I obeyed my Church and walked in her ways?

With these sentiments of a most profound and perfect respect for my Church, I irrevocably consecrated myself to her service on the 4th of May, 1832, by making the vow of celibacy and accepting the office of sub-deacon.

CHAPTER XV.

"The mother of harlots and abominations."—REV. xvii. 5.

CONSTRAINED by the voice of my conscience to reveal the impurities of the theology of the Church of Rome, I feel, in doing so, a sentiment of inexpressible shame. They are of such a loathsome nature, that often they cannot be expressed in any living language.

However great may have been the corruptions in the theologies and priests of paganism, there is nothing in their records which can be compared with the depravity of those of the Church of Rome. Before the day on which the theology of Rome was inspired by Satan, the world had certainly witnessed many dark deeds ; but vice had never been clothed with the mantle of theology :—the most shameful forms of iniquity had never been publicly taught in the schools of the old pagan priest, under the pretext of saving the world. No! neither had the priests nor the idols been forced to attend meetings where the most degrading forms of iniquity were objects of the most minute study, and that under the pretext of glorifying God.

Let those who understand Latin read "The Priest, the Woman, and the Confessional," and decide as to whether or not the sentiments therein contained are not enough to shock the feelings of the most depraved. And let it be remembered that all those abominations have to be studied, learned by heart and thoroughly understood by men who have to make a vow never to marry ! For it is not till after his vow of celibacy that the student in theology is *initiated* into those mysteries of iniquity.

Has the world ever witnessed such a sacrilegious comedy? A young man about twenty years of age has been enticed to make a vow of perpetual celibacy, and the very next day the Church of Rome puts under the eye of his soul the most infamous spectacle! She fills his memory with the most disgusting images! She tickles all his senses and pollutes his ears, not by imaginary representations, but by realities which would shock the most abandoned in vice!

For, let it be well understood, that it is absolutely impossible for one to study those questions of Roman Theology, and fathom those forms of iniquity without having his body as well as his mind plunged into a state the most degrading. Moreover, Rome does not even try to conceal the overwhelming power of this kind of teaching; she does not even attempt to make it a secret from the victims of her incomparable depravity, but BRAVELY TELLS them that the study of those questions will act with an irresistible power upon their organs, and without a blush says "that pollution must follow!!!"

But in order that the Church of Rome may more certainly destroy her victims, and that they may not escape from the abyss which she has dug under their feet, she tells them, "There is no sin for you in those pollutions!" (Dens, vol. i. p. 315.)

But Rome must bewitch so as the better to secure their destruction. She puts to their lips the cup of her enchantments, the more certainly to kill their souls, dethrones God from their consciences, and abrogates His eternal laws of holiness. What answer does Rome give to those who reproach her with the awful impurity of theology. "My theological works," she answers, "are all written in Latin; the people cannot read them. No evil, no scandal, therefore, can come from them!" But this answer is a miserable subterfuge. Is this not the public acknowledgment that her theology would be exceedingly injurious to the people if it were read and understood by them?

By saying, "My theological works are written in Latin, therefore the people cannot be defiled, as they do not understand them," Rome does acknowledge that these works would only act as a pestilence among the people, were they read and understood by them. But are not the one hundred thousand priests of Rome bound to explain in every known tongue, and present to the mind of every nation, the theology contained in those books? Are they not bound to make every polluting sentence in them flow into the ears, imaginations, hearts and minds of all the married and unmarried women whom Rome holds in her grasp?

I exaggerate nothing when I say that not fewer than half a million

women every day are compelled to hear in their own language, almost
every polluting sentence and impure notion of the diabolical sciences.

And here I challenge, most fearlessly, the Church of Rome to
deny what I say, when I state that the daily average of women who
go to confession to each priest, is ten. But let us reduce the number
to five. Then the one hundred thousand priests who are scattered
over the whole world, hear the confessions of five hundred thousand
women every day! Well, now, out of one hundred women who
confess, there are at least ninety-nine whom the priest is bound in
conscience to pollute, by questioning them on the matters mentioned
in the Latin pages at the end of this chapter. How can one be
surprised at the rapid downfall of the nations who are under the yoke
of the Pope.

The public statistics of the European, as well of American nations,
show that there is among Roman Catholics nearly double the amount
of prostitution, bastardy, theft, perjury, and murder than is found
among Protestant nations. Where must we, then, look for the cause
of those stupendous facts, if not in the corrupt teachings of the
theology of Rome. How can the Roman Catholic nations hope to
raise themselves in the scale of Christian dignity and morality as long
as there remain one hundred thousand priests in their midst, bound
in conscience every day to pollute the minds and the hearts of their
mothers, their wives and their daughters!

And here let me say, once for all, that I am not induced to speak
as I do from any motive of contempt or unchristian feeling against the
theological professors who have initiated me into those mysteries of
iniquity. The Rev. Messrs. Raimbault and Leprohon were, and in my
mind they still are, as respectable as men can be in the Church of
Rome. As I have been myself, and as all the priests of Rome are,
they were plunged without understanding it, into the abyss of the
most stolid ignorance. They were crushed, as I was myself, under a
yoke which bound their understanding to the dust, and polluted
their hearts without measure. We were embarked together on a ship,
the first appearance of which was really magnificent, but the bottom of
which was irremediably rotten. Without the true Pilot on board we
were left to perish on unknown shoals. Out of this sinking ship the
hand of God alone, in His providence rescued me. I pity those friends
of my youth, but despise them? hate them? No! Never! Never!

Every time our theological teachers gave us our lessons, it was
evident that they blushed in the inmost part of their souls. Their
consciences as honest men were evidently forbidding them, on the one
hand, to open their mouths on such matters, while, on the other hand,
as slaves and priests of the Pope, they were compelled to speak without
reserve.

After our lessons in theology, we students used to be filled with such a sentiment of shame that sometimes we hardly dared to look at each other: and, when alone in our rooms, those horrible pictures were affecting our hearts, in spite of ourselves, as the rust affects and corrodes the hardest and purest steel. More than one of my fellow-students told me, with tears of shame and rage, that they regretted to have bound themselves by perpetual oaths to minister at the altars of the Church.

One day one of the students, called Desaulnier, who was sick in the same room with me, asked me: "Chiniquy, what do you think of the matters which are the objects of our present theological studies? Is it not a burning shame that we must allow our minds to be so polluted?"

"I cannot sufficiently tell you my feelings of disgust," I answered. "Had I known sooner that we were to be dragged over such a ground, I certainly never would have nailed my future to the banners under which we are irrevocably bound to live."

"Do you know," said Desaulnier, "that I am determined never to consent to be ordained a priest; for when I think of the fact that the priest is bound to confer with women on all these polluting matters, I feel an insurmountable disgust and shame."

"I am not less troubled," I replied. "My head aches and my heart sinks within me when I hear our theologians telling us that we will be in conscience bound to speak to females on these impure subjects. But sometimes this looks to me as if it were a bad dream, the impure phantoms of which will disappear at the first awakening. Our Church, which is so pure and holy that she can only be served by the spotless virgins, surely cannot compel us to pollute our lips, thoughts, souls, and even our bodies, by speaking to strange women on matters so defiling!"

"But we are near the hour at which the good Mr. Leprohon is in the habit of visiting us. Will you," I said, "promise to stand by me in what I will ask him on this subject? I hope to get from him a pledge that we will not be compelled to be polluted in the confessional by the women who will confess to us. The purity and holiness of our superior is of such a high character, that I am sure he has never said a word to females on those degrading matters. In spite of all the theologians, Mr. Leprohon will allow us to keep our tongues and our hearts, as well as our bodies, pure in the confessional."

"I have had the desire to speak to him upon this subject for some time," rejoined Desaulnier, "but my courage failed me every time I attempted to do so. I am glad, therefore, that you are to break the ice, and I will certainly support you, as I have a longing desire to know something more in regard to the mysteries of the confessional.

If we are at liberty never to speak to women on these horrors, I will consent to serve the Church as a priest; but if not, I WILL NEVER BE A PRIEST."

A few minutes after this our superior entered to kindly enquire how we had rested the night before. Having thanked him for his kindness, I opened the volumes of Dens and Liguori which were on our table, and, with a blush, putting my fingers on one of the infamous chapters referred to, I said to him :

"After God, you have the first place in my heart since my mother's death, and you know it. I take you, not only as my benefactor, but also, as it were, as my father and mother. You will therefore tell me all I want to know in these my hours of anxiety, through which God is pleased to make me pass. To follow your advice, not to say your commands, I have lately consented to receive the order of sub-deacon, and I have in consequence taken the vow of perpetual celibacy. But I will not conceal the fact from you, I had not a clear understanding of what I was then doing; and Desaulnier has just stated to me, that until recently he had no more idea of the nature of that promise, nor of the difficulties which we now see ahead of us in our priestly life than I had.

"But Dens, Liguori and St. Thomas have given us notions quite new in regard to many things. They have directed our minds to the knowledge of the laws which are in us, as well as in every other child of Adam. They have, in a word, directed our minds into regions which were quite new and unexplored by us; and I dare say that every one of those whom we have known, whether in this house or elsewhere, who have made the same vow, could tell the same tale.

"However, I do not speak for them; I speak only for myself and Desaulnier. For God's sake, please tell us if we will be bound in conscience to speak in the confessional, to the married and unmarried females, on such impure and defiling questions as are contained in the theologians before us ? "

"Most undoubtedly," replied Rev. Mr. Leprohon; "because the learned and holy theologians whose writings are in your hands are positive on that question. It is absolutely necessary that you should question your female penitents on such matters; for, as a general thing, girls and married women are too timid to confess those sins, of which they are even more frequently guilty than men, therefore they must be helped by questioning them."

"But have you not," I rejoined, "induced us to make an oath that we should always remain pure and undefiled ? How is it, then, that to-day you put us in such a position that it is almost an impossibility for us to be true to our sacred promise ? For the theologians are unanimous that those questions put by us to our female penitents, together with the recital of their secret sins, will act with such an irresistible power upon us that we will be polluted.

" Would it not be better for us to experience those things in the holy bonds of marriage, with our wives, and according to the laws of God, than in company and conversation with strange women ? Because, if we are to believe the theologians which are in our hands, no priest—not even you, my dear Mr. Leprohon—can hear the confessions of women without being defiled."

Here Desaulnier interrupted me, and said : " My dear Mr. Leprohon, I concur in everything Chiniquy has just been telling you. Would we not be more chaste and pure by living with our lawful wives, than by daily exposing ourselves in the confessional in company of women whose presence will irresistibly drag us into the most shameful pit of impurity ? I ask you, my dear sir, what will become of my vow of perfect and perpetual chastity, when the seducing presence of my neighbour's wife, or the enchanting words of his daughter, will have defiled me through the confessional. After all, I may be looked upon by the people as a chaste man ; but what will I be in the eyes of God ? The people may entertain the thought that I am a strong and honest man ; but will I not be a broken reed ? Will God not be the witness that the irresistible temptations which will have assailed me when hearing the secret sins of some sweet and tempting woman, will have deprived me of that glorious crown of chastity for which I have so dearly paid ? Men will think that I am an angel of purity ; but my own conscience will tell me that I am nothing but a skilful hypocrite. For according to all the theologians, the confessional is the tomb of the chastity of priests ! ! If I hear the confession of women, I will be like all other priests, in a tomb, well painted and gilded on the outside, but within full of corruption."

Francis Desaulnier, just as he had foretold me, refused to be a priest. He remained all his life in the orders of sub-deaconate, in the College of Nicolet, as a Professor of Philosophy. He was a man who seldom spoke in conversation, but thought very much. It seems to me that I still see him there, under that tall centenary tree, alone, during the long hours of intermission, and many long days during our holidays, while the rest of the students passed hither and thither, singing and playing, on the enchanting banks of the river of Nicolet.

He was a good logician and a profound mathematician ; and although affable to everyone, he was not communicative. I was probably the only one to whom he opened his mind concerning the great questions of Christianity—faith, history, the Church and her discipline. He repeatedly said to me : " I wish I had never opened a book of theology. Our theologians are without heart, soul or logic. Many of them approve of theft, lies and perjury ; others drag us without a blush, into the most filthy pits of iniquity. Every one of them would like to make an assassin of every Catholic. According to their doctrine, Christ is nothing but a Corsican brigand, whose blood-thirsty disciples are bound to destroy all the heretics with fire and sword. Were we acting according to the principles of those theologians, we would slaughter all Protestants with the same coolness of blood as we would shoot down the wolf which crosses our path. With their hand still reddened with the blood of St. Bartholomew, they speak to us of charity, religion and God, as if there were neither of them in the world."

Desaulnier was looked upon as "*un homme singulier*" at Nicolet. He was really an exception to all the men in the seminary. For example: Though it was the usage and the law that ecclesiastics should receive the communion every month, and upon every great feast day of the Church, yet he would scarcely take the communion once a year. But let me return to the interview with our superior.

Desaulnier's fearless and energetic words had evidently made a very painful impression upon our superior. It was not a usual thing for His disciples in theology thus to take upon themselves to speak with such freedom as we both did on this occasion. He did not conceal his pain at what he called our unbecoming and unchristian attack upon some of the most holy ordinances of the Church; and after he had refuted Desaulnier in the best way he could, he turned to me and said: "My dear Chiniquy, I have repeatedly warned you against the habit you have of listening to your own frail reasoning, when you should only obey as a dutiful child. Were we to believe you, we would immediately set ourselves to work to reform the Church and abolish the confession of women to priests; we would throw all our theological books into the fire and have new ones written, better adapted to your fancy. What does all this prove? Only one thing, and that is, that the devil of pride is tempting you as he has tempted all the so-called Reformers, and destroyed them as he would you. If you do not take care, you will become another Luther!

"The Theological books of St. Thomas, Liguori and Dens have been approved by the Church. How, therefore, do you not see the ridicule and danger of your position. On one side, then, I see all our holy popes, the two thousand Catholic bishops, all our learned theologians and priests, backed up by over two hundred millions of Roman Catholics drawn up as an innumerable army to fight the battles of the Lord; and on the other side what do I see? Nothing but my small, though very dear Chiniquy!

"How, then, is it that you do not fear, when with your weak reasoning you oppose the mighty reasoning and light of so many holy popes, and venerable bishops and learned theologians? Is it not just

as absurd for you to try to reform the Church by your small reason, as
it is for the grain of sand which is found at the foot of the great
mountain to try to turn that mighty mountain out of its place? or for
the small drop of water to attempt to throw the boundless ocean out
of its bed, or try to oppose the running tides of the Polar seas?

"Believe me, and take my friendly advice," continued our superior,
"before it is too late. Let the small grain of sand remain still at the
foot of the majestic mountain; and let the humble drop of water
consent to follow the irresistible currents of the boundless seas, and
everything will be in order.

"All the good priests who have heard the confessions of women
before us have been sanctified and have had their souls saved, even
when their bodies were polluted; for those carnal pollutions are
nothing but human miseries, which cannot defile a soul which desires
to remain united to God. Are the rays of the sun defiled by coming
down into the mud? No! The rays remain pure, and return
spotless to the shining orb whence they came. So the heart of a good
priest—as I hope my dear Chiniquy will be—will remain pure and
holy in spite of the accidental and unavoidable defilement of the
flesh.

"Apart from those things, in your ordination you will receive a
special grace which will change you into another man; and the Virgin
Mary, to whom you will constantly address yourself, will obtain for
you a perfect purity from her Son.

"The defilement of the flesh spoken of by the theologians, and
which, I confess, is unavoidable when hearing the confessions of
women, must not trouble you; for they are not sinful, as Dens and
Liguori assure us. (Dens. vol. i., pages 299, 300.)

"But enough on that subject. I forbid you to speak to me any
more on those idle questions, and, as much as my authority is anything to you both, I forbid you to say a word more to each other on
that matter!!"

It was my fond hope that my dear and so much venerated Mr.
Leprohon would answer me with some good and reasonable arguments; but he, to my surprise, silenced the voice of our conscience by
un coup d'etat.

Nevertheless, the idea of that miserable grain of sand which so
ridiculously attempted to remove the stately mountain, and also of
that all but imperceptible drop of water which attempted to oppose
itself to the onward motion of the vast ocean, singularly struck and
humbled me. I remained silent and confused, though not convinced.

This was not all. Those rays of the sun, which could not be defiled
even when going down into the mud, after bewildering one by their
glittering appearance, left my soul more in the dark than ever. I

could not resist the presentiment that I was in the presence of an imposition, and of a glittering sophism. But I had neither sufficient learning, moral courage, nor grace from God clearly to see through that misty cloud and to expel it from my mind.

Almost every month of the ten years which I had passed in the seminary of Nicolet, priests of the district of Three Rivers and elsewhere were sent by the bishops to spend two or three weeks in doing penances for having bastards by their nieces, their housekeepers, or their fair penitents. Even not long before this conversation with our director, the curate of St. Francois, the Rev. Mr. Amiot, had in the very same week two children by two of his fair penitents, both of whom were sisters. One of those girls gave birth to her child at the parsonage the very night on which the bishop was on his episcopal visit to that parish. These public and undeniable facts were not much in harmony with those beautiful theories of our venerable director concerning the rays of the sun, which "remained pure and undefiled even when warming and vivifying the mud of our planet." The facts had frequently occurred to my mind while Mr. Leprohon was speaking, and I was tempted more than once to ask him respectfully if he really thought these "shining rays," the priests, had thus come into the mire, and would then return, like the rays of the sun, without taking back with them something of the mire in which they had been so strangely wallowing. But my respect for Mr. Leprohon sealed my lips.

When I returned to my room I fell on my knees to ask God to pardon me for having, for a moment, thought otherwise than the popes and theologians of Rome. I again felt angry with myself for having dared, for a single moment, to have arrayed my poor little and imperceptible grain of sand—drop of water—and personal and con- temptible understanding against that sublime mountain of strength, that vast ocean of learning, and that immensely divine wisdom of the popes!

But, alas! I was not yet aware that when Jesus in His mercy sends into a perishing soul a single ray of His grace, that there is more light and wisdom in that soul than in all the popes and their theologians!

I was then taught what the real foundation of the Church of Rome is, and sincerely believed that to think for myself was a damnable impiety—that to look and see with my own eyes, and understand with my own mind, was an unpardonable sin. To be saved I had to believe, not what I considered to be the truth, but what the popes told me to be the truth. I had to look and see every object of faith, just as every true Roman Catholic of to-day has to look and see the same, through the Pope's eyes or those of his theologians.

However absurd and impious this belief may be, yet it was mine, and it is also the belief of every true member of the Church of Rome to-day. The glorious light and grace of God could not possibly flow directly from Him to me; they had to pass through the Pope and his Church, which were my only mountain of strength and only ocean of light. It was, then, my firm belief that there was an impassable abyss between myself and God, and that the Pope and his Church were the only bridge by which I could have communication with Him. That stupendously high and most sublime mountain, the Pope, was between myself and God : and all that was allowed my poor soul was to raise itself and travel with great difficulty till it attained the foot of that holy mountain, the Pope, and, prostrating itself there in the dust, ask him to let me know what my yet distant God would have me to do. The promises of mercy, truth, light, and life were all vested in this great mountain, the Pope, from whom alone they could descend upon my poor lost soul!

Darkness, ignorance, uncertainty, and eternal loss were my lot, the very moment I ceased worshipping at the feet of the Pope! The God of Heaven was not *my* God ; He was only the God of the Pope! The Saviour of the world was not my Saviour; He was only the Pope's. Therefore it was through the Pope only that I could receive Christ as my Saviour, and to the Pope alone had I to go to know the way, the truth, and the life of my soul!

God alone knows what a dark and terrible night I passed after this meeting! I had again to smother my conscience, dismantle my reason, and bring them all under the turpitudes of the theologies of Rome, which are so well calculated to keep the world fettered in ignorance and superstition.

But God saw the tears with which I bedewed my pillow that night. He heard the cry of my agonizing soul, and in His infinite love and mercy determined to come to my rescue, and save me. If He saw fit to leave me many years more in the slavery of Egypt, it was that I might better know the plagues of that land of darkness, and the iron chains which are there prepared for poor lost souls.

When the hour of my deliverance came, the Lord took me by the hand and helped me to cross the Red Sea. He brought me to the Land of Promise—a land of peace, life, and joy which passeth all understanding.

CHAPTER XVI.

THERE are several imposing ceremonies at the ordination of a priest; and I will never forget the joy I felt when the Roman Pontiff, presenting to me the Bible, ordered me, with a solemn voice, to study and preach it. That order passed through my soul as a beam of light.

But, alas! those rays of light and life were soon to be followed, as a flash of lightning in a stormy night, by the most sudden and distressing darkness!

When holding the sacred volume, I accepted with unspeakable joy the command of studying and preaching its saving truth; but I felt as if a thunderbolt had fallen upon me when I pronounced the awful oath which is required from every priest: "*I will never interpret the Holy Scriptures except according to the unanimous consent of the Holy Fathers.*"

Many times, with the other students in theology, I had discussed the nature of that strange oath; still more often, in the silence of my meditations, alone in the presence of God, I had tried to fathom the bottomless abyss which, it seemed to me, was dug under my feet by it, and every time my conscience had shrunk in terror from its consequences. But I was not the only one in the seminary who contemplated, with an anxious mind, its evidently blasphemous nature.

About six months before our ordination, Stephen Baillargeon, one of my fellow theological students, had said in my presence to our superior, the Rev. Mr. Raimbault: " Allow me to tell you that one of the things with which I cannot reconcile my conscience is the solemn oath we will have to take, ' That we will never interpret the Scriptures except according to the *unanimous* consent of the Holy Fathers !' We have not given a single hour yet to the serious study of the Holy Fathers. I know many priests, and not a single one of them has ever studied the Holy Fathers; they have not even got them in their libraries! We will probably walk in their footsteps. It may be that not a single volume of the Holy Fathers will ever fall into our hands! In the name of common sense, how can we swear that we will follow the sentiments of men of whom we know absolutely nothing, and about whom, it is more probable, we will never know anything, except by mere vague hearsay ?"

Our superior gave evident signs of weakness in his answer to that unexpected difficulty. But his embarrassment grew much greater when I said: "Baillargeon cannot contemplate that oath without anxiety, and he has given you some of his reasons; but he has not said the last word on that strange oath. If you will allow me, Mr. Superior, I will present you some more formidable objections. It is not so much on account of our ignorance of the doctrines of the Holy Fathers that I tremble when I think I will have ' to swear never to interpret the Scriptures, except according to their unanimous consent.' Would to God that I could say, with Baillargeon, ' I know nothing of the Holy Fathers: how can I swear they will guide me in all my ways?' It is true that we know so little of them that it is supremely ridiculous, if it is not an insult to God and man, that we take them for our guides. But my regret is that we know already too much of the Holy Fathers to be exempt from perjuring ourselves, when we swear that we will not interpret the Holy Scriptures except according to their unanimous consent.

"Is it not a fact that the Holy Fathers' writings are so perfectly kept out of sight, that it is absolutely impossible to read and study them? But even if we had access to them, have we sufficient time at our disposal to study them so perfectly that we could conscientiously swear that we will follow them? And if we do not study them, how can we be exempted from wilful perjury the day that we will swear to follow them? How can we follow a thing we do not see, which we cannot hear, and about which we do not know more than the man in the moon? Our shameful ignorance of the Holy Fathers is a sufficient reason to make us fear at the approach of the solemn hour that we will swear to follow them. Yes! But we know enough of the Holy Fathers to chill the blood in our veins when swearing to interpret the Holy Scriptures only according to their unanimous consent. Please, Mr. Superior, tell us what are the texts of Scripture on which the Holy Fathers are *unanimous*. You respect yourself too much to try to answer a question which no honest man has, or will ever dare to answer. And if you, one of the most learned men of France, cannot put your finger on the texts of the Holy Bible and say, 'The Holy Fathers are perfectly unanimous on these texts!' how can we, poor young ecclesiastics of the humble College of Nicolet, say 'The Holy Fathers are *unanimously* of the same mind on those texts?' But if we cannot distinguish to-day, and if we shall never be able to distinguish between the texts on which the Holy Fathers are unanimous and the ones on which they differ, how can we *dare* to swear before God and men to interpret *every text of the Scriptures* only according to the unanimous consent of those Holy Fathers?

"By that awful oath, will we not be absolutely bound to remain mute as dead men on every text on which the Holy Fathers have differed, under the evident penalty of becoming perjured? Will not every text on which the Holy Fathers have differed become as the dead carcass which the Israelites could not touch, except by defiling themselves? After that strange oath, to interpret the Scripture *only* according to the *unanimous* consent of the Holy Fathers, will we not be absolutely deprived of the privilege of studying or preaching on a text on which they have differed?

"The consequences of that oath are *legion*, and every one of them seems to me the death of our ministry, the damnation of our souls! You have read the history of the Church, as we have it here, written by Henrion, Berrault, Bell, Costel, and Fleury. Well, what is the

prominent fact in those reliable histories of the Church? Is it not
that the Church has constantly been filled with the noise of the controversies of Holy Fathers with Holy Fathers? Do we not find, on
every page, that the Holy Fathers of one century very often differed
from the Holy Fathers of another century in very important matters?
Is it not a public and undeniable fact, that the history of our Holy
Church is almost nothing else than the history of the hard conflict,
stern divisions, unflinching contradictions and oppositions of Holy
Fathers to Holy Fathers?

"Here is a big volume of manuscript written by me, containing
only extracts from our best Church historians, filled with the public
disputes of Holy Fathers among themselves on almost every subject of
Christianity.

"There are Holy Fathers who say, with our best modern
theologians—St. Thomas, Bellarmine and Liguori—that we must kill
heretics as we kill wild beasts; while many others say that we must
tolerate them! You all know the name of the Holy Father who sends
to hell all the widows who marry a second time, while other Holy
Fathers are of a different mind. Some of them, you know well, had
very different notions from ours about purgatory. Is it necessary for
me to give you the names of the Holy Fathers, in Africa and Asia,
who refused to accept the supreme jurisdiction we acknowledge in the
Pope over all churches? Several Holy Fathers have denied the
supreme authority of the Church of Rome—you know it; they have
laughed at the excommunications of the Popes! Some even have
gladly died, when excommunicated by the Pope, without doing
anything to reconcile themselves to him! What do we find, in the
six volumes of letters we have still from St. Jerome, if not the
undeniable fact that he filled the Church with the noise of his harsh
denunciations of the scriptural views of St. Augustine on many
important points. You have read those letters? Well, have you not
concluded that St. Jerome and St. Augustine agreed almost only on
one thing, which was, to disagree on every subject they treated?

"Did not St. Jerome knock his head against nearly all the Holy
Fathers of his time? And has he not received hard knocks from
almost all the Holy Fathers with whom he was acquainted? Is it
not a public fact that St. Jerome and several other Holy Fathers
rejected the sacred books of the Maccabees, Judith, Tobias, just as the
heretics of our time reject them?

"And now we are gravely asked, in the name of the God of Truth,
to swear that we will interpret the Holy Scriptures only according
to the unanimous consent of those Holy Fathers, who have been
unanimous but in one thing, which was never to agree with each
other, and sometimes not even with themselves.

" For it is a well-known fact, though it is a very deplorable one, for instance, that St. Augustine did not always keep to the same correct views on the text " Thou art Peter, and upon that rock I will build My church.' After holding correct views on that fundamental truth he gave it up, at the end of his life, to say, with the Protestants of our day, that ' upon that rock means only Christ, and not Peter.' Now, how can I be bound by an oath to follow the views of men who have themselves been wavering and changing, when the Word of God must stand as an unmoving rock to my heart ? If you require from us an oath, why put into our hands the history of the Church, which has stuffed our memory with the undeniable facts of the endless fierce divisions of the Holy Fathers on almost every question which the Scriptures present to our faith ?

Would to God that I could say, with Baillargeon, I know nothing of the Holy Fathers ! Then I could perhaps be at peace with my conscience, after perjuring myself by promising a thing that I cannot do.

" I was lately told by the Rev. Mr. Leprohon, that it is absolutely necessary to go to the Holy Fathers in order to understand the Holy Scriptures ! But I will respectfully repeat to-day what I then said on that subject.

" If I am too ignorant or too stupid to understand St. Mark, St. Luke and St. Paul, how can I be intelligent enough to understand Jerome, Augustine and Tertullian ? And if St. Matthew, St. John and St. Peter have not got from God the grace of writing with a sufficient degree of light and clearness to be understood by men of good-will, how is it that Justin, Clemens and Cyprian have received from our God a favour of lucidity and clearness which He denied to His apostles and evangelists? If I cannot rely upon my private judgment when studying, with the help of God, the Holy Scriptures, how can I rely on my private judgment when studying the Holy Fathers ? You constantly tell me I cannot rely on my private judgment to understand and interpret the Holy Scriptures ; but will you please tell me with what judgment and intelligence I shall have to interpret and understand the writings of the Holy Fathers, if it be not with my own private judgment? Must I borrow the judgment and intelligence of some of my neighbours in order to understand and interpret, for instance, the writings of Origen ? or shall I be allowed to go and hear what that Holy Father wants from me, with my own private intelligence ? But again, if you are forced to confess that I have nothing else but my *private judgment and intelligence* to read, understand and follow the Holy Fathers, and that I not only can but must rely on my own private judgment, without any fear, in that case, how is it that I will be lost if I make use of that same *private and personal judgment* when at the feet of Jesus, listening to His eternal and life-giving words ?

"Nothing distresses me so much in our holy religion as that want of confidence in God when we go to the feet of Jesus to hear or read His soul-saving words, and the abundance of self-confidence, when we go among sinful and fallible men, to know what they say.

"It is not to the Holy Scriptures that we are invited to go to know what the Lord saith : it is to the Holy Fathers !

"Would it be possible that, in our Holy Church, the Word of God would be darkness, and the words of men light!

"This dogma, or article of our religion, by which we must go to the Holy Fathers in order to know what ' The Lord saith,' and not to the Holy Scriptures, is to my soul what a handful of sand would be to my eyes—it makes me perfectly blind.

"When our venerable bishop places the Holy Scriptures in my hands and commands me to study and preach them, I shall understand what he means, and he will know what he says. He will give me a most sublime work to perform ; and, by the grace of God, I hope to do it. But when he orders me to swear that I will *never* interpret the Holy Scriptures except according to the unanimous consent of the Holy Fathers, will he not make a perjured man of me, and will he not say a thing to which he has not given sufficient attention ? For to swear that we will never interpret anything of the Scriptures, except according to the unanimous consent of the Holy Fathers, is to swear to a thing as impossible and ridiculous as to take the moon with our hands. I say more, it is to swear that we will never study nor interpret a single chapter of the Bible. For it is probable that there are very few chapters of that Holy Book which have not been a cause of serious differences between some of the Holy Fathers.

"As the writings of the Holy Fathers fill at least two hundred volumes in folio, it will not take us less than ten years of constant study to know on what question they are or are not unanimous ! If, after that time of study, I find that they are *unanimous* on the question of orthodoxy which I must believe and preach, all will be right with me. I will walk with a fearless heart to the gates of eternity, with the certainty of following the true way of salvation. But if among fifty Holy Fathers there are forty-nine on one side and one only on the opposite side, in what awful state of distress will I be plunged ! Shall I not be then as a ship in a stormy night, after she has lost her compass, her masts, and her helm. If I were allowed to follow the majority, there would always be a plank of safety to rescue me from the impending wreck. But the Pope has inexorably tied us to the unanimity. If my faith is not the faith of *unanimity*, I am for ever damned. I am out of the Church !

"What a frightful alternative is just before us! We must either perjure ourselves, by swearing to follow a unanimity which is a fable, in order to remain Roman Catholics, or we must plunge into the abyss of impiety and atheism by refusing to swear that we will adhere to a unanimity which never existed."

It was visible, at the end of that long and stormy conference, that the fears and anxieties of Baillargeon and mine were partaken of by every one of the students in theology. The boldness of our expressions brought upon us a real storm. But our Superior did not dare to face or answer a single one of our arguments; he was evidently embarrassed, and nothing could surpass his joy when the bell told him that the hour of the conference was over. He promised to answer us the next day; but the next day he did nothing but throw dust into our eyes, and abuse us to his heart's content. He began by forbidding me to read any more of the controversial books I had bought a few months before, among which was the celebrated Derry discussion between seven priests and seven Protestants. I had to give back the well-known discussion between "Pope and Maguire," and between Gregg and the same Maguire. I had also to give up the numbers of the *Avenir* and other books of Lamenais, which I had got the liberty, as a privilege, to read. It was decided that my intelligence was not clear enough, and that my faith was not sufficiently strong to read those books. I had nothing to do but to bow my head under the yoke and obey, without a word of murmur. The darkest night was made around our understandings, and we had to believe that that awful darkness was the shining light of God! We rejected the bright truth which had so nearly conquered our mind in order to accept the most ridiculous sophisms as gospel truths! We did the most degrading action a man can do—we silenced the voice of our conscience, and we consented to follow our superior's views, as a brute follows the order of his master; we consented to be in the hands of our superiors like a stick in the hands of the traveller.

During the months which elapsed between that hard fought, though lost battle, and the solemn hour of my priestly ordination, I did all I could to subdue and annihilate my thoughts on that subject. My hope was that I had entirely succeeded. But, to my dismay, that reason suddenly awoke, as from a long sleep, when I had perjured myself, as every priest has to do. A chill of horror and shame ran through all my frame in spite of myself. In my inmost soul a cry was heard from my wounded conscience, "You annihilate the Word of God! You rebel against the Holy Ghost! You deny the Holy Scriptures to follow the steps of sinful men! You reject the pure waters of eternal life, to drink the waters of death."

In order to choke again the voice of my conscience, I did what my

Church advised me to do—I cried to my wafer god and to the blessed Virgin Mary that they might come to my help, and silence the voices which were troubling my peace by shaking my faith.

With the utmost sincerity, the day of my ordination, I renewed the promise that I had already so often made, and said in the presence of God and His angels, "I promise that I will never believe anything except according to the teachings of my Holy and Apostolic Church of Rome."

And on that pillow of folly, ignorance, and fanaticism I laid my head to sleep the sleep of spiritual death, with the two hundred millions of slaves whom the Pope sees at his feet.

And I slept that sleep till the God of our salvation, in His great mercy, awoke me, by giving to my soul the light, the truth, and the life which are in Jesus Christ.

CHAPTER XVII.

I was ordained a priest of Rome in the Cathedral of Quebec, on the 21st of September, 1833, by the Right Reverend Signaie, first Archbishop of Canada. No words can express the solemnity of my thoughts, the superhuman nature of my aspirations, when the delegate of the Pope, imposing his hands on my head, gave me the power of converting a real wafer into the real substantial body, blood, soul and divinity of Jesus Christ! The bright illusion of Eve, as the deceiver told her "Ye shall be as gods," was child's play compared with what I felt when, assured by the infallible voice of my Church that I was not only on equal terms with my Saviour and God, but I was in reality above Him! and that hereafter I would not only command, but *create* Him!!

The aspirations to power and glory which had been such a terrible temptation in Lucifer were becoming a reality in me! I had received the power of commanding God, not in a spiritual and mystical, but in a real, personal and most irresistible way.

With my heart full of an inexpressible joy and gratitude to God, and with all the faculties of my soul raised to exaltation, I withdrew from the feet of the pontiff to my oratory, where I passed the rest of the day in meditation on the great things which my God had wrought in me.

I had, at last, attained the top of that power and holiness which my Church had invited me to consider from my infancy as the most glorious gift which God had ever given to man! The dignity which I had just received was above all the dignities and the thrones of this world. The holy character of the PRIESTHOOD had been impressed on my soul, with the blood of Christ, as an imperishable and celestial glory. Nothing could ever take it away from me, in time or eternity. I was to be a priest of my God for ever and ever. Not only had Christ let His divine and priestly mantle fall on my shoulders, but He had so perfectly associated me with Himself as the great and eternal Sacrificer, that I was to renew, every day of my life, His atoning SACRIFICE! At my bidding, the only and eternally begotten Son of my God was now to come into my hands in Person! The same Christ who sits at the right hand of the Father was to come down every day into my breast, to unite His flesh to my flesh, His blood to my blood, His divine soul to my poor sinful soul, in order to walk, work and live in me and with me in the most perfect unity and intimacy!

I passed that whole day and the greater part of the night in contemplating the superhuman honours and dignities which my beloved Church had conferred on me. Many times I fell on my knees to thank God for His mercies towards me, and I could hardly speak to Him except with tears of joy and gratitude. I often repeated the words of the Holy Virgin Mary: " My soul doth magnify the Lord, and my spirit doth rejoice in God my Saviour."

The privileges granted to me were of a more substantial kind than those bestowed upon Mary. She had been obeyed by Christ *only* when He was a child. He had to obey me now, although He was in the full possession of His eternal glory!

In the presence of God and His angels, I promised to live a holy life as a token of my gratitude to Him. I said to my lips and my tongue, " Be holy now ; for you will not only speak to your God : you will give Him a new birth every day!" I said to my heart, " Be holy and pure now ; for you will bear every day the Holy of Holies!" To my soul I said, " Be holy now ; for you will henceforth be most intimately and personally united to Christ Jesus. You will be fed with the body, blood, soul and divinity of Him before whom the angels do not find themselves pure enough!"

Looking on my table, where my pipe, filled with tobacco, and my snuff-box were lying, I said : " Impure and noxious weeds, you will no more defile me! I am the priest of the Almighty. It is beneath my dignity to touch you any more!" and opening the window I threw them into the street, never to make use of them again.

On the 21st of September, 1833, I had thus been raised to the priesthood ; but I had not yet made use of the divine powers with which I had been invested. The next day I was to say my first Mass, and work that incomparable miracle which the Church of Rome calls TRANSUBSTANTIATION.

As I have already said, I had passed the greater part of the night between the 21st and 22nd in meditation and thanksgivings. On the morning of the 22nd, long before the dawn of day, I was dressed and on my knees. This was to be the most holy and glorious day of my life! Raised, the day before, to a dignity which was above the kingdoms and empires of the world, I was now, for the first time, to work a miracle at the altar which no angel or seraph could do.

At my bidding Christ was to receive a new existence! The miracle wrought by Joshua, when he commanded the sun and moon to stop, on the bloody plain of Gibeon, was nothing compared to the miracle that I was to perform that day. When the eternal Son of God would be in my hands, I was to present myself at the throne of mercy, with that expiatory victim of the sins of the world pay the debt, not only of my guilty soul, but of all those for whom I should speak! The ineffable sacrifice of Calvary was to be renewed by me that day with the utmost perfection!

When the bell rang to tell me that the hour was come to clothe myself with the golden priestly robes and go to the altar, my heart beat with such a rapidity that I came very near fainting. The holiness of the action I was to do, the infinite greatness of the sacrifice I was about to make, the divine victim I was to hold in my hands and present to God the Father! the wonderful miracle I was to perform, filled my soul and my heart with such sentiments of terror, joy and awe, that I was trembling from head to foot; and if very kind friends, among whom was the venerable secretary of the Archbishop of Quebec, now the Grand Vicar Cazault, had not been there to help and encourage me, I think I would not have dared to ascend the steps of the altar.

It is not an easy thing to go through all the ceremonies of a Mass. There are more than *one hundred different ceremonies and positions* of the body, which must be observed with the utmost perfection. To omit *one* of them willingly, or through a culpable neglect or ignorance, is eternal damnation. But thanks to a dozen exercises through which I had gone the previous week, and thanks be to the kind friends who helped and guided me, I went through the performances of that first Mass much more easily than I expected. It lasted about an hour. But when it was over, I was really exhausted by the effort made to keep my mind and heart in unison with the infinite greatness of the mysteries accomplished by me.

To make one's self believe that he can convert a piece of bread into God requires such a supreme effort of the will, and complete annihilation of intelligence, that the state of the soul, after the effort is over, is more like death than life.

I had really persuaded myself that I had done the most holy and sublime action of my life, when, in fact, I had been guilty of the most outrageous act of idolatry! My eyes, my hands and lips, my mouth and tongue, and all my senses, as well as the faculties of my intelligence, were telling me that what I had seen, touched, eaten, was nothing but a wafer ; but the voices of the Pope and his Church were telling me that it was the real body, blood, soul and divinity of Jesus Christ. I had persuaded myself that the voices of my senses and intelligence were the voices of Satan, and that the deceitful voice of the Pope was the voice of the God of Truth ! Every priest of Rome has come to that strange degree of folly and perversity, every day of his life, to remain a priest of Rome.

The great imposture taught under the modern word TRANSUB-STANTIATION, when divested of the glare which Rome, by her sorceries, throws around it, is soon seen to be what it is—a *most impious and idolatrous doctrine.*

"I must carry the 'good God' to-morrow to a sick man," says the priest to his servant girl. In plain French: "Je dois porter le 'Bon Dieu' demain à un malade," dit le prêtre à sa servante; "mais il n'y en a plus dans le tabernacle." "But there are no more particles in the tabernacle. Make some small cakes that I may consecrate them to-morrow." And the obedient domestic takes some wheat flour, for no other kind of flour is fit to make the god of the Pope. A mixture of any other kind would make the miracle of "transubstantiation" a great failure. The servant girl accordingly takes the dough, and bakes it between two heated irons, on which are graven the following figures, c. h. s. When the whole is well baked, she takes her scissors and cuts those wafers, which are about four or five inches large, into smaller ones of the size of an inch, and respectfully hands them over to the priest.

The next morning the priest takes the newly-baked wafers to the altar, and changes them into the body, blood, soul, and divinity of Jesus Christ. It was one of those wafers that I had taken to the altar in that solemn hour of my first Mass, and which I had turned into my Saviour by the five magical words—HOC EST ENIM CORPUS MEUM !

What was the difference between the incredible folly of Aaron, on the day of his apostasy in the wilderness, and the action I had done when I worshipped the god whom I made myself, and got my friends to worship ? Where, I ask, is the difference between the adoration of the calf-god of Aaron and the wafer-god which I had made on the 22nd September, 1833. The only difference was, that the idolatry of Aaron lasted but one day, while the idolatry in which I lived lasted a quarter of a century, and has been perpetuated in the Church of Rome for more than a thousand years.

What has the Church of Rome done by giving up the words of Christ, "Do this in remembrance of Me," and substituting her dogma of Transubstantiation ? She has brought the world back to the old heathenism. The priest of Rome worships a Saviour called Christ. Yes; but that Christ is not the Christ of the gospel. It is a false and newly-invented Christ whom the Popes have smuggled from the Pantheon of Rome, and sacrilegiously called by the adorable name of our Saviour, Jesus Christ.

I have often been asked : " Was it possible that you sincerely believed that the wafer could be changed into God by you?" And, " Have you really worshipped that water as your Saviour ?"

To my shame, and to the shame of poor humanity, I must say " Yes." I believed as sincerely as every Roman Catholic priest is bound to believe it, that I was creating my own Saviour-God every morning by the assumed consecration of the wafer; and I was saying to the people, as I presented it to them, "Ecce Agnus Dei"—" This is the Lamb of God, who takes away the sins of the world ; let us adore Him ;" and prostrating myself on my knees I was adoring the god made by myself, with the help of my servant; and all the people prostrated themselves to adore the newly-made god!

I must confess, further, that though I was bound to believe in the existence of Christ in heaven, and was invited by my Church to worship Him as my Saviour and my God, I had, as every Roman Catholic has, more confidence, faith, and love towards the Christ which I had created with a few words of my lips than towards the Christ of heaven.

My Church told me, every day of my life, and I had to believe and preach it, that though the Christ of heaven was my Saviour, He was angry against me on account of my sins; that He was constantly disposed to punish me, according to His terrible justice; that He was armed with lightning and thunder to crush me; and that, were it not for His mother, who day and night was interceding for me, I should be cast into that hell which my sins had so richly deserved. All the theologians, with St. Liguori at their head, whose writings I was earnestly studying, and which had received the approbation of infallible Popes, persuaded me that it was Mary whom I had to thank and bless, if I had not yet been punished as I deserved. Not only had I to believe this doctrine, but I had to preach it to the people. The result was for me, as it is for every Roman Catholic, that my heart was really chilled, and I was filled with terror every time I looked to the Christ of heaven through the lights and teachings of my Church. He could not, as I believed, look to me except with an angry face; He could not stretch out His hand towards me except to crush me, unless His merciful mother or some other mighty saint interposed their saving supplications to appease His just indignation. When I was praying to that Christ of the Church of Rome, my mind was constantly perplexed about the choice I should make of some powerful protector, whose influence could get me a favourable hearing from my irritated Saviour.

Besides this, I was told, and I had to believe it, that the Christ of heaven was a mighty monarch, a most glorious king, surrounded by innumerable hosts of servants, officers and friends, and that, as it would not do for a poor rebel to present himself before his irritated King to get His pardon, but he must address himself to some of His most influential courtiers, or to His beloved mother, to whom nothing can be refused, that they might plead his cause; so I sincerely believed that it was better for me not to speak myself to Jesus Christ, but to look for some one who would speak for me.

But there were no such terrors or fears in my heart when I approached the Saviour whom I had created myself! Such an humble and defenceless Saviour, surely, had no thunder in His hands to punish His enemies. He could have no angry looks for me. He was my friend, as well as the work of my hands. There was nothing in Him which could inspire me with any fear. Had I not brought Him down from heaven? And had He not come into my hands that He might hear, bless, and forgive me?—that He might be nearer to me, and I nearer to Him?

When I was in His presence, in that solitary church, there was no need of officers, of courtiers, of mothers to speak to Him for me. He was no longer there a mighty monarch, an angry king, who could be approached only by the great officers of His court; He was now the rebuked of the world, the humble and defenceless Saviour of the manger, the forsaken Jesus of Calvary, the forgotten Christ of Gethsemane.

No words can give any idea of the pleasure I used to feel when alone, prostrated before the Christ whom I had made at the morning Mass, I poured out my heart at His feet. It is impossible for those who have not lived under those terrible illusions to understand with what confidence I spoke to the Christ who was then before me, bound by the ties of His love for me! How many times, in the colder days of winter, in churches which had never seen any fire, with an atmosphere 15 degrees below zero, had I passed whole hours alone, in adoration of the Saviour whom I had made only a few hours before! How often have I looked with silent admiration to the Divine Person who was there alone, passing the long hours of the day and night, rebuked and forsaken, that I might have an opportunity of approaching Him, and of speaking to Him as a friend to his friend, as a repenting sinner to his merciful Saviour. My faith—I should rather say my awful delusion, was then so complete that I scarcely felt the biting of the cold! I may say with truth, that the happiest hours I ever had, during the long years of darkness into which the Church of Rome had plunged me, were the hours which I passed in adoring the Christ whom I had made with my own lips. And every priest of Rome

would make the same declaration were they questioned on the
subject.

It is a similar principle of monstrous faith that leads widows in
India to leap with cries of joy into the fire which will burn them into
ashes with the bodies of their deceased husbands. Their priests have
assured them that such a sacrifice will secure eternal happiness to
themselves and their departed husbands.

In fact, the Roman Catholics have no other Saviour to whom they
can betake themselves than the one made by the consecration of the
wafer. He is the only Saviour who is not angry with them, and who
does not require the mediation of virgins and saints to appease His
wrath. This is the reason why Roman Catholic churches are so well
filled by the poor blind Roman Catholics. See how they rush to the
foot of their altars at almost every hour of the day, sometimes long
before the dawn! Go to some of their churches, even on a rainy and
stormy morning, and you will see crowds of worshippers, of every age
and from every grade of society, braving the storm and the rain,
walking through the mud to pass an hour at the foot of their
tabernacles!

How is it that the Roman Catholics, alone, offer such a spectacle
to the civilized world? The reason is very simple and plain. Every
soul yearns for a God to whom it can speak, and who will hear its
supplications with a merciful heart, and who will wipe away her
penitential tears. Just as the flowers of our gardens turn naturally
towards the sun which gives them their colour, their fragrance and
their life, so every soul wants a Saviour who is not angry but
merciful towards those who come unto Him. A Saviour who will
say to the weary and heavy laden : "Come unto Me and I will give
you rest." A God, in fine, who is not armed with Thunder and Lightning, and does not require to be approached only by saints, virgins,
and martyrs; but who, through his son Jesus, is the real, the true,
and the only friend of Sinners.

When the people think there is such a God — such a loving
Saviour to be found in the tabernacle, it is but natural that they should
brave the storms and the rains, to worship at His feet, to receive the
pardon of their sins.

The children of light, the disciples of the gospel, who protest
against the errors of Rome, know that their Heavenly Father is *everywhere* ready to hear, forgive, and help them. They know that it is no
more at Jerusalem, nor on this or that mountain, or at Church that
God wants to be worshipped (John iv. 21). They know that their
Saviour liveth, and is everywhere ready to hear those who invoke His
name; that He is no more in that desert, or in that secret chamber
(Matt. xxiv. 26). They know that He is everywhere—that He is ever

near to those who look to His bleeding wounds, and whose robes are washed in His blood. They find Jesus in their most secret closets when they enter them to pray ; they meet Him and converse with Him when in the fields, behind the counter, travelling on railroads or steamers—everywhere they meet with Him, and speak to Him as friend to friend.

It is not so with the followers of the Pope. They are told contrary to the gospel (Matt. xxiv. 23), that Christ is in this Church—in that secret chamber or tabernacle! Cruelly deceived by their priests, they run, they brave the storms to go as near as possible to that place where their merciful Christ lives. They go to the Christ who will give them a hearty welcome—who will listen to their humble prayers, and be compassionate to their tears of repentance.

Let Protestants cease to admire poor deluded Roman Catholics who dare the storm and go to church even before the dawn of day. This devotion, which so dazzles them, should excite compassion, and not admiration ; for it is the logical result of the most awful spiritual darkness. It is the offspring of the greatest imposture the world has ever seen ; it is the natural consequence of the belief that the priest of Rome can create Christ and God by the consecration of a wafer, and keep Him in a secret chamber.

The Egyptians worshipped God under the form of crocodiles and calves. The Greeks made their gods of marble or of gold. The Persian made the sun his god. The Hottentots make their gods with whalebone, and go far through the storms to adore them. The Church of Rome makes her god out of a piece of bread! Is this not Idolatry ?

From the year 1833, to the day that God in His mercy opened my eyes, my servant had used more than a bushel of wheat flour, to make the little cakes which I had to convert into the Christ of the Mass. Some of these I ate; others I carried about with me for the sick, and others I placed in the tabernacle for the adoration of the people.

I am often asked, "How is it that you could be guilty of such a gross act of idolatry ?" My only answer is the answer of the blind man of the gospel : "I know not; one thing I know, that, whereas I was blind, now I see" (John ix. 25).

CHAPTER XVIII.

ON the day of my ordination to the priesthood, I had to believe, with all the priests of Rome, that it was within the limits of my powers to go into all the bakeries of Quebec, and change all the loaves and biscuits in that old city, into the body, blood, soul, and divinity of our

8

Lord Jesus Christ, by pronouncing over them the five-words : HOC EST
ENIM CORPUS MEUM. Nothing would have remained of these loaves and
biscuits but the smell, the colour, the taste.

Every bishop and priest of the cities of New York and Boston,
Chicago, Montreal, Paris, and London, etc., firmly believes and teaches
that he has the power to turn all the loaves of their cities, of their
dioceses, nay, of the whole world, into the body, blood, soul, and
divinity of our Saviour, Jesus Christ. And, though they have never
yet found it advisable to do that wonderful miracle, they consider, and
say, that to entertain any doubt about the power to perform that
marvel, is as criminal as to entertain any doubt about the existence of
God.

When in the Seminary of Nicolet, I heard, several times, our
Superior, the Rev. Mr. Raimbault, tells us that a French priest
having been condemned to death in Paris, when dragged to the
scaffold had, through revenge, consecrated and changed into Jesus
Christ all the loaves of the bakeries which were along the streets
through which he had to pass ; and though our learned Superior
condemned that action in the strongest terms, yet he told us that the
consecration was valid, and that the loaves were really changed into
the body, blood, soul and divinity of the Saviour of the world. And
I was bound to believe it under pain of eternal damnation.

Before my ordination I had been obliged to learn by heart, in one
of the most sacred books of the Church of Rome (Missale Romanum,
p. 63) the following statement :—"If the host after consecration disappear, either by any accident, as by the wind, or a miracle, or being
taken and carried off by any animal ; and if it cannot be recovered,
then he shall consecrate another."

And at page 57 I had learned, "If after consecration a fly has
fallen in, or anything of that sort, and a nausea be occasioned to the
priest, he shall draw it out and wash it with wine, and when the
mass is finished, burn it, and the ashes and lotion shall be thrown
into the sacrarium. But if he have not a nausea, nor fear any danger,
he shall drink them [ashes and lotion] with the blood."

In the month of January, 1834, I heard the following fact from the
Rev. Mr. Paquette, curate of St. Gervais, at a grand dinner which he
had given to the neighbouring priests :—

"When young, I was the vicar of a curate who could eat as
much as two of us, and drink as much as *four*. He was tall and
strong, and he has left the dark marks of his hard fists on the nose of
more than one of his beloved sheep; for his anger was really terrible
after he had drank his bottle of wine.

"One day, after a sumptuous dinner, he was called to carry the
good god (Le Bon Dieu), to a dying man. It was in midwinter. The

cold was intense. The wind was blowing hard. There were at least
five or six feet of snow, and the roads were almost impassable. It was
really a serious matter to travel nine miles on such a day, but there
was no help. The messenger was one of the first marguilliers (elders)
who was very pressing, and the dying man was one of the first
citizens of the place. The curate, after a few grumblings, drank a
tumbler of good Jamaica with his marguillier, as a preventive against
the cold; went to church, took the good god (Le Bon Dieu), and
threw himself into the sleigh, wrapped as well as possible in his large
buffalo robes.

" Though there were two horses, one before the other, to drag the
sleigh, the journey was a long and tedious one, which was made still
worse by an unlucky circumstance. They were met half-way by
another traveller coming from the opposite direction. The road was
too narrow to allow the two sleighs and horses to remain easily on
firm ground when passing by each other, and it would have required
a good deal of skill and patience in driving the horses to prevent them
from falling into the soft snow. It is well known that when once
horses are sunk into five or six feet of snow, the more they struggle
the deeper they sink.

" The marguillier, who was carrying the ' good god,' with the
curate, naturally hoped to have the privilege of keeping the middle
of the road, and escaping the danger of getting his horses wounded
and his sleigh broken. He cried to the other traveller in a high tone
of authority, ' Traveller! let me have the road. Turn your horses
into the snow. Make haste, I am in a hurry. I carry the good god!'

" Unfortunately that traveller was a heretic, who cared much more
for his horses than for the ' good god.' He answered:

" ' Le Diable emporte ton Bon Dieu avant que je ne casse le cou
de mon cheval!' 'The d—— take your " good god " before I break
the neck of my horse. If your god has not taught you the rules of
law and of common sense, I will give you a free lecture on that
matter,' and jumping out of his sleigh he took the reins of the
front horse of the marguillier to help him to walk on the side of the
road, and keep the half of it for himself.

" But the marguillier, who was naturally a very impatient and
fearless man, had drank too much with my curate, before he left the
parsonage, to keep cool, as he ought to have done. He also jumped
out of his sleigh, ran to the stranger, took his cravat in his left hand
and raised his right to strike him in the face.

" Unfortunately for him, the heretic seemed to have foreseen all
this. He had left his overcoat in the sleigh, and was more ready for
the conflict than his assailant. He was also a real giant in size and
strength. As quick as lightning his right and left fists fell like iron

masses on the face of the poor marguillier, who was thrown upon his back in the soft snow, where he almost disappeared.

"Till then the curate had been a silent spectator; but the sight and cries of his friend, whom the stranger was pommelling without mercy, made him lose his patience. Taking the little silk bag which contained the 'good god' from about his neck, where it was tied, he put it on the seat of the sleigh, and said, 'Dear good god! Please remain neutral; I must help my marguillier. Take no part in this conflict, and I will punish that infamous Protestant as he deserves.'

"But the unfortunate marguillier was entirely put *hors de combat* before the curate could go to his help. His face was horribly cut—three teeth were broken—the lower jaw dislocated, and the eyes were so terribly damaged that it took several days before he could see anything.

"When the heretic saw the priest coming to renew the battle, he threw down his other coat, to be freer in his movements. The curate had not been so wise. Relying too much on his herculean strength, covered with his heavy overcoat, on which was his white surplice, he threw himself on the stranger, like a big rock which falls from the mountain and rolls upon the oak below.

"Both of these combatants were real giants, and the first blows must have been terrible on both sides. But the 'infamous heretic' probably had not drank so much as my curate before leaving home, or perhaps he was more expert in the exchange of these savage jokes. The battle was long, and the blood flowed pretty freely on both sides. The cries of the combatants might have been heard at a long distance, were it not for the roaring noise of the wind which at that instant was blowing a hurricane.

"The storm, the cries, the blows, the blood, the surplice, and the overcoat of the priest torn to rags; the shirt of the stranger reddened with gore, made such a terrible spectacle, that in the end the horses of the marguillier, though well trained animals, took fright and threw themselves into the snow, turned their backs to the storm and made for home. They dragged the fragments of the upset sleigh a pretty long distance, and arrived at the door of their stable with only some diminutive parts of the harness.

"The 'good god' had evidently heard the prayer of my curate, and he had remained neutral; at all events, he had not taken the part of his priest, for he lost the day, and the infamous Protestant remained master of the battle-field.

"The curate had to help his marguillier out of the snow in which he was buried, and where he had lain like a slaughtered ox. Both had to walk, or rather crawl, nearly half a mile in snow to the knees, before they could reach the nearest farmhouse, where they arrived when it was dark.

"But the worst is not told. You remember when my curate had put the box containing the 'good god' on the seat of the sleigh, before going to fight. The horses had dragged the sleigh a certain distance, upset and smashed it. The little silk bag, with the silver box and its precious contents, was lost in the snow, and though several hundred people had looked for it, several days at different times, it could not be found. It was only late in the month of June, that a little boy, seeing some rags in the mud of the ditch, along the highway, lifted them and a little silver box fell out. Suspecting that it was what the people had looked for so many days during the last winter, he took it to the parsonage.

"I was there when it was opened; we had the hope that the 'good god' would be found pretty intact, but we were doomed to be disappointed. *The good god was entirely melted away. Le Bon Dieu etait fondu!*"

During the recital of that spicy story, which was told in the most amusing and comical way, the priests had drunk freely and laughed heartily. But when the conclusion came: "Le Bon Dieu etait fondu!"

"The good god was melted away!" There was a burst of laughter such as I never heard—the priests striking the floor with their feet, and the table with their hands, filled the house with the cries, "The good god melted away!"

"The good god melted away!"

"Le Bon Dieu est fondu!" "Le Bon Dieu est fondu!" Yes, the god of Rome, dragged away by a drunken priest, had really melted away in the muddy ditch. This glorious fact was proclaimed by his own priests in the midst of convulsive laughter, and at tables covered with scores of bottles just emptied by them!

About the middle of March, 1839, I had one of the most unfortunate days of my Roman Catholic priestly life. At about two o'clock in the afternoon, a poor Irishman had come in haste from beyond the high mountains, between Lake Beauport and the River Morency, to ask me to go and anoint a dying woman. It took me ten minutes to run to the church, put the "good god" in the little silver box, shut the whole in my vest pocket and jump into the Irishman's rough sleigh. The roads were exceeding bad, and we had to go very slowly. At 7 p.m. we were yet more than three miles from the sick woman's house. It was very dark, and the horse was so exhausted that it was impossible to go any further through the gloomy forest. I determined to pass the night at a poor Irish cabin which was near the road. I knocked at the door, asked hospitality, and was welcomed

with that warm-hearted demonstration of respect which the Roman
Catholic Irishman knows, better than any other man, how to pay to
his priests.

The shanty, twenty-four feet long by sixteen wide, was built with
round logs, between which a liberal supply of clay, instead of mortar,
had been thrown, to prevent the wind and cold from entering. Six
fat, though not absolutely well-washed, healthy boys and girls, half-
naked, presented themselves around their good parents, as the living
witnesses that this cabin, in spite of its ugly appearance, was really a
happy home for its dwellers.

Besides the eight human beings sheltered beneath that hospitable
roof, I saw, at one end, a magnificent cow, with her new-born calf,
and two fine pigs. These last two boarders were separated from the
rest of the family only by a branch partition two or three feet high.

"Please your reverence," said the good woman, after she had prepared her supper, "excuse our poverty, but be sure that we feel
happy and much honoured to have you in our humble dwelling for the
night. My only regret is that we have only potatoes, milk and butter
to give you for your supper. In these backwoods, tea, sugar, and
wheat flour are unknown luxuries."

I thanked that good woman for her hospitality, and caused her to
rejoice not a little by assuring her that good potatoes, fresh butter and
milk, were the best delicacies which could be offered to me in any
place. I sat at the table, and ate one of the most delicious suppers of
my life. The potatoes were exceedingly well-cooked—the butter,
cream and milk of the best quality, and my appetite was not a little
sharpened by the long journey over the steep mountains.

I had not told these good people, nor even my driver, that I had
" Le Bon Dieu," the good god, with me in my vest pocket. It would
have made them too uneasy, and would have added too much to my
other difficulties. When the time of sleeping arrived I went to bed
with all my clothing, and I slept well; for I was very tired by the
tedious and broken roads from Beauport to these distant mountains.

Next morning, before breakfast and the dawn of day, I was up,
and as soon as we had a glimpse of light to see our way, I left for the
house of the sick woman after offering a silent prayer.

I had not travelled a quarter of a mile when I put my hand into
my vest pocket, and to my indescribable dismay I found that the little
silver box, containing the "good god," was missing. A cold sweat
ran through my frame. I told my driver to stop and turn back immediately, that I had lost something which might be found in the
bed where I had slept. It did not take five minutes to retrace our
way.

On opening the door I found the poor woman and her husband

almost beside themselves, and distressed beyond measure. They were
pale and trembling as criminals who expected to be condemned.

" Did you not find a little silver box after I left," I said.

" O my God! " answered the desolate woman ; " yes, I have found
it, but would to God I had never seen it. There it is."

" But why do you regret finding it, when I am so happy to find it
here, safe in your hands! " I replied.

" Ah ; your reverence, you do not know what a terrible misfortune
has just happened to me, not more than half a minute before you
knocked at the door."

" What misfortune can have fallen upon you in so short a time," I
answered.

" Well, please your reverence, open the little box and you will
understand me."

I opened it, but the " good god" was not in it!! Looking in the
face of the poor distressed woman, I asked her, " What does this
mean? It is empty! "

" It means," answered she, " that I am the most unfortunate of
women! Not more than five minutes after you had left the house, I
went to your bed and found that little box. Not knowing what it
was I showed it to my children and to my husband. I asked him to
open it, but he refused to do it. I then turned it on every side, trying
to guess what it could contain ; till the devil tempted me so much that
I determined to open it. I came to this corner, where this pale lamp
is used to remain on that little shelf, and I opened it. But, oh my
God! I do not dare to tell the rest."

At these words she fell on the floor in a fit of nervous excitement
—her cries were piercing, her mouth was foaming. She was cruelly
tearing her hair with her own hands. The shrieks and lamentations
of the children were so distressing that I could hardly prevent myself
from crying also.

After a few moments of the most agonizing anxiety, seeing that the
poor woman was becoming calm, I addressed myself to the husband,
and said : " Please give me the explanation of these strange things? "
He could hardly speak at first, but as I was very pressing he told me
with a trembling voice : " Please your reverence ; look into that
vessel which the children use, and you will perhaps understand our
desolation ! When my wife opened the little silver box she did not
observe the vessel was there, just beneath her hands. In the opening,
what was in the silver box fell into that vase, and sank ! We were
all filled with consternation when you knocked at the door and
entered."

I felt struck with such unspeakable horror at the thought that the
body, blood, soul and divinity of my Saviour, Jesus Christ, was there,

sunk into that vase, that I remained speechless, and for a long time did not know what to do. At first it came into my mind to plunge my hands into the vase and try to get my Saviour out of that sepulchre of ignominy. But I could not muster courage to do so.

At last I requested the poor desolated family to dig a hole three feet deep in the ground, and deposit it, with its contents, and I left the house, after I had forbidden them from ever saying a word about that awful calamity.

In one of the most sacred books of the laws and regulations of the Church of Rome (Missale Romanum), we read, page 58, " If the priest vomit the Eucharist, if the species appear entire, let them be reverently swallowed, unless sickness arise; for then let the consecrated species be cautiously separated and laid up in some sacred place till they are corrupted; and afterwards let them be cast into the sacrarium. But if the species do not appear, let the vomit be burned, and the ashes cast into the sacrarium."

When a priest of Rome, I was bound, with all the Roman Catholics, to believe that Christ had taken His own body, with His own hands, to His mouth; and that He had eaten Himself, not in a spiritual, but in a substantial material way! After eating Himself, He had given it to each of His apostles, who then ate Him also!!

Before closing this chapter, let the reader allow me to ask him, if the world, in its darkest ages of paganism, has ever witnessed such a system of idolatry, so debasing, impious, ridiculous and diabolical in its consequences as the Church of Rome teaches in the dogma of transubstantiation!

When, with the light of the gospel in hand, the Christian goes into those horrible recesses of superstition, folly, and impiety, he can hardly believe what his eyes see and his ears hear. It seems impossible that men can consent to worship a god whom the rats can eat! A god who can be dragged away and lost in a muddy ditch by a drunken priest! A god who can be eaten, vomited, and eaten again by those who are courageous enough to eat again what they have vomited!!

The religion of Rome is not a religion: it is the mockery, the destruction, the ignominious caricature of religion. The Church of Rome, as a public fact, is nothing but the accomplishment of the awful prophecy: "Because they received not the love of the truth that they might be saved. And for this cause God shall send them strong delusion, that they should believe a lie." (2 Thess. ii. 10, 11.)

CHAPTER XIX.

On the 24th September, 1833, the Rev. Mr. Casault, secretary of the Bishop of Quebec, presented to me the official letters which named me the vicar of the Rev. Mr. Perras, arch-priest, and curate of St. Charles, Rivierre Boyer, and I was soon on my way, with a cheerful heart, to fill the post assigned to me by my Superior.

The parish of St. Charles is beautifully situated about twenty miles south-west of Quebec, on the banks of a river, which flows in its very midst, from north to south. Its large farm-houses and barns, neatly white-washed with lime, were the symbols of peace and comfort. The vandal axe had not yet destroyed the centenary forests which covered the country. On almost every farm a splendid grove of maples had been reserved as the witness of the intelligence and tastes of the people.

I had often heard of the Rev. Mr. Perras as one of the most learned, pious, and venerable priests of Canada. I had even been told that several of the governors of Quebec had chosen him for the French teacher of their children. When I arrived, he was absent on a sick call, but his sister received me with every mark of refined politeness. Under the burden of her five-and-fifty years she had kept all the freshness and amiability of youth. After a few words of welcome, she showed me my study and sleeping room. They were both perfumed with the fragrance of two magnificent bouquets of the choicest flowers, on the top of one of which were written the words: " Welcome to the angel whom the Lord sends to us as His messenger." The two rooms were the perfection of neatness and comfort. I shut the doors and fell on my knees to thank God and the blessed Virgin for having given me such a home. Ten minutes later I came back to the large parlour, where I found Miss Perras waiting for me, to offer me a glass of wine and some excellent " pain de savoie," as it was the universal custom, then, to do in every respectable house. She then told me how her brother, the curate, and herself were happy when they heard that I was to come and live with them. She had known my mother before her marriage, and she told me how she had passed several happy days in her company.

She could not speak to me of any subject more interesting than my mother; for, though she had died a few years before, she had never ceased to be present to my mind, and near and dear to my heart.

Miss Perras had not spoken long when the curate arrived. I rose to meet him, but it is impossible to adequately express what I felt at that moment. The Israelites were hardly struck with more awe when they saw Moses coming down from Mount Sinai, than I was at the first sight I had of that venerable man.

Rev. Mr. Perras was then about sixty-five years old. He was a tall man—almost a giant. No army officer, no king ever bore his head with more dignity. But his beautiful blue eyes, which were the embodiment of kindness, tempered the dignity of his mien. His hair, which was beginning to whiten, had not yet lost its golden lustre. It seemed as if silver and gold were mixed on his head to adorn and beautify it. There was on his face an expression of peace, calm, piety and kindness, which entirely won my heart and my respect. When, with a smile on his lips, he extended his hands towards me, I felt beside myself, I fell on my knees and said : " Mr. Perras, God sends me to you that you may be my teacher and my father. You will have to guide my first and inexperienced steps in the holy ministry. Do bless me, and pray that I may be a good priest as you are yourself."

That unpremeditated and earnest act of mine so touched the good old priest, that he could hardly speak. Leaning towards me he raised me up and pressed me to his bosom, and with a voice trembling with emotion he said : " May God bless you, my dear sir, and may He also be blessed for having chosen you to help me to carry the burden of the holy ministry in my old age." After half-an-hour of the most interesting conversation, he showed me his library, which was very large, and composed of the best books which a priest of Rome is allowed to read ; and he very kindly put it at my service.

Next morning, after breakfast, he handed me a large and neat sheet of paper, headed by these latin words:

" ORDO DUCIT AD DEUM."

It was the rule of life which he had imposed upon himself, to guide all the hours of the day in such a way that not a moment could be given to idleness or vain pastime.

"Would you be kind enough," he said, " to read this and tell me if it suits your views ? I have found great spiritual and temporal benefits in following these rules of life, and would be very happy if my dear young coadjutor would unite with me in walking in the ways of an orderly, Christian and priestly life.

I read this document with interest and pleasure, and handed it back to him saying: "I will be very happy, with the help of God, to follow, with you, the wise rules set down here for a holy and priestly life."

Thinking that these rules might be interesting to the reader, I give them here in full :

1. Rising - - - - - - - 5.30 a.m.
2. Prayer and Meditation - - - - - 6 to 6.30 a.m.

3. Mass, hearing confessions and recitation of breva-
   rium - - - - - - - 6.30 to 8 a.m.
4. Breakfast - - - - - - - 8 a.m.
5. Visitation of the sick, and reading the lives of
   the saints - - - - - - 8.30 to 10 a.m.
6. Study of philosophical, historical, or theological
   books - - - - - - 11 a.m. to 12.
7. Dinner - - - - - - - 12 to 12.30.
8. Recreation and conversation - - - - 12.30 to 1.30.
9. Recitation and vespers - - - - 1.30 to 2 p.m.
10. Study of history, theology or philosophy - - 2 to 4 p.m.
11. Visit to the holy sacrament and reading "Imita-
    tion of Jesus Christ" - - - - 4 to 4.30.
12. Hearing of confessions, or visit to the sick, or study 4.30 to 6 p.m.
13. Supper - - - - - - - 6 to 6.30 p.m.
14. Recreation, - - - - - - 6.30 to 8 p.m.
15. Chaplet—reading of the Holy Scriptures and
    prayer - - - - - - 8 to 9 p.m.
16. Going to bed - - - - - - 9 p.m.

Such was our daily life during the eight months which it was my privilege to remain with the venerable Mr. Perras, except that Thursdays were invariably given to visit some of the neighbouring curates, and the Sabbath days spent in hearing confessions, and performing the public services of the church.

The conversation of Mr. Perras was generally exceedingly interesting. I never heard from him any idle, frivolous talking, as is so much the habit among the priests. He was well versed in the literature, philosophy, history and theology of Rome. He had personally known almost all the bishops and priests of the last fifty years, and his memory was well stored with anecdotes and facts concerning the clergy, from almost the days of the conquest of Canada. I could write many interesting things, were I to publish what I heard from him, concerning the doings of the clergy. I will only give two or three of the facts of that interesting period of the church in Canada.

A couple of months before my arrival at St. Charles, the vicar who preceded me, called Lajus, had publicly eloped with one of his beautiful penitents, who, after three months of public scandal, had repented and come back to her heartbroken parents. About the same time a neighbouring curate, in whom I had great confidence, compromised himself also, with one of his fair parishioners, in a most shameful, though less public way. These two scandals, which came to my knowledge almost at the same time, distressed me exceedingly, and for nearly a week I felt so overwhelmed with shame, that I dreaded to show my face in public, and I almost regretted that I ever became a priest. My nights were sleepless; the best viands of the table had lost their relish. I could hardly eat anything. My conversations

with Mr. Perras had lost their charms. I even could hardly talk with
him or anybody else.

"Are you sick, my young friend?" said he to me one day.

"No, sir, I am not sick, but I am sad."

He replied, "Can I know the cause of your sadness? You used
to be so cheerful and happy since you came here. I must bring you
back to your former happy frame of mind. Please tell me what is the
matter with you? I am an old man, and I know many remedies for
the soul as well as for the body. Open your heart to me, and I hope
soon to see that dark cloud which is over you pass away."

"The two last awful scandals given by the priests," I answered,
"are the cause of my sadness. The news of the fall of these two confreres, one of whom seemed to me so respectable, has fallen upon me
like a thunderbolt. Though I had heard something of that nature when
I was a simple ecclesiastic in the college, I had not the least idea that
such was the life of so many priests. The fact of the human frailty
of so many, is really distressing. How can one hope to stand up on
one's feet when one sees such strong men fall by one's side? What
will become of our holy church in Canada, and all over the world, if
her most devoted priests are so weak and have so little self-respect,
and so little fear of God?"

"My dear young friend," answered Mr. Perras. "Our holy
church is infallible. The gates of hell can not prevail against her;
but the assurance of her perpetuity and infallibility does not rest on
any human foundation. It does not rest on the personal holiness of
her priests; but it rests on the promises of Jesus Christ. Her perpetuity and infallibility are a perpetual miracle. It requires the constant working of Jesus Christ to keep her pure and holy, in spite of
the sins and scandals of her priests. Even the clearest proof that our
holy church has a promise of perpetuity and infallibility is drawn
from the very sins and scandals of her priests; for those sins and
scandals would have destroyed her long ago, if Christ was not in the
midst to save and sustain her. Just as the ark of Noah was
miraculously saved by the mighty hand of God, when the waters of
the deluge would otherwise have wrecked it, so our holy church is
miraculously prevented from perishing in the flood of iniquities by
which too many priests have deluged the world. By the great mercy
and power of God, the more the waters of the deluge were flowing on
the earth, the more the ark was raised towards heaven by these very
waters. So it is with our holy church. The very sins of the priests
make that spotless spouse of Jesus Christ fly away higher and higher
towards the regions of holiness, as it is in God. Let, therefore, your
faith and confidence in our holy church, and your respect for her,
remain firm and unshaken in the midst of all these scandals. Let your

zeal be rekindled for her glory and extension, at the sight of the unfortunate confreres who yield to the attacks of the enemy. Just as the valiant soldier makes superhuman efforts to save the flag, when he sees those who carried it fall on the battlefield. Oh! you will see more of our flag bearers slaughtered before you reach my age. But be not disheartened or shaken by that sad spectacle; for once more our holy church will stand for ever, in spite of all those human miseries, for her strength and her infallibility do not lie in men, but in Jesus Christ, whose promises will stand in spite of all the efforts of hell.

"I am near the end of my course, and, thanks be to God, my faith in our holy church is stronger than ever, though I have seen and heard many things, compared with which, the facts which just now distress you are mere trifles. In order the better to inure you to the conflict, and to prepare you to hear and see more deplorable things than what is now troubling you, I think it is my duty to tell you a fact which I got from the late Lord Bishop Plessis. I have never revealed it to anybody, but my interest in you is so great that I will tell it to you, and my confidence in your wisdom is so absolute, that I am sure you will never abuse it. What I will reveal to you is of such a nature that we must keep it among ourselves, and never let it be known to the people, for it would diminish, if not destroy their respect and confidence in us, respect and confidence, without which, it would become almost impossible to lead them.

"I have already told you that the late venerable Bishop Plessis was my personal friend. Our intimacy had sprung up when we were studying under the same roof in the seminary of St. Sulpice, Montreal, and it had increased year after year till the last hour of his life. Every summer, when he had reached the end of the three months of episcopal visitation of his diocese, he used to come and spend eight or ten days of absolute rest and enjoyment of private and solitary life with me in this parsonage. The two rooms you occupy were his, and he told me many times that the happiest days of his episcopal life were those passed in this solitude.

"One day he had come from his three months' visit, more worn out than ever, and when I sat down with him in this parlour, I was almost frightened by the air of distress which covered his face. Instead of finding him the loquacious, amiable and cheerful guest I used to have in him, he was taciturn, cast down, distressed. I felt really uneasy, for the first time, in his presence, but as it was the last hour of the day, I supposed that this was due to his extreme fatigue, and I hoped that the rest of the night would bring about such a change in my venerable friend, that I would find him, the next morning, what he used to be, the most amiable and interesting of men.

"I was, myself, completely worn out. I had travelled nearly thirty miles that day, to go to receive him at St. Thomas. The heat was oppressive, the roads very bad, and the dust awful. I was in need of rest, and I was hardly in my bed when I fell into a profound sleep, and slept till three o'clock in the morning. I was then suddenly awakened by sobs and half-suppressed lamentations and prayers, which were evidently coming from the bishop's room. Without losing a moment, I went and knocked at the door, inquiring about the cause of these sobs. Evidently the poor bishop had not suspected that I could hear him.

"'Sobs! sobs!' he answered, 'What do you mean by that. Please go back to your room and sleep. Do not trouble yourself about me, I am well,' and he absolutely refused to open the door of his room. The remaining hours of the night, of course, were sleepless ones for me. The sobs of the bishop were more suppressed, but he could not sufficiently suppress them to prevent me from hearing them. The next morning his eyes were reddened with weeping, and his face was that of one who had suffered intensely all the night. After breakfast I said to him : ' My lord, last night has been one of desolation to your lordship ; for God's sake, and in the name of the sacred ties of friendship, which has united us during so many years, please tell me what is the cause of your sorrow. It will become less the very moment you share it with your friend.'

"The bishop answered me : 'You are right when you think that I am under the burden of a great desolation ; but its cause is of such a nature, that I cannot reveal it even to you, my dear friend. It is only at the feet of Jesus Christ and His holy mother, that I must go to unburden my heart. If God does not come to my help, I must certainly die from it. But I will carry with me into my grave, the awful mystery which kills me.'

"In vain, during the rest of the day, I did all that I could to per-suade Monseigneur Plessis to reveal the cause of his grief. I failed. At last, through respect for him, I withdrew to my own room, and left him alone, knowing that solitude is sometimes the best friend of a desolated mind. His lordship, that evening, withdrew to his sleeping room sooner than usual, and I retired to my room much later. But sleep was out of the question for me that night, for his desolation seemed to be so great, and his tears so abundant, that when he bade me ' good-night,' I was in fear of finding my venerable, and more than ever dear friend, dead in his bed the next morning. I watched him, without closing my eyes, from the adjoining room, from ten o'clock till the next morning. Though it was evident that he was making great efforts to suppress his sobs, I could see that his sorrow was still more intense that night, than the last one, and my mental agony was not much less than his, during those distressing hours.

"But I formed an extreme resolution, which I put into effect the very moment that he came out of his room the next morning, to salute me.

"'My Lord,' said I, 'I thought till the night before last, that you honoured me with your friendship, but I see to-day that I was mistaken. You do not consider me as your friend, for if you would look upon me as a friend worthy of your confidence, you would unburden your heart into mine. A true friend has no secret from a true friend. What is the use of friendship if it be not to help each other to carry the burdens of life! I found myself honoured by your presence in my house, so long as I considered myself as your own friend. But now, that I see I have lost your confidence, please allow me frankly to say to your lordship, that I do not feel the same at your presence here. Besides, it seems to me very probable that the terrible burden which you want to carry alone, will kill you, and that very soon. I do not at all like the idea of finding you suddenly dead in my parsonage, and having the coroner holding his inquest upon your body, and making the painful inquiries which are always made upon one suddenly taken by death, particularly when he belongs to the highest ranks of society. Then, my lord, be not offended if I respectfully request your lordship to find another lodging as soon as possible.'

"My words fell upon the bishop like a thunderbolt. He seemed to awaken from a profound sleep. With a deep sigh he looked in my face with his eyes rolling in tears, and said :

"'You are right, Perras, I ought never to have concealed my sorrow from such a friend as you have always been for more than half a century to me. But you are the only one to whom I can reveal it. No doubt your priestly and Christian heart will not be less broken than mine; but you will help me with your prayers and wise counsels to carry it. However, before I initiate you into such an awful mystery, we must pray.'

"We then knelt down, and we said together a chaplet to invoke the power of the Virgin Mary, after which we recited Psalm li. : 'Miserere mihi.' Have mercy upon me, O Lord!

"Then, sitting by me on this sofa, the bishop said: 'My dear Mr. Perras, you are the only one to whom I could reveal what you are about to hear, for I think you are the only one who can hear such a terrible secret without revealing it, and because, also, you are the only friend whose advice can guide me in this terrible affliction.

"'You know that I have just finished the visit of my immense diocese of Quebec. It has taken me several years of hard work and fatigue, to see by my own eyes, and know by myself, the gains and losses—in a word, the strength and life of our holy church. I will not speak to you of the people. They are, as a general thing, truly religious and faithful to the church. But the priests. O Great God! will I tell you what they are? My dear Perras, I would almost die with joy, if God would tell me that I am mistaken. But, alas! I am not mistaken. The sad, the terrible truth is this' (putting his right hand on his forehead), 'the priests! Ah! with the exception of you and three others, are infidels and atheists! O my God! my God! what will become of the church, in the hands of such wicked men!' and covering his face with his hands, the bishop burst into tears, and for one hour could not say a word. I myself remained mute.

"At first I regretted having pressed the bishop to reveal such an unexpected 'mystery of iniquity.' But, taking counsel of our very fathomless humiliation and distress, after an hour of silence, spent in pacing the walks of the garden, almost unable to look each other in the face, I said: 'My lord, what you have told me is surely the saddest thing that I ever heard; but allow me to tell you that your sorrows are out of the limits of your high intelligence and your profound science. If you read the history of our holy church, from the seventh to the fifteenth century, you will know that the spotless spouse of Christ has seen as dark days, if not darker, in Italy, France, Spain and Germany, as she does in Canada, and though the saints of those days deplored the errors and crimes of those dark ages, they have not killed themselves with their vain tears, as you are doing.'

"Taking the bishop by the hand, I led him to the library, and opened the pages of the history of the church, by Cardinals Baronius and Fleury, and I showed him the names of more than fifty Popes who had evidently been atheists and infidels. I read to him the lives of Borgia, Alexander VI., and a dozen others, who would surely and justly be hanged to-day by the executioner of Quebec, were they, in that city, committing one-half of the public crimes of adultery, murder, debauchery of every kind, which they committed in Rome, Avignon, Naples, etc., etc. I read to him some of the public and undeniable crimes of the successors of the apostles, and of the inferior clergy, and I easily and clearly proved to him that his priests, though infidels and atheists, were angels of pity, modesty, purity, and religion, when compared with a Borgia, who publicly lived as a married man with his own daughter, and had a child by her. He agreed with me that several of the Alexanders, the Johns, the Piuses, and the Leos were sunk much deeper in the abyss of every kind of iniquity than his priests.

"Five hours passed in so perusing the sad but irrefutable pages of the history of our holy church, wrought a marvellous and beneficial change in the mind of Monseigneur Plessis.

" My conclusion was, that if our holy church had been able to resist the deadly influence of such scandals during so many centuries in Europe, she would not be destroyed in Canada, even by the legion of atheists by whom she is served to-day.

" The bishop acknowledged that my conclusion was correct. He thanked me for the good I had done him, by preventing him from despairing of the future of our holy church in Canada, and the rest of the days which he spent with me, he was almost as cheerful and amiable as before.

" Now, my dear young friend," added Mr. Perras, " I hope you will be as reasonable and logical in your religion as bishop Plessis, who was probably the greatest man Canada has ever had. When Satan tries to shake your faith by the scandals you see, remember that Stephen, after having fought with his adversary, Pope Constantine II., put out his eyes and condemned him to die. Remember that other Pope, who through revenge against his predecessor, had him exhumed, brought his dead body before judges, then charged him with the most horrible crimes, which he proved by the testimony of scores of eye-witnesses, got him (the dead Pope), to be condemned to be beheaded and dragged with ropes through the muddy streets of Rome, and thrown into the river Tiber. Yes, when your mind is oppressed by the secret crimes of the priests, which you will know, either through the confessional or by public rumour, remember that more than twelve Popes have been raised to that high and holy dignity by the rich and influential prostitutes of Rome, with whom they were publicly living in the most scandalous way. Remember that young bastard, John XI., the son of Pope Sergius, who was consecrated Pope when only twelve years old by the influence of his prostitute mother, Marosia, but who was so horribly profligate that he was deposed by the people and the clergy of Rome.

" Well, if our holy church has been able to pass through such storms without perishing, is it not a living proof that Christ is her pilot, that she is imperishable and infallible because St. Peter is her foundation, ' Tu es Petrus, et super hanc petram aedificabo Ecclesiam meam, et portae inferi non prevalebunt adversus eam.' "

Oh, my God! Shall I confess, to my confusion, what my thoughts were during that conversation, or rather that lecture of my curate, which lasted more than an hour! Yes, to thy eternal glory, and to my eternal shame, I must say the truth. When the priest was exhibiting to me the horrible unmentionable crimes of so many of our Popes, to calm my fears and strengthen my shaken faith, a mysterious voice was repeating to the ears of my soul the dear Saviour's words : " A good tree cannot bring forth evil fruit, neither can a corrupt tree bring forth good fruit. Every tree that bringeth not good fruit is hewn

9

down and cast into the fire. Wherefore by their fruits ye shall know them" (Matt. vii. 18—20), and in spite of myself the voice of my conscience cried in thundering tones that a church, whose head and members were so horribly corrupt, could not, by any means, be the Church of Christ.

But the most sacred and imperative law of my church, which I had promised by oaths, was that I would never obey the voice of my conscience, nor follow the dictates of my private judgment, when they were in opposition to the teachings of my church. Too honest to admit the conclusions of Mr. Perras, which were evidently the conclusions of my church, I was too cowardly and too mean to bravely express my own mind, and repeat the words of the Son of God: "By their fruits ye shall know them! A good tree cannot bring forth evil fruit!"

CHAPTER XX.

THE name of Louis Joseph Papineau will be for ever dear to the French Canadians; for whatever may be the political party to which one belongs in Canada, he cannot deny that it is to the ardent patriotism, the indomitable energy, and the remarkable eloquence of that great patriot, that Canada is indebted for the greater part of the political reforms which promise in a near future to raise the country of my birth to the rank of a great and free nation.

It is not my intention to speak of the political parties which divided the people of Canada into two camps in 1833. The long and trying abuses under which our conquered race was groaning, and which at last brought about the bloody insurrections of 1837 and 1838, are matters of history, which do not pertain to the plea of this work. I will speak of Papineau, and the brilliant galaxy of talented young men by whom he was surrounded and supported, only in connection with their difficulties with the clergy and the Church of Rome.

Papineau, Lafontaine, Bedard, Cartier and others, though born in the Church of Rome, were only nominal Romanists. I have been personally acquainted with every one of them, and I know they were not in the habit of confessing. Several times I invited them to fulfil that duty, which I considered, then, of the utmost importance to be saved. They invariably answered me with jests which distressed me; for I could see that they did not believe in the efficacy of auricular confession. These men were honest and earnest in their efforts to raise their countrymen from the humiliating and inferior position which they occupied compared with the conquering race. They well understood that the first thing to be done, in order to put the French Canadians on a level with their British compatriots, was to give good

schools to the people; and they bravely set themselves to show the
necessity of having a good system of education, for the country as
well as for the city. But at the very first attempt they found an
insurmountable barrier to their patriotic views in the clergy. The
priests had everywhere the good common sense to understand that
their absolute power over the people was due to its complete
ignorance. They felt that that power would decrease in the same
proportion that light and education would spread among the masses.
Hence the almost insurmountable obstacles put by the clergy before
the patriots, to prevent them from reforming the system of education.
The only source of education, then in Canada, with the exception of
the colleges of Quebec, Montreal and Nicolet, consisted in one or two
schools in the principal parishes, entirely under the control of the
priests and kept by their most devoted servants, while the new
parishes had none at all. The greater part of these teachers knew
very little more, and required nothing more from their pupils, than
the reading of the A, B, C, and their little catechism. When once
admitted to their first communion the A, B, C, and the little catechism
were soon forgotten, and 95 in 100 of the French Canadian people
were not even able to sign their names! In many parishes, the
curate, with his school teacher, the notary, and half-a-dozen others,
were the only persons who could read or write a letter. Papineau and
his patriotic friends understood that the French Canadian people were
doomed to remain an inferior race in their own country, if they were
left in that shameful state of ignorance. They did not conceal their
indignation at the obstacles placed by the clergy to prevent them from
amending the system of education. Several eloquent speeches were
made by Papineau, who was their "Parliament Speaker," in answer
to the clergy. The curates, in their pulpits, as well as by the press,
tried to show that Canada had the best possible system of education—
that the people were happy—that too much education would bring
into Canada the bitter fruits which had grown in France—infidelity,
revolution, riots, bloodshed; that the people were too poor to pay
the heavy taxes which would be imposed for the new system of
education. In one of his addresses, Papineau answered this last
argument, showing the immense sums of money foolishly given by
those so-called poor people to gild the ceilings of the church (as was
the usage then). He made a calculation of the tithes paid to the
priests; of the costly images and statues of saints, which were to be
seen then, around all the interior of the churches, and he boldly said
that the priests would do better to induce the people to establish
good schools, and pay respectable teachers, than to lavish their money
on objects which were of so little benefit.

That address, which was reproduced by the only French paper of

Quebec, " Le Canadien," fell upon the clergy like a hurricane upon a rotten house, shaking it to its foundation. Everywhere Papineau and his party were denounced as infidels, more dangerous than Protestants, and plans were immediately laid down to prevent the people from reading " Le Canadien," the only French paper they could receive. Not more than half-a-dozen were receiving it in St. Charles ; but they used to read it to their neighbours, who gathered on Sabbath afternoons to hear its contents. We at first tried, through the confessional, to persuade the subscribers to reject it, under the pretext that it was a bad paper ; that it spoke against the priests and would finally destroy our holy religion. But, to our great dismay, our efforts failed. The curates then had recourse to a more efficacious way of preserving the faith of their people.

The postmaster of St. Charles was, then, a man whom Mr. Perras had got educated at his own expense in the seminary of Quebec. His name was Chabot. That man was a perfect machine in the hands of his benefactor. Mr. Perras forbade him to deliver any more of the numbers of that journal to the subscribers, when there would be anything unfavourable to the clergy in its columns. " Give them to me," said he, " that I may burn them, and when the people come to get them, give them such evasive answers, that they may believe that it is the editor's fault, or of some other post-offices, if they have not received it." From that day, every time there was any censure of the clergy, the poor paper was consigned to the flames. One evening, when Mr. Perras had, in my presence, thrown a bundle of these papers into the stove, I told him : " Please allow me to express to you my surprise at this act. Have we really the right to deprive the subscribers of that paper of their property ! That paper is theirs, they have paid for it. How can we take upon ourselves to destroy it without their permission ! Besides, you know the old proverb : *Les pierres parlent*. (Stones speak.) If it were known by our people that we destroy their papers, would not the consequences be very serious ? Now, Mr. Perras, you know my sincere respect for you, and I hope I do not go against that respect by asking you to tell me by what right or authority you do this ? I would not put this question to you, if you were the only one who does it. But I know several others who do just the same thing. I will, probably, be obliged, when a curate, to act in the same manner, and I wish to know on what grounds I shall be justified in acting as you do."

" Are we not the spiritual fathers of our people ?" answered Mr. Perras.

I replied, " Yes sir, we are surely the spiritual fathers of our people."

" Then," rejoined Mr. Perras, " we have in spiritual matters, all the rights and duties which temporal fathers have, in temporal things, towards their children. If a father sees a sharp knife in the hands of his beloved but inexperienced child, and if he has good reason to fear that the dear child may wound himself, nay, destroy his own life with that knife, is it not his duty, before God and man, to take it from his hands, and prevent him from touching it any more ?"

"Yes," I answered, "but allow me to draw your attention to a little difference which I see between the corporal and the spiritual children of your comparison. In the case you bring forward, of a father who takes away the knife from the hands of a young and inexperienced child, that knife has, very probably, been bought by the father. It has been paid for with that father's money. It is, then, the father's knife. But the papers of your spiritual children, which you have thrown into your stove, have been paid for by them, and not by you. They are theirs, then, before the laws of God and man, and they are not yours."

I saw that my answer had cut the good old priest to the quick, and he became more nervous than I had ever seen him. "I see that you are young," answered he; "you have not yet had time to meditate on the great and broad principles of our holy church. I confess there is a difference in the rights of the two children to which I had not paid attention, and which, at first sight, may seem to diminish the strength of my argument. But I have here an argument which will satisfy you, I hope. Some weeks ago I wrote to our venerable bishop Panet about my intention of burning that miserable and impious paper, 'Le Canadien,' to prevent it from poisoning the minds of our people against us, and he has approved me, adding the advice, to be very prudent, and to act so secretly that there would be no danger in being detected. Here is the letter of the holy bishop; you may read it if you like."

"I thank you," I replied. "I believe that what you say in reference to that letter is correct. But suppose that our good bishop has made a mistake in advising you to burn those papers, would you not have some reasons to regret that burning, should you, sooner or later, detect that mistake?"

"A reason of regretting to follow the advice of my superiors! Never! Never! I fear, my dear young friend, that you do not sufficiently understand the duties of an inferior, and the sacred rights of superiors in our holy church. Have you not been told by your superiors in the College of Nicolet, that there can be no sin in an inferior who obeys the orders or counsels of his legitimate superiors?"

"Yes, sir," I answered, "the Rev. Mr. Leprohon has told us that in the college of Nicolet."

"But," rejoined Mr. Perras, "your last question makes me fear that you have forgotten what you have learned there. My dear young friend, do not forget that it was the want of respect to their ecclesiastical superiors which caused the apostacy of Luther and Calvin, and damned so many millions of heretics who have followed them. But in order to bring your rebellious mind under the holy yoke of a perfect submission to your superiors, I will show you, by our greatest and most approved theologian, that I can burn these papers, without doing anything wrong before God."

He then went to his library, and brought me a volume of Liguori, from which he read to me the following Latin words : "Docet Sanchez, etc., parato aliquem occidere, licite posse suaderi, ut ab eo furetur, vel ut fornicetur." *   With an air of triumph he said, " Do you see now that I am absolutely justifiable in destroying these pestilential papers.   According to those principles of our holy church, you know well that even a woman is allowed to commit the sin of adultery with a man who threatens to kill her, or himself, if she rebukes him ; because murder and suicide are greater crimes, and more irremediable than adultery.   So the burning of those papers, though a sin, if done through malice, or without legitimate reasons, ceases to be a sin ; it is a holy action the moment I do it, to prevent the destruction of our holy religion, and to save immortal souls."

I must confess, to my shame, that the degrading principles of absolute submission of the inferior to the superiors, which flattens everything to the ground in the Church of Rome, had so completely wrought their deadly work on me, that it was my wish to attain to that supreme perfection of the priest of the Church of Rome, to become like a stick in the hands of my superiors—like a corpse in their presence. But my God was stronger than His unfaithful and blind servant, and He never allowed me to go down to the bottom of that abyss of folly and impiety. In spite of myself, I had left in me sufficient manhood to express my doubts about that awful doctrine of my Church.

"I do not want to revolt against my superiors," I answered, "and I hope God will prevent me from falling into the abyss where Luther and Calvin lost themselves. I only respectfully request you to tell me, if you would not regret the burning of these papers, in case you would know that Bishop Panet made a mistake in granting you the power of destroying a property which is neither yours nor his—a property over which neither of you has any control ? "

* "Hence Sanchez teaches, n. 19, with Cajet. Sot. Covar. Valent, that it is lawful to persuade a man, determined to slay some one, that he should commit theft or fornication." (Mor. Theol. lib. iii. t. ii. cap. 2, p. 175, n. 157. Mech. 1845.)

It was the first time that I was not entirely of the same mind with Mr. Perras. Till then, I had not been brave, honest, or independent enough to oppose his views and his *ipse dixit*, though often tempted to do so. The desire of living in peace with him ; the sincere respect which his many virtues and venerable age commanded in me; the natural timidity, not to say cowardice, of a young, inexperienced man, in the presence of a learned and experienced priest, had kept me, till then, in perfect submission to the views of my aged curate. But it seemed impossible to yield any longer, and to bow my conscience before principles, which seemed to me then, as I am sure they are now, subversive of everything which is good and holy among men. I took the big Bible, which was on the table, and I opened it at the history of Susanna, and I answered: " My dear Mr. Perras, God has chosen you to be my teacher, and I have learned many things since it has been my privilege to be with you. But I have much more to learn, before I know all that your books and your long experience have taught you. I hope you will not find fault with me, if I honestly tell you that in spite of myself, there is a doubt in my mind about this doctrine of our theologians," and I said, " is there anything more sublime, in the whole Bible, than that feeble woman, Susanna, in the hands of those two infamous men ? With a diabolical impudence and malice, they threaten to destroy her, and to take her before a tribunal which will surely condemn her to the most ignoble death, if she does not consent to satisfy their criminal desires. She is just in the position alluded to by Liguori. What will she do ? Will she be guided by the principles of our theologians ? Will she consent to become an adulteress in order to prevent those two men from perjuring themselves, and becoming murderers, by causing her to be stoned to death, as was required by the law of the Jews ? No ! She raises her eyes and her soul towards the God whom she loves and fears more than anything in the world, and she says, ' I am straitened on every side, for if I do this thing it is death unto me ; and if I do it not, I cannot escape your hands. It is better for me to fall into your hands, and not to do it, than to sin in the sight of the Lord.' Has not God Almighty Himself shown that He approved of that heroic resolution of Susanna, to die rather than commit adultery. Does He not show that He Himself planted, in that noble soul, the principle that it is better to die than break the laws of God, when He brought His prophet Daniel, and gave him a supernatural wisdom to save the life of Susanna ? If that woman had been guided by the principles of Liguori, which, I confess to you with regret, are the principles accepted everywhere in our Church (principles which have guided you in the burning of ' Le Canadien '), she would have consented to the desires of those infamous men. Nay, if she had been interrogated by her husband, or by the judges on that action, she would have been allowed to swear before God and men, that she was not guilty of it. Now, my dear Mr. Perras, do you not find that there is some clashing between the Word of God, as taught in the Holy Scriptures, and the teachings of our Church, through the theologians ? "

Never have I seen such a sudden change in the face and manners of a man, as I saw in that hour. That Mr. Perras, who had, till then, spoken with so much kindness and dignity, completely lost his temper. Instead of answering me, he abruptly rose to his feet, and began to pace the room with a quick step. After some time he told me : "Mr. Chiniquy, you forget that when you were ordained a priest, you swore that you would never interpret the Holy Scriptures according to your own fallible private judgment; you solemnly promised that you would take them only according to the unanimous consent of the Holy Fathers speaking to you through your superiors. Has not Liguori been approved by the Popes — by all the bishops of the Church ? We have then, here, the true doctrine which must guide us. But instead of submitting yourself with humility, as it becomes a young and inexperienced priest, you boldly appeal to the Scriptures, against the decisions of Popes and bishops—against the voice of all your superiors, speaking. to you through Liguori. Where will that boldness end ? Ah ! I tremble for you, if you do not speedily change : you are on the high road to heresy ! "

These last words had hardly fallen from his lips, when the clock struck 9 p.m. He abruptly stopped speaking, and said, " This is the hour of prayer." We knelt and prayed.

I need not say that that night was a sleepless one to me. I wept and prayed all through its long dark hours. I felt that I had lost, and for ever, the high position I had in the heart of my old friend, and that I had probably compromised myself, for ever, in the eyes of my superiors, who were the absolute masters of my destinies. I condemned myself for that inopportune appeal to the Holy Scriptures, against the *ipse dixit* of my superiors. 1 asked God to destroy in me, that irresistible tendency, by which I was constantly going to the Word of God to know the truth, instead of remaining at the feet of my superiors, with the rest of the clergy, as the only fountain of knowledge and light.

But thanks be to God that blasphemous prayer was never to be granted.

CHAPTER XXI.

It was the custom in those days, in the Church of Rome, to give the title of arch-priest to one of the most respectable and able priests, among twelve or fifteen others, by whom he was surrounded. That title was the token of some superior power, which was granted to him over his confrères, who, in consequence, should consult him in certain difficult matters.

As a general thing, those priests lived in the most cordial and fraternal unity, and, to make the bond of that union stronger and more pleasant, they were, in turn, in the habit of giving a grand dinner every Thursday.

In 1834 those dinners were really *state affairs*. Several days in advance, preparations were made on a grand scale, to collect everything that could please the taste of the guests. The best wines were purchased. The fattest turkeys, chickens, lambs, or sucking pigs were hunted up. The most delicate pastries were brought from the city, or made at home, at any cost. The rarest and most costly fruits and desserts were ordered. There was a strange emulation among those curates, who would surpass his neighbours. Several extra hands were engaged, some days before, to help the ordinary servants to prepare the "GRAND DINNER."

The second Thursday of May, 1834, was Mr. Perras' turn, and at twelve o'clock noon, we were fifteen priests seated around the table.

I must here render homage to the sobriety and perfect moral habits of the Rev. Mr. Perras. Though he took his social glass of wine, as it was the universal usage at that time, I never saw him drink more than a couple of glasses at the same meal. I wish I could say the same thing of all those who were at his table that day.

Never did I see, before nor after, a table covered with so many tempting and delicate viands. The good curate had surpassed himself, and I would hardly be believed, were I to give the number of dishes and covers, *plates et entreplates,* which loaded the table. I will only mention a splendid salmon, which was the first brought to Quebec that year, for which Mr. Amiot, the purveyor for the priests around the capital, had paid twelve dollars.

There was only one lady at that dinner, Miss Perras, sister of the curate. However, she was not at all embarrassed by finding herself alone among those jolly celebataires, and she looked like a queen at the head of the table. Her sweet and watchful eyes were everywhere to see the wants of her guests. She had an amiable word for every one of them. With the utmost grace she pressed the Rev. Mr. *A.* to try that wing of turkey—she was so gently remonstrating with the Rev. Mr. *B.* for his not eating more, and she was so eloquent in requesting them all to taste of this dish, or of that; which was quite a new thing in Canada. And her young chickens! who could refuse to accept one of them, after she had told their story : how, three months before, in view of this happy day, she had so cajoled the big black hen to hatch over sixteen eggs in the kitchen ; what a world of trouble she had, when the little dog was coming in, and she (the hen) was rushing at him! how, many times, she had to stop the combatants, and force them to live in peace ! and what desolation swept over her mind, when, in a dark night, the rats had dragged into their holes, three of her newly-hatched chickens ! how she had got a cat to destroy the rats; and, how in escaping Scylla, she was thrown on Charybdis, when, three days after, the cat made his dinner of two of her dear little chickens ; for which crime, committed in open day, before several witnesses, the sentence of death was passed and executed, without benefit of clergy.

Now where would they find young chickens in the month of May, in the neighbourhood of Quebec, when the snow had scarcely disappeared ?

These stories, given with an art which no pen can reproduce, were not finished before the delicate chickens had disappeared in the hungry mouths of the cheerful guests.

One of the most remarkable features of these dinners was the levity, the absolute want of seriousness and gravity. Not a word was said in my presence, there, which could indicate that these men had anything else to do in this world but to eat and drink, tell and hear merry stories, laugh and lead a jolly life !

I was the youngest of those priests. Only a few months before, I was in the Seminary of Nicolet, learning from my grave old superior, lessons of priestly life, very different from what I had there under my eyes. I had not yet forgotten the austere preaching of self-denial, mortification, austerity and crucifixion of the flesh, which were to fill up the days of a priest !

Though, at first, I was pleased with all I saw, heard and tasted ; though I heartily laughed with the rest of the guests, at their *bon mots,* their spicy stories about their fair penitents, or at the funny caricatures they drew of each other, as well as of absent ones, I felt, by turns, uneasy. Now and then the lessons of priestly life, received from the lips of my venerable and dear Mr. Leprohon, were knocking hard at the door of my conscience. Some words of the Holy Scriptures which, more than others, had adhered to my memory, were also making a strange noise in my soul. My own common sense was

telling me, that this was not quite the way Christ taught His disciples
to live.

I made a great effort to stifle those troublesome voices. Sometimes I succeeded, and then I became cheerful : but a moment after I
was overpowered by them, and I felt chilled, as if I had perceived on the
walls of the festive room, the finger of my angry God, writing " MENE,
MENE, TEKEL, UPHARSIN." Then all my cheerfulness vanished, and I
felt so miserable that, in spite of all my efforts to look happy, the Rev.
Mr. Paquette, curate of St. Gervais, observed it on my face. That
priest was probably the one who most enjoyed everything of that
feast. Under the snowy mantle of sixty-five years, he had kept the
warm heart and the joviality of youth. He was considered one of
our most wealthy curates, and he richly deserved the reputation of
being the most epicurean of them all. He was a perfect cook, and
with his chaplet or his breviarium in hand, he used to pass a great
part of the day in his kitchen, giving orders about broiling this beef-
steak, or preparing this fricassee, and that gravy à la Française. He
was loved by all his confrères, but particularly by the young priests,
who were the objects of his constant attentions. He had always been
exceedingly kind to me, and when in his neighbourhood, I dare say
that my most pleasant hours were those passed in his parsonage.

Looking at me in the very moment when my whole intellectual
being was, in spite of myself, under the darkest cloud, he said : " My
dear little Father Chiniquy, are you falling into the hands of some
blue devils, when we are all so happy ? You were so cheerful half-
an-hour ago ! What is the matter with you now ? Are you sick ?
You look as grave and anxious as Jonah, when in the big whale's
stomach ! What is the matter with you ? Has any of your fair
penitents left you, to go to confess to another, lately ? "

At these funny questions, the dining-room was shaken with the
convulsive laughter of the priests. I wished I could join in with the
rest of my confrères ; for it seemed to me very clear that I was
making a fool of myself by this singularity of demeanour. But there
was no help for it : for a moment before I had seen that the servant
girls had blushed ; they had been scandalized by a very improper
word from the lips of a young priest about one of his young female
penitents ; a word which he would, surely, never have uttered, had he
not drank too much wine. I answered : " I am much obliged to you
for your kind interest, I find myself much honoured to be here in
your midst ; but as the brightest days are not without clouds, so it is
with us all sometimes. I am young, and without experience ; I have
not yet learned to look at certain things in their proper light. When
older, I hope I shall be wiser, and not make an ass of myself as I do
to-day."

"Tah! tah! tah!" said old Mr. Paquette, "this is not the hour of dark clouds and blue devils. Be cheerful, as it behoves your age. There will be hours enough in the rest of your life for sadness and sombre thoughts. This is the hour for laughing and being merry. Sad thoughts for to-morrow." And appealing to all, he asked, "Is not this correct, gentlemen?"

"Yes, yes," unanimously rejoined all the guests.

"Now," said the old priest, "you see that the verdict of the jury is unanimously in my favour and against you. Give up those airs of sadness, which do not answer in the presence of those bottles of champagne. Your gravity is an anachronism when we have such good wines before us. Tell me the reason of your grief, and I pledge myself to console you, and make you happy as you were at the beginning of the dinner."

"I would have liked better that you should have continued to enjoy this pleasant hour without noticing me," I answered. "Please excuse me if I do not trouble you with the causes of my personal folly."

"Well, well," said Mr. Paquette, "I see it, the cause of your trouble is that we have not yet drank together a single glass of sherry. Fill your glass with that wine, and it will surely drown the blue devil which I see at its bottom."

"With pleasure," I said; "I feel much honoured to drink with you," and I put some drops of wine into my glass.

"Oh! oh! what do I see you doing there? Only a few drops in your glass! This will not even wet the cloven feet of the blue devil which is tormenting you. It requires a full glass, an over-flowing glass to drown and finish him. Fill, then, your glass with that precious wine—the best I ever tasted in my whole life."

"But I cannot drink more than those few drops," I said.

"Why not?" he replied.

"Because, eight days before her death, my mother wrote me a letter, requesting me to promise her that I would never drink more than two glasses of wine at the same meal. I gave her that promise in my answer, and the very day she got my pledge, she left this world to convey it, written on her heart, into heaven, to the feet of her God!"

"Keep that sacred pledge," answered the old curate; "but tell me why you are so sad when we are so happy?"

"You already know part of my reasons—if I had drunk as much wine as my neighbour, the vicar of St. Gervais, I would probably have filled the room with my shouts of joy as he does; but you see now that the hands of my deceased, though always dear mother, are on my glass to prevent me from filling it any more, for I have already drank two glasses of wine."

"But your sadness, in such a circumstance, is so strange, that we would all like to know its cause."

"Yes, yes," said all the priests. "You know that we like you, and we deeply feel for you. Please tell us the reason of this sadness."

I then answered, "It would be better for me to keep my own secret : for I know I will make a fool of myself here : but as you are unanimous in requesting me to give you the reasons of the mental agony through which I am just passing, you will have them.

"You well know that, through very singular circumstances, I have been prevented, till this day, from attending any of your grand dinners. Twice I had to go to Quebec on these occasions, sometimes I was not well enough to be present—several times I was called to visit some dying person, and at other times the weather, or the roads were too bad to travel ; this, then is the first grand dinner, attended by you all, which I have the honour of attending.

"But before going any further, I must tell you that, during the eight months it has been my privilege to sit at Rev. Mr. Perras' table, I have never seen anything which could make me suspect that my eyes would see, and my ears would hear such things in this parsonage, as have just taken place. Sobriety, moderation, truly evangelical temperance in drink and food were the invariable rule. Never a word was said which could make our poor servant girls, or the angels of God blush. Would to God that I had not been here to-day ! For, I tell you, honestly, that I am scandalized by the epicurean table which is before us ; by the enormous quantity of delicate viands and the incredible number of bottles of most costly wines, emptied at this dinner.

"However, I hope I am mistaken in my appreciation of what I have seen and heard—I hope you are all right and that I am wrong. I am the youngest of you all. It is not my business to teach you, but it is my duty to be taught by you.

"Now, I have given you my mind, because you so pressingly requested me to do it, as honestly as human language will allow me to do. I have the right, I hope, to request you to tell me, as honestly, if I am, and in what I am wrong or right ! "

"Oh ! oh ! my dear Chiniquy," replied the old curate, "you hold the stick by the wrong end. Are we not the children of God ? "

"Yes, sir," I answered, "we are the children of God."

"Now, does not a loving father give what he considers the best part of his goods to his beloved children ? "

"Yes, sir," I replied.

"Is not that loving father pleased when he sees his beloved children eat and drink the good things he has prepared for them ? "

"Yes, sir," was my answer.

"Then," rejoined the logical priest, "the more we, the beloved children of God, eat of these delicate viands, and drink of those precious wines, which our heavenly Father puts into our hands, the more He is pleased with us. The more we, the most beloved ones of God, are merry and cheerful, the more He is Himself pleased and rejoiced in His heavenly kingdom.

"But if God our Father is so pleased with what we have eaten and drunk to-day, why are you so sad?"

This masterpiece of argumentation was received by all (except Mr. Perras), with convulsive cries of approbation, and repeated "Bravo! bravo!"

I was too mean and too cowardly to say what I felt. I tried to conceal my increased sadness under the forced smiles of my lips, and I followed the whole party, who left the table, and went to the parlour to drink a cup of coffee. It was then half-past one p.m. At two o'clock, the whole party went to the church, where, after kneeling for a quarter of an hour before their wafer God, they fell on their knees to the feet of each other, to confess their sins, and get their pardon, in the absolution of their confessors!

At three p.m. they were all gone, and I remained alone with my venerable old curate Perras. After a few moments of silence, I said to him: "My dear Mr. Perras, I have no words to express to you my regret for what I have said at your table. I beg your pardon for every word of that unfortunate and unbecoming conversation, into which I was dragged in spite of myself; you know it. It does not do for a young priest, as I am, to criticise those whom God has put so much above him by their science, their age, and their virtues. But I was forced to give my mind, and I have given it. When I requested Mr. Paquette to tell me in what I might be wrong, I had not the least idea that we would hear, from the lips of one of our veterans in the priesthood, the blasphemous jokes he has uttered. Epicurus himself would have blushed, had he been among us, in hearing the name of God connected with such deplorable and awful impieties."

Mr. Perras answered me: "Far from being displeased with what I have heard from you at this dinner, I must tell you that you have gained much in my esteem by it. I am, myself, ashamed of that dinner. We priests are the victims, like the rest of the world, of the fashions, vanities, pride and lust of that world against which we are sent to preach. The expenditure we make at those dinners is surely a crime, in the face of the misery of the people by whom we are surrounded. This is the last dinner I give with such foolish extravagance. The next time my neighbours will meet here, I will not expose them to stagger, as the greater part of them did when they rose from the table. The brave words you have uttered have done me good. They will do them good also; for though they had all eaten and drunk too much, they were not so intoxicated as not to remember what you have said."

Then, pressing my hand in his, he said, "I thank you, my good little Father Chiniquy, for the short but excellent sermon you have given us. It will not be lost. You have drawn my tears when you have shown us your saintly mother going to the feet of God in heaven, with your sacred promise written in her heart. Oh! you must have had a good mother! I knew her when she was very young. She was then, already, a very remarkable girl, for her wisdom and the dignity of her manners."

Then he left me alone in the parlour, and he went to visit a sick man in one of the neighbouring houses.

When alone I fell on my knees, to pray and weep. My soul was filled with emotions which it is impossible to express. The remembrance of my beloved mother, whose blessed name had fallen from my lips when her sacred memory filled my mind with the light and strength I needed in that hour of trial—the gluttony and drunkenness of those priests, whom I was accustomed to respect and esteem so much—their scandalous conversation—their lewd expressions—and more than all, their confessions to each other after two such hours of profanity and drinking, were more than I could endure. I could not contain myself. I wept over myself, for I felt also the burden of my sins, and I did not find myself much better than the rest, though I had not eaten or drunk quite so much as several of them—I wept over my friends, whom I had seen so weak; for they were my friends. I loved them, and I knew they loved me. I wept over my church, which was served by such poor, sinful priests. Yes! I wept there, when on my knees, to my heart's content, and it did me good. But my God had another trial in store for his poor unfaithful servant.

I had not been ten minutes alone, sitting in my study, when I heard strange cries, and such a noise as if a murderer were at work to strike his victim. A door had evidently been broken open, upstairs, and someone was running down stairs as if one was wanting to break down everything. The cries of "Murder, murder!" reached my ears, and the cries of "Oh! my God! my God! where is Mr. Perras?" filled the air.

I quickly ran to the parlour to see what was the matter, and there I found myself face to face with a woman absolutely naked! Her long black hair was flowing on her shoulders; her face was pale as death—her dark eyes fixed in their sockets. She stretched her hands towards me with a horrible shriek, and before I could move a step,

terrified, and almost paralyzed as I was, she seized my two arms with
her hands, with such a terrible force as if my arms had been grasped
in a vice. My bones were cracking under her grasp, and my flesh
was torn by her nails. I tried to escape, but it was impossible. I
soon found myself as if nailed to the wall, unable to move any further.
I cried then to the utmost compass of my voice for help. But the
living spectre cried still louder: "You have nothing to fear. Be
quiet. I am sent by God Almighty and the blessed Virgin Mary, to
give you a message. The priests whom I have known, without a
single exception, are a band of vipers; they destroy their female
penitents through auricular confession. They have destroyed me, and
killed my female child! Do not follow their example!" Then she
began to sing with a beautiful voice, to a most touching tune, a kind
of poem she had composed herself, which I secretly got afterwards
from one of her servant maids, the translation of which is as follows:

> " Satan's priests have defiled my heart!
> Damned my soul! murdered my child!
> O my child! my darling child!
> From thy place in heaven, dost thou see
>   Thy guilty mother's tears?
> Canst thou come and press me in thine arms?
>   My child! my darling child!
> Will never thy smiling face console me?"

When she was singing these words, big tears were rolling down
her pale cheeks, and the tone of her voice was so sad that she could
have melted a heart of stone. She had not finished her song when I
cried to the girl: "I am fainting, for God's sake bring me some
water!" The water was only passed to my lips, I could not drink. I
was choked, and petrified in the presence of that living phantom! I
could not dare to touch her in any way with my hands. I felt horrified
and paralyzed at the sight of that livid, pale, cadaverous, naked
spectre. The poor servant girl had tried in vain, at my request, to
drag her away from me. She had struck her with terror, by crying,
"If you touch me, I will instantly strangle you!"

"Where is Mr. Perras? Where is Mr. Perras and the other
servants? For God's sake call them," I cried out to the servant girl,
who was trembling and beside herself.

"Miss Perras is running to the church after the curate," she answered, "and I do not know where the other girl is gone."

In that instant Mr. Perras entered, rushed towards his sister, and
said, "Are you not ashamed to present yourselves naked before such a
gentleman?" and with his strong arms he tried to force her to give
me up.

Turning her face towards him, with tigress eyes, she cried out

" Wretched brother! what have you done with my child? I see her blood on your hands! "

When she was struggling with her brother, I made a sudden and extreme effort to get out of her grasp; and this time I succeeded: but seeing that she wanted to throw herself again upon me, I jumped through a window which was opened.

Quick as lightning she passed out of the hands of her brother, and jumped also through the window to run after me. She would, surely, have overtaken me; for I had not run two rods, when I fell headlong, with my feet entangled in my long, black, priestly robe. Providentially, two strong men, attracted by my cries, came to my rescue. They wrapped her in a blanket, taken there by her sister, and brought her back into her upper chambers, where she remained safely locked, under the guard of two strong servant maids.

The history of that woman is sad indeed. When in her priest-brother's house, when young and of great beauty, she was seduced by her father confessor, and became mother of a female child, which she loved with a real mother's heart. She determined to keep it and bring it up. But this did not meet the views of the curate. One night, when the mother was sleeping, the child had been taken away from her. The awakening of the unfortunate mother was terrible. When she understood that she could never see her child any more, she filled the parsonage with her cries and lamentations, and, at first, refused to take any food, in order that she might die. But she soon became a maniac.

Mr. Perras, too much attached to his sister to send her to a lunatic asylum, resolved to keep her in his own parsonage, which was very large. A room in its upper part had been fixed in such a way that her cries could not be heard, and where she would have all the comfort possible in her sad circumstances. Two servant maids were engaged to take care of her. All this was so well arranged, that I had been eight months in that parsonage, without even suspecting that there was such an unfortunate being under the same roof with me. It appears that occasionally, for many days, her mind was perfectly lucid, when she passed her time in praying, and singing a kind of poem which she had composed herself, and which she sang while holding me in her grasp. In her best moments she had fostered an invincible hatred of the priests whom she had known. Hearing her attendants often speak of me, she had, several times, expressed the desire to see me, which, of course, had been denied her. Before she had broken her door, and escaped from the hands of her keeper, she had passed several days in saying that she had received from God a message for me which she would deliver, even if she had to pass on the dead bodies of all in the house.

10

Unfortunate victim of auricular confession! How many others could sing the sad words of thy song,

> " Satan's priests have defiled my heart,
>   Damned my soul ! murdered my child ! "

CHAPTER XXII.

THE grand dinner previously described had its natural results. Several of the guests were hardly at home, when they complained of various kinds of sickness, and none was so severely punished as my friend Paquette, the curate of St. Gervais. He came very near dying, and for several weeks was unable to work. He requested the Bishop of Quebec to allow me to go to his help, which I did to the end of May, when I received the following letter :

CHARLESBOURGH, May 25th, 1834.

REV. MR. C. CHINIQUY :

MY DEAR SIR : My Lord Panet has again chosen me, this year, to accompany him in his episcopal visit. I have consented, with the condition that you should take my place, at the head of my dear parish, during my absence. For I will have no anxiety when I know that my people are in the hands of a priest who, though so young, has raised himself so high in the esteem of all those who know him.

Please come as soon as possible to meet me here, that I may tell you many things which will make your ministry more easy and blessed in Charlesbourgh.

His Lordship has promised me that when you pass through Quebec, he will give you all the powers you want to administer my parish, as if you were its curate during my absence.

Your devoted brother priest, and friend in the love and heart of Jesus and Mary,

ANTOINE BEDARD.

I felt absolutely confounded by that letter. I was so young and so deficient in the qualities required for the high position to which I was so unexpectedly called. I know it was against the usages to put a young and untried priest in such a responsible post. It seemed evident to me that my friends and my superiors had strangely exaggerated to themselves my feeble capacity.

In my answer to the Rev. Mr. Bedard, I respectfully remonstrated against such a choice. But a letter received from the bishop himself, ordering me to go to Charlesbourgh, without delay, to administer that parish during the absence of its pastor, soon forced me to consider that sudden and unmerited elevation as a most dangerous, though providential trial of my young ministry. Nothing remained to be done by me but to accept the task in trembling, and with a desire to do my duty. My heart, however, fainted within me, and I shed bitter tears of anxiety. When entering into that parish for the first time,

I saw its magnitude and importance. It seemed, then, more than ever
evident to me that the good Mr. Bedard, and my venerable superiors,
had made a sad mistake in putting such a heavy burden on my young
and feeble shoulders. I was hardly twenty-four years old, and had
not more than nine months' experience of the ministry.

Charlesbourgh is one of the most ancient and important parishes
of Canada. Its position, so near Quebec, at the feet of the Laurentide
Mountains, is peculiarly beautiful. It has an almost complete command of the city, and of its magnificent port, where not less than 900
ships then received their precious cargoes of lumber. On our left,
numberless ranges of white houses extended as far as the Falls of
Montmorency. At our feet the majestic St. Lawrence, dashing its
rapid waters on the beautiful " Isle d'Orleans." To the right, the
parishes of Lorette, St. Foy, St. Roch, etc., with their high church
steeples, reflected the sun's glorious beams; and beyond, the impregnable citadel of Quebec, with its tortuous ranges of black walls, its
numerous cannon, and its high towers, like fearless sentinels, presented a spectacle of remarkable grandeur.

The Rev. Mr. Bedard welcomed me on my arrival with words of
such kindness that my heart was melted and my mind confounded.
He was a man about sixty-five years of age, short in stature, with a
well-formed breast, large shoulders, bright eyes, and a face where the
traits of indomitable energy were coupled with an expression of unsurpassed kindness.

One could not look on that honest face without saying to himself,
" I am with a really good and upright man ! " Mr. Bedard is one of
the few priests in whom I have found a true honest faith in the Church
of Rome. With an irreproachable character, he believed, with a
child's faith, all the absurdities which the Church of Rome teaches,
and he lived according to his honest and sincere faith.

Though the actions of our daily lives were not subjected to a
regular and inexorable rule in Charlesbourgh's as in St. Charles' parsonage, there was yet far more life and earnestness in the performance
of our ministerial duties.

There was less reading of learned, theological, philosophical, and
historical books, but much more real labour in Mr. Bedard's than in
Mr. Perras' parish ; there was more of the old French aristocracy in
the latter priest, and more of the good religious Canadian habitant in
the former. Though both could be considered as men of the most
exalted faith and piety in the Church of Rome, their piety was of a
different character. In Mr. Perras' religion there was real calmness
and serenity, while the religion of Mr. Bedard had more of the flash
of lightning and the noise of thunder. The private religious conversations with the curate of St. Charles were admirable, but he could

not speak common sense for ten minutes when preaching from his pulpit. Only once did he preach while I was his vicar, and then he was not half through his sermon before the greater part of his auditors were soundly sleeping. But who could hear the sermons of Rev. Mr. Bedard without feeling his heart moved and his soul filled with terror? I never heard anything more thrilling than his words when speaking of the judgments of God and the punishment of the wicked. Mr. Perras never fasted, except on the days appointed by the church: Mr. Bedard condemned himself to fast besides twice every week. The former never drank, to my knowledge, a single glass of rum or any other strong drink, except his two glasses of wine at dinner; but the latter never failed to drink full glasses of rum three times a day, besides two or three glasses of wine at dinner. Mr. Perras slept the whole night as a guiltless child. Mr. Bedard, almost every night I was with him, rose up, and lashed himself in the most merciless manner with leather thongs, at the end of which were small pieces of lead. When inflicting upon himself those terrible punishments, he used to recite, by heart, the fifty-first Psalm, in Latin, " Miserere mei, Deus, secundam magnam misericordiam tuam " (Have mercy upon me, O Lord, according to Thy lovingkindness); and though he seemed to be unconscious of it, he prayed with such a loud voice, that I heard every word he uttered; he also struck his flesh with such violence that I could count all the blows he administered.

One day I respectfully remonstrated against such a cruel self-infliction as ruining his health and breaking his constitution: " Cher petit Frère " (dear little brother), he answered, " our health and constitution cannot be impaired by such penances, but they are easily and commonly ruined by our sins. I am one of the healthiest men of my parish, though I have inflicted upon myself those salutary and too well-merited chastisements for many years. Though I am old, I am still a great sinner. I have an implacable and indomitable enemy in my depraved heart, which I cannot subdue except by punishing my flesh. If I do not do those penances for my numberless transgressions, who will do penance for me? If I do not pay the debts I owe to the justice of God, who will pay them for me? "

" But," I answered, " has not our Saviour, Jesus Christ, paid our debts on Calvary? Has He not saved and redeemed us all by His death on the cross? Why, then, should you or I pay again to the justice of God that which has been so perfectly and absolutely paid by our Saviour? "

" Ah! my dear young friend," quickly replied Mr. Bedard, " that doctrine you hold is Protestant, which has been condemned by the Holy Council of Trent. Christ has paid our debts certainly; but not in such an absolute way that there is nothing more to be paid by us.

Have you never paid attention to what St. Paul says in his Epistle to the Colossians, 'I fill up that which is behind of the sufferings of Christ in my flesh for His body's sake, which is the Church.' Though Christ could have entirely and absolutely paid our debts, if it had been His will, it is evident that such was not His holy will—He left something behind which Paul, you, I, and every one of His disciples, should take and suffer in our flesh for His Church. When we have taken and accomplished in our flesh what Christ has left behind, then the surplus of our merits goes to the treasury of the Church. For instance, when a saint has accomplished in his flesh what Christ has left behind for his perfect sanctification, if he accomplishes more than the justice of God requires, that surplus of merits not being of any use to him, is put by God into the grand and common treasure, where it makes a fund of merits of infinite value, from which the Pope and the bishops draw the indulgences which they scatter all over the world as a dew from heaven. By the mercy of God, the penances which I impose upon myself, and the pains I suffer from these flagellations, purify my guilty soul, and raising me up from this polluting world, they bring me nearer and nearer to my God every day. I am not yet a saint, unfortunately, but if by the mercy of God, and my penances united to the sufferings of Christ, I arrive at the happy day when all my debts shall be paid, and my sins cleansed away, then if I continue those penances and acquire new merits, more than I need, and if I pay more debts than I owe to the justice of God, this surplus of merits which I shall have acquired will go to the rich treasure of the Church, from which she will draw merits to enrich the multitude of good souls who cannot do enough for themselves to pay their own debts, and to reach that point of holiness which will deserve a crown in heaven. Then the more we do penance and inflict pains on our bodies, by our fastings and floggings, the more we feel happy in the assurance of thus raising ourselves more and more above the dust of this sinful world, of approaching more and more to that state of holiness of which our Saviour spoke when He said, 'Be holy as I am holy Myself.' We feel an unspeakable joy when we know that by those self-inflicted punishments we acquire incalculable merits, which enrich not only ourselves, but our Holy Church, by filling her treasures for the benefit and salvation of the souls for which Christ died on Calvary."

When Mr. Bedard was feeding my soul with these husks, he was speaking with great animation and sincerity. Like myself, he was far away from the good Father's house. He had never tasted of the bread of the children. Neither of us knew anything of the sweetness of that bread. We had to accept those husks as our only food, though it did not remove our hunger.

I answered him : " What you tell me here is what I find in all our ascetic books and theological treatises, and in the lives of all our saints. I can hardly reconcile that doctrine with what I read this morning in the 2nd chapter of Ephesians. Here is the verse in my New Testament : ' But God who is rich in mercy, for His great love wherewith He loved us, even when we were dead in sins, hath quickened us together with Christ. By grace ye are saved . . . . for by grace are ye saved, through faith, and that not of ourselves, it is the gift of God ; not of works, lest any man should boast.'

" Now, my dear and venerable Mr. Bedard, allow me respectfully to ask, how is it possible that your salvation is only by grace, if you have to purchase it every day by tearing your flesh and lashing your body in such a fearful manner ? Is it not a strange favour—a very singular grace—which reddens your skin with your blood, and bruises your flesh every night ? "

" Dear little brother," answered Mr. Bedard, " when Mr. Perras spoke to me, in the presence of the bishop, with such deserved eulogium of your piety, he did not conceal that you had a very dangerous defect, which was to spend too much time in reading the Bible, in preference to every other of our holy books. He told us more than this. He said that you had a fatal tendency to interpret the Holy Scriptures too much according to your own mind, and in a sense which is rather more Protestant than Catholic. I am sorry to see that the curate of St. Charles was but too correct in what he told us of you. But, as he added that, though your reading too much the Holy Scriptures brought some clouds in your mind, yet when you were with him, you always ended by yielding to the sense given by our holy Church. This did not prevent me from desiring to have you in my place during my absence, and I hope I will not regret it, for we are sure that our dear young Chiniquy will never be a traitor to our holy Church."

These words, which were given with a great solemnity, mixed with the good manners of the most sincere kindness, went through my soul as a two-edged sword. I felt an inexpressible confusion and regret, and, biting my lips, I said : " I have sworn never to interpret the Holy Scriptures except according to the unanimous consent of the Holy Fathers, and with the help of God, I will fulfil my promise. I regret exceedingly to have differed for a moment from you. You are my superior by your age, your science and your piety. Please pardon me that momentary deviation from my duty, and pray that I may be as you are—a faithful and a fearless soldier of our holy Church to the end."

At that moment the niece of the curate came to tell us that the dinner was ready. We went to the modest, though exceedingly well-spread table, and to my great pleasure that painful conversation was dropped. We had not sat at the table five minutes, when a poor man knocked at the door and asked a piece of bread for the sake of Jesus and Mary. Mr. Bedard rose from the table, went to the poor stranger, and said : " Come, my friend, sit between me and our dear little Father Chiniquy. Our Saviour was the friend of the poor : He was the father of the widow and the orphan, and we, His priests, must walk after Him. Be not troubled ; make yourself at home. Though I am the curate of Charlesbourgh, I am your brother. It may be that in heaven you will sit on a higher throne than mine, if you love our Saviour Jesus Christ and His holy mother Mary, more than I do."

With these words, the best things that were on the table were put by the good old priest in the plate of the poor stranger, who with some hesitation finished by doing honour to the excellent viands.

After this, I need not say that Mr. Bedard was charitable to the poor: he always treated them as his best friends. So also was my former curate of St. Charles ; and, though his charity was not so demonstrative and fraternal as that of Mr. Bedard, I had yet never seen a poor man go out of the parsonage of St. Charles whose breast ought not to have been filled with gratitude and joy.

Mr. Bedard was as exact as Mr. Perras in confessing once, and sometimes twice, every week ; and, rather than fail in that humiliating act, they both, in the absence of their common confessors, and much against my feelings, several times humbly knelt at my youthful feet to confess to me.

Those two remarkable men had the same views about the immorality and the want of religion of the greater part of the priests. Both have told me, in their confidential conversations, things about the secret lives of the clergy which would not be believed were I to publish them ; and both repeatedly said that auricular confession was the daily source of unspeakable depravities between the confessors and their female as well as male penitents ; but neither of them had sufficient light to conclude from those deeds of depravity that auricular confession was a diabolical institution. They both sincerely believed as I did then, that the institution was good, necessary and divine, and that it was a source of perdition to so many priests only on account of their want of faith and piety ; and principally from their neglect of prayers to the Virgin Mary.

They did not give me those terrible details with a spirit of criticism against our weak brethren. Their intention was to warn me against the dangers, which were as great for me as for others. They both invariably finished those confidences by inviting me more and more to pray constantly to the mother of God, the blessed Virgin

Mary, and to watch over myself, and avoid remaining alone with a female penitent; advising me also to treat my own body as my most dangerous enemy, by reducing it into subjection to the law, and crucifying it day and night.

Mr. Bedard had accompanied the Bishop of Quebec in his episcopal visits during many years, and had seen with his eyes the unmentionable plague, which was then, as it is now, devouring the very vitals of the Church of Rome. He very seldom spoke to me of those things without shedding tears of compassion over the guilty priests. My heart and my soul were also filled with an unspeakable sadness when hearing the details of such iniquities. I also felt struck with terror lest I might perish myself, and fall into the same bottomless abyss.

One day I told him what Mr. Perras had revealed to me about the distress of Bishop Plessis, when he had found that only three priests besides Mr. Perras believed in God, in his immense diocese. I asked him if there was not some exaggeration in this report. He answered, after a profound sigh : "My dear young friend : the angel could not find ten just men in Sodom—my fear is that they would not find more among the priests! The more you advance in age, the more you will see that awful truth—Ah! let those who stand fear, lest they fall!"

After these last words he burst into tears, and went to church to pray at the feet of his wafer god!

The revelations which I received from those worthy priests did not in any way shake my faith in my Church. She even became dearer to me; just as a dear mother gains in the affection and devotedness of a dutiful son as her trials and afflictions increase. It seemed to me that after this knowledge it was my duty to do more than I had ever done to show my unreserved devotedness, respect and love to my holy and dear mother, the Church of Rome, out of which (I sincerely believed then) there was no salvation. These revelations became to me, in the good providence of God, like the light-houses raised on the hidden and dreadful rocks of the sea, to warn the pilot during the dark hours of the night to keep at a distance, if he does not want to perish.

Though these two priests professed to have a most profound love and respect for the Holy Scriptures, they gave very little time to their study, and both several times rebuked me for passing too many hours in their perusal ; and repeatedly warned me against the habit of constantly appealing to them against certain practices and teachings of our theologians. As good Roman Catholic priests they had no right to go to the Holy Scriptures alone to know what "the Lord saith!" The traditions of the Church were their fountain of science and light! Both of them often distressed me with the facility with which they buried out of view, under the dark clouds of their traditions, the clearest texts of Holy Scriptures which I used to quote in defence of my positions in our conversations and debates.

They both, with an equal zeal, and unfortunately with too much success, persuaded me that it was right for the Church to ask me to swear that I would never interpret the Holy Scriptures, except according to the unanimous consent of the Holy Fathers. But when I showed them that the Holy Fathers had never been unanimous in anything except in differing from one another on almost every subject they had treated; when I demonstrated by our Church historians that some Holy Fathers had very different views from ours on many subjects, they never answered my questions except by silencing me by the text: "If he does not hear the Church let him be as a heathen or a publican," and by giving me long lectures on the danger of pride and self-confidence.

Mr. Bedard had many opportunities of giving me his views about the submission which an inferior owes to his superiors. He was or one mind with Mr. Perras and all the theologians who had treated that subject. They both taught me that the inferior must blindly obey his superior, just as the stick must obey the hand which holds it; assuring me at the same time that the inferior was not responsible for the errors he commits when obeying his legitimate superior.

Mr. Bedard and Mr. Perras had a great love for their Saviour, Jesus; but the Jesus Christ whom they loved and respected and adored was not the Christ of the Gospel, but the Christ of the Church of Rome.

Mr. Perras and Mr. Bedard had a great fear, as well as a sincere love for their god, while yet they professed to make him every morning by the act of consecration. They also most sincerely believed and preached that idolatry was one of the greatest crimes a man could commit, but they themselves were every day worshipping an idol of their own creating. They were forced by their Church to renew the awful iniquity of Aaron, with this difference only, that while Aaron made his gods of melted gold, and moulded them into the figure of a calf, they made theirs with flour, baked between two heated and well polished irons, and in the form of a crucified man.

When Aaron spoke of his golden calf to the people, he said: "These are thy gods, O Israel, which brought thee out of the land of Egypt." So likewise Mr. Bedard and Mr. Perras, showing the wafer to the deluded people, said: "Ecce agnus Dei qui tollit peccata mundi!" ("Behold the Lamb of God which taketh away the sins of the world!")

These two sincere and honest priests placed the utmost confidence

also in relics and scapularies. I have heard both say that no fatal
accident could happen to one who had a scapular on his breast—no
sudden death would overtake a man who was faithful in keeping
those blessed scapularies about his person. Both of them, nevertheless, died suddenly, and that too of the saddest of deaths. Mr.
Bedard dropped dead on the 19th of May, 1837, at a great dinner
given to his friends. He was in the act of swallowing a glass of that
drink of which God says: "Look not upon the wine when it is red,
when it giveth its colour in the cup, when it moveth itself aright. At
the last it biteth like a serpent and stingeth like an adder."

The Rev. Mr. Perras, sad to say, became a lunatic in 1845, and
died on the 29th of July, 1347, in a fit of delirium.

CHAPTER XXIII.

I HAD not been more than three weeks the administrator of the parish
of Charlesbourgh, when the terrible words, " The cholera morbus is in
Quebec!" sent a thrill of terror from one end to the other of Canada.

The cities of Quebec and Montreal, with many surrounding country
places, had been decimated in 1832 by the same terrible scourge.
Thousands upon thousands had fallen its victims; families in every
rank of society had disappeared ; for the most skilful physicians of
both Europe and America had been unable to stop its march and
ravages. But the year 1833 had passed without hearing almost of a
single case of that fatal disease : we had all the hope that the justice
of God was satisfied, and that He would no more visit us with that
horrible plague. In this, however, we were to be sadly disappointed.

Charlesbourgh is a kind of suburb of Quebec, the greatest part of
its inhabitants had to go within its walls to sell their goods several
times every week. It was evident that we were to be among the first
visited by that messenger of a just, but angry God. I will never
forget the hour after I had heard : " The cholera is in Quebec!" It
was, indeed, a most solemn hour to me. At a glance, I measured
the bottomless abyss which was dug under my feet. We had no
physicians, and there was no possibility of having any one—for they
were to have more work than they could do in Quebec. I saw that I
would have to be both the body and soul-physician of the numberless
victims of this terrible disease.

The tortures of the dying, the cries of the widows and of the
orphans, the almost unbearable stench of the houses attacked by the
scourge, the desolation and the paralyzing fears of the whole people,
the fatherless and motherless orphans by whom I was to be

surrounded, the starving poor for whom I would have to provide food and clothing when every kind of work and industry was stopped ; but above all, the crowds of penitents whom the terrors of an impending death would drag to my feet to make their confessions, that I might forgive their sins, passed through my mind as so many spectres. I fell on my knees, with a heart beating with emotions that no pen can describe, and prostrating myself before my too justly angry God, I cried for mercy : with torrents of tears I asked Him to take away my life as a sacrifice for my people, but to spare them : raising my eyes towards a beautiful statue of Mary, whom I believed to be then the Mother of God, I supplicated her to appease the wrath of her Son.

I was still on my knees, when several knocks at the door told me that some one wanted to speak to me—a young woman was there, bathed in tears and pale as death, who said to me : " My father has just returned from Quebec, and is dying from the cholera—please come quick to hear his confession before he expires !"

No tongue will ever be able to tell half of the horrors which strike the eyes and the mind the first time one enters the house of a man struggling in the agonies of death from cholera. The other diseases seem to attack only one part of the body at once, but the cholera is like a furious tiger whose sharp teeth and nails tear his victim from head to feet without sparing any part. The hands and the feet, the legs and the arms, stomach, the breast and the bowels are at once tortured. I had never seen anything so terrific as the fixed eyes of that first victim whom I had to prepare for death. He was already almost as cold as a piece of ice. He was vomiting and ejecting an incredible quantity of a watery and blackish matter, which filled the house with an unbearable smell. With a feeble voice he requested me to hear the confession of his sins, and I ordered the family to withdraw and leave me alone, that they might not hear the sad story of his transgressions. But he had not said five words before he cried out : "Oh my God ! what horrible cramps in my leg ! For God's sake, rub it." And when I had given up hearing his confession to rub the leg, he cried again : " Oh ! what horrible cramps in my arms ! —in my feet !—in my shoulders !—in my stomach !" And to the utmost of my capacity and my strength, I rubbed his arms, his feet, his shoulders, his breast, till I felt so exhausted and covered with perspiration, that I feared I should faint. During that time the fetid matter ejected from his stomach, besmeared me almost from head to foot. I called for help, and two strong men continued with me to rub the poor dying man.

It seemed evident that he could not live very long : his sufferings looked so terrible and unbearable ! I administered him the sacrament of extreme unction. But I did not leave the house after that ceremony

as it is the custom of the priests. It was the first time that I had met
face to face with that giant which had covered so many nations with
desolation and ruin, caused so many torrents of tears to flow. I had
heard so much of him! I knew that, till then, nothing had been able
to stop his forward march! He had scornfully gone through the
obstacles which the most powerful nations had placed before him to
retard his progress. He had mocked the art and science of the
most skilful physicians all over the world! In a single step he had
gone from Moscow to Paris!—and in another month he had crossed
the bottomless seas which the hands of the Almighty have spread
between Europe and America! That king of terrors, after piling in
their graves, by millions, the rich and the poor, the old and the young,
whom he had met on his march through Asia, Africa, Europe,
and America, was now before me! Nay, he was torturing, before my
eyes, the first victim he had chosen among my people! But the more
I felt powerless in the presence of that mighty giant, the more I
wanted to see him face to face. I had a secret pleasure, a holy
pride, in daring him. I wanted to tell him : "I do not fear you! You
mercilessly attack my people, but with the help of God, in the
strength of the One who died on Calvary for me, and who told me that
nothing is more sweet and glorious than to give my life for my friends,
I will meet and fight you everywhere when you attack any one of
those sheep who are dearer to me than my own life!"

Standing by the bedside of the dying man whilst I rubbed his
limbs to alleviate his tortures, I exhorted him to repent. But I
closely watched that hand-to-hand battle—that merciless and unequal
struggle between the giant and his poor victim. His agony was long
and terrible, for he was a man of great bodily strength. But after
several hours of the most frightful pains, he quietly breathed his last.
The house was crowded with the neighbours and relations, who,
forgetful of the danger of catching the disease, had come to see him.
We all knelt and prayed for the departed soul, after which I gave
them a few words about the necessity of giving up their sins and
keeping themselves ready to die and go at the Master's call.

I then left that desolated house with feelings of distress which no
pen can portray. When I got back to the parsonage, after praying and
weeping alone in my chamber, I took a bath, and washed myself with
vinegar and a mixture of camphor, as a preventive against the
epidemic. The rest of the day, till ten at night, was spent in hearing
the confessions of a great number of people whom the fear of death
had dragged around my confessional box that I might forgive their
sins. This hearing of confession was interrupted only at ten o'clock
at night, when I was called to the cemetery to bury the first victim of
the cholera in Charlesbourgh. A great number of people had accom-

panied the corpse to his last resting-place : the night was beautiful, the atmosphere balmy, and the moon and stars had never appeared to me so bright. The stillness of the night was broken only by the sobs of the relations and friends of the deceased. It was one of the best opportunities God had ever given me of exhorting the people to repentance. I took for my text : " Therefore, be ye also ready ; for in such an hour as ye think not, the Son of Man cometh." The spectacle of that grave, filled by a man who, twenty-four hours before, was full of health and life in the midst of his happy family, was speaking more eloquently than the words of my lips, to show that we must be always ready. And never any people entered the threshold of their homes with more solemn thoughts than those to whom I spoke, that night, in the midst of the graveyard.

The history of that day is the history of the forty days which followed—for not a single one of them passed without my being called to visit a victim of the cholera—more than one hundred people were attacked by the terrible disease, nearly forty of whom died !

I cannot sufficiently thank my merciful God for having protected me in such a marvellous way that I had not a single hour of disease during those two months of hard labours and sore trials. I had to visit the sick not only as a priest, but as physician also ; for seeing, at first, the absolute impossibility of persuading any physician from Quebec to give up their rich city patients for our more humble farmers, I felt it was my duty to make myself as expert as I could in the art of helping the victims of that cruel and loathsome disease : I studied the best authors on that subject, consulted the most skilful physicians, got a little pharmacy which would have done honour to an old physician, and I gave my care and my medicine gratis. Very soon the good people of Charlesbourgh put as much, if not more confidence, in my medical care, as in any other of the best physicians of the country. More than once I had to rub the limbs of so many patients in the same day, that the skin of my hands was taken away, and several times the blood came out from the wounds. Dr. Painchaud, one of the ablest physicians of Quebec, who was my personal friend, told me after, that it was a most extraordinary thing that I had not fallen a victim to that disease.

I would never have mentioned what I did, in those never-to-be-forgotten days of the cholera of 1834, when one of the most horrible epidemics which the world has ever seen spread desolation and death almost all over Canada, if I had been alone to work as I did ; but I am happy and proud to say that, without a single exception, the French Canadian priests, whose parishes were attacked by that pestilence, did the same. I could name hundreds of them who, during several months, also, day after day and night after night, bravely met and fought the enemy, and fearlessly presented their breast to its blows. I could even name scores of them who heroically fell and died when facing the foe on that battlefield!

We must be honest and true towards the Roman Catholic priests of Canada. Few men, if even any, have shown more courage and self-denial in the hour of danger than they did. I have seen them at work during the two memorable years of 1832 and 1834, with a courage and self-denial worthy of the admiration of heaven and earth. Though they knew well that the most horrible tortures and death might be the price of their devotedness, I have not known a single one of them who ever shrank before the danger. At the first appeal, in the midst of the darkest and stormiest nights, as well as in the light of the brightest days, they were always ready to leave their warm and comfortable beds to run to the rescue of the sick and dying.

But, shall we conclude from that, as the priests of Rome want us to do, that their religion is the true and divine religion of Christ? Must we believe that because the priests are brave, admirably brave, and die the death of heroes on the battlefields, they are the true, the only priests of Christ, the successors of the apostles— the ministers of the religion out of which there is no salvation? No!

Was it because his religion was the divine and only true one that the millionaire, Stephen Gerard, when in 1793 Philadelphia was decimated by a most frightful epidemic, went from house to house, visiting the sick, serving, washing them with his own hands, and even helping to put them into their coffins? I ask it again, is it because his religion was the divine religion of Jesus that that remarkable man, during several months, lived among the dying and the dead, to help them, when his immense fortune allowed him to put a whole world between him and the danger? No; for every one knows that Stephen Gerard was a deist, who did not believe in Christ.

Was it because they followed the true religion that, in the last war between Russia and Turkey, a whole regiment of Turks heroically ran to a sure death to obey the order of their general, who commanded them to charge bayonets on a Russian battery, which was pouring upon them a real hail of bullets and canister? No! surely no!

These Turks were brave, fearless, heroic soldiers, but nothing more. So the priests of the Pope, who expose themselves in the hour of danger, are brave, fearless, heroic soldiers of the Pope—but they are nothing more.

Was it because they were good Christians that the soldiers of a French regiment, at Austerlitz, consented to be slaughtered to the last, at the head of a bridge where Napoleon had ordered them to remain, with these celebrated words : "Soldiers ! stand there and fight to the last; you will all be killed, but you will save the army, and we will gain the day ! "

Those soldiers were admirably well disciplined—they loved their flag more than their lives—they knew only one thing in the world: " Obey the command of Napoleon ! " They fought like giants, and died like heroes. So the priests are a well disciplined band of soldiers; they are trained to love their church more than their own life ; they also know only one thing: " Obey your superior, the Pope ! " they fight the battle of their church like giants, and they die like heroes !

Who has not read the history of the renowned French man-of-war, the " Tonnant ? " When she had lost her masts, and was so crippled by the red-hot shot of the English fleet that there was no possibility of escape, what did the soldiers and mariners of that ship answer to the cries of " Surrender ! " which came from the English admiral ? " We die, but do not surrender ! "

They all went to the bottom of the sea, and perished rather than see their proud banners fall into the hands of the foe !

Is it because those French warriors were good Christians that they preferred to die rather than give up their flag ? No ! But they knew that the eyes of their country, the eyes of the whole world were upon them. Life became to them a trifle : it became nothing when placed in the balance against what they considered their honour, and the honour of their fair and noble country ;—nay, life became an undesirable thing, when it was weighted against the glory of dying at the post of duty and honour.

So it is with the priest of Rome. He knows that the eyes of his people, and of his superiors—the eyes of his whole church are upon him. He knows that if he shrinks in the hour of danger, he will for ever lose their confidence and their esteem; that he will lose his position and live the life of a degraded man ! Death seems preferable to such a life.

Yes ! let the people of Canada read the history of " La Nouvelle France," and they will cease from presenting to us the courage of their priests as an indication of the divinity of their religion. For there they will see that the worshippers of the wooden gods of the forests have equalled, if not surpassed, in courage and self-denial in the face of death, the courage and self-denial of the priests of the wafer god of Rome.

CHAPTER XXIV.

In the beginning of September, 1834, the Bishop Synaie gave me the enviable position of one of the vicars of St. Roch, Quebec, where the Rev. Mr. Tetu had been curate for about a year. He was one of the seventeen children of Mr. Francis Tetu, one of the most respectable and wealthy farmers of St. Thomas. Such was the amiability of character of my new curate, that I never saw him in bad humour a single time during the four years that it was my fortune to work under him in that parish. And although in my daily intercourse with him I sometimes unintentionally sorely tried his patience, I never heard an unkind word proceed from his lips.

He was a fine looking man, tall and well built, large forehead, blue eyes, a remarkably fine nose and rosy lips, only a little too feminine. His skin was very white for a man, but his fine short whiskers, which he knew so well how to trim, gave to his whole mien a manly and pleasant appearance.

He was the finest penman I ever saw ; and by far the most skilful skater of the country. Nothing could surpass the agility and perfection with which he used to write his name on the ice with his skates. He was also fond of fast horses, and knew, to perfection, how to handle the most unmanageable steeds of Quebec. He really looked like Phaeton when, in a light and beautiful buggy, he held the reins of the fiery coursers which the rich bourgeois of the city liked to trust to him once or twice a week, that he might take a ride with one of his vicars to the surrounding country. Mr. Tetu was also fond of fine cigars and choice chewing tobacco. Like the late Pope Pius IX., he also constantly used the snuff box. He would have been a pretty good preacher, had he not been born with a natural horror of books. I very seldom saw in his hands any other books than his breviary, and some treatises on the catechism : a book in his hands had almost the effect of opium on one's brains, it put him to sleep. One day, when I had finished reading a volume of Tertullian, he felt much interested in what I said of the eloquence and learning of that celebrated Father of the Church, and expressed a desire to read it. I smilingly asked him if he were more than usual in need of sleep. He seriously answered me that he really wanted to read that work, and that he wished to begin its study just then. I lent him the volume, and he went immediately to his room in order to enrich his mind with the treasures of eloquence and wisdom of that celebrated writer of the primitive church. Half an hour after, suspecting what would occur, I went down to his room, and noiselessly opening the door, I found my dear Mr. Tetu sleeping on his soft sofa, and snoring to his heart's content, while Tertullian was lying on the floor! I ran to the rooms of the other vicars, and told them: "Come and see how our good curate is studying Tertullian!"

There is no need to say that we had a hearty laugh at his expense. Unfortunately, the noise we made awoke him, and we then asked him: "What do you think of Tertullian?"

He rubbed his eyes, and answered, "Well, well! what is the matter? Are you not four very wicked men to laugh at the human frailties of your curate?" We for a while called him Father Tertullian.

Another day he requested me to give him some English lessons. For, though my knowledge of English was then very limited, I was the only one of five priests who understood and could speak a few words in that language. I answered him that it would be as pleasant as it was easy for me to teach the little I knew of it, and I advised him to subscribe for the "Quebec Gazette," that I might profit by the interesting matter which that paper used to give to its readers; and at the same time I should teach him to read and understand its contents.

The third time that I went to his room to give him his lesson, he gravely asked me: "Have you ever seen 'General Cargo?'"

I was at first puzzled by that question, and answered him: "I never heard that there was any military officer by the name of 'General Cargo.' How do you know that there is such a general in the world?"

He quickly answered: "There is surely a 'General Cargo' somewhere in England or America, and he must be very rich; for see the large number of ships which bear his name, and have entered the port of Quebec, these last few days!"

Seeing the strange mistake, and finding his ignorance so wonderful, I burst into a fit of uncontrollable laughter. I could not answer a word, but cried at the top of my voice: "General Cargo! General Cargo!"

The poor curate, stunned by my laughing, looked at me in amazement. But, unable to understand its cause, he asked me: "Why do you laugh?" But the more stupefied he was, the more I laughed, unable to say anything but "General Cargo! General Cargo!"

The three other vicars, hearing the noise, hastily came from their rooms to learn its cause, and get a good laugh also. But I was so completely beside myself with laughing, that I could not answer their questions in any other way than by crying, "General Cargo! General Cargo!"

The puzzled curate tried then to give them some explanation of that mystery, saying with the greatest naïveté: "I cannot see why our little Father Chiniquy is laughing so convulsively. I put to him a very

11

simple question, when he entered my room to give me my English lesson. I simply asked him if he had ever seen ' General Cargo,' who has sent so many ships to our port these last few days, and added that that general must be very rich, since he has so many ships on the sea!'" The three vicars saw the point, and without being able to answer him a word, they burst also into such fits of laughter, that the poor curate felt more than ever puzzled.

"Are you crazy?" he said. "What makes you laugh so when I put to you such a simple question? Do you not know anything about that ' General Cargo,' who surely must live somewhere, and be very rich, since he sends so many vessels to our port that they fill nearly two columns of the ' Quebec Gazette ' ? "

These remarks of the poor curate brought such a new storm of irrepressible laughter from us all as we never experienced in our whole lives. It took us some time to sufficiently master our feelings to tell him that " General Cargo " was not the name of any individual, but only the technical words to say that the ships were laden with general goods.

The next morning, the young and jovial vicars gave the story to their friends, and the people of Quebec had a hearty laugh at the expense of our friend. From that time we called our good curate by the name of " General Cargo," and he was so good-natured that he joined with us in joking at his own expense. It would require too much space were I to publish all the comic blunders of that good man, and so I shall give only one more.

On one of the coldest days of January, 1835, a merchant of seal skins came to the parsonage with some of the best specimens of his merchandise, that we might buy them to make overcoats, for in those days the overcoats of buffalo or raccoon skins were not yet thought of. Our richest men used to have beaver overcoats, but the rest of the people had to be contented with Canada seal skins; a beaver overcoat could not be had for less than 200 dollars.

Mr. Tetu was anxious to buy the skins; his only difficulty was the high price asked by the merchant. For nearly an hour he had turned over and over again the beautiful skins, and had spent all his eloquence on trying to bring down their price, when the sexton arrived, and told him, respectfully, "Mr. le Cure, there are a couple of people waiting for you with a child to be baptized."

"Very well," said the curate, "I will go immediately;" and addressing the merchant, he said, " Please wait a moment; I will not be long absent."

In two minutes after the curate had donned the surplice, and was going at full speed through the prayers and ceremonies of baptism. For, to be fair and true towards Mr. Tetu (and I might say the same thing of the greatest part of the priests I have known), it must be acknowledged that he was very exact in all his ministerial duties; yet he was, in this case, going through them by steam, if not by electricity. He was soon at the end. But, after the sacrament was administered, we were enjoined, then, to repeat an exhortation to the godfathers and godmothers, from the ritual which we all knew by heart, and which began with these words: "Godfathers and Godmothers: You have brought a sinner to the church, but you will take back a saint!"

As the vestry was full of people who had come to confess, Mr. Tetu thought that it was his duty to speak with more emphasis than usual, in order to have his instructions heard and felt by everyone, but instead of saying, "Godfather and Godmother, You have brought a sinner to the church, you will take back a saint!" he, with great force and unction said: "Godfather and Godmother, You have brought a sinner to the church, you will take back a *seal skin!*"

No words can describe the uncontrollable burst and roar of laughter among the crowd, when they heard that the baptized child was just changed into a "seal skin." Unable to contain themselves, or do any serious thing, they left the vestry to go home and laugh to their heart's content.

But the most comic part of this blunder was the *sang froid* and the calmness with which Mr. Tetu, turning towards me, asked: "Will you be kind enough to tell me the cause of that indecent and universal laughing in the midst of such a solemn action as the baptism of this child?"

I tried to tell him his blunder, but for some time it was impossible to express myself. My laughing propensities were so much excited, and the convulsive laughter of the whole multitude made such a noise, that he would not have heard me had I been able to answer him. It was only when the greatest part of the crowd had left that I could reveal to Mr. Tetu that he had changed the baptized baby into a "seal skin!" He heartily laughed at his own blunder, and calmly went back to buy his seal skins. The next day the story went from house to house in Quebec, and caused everywhere such a laugh as they had not had since the birth of "General Cargo."

That priest was a good type of the greatest part of the priests of Canada. Fine fellows — social and jovial gentlemen — as fond of smoking their cigars as of chewing their tobacco and using their snuff; fond of fast horses; repeating the prayers of their breviary and going through the performance of their ministerial duties with as much speed as possible. With a good number of books in their libraries, but knowing nothing of them but the titles. Possessing the Bible, but ignorant of its contents, believing that they had the light, when they were in awful darkness; preaching the most monstrous doctrines as the gospel of truth; considering themselves the only true Christians in the world, when they worshipped the most contemptible idols made with hands. Absolutely ignorant of the Word of God, while they proclaimed and believed themselves to be the lights of the world. Unfortunate, blind men, leading the blind into the ditch!

CHAPTER XXV.

IN one of the pleasant hours which we used invariably to pass after dinner, in the comfortable parlour of our parsonage, one of the vicars, Mr. Louis Parent, said to the Rev. Mr. Tetu, "I have handed this morning more than one hundred dollars to the bishop, as the price of the masses which my pious penitents have requested me to celebrate, the greatest part of them for the souls in purgatory. Every week I have to do the same thing, just as each of you, and every one of the hundreds of priests in Canada have to do. Now I would like to know how the bishops can dispose of all these masses, and what they do with the large sums of money which go into their hands from every part of the country to have masses said. This question vexes me, and I would like to know your mind about it."

The good curate answered in a joking manner, as usual: "If the masses paid into our hands, which go to the bishop, are all celebrated, purgatory must be emptied twice a day. For I have calculated that the sums given for those masses in Canada cannot be less than 4,000 dollars every day, and, as there are three times as many Catholics in the United States as here, and as those Irish Catholics are more devoted to the souls in purgatory than the Canadians, there is no exaggeration in saying that they give as much as our people; 16,000 dollars at least will thus be given every day in these two countries to throw cold water on the burning flames of that fiery prison. Now these 16,000 dollars given every day, multiplied by the 365 days of the year, make the handsome sum of 5,840,000 dollars paid for that object in low masses every year. But, as we all know, that more than twice as much is paid for high masses than for the low, it is evident that more than 10,000,000 dollars are expended to help the souls of purgatory end their tortures every twelve months, in North America alone. If those millions of dollars do not benefit the good souls in purgatory, they at all events are of some benefit to our pious bishops and holy popes, in whose hands the greatest part must remain till the day of judgment. For there is not a sufficient number of priests in the world to say all the masses which are paid for by the people. I do not know any more than you do about what the bishops do with those millions of dollars; they keep that among their secret good works. But it is evident there is a serious mystery here. I do not mean to say that the Yankee and the Canadian bishops swallow those huge piles of dollars as sweet oranges; or that they are a band of big swindlers, who employ smaller ones, called Revs. Tetu, Baillargeon, Chiniquy, Parent, etc., to fill their treasures. But, if you want to know my mind on that delicate subject, I will tell you that the least we think and speak of it the better it is for us. Every time my thoughts turn to those streams of money which day and night flow from the small purses of our pious and unsuspecting people into our hands, and from ours into those of the bishops, I feel as if I were choking. If I am at the table I can neither eat nor drink, and if in my bed at night, I cannot sleep. But as I like to eat, drink, and sleep, I reject those thoughts as much as possible, and I advise you to do the same thing."

The other vicars seemed inclined, with Mr. Parent, to accept that conclusion; but, as I had not said a single word, they requested me to give them my views on that vexatious subject, which I did in the following brief words:—

"There are many things in our holy church which look like dark spots; but I hope that this is due only to our ignorance. No doubt these very things would look as white as snow, were we to see and know them just as they are. Our holy bishops, with the majority of the Catholic priests of the United States and Canada, cannot be that band of thieves and swindlers whose phantoms chill the blood of our worthy curate. So long as we do not know what the bishops do with those numberless masses paid into their hands, I prefer to believe that they act as honest men."

I had hardly said these few words, when I was called to visit a sick parishioner, and the conversation was ended.

Eight days later, I was alone in my room, reading the " L'Ami de la Religion et du Roi," a paper which I received from Paris, edited by Picot. My curiosity was not a little excited, when I read, at the head of a page, in large letters: "Admirable Piety of the French Canadian People." The reading of that page made me shed tears of shame, and shook my faith to its foundation. Unable to contain myself, I ran to the rooms of the curate and the vicars, and said to them : " A few days ago we tried, but in vain, to find what becomes of the large sums of money which pass from the people, through our hands, into those of the bishop, to say masses; but here is the answer, I have the key to that mystery, which is worthy of the darkest ages of the Church. I wish I were dead, rather than see with my own eyes such abominations." We then read that long chapter, the substance of which was that the venerable bishops of Quebec had sent not less than one hundred thousand francs, at different times, to the priests of Paris, that they might say four hundred thousand masses at five cents each! Here we had the sad evidence that our bishops had taken four hundred thousand francs from our poor people, under the pretext of saving the souls from purgatory! That article fell upon us as a thunderbolt. For a long time we looked at each other without being able to utter a single word; our tongues were as paralyzed by our shame: we felt as vile criminals when detected on the spot.

At last, Baillargeon, addressing the curate, said: "Is it possible that our bishops are swindlers, and we, their tools to defraud our people? What would that people say, if they knew that not only we do not say the masses for which they constantly fill our hands with their hard-earned money, but that we send those masses to be said in Paris for five cents! What will our good people think of us all when they know that our bishop pockets twenty cents out of each mass they ask us to celebrate according to their wishes."

The curate answered: "It is very lucky that the people do not know that sharp operation of our bishops, for they would surely throw us all into the river. Let us keep that shameful trade as secret as possible. For what is the crime of simony if this be not an instance of it?"

I replied: "How can you hope to keep that traffic of the body and blood of Christ a secret, when not less than 40,000 copies of this paper are circulated in France, and more than 100 copies come to the United States and Canada! The danger is greater than you suspect; it is even at our doors. Is it not on account of such public and undeniable crimes and vile tricks of the clergy of France, that the French people in general, not only have lost almost every vestige of religion, but, not half a century ago, condemned all the bishops and priests of France to death as public malefactors?

"But that sharp mercantile operation of our bishops takes a still darker colour, when we consider that those 'five-cent masses' which are said in Paris are not worth a cent. For who among us is ignorant of the fact that the greatest part of the priests of Paris are infidels, and that many of them live publicly with concubines? Would our people put their money in our hands if we were honest enough to tell them that their masses would be said for five cents in Paris by such priests? Do we not deceive them when we accept their money, under the well understood condition that we shall offer the holy sacrifice according to their wishes? But, instead of that, we get it sent to France, to be disposed of in such a criminal way. But, if you allow me to speak a little more, I have another strange fact to consider with you, which is closely connected with this simoniacal operation?"

"Yes! speak, speak!" answered all four priests.

I then resumed: "Do you remember how you were enticed into the 'Three Masses Society'? Who among us had the idea that the new obligations we were then assuming were such that the greatest part of the year would be spent in saying masses for the priests, and that it would thus become impossible to satisfy the pious demands of the people who support us ? We already belonged to the societies of the Blessed Virgin Mary and of St. Michael, which raised to five the number of masses we had to celebrate for the dead priests. Dazzled by the idea that we would have two thousand masses said for us at our death, we bit at the bait presented to us by the bishop as hungry fishes, without suspecting the hook. The result is that we have had to say 165 masses for the 33 priests who died during the past year, which means that each of us has to pay forty-one dollars to the bishop for masses which he has had said in Paris for eight dollars. Each mass which we celebrate for a dead priest here, is a mass which the bishop sends to Paris, on which he gains twenty cents. Then the more priests he enrols in his society of 'Three Masses,' the more twenty cents he pockets from us and from our pious people. Hence his admirable zeal to enrol every one of us. It is not the value of the money which our bishop so skilfully got from our hands which I consider, but I feel desolate when I see that by these societies we become the accomplices of his simoniacal trade. For, being forced the greatest part of the year to celebrate the holy sacrifice for the benefit of the dead priests, we cannot celebrate the masses for which we are daily paid by the people, and are therefore forced to transfer them into the hands of the bishop, who sends them to Paris, after spiriting away twenty cents from each of them. However, why should we lament over the past ? It is no more within our reach. There is no remedy for it. Let us then learn from the past errors how to be wise in the future."

Mr. Tetu answered : "You have shown us our error. Now, can you indicate any remedy ? "

"I cannot say that the remedy we have in hand is one of those patented medicines which will cure all the diseases of our sickly church in Canada, but I hope it will help to bring a speedy convalescence. That remedy is to abolish the society of 'Three Masses,' and to establish another of 'One Mass,' which will be said at the death of every priest. In that way it is true that instead of 2,000 masses, we shall have only 1,200 at our death. But if 1,200 masses do not open to us the gates of heaven, it is because we shall be in hell. By that reduction we shall be enabled to say more masses at the request of our people, and shall diminish the number of five cent masses said by the priests of Paris at the request of our bishop. If you take my advice, we will immediately name the Rev. Mr. Tetu president of the new society, Mr. Parent will be its treasurer, and I consent to act as your secretary, if you like it. When our society is organized, we will send our resignations to the president of the other society, and we shall immediately address a circular to all the priests, to give them the reason for the change, and respectfully ask them to unite with us in this new society, in order to diminish the number of masses which are celebrated by the five cent priests of Paris."

Within two hours the new society was fully organized, the reasons of its formation written in a book, and our names were sent to the bishop, with a respectful letter informing him that we were no more members of the ' Three Masses Society.' That letter was signed, C. Chiniquy, Secretary. Three hours later, I received the following note from the bishop's palace :

"My Lord Bishop of Quebec wants to see you immediately upon important affairs. Do not fail to come without delay. Truly yours,

"CHARLES F. CAZEAULT, Secy."

I showed the missive to the curate and the vicars, and told them : " A big storm is raging on the mountain ; this is the first peal of thunder—the atmosphere looks dark and heavy. Pray for me that I may speak and act as an honest and fearless priest, when in the presence of the bishop."

In the first parlour of the bishop I met my personal friend, Secretary Cazeault. He said to me : " My dear Chiniquy, you are sailing on a rough sea—you must be a lucky mariner if you escape the wreck. The bishop is very angry at you ; but be not discouraged, for the right is on your side." He then kindly opened the door of the bishop's parlour, and said : " My lord, Mr. Chiniquy is here, waiting for your orders."

" Let him come, sir," answered the bishop.

I entered and threw myself at his feet, as it is the usage of the priests. But, stepping backward, he told me in a most excited manner : " I have no benediction for you till you give me a satisfactory explanation of your strange conduct."

I arose to my feet and said : " My lord, what do you want from me ? "

" I want you, sir, to explain to me the meaning of this letter signed by you as secretary of a new-born society called, ' One Mass Society.' " At the same time he showed me my letter.

I answered him : " My lord—the letter is in good French—your lordship must have understood it well. I cannot see how any explanation on my part could make it clearer."

" What I want to know from you, is what you mean, and what is your object in leaving the old and respectable ' Three Mass Society ' ? Is it not composed of your bishops and of all the priests of Canada ?

Did you not find yourself in sufficiently good company? Do you object to the prayers said for the souls in purgatory?"

I replied: "My lord, I will answer by revealing to your lordship a fact which has not sufficiently attracted your attention. The great number of masses which we have to say for the souls of the dead priests makes it impossible for us to say the masses for which the people pay into our hands; we are, then, forced to transfer this money into your hands; and then instead of having these holy sacrifices offered by the good priests of Canada, your lordship has recourse to the priests of France, where you get them said for five cents. We see two great evils in this: First, our masses are said by priests in whom we have not the least confidence; and though the masses they say are very cheap, they are too dearly purchased; for between you and me, we can say that, with very few exceptions, the masses said by the priests of France, particularly of Paris, are not worth one cent. The second evil is still greater, for in our eyes, it is one of the greatest crimes which our holy church has always condemned, the crime of simony."

"Do you mean to say," indignantly replied the bishop, "that I am guilty of the crime of simony?"

"Yes! my lord; it is just what I mean to say, and I do not see how your lordship does not understand that the trade in masses by which you gain 400,000 francs on a spiritual merchandise, which you get for 100,000, is not simony."

"You insult me! You are the most impudent man I ever saw. If you do retract what you have said, I will suspend and excommunicate you!"

"My suspension and my excommunication will not make the position of your lordship much better. For the people will know that you have excommunicated me because I protested against your trade in masses. They will know that you pocket twenty cents on every mass, and that you get them said for five cents in Paris by priests, the greatest part of whom live with concubines, and you will see that there will be only one voice in Canada to bless me for my protest and to condemn you for your simoniacal trade on such a sacred thing as the holy and tremendous sacrifice of the body, blood, soul and divinity of Jesus Christ."

I uttered these words with such perfect calmness that the bishop saw that I had not the least fear of his thunders. He began to pace the room, and he heaped on my devoted head all the epithets by which I could learn that I was an insolent, rebellious and dangerous priest.

"It is evident to me," said he, "that you aim to be a reformer, a Luther, *au petit pied*, in Canada. But you will never be anything else than a monkey!"

I saw that my bishop was beside himself, and that my perfect calmness added to his irritation. I answered him: "If Luther had never done anything worse than I do to-day, he ought to be blessed by God and man. I respectfully request your lordship to be calm. The subject on which I speak to you is more serious than you think. Your lordship, by asking twenty-five cents for a mass which can be said for five cents, does a thing which you would condemn if it were done by another man. You are digging under your own feet, and under the feet of your priests the same abyss in which the Church of France nearly perished, not half a century ago. You are destroying with your own hands every vestige of religion in the hearts of the people, who will sooner or later know it. I am your best friend, your most respectful priest, when I fearlessly tell you this truth before it is too late. Your lordship knows that he has not a priest who loves and cherishes him more than I do—God knows, it is because I love and respect you, as my own father, that I profoundly deplore the illusions which prevent you from seeing the terrible consequences that will follow, if our pious people learn that you abuse their ignorance and their good faith, by making them pay twenty-five cents for a thing which costs only five. Woe to your lordship! Woe to me, woe to our holy church, the day that our people know that in our holy religion the blood of Christ is turned into merchandise to fill the treasury of the bishops and popes!"

It was evident that these last words, said with the most perfect self-possession, had not all been lost. The bishop had become calmer. He answered me: "You are young and without experience; your imagination is easily fed with phantoms; when you know a little more, you will change your mind and will have more respect for your superiors. I hope your present error is only a momentary one. I could punish you for this freedom with which you have dared to speak to your bishop, but I prefer to warn you to be more respectful and obedient in future. Though I deplore for your sake, that you have requested me to take away your name from the 'Three Mass Society'—you and the four simpletons who have committed the same act of folly, are the only losers in the matter. Instead of two thousand masses said for the deliverance of your souls from the flames of Purgatory, you will have only twelve hundred. But, be sure of it, there is too much wisdom and true piety in my clergy to follow your example. You will be left alone, and, I fear, covered with ridicule. For they will call you the 'little reformer.'"

I answered the bishop: "I am young, it is true, but the truths I have said to your lordship are as old as the Gospel. I have such confidence in the infinite merits of the holy sacrifice of the mass, that I sincerely believe, that twelve hundred masses said by good priests, are enough to cleanse my soul and extinguish the flames of purgatory. But, besides, I prefer twelve hundred masses said by one hundred sincere Canadian priests, to a million said by the five cent priests of Paris."

These last words, spoken with a tone half serious, half jocose, brought a change on the face of my bishop. I thought it was a good moment to get my benediction and take leave of him. I took my hat, knelt at his feet, obtained his blessing, and left.

CHAPTER XXVI.

THE hour of my absence had been one of anxiety for the curate and the vicars. But my prompt return filled them with joy.

" What news ? " they all exclaimed.

" Good news," I answered; " the battle has been fierce but short. We have gained the day; and if we are only true to ourselves, another great victory is in store for us. The bishop is so sure that we are the only ones who think of that reform, that he will not move a finger to prevent the other priests from following us. This security will make our success infallible. But we must not lose a moment. Let us address our circular to every priest in Canada."

One hour later there were more than twenty writers at work, and before twenty-four hours, more than three hundred letters were carried to all the priests, giving them the reasons why we should try, by all fair means, to put an end to the shameful simoniacal trade in masses which was going on between Canada and France.

The week was scarcely ended, when letters came from almost all curates and vicars to the bishop, respectfully requesting him to withdraw his name from " The Society of the Three Masses." Only fifty refused to comply with our request.

Our victory was more complete than we had expected. But the Bishop of Quebec, hoping to regain his lost ground, immediately wrote to the Bishop of Montreal, my Lord Telemesse, to come to his help and show us the enormity of the crime we had committed, in rebelling against the will of our ecclesiastical superiors.

A few days later, to my great dismay, I received a short and very cold note from the bishops' secretary, telling me that their lordships, the Bishops of Montreal and Quebec, wanted to see me at the palace, without delay. I had never seen the Bishop of Montreal, and my surprise and disappointment were great in finding myself in the presence of a man, my idea of whom was of gigantic proportions, when in reality, he was very small. But I felt exceedingly well pleased by the admirable mixture of firmness, intelligence, and honesty of his whole demeanour. His eyes were piercing as the eagle's; but when fixed on me, I saw in them the marks of a noble and honest heart.

The motions of his head were rapid, his sentences short, and he seemed to know only one line, the straight one, when approaching a subject or dealing with a man. He had the merited reputation of being one of the most learned and eloquent men of Canada. The Bishop of Quebec had remained on his sofa, and left the Bishop of Montreal to receive me. I fell at his feet and asked his blessing, which he gave me in the most cordial way. Then, putting his hand upon my shoulder, he said, in a Quaker style: "Is it possible that *thou* art Chiniquy—that young priest who makes so much noise? How can such a small man make so much noise?"

There being a smile on his countenance as he uttered these words, I saw at once that there was no anger or bad feeling in his heart; I replied: "My lord; do you not know that the most precious pearls and perfumes are put up in the smallest vases?"

The bishop saw that this was a compliment to his address; he smilingly replied: "Well, well, if thou art a noisy priest, thou art not a fool. But, tell me, why dost thou want to destroy our 'Three Mass Society' and establish that new one on its ruins, in spite of thy superiors?"

"My lord, my answer will be as respectful, short, and plain as possible. I have left the 'Three Mass Society' because it was my right to do it, without anybody's permission. I hope our venerable Canadian bishops do not wish to be served by slaves!"

"I do not say," replied the bishop, "that thou wert bound in conscience to remain in the 'Three Mass Society;' but, can I know why thou hast left such a respectable association, at the head of which thou seest thy bishops and the most venerable priests in Canada?"

"I will again be plain in my answer, my lord. If your lordship wants to go to hell with your venerable priests by spiriting away twenty cents from every one of our honest and pious penitents, for masses which you get said for five, by bad priests in Paris, I will not follow you. Moreover, if your lordship wants to be thrown into the river by the furious people, when they know how long and how cunningly we have cheated them, with our simoniacal trade in masses, I do not want to follow you into the cold stream."

"Well! well," answered the bishop, "let us drop that matter for ever."

He uttered this short sentence with such an evidence of sincerity and honesty, that I saw he really meant it. He had, at a glance, seen that his ground was untenable, in the presence of priests who knew their rights, and had a mind to stand by them.

My joy was great indeed at such a prompt and complete victory. I fell again at the bishop's feet, and asked his benediction before taking leave of him—I then left to go and tell the curates and vicars the happy issue of our interview with the bishop of Montreal.

From that time till now, at the death of every priest, the Clerical Press never failed mentioning whether the deceased priest belonged to the " Three " or " One Mass Society."

We had, to some extent, diminished the simoniacal and infamous trade in masses ; but unfortunately we had not destroyed it ; and I know that to-day it has revived.   Since I left the Church of Rome, the Bishops of Quebec have raised the "Three Mass Society" from its grave.

It is a public fact, that no priest will dare deny, that the trade in masses is still conducted on a large scale with France.   There are in Paris and other large cities in that country, public agencies to carry on that shameful traffic.   It is, generally, in the hands of booksellers or merchants of church ornaments.   Every year their houses send a large number of prospectuses through France and Belgium and other catholic countries, in which they say that, in order to help the priests, who having received money for their masses, don't know where to have them said ; they offer a premium of twenty-five or thirty per cent. to those who will send them the surplus of the money they have in hand, to offer the Holy Sacrifice of the Mass.

The priests who have such surplus, tempted by that premium, which is usually paid with a watch or a chain, or a chalice, disgorge a part, or the whole of the large sums they possess, into the hands of the pious merchants, who take this money and use it as they please.

But they never pay the masses in money, they give only merchandise.   For instance, that priest will receive a watch, if he promises to celebrate one or two hundred masses, or a chalice to celebrate three or four hundred masses.   I have, here in hand, several of the contracts or promissory notes sent by those merchants of masses to the priests. The public will, no doubt, read the following documents with interest. They were handed me by a priest lately converted from the Church of Rome :

RUE DE REIMES—PARIS.

Ant. Levesques, editor of the works of Mr. Dufriche—Desgenettes.
Cure of Notre Dame des Victoires.
Delivered to the Rev. Mr. Camerle, curate of Ansibeau (Basses Alpes).

PARIS, October 12, 1874.

	F.
10 metres of Satin Cloth at 22 francs	220.
8 „ of Merino, all wool	123.
Month of May	2.
History of Mary Christina...................................	1.40
Life of St. Stanislas Koska	2.
Meditations of the Soul	4.
Jesus Christ, the Light of the World	2.
Packing and Freight	9.30
Total ....,....................	363.70

MR. CURATE; We have the honour of informing you that the packages containing the articles you have ordered on the 4th of October, were shipped on the 12th of October, to Digne, where we respectfully request you to go and ask for them. For the payment of these articles, we request you to say the following masses:

58 ad intentionem of the giver, for the discharge of Rev. Mr. Montet.
58 ad intentionem of the givers, for the discharge of Rev. Mr. Hœg.
100—188 for the dead, for the discharge of Rev. Mr. Wod.

MR. CURATE: Will you be kind enough to say or have said all those masses in the shortest time possible, and answer these Revd. gentlemen, if they make any inquiries about the acquittal of those masses.

Respectfully yours,
(Signed)   ANT. LEVESQUES.

PARIS, November 11th, 1874.

REV. MR. CAMERLE; We have the honour of addressing you the invoice of what we forwarded to you on the 12th of October. On account we have put to your credit 188 masses. We respectfully request you to get said the following intentions:

73 for the dead, to the acquittal of Rev. Mr. Watters,
70 pro defuncto,
20 ad intentionem donatis,
13 ad intentionem donatis,

For the discharge of Rev. Mr. C.

176

MR. CURATE; Be kind enough to say these masses, or have them said as soon as possible, and answer the reverend gentleman who may inquire from you about their acquittal. The 188 masses mentioned in our letter of the 3rd inst., added to the 176 here mentioned, make 364 francs, the value of the goods sent you. We thought you would like to have the pamphlets of propaganda we address you.

Respectfully yours,
(Signed)   ANT. LEVESQUES.

Hence, it is that priests, in France and elsewhere, have gold watches, rich house furniture, and interesting books, purchased with the money paid by our poor deluded Canadian Catholics to their priests, for masses which are turned into mercantile commodities in other places. It would be difficult to say who makes the best bargain between those merchants of masses, the priests to whom they are sold, or those from whom they are bought at a discount of twenty-five to thirty per cent.

The only evident thing is the cruel deception practised on the credulity and ignorance of the Roman Catholics by their priests and bishops. To-day, the houses of Dr. Anthony Levesques in Paris are the most accredited in France. In 1874, the house of Mesme was doing an immense business with its stock of masses, but in an evil day, the government suspected that the number of masses paid into their hands, exceeded the number of those celebrated through their hired priests. The suspicions soon turned into certainty when the books were examined. It was then found that an incredible number of masses, which were to empty the large room of purgatory, never reached their destination, but only filled the purse of the Parisian mass merchant; and so the unlucky Mesme was unceremoniously sent to the penitentiary to meditate on the infinite merits of the Holy Sacrifice of the Mass, which had been engulfed in his treasures.

But these facts are not known by the poor Roman Catholics of Canada, who are fleeced more and more by their priests, under the pretext of saving souls from purgatory.

A new element of success in the large swindling operations of the Canadian priests has lately been discovered. It is well known that in the greater part of the United States, the poor deluded Irish pay one dollar to their priest, instead of a shilling, for a low mass. Those priests whose conscience are sufficiently elastic (as is often the case), keep the money without ever thinking of having the masses said, and soon get rich. But there are some whose natural honesty shrinks from the idea of stealing; but unable to celebrate all the masses paid for and requested at their hands, they send the dollars to some of their clerical friends in Canada, who, of course, prefer these one dollar masses to the twenty-five cent ones paid by the French Canadians. However, they keep that secret and continue to fill their treasury.

There are, however, many priests in Canada who think it less evil to keep those large sums of money in their own hands, than to give them to the bishops to traffic with the merchants of Paris. At the end of one of the ecclesiastical retreats in the seminary of St. Sulpice in 1850, Bishop Bourget told us that one of the priests who had lately died, had requested him, in the name of Jesus Christ, to ask every priest to take a share in the four thousand dollars which he had received for masses he had never said. We refused to grant him that favour, and those four thousand dollars received by that priest, like the millions put into the hands of other priests and the bishops, turned to be nothing less than an infamous swindling operation under the mask of religion.

To understand what the priests of Rome are, let the readers note what is said in the Roman Catholic Bible, of the priest of Babylon :—

"And King Astyges was gathered to his fathers, and Cyrus, of Persia, received his kingdom, and Daniel conversed with the king, and was honoured above all his friends. Now the Babylonians had an idol, called Bel, and there were spent upon him, every day, twelve measures of fine flour, and forty sheep and six vessels of wine. And the king worshipped it and went daily to adore: but Daniel worshipped his own God, and the king said unto him : ' Why dost thou not worship Bel ? ' who answered and said : ' Because I may not worship idols made with hands, but the living God, who hath created the heavens and the earth, and hath sovereignty over all flesh.' Then the king said : ' Thinkest thou not that Bel is a living God ! Seest thou not how much he eateth and drinketh every day ? '

" Then Daniel smiled and said : ' Oh, king ! be not deceived ; for this is but clay within and brass without, and did never eat or drink anything.'

" So that king was wroth, and called for his priests and said : ' If ye tell me not who this is that devoureth these expenses, ye shall die ; but if ye can certify me that Bel devoureth them, then Daniel shall die, for he has spoken blasphemy against Bel.' And Daniel said unto the king ; ' Let it be according to thy word.'

" Now the priests of Bel were three score and ten, besides their wives and children.

" And the king went with Daniel to the temple of Bel—so Bel's priests said : ' Lo ! we got out, but thou, O king, set on the meat, and make ready the wine, and shut the door fast, and seal it with thine own signet ; and to-morrow when thou comest in, if thou findest not that Bel had eaten up all, we will suffer death ; or else, Daniel, that speaketh falsely against Bel, shall die—and they little regarded it, for under the table they had made a privy entrance, whereby they entered continually and consumed those things.'

" So when they were gone forth, the king set meats before Bel.

" Now Daniel had commanded his servants to bring ashes, and those they strewed throughout all the temple, in the presence of the king alone : then went they out, and shut the door, and sealed it with the king's signet, and so departed.

" Now in the night came the priests, with their wives and children, as they were wont to do, and did eat and drink up all.

" In the morning betimes the king arose, and Daniel with him.

" And the king said, ' Daniel, are the seals whole ? ' And he said, ' Yea, O king, they be whole.' And as soon as they had opened the door, the king looked upon the table, and cried with a loud voice : ' Great art thou, O Bel ! and with thee there is no deceit at all.' Then laughed Daniel, and held the king that he should not go in, and said : ' Behold now the pavement, and mark well whose footsteps are these.' And the king said : ' I see the footsteps of men, women, and children.' And then the king was angry, and took the priests, with their wives and children, who showed him the privy doors, where they came in and consumed such things as were on the tables.

" Therefore the king slew them, and delivered Bel into Daniel's power, who destroyed him and his temple."

Who does not pity the king of Babylon, who, when looking at his clay and brass god, exclaimed : " Great art thou, O Bel, and with thee there is no deceit ! "

But, is the deception practised by the priests of the Pope on their poor, deluded dupes, less cruel and infamous? Where is the difference between that Babylonian god, made with brass and baked clay, and the god of the Roman Catholics, made with a handful of wheat and flour, baked between two hot polished irons?

How skilful were the priests in keeping the secret of what became of the rich daily offerings brought to the hungry god! Who could suspect that there was a secret trap through which they came with their wives and children to eat the rich offerings?

So, to-day, among the simple and blind Roman Catholics, who could suppose that the immense sums of money given every day to the priests to glorify God, purify the souls of men, and bring all kinds of blessings upon the donors, were, on the contrary, turned into the most ignominious and swindling operation the world has ever seen?

Though the brass god of Babylon was a contemptible idol, is not the wafer god of Rome still more so? Though the priests of Bel were skilful deceivers, are they not surpassed in the art of deception by the priests of Rome! Do not these carry on their operations on a much larger scale than the former?

But, as there is always a day of retribution for the great iniquities of this world, when all things will be revealed; and just as the cunning of the priests of Babylon could not save them, when God sent His prophet to take away the mask, behind which they deceived their people, so let the priests of Rome know that God will, sooner or later, send His prophet, who will tear off the mask, behind which they deceive the world. Their big, awkward, and flat feet will be seen and exposed, and the very people whom they keep prostrated before their idols, crying: " O God! with Thee there is no deceit at all!" will become the instruments of the justice of God in the great day of retribution.

CHAPTER XXVII.

ONE of the first things done by the curate Tetu, after his new vicars had been chosen, was to divide, by casting lots, his large parish into four parts, that there might be more regularity in our ministerial labours, and my lot gave me the north-east of the parish, which contained the Quebec Marine Hospital.

The number of sick sailors I had to visit almost every day in that noble institution, was between twenty-five and a hundred. The Roman Catholic chapel, with its beautiful altar, was not yet completed. It was only in 1837 that I could persuade the hospital authorities to fix

12

it as it is to-day. Having no place there to celebrate mass and keep the Holy Sacrament, I soon found myself in presence of a difficulty which, at first, seemed to me of a grave character. I had to administer the viaticum (holy communion) to a dying sailor. As every one knows, all Roman Catholics are bound to believe that by the consecration, the wafer is transformed into the body, soul and divinity of Jesus Christ. Hence, they call that ceremony : " Porter le bon dieu au malade " (carry the good god to the sick). Till then, when in Charlesbourgh or St. Charles, I, with the rest of Roman Catholic priests, always made use of pomp and exterior marks of supreme respect for the Almighty God I was carrying in my hands to the dying.

I had never carried the good God without being accompanied by several people, walking or riding on horseback. I then wore a white surplice over my long black robe (soutane) to strike the people with awe. There was also a man ringing a bell before me, all along the way, to announce to the people that the great God, who had not only created them, but had made Himself man to save them, by dying on Calvary, was passing by ; that they had to fall on their knees in their houses, or along the public roads, or in their fields, and prostrate themselves and adore Him.

But could I do that in Quebec, where so many miserable heretics were more disposed to laugh at my god than to adore him ?

In my zeal and sincere faith, I was, however, determined to dare the heretics of the whole world, and to expose myself to their insults, rather than give up the exterior marks of supreme respect and adoration which were due to my god everywhere ; and twice I carried him to the hospital with the usual solemnity.

In vain, my curate tried to persuade me to change my mind. I closed my ears to his arguments. He then kindly invited me to go with him to the bishop's palace, in order to confer with him on that grave subject. How can I express my dismay when the bishop told me, with a levity which I had not yet observed in him, "that on account of the Protestants whom we had to meet everywhere, it was better to make our 'god' travel *incognito* in the streets of Quebec." He added in a high and jocose tone : " Put him in your vest pocket, as do the rest of the city priests. Carry him to your dying patients without any scruples. Never aim at being a reformer and doing better than your venerable brethren in the priesthood. We must not forget that we are a conquered people. If we were masters, we would carry him to the dying with the public honours we used to give him before the conquest ; but the Protestants are the stronger. Our governor is a Protestant, as well as our Queen. The garrison, which is inside the walls of their impregnable citadel, is composed chiefly of Protestants. According to the laws of our holy church, we have the right to punish, even by death, the miserable people who turn into ridicule the mysteries of our holy religion. But though we have that right, we are not strong enough to enforce it. We must, then, bear the yoke in silence. After all, it is our god himself, who in his inscrutable judgment, has deprived us of the power of honouring him as he deserves; and to tell you my whole mind as plainly as possible, it is not our fault, but his own doing, so to speak, if we are forced to make him travel *incognito* through our streets. It is one of the sad results of the victory which the God of battles gave to the heretics over us on the plains of Abraham. If, in his good providence, we could break our fetters, and become free to pass again the laws which regulated Canada before the conquest, to prevent the heretics from settling among us, then we would carry him as we used to do in those happy days."

"But," said I, "when I walk in the streets with my good god in my vest pocket, what will I do if I meet any friend who wants to shake hands and have a joke with me?"

The bishop laughed and answered: "Tell your friend you are in a hurry, and go your way as quickly as possible; but if there is no help, have your talk and your joke with him, without any scruple of conscience. The important point in this delicate matter is that the people should not know we are carrying our god through the streets *incognito,* for this knowledge would surely shake and weaken their faith. The common people are, more than we think, kept in our holy church, by the impressing ceremonies of our processions and public marks of respect we give to Jesus Christ, when we carry Him to the sick; for the people are more easily persuaded by what they see with their eyes and touch with their hands, than by what they hear with their ears."

I submitted to the order of my ecclesiastical superior; but I would not be honest, were I not to confess that I lost much of my spiritual joy for some time in the administration of the viaticum. I continued to believe as sincerely as I could, but the laughing words and light tone of my bishop had fallen upon my soul as an icy cloud. The jocose way in which he had spoken of what I had been taught to consider as the most awful and adorable mystery of the church, left the impression on my mind that he did not believe one iota of the dogma of transubstantiation. And in spite of all my honest efforts to get rid of that suspicion, it grew in my mind every time I met him to talk on any ministerial subject.

It took several years before I could accustom myself to carry my god in my vest pocket as the other priests did, without any more ceremony than with a piece of tobacco. So long as I was walking alone I felt happy. I could then silently converse with my Saviour, and give Him all the expression of my love and adoration. It was my custom, then, to repeat the 103rd or 50th Psalm of David, or the Te Deum, or some other beautiful hymn, or the *Pange Lingua*, which I knew by heart. But no words can express my sadness when, as it was very often the case, I met some friends forcing me to shake hands with them, and began one of those idle and commonplace talks, so common everywhere.

With the utmost efforts, I had then to put a smiling mask on my face, in order to conceal the expressions of faith which are infallibly seen, in spite of one's self, if one is in the very act of adoration.

How, then, I earnestly cursed the day when my country had fallen under the yoke of Protestants, whose presence in Quebec prevented me from following the dictates of my conscience! How many times did I pray my wafer god, whom I was personally pressing on my heart, to grant us an opportunity to break those fetters, and destroy for ever the power of Protestant England over us! Then we should be free again, to give our Saviour all the public honours which were due to His Majesty. Then we should put in force the laws by which no heretic had any right to settle and live in Canada.

Not long after that conversation with the bishop, I found myself in a circumstance which added much to my trouble and confusion of conscience on that matter.

There was then, in Quebec, a merchant who had honourably raised himself from a state of poverty, to the first rank among the wealthy merchants of Canada. Though, a few years after, he was ruined by a series of most terrible disasters, his name is still honoured in Canada, as one of the most industrious and honest merchants of our young country. His name was James Buteau. He had built a magnificent house, and furnished it in a princely style.

In order to celebrate his "house warming" in a becoming style, he invited a hundred guests from the élite of the city, among whom were all the priests of the parishes. But in order not to frighten their prudery—though that party was to be more of the nature of a ball than anything else—Mr. Buteau had given it the modest name of an Oyster Soirée.

Just as the good curate, Tetu, with his cheerful vicars was starting, a messenger met us at the door, to say that Mr. Parent, the youngest vicar, had been called to carry the "good god" to a dying woman.

Mr. Parent was born, and had passed his whole life in Quebec, in whose seminary he had gone through a complete and brilliant course of study. I think there was scarcely a funny song in the French language which he could not sing. With a cheerful nature, he was the delight of the Quebec society, by almost every member of which he was personally known.

His hair was constantly perfumed with the richest pomade, and the most precious eau de cologne surrounded him with an atmosphere of the sweetest odours. With all these qualities and privileges, it is no wonder that he was the confessor, *à la mode*, of the young ladies of Quebec.

The bright luminaries which hover around Jupiter are not more exact in converging toward that brilliant star than those pious young ladies were in gathering around the confessional box of Mr. Parent every week or fortnight.

The unexpected announcement of a call to the death-bed of one of his poorest penitents, was not quite the most desirable thing for our dear young friend, at such an hour. But he knew too well his duty to grumble. He said to us, " Go before me and tell Mrs. Buteau that I will be in time to get my share of the oysters."

By chance, the sick house was on the way and not far from. Mr. Buteau's splendid mansion. He left us to run to the altar and take the "good god" with him. We started for the soirée, but not sympathizing with our dear Mr. Parent, who would lose the most interesting part, for the administration of the viaticum. The extreme unction, with the giving of indulgences, *in articulo mortis*, and the exhortations to the dying, and the people gathered from the neighbourhood to witness those solemn rites, could not take much less than three quarters, or even an hour of his time. But, to my great surprise, we had not yet been ten minutes in the magnificent parlour of our host, when I saw Mr. Parent, who like a new-born butterfly, flying from flower to flower, was running from lady to lady, joking, laughing, surpassing himself with his inimitable and refined manners. I said to myself, " How is it possible that he has so quickly got rid of his unpalatable task with his dying penitent ? " and I wanted an opportunity of being alone with him, to satisfy my curiosity on that point; but it was pretty late in the evening when I found a chance to say to him : " We all feared lest your dying patient may deprive us of the pleasure of your company the greatest part of the soirée ! "

" Oh ! oh ! " answered he, with a hearty laugh, " that intelligent woman had the good common sense to die just two minutes before I entered her house. I suppose that her guardian angel, knowing all about this incomparable party, had despatched the good soul to heaven a little sooner than she expected, in my behalf."

I could not but smile at his answer, which was given in a manner to make a stone laugh. " But," said I, " what have you done with the ' good god ' you had carried with you ? "

" Ah ! ah ! the ' good god,' " he replied, in a jocose and subdued tone. " Well, well ; the ' good god ! ' He stands very still in my vest pocket ; and if he enjoys this princely festivity as well as we all do, he will surely thank me for having brought him here, even *en sur-*

venant. But do not say a word of his presence here ; it would spoil everything."

That priest, who was only one year younger than myself, was one of my dearest friends. Though his words rather smelt of the unbeliever and blasphemer, I preferred to attribute them to the sweet champagne he had drank than to a real want of faith.

But I must confess that, though I had laughed very heartily at first, his last utterance pained me so much that, from that moment to the end of the soiree, I felt uneasy and confounded. My firm belief that my Saviour, Jesus Christ, was there in person, kept a prisoner in my young friend's vest pocket, going to and fro from one young lady to the other, witnessing the constant laughing, hearing the idle words, the light and funny songs, made my whole soul shudder, and my heart sunk within me. By times I wished I could fall on my knees to adore my Saviour, whom I believed to be there. However, a mysterious voice was whispering in my ear : "Are you not a fool to believe that you can make a God with a wafer ; and that Jesus Christ, your Saviour and your God, can be kept a prisoner, in spite of himself, in the vest pocket of a man ? Do you not see that your friend, Parent, who has much more brains and intelligence than you, does not believe a word of that dogma of transubstantiation ? Have you forgotten the unbeliever's smile, which you saw on the lips of the bishop himself only a few days ago ? Was not that laugh the infallible proof that he also does not believe a particle of that ridiculous dogma ? "

With superhuman effort I tried, and succeeded partly, to stifle that voice. But that struggle could not last long within my soul, without leaving its exterior marks on my face. Evidently a sad cloud was over my eyes, for several of my most respectable friends, with Mr. and Mrs. Buteau, kindly asked if I were sick.

At last I felt so confused at the repetition of the same suggestion by so many, that I felt I was only making a fool of myself by remaining any longer in their midst. Angry with myself for my want of moral strength in this hour of trial, I respectfully asked pardon from my kind host for leaving their party before the end, on account of a sudden indisposition.

The next day there was only one voice in Quebec saying that young Parent had been the lion of that brilliant soirée, and that the poor young priest, Chiniquy, had been its fool.

CHAPTER XXVIII.

GOD controls the greatest as well as the smallest of the events of this world. Our business during the few days of our pilgrimage, then, is to know His will and do it. Our happiness here, as in heaven, rests on this foundation, just as the success and failures of our lives come entirely from the practical knowledge or ignorance of this simplest and sublimest truth. I dare say that there is not a single fact of my long and eventful life which has not taught me that there is a special providence in our lives. Particularly was this apparent in the casting of the lots by which I became the first chaplain of the Quebec Marine Hospital. After the other vicars had congratulated each other for having escaped the heavy burden of work and responsibilities connected with that chaplaincy, they kindly gave me the assurance of their sympathies for what they called my bad luck. In thanking them for their friendly feeling, I confessed that this occurrence appeared to me in a very different light. I was sure that God had directed this for my good and His own glory, and I was right. In the beginning of November, 1834, a slight indisposition having kept me a few days at home, Mr. Glackmayer, the superintendent of the hospital, came to tell me that there was an unusually large number of sick, left by the Fall fleets, in danger of death, who were day and night calling for me. He added, in a secret way, that there were several cases of small-pox of the worst type; that several had already died, and many were dying from the terrible cholera morbus, which was still raging among the sailors.

This sad news came to me as an order from heaven to run to the rescue of my dear sick seamen. I left my room, despite my physician, and went to the hospital.

The first man I met was Dr. Douglas, who was waiting for me at Mr. C. Glackmayer's room. He confirmed what I had known before of the number of sick, and added that the prevailing diseases were of the most dangerous kind.

Dr. Douglas, who was one of the founders and governors of the hospital, had the well-merited reputation of being one of the ablest surgeons of Quebec. Though a staunch Protestant by birth and profession, he honoured me with his confidence and friendship from the first day we met. I may say I have never known a nobler heart, a larger mind and a truer philanthropist.

After thanking him for the useful though sad intelligence he had given me, I requested Mr. Glackmayer to give me a glass of brandy, which I immediately swallowed.

"What are you doing there?" said Dr. Douglas.

"You see," I answered; "I have drunk a glass of excellent brandy."

"But please tell me why you drank that brandy."

"Because it is a good preservative against the pestilential atmosphere I will breathe all day," I replied. "I will have to hear the confessions of all those people dying from small-pox or cholera, and breathe the putrid air which is around their pillows. Does not common sense warn me to take some precautions against the contagion?"

"Is it possible," rejoined he, "that a man for whom I have such a sincere esteem is so ignorant of the deadly workings of alcohol in the human frame? What you have just drank is nothing but poison; and, far from protecting yourself against the danger, you are now much more exposed to it than before you drank that beverage."

"You poor Protestants," I answered, in a jocose way, "are a band of fanatics, with your extreme doctrines on temperance; you will never convert me to your views on that subject. Is it for the use of the dogs that God has created wine and brandy? No; it is for the use of men who drink them with moderation and intelligence."

"My dear Mr. Chiniquy, you are joking; but I am in earnest when I tell you that you have poisoned yourself with that glass of brandy," replied Dr. Douglas.

"If good wine and brandy were poisons," I answered, "you would be long ago the only physician in Quebec, for you are the only one of the medical body whom I know to be an abstainer. But, though I am much pleased with your conversation, excuse me if I leave you to visit my dear sick sailors, whose cries for spiritual help ring in my ears."

"One word more," said Dr. Douglas, "and I have done. To-morrow morning we will make the autopsy of a sailor who has just died suddenly here. Have you any objection to come and see with your eyes, in the body of that man, what your glass of brandy has done in your own body."

"No, sir; I have no objection to see that," I replied. "I have been anxious for a long time to make a special study of anatomy. It will be my first lesson; I cannot get it from a better master."

I then shook hands with him and went to my patients, with whom I passed the remainder of the day and the greater part of the night. Fifty of them wanted to make general confessions of all the sins of their whole lives; and I had to give the last sacraments to twenty-five who were dying from small-pox or cholera morbus. The next morning I was, at the appointed hour, by the corpse of the dead man, when Dr. Douglas kindly gave me a very powerful microscope, that I might more thoroughly follow the ravages of alcohol in every part of the human body.

"I have not the least doubt," said he, "that this man has been instantly killed by a glass of rum, which he drank one hour before he fell dead. That rum has caused the rupture of the aorta" (the big vein which carries the blood to the heart).

While talking thus the knife was doing its work so quickly that the horrible spectacle of the broken artery was before our eyes almost as the last word fell from his lips.

"Look here," said the doctor, "all along the artery, and you will see thousands, perhaps millions, of reddish spots, which are as many holes perforated through it by alcohol. Just as the musk rats of the Mississippi river, almost every spring, dig little holes through the dams which keep that powerful river within its natural limits, and cause the waters to break through the little holes, and thus carry desolation and death along its shores, so alcohol every day causes the sudden death of thousands of victims by perforating the veins and opening small issues through which the blood rushes out of its natural limits. It is not only this big vein which alcohol perforates; it does the same deadly work in the veins of the lungs and the whole body. Look at the lungs with attention, and count, if you can, the thousands and thousands of reddish, dark and yellow spots, and little ulcers with which they are covered. Every one of them is the work of alcohol, which has torn and cut the veins and caused the blood to go out of its canals, to carry corruption and death all over these marvellous organs. Alcohol is one of the most dangerous poisons—I dare say it is the most dangerous. It has killed more men than all the other poisons together. Alcohol cannot be changed or assimilated to any part or tissue of our body, it cannot go to any part of the human frame without bringing disorder and death to it. For it cannot in any possible way unite with any part of our body. The water we drink, and the wholesome food and bread we eat, by the laws and will of God are transformed into the different parts of the body, to which they are sent through the millions of small canals which take them from the stomach to every part of our frame. When the water has been drunk, or the bread we have eaten is, for instance, sent to the lungs, to the brain, the nerves, the muscles, the bones—wherever it goes it receives, if I can so speak, letters of citizenship; it is allowed to remain there in peace and work for the public good. But it is not so with alcohol. The very moment it enters the stomach it more or less brings disorder, ruin and death, according to the quantity taken. The stomach refuses to take it, and makes a supreme effort to violently throw it out, either through the mouth, or by indignantly pushing it to the brain or into the numberless tubes by which it discharges its contents to the surface through all the tissues. But will alcohol be welcome in any of these tubes or marvellous canals, or in any part or tissue of the body it will visit on its passage to the surface? No! Look here with your microscope, and you will see with your own eyes that everywhere alcohol has gone in the body there has been a hand-to-hand struggle and a bloody battle fought to get rid of it. Yes! every place where King Alcohol has put his foot has been turned into a battlefield, spread with ruin and death, in order to ignominiously turn it out. By a most extraordinary working of nature, or rather by the order of God, every vein and artery through which alcohol has to pass suddenly contracts, as if to prevent its passage or choke it as a deadly foe. Every vein and artery has evidently heard the voice of God: "Wine is a mocker; it bites like a serpent and stings as an adder!" Every nerve and muscle which alcohol touched, trembled and shook as if in the presence of an implacable and unconquerable enemy. Yes, at the presence of alcohol every nerve and muscle loses its strength, just as the bravest man, in the presence of a horrible monster or demon, suddenly loses his natural strength, and shakes from head to foot."

I cannot repeat all I heard that day from the lips of Dr. Douglas, and what I saw with my own eyes of the horrible workings of alcohol through every part of that body. It would be too long. Suffice to say that I was struck with horror at my own folly, and at the folly of so many people who make use of intoxicating drinks.

What I learned that day was like the opening of a mysterious door, which allowed me to see the untold marvels of a new and most magnificent world. But though I was terror-stricken with the ravages of strong drink in that dead man, I was not yet convinced of the necessity of being a total abstainer from wine and beer, and a little brandy now and then, as a social habit. I did not like to expose myself to ridicule by the sacrifice of habits which seemed then, more than now, to be among the sweetest and most common links of society. But I determined to lose no opportunity of continuing the study of the working of alcohol in the human body. At the same time I resolved to avail myself of every opportunity of making a complete study of anatomy under the kind and learned Dr. Douglas.

It was from the lips and works of Dr. Douglas that I learned the following startling facts:

1st. The heart of man, which is only six inches long by four inches wide, beats seventy times in a minute, 4,200 in one hour, 100,300 in a day, 36,792,000 in a year. It ejects two ounces and a half of blood out of itself every time it beats, which makes 175 ounces every minute, 656 pounds every hour, seven tons and three-quarters of blood which goes out of the heart every day! The whole blood of a man runs through his heart in three minutes.

2nd. The skin is composed of three parts placed over each other, whose thickness varies from a quarter to an eighth of a line. Each square inch contains 3,500 pores, through which the sweat goes out. Every one of them is a pipe a quarter of an inch long. All those small pipes united together would form a canal 201,166 feet long— equal to forty miles, or nearly thirteen leagues!

3rd. The weight of the blood in an ordinary man is between thirty and forty pounds. That blood runs through the body in 101 seconds, or one minute and forty-one seconds. Eleven thousand (11,000) pints of blood pass through the lungs in twenty-four hours.

4th. There are 246 bones in the human body; 63 of them are in the head, 24 in the sides, 16 in the wrist, 14 in the joints, and 108 in the hands and feet!

The heart of a man who drinks nothing but pure water beats about 100,300 a day, but will beat from 25,000 to 30,000 times more if he drinks alcoholic drinks. Those who have not learned anatomy know little of the infinite power, wisdom, love and mercy of God. No book except the Bible, and no science except the science of astronomy is like the body of man *to tell us what our God is, and what we are.* The body of man is a book written by the hand of God, to speak to us of Him as no man can speak. After studying the marvellous working of the heart, the lungs, the eyes and the brain of man, I could not speak; I remained mute, unable to say a single word to tell my admiration and awe. I wept as overwhelmed with my feelings. I should have liked to speak of those things to the priests with whom I lived, but I saw at first they could not understand me; they thought I was exaggerating. How many times, when alone with God in my little closet, when thinking of those marvels, I fell on my knees and said: " Thou art great, O my God! The works of Thy hands are above the works of man! But the works of Thy love and mercy are above all Thy other works!"

During the four years I was chaplain of the Marine Hospital, more than one hundred corpses were opened before me, and almost as many outside the hospital. For when, by the order of the jury and the coroner, an autopsy was to be made, I seldom failed to attend. In that way I have had a providential opportunity of acquiring the knowledge of one of the most useful and admirable sciences as no priest or minister probably ever had on this continent. It is my conviction that the first thing a temperance orator ought to do is to study anatomy; get the bodies of drunkards, as well those of so-called temperate drinkers, opened before him, and study there the working of alcohol in the different organs of man. So long as the orators on temperance will not do that, they cannot understand the subject on which they speak. Though I have read the best books written by the most learned physicians of England, France, and United States on the ravages of rum, wines and beer of every kind and name in the body of men, I have never read anything which enlightened me so much, and brought such profound convictions to my intelligence, as the study I have made of the brain, the lungs, the heart, veins, arteries, nerves and muscles of a single man or woman. These bodies, opened before me, were books written by the hand of God Himself, and they spoke to me as no man could speak. By the mercy of God, to that study is due the irresistible power of my humble efforts in persuading my countrymen to give up the use of intoxicating drinks. But here is the time to tell how my merciful God forced me, His unprofitable and rebellious servant, almost in spite of myself, to give up the use of intoxicating drinks.

Among my penitents there was a young lady belonging to one of the most respectable families of Quebec. She had a child, a girl, almost a year old, who was a real beauty. Nothing this side of heaven could surpass the charms of that earthly angel. Of course that young mother idolized her; she could hardly consent to be without her sweet angel, even to go to church. She carried her everywhere, to kiss her at every moment and press her to her heart. Unfortunately that lady, as it was then and is still now too often the case, even among the most refined, had learned in her father's house, and by the example of her own mother, to drink wine at table, and when receiving the visits of her friends or when visiting them herself. Little by little she began to drink, when alone, a few drops of wine, at first by the advice of her physician, but soon only to satisfy the craving appetite, which grew stronger day by day. I was the only one, excepting her husband, who knew this fact. He was my intimate friend, and several times, with tears trickling down his cheeks, he had requested me, in the name of God, to persuade her to abstain from drinking. That young man was so happy with his accomplished wife and his incomparably beautiful child! He was rich, had a high position in the world, numberless friends, and a palace for his home! Every time I had spoken to that young lady, either when alone or in the presence of her husband, she had shed tears of regret; she had promised to reform, and take only the few glasses prescribed by her doctor. But, alas! that fatal prescription of the doctor was like the oil poured on burning coals; it was kindling a fire which nothing could quench. One day, which I will never forget, a messenger came in haste and said: "Mr. A. wants you to come to his home immediately. A terrible misfortune has just happened—his beautiful child has just been killed. His wife is half crazy; he fears lest she will kill herself."

I leaped into the elegant carriage drawn by two fine horses, and in a few minutes I was in the presence of the most distressing spectacle I ever saw. The young lady, tearing her robes into fragments, tearing her hair with her hands, and cutting her face with the nails of her fingers, was crying, "Oh! for God's sake, give me a knife that I may cut my throat? I have killed my child! My darling is dead! I am the murderess of my own dear Lucy! My hands are reddened with her blood. Oh! may I die with her!"

I was thunderstruck, and at first remained mute and motionless. The young husband, with two other gentlemen, Dr. Blanchet and Coroner Panet, were trying to hold the hands of his unfortunate wife. He did not dare to speak. At last the young wife, casting her eyes upon me, said: "Oh, dear Father Chiniquy, for God's sake give me a knife that I may cut my throat! When drunk, I took my precious darling in my arms to kiss her; but I fell—her head struck the sharp corner of the stove. Her brain and blood are there spread on the floor! My child! my own child is dead! I have killed her! Cursed liquor! Cursed wine! My child is dead! I am damned! Cursed drink!"

I could not speak, but I could weep and cry. I wept, and mingled my tears with those of that unfortunate mother. Then, with an expression of desolation which pierced my soul as with a sword, she said: "Go and see." I went to the next room, and there I saw that once beautiful child, dead, her face covered with her blood and brains! There was a large gap made in the right temple. The drunken mother, by falling with her child in her arms, had caused the head to strike with such a terrible force on the stove that it upset on the floor. The burning coals were spread on every side, and the house had been very nearly on fire. But that very blow, with the awful death of her child, had suddenly brought her to her senses, and put an end to her intoxication. At a glance she saw the whole extent of her misfortune. Her first thought had been to run to the sideboard, seize a large, sharp knife, and cut her own throat. Providentially, her husband was on the spot. With great difficulty, and after a terrible struggle, he took the knife out of her hands, and threw into the street through the window. It was then about five o'clock in the afternoon. After an hour passed in indescribable agony of mind and heart, I attempted to leave and go back to the parsonage. But my unfortunate young friend requested me, in the name of God, to spend the night with him. "You are the only one," he said, "who can help us in this awful night. My misfortune is great enough, without destroying our good name by spreading it in public. I want to keep it as secret as possible. With our physician and coroner, you are the only man on earth whom I trust to help me. Please pass the night with us."

I remained, but tried in vain to calm the unfortunate mother. She was constantly breaking our hearts with her lamentations—her convulsive efforts to take her own life. Every minute she was crying, "My child! my darling Lucy! Just when thy little arms were so gently caressing me, and thy angelic kisses were so sweet on my lips, I have slaughtered thee! When thou wert pressing me on thy loving heart and kissing me, I, thy drunken mother, gave thee the death-blow! My hands are reddened with thy blood! My breast is covered with thy brains! Oh! for God's sake, my dear husband, take my life. I cannot consent to live a day longer! Dear Father Chiniquy, give me a knife that I may mingle my blood with the blood of my child! Oh that I could be buried in the same grave with her!"

In vain I tried to speak to her of the mercies of God towards sinners; she would not listen to anything I could say; she was absolutely deaf to my voice. At about ten o'clock she had a most terrible fit of anguish and terror. Though we were four men to keep her quiet, she was stronger than we all. She was strong as a giant. She slipped from our hands and ran to the room where the dead child was lying in her cradle. Grasping the cold body in her hands, she tore the bands of white linen which had been put round the head to cover the horrible wound, and with cries of desolation she pressed her lips, her cheeks, her very eyes on the horrible gap from which the brain and blood were oozing, as if wanting to heal it and recall the poor dear one to life.

"My darling, my beloved, my own dear Lucy," she cried, "open thy eyes—look again at thy mother! Give me a kiss! Press me again to thy bosom! But thine eyes are shut! Thy lips are cold! Thou dost not smile on me any longer! Thou art dead, and I, thy mother, have slaughtered thee! Canst thou forgive me thy death? Canst thou ask Jesus Christ, our Saviour, to forgive me? Canst thou ask the blessed Virgin Mary to pray for me? Will I never see thee again? Ah, no! I am lost—I am damned! I am a drunken mother who has murdered her own darling Lucy! There is no mercy for the drunken mother, the murderess of her own child."

And when speaking thus to her child she was sometimes kneeling down, then running around the room as if flying before a phantom.

But even then she was constantly pressing the motionless body to her bosom or convulsively passing her lips and cheeks over the horrible wound, so that her lips, her whole face, her breast and hands were literally besmeared with the blood flowing from the wound. I will not say that we were all weeping and crying, for the words "weeping and crying" cannot express the desolation—the horror we felt. At about eleven o'clock, when on her knees, clasping her child to her bosom, she lifted her eyes towards me, and said:

"Dear Father Chiniquy, why is it that I have not followed your charitable advice when, still more with your tears than with words, you tried so often to persuade me to give up the use of those cursed intoxicating wines ? How many times you have given me the very words which come from heaven : ' Wine is a mocker; it bites as a serpent, and stings as an adder ! ' How many times, in the name of my dear child, in the name of my dear husband, in the name of God, you have asked me to give up the use of those cursed drinks ! But listen now to my prayer. Go all over Canada ; tell all the fathers never to put any intoxicating drink before the eyes of their children. It was at my father's table that I first learned to drink that wine which I will curse during all eternity ! Tell all the mothers never to taste these abominable drinks. It was my mother who first taught me to drink that wine which I will curse as long as God is !

"Take the blood of my child, and go redden with it the top of the doors of every house in Canada, and say to all those who dwell in those houses that that blood was shed by the hand of a murderess mother when drunk. With that blood write on the walls of every house in Canada that ' wine is a mocker.' Tell the French Canadians how, on the dead body of my child, I have cursed that wine which has made me so wretchedly miserable and guilty."

She then stopped, as if to breathe a little for a few minutes. She added :

"In the name of God, tell me, can my child forgive me her death ? Can she ask God to look upon me with mercy ? Can she cause the blessed Virgin Mary to pray for me and obtain my pardon ? "

But before I could answer, she horrified us by the cries, "I am lost ! When drunk I killed my child ! Cursed wine ! "

And she fell a corpse on the floor. Torrents of blood were flowing from her mouth on her dead child, which she was pressing to her bosom even after her death !

That terrible drama was never revealed to the people of Quebec. The coroner's verdict was that the child's death was accidental, and that the distressed mother died from a broken heart six hours after. Two days later the unfortunate mother was buried, with the body of her child clasped in her arms.

After such a terrible storm I was in need of solitude and rest, but above everything I was in need of praying. I shut myself in my little room for two days, and there, alone, in the presence of God, I meditated on the terrible justice and retribution which He had called me to witness. That unfortunate woman had not only been my penitent : she had been, with her husband, among my dearest and most devoted friends. It was only lately that she had become a slave to drunkenness. Before that, her piety and sense of honour were of the most exalted kind known in the Church of Rome. Her last words were not the commonplace expressions which ordinary sinners proffer at the approach of death ; her words had a solemnity for me which almost transformed them into oracles of God in my mind. Each of them sounded in my ears as if an angel of God had touched the thousand strings of my soul, to call my attention to a message from heaven. Sometimes they resembled the terrible voice of thunder; and again it seemed as if a seraph, with his golden harp, were singing them in my ears, that I might prepare to fight faithfully for the Lord against His gigantic enemy, alcohol.

In the middle of that memorable night, when the darkness was most profound and the stillness fearful, was I awake, was I sleeping ? I do not know. But I saw the calm, beautiful, and cherished form of my dear mother standing by me, holding by the hand the late murderess, still covered with the blood of her child. Yes ! my beloved mother was standing before me ; and she said, with power and authority which engraved every one of her words on my soul, as if written with letters of tears, blood, and fire : " Go all over Canada ; tell every father of a family never to put any intoxicating drink before his children. Tell all the mothers never to take a drop of those cursed wines and drinks. Tell the whole people of Canada never to touch nor look at the poisoned cup, filled with those cursed intoxicating drinks. And thou, my beloved son, give up for ever the use of those detestable beverages, which are cursed in hell, in heaven, and on earth. It bites like a serpent; it stings like an adder."

When the sound of that voice, so sweet and powerful, was hushed, and my soul had ceased seeing that strange vision of the night, I remained for some time exceedingly agitated and troubled. I said to myself, " Is it possible that the terrible things I have seen and heard these last few days will destroy my mind, and send me to the lunatic asylum ? "

I had hardly been able to take any sleep or food for the last three days and nights, and I seriously feared lest the weakness of my body would cause me to lose my reason. I then threw myself on my knees to weep and pray. This did me good. I soon felt myself stronger and calmer.

Raising again my mind to God, I said : " O my God, let me know Thy holy will, and grant me the grace to do it. Do the voices I have just heard come from Thee ? Hast Thou really sent one of the angels of Thy mercy, under the form of my beloved mother ? or is all this nothing but the vain dreams of my distressed mind ?

" Is it Thy will, O my God, that I should go and tell my country what Thou hast so providentially taught me of the horrible and unsuspected injuries which wine and strong drink cause to the bodies as well as the souls of men ? Or is it Thy will that I should conceal from the eyes of the world the wonderful things Thou hast made known to me, and that I might bury them with me in my grave ?"

As quick as lightning the answer was suggested to me. " What I have taught thee in secret, go and tell it on the housetops!" Overwhelmed with an unspeakable emotion, and my heart filled with a power which was not mine, I raised my hands toward heaven and said to my God:

"For my dear Saviour Jesus' sake, and for the good of my country, O my God, I promise that I will never make any use of intoxicating drinks; I will, moreover, do all in my power to persuade the other priests and the people to make the same sacrifice!"

Fifty years have passed since I took that pledge, and, thanks be to God, I have kept it.

For the next two years I was the only priest in Canada who abstained from the use of wine and other intoxicating drinks; and God only knows what I had to suffer all that time—what sneers, and rebukes and insults of every kind I had silently to bear! How many times the epithets of *fanatic, hypocrite, reformer, half-heretic*, have been whispered into my ear, not only by the priests, but also by the bishops.

But I was sure that my God knew the motives of my actions, and by His grace I remained calm and patient. In His infinite mercy *He* has looked down upon His unprofitable servant and has taken his part. He had Himself chosen the day when my humiliations were to be turned into great joy. The day came when I saw those same priests and bishops, at the head of their people, receiving the pledge and blessing of temperance from my hands. Those very bishops who had unanimously, at first, condemned me, soon invited the first citizens of their cities to present me with a golden medal, as a token of their esteem, after giving me, officially, the title of " Apostle of Temperance of Canada." The Governor and the two Chambers of Parliament of Canada voted me public thanks in 1851, and presented me £500 as a public testimony of their kind feeling for what had been done in the cause of temperance. It was the will of my God that I should see, with my own eyes, my dear Canada taking the pledge of temperance and giving up the use of intoxicating drinks. How many tears were dried in those days ! Thousands and thousands of broken hearts were consoled and filled with joy. Happiness and abundance reigned in many once desolate homes, and the name of our merciful God was blessed everywhere in my beloved country. Surely this was not the work of poor Chiniquy !

It was the Lord's work, for the Lord, who is wonderful in all His doings, had once more chosen the weakest instrument to show His

13

mercy towards the children of men. He has called the most unprofitable of His servants to do the greatest work of reform Canada
has ever seen, that the praise and glory might be given to Him, and
Him alone!

CHAPTER XXIX.

"OUT of the Church of Rome there is no salvation," is one of the
doctrines which the priests of Rome have to believe and teach to the
people, That dogma, once accepted, caused me to devote all my
energies to the conversion of Protestants. To prevent one of those
immortal and precious souls from going into hell seemed to me more
important and glorious than the conquest of a kingdom. In view of
showing them their errors, I filled my library with the best controversial books which could be got in Quebec, and I studied the Holy
Scriptures with the utmost attention. In the Marine Hospital, as
well as in my intercourse with the people of the city, I had several
occasions of meeting Protestants and talking to them; but I found at
once that, with very few exceptions, they avoided speaking with me on
religion. This distressed me. Having been told one day that the
Rev. Mr. Anthony Parent, superior of the Seminary of Quebec, had
converted several hundred Protestants during his long ministry, I went
to ask him if this were true. For answer he showed me the list of
his converts, which numbered more than two hundred, among whom
were some of the most respectable English and Scotch families of the
city. I looked upon that list with amazement; and from that day I
considered him the most blessed priest of Canada. He was a perfect
gentleman in his manners, and was considered our best champion on all
points of controversy with Protestants. He could have been classed
also among the handsomest men in his time, had he not been so fat.
But, when the high classes called him by the respectable name of
"Mr. Superior of the Seminary," the common people used to name
him Père Cocassier ("Cock-fighting Father"), on account of his long-
cherished habit of having the bravest and strongest fighting-cocks of
the country. In vain had the Rev. Mr. Renvoyze, curate of the
"Good St. Anne," that greatest miracle-working saint of Canada,
expended fabulous sums of money in ransacking the whole country to
get a cock who would take away the palm of victory from the hands of
the Superior of the Seminary of Quebec. He had almost invariably
failed; with very few exceptions his cocks had fallen bruised, bleeding,
and dead on the many battlefields chosen by those two priests.
However, I feel happy in acknowledging that, since the terrible
epidemic of cholera, that cruel and ignominious *passe temps* has
been entirely given up by the Roman Catholic clergy of this country.

Playing cards and checkers is now the most usual way the majority of curates and vicars have recourse to spend their long and many idle hours, both of the week and Sabbath days.

After reading over and over again that long list of converts, I said to Mr. Parent: "Please tell me how you have been able to persuade these Protestant converts to consent to speak with you on the errors of their religion. Many times I have tried to show the Protestants whom I met that they would be lost if they do not submit to our holy church, but, with few exceptions, they laughed at me as politely as possible, and turned the conversation to other matters. You must have some secret way of attracting their attention and winning their confidence. Would you not be kind enough to give me that secret, that I may be able also to prevent some of those precious souls from perishing?"

"You are right when you think that I have a secret to open the doors of the Protestants, and conquer and tame their haughty minds," answered Mr. Parent. "But that secret is of such a delicate nature, that I have never revealed it to anybody except my confessor. Nevertheless, I see that you are so in earnest for the conversion of Protestants, and I have such a confidence in your discretion and honour, that for the sake of our holy church I consent to give you my secret; only you must promise that you will never reveal it, during my lifetime, to anybody—and even after my death you will not mention it, except when you are sure it is for the greatest glory of God. You know that I was the most intimate friend your father ever had; I had no secret from him, and he had none from me. But God knows that the friendly feelings and the confidence I had in him are now bestowed upon you, his worthy son. If you had not in my heart and esteem the same high position your father occupied, I would not trust you with my secret."

He then continued: "The majority of Protestants in Quebec have Irish Roman Catholic servant girls; these, particularly before the last few years, used to come to confess to me, as I was almost the only priest who spoke English. The first thing I used to ask them, when they were confessing, was if their masters and mistresses were truly devoted and pious Protestants, or if they were indifferent and cold in performing their duties. The second thing I wanted to know was if they were on good terms with their ministers? whether or not they were visited by them? From the answers of the girls I knew both the moral and immoral, the religious or irreligious habits of their masters as perfectly as if I had been an inmate of their households. It is thus that I learned that many Protestants have no more religion and faith than our dogs. They awake in the morning and go to bed at night without praying to God any more than the horses in their stables. Many of them go to church on the Sabbath day more to laugh at their ministers and criticise their sermons than for anything else. A part of the week is passed in turning them into ridicule; nay, through the confessions of these honest girls, I learned that many Protestants liked the fine ceremonies of our Church; that they often favourably contrasted them with the cold performances of their own, and expressed their views in glowing terms about the superiority of our educational institutions, nunneries, etc., over their own high schools or colleges. Besides, you know that a great number of our most respectable and wealthy Protestants trust their daughters to our good nuns for their education. I took notes of all these things, and formed my plans of battle against Protestantism, as a general who knows his ground and the weak points of his adversaries, and I fought as a man who is sure of an easy victory. The glorious result you have under your eyes is the proof that I was correct in my plans. My first step with the Protestants whom I knew to be without any religion, or even already well disposed towards us, was to go to them with sometimes £5, or even £25, which I presented to them as being theirs. They, at first, looked at me with amazement, as a being coming from a superior world. The following conversation then almost invariably took place between them and me:

"'Are you positive, sir, that this money is mine?'

"'Yes, sir,' I answered, 'I am certain that this money is yours.'

"'But,' they replied, 'please tell me how you know that it belongs to me? It is the first time I have the honour of talking with you, and we are perfect strangers to each other.'

"I answered: 'I cannot say, sir, how I know that this money is yours, except by telling you that the person who deposited it in my hands for you has given me your name and your address so correctly that there is no possibility of any mistake.'

"'But can I not know the name of the one who has put that money into your hands for me?' rejoined the Protestant.

"'No, sir; the secret of confession is inviolable,' I replied. 'We have no example that it has ever been broken; and I, with every priest of our Church, would prefer to die rather than betray our penitents and reveal their confession. We cannot even act from what we have learned through their confession, except at their own request.'

"'But this auricular confession must then be a most admirable thing,' added the Protestant; 'I had no idea of it before this day.'

"'Yes, sir, auricular confession is a most admirable thing,' I used to reply, 'because it is a divine institution. But, sir, please excuse me; my ministry calls me to another place. I must take leave of you, to go where my duty calls me.'

" ' I am very sorry that you go so quickly,' generally answered the Protestant. 'Can I have another visit from you? Please do me the honour of coming again. I would be so happy to present you to my wife; and I know she would be happy also, and much honoured to make your acquaintance.'

" ' Yes, sir, I accept with gratitude your invitation. I will feel much pleased and honoured to make the acquaintance of the family of a gentleman whose praises are in the mouth of everyone, and whose industry and honesty are an honour to our city. If you allow me, next week, at the same hour, I will have the honour of presenting my respectful homage to your lady.'

" The very next day all the papers reported that Mr. So-and-So had received £5, or £10, or even £25 as a restitution, through auricular confession, and even the staunch Protestant editors of those papers could not find words sufficiently eloquent to praise me and our sacrament of penance.

" Three or four days later I was sure that the faithful servant girls were in the confessional box, glowing with joy to tell me that now their masters and mistresses could not speak of anything else than the amiability and honesty of the priests of Rome. They raised them a thousand miles over the heads of their own ministers. From those pious girls they invariably learned that they had not been visited by a single friend without making the eulogium of auricular confession, and even sometimes expressing the regret that the reformers had swept away such a useful institution.

" Now, my dear young friend, you see how, by the blessing of God, the little sacrifice of a few pounds brought down and destroyed all the prejudices of those poor heretics against auricular confession and our holy church in general. You understand how the doors were opened to me, and how their hearts and intelligences were like fields prepared to receive the good seed. At the appointed hour I never failed from paying the requested visit, and I was invariably received like a Messiah. Not only the gentlemen, but the ladies overwhelmed me with marks of the most sincere gratitude and respect; even the dear little children petted me, and threw their arms around my neck to give me their sweetly angelic kisses. The only topic on which we could speak, of course, was the great good done by auricular confession. I easily showed them how it works as a check to all the evil passions of the heart; how it is admirably adapted to all the wants of the poor sinners, who find a friend, a counsellor, a guide, a father, a real saviour in their confessor.

" We had not talked half an hour in that way, when it was generally evident to me that they were more than half way out of their Protestant errors. I very seldom left those houses without being sure of a new, glorious victory for our holy religion over its enemies. It is very seldom that I do not succeed in bringing that family to our holy church before one or two years; and if I fail from gaining the father or mother, I am nearly sure to persuade them to send their daughters to our good nuns and their boys to our colleges, where they sooner or later become our most devoted Catholics. So you see that the few dollars I spend every year for that holy cause are the best investments ever made. They do more to catch the Protestants of Quebec than the baits of the fishermen do to secure the cod fishes of the Newfoundland banks."

In ending this last sentence, Mr. Parent filled his room with laughter.

I thanked him for these interesting details. But I told him: "Though I cannot but admire your perfect skill and shrewdness in breaking the barriers which prevent Protestants from understanding the divine institution of auricular confession, will you allow me to ask you if you do not fear to be guilty of an imposture and a gross imposition in the way you make them believe that the money you hand them has come to you through auricular confession?"

"I have not the least fear of that," promptly answered the old priest, "for the good reason, that if you had paid attention to what I have told you, you must acknowledge that I have not said positively that the money was coming from auricular confession. If those Protestants have been deceived, it is only due to their own want of a more perfect attention to what I said. I know that there were things that I kept in my mind which would have made them understand the matter in a very different way if I had said them. But Liguori and all our theologians, among the most approved of our holy church, tell us that these reservations of the mind (*mentis reservationes*) are allowed, when they are for the good of souls and the glory of God."

"Yes," answered I, "I know that such is the doctrine of Liguori, and it is approved by the popes. I must confess that this seems to me, entirely opposed to what we read in the sublime gospel. The simple and sublime 'Yea, yea' and 'Nay, nay' of our Saviour seems to me in contradiction with the art of deceiving, even when not saying absolute and direct falsehoods; and if I submit myself to those doctrines, it is always with a secret protest in my inmost soul."

In an angry manner, Mr. Parent replied: "Now, my dear young friend, I understand the truth of what the Rev. Messrs. Perras and Bedard told me lately about you. Though these remarkable priests are full of esteem for you, they see a dark cloud on your horizon; they say that you spend too much time in reading the Bible, and not enough in studying the doctrines and holy traditions of the Church. You are too much inclined also to interpret the Word of God according to your own fallible intelligence, instead of going to the Church *alone* for that interpretation. This is the dangerous rock on which Luther and Calvin were wrecked. Take my advice. Do not try to be wiser than the Church. Obey her voice when she speaks to you through her holy theologians. This is your only safeguard. The bishop would suspend you at once were he aware of your want of faith in the Church."

These last words were said with such emphasis, that they seemed more like a sentence of condemnation from the lips of an irritated judge than anything else. I felt that I had again seriously compromised myself in his mind; and the only way of preventing him from denouncing me to the bishop as a heretic and a Protestant was to make an apology, and withdraw from the dangerous ground on which I had again so imprudently put myself. He accepted my explanation, but I saw that he bitterly regretted having trusted me with his secret. I withdrew from his presence, much humiliated by my want of prudence and wisdom. However, though I could not approve of all the *modus operandi* of the Superior of Quebec, I could not but admire then the glorious results of his efforts in converting Protestants ; and I took the resolution of devoting myself more than ever to show them their errors and make them good Catholics. In this I was too successful; for during my twenty-five years of priesthood I have persuaded ninety-three Protestants to give up their gospel light and truth in order to follow the dark and lying traditions of Rome. I cannot enter into the details of their conversions, or rather perversions ; suffice to say that I soon found that my only chance of success in that proselytizing work was among the Ritualists. I saw at first that Calvin and Knox had dug a really impassable abyss between the Presbyterians, Methodists, Baptists, and the Church of Rome. If these Ritualists remain Protestants, and do not make the very short step which separates them from Rome, it is a most astonishing fact, when they are logical men. Some people are surprised that so many eminent and learned men, in Great Britain and America, give up their Protestantism to submit to the Church of Rome ; but my wonder is that there are so few among them who fall into that bottomless abyss of idolatry and folly, when they are their whole life on the very brink of the chasm. Put millions of men on the very brink of the Falls of Niagara, force them to cross to and fro in small canoes between both shores, and you will see that, every day, some of them will be dragged, in spite of themselves, into the yawning abyss. Nay, you will see that, sooner or later, those millions of people will be in danger of being dragged in a whole body, by the irresistible force of the dashing waters, into the fathomless gulf. Through a sublime effort the English people, helped by the mighty and merciful hand of God, has come out from the abyss of folly, impurity, ignorance, slavery, and idolatry, called the Church of Rome. But many, alas! in the present day, instead of marching up to the high regions of unsullied Gospel truth and light—instead of going up to the high mountains where true Christian simplicity and liberty have for ever planted their glorious banners—have been induced to walk only a few steps out of the pestiferous regions of Popery. They have remained so near the pestilential atmosphere of the stagnant waters of death which flow from Rome, that the atmosphere they breathe is still filled with the deadly emanations of that modern Sodom. Who, without shedding tears of sorrow, can look at those misguided ministers of the Gospel who believe and teach in the Episcopal Church that they have the power to make their God with a wafer, and who bow down before that wafer God and adore him! Who can refrain from indignation at the sight of so many Episcopal ministers who consent to have their ears, minds, and souls polluted at the confessional by the stories of their penitents, whom in their turn they destroy by their infamous and unmentionable questions? When I was lecturing in England in 1860, the late Archbishop of Canterbury, then Bishop of London, invited me to his table, in company with Rev. Mr. Thomas, now Bishop of Goulburn, Australia, and put to me the following questions, in the presence of his numerous and noble guests :—

"Father Chiniquy, when you left the Church of Rome, why did you not join the Episcopalian rather than the Presbyterian Church?"

I answered : "Is it the desire of your lordship that I should speak my mind on that delicate subject?"

"Yes, yes," said the noble lord bishop.

"Then, my lord, I must tell you that my only reason is that I find in your Church several doctrines which I have to condemn in the Church of Rome."

"How is that?" replied his lordship.

"Please," I answered, "let me have one of your Common Prayer Books."

Taking the book, I read slowly the article on the visitation of the sick: "Here shall the sick person be moved to make a special confession of his sins, if he feel his conscience troubled with any weighty matter. After which confession the priest shall absolve him if he humbly and heartily desire it after this sort : 'Our Lord Jesus Christ, who hath left power to His Church to absolve all sinners who repent and believe in Him, of His great mercy forgive thee thine offences : and, by His authority committed to me, I absolve thee from all thy sins, in the name of the Father and of the Son, and of the Holy Ghost. Amen.'" I then added : "Now, my lord, where is the difference between the errors of Rome and your Church on this subject?"

"The difference is very great," he answered. "The Church of Rome is constantly pressing the sinners to come to her priests all their lifetime, when we subject the sinner to this humiliation only once in his life, when he is near his last hour."

"But, my lord, let me tell you that it seems to me the Church of Rome is much more logical and consistent in this than the Episcopal Church. Both churches believe and teach that they have received from Christ the power to forgive the sins of those who confess to their priests, and you think yourself wiser because you invite the sinner to confess and receive His pardon only when he is tied to a bed of suffering, at the last hour before his death. But will your lordship be kind enough to tell me when I am in danger of death? If I am constantly in danger of death, must you not, with the Church of Rome, induce me constantly to confess to your priests, and get my pardon and make my peace with God? Has our Saviour said anywhere that it was only for the dying, at the last extremity of life, that He gave the power to forgive my sins? Has He not warned me many times to be always ready; to have always our peace made with God, and not to wait till the last day, to the last hour?"

The noble bishop did not think fit to give me any other answer than these very words: "We all agree that this doctrine ought never to have been put in our Common Prayer Book. But you know that we are at work to revise that book, and we hope that this clause, with several others, will be taken away."

"Then," I answered in a jocose way, "my lord, when this obnoxious clause has been removed from your Common Prayer Book it will be time for me to have the honour of belonging to your great and noble Church."

When the Church of England went out of the Church of Rome, she did as Rachel, the wife of Jacob, who left the house of her father Laban and took his gods with her. So the Episcopal Church of England, unfortunately, when she left Rome, concealed in the folds of her mantle some of the false gods of Rome; she kept to her bosom some vipers engendered in the marshes of the modern Sodom. Those vipers, if not soon destroyed, will kill her. They are already eating up her vitals. They are covering her with most ugly and mortal wounds. They are rapidly taking away her life. May the Holy Ghost rebaptize and purify that noble Church of England, that she may be worthy to march at the head of the armies of the Lord to the conquest of the world, under the banners of the great Captain of our Salvation.

CHAPTER XXX.

THE three years which followed the cholera will be long remembered in Quebec for the number of audacious thefts and the murders which kept the whole population in constant terror. Almost every week the public press had to give us the account of the robbery of the houses of some of our rich merchants or old wealthy widows.

Many times the blood was chilled in our veins by the cruel and savage assassinations which had been committed by the thieves when resistance had been offered. The number of these crimes, the audacity with which they were perpetrated, the ability with which the guilty parties escaped from all the researches of the police, indicated that they were well organized, and had a leader of uncommon shrewdness.

But in the eyes of the religious population of Quebec, the thefts of the 10th February, 1835, surpassed all the others by its sacrilegious character. That night the chapel dedicated to the blessed Virgin Mary was entered, a silver statue of the Virgin—the gift of the King of France—a massive lamp, a silver candlestick, and the silver vases which contained the bread which the Roman Catholics believe to be the body, blood, and divinity of Jesus Christ, were stolen, and the holy sacrament impiously thrown and scattered on the floor.

Nothing can express the horror and indignation of the whole Catholic population at this last outrage. Large sums of money were offered in order that the brigands might be detected. At last five of them—Chambers, Mathieu, Gagnon, Waterworth, and Lemoine, were caught in 1836, tried, found guilty, and condemned to death in the month of March, 1837.

During the trial, and when public attention was most intensely fixed on its different aspects, in a damp, chilly, dark night, I was called to visit a sick man. I was soon ready, and asked the name of the sick from the messenger. He answered that it was Francis Oregon. As a matter of course, I said that that sick man was a perfect stranger to me, and that I had never heard that there was even such a man in the world. But when I was near the carriage which was to take me, I was not a little surprised to see that the first messenger left abruptly and disappeared. Looking with attention, then, at the faces of the two men who had come for me in the carriage, it seemed that they both wore masks.

" What does this mean ? " I said; " each of you wear a mask. Do you mean to murder me ? "

"Dear Father Chiniquy," answered one of them, in a low, trembling voice, and in a supplicating tone, " fear not. We swear before God that no evil will be done to you. On the contrary, God and man

will, to the end of the world, praise and bless you if you come to our
help and save our souls, as well as our mortal bodies.   We have in our
hands a great part of the silver articles stolen these last three years.
The police are on our track, and we are in great danger of being caught.
For God's sake come with us.   We will put all those stolen things in
your hands, that you may give them back to those who have lost
them.   We will then immediately leave the country, and lead a better
life.   We are Protestants, and the Bible tells us that we cannot be
saved if we keep in our hands what is not ours.   You do not know us,
but we know you well.   You are the only man in Quebec to whom we
can so trust our lives and this terrible secret.   We have worn these
masks that you may not know us, and that you may not be compromised if you are ever called before a court of justice."

My first thought was to leave them and run back to the door of the
parsonage; but such an act of cowardice seemed to me, after a
moment's reflection, unworthy of a man.   I said to myself, these two
men cannot come to steal from me : it is well known in Quebec that
I keep myself as poor as a church mouse, by giving all I have to the
poor.   I have never offended any man in my life, that I know.   They
cannot come to punish or murder me.   They are Protestants, and
they trust me.   Well, well, they will not regret to have put their
trust in a Catholic priest."

I then answered them : "What you ask from me is of a very
delicate, and even dangerous nature.   Before I do it, I want to take
the advice of one whom I consider the wisest man of Quebec—the old
Rev. Mr. Demars, ex-president of the seminary of Quebec.   Please
drive me as quickly as possible to the seminary.   If that venerable
man advises me to go with you I will go; but I cannot promise to
grant you your request if he tells me not to go."

"All right," they both said, and in a very short time I was knocking at the door of the seminary.   A few moments after I was alone in
the room of Mr. Demars.   It was just half-past twelve at night.

"Our little Father Chiniquy here on this dark night, at half-past
twelve!   What does this mean?   What do you want from me?" said
the venerable old priest.

"I come to ask your advice," I answered, "on a very strange
thing.   Two Protestant thieves have in their hands a great quantity
of the silver ware stolen these last three years.   They want to deposit
them in my hands, that I may give them back to those from whom
they have been stolen, before they leave the country and lead a better
life.   I cannot know them, for they both wear masks.   I cannot even
know where they take me, for the carriage is so completely wrapped
up by curtains that it is impossible to see outside.   Now, my dear Mr.
Demars, I come to ask your advice.   Shall I go with them or not?

But remember that I trust you with these things under the seal of confession, that neither you nor I may be compromised."

Before answering me the venerable priest said : "I am very old, but I have never heard of such a strange thing in my life. Are you not afraid to go alone with these two thieves in that covered carriage ?"

"No, sir," I answered; "I do not see any reason to fear anything from these two men."

"Well! well," rejoined Mr. Demars, "If you are not afraid under such circumstances, your mother has given you a brain of diamond and nerves of steel."

"Now, my dear sir," I answered, "time flies, and I may have a long way to travel with these two men. Please, in the shortest possible way, tell me your mind? Do you advise me to go with them ?"

He replied, "You consult me on a very difficult matter; there are so many considerations to make, that it is impossible to weigh them all. The only thing we have to do is to pray God and His Holy Mother for wisdom. Let us pray."

We knelt and said the "Veni Sancte Spiritus;" "Come Holy Spirit," etc., which prayer ends by an invocation to Mary as Mother of God.

After the prayer Mr. Demars again asked me : "Are you not afraid ?"

"No, sir, I do not see any reason to be afraid. But, please, for God's sake, hurry on, tell me if you advise me to go and accept this message of mercy and peace."

"Yes! go! go! If you are not afraid," answered the old priest, with a voice full of emotion, and tears in his eyes.

I fell on my knees and said : "Before I start, please, give me your blessing, and pray for me, when I shall be on the way to that strange, but, I hope, good work."

I left the seminary and took my seat at the right hand of one of my unknown companions, while the other was on the front seat driving the horse.

Not a word was said by any of us on the way. But I perceived that the stranger who was at my left, was praying to God; though in such a low voice that I understood only these words twice repeated : "O Lord! have mercy upon me—such a sinner!"

These words touched me to the heart, and brought to my mind the dear Saviour's words : "The publicans and harlots shall go into the kingdom of God before you," and I also prayed for that poor repenting sinner and for myself, by repeating the sublime 50th Psalm :

" Have mercy upon me, O Lord !"

It took about half an hour to reach the house. But, there, again, it was impossible for me to understand where I was. For the carriage was brought so near the door that there was no possibility of seeing anything beyond the carriage and the horse through the terrible darkness of that night.

The only person I saw, when in the house, was a tall woman covered with a long black veil, whom I took to be a disguised man, on account of her size and her strength ; for she was carrying very heavy bags with as much ease as if they had been a handful of straw.

There was only a small candle behind a screen, which gave so little light that everything looked like phantoms around us. Pictures and mirrors were all turned to the wall, and presented the wrong side to view. The sofa and the chairs were also upset in such a way that it was impossible to identify anything of what I had seen. In fact, I could see nothing in that house. Not a word was said, except by one of my companions, who whispered in a very low voice, " Please, look at the tickets which are on every bundle ; they will indicate to whom these things belong."

There were eight bundles. The heaviest of which was composed of the melted silver of the statue of the virgin, the candlesticks, the lamp of the chapel, the ciborium, a couple of chalices, and some dozens of spoons and forks. The other bundles were made up of silver plates, fruit baskets, tea, coffee, cream and sugar pots, silver spoons and forks, etc.

As soon as these bundles were put into the carriage we left for the parsonage, where we arrived a little before the dawn of day. Not a word was exchanged between us on the way, and my impression was, that my penitent companions were sending their silent prayers, like myself, to the feet of that merciful God who has said to all sinners, " Come unto Me, all ye who are heavy laden, and I will give you rest."

They carried the bundles into my trunk, which I locked with peculiar attention. When all was over I accompanied them to the door to take leave of them. Then, each seizing one of my hands, by a spontaneous movement of gratitude and joy, they pressed them on their lips, shedding tears, and saying in a low voice : " God bless you a thousand times for the good work you have just performed. After Christ, you are our saviour."

As these two men were speaking, it pleased God to send forth into my soul one of those rays of happiness which He gives us only at great intervals.

I believe our fragile existence would soon be broken up were we by such joys incessantly inundated. These two men had ceased to be robbers in my eyes. They were dear brethren, precious friends, such as are seldom to be seen. The narrow and shameful prejudices of my religion were silent before the fervent prayers that I had heard from their lips ; they disappeared in those tears of repentance, gratitude and love, which fell from their eyes on my hands. Night surrounded us with its deepest shades; but our souls were illuminated by a light purer than the rays of the sun. The air that we breathed was cold and damp; but one of these sparks brought down from heaven by Jesus to warm the earth, had fallen into our hearts, and we were all penetrated by its glow. I pressed their hands in mine, saying to them :

"I thank and bless you for choosing me as the confident of your misfortunes and repentance. To you I owe three of the most precious hours of my life. Adieu ! We shall see one another no more on this earth; but we shall meet in heaven. Adieu !"

It is unnecessary to add that it was impossible to sleep the remainder of that memorable night. Besides, I had in my possession more stolen articles than would have caused fifty men to be hanged. I said to myself: "What would become of me if the police were to break in on me, and find all that I have in my hands. What could I answer if I were asked, how all these had reached me ?"

Did I not go beyond the bounds of prudence in what I have just done ? Have I not, indeed, slipped a rope around my neck ?

Though my conscience did not reproach me with anything, especially when I had acted on the advice of a man as wise as Mr. Demars, yet was I not without some anxiety, and I longed to get rid of all the things I had by giving them to their legitimate owners.

At ten o'clock in the morning I was at Mr. Amiot's, the wealthiest goldsmith of Quebec, with my heavy satchel of melted silver. After obtaining from him the promise of secrecy, I handed it over to him, giving him at the same time its history. I asked him to weigh it, keep its contents, and let me have its value, which I was to distribute according to its label.

He told me that there was in it a thousand dollars worth of melted silver, which amount he immediately gave me. I went down directly to give about half of it to Rev. Mr. Cazeault, chaplain of the congregation which had been robbed, and who was then the secretary of the Archbishop of Quebec; and I distributed the remainder to the parties indicated on the labels attached to this enormous ingot.

The good Lady Montgomery could scarcely believe her eyes when, after obtaining also from her the promise of the most inviolable secrecy on what I was going to show her, I displayed on her table the magnificent dishes of massive silver, fruit baskets, tea and coffee pots, sugar bowls, cream jugs, and a great quantity of spoons and forks of the finest silver, which had been taken from her in 1835. It seemed to her a dream which brought before her eyes these precious family relics.

She then related in a most touching manner what a terrible moment she had passed, when the thieves, having seized her, with her maid and a young man, rolled them in carpets to stifle their cries, whilst they were breaking locks, opening chests and cupboards to carry off their rich contents. She had told me how nearly she had been stifled with her faithful servants under the enormous weight of carpets heaped upon them by the robbers.

This excellent lady was a Protestant, and it was the first time in my life that I met a Protestant whose piety seemed so enlightened and sincere. I could not help admiring her.

When she had most sincerely thanked and blessed me for the service I had done her, she asked if I would have any objection to pray with her, and to aid her in thanking God for the favour He had just shown her. I told her, I should be happy in uniting with her to bless the Lord for His mercies. Upon this she gave me a Bible, magnificently bound, and we read each in turn a verse, slowly and on our knees the sublime Psalm 103: "Bless the Lord, O my soul," etc.

As I was about to take leave of her she offered me a purse containing one hundred dollars in gold, which I refused, telling her that I would rather lose my two hands than receive a cent for what I had done.

"You are," said she, "surrounded with poor people. Give them this that I offer to the Lord as a feeble testimony of my gratitude, and be assured that as long as I live I will pray God to pour His most abounding favours upon you."

In leaving that house I could not hide from myself that my soul had been embalmed with the true perfume of a piety that I had never seen in my own church.

Before the day closed I had given back to their rightful owners the effects left in my hands, whose value amounted to more than 7,000 dollars, and had my receipts in good form.

I am glad to say here, that the persons, most of whom were Protestants, to whom I made these restitutions, were perfectly honourable, and that not a single one of them ever said anything to compromise me in this matter, nor was I ever troubled on this subject.

I thought it my duty to give my venerable friend, the Grand Vicar Demars, a detailed account of what had just happened. He heard me with the deepest interest, and could not retain his tears when I related the touching scene of my separation from my two new friends that night, one of the darkest—which, nevertheless, has remained one of the brightest of my life.

My story ended, he said: "I am, indeed, very old, but I must confess that never did I hear anything so strange and so beautiful as this story. I repeat, however, that your mother must have given you a brain harder than diamond and nerves more solid than brass, not to have been afraid during this very singular adventure in the night."

After the fatigues and incidents of the last twenty-four hours, I was in great need of rest, but it was impossible for me to sleep a single instant during the night which followed. For the first time I stood face to face with that Protestantism which my Church had taught me to hate and fight with all the energy that heaven had bestowed on me, and when that faith had been, by the hand of Almighty God, placed in the scale against my own religion, it appeared to me as a heap of pure gold opposite a pile of rotten rags. In spite of myself, I could hear incessantly the cries of grief of that penitent thief: "Lord, have mercy on me, so great a sinner!"

Then, the sublime piety of Lady Montgomery, the blessings she had asked God to pour on me, His unprofitable servant, seemed, as so many coals of fire heaped upon my head by God, to punish me for having said so much evil of Protestants, and so often decried their religion.

A secret voice arose within me: "Seest thou not how these Protestants, whom thou wishest to crush with thy disdain, know how to pray, repent, and make amends for their faults much more nobly than the unfortunate wretches whom thou holdest as so many slaves at thy feet by means of the confessional?

"Understandest thou not that the Spirit of God, the grace and love of Jesus Christ, produces effectually in the hearts and minds of these Protestants a work much more durable than thy auricular confession? Compare the miserable wiles of Mr. Parent, who makes false restitutions, to cast dust into the eyes of the unsuspecting multitude, with the straightforwardness, noble sincerity, and admirable wisdom of these Protestants, in making amends for their wrongs before God and men, and judge for thyself which of those two religions raise, in order to save, and which degrades, in order to destroy the guilty.

"Has ever auricular confession worked as efficiently on sinners as the Bible on these thieves to change their hearts?

"Judge, this day, by their fruits, which of the two religions is led by the spirit of darkness, or the Holy Ghost?"

Not wishing to condemn my religion, nor allow my heart to be attracted by Protestantism during the long hours of that restless night, I remained anxious, humiliated, and uneasy.

It is thus, O my God, that Thou madest use of everything, even these thieves, to shake the wonderful fabric of errors, superstitions, and falsehoods that Rome had raised in my soul. May Thy name be for ever blessed for Thy mercies towards me, Thy unprofitable servant.

CHAPTER XXXI.

A FEW days after the strange and providential night spent with the repentant thieves, I received the following letter signed by Chambers and his unfortunate criminal friends:

"DEAR FATHER CHINIQUY:—We are condemned to death. Please come and help us to meet our sentence as Christians."

I will not attempt to say what I felt when I entered the damp and dark cells where the culprits were enchained. No human words can express those things. Their tears and their sobs were going through my heart as a two-edged sword. Only one of them had, at first, his eyes dried, and kept silent: Chambers, the most guilty of all.

After the others had requested me to hear the confession of their sins, and prepare them for death, Chambers said: "You know that I am a Protestant. But I am married to a Roman Catholic, who is your penitent. You have persuaded my two so dear sisters to give up their Protestantism and become Catholics. I have many times desired to follow them. My criminal life alone has prevented me from doing so. But now I am determined to do what I consider to be the will of God in this important matter. Please, tell me what I must do to become a Catholic."

I was a sincere Roman Catholic priest, believing that out of the Church of Rome there was no salvation. The conversion of that great sinner seemed to me a miracle of the grace of God; it was for me a happy distraction in the desolation I felt in that dungeon.

I spent the next eight days in hearing their confessions, reading the lives of some saints, with several chapters of the Bible, as the Seven Penitential Psalms, the sufferings and death of Christ, the history of the Prodigal Son, etc. And I instructed Chambers, as well as the shortness of the time allowed me, in the faith of the Church of Rome. I usually entered the cells at about 9 a.m., and left them only at 9 p.m.

After I had spent much time in exhorting them, reading and praying, several times, I asked them to tell me some of the details of the murders and thefts they had committed, which might be to me as a lesson of human depravity, which would help me when preaching on the natural corruption and malice of the human heart, when once the fear and the love, or even the faith in God, were completely set aside.

The facts I then heard very soon convinced me of the need we have of a religion, and what would become of the world if the atheists could succeed in sweeping away the notions of a future punishment after death, or the fear and the love of God from among men.

When absolutely left to his own depravity, without any religion to stop him on the rapid declivity of his uncontrollable passions, man is

14

more cruel than the wild beasts. The existence of society would be impossible without a religion and a God to protect it.

Though I am in favour of liberty of conscience in its highest sense, I think that the atheist ought to be punished like the murderer and the thief—for his doctrines tend to make a murderer and a thief of every man. No law, no society is possible if there is no God to sanction and protect them.

But the more we were approaching the fatal day, when I had to go on the scaffold with those unfortunate men, and to see them launched into eternity, the more I felt horrified. The tears, the sobs, and the cries of those unfortunate men had so melted my heart, my soul, and my strong nerves, they had so subdued my unconquerable will, and that stern determination to do my duty at any cost, which had been my character till then, that I was shaking from head to feet, when thinking of that awful hour.

Besides that, my constant intercourse with those criminals these last few days, their unbounded confidence in me, their gratitude for my devotedness to them, their desolation, and their cries when speaking of their fathers or mothers, wives or children, had filled my heart with a measure of sympathy which I would vainly try to express. They were no more thieves and murderers to me, whose bloody deeds had at first chilled the blood in my veins; they were the friends of my bosom—the beloved children whom cruel beasts had wounded. They were dearer to me than my own life—not only I felt happy to mix my tears with theirs, and unite my ardent prayers to God for mercy with them, but I would have felt happy to shed my blood in order to save their lives. As several of them belonged to the most reputable families of Quebec and vicinity, I thought I could easily interest the clergy and the most respectable citizens to sign a petition to the governor, Lord Gosford, asking him to change their sentence of death into one of perpetual exile to the distant penal colony of Botany Bay in Australia. The governor was my friend. Colonel Vassal, who was my uncle, and the adjutant-general of the militia of the whole country, had introduced me to his Excellency, who many times had overloaded me with the marks of his interest and kindness, and my hope was that he would not refuse me the favour I was to ask him, when the petition would be signed by the Bishop, the Catholic priests, the ministers of the different Protestant denominations of the city, and hundreds of the principal citizens of Quebec. I presented the petition myself, accompanied by the secretary of the Archbishop. But to my great distress the Governor answered me that those men had committed so many murders, and kept the country in terror for so many years, that it was absolutely necessary they should be punished according to the sentence of the court. Who can tell the desolation of those unfortunate men, when, with a voice choked by my sobs and my tears, I told them that the governor had refused to grant the favour I had asked him for them. They fell on the ground and filled their cells with cries which would have have broken the hardest heart. From those very cells we were hearing the noise of the men who were preparing the scaffold where they were to be hanged the next day. I tried to pray and read, but I was unable to do so. My desolation was too great to utter a single word. I felt as if I were to be hanged with them—and to say the whole truth, I think I would have been glad to hear that I was to be hanged the next day to save their lives. For there was a fear in me, which was haunting me as a phantom from hell, the last three days. It seemed that, in spite of all my efforts, prayers, confessions, absolutions, and sacraments, these men were not converted, and that they were to be launched into eternity with all their sins.

When I was comparing the calm and true repentance of the two thieves, with whom I spent the night a few weeks before in the carriage, with the noisy expressions of sorrow of those newly converted sinners, I could not help finding an immeasurable distance between the first and second of those penitents. No doubt had remained in my mind about the first, but I had serious apprehensions about the last. Several circumstances, which it would be too long and useless to mention here, were distressing me by the fear that all my chaplets, indulgences, medals, scapulars, holy waters, signs of the cross, prayers to the Virgin, auricular confession, absolutions, used in the conversion of these sinners, had not the divine and perfect power of a simple look to the dying Saviour on the cross. I was saying to myself with anxiety: " Would it be possible that those Protestants, who were with me in the carriage, had the true ways of repentance, pardon, peace, and life eternal in that simple look to the great victim, and that we Roman Catholics with our signs of the cross and holy waters, our crucifixes and prayers to the saints, our scapulars and medals, our so humiliating auricular confession, were only distracting the mind, the soul, and the heart of the sinner from the true and only source of salvation, Christ! " In the midst of those distressing thoughts I almost regretted having helped Chambers in giving up his Protestantism for my Romanism.

At about 4 p.m. I made a supreme effort to shake off my desolation, and nerve myself for the solemn duties God had entrusted to me. I put a few questions to those desolated men, to see if they were really repentant and converted. Their answers added to my fear that I had spoken too much of the virgins and the saints, the indulgences, medals and scapulars, integrity of confession, and not enough of Christ dying on the cross for them. It is true I had spoken of Christ and His death to them, but this had been so much mixed up with exhortation to trust in Mary, put their confidence in their medals, scapulars, confessions, etc., that it became almost evident to me that in our religion Christ was like a precious pearl lost in a mountain of sand and dust. This fear soon caused my distress to be unbearable.

I then went to the private, neat little room, which the gaoler had kindly allotted to me, and I fell on my knees to pray God for myself and for my poor convicts. Though this prayer brought some calm to my mind, my distress was still very great. It was then that the thought came again to my mind to go to the governor and make a new and supreme effort to have the sentence of death changed into that of perpetual exile to Botany Bay, and without a moment of delay I went to his palace.

It was about 7 p.m. when he reluctantly admitted me to his presence, telling me, when shaking hands, "I hope, Mr. Chiniquy, you are not coming to renew your request of the morning, for I cannot grant it."

Without a word to answer I fell on my knees, and for more than ten minutes I spoke as I had never spoken before. I spoke as we speak when we are the ambassadors of God in a message of mercy. I spoke with my lips. I spoke with my tears. I spoke with my sobs and my cries. I spoke with my supplicating hands lifted to heaven. For some time the governor was mute and as if stunned. He was not only a noble-minded man, but he had a most tender, affectionate, and kind heart. His tears soon began to flow with mine, and his sobs mixed with my sobs ; with a voice half-suffocated by his emotion, he extended his friendly hand and said :

"Father Chiniquy, you ask me a favour which I ought not to give, but I cannot resist your arguments, when your tears, your sobs, and your cries are like arrows which pierce and break my heart. I will give you the favour you ask."

It was nearly 10 p.m. when I knocked at the door of the gaoler, asking his permission to see my dear friends in their cells, to tell them that I had obtained their pardon, that they would not die. That gentleman could hardly believe me. It was only after reading twice the document I had in my hands that he saw that I told him the truth.

Looking at that parchment again, he said : "Have you noticed that it is covered and almost spoiled by the spots evidently made with the tears of the governor. You must be a kind of sorcerer to have melted the heart of such a man, and have wrenched from his hands the pardon of such convicts ; for I know he was absolutely unwilling to grant the pardon."

"I am not a sorcerer," I answered. "But you remember that our Saviour Jesus Christ had said, somewhere, that He had brought a fire from heaven—well, it is evident that He has thrown some sparks of that fire into my poor heart, for it was so fiercely burning when I was at the feet of the governor, that I think I would have died at his feet, had he not granted me that favour. No doubt that some sparks of that fire have also fallen on his soul and in his heart when I was speaking, for his cries, his tears, and his sobs were filling his room, and showing that he was suffering as much as myself. It was that he might not be consumed by that fire that he granted my request. I am now the most happy man under heaven. Please, make haste. Come with me and open the cells of those unfortunate men that I may tell what our merciful God has done for them." When entering their desolated cells I was unable to contain myself; I cried out: "Rejoice and bless the Lord, my dear friends! You will not die to-morrow! I bring you your pardon with me!"

Two of them fainted, and came very near dying from excess of surprise and joy. The others, unable to contain their emotions, were crying and weeping for joy. They threw their arms around me to press me to their bosom, kiss my hands and cover them with their tears of joy. I knelt with them and thanked God, after which I told them how they must promise to God to serve Him faithfully after such a manifestation of His mercies. I read to them the 100th, 101st, 102d, and 103d Psalms, and I left them after twelve o'clock at night to go and take some rest. I was in need of it after a whole day of such work and emotions.

The next day I wanted to see my dear prisoners early, and I was with them before 7 a.m. As the whole country had been glad to hear that they were to be hanged that very day, the crowds were beginning to gather at that early hour to witness the death of those great culprits. The feelings of indignation were almost unmanageable when they heard that they were not to be hanged, but only to be exiled for their life to Botany Bay. For a time it was feared that the mob would break the doors of the gaol and lynch the culprits. Though very few priests were more respected and loved by the people, they would have probably torn me to pieces when they heard that it was I who had deprived the gibbet of its victims that day. The chief of police had to take extraordinary measures to prevent the wrath of the mob from doing mischief. He advised me not to show myself for a few days in the streets.

More than a month passed before all the thieves and murderers in Canada, to the number of about seventy, who had been sentenced to be exiled to Botany Bay, could be gathered into the ship which was to take them into that distant land. I thought it was my duty during that interval to visit my penitents in gaol every day, and instruct them on the duties of the new life they were called upon to live. When the day of their departure arrived I gave a Roman Catholic New

Testament, translated by De Sacy, to each of them to read and meditate on their long and tedious journey, and I bade them adieu, recommending them to the mercy of God, and the protection of the Virgin Mary and all the Saints. Some months later I heard, that on the sea Chambers had broken his chains and those of some of his companions, with the intention of taking possession of the ship, and escaping on some distant shore. But he had been betrayed, and was hanged on his arrival at Liverpool.

I had almost lost sight of those emotional days of my young years of priesthood. Those facts were silently lying among the big piles of the daily records which I had faithfully kept since the very days of my collegiate life at Nicolet, when, in 1878, I was called by the providence of God to go and lecture on Romanism in the noble and grand English colony of Australia, formerly known by me only as the penal colony of Botany Bay.

Some time after my arrival, when I was lecturing in one of the young and thriving cities of that country, whose future destinies promise to be so great, a rich carross, drawn by two splendid English horses, with two men in livery, stopped before the house where I had put up for a few days. A venerable gentleman alighted from the carriage and knocked at the door as I was looking at him from the window. I went to the door, to save trouble to my host, and I opened it. In saluting me, the stranger said : " Is Father Chiniquy here ? "

"Yes, sir," I answered. "Father Chiniquy is the guest of this family."

" Could I have the honour of a few minutes' conversation with him ? " replied the old gentleman.

" As I am Father Chiniquy, I can at once answer you that I will feel much pleasure in granting your request."

" Oh, dear Father Chiniquy," quickly replied the stranger, " is it possible that it is you ? Can I be absolutely alone with you for half an hour, without any one to see and hear us ? "

" Certainly," I said ; " my comfortable rooms are upstairs, and I am absolutely alone there. Please, sir, come and follow me."

When alone with me the stranger said :

" Do you not know me ? "

"How can I know you, sir ? " I answered. " I do not even remember ever having seen you ? "

" You have not only seen me, but you have heard the confession of my sins many times; and you have spent many hours in the same room with me," replied the old gentleman.

"Please tell me where and when I have seen you, and also be kind enough to give me your name; for all those things have escaped from my memory."

"Do you remember the murderer and thief, Chambers, who was condemned to death in Quebec, in 1837, with eight of his accomplices?" asked the stranger.

"Yes, sir; I remember well Chambers and the unfortunate men he was leading in the ways of iniquity," I replied.

"Well, dear Father Chiniquy, I am one of the criminals who filled Canada with terror for several years, and who were caught and rightly condemned to death. When condemned, we selected you for our father confessor, with the hope that through your influence we might escape the gallows; and we were not disappointed. You obtained our pardon; the sentence of death was commuted into a life of exile to Botany Bay. My name in Canada was A——, but here they call me B——. God has blessed me since in many ways; but it is to you I owe my life, and all the privileges of my present existence. After God, you are my saviour. I come to thank and bless you for what you have done for me."

In saying that, he threw himself into my arms, pressed me to his heart, and bathed my face and my hands with his tears of joy and gratitude.

But his joy did not exceed mine, and my surprise was equal to my joy to find him apparently in such good circumstances. After I had knelt with him to thank and bless God for what I had heard, I asked him to relate to me the details of his strange and marvellous story. Here is a short *résumé* of his answer:

"After you had given us your last benediction when on board the ship which was to take us from Quebec to Botany Bay, the first thing I did was to open the New Testament you had given me and the other culprits, with the advice to read it with a praying heart. It was the first time in my life I had that book in my hand. You were the only priest in Canada who would put such a book in the hands of common people. But I must confess that its first reading did not do me much good, for I read it more to amuse myself and satisfy my curiosity than through any good and Christian motive. The only good I received from that first reading was that I clearly understood, for the first time, why the priests of Rome fear and hate that book, and why they take it out of the hands of their parishioners when they hear that they have it. It was in vain that I looked for mass, indulgences, chaplets, purgatory, auricular confession, Lent, holy water, the worship of Mary, or prayers in an unknown tongue. I concluded from my first reading of the Gospel that our priests were very wise to prevent us from reading a book which was really demolishing our Roman Catholic Church, and felt surprised that you had put in our hands a book which seemed to me so opposed to the belief and practice of our religion as you taught it to us when in gaol, and my confidence in your good judgment was much shaken. To tell you the truth, the first reading of the Gospel went far to demolish my Roman Catholic faith, and to make a wreck of the religion taught me by my parents and at the college, and even by you. For a few weeks I became more of a sceptic than anything else. The only good that first reading of the Holy Book did me was to give me more serious thoughts, and prevent me from uniting myself to Chambers and his conspirators in their foolish plot for taking possession of the ship and escaping to some unknown and distant shore. He had been shrewd enough to conceal a very small but exceedingly sharp saw between his toes before coming to the ship, with which he had already cut the chains of eighteen of the prisoners, when he was betrayed, and hanged on his arrival at Liverpool.

"But if my first reading of the Gospel did not do me much good, I cannot say the same thing of the second. I remember that, when handing to us that holy book, you had told us never to read it except after a fervent prayer to God for help and light to understand it. I was really tired of my former life. In giving up the fear and the love of God I had fallen into the deepest abyss of human depravity and misery, till I had come very near ending my life on the scaffold. I felt the need of a change. You had often repeated to us the words of our Saviour, 'Come unto Me, all ye who are weary and heavy laden, and I will give you rest;' but, with all the other priests, you had always mixed those admirable and saving words with the invocation to Mary, the confidence in our medals, scapulars, signs of the cross, holy waters, indulgences, auricular confessions, that the sublime appeal of Christ had always been, as it always will be, drowned in the Church of Rome by those absurd and impious superstitions and practices.

"One morning, after I had spent a sleepless night, and feeling as pressed down under the weight of my sins, I opened my Gospel book, after an ardent prayer for light and guidance, and my eyes fell on these words of John, 'Behold, the Lamb of God, who taketh away the sin of the world!' (John i. 29). These words fell upon my poor guilty soul with a divine, irresistible power. With tears and cries of an unspeakable desolation I spent the day in crying, 'O Lamb of God, who taketh away the sins of the world, have mercy upon me! Take away my sins!' The day was not over when I felt and knew that my cries had been heard at the mercy-seat. The Lamb of God had taken away my sins! He had changed my heart and made quite a new man of me. From that day the reading of the Gospel was to my soul what bread is to the poor hungry man, and what pure and refreshing waters are to the thirsty traveller. My joy, my unspeakable joy, was to read the holy book and speak with my companions in chains of the dear Saviour's love for the poor sinners; and, thanks be to God, a good number of them have found Him altogether precious, having been sincerely converted in the dark holes of that ship. When working hard at Sydney with the other culprits, I felt my chains to be as light as feathers when I was sure that the heavy chains of my sins were gone ; and though working hard under a burning sun from morning till night, I felt happy, and my heart was full of joy when I was sure that my Saviour had prepared a throne for me in His kingdom, and that He had bought a crown of eternal glory for me by dying on the cross to redeem my guilty soul.

"I had hardly spent a year in Australia, in the midst of the convicts, when a minister of the Gospel, accompanied by another gentleman, came to me and said : 'Your perfectly good behaviour and your Christian life have attracted the attention and admiration of the authorities, and the governor sends us to hand you this document, which says that you are no more a criminal before the law, but that you have your pardon, and you can live the life of an honourable citizen, by continuing to walk in the ways of God.' After speaking so, the gentleman put one hundred dollars in my hands, and added : 'Go and be a faithful follower of the Lord Jesus, and God Almighty will bless you and make you prosper in all your ways.' All this seemed to me as a dream or vision from heaven. I would hardly believe my ears and my eyes. But it was not a dream, it was a reality. My merciful Heavenly Father had again heard my humble supplications ; after having taken away the heavy chains of my sins, He had mercifully taken away the chains which wounded my feet and my hands. I spent several days and nights in weeping and crying for joy, and in blessing the God of my salvation, Jesus the Redeemer of my soul and my body.

"Some years after that we heard of the discoveries of the rich gold mines in several parts of Australia.

"After having prayed God to guide me, I bought a bag of hard crackers, a ham and cheese, and started for the mines in company with several who were going, like myself, in search of gold. But I soon preferred to be alone. For I wanted to pray and to be united to my God, even when walking. After a long march, I reached a beautiful spot, between three small hills, at the foot of which a little brook was running down towards the plain below. The sun was scorching, there was no shade, and I was much tired, I sat on a flat stone to take my dinner, and quenching my thirst with the water of the brook, I was eating and blessing my God at the same time for His mercies, when suddenly my eyes fell on a stone by the brook, which was about the size of a goose egg. But the rays of the sun was dancing on the stone, as if it had been a mirror. I went and picked it up. The stone was almost all gold of the purest kind! It was almost enough to make me rich. I knelt to thank and bless God for this new token of His mercy toward me, and I began to look around and see if I would not find some new piece of the precious metal, and you may imagine my joy when I found that the ground was not only literally covered with pieces of gold of every size from half an inch to the smallest dimensions, but that the very sand was in great part composed of gold. In a very short time it was the will of God that I could carry to the bank particles of gold to the value of several thousand pounds. I continued to cover myself with rags, and have old boots on in order not to excite the suspicion of any one on the fortune which I was accumulating so rapidly. When I had about £80,000 deposited in the banks, a gentleman offered me £80,000 more for my claim, and I sold it. The money was invested by me on a piece of land which soon became the site of an important city, and I soon became one of the wealthy men of Australia. I then begun to study hard and improve the little education I had received in Canada. I married, and my God has made me father of several children. The people where I settled with my fortune and wife, not knowing my antecedents, have raised me to the first dignities of the place. Please, dear Mr. Chiniquy, come and take dinner with me to-morrow, that I may show you my house and some of my other properties, and also that I may introduce you to my wife and children. Let me ask the favour not to make them suspect that you have known me in Canada, for they think that I am an European." When telling me his marvellous adventures, which I am obliged to condense and abridge, his voice was many times choked by his emotion, his tears and sobs, and more than once he had to stop. As for me, I was absolutely beside myself with admiration at the mysterious ways through which God leads His elect in all ages. "Now, I understood why my God had given me such a marvellous power over the Governor of Canada when I wrenched your pardon from his hands almost in spite of himself." I said : "That merciful God willed to save you, and you are saved! May His name be for ever blessed."

The next day, it was my privilege to be with his family, at dinner. And never in my life, have I seen a more happy mother, and a more interesting family. The long table was actually surrounded by them. After dinner he showed me his beautiful garden and his rich palace, after which, throwing himself into my arms, he said : "Dear Father Chiniquy, all those things belong to you. It is to you after God that I owe my life, all the blessings of a large and Christian family, and the honour of the high position I have in this country. May the God of heaven for ever bless you for what you have done for me." I answered him: "Dear friend, you owe me nothing, I have been nothing but a feeble instrument of the mercies of God towards you.

To that great merciful God alone be the praise and the glory. Please ask your family to come here and join with us in singing to the praise of God the 103rd Psalm." And we sung together: "Bless the Lord, O my soul, and all that is within me bless His holy name. He hath not dealt with us after our sins; nor rewarded us according to our iniquities. For as the heaven is high above the earth, so great is His mercy toward them that fear Him. As far as the east is from the west, so far hath He removed our transgressions from us. Like as a father pitieth his children, so the Lord pitieth them that fear Him." After the singing of that Psalm, I bade him adieu for the second time, never to meet him again except in that Promised Land, where we shall sing the eternal Hallelujah around the throne of the Lamb, who was slain for us, and who redeemed us in His blood.

CHAPTER XXXII.

The merchant fleet of the Fall of 1836 had filled the Marine Hospital of Quebec with the victims of a ship-typhoid fever of the worst kind, which soon turned into an epidemic. Within the walls of that institution Mr. Glackmeyer, the superintendent, with two of the attending doctors, and the majority of the servants were swept away during the winter months.

I was, in the spring of 1837, almost the only one spared by that horrible pest. In order not to spread terror among the citizens of Quebec, the physicians and I had determined to keep that a secret. But, at the end of May, I was forced to reveal it to Bishop Signaie, of Quebec; for I felt in my whole frame the first symptoms of the merciless disease. I prepared myself to die, as very few who had been attacked by it had escaped. I went to the bishop, told him the truth about the epidemic, and requested him to appoint a priest immediately, as chaplain in my place; for, I added, "I feel the poison running through my veins, and it is very probable that I have not more than ten or twelve days to live."

The young Mons. D. Estimanville was chosen, and though I felt very weak, I thought it was my duty to initiate him in his new and perilous work. I took him immediately to the hospital, where he never had been before, and when at a few feet from the door, I said: "My young friend, it is my duty to tell you that there is a dangerous epidemic raging in that house since last Fall, nothing has been able to stop it. The superintendent, two physicians, and most of the servants have been its victims. My escape till now is almost miraculous. But these last ten hours I feel the poison running through my whole body. You are called by God to take my place ; but before you cross the threshold of that hospital, you must make the generous sacrifice of your life ; for you are going on the battle-field from which only few have come out with their lives." The young priest turned pale, and said, " Is it possible that such a deadly epidemic is raging where you are taking me ? " I answered, " Yes ; my dear young brother, it is a fact, and I consider it my duty to tell you not to enter that house, if you are afraid to die ! " A few minutes of silence followed, and it was a solemn silence indeed ! He then took his handkerchief and wiped away some big drops of sweat which were rolling from his forehead on his cheeks, and said : " Is there a more holy and desirable way of dying than in ministering to the spiritual and temporal wants of my brethren ? No ! If it is the will of God that I should fall when fighting at this post of danger, I am ready. Let His holy will be done."

He followed me into the pestilential house with the heroic step of the soldier who runs at the command of his general to storm an impregnable citadel when he is sure to fall. It took me more than an hour to show him all the rooms, and introduce him to the poor, sick, and dying mariners.

I felt then so exhausted that two friends had to support me on my return to the parsonage of St. Roche. My physicians were immediately called (one of them, Dr. Rosseau, is still living), and soon pronounced my case so dangerous that three other physicians were called in consultation. For nine days I suffered the most horrible tortures in my brains, and the very marrow of my bones, from the fever which so devoured my flesh as to seemingly leave but the skin. On the ninth day, the physicians told the bishop who had visited me, that there was no hope of my recovery. The last sacraments were administered to me, and I prepared myself to die, as taught by the Church of Rome. The tenth day I was absolutely motionless, and not able to utter a word. My tongue was parched like a piece of dry wood.

Through the terrible ravage on the whole system, my very eyes were so turned inside their orbits, the white part only could be seen ; no food could be taken from the beginning of the sickness, except a few drops of cold water, which were dropped through my teeth with much difficulty. But though all my physical faculties seemed dead, my memory, intelligence, and soul were full of life, and acting with more power than ever. Now and then, in the paroxysms of the fever, I used to see awful visions. At one time, suspended by a thread at the top of a high mountain, with my head down over a bottomless abyss ; at another, surrounded by merciless enemies, whose daggers and swords were plunged through my body. But these were of short duration, though they have left such an impression on my mind that I still remember the minutest details. Death had, at first, no terror for me. I had done, to the best of my ability, all that my Church had told me to do, to be saved. I had, every day, given my last cent to the poor, fasted and done penance almost enough to kill myself; made my confessions with the greatest care and sincerity ; preached with such zeal and earnestness as to fill the whole city with admiration.

My pharisaical virtues and holiness, in a word, were of such a glaring and deceitful character, and my ecclesiastical superiors were so taken by them, that they made the greatest efforts to persuade me to become the first Bishop of Oregon and Vancouver.

One after the other, all the saints of heaven, beginning with the Holy Virgin Mary, were invoked by me that they might pray God to look down upon me in mercy and save my soul. On the thirteenth night, as the doctors were retiring, they whispered to the Revs. Baillargeon and Parent, who were at my bedside: " He is dead, or if not, he has only a few minutes to live. He is already cold and breathless, and we cannot feel his pulse." Though these words had been said in a very low tone, they fell upon my ears as a peal of thunder. The two young priests, who were my devoted friends, filled the room with such cries that the curate and the priest who had gone to rest, rushed to my room and mingled their tears and cries with theirs.

The words of the doctor, " He is dead ! " were ringing in my ears as the voice of a hurricane. I suddenly saw that I was in danger of being buried alive ; no words can express the sense of horror I felt at that idea. A cold icy wave began to move slowly, but it seemed to me, with irresistible force, from the extremities of my feet and hands towards the heart, as the first symptoms of approaching death. At that moment I made a great effort to see what hope I might have of being saved, invoking the help of the blessed Virgin Mary. With lightning rapidity, a terrible vision struck my mind; I saw all my good works and penances, in which my Church had told me to trust for salvation, in the balance of the justice of God. These were in one side of the scales, and my sins on the other. My good works seemed only as a grain of sand compared with the weight of my sins.*

This awful vision entirely destroyed my false and pharisaical

* In order to be understood by those of my readers who have never been deceived by the diabolical doctrines of the Church of Rome, I must say here, that when young I had learned in my catechism, and when a priest I had believed and preached what Rome says on that subject. Here is her doctrine as taught in her Catechism :—

" Who are those who go to heaven ? "

ANS. " Those only who have never offended God, or who, having offended Him, have done penance."

security, and filled my soul with an unspeakable terror. I could not
cry to Jesus Christ, nor to God, His Father, for mercy; for I sincerely
believed what my Church had taught me on that subject, that they
were both angry with me on account of my sins. With much anxiety
I turned my thoughts, my soul, and hopes, towards St. Anne and St.
Philomene. The first was the object of my confidence, since the first
time I had seen the numberless crutches and other "Ex Votis" which
covered the church of "La Bonne St. Anne du Nord," and the second
was the saint *a la mode*. It was said that her body had lately been
miraculously discovered, and the world was filled with the noise of the
miracles wrought through her intercession. Her medals were on
every breast, her pictures in every house, and her name on all lips.
With entire confidence in the will and power of these two saints to
obtain any favour for me, I invoked them to pray God to grant me a
few years more of life; and with the utmost honesty of purpose, I promised to add to my penances, and to live a more holy life, by consecrating myself with more zeal than ever to the service of the poor and
the sick. I added to my former prayer the solemn promise to have a
painting of the two saints put in St. Anne's Church, to proclaim to
the end of the world their great power in heaven, if they would obtain
my cure and restore my health. Strange to say! The last words of
my prayer were scarcely uttered, when I saw above my head St. Anne
and St. Philomene sitting in the midst of a great light, on a beautiful
golden cloud. St. Anne was very old and grave, but St. Philomene
was very young and beautiful. Both were looking at me with great
kindness.

However, the kindness of St. Anne was mixed with such an air of
awe and gravity that I did not like her looks; while St. Philomene
had such an expression of superhuman love and kindness that I felt
myself drawn to her by a magnetic power, when she said, distinctly:
"You will be cured," and the vision disappeared.

But I was cured, perfectly cured! At the disappearance of the
two saints, I felt as though an electric shock went through my whole
frame; the pains were gone, the tongue was untied, the nerves were
restored to their natural and usual power; my eyes were opened, the
cold and icy waves which were fast going from the extremities to the
regions of my heart, seemed to be changed into a most pleasant warm
bath, restoring life and strength to every part of my body. I raised
my head, stretched out my hands, which I had not moved for three
days, and looking around, I saw the four priests. I said to them:
"I am cured, please give me something to eat, I am hungry."

Astonished beyond measure, two of them threw their arms around
my shoulders to help me to sit a moment, and change my pillow;
when two others ran to the table, which the kind nuns of Quebec had

covered with delicacies in case I might want them. Their joy was mixed with fear, for they all confessed to me afterwards that they had at once thought that all this was nothing but the last brilliant flash of light which the flickering lamp gives before dying away. But they soon changed their minds when they saw that I was eating raven- ously, and that I was speaking to them and thanking God with a cheerful, though very feeble voice. "What does this mean?" they all said. "The doctors told us last evening that you were dead; and we have passed the night not only weeping over your death, but pray- ing for your soul, to rescue it from the flames of purgatory, and now you look so hungry, so cheerful and well."

I answered: "It means that I was not dead, but very near dying, and when I felt that I was to die, I prayed to St. Anne and St. Philomene to come to my help and cure me; and they have come. I have seen them both, there above my head. Ah! if I were a painter, what a beautiful picture I could make of that dear old St. Anne and the still dearer Philomene! for it is St. Philomene who has spoken to me as the messenger of the mercies of God. I have promised to have their portraits painted and put into the church of The Good St. Anne du Nord."

While I was speaking thus, the priests, filled with admiration and awe, were mute; they could not speak except with tears of gratitude. They honestly believed with me that my cure was miraculous, and consented with pleasure to sing that beautiful hymn of gratitude, the "Te Deum."

The next morning, the news of my miraculous cure spread through the whole city with the rapidity of lightning, for besides a good number of the first citizens of Quebec who were related to me by blood, I had not less than 1,800 penitents who loved and respected me as their spiritual father.

To give an idea of the kind interest of the numberless friends whom God had given me when in Quebec, I will relate a single fact. The citizens who were near our parsonage, having been told, by a physician, that the inflammation of my brain was so terrible that the least noise, even the passing of carriages or the walking of horses on the streets, was causing me real torture, they immediately covered all the surrounding streets with several inches of straw to prevent the possibility of any more noise.

The physicians, having heard of my sudden cure, hastened to come and see what it meant. At first, they could scarcely believe their eyes. The night before they had given me up for dead, after thirteen days' suffering with the most horrible and incurable of diseases! And, there I was, the very next morning, perfectly cured! No more pain, not the least remnant of fever, all the faculties of my body and mind perfectly restored! They minutely asked me all the circumstances connected with that strange, unexpected cure; and I told them simply but plainly, how, at the very moment I expected to die, I had fervently prayed to St. Anne and St. Philomene, and how they had come, spoken to me and cured me. Two of my physicians were Roman Catholics, and three Protestants. They at first looked at each other without saying a word. It was evident they were not all partakers of my strong faith in the power of the two saints. While the Roman Catholic doctors, Messrs. Parent and Rousseau, seemed to believe in my miraculous cure, the Protestants energetically protested against that view in the name of science and common sense.

Dr. Douglas put me the following questions, and received the following answers. He said:

"Dear Father Chiniquy, you know you have not a more devoted friend in Quebec than I, and you know me too well to suspect that I want to hurt your religious feelings when I tell you that there is not the least appearance of a miracle in your so happy and sudden cure. If you will be kind enough to answer my questions, you will see that you are mistaken in attributing to a miracle a thing which is most common and natural. Though you are perfectly cured, you are very weak; please answer only 'yes' or 'no' to my questions, in order not to exhaust yourself. Will you be so kind as to tell us if this is the first vision you have had during the period of that terrible fever?"

Ans. "I have had many other visions, but I took them as being the effect of the fever."

Doctor. "Please make your answers shorter, or else I will not ask you another question, for it would hurt you. Tell us simply, if you have not seen in those visions, at times, very frightful and terrible, and at others, very beautiful things."

Ans. "Yes, sir."

Doctor. "Have not those visions stamped themselves on your mind with such a power and vividness that you never forget them, and that you deem them more realities than mere visions of a sickly brain?"

Ans. "Yes, sir."

Doctor. "Did you not feel sometimes much worse, and sometimes much better after those visions, according to their nature?"

Ans. "Yes, sir."

Doctor. "When at ease in your mind during that disease, were you not used to pray to the saints, particularly to St. Anne and St. Philomene?"

Ans. "Yes, sir."

Doctor. "When you considered that death was very near (and it was indeed) when you had heard my imprudent sentence that you had only a few minutes to live, were you not taken suddenly, by such a fear of death as you never felt before?"

ANS. "Yes, sir."

DOCTOR. "Did you not then make a great effort to repel death from you?"

ANS. "Yes, sir."

DOCTOR. "Do you know that you are a man of an exceedingly strong will, and that very few men can resist you when you want to do something? Do you not know that your will is such an exceptional power that mountains of difficulties have disappeared before you, here in Quebec? Have you not seen even me, with many others, yielding to your will almost in spite of ourselves, to do what you wanted?"

With a smile I answered, "Yes, sir."

DOCTOR. "Do you not know that the will, or if you like it better, the soul, has a real, mysterious, and sometimes an irresistible power over the body, to silence its passions, calm its sufferings, and really heal its diseases, particularly when they are of a nervous nature, and in all cases of fever?"

ANS. "Yes, sir! I know that."

DOCTOR. "Do you not remember seeing, many times, people suffering dreadfully from toothache coming to us to have their teeth extracted, who were suddenly cured at the sight of the knives and other surgical instruments we put upon the table for use?"

I answered with a laugh, "Yes, sir. I have seen that very often, and it has occurred to me once."

DOCTOR. "Do you think that there was a supernatural power, then, in the surgical implements, and that those sudden cures of toothache were miraculous?"

ANS. "No, sir!"

DOCTOR. "Have you not read the volume of the 'Medical Directory' I lent you on typhoid fever, where several cures exactly like yours are reported?"

ANS. "Yes, sir."

Then addressing the physicians, Doctor Douglas said to them:

"We must not exhaust our dear Father Chiniquy. We are too happy to see him full of life again, but from his answers you understand that there is no miracle here. His happy and sudden cure is a very natural and common thing. The vision was what we call the turning-point of the disease, when the mind is powerfully bent on some very exciting object, when that mysterious thing of which we know so little as yet, called the will, the spirit, the soul, fights as a giant against death, in which battle, pains, diseases, and even death are put to flight and conquered.

"My dear Father Chiniquy, from your own lips, we have it; you

15

have fought, last night, the fever and approaching death, as a giant. No wonder that you won the victory, and I confess, it is a great victory. I know it is not the first victory you have gained, and I am sure it will not be the last. It is surely God who has given you that irresistible will. In that sense only does your cure come from Him. Continue to fight and conquer as you have done last night, and you will live a long life. Death will long remember its defeat of last night, and will not dare approach you any more, except when you will be so old that you will ask it to come as a friend to put an end to the miseries of this present life. Good-bye."

And with friendly smiles, all the doctors pressed my hand and left me just as the bishop and curate of Quebec, Mons. Baillargeon, my confessor, were entering the room.

An old proverb says : " There is nothing so difficult as to persuade a man who does not want to be persuaded." Though the reasoning and kind words of the doctor ought to have been gladly listened to by me, they had only bothered me. It was infinitely more pleasant, and it seemed then, more agreeable to God, and more according to my faith in the power of the saints in heaven, to believe that I had been miraculously cured. Of course, the bishop, with his coadjutor and my Lord Turgeon, as well as my confessor, with the numberless priests and Roman Catholics who visited me during my convalescence, confirmed me in my views.

The skilful painter, Mr. Plamonon, recently from Rome, was called and painted, at the price of two hundred dollars (£50) the tableau I had promised to put in the church of St. Anne du Nord. It was one of the most beautiful and remarkable paintings of that artist, who had passed several years in the Capital of Fine Arts in Italy, where he had gained a very good reputation for his ability.

Three months after my recovery, I was at the parsonage of the curate of St. Anne, the Rev. Mr. Ranvoize, a relative of mine. He was about sixty-five years of age, very rich, and had a magnificent library. When young, he had enjoyed the reputation of being one of the best preachers in Canada. Never had I been so saddened and scandalized as I was by him on this occasion. It was evening when I arrived with my tableau. As soon as we were left alone, the old curate said: " Is it possible, my dear young cousin, that you will make such a fool of yourself to-morrow ? That so-called miraculous cure is nothing but '*naturæ suprema vis*,' as the learned of all ages have called it. Your so-called vision was a dream of your sickly brain, as it generally occurs in the moment of the supreme crisis of the fever. It is what is called 'the turning-point' of the disease, when a desperate effort of nature kills or cures the patient. As for the vision of that beautiful girl, whom you call St. Philomene, who has done you so much good, she is not the first girl, surely, who has come to you in your dreams, and done you good ! " At these words he laughed so heartily that I feared he would split his sides. Twice he repeated this unbecoming joke.

I was, at first, so shocked at this unexpected rebuke, which I considered as bordering on blasphemy, that I came very near taking my hat without answering a word, to go and spend the night at his brother's; but after a moment's reflection, I said to him : " How can you speak with such levity on so solemn a thing ? Do you not believe in the power of the saints, who being more holy and pure than we are, see God face to face, speak to Him and obtain favours which He would refuse us rebels ? Are you not the daily witness of the miraculous cures wrought in your own church, under your own eyes ? Why those thousands of crutches which literally cover the walls of your church ? " My strong credulity, and the earnestness of my appeal to the daily miracles of which he was the witness, and above all, the mention of the numberless crutches suspended all over the walls of his church, brought again from him such a Homeric laugh, that I was disconcerted and saddened beyond measure. I remained absolutely mute ; I wished I had never come into such company.

When he had laughed at me to his heart's content, he said: "My dear cousin, you are the first one to whom I speak in this way. I do it because, first : I consider you a man of intelligence, and hope you will understand me. Secondly : because you are my cousin. Were you one of those idiotic priests, real blockheads, who form the clergy to-day; or, were you a stranger to me, I would let you go your way, and believe in those ridiculous, degrading superstitions of our poor ignorant and blind people, but I know you from your infancy, and I have known your father, who was one of my dearest friends ; the blood which flows in your veins, passes thousands of times every day through my heart. You are very young and I very old. It is a duty of honour and conscience in me to reveal to you a thing which I have thought better to keep till now, a secret between God and myself. I have been here more than thirty years, and though our country is constantly filled with the noise of the great and small miracles wrought in my church every day, I am ready to swear before God, and to prove to any man of common sense, that not a single miracle has been wrought in my church since I have come here. Every one of the facts given to the Canadian people as miraculous cures are sheer impositions, deceptions, the work of either fools, or the work of skilful impostors and hypocrites, whether priests or laymen. Believe me, my dear cousin, I have studied carefully the history of all those crutches. Ninety-nine out of a hundred have been left by poor, lazy beggars, who, at first, thought with good reason that by walking from door to door with one or two crutches, they would create more sympathy and bring more into their purses ; for how many will indignantly turn out of doors a lazy, strong and healthful beggar, who will feel great compassion, and give largely to a man who is crippled, unable to work, and forced to drag himself painfully on crutches ? Those crutches are then passports from door to door. They are the very keys to open both the hearts and purses. But the day comes when that beggar has bought a pretty good farm with his stolen alms ; or when he is really tired, disgusted with his crutches and wants to get rid of them ! How can he do that without compromising himself ? By a miracle ! Then he will sometimes travel again hundreds of miles from door to door, begging as usual, but this time he asks the prayers of the whole family, saying : ' I am going to the " good St. Anne du Nord" to ask her to cure my leg (or legs). I hope she will cure me, as she has cured so many others. I have great confidence in her power ! ' Each one gives twice, nay, ten times as much as before to the poor cripple, making him promise that if he is cured, he will come back and show himself, that they may bless the good St. Anne with him. When he arrives here, he gives me sometimes one, sometimes five dollars, to say mass for him. I take the money, for I would be a fool to refuse it when I know that his purse has been so well filled. During the celebration of the mass, when he receives the communion, I hear generally, a great noise, cries of joy ! A miracle ! A miracle ! ! The crutches are thrown on the floor, and the cripple walks as well as you or I ! And the last act of that religious comedy is the most lucrative one, for he fulfils his promise of stopping at every house he had ever been seen with his crutches. He narrates how he was miraculously cured, how his feet and legs became suddenly all right. Tears of joy and admiration flow from every eye. The last cent of that family is generally given to the impostor, who soon grows rich at the expense of his dupes. This is the plain but true story of ninety-nine out of every hundred of the cures wrought in my church. The hundredth, is upon people as honest, but, pardon me the expression, as blind and superstitious as you are ; they are really cured, for they were really sick. But their cures are the natural effects of the great effort of the will. It is the result of a happy combination of natural causes which work together on the frame, and kill the pain, expel the disease and restore the health, just as I was cured of a most horrible toothache, some years ago. In the paroxysm I went to the dentist and requested him to extract the affected tooth. Hardly had his knife and other surgical instruments come before my eyes than the pain disappeared. I quietly took my hat and left, bidding a hearty ' good-bye ' to the dentist, who laughed at me every time we met, to his heart's content.

" One of the weakest points of our religion is in the ridiculous, I venture to say, diabolical miracles, performed and believed every day among us, with the so-called relics and bones of the saints. But, don't you know that, for the most part, these relics are nothing but chickens' or sheeps' bones. And what could I not say, were I to tell you what I know of the daily miraculous impostures of the scapulars, holy water, chaplets and medals of every kind. Were I a pope, I would throw all these mummeries, which come from paganism, to the bottom of the sea, and would present to the eyes of the sinners, nothing but Christ and Him crucified as the object of their faith, invocation and hope, for this life and the next, just as the Apostles Paul, Peter and James do in their Epistles."

I cannot repeat here, all that I heard that night from that old relative, against the miracles, relics, scapulars, purgatory, false saints and ridiculous practices of the Church of Rome. It would take too long, for he spoke three hours as a real Protestant. Sometimes what he said seemed to me according to common sense, but as it was against the practices of my church, and against my personal practices, I was exceedingly scandalized and pained, and not at all convinced. I pitied him for having lost his former faith and piety. I told him at the end, without ceremony : " I heard, long ago, that the bishops did not like you, but I knew not why. However, if they could hear what you think and say here about the miracles of St. Anne, they would surely interdict you." " Will you betray me ? " he added, " and will you report our conversation to the bishop ? " " No," my cousin," I replied, " I would prefer to be burnt to ashes. I will not sell your kind hospitality for the traitor's money." It was two o'clock in the morning when we parted to go to our sleeping rooms. But that night was again a sleepless one to me. Was it not too sad and strange for me to see that that old and learned priest was secretly a Protestant !

The next morning the crowds began to arrive, not by hundreds, but by thousands, from the surrounding parishes. The channel between " L'Isle d'Orleans " and St. Anne, was literally covered with boats of every size, laden with men and women who wanted to hear from my own lips, the history of my miraculous cure, and see, with their own eyes, the picture of the two saints who had appeared to me. At ten a.m., more than 10,000 people were crowded inside and outside the wall of the church.

No words can give an idea of my emotion and of the emotion of the multitude when, after telling them in a simple and plain way, what I then considered a miraculous fact, I disclosed the picture, and presented it to their admiration and worship. There were tears rolling on every cheek and cries of admiration and joy from every lip.

The picture represented me dying in my bed of sufferings, and the two saints seen at a distance above me and stretching their hands as if to say : " You will be cured." It was hung on the walls, in a conspicuous place, where thousands and thousands have come to worship it from that day to the year 1858, when the curate was ordered by the bishop to burn it, for it had pleased our merciful God that very year, to take away the scales which were on my eyes and show me His saving light, and I had published all over Canada, my terrible, though unintentional error, in believing in that false miracle. I was so honest in my belief in a miraculous cure, and the apparition of the two saints had left such a deep impression on my mind, that, I confess it to my shame, the first week after my conversion, I very often said to myself : " How is it that I now believe that the Church of Rome is false, when such a miracle has been wrought on me as one of her priests ? " But, our God, whose mercies are infinite, knowing my honesty when a slave of Popery, was determined to give me the full understanding of my errors in this way.

About a month after my conversion, in 1858, I had to visit a dying Irish convert from Romanism, who had caught in Chicago, the same fever which so nearly killed me at the Marine Hospital of Quebec. I again caught the disease, and during twelve days, passed through the same tortures and suffered the same agonies as in 1837. But this time, I was really happy to die ; there was no fear for me to see the good works as a grain of sand in my favour, and the mountains of my iniquities in the balance of God against me. I had just given up my pharisaical holiness of old ; it was no more in my good works, my alms, my penances, my personal efforts, I was trusting to be saved ; it was in Jesus alone. My good works were no more put by me in the balance of the justice of God to pay my debts, and to appeal for mercy. It was the blood of Jesus, the Lamb slain from the foundation of the world for me, which was in the balance. It was the tears of Jesus, the nails, the crown of thorns, the heavy cross, the cruel death of Jesus only, which was there to pay my debts and to cry for mercy. I had no fear then, for I knew that I was saved by Jesus, and that that salvation was a perfect act of His love, His mercy, and His power ; consequently I was glad to die.

But when the doctor had left me, the thirteenth day of my sufferings, saying the very same words of the doctors of Quebec : " He has only a few minutes to live, if he be not already dead," the kind friends who were around my bed, filled the room with their cries ! Although for three or four days I had not moved a finger, said a single word, or given any sign of life, I was perfectly conscious. I had heard the words of the doctor, and I was glad to exchange the miseries of this short life for that eternity of glory which my Saviour had bought for me. I only regretted to die before bringing more of my dear country-men out of the idolatrous religion of Rome, and from the lips of my soul, I said : " Dear Jesus, I am glad to go with Thee just now, but if it be Thy will to let me live a few years more, that I may spread the light of the Gospel among my countrymen ; grant me to live a few years more, and I will bless Thee eternally, with my converted country-men, for Thy mercy." This prayer had scarcely reached the mercy-seat, when I saw a dozen bishops marching toward me, sword in hand to kill me. As the first sword raised to strike was coming down to split my head, I made a desperate effort, wrenched it from the hand of my would-be murderer, and struck such a blow on his neck that his head rolled on to the floor. The second, third, fourth, and so on to the last, rushed to kill me ; but I struck such terrible blows on the necks of every one of them, that twelve heads were rolling on the floor and swimming in a pool of blood. In my excitement I cried to my friends around me : " Do you not see the heads rolling and the blood flowing on the floor ? "

And suddenly I felt a kind of electric shock from head to foot. I was cured! perfectly cured ! ! I asked my friends for something to eat ; I had not taken any food for twelve days. And with tears of joy and gratitude to God, they complied with my request. This last was not only the perfect cure of the body, but it was a perfect cure of the soul. I understood then clearly that the first was not more miracu-lous than the second. I had a perfect understanding of the diabolical forgeries and miracles of Rome. It was in both cases, I was not cured or saved by the saints, the bishops or the Popes, but by my God, through His Son Jesus.

CHAPTER XXXIII.

The 21st of September, 1838, was a day of desolation to me. On that day I received the letter of my bishop appointing me curate of Beauport. Many times, I had said to the other priests, when talking about our choice of the different parishes, that I would never consent to be curate of Beauport. That parish, which is a kind of suburb of Quebec, was too justly considered the very nest of the drunkards of Canada. With a soil of unsurpassed fertility, inexhaustible lime quarries, gardens covered with most precious vegetables and fruits, forests near at hand, to furnish wood to the city of Quebec, at their doors, the people of Beauport, were, nevertheless, classed among the poorest, most ragged and wretched people of Canada. For almost every cent they were getting at the market went into the hands of the saloon-keepers. Hundreds of times I had seen the streets which led from St. Roch to the upper town of Quebec almost impassable, when the drunkards of Beauport were leaving the market to go home. How many times I heard them fill the air with their cries and blasphemies; and saw the streets reddened with their blood when fighting with one another, like mad dogs!

The Rev. Mr. Begin, who was their cure since 1825, had accepted the moral principles of the great Roman Catholic theologian Liguori, who says, "that a man is not guilty of the sin of drunkenness, so long as he can distinguish between a small pin and a load of hay." Of course the people would not find themselves guilty of sin, so long as their eyes could make that distinction. After weeping to my heart's content at the reading of the letter from my bishop, which had come to me as a thunderbolt, my first thought was that my misfortune, though very great, was not irretrievable. I knew that there were many priests who were as anxious to become curates of Beauport as I was opposed to it. My hope was that the bishop would be touched by my tears, if not convinced by my arguments, and that he would not persist in putting on my shoulders a burden which they could not carry. I immediately went to the palace, and did all in my power to persuade his lordship to select another priest for Beauport. He listened to my arguments with a great deal of patience and kindness, and answered:

"My dear Mr. Chiniquy, you forget too often, that 'implicit and perfect obedience to his superiors is the virtue of a good priest. You have given me a great deal of trouble and disappointment by refusing to relieve the good bishop Provencher of his too heavy burden. It was at my suggestion, you know very well, that he had selected you to be his co-worker along the coasts of the Pacific, by consenting to become the first Bishop of Oregon. Your obstinate resistance to your superiors in that circumstance, and in several other cases, is one of your weak points. If you continue to follow your own mind rather than obey those whom God has chosen to guide you, I really fear for your future. I have already too often yielded to your rebellious character. Through respect to myself, and for your own good, to-day I must force you to obey me. You have spoken of the drunkenness of the people of Beauport, as one of the reasons why I should not put you at the head of that parish; but this is just one of the reasons why I have chosen you. You are the only priest I know, in my diocese, able to struggle against the long-rooted and detestable evil, with a hope of success.

"'Quod scriptum scriptum est.' Your name is entered in our official registers as the curate of Beauport; it will remain there till I find better reasons than those you have given me to change my mind. After all, you cannot complain; Beauport is not only one of the most beautiful parishes of Canada, but it is one of the most splendid spots in the world. It is, besides, a parish which gives great revenues to its curate. In your beautiful parsonage, at the door of the old capital of Canada, you will have the privileges of the city, and the enjoyments of some of the most splendid sceneries of this continent. If you are not satisfied with me to-day, I do not know what I can do to please you."

Though far from being reconciled to my new position, I saw there was no help; I had to obey, As my predecessor, Mr. Begin, was to sell all his house furniture, before taking charge of his far distant parish, La Riviere Ouelle, he kindly invited me to go and buy, on long credit, what I wished for my own use, which I did. The whole parish was on the spot long before me, partly to show their friendly sympathy for their last pastor, and partly to see their new curate. I was not long in the crowd without seeing that my small stature and my leanness were making a very bad impression on the people, who were accustomed to pay their respects to a comparatively tall man, whose large and square shoulders were putting me in the shade. Many jovial remarks, though made in half-suppressed tones, came to my ears, to tell me that I was cutting a poor figure by the side of my jolly predecessor.

"He is hardly bigger than my tobacco box," said one not far from me: "I think I could put him in my vest pocket."

"Has he not the appearance of a salted sardine!" whispered a woman to her neighbour, with a hearty laugh.

Had I been a little wiser, I could have redeemed myself by some amiable or funny words, which would have sounded pleasantly in the ears of my new parishioners. But, unfortunately for me, that wisdom is not among the gifts I received. After a couple of hours of auction, a large cloth was suddenly removed from a long table, and presented to our sight an incredible number of wine and beer glasses, of empty decanters and bottles, of all sizes and quality. This brought a burst of laughter and clapping of hands from almost every one. All eyes were turned towards me, and I heard from hundreds of lips: "This is for you, Mr. Chiniquy." Without weighing my words, I instantly answered: "I do not come to Beauport to buy wine glasses and bottles, but to break them."

These words fell upon their ears as a spark of fire on a train of powder. Nine-tenths of that multitude, without being very drunk, had emptied from four to ten glasses of beer or rum, which Rev. Mr. Begin himself was offering them in a corner of the parsonage. A real deluge of insults and cursings overwhelmed me; and I soon saw that the best thing I could do was to leave the place without noise, and by the shortest way.

I immediately went to the bishop's palace, to try again to persuade his lordship to put another curate at the head of such a people. "You see, my lord," I said, "that by my indiscreet and rash answer I have for ever lost the respect and confidence of that people. They already hate me; their brutal cursings have fallen upon me like balls of fire. I prefer to be carried to my grave next Sabbath, than have to address such a degraded people. I feel that I have neither the moral nor the physical power to do any good there."

"I differ from you," replied the bishop. "Evidently the people wanted to try your mettle, by inviting you to buy those glasses, and you would have lost yourself by yielding to their desire. Now they have seen that you are brave and fearless. It is just what the people of Beauport want; I have known them for a long time. It is true that they are drunkards; but, apart from that vice, there is not a nobler people under heaven. They have, literally, no education, but they possess marvellous common sense, and have many noble and redeeming qualities, which you will soon find out. You took them by surprise when you boldly said you wanted to break their glasses and decanters. Believe me, they will bless you, if by the grace of God, you fulfil your prophecy; though it will be a miracle if you succeed in making the people of Beauport sober. But you must not despair. Trust in God; fight as a good soldier, and Jesus Christ will win the victory." Those kind words of my bishop did me good, though I would have preferred being sent to the backwoods of Canada, than to the great parish of Beauport. I felt that the only thing that I had to do was to trust in God for success, and to fight as if I were to gain the day. It came to my mind that I had committed a great sin by obstinately refusing to become Bishop of Oregon, and my God, as a punishment, had given me the very parish for which I felt an almost insurmountable repugnance.

Next Sunday was a splendid day, and the church of Beauport was filled to its utmost capacity by the people, eager to see and hear, for the first time, their new pastor. I had spent the last three days in prayers and fastings. God knows that never a priest, nor any minister of the Gospel, ascended the pulpit with more exalted views of his sublime functions than I did that day, and never a messenger of the Gospel had been more terrified than I was, when in that pulpit, by the consciousness of his own demerits, inability and incompetency, in the face of the tremendous responsibilities of his position. My first sermon was on the text: "Woe is unto me, if I preach not the Gospel" (1 Cor. ix. 16). With a soul and heart filled with the profoundest emotions, a voice many times suffocated by uncontrollable sobs, I expounded to them some of the awful responsibilities of a pastor. The effect of the sermon was felt to the last day of my priestly ministry in Beauport.

After the sermon, I told them: "I have a favour to ask of you. As it is the first, I hope you will not rebuke me. I have just now given you some of the duties of your poor young curate towards you; I want you to come again this afternoon at half-past two o'clock, that I may give you some of your duties towards your pastor." At the appointed hour the church was still more crowded than in the morning, and it seemed to me that my merciful God blessed still more that second address than the first.

The text was: "When he (the shepherd) putteth forth his own sheep, he goeth before them, and the sheep follow him; for they know his voice" (Jno. x. 4).

Those two sermons on the Sabbath were a startling innovation in the Roman Catholic Church of Canada, which brought upon me, at once, many bitter remarks from the bishop and surrounding curates. Their unanimous verdict was that I wanted to become a little reformer. They had not the least doubt that in my pride I wanted to show the people "that I was the most zealous priest of the country." This was not only whispered from ear to ear among the clergy, but several times it was thrown into my face in the most insulting manner. However, my God knew that my only motives were, first, to keep my people away from the taverns, by having them before their altars during the greatest part of the Sabbath day ; second, to impress more on their minds the great saving and regenerating truths I preached, by presenting them twice on the same day under different aspects. I found such benefits from those two sermons, that I continued the practice during the four years I remained in Beauport, though I had to suffer and bear, in silence, many humiliating and cutting remarks from many co-priests.

I had not been more than three months at the head of that parish, when I determined to organize a temperance society on the same principles as Father Mathew, in Ireland. I opened my mind, at first, on that subject to the bishop, with the hope that he would throw the influence of his position in favour of the new association, but, to my great dismay and surprise, not only did he turn my project into ridicule, but absolutely forbade me to think any more of such an innovation. "These temperance societies are a Protestant scheme," he said. "Preach against drunkenness, but let the respectable people who are not drunkards alone. St. Paul advised his disciple Timothy to drink wine. Do not try to be more zealous than they were in those apostolic days."

I left the bishop much disappointed, but did not give up my plan. It seemed to me if I could gain the neighbouring priests to join with me in my crusade I wanted to preach against the usage of intoxicating drinks, we might bring about a glorious reform in Canada, as Father Mathew was doing in Ireland. But the priests, without a single exception, laughed at me, turned my plans into ridicule, and requested me, in the name of common sense, never to speak any more to them of giving up their social glass of wine. I shall never be able to give any idea of my sadness, when I saw that I was to be opposed by my bishop and the whole clergy in the reform which I considered then, more and more every day, the only plank of salvation, not only of my dear people of Beauport, but of all Canada. God only knows the tears I shed, the long sleepless nights I have passed in studying, praying, meditating on that great work of Beauport. I had recourse to all the saints of heaven for more strength and light; for I was determined, at any cost, to try and form a temperance society. But every time I wanted to begin, I was frightened by the idea, not only of the wrath of the whole clergy, which would hunt me down, but still more of the ridicule of the whole country, which would overwhelm me in case of a failure. In these perplexities, I thought I would do well to write to Father Mathew and ask him his advice and the help of his prayers. That noble apostle of temperance of Ireland answered me in an eloquent letter, and pressed me to begin the work in Canada as he had done in Ireland, relying on God, without paying any attention to the opposition of man.

The wise and Christian words of that great and worthy Irish priest, came to me as the voice of God; and I determined to begin the work at once, though the whole world should be against me. I felt that if God was in my favour, I would succeed in reforming my parish and my country in spite of all the priests and bishops of the world, and I was right. Before putting the plough into the ground, I had not only prayed to God and all His saints, almost day and night, during many months, but I had studied all the best books written in England, France and the United States, on the evils wrought by the use of intoxicating drinks. I had taken a pretty good course of anatomy in the Marine Hospital under the learned Dr. Douglas.

I was then well posted on the great subject I was to bring before my country. I knew the enemy I was to attack. And the weapons which would give him the death blow were in my hands. I only wanted my God to strengthen my hands and direct my blows. I prayed to Him, and in His great mercy He heard me.

CHAPTER XXXIV.

" My thoughts are not your thoughts," saith the Lord. And, we may add, His works are not like the works of man. This great truth has never been better exemplified than in the marvellous rapidity with which the great temperance reformation grew in Canada, in spite of the most formidable obstacles. To praise any man for such a work seems to me a kind of blasphemy, when it is so visibly the work of the Lord. I had hardly finished reading the letter of Ireland's Apostle of Temperance, when I fell on my knees and said : " Thou knowest, O my God, that I am nothing but a sinner. There is no light, no strength in Thy poor unprofitable servant. Therefore, come down into my heart and soul, to direct me in that temperance reform which Thou hast put into my mind to establish. Without Thee I can do nothing, but with Thee I can do all things."

This was on a Saturday night, March 20, 1839. The next morning was the first Sabbath of Lent. I said to the people after the sermon :

" I have told you, many times, that I sincerely believe it is my mission from God to put an end to the unspeakable miseries and crimes engendered every day, here and in our whole country, by the use of intoxicating drinks. Alcohol is the great enemy of your souls and your bodies. It is the most implacable enemy of your wives, your husbands, and your children. It is the most formidable enemy of our dear country and our holy religion. I must destroy that enemy. But I cannot fight alone. I must form an army and raise a banner in your midst, around which all the soldiers of the Gospel will rally. Jesus Christ Himself will be our general. He will bless and sanctify us—He will lead us to victory. The next three days will be consecrated by you and by me in preparing to raise that army. Let all those who wish to fill its ranks, come and pass these three days with me in prayer and meditation before our sacred altars. Let even those who do not want to be soldiers of Christ, or to fight the great and glorious battles which are to be fought, come through curiosity, to see a most marvellous spectacle. I invite every one of you, in the name of our Saviour, Jesus Christ, whom alcohol nails anew to the cross every day. I invite you in the name of the holy Virgin Mary, and of all the saints and angels of God, who are weeping in heaven for the crimes committed every day by the use of intoxicating drinks. I invite you in the names of the wives whom I see here in your midst, weeping because they have drunken husbands. I invite you to come in the names of the fathers whose hearts are broken by drunken children. I invite you to come in the name of so many children who are starving, naked, and made desolate by their drunken parents. I invite you to come in the name of your immortal souls, which are to be eternally damned if the giant destroyer, Alcohol, be not driven from our midst."

The next morning, at eight o'clock, my church was crammed by the people. My first address was at half-past eight o'clock, the second at 10.30 a.m., the third at 2.0 p.m., and the fourth at five. The intervals between the addresses were filled by beautiful hymns selected for the occasion. Many times during my discourse the sobs and the cries of the people were such that I had to stop speaking, to mix my sobs and my tears with those of my people. That first day seventy-five men, from among the most desperate drunkards, enrolled themselves under the banner of temperance. The second day I gave again four addresses, the effects of which were still more blessed in their result. Two hundred of my dear parishioners were enrolled in the grand army which was to fight against their implacable enemy. But it would require the hand of an angel to write the history of the third day, at the end of which, in the midst of tears, sobs, and cries of joy, three hundred more of that noble people swore, in the presence of their God, never to touch, taste, nor handle the cursed drinks with which Satan inundates the earth with desolation, and fills hell with eternal cries of despair. During these three days more than two-thirds of my people had publicly taken the pledge of temperance, and had solemnly said in the presence of God, before their altars, " For the love of Jesus Christ, and by the grace of God, I promise that I will never take any intoxicating drink, except as a medicine. I also pledge myself to do all in my power, by my words and example, to persuade others to make the same sacrifice." The majority of my people, among whom we counted the most degraded drunkards, were changed and reformed, not by me, surely, but by the visible, direct work of the great and merciful God, who alone can change the heart of man.

As a great number of people from the surrounding parishes, and even from Quebec, had come to hear me the third day through curiosity, the news of that marvellous work spread very quickly throughout the whole country. The press, both French and English, were unanimous in their praises and felicitations. But when the Protestants of Quebec were blessing God for that reform, the French Canadians, at the example of their priests, denounced me as a fool and heretic.

The second day of our revival I had sent messages to four of the neighbouring curates, respectfully requesting them to come and see what the Lord was doing, and help me to bless Him. But they refused. They answered my note with their contemptuous silence.

One only, the Rev. Mr. Roy, curate of Charlesbourg, deigned to write me a few words, which I copy here :

Rev. MR. CHINIQUY, Curate of Beauport.

My dear Confrère :—Please forgive me if I cannot forget the respect I owe to myself, enough to go and see your fooleries.

Truly yours,
PIERRE ROY.

Charlesbourg, March 5th, 1839.

The indignation of the bishop knew no bounds. A few days after, he ordered me to go to his palace and give an account of what he called my " strange conduct." When alone with me he said : " Is it possible, Mr. Chiniquy, that you have so soon forgotten my prohibition not to establish that ridiculous temperance society in your parish ? Had you compromised yourself alone by that Protestant comedy—for it is nothing but that—I would remain silent, in my pity for you. But you have compromised our holy religion by introducing a society whose origin is clearly heretical.   Last evening, the venerable Grand Vicar Demars told me that you would sooner or later become a Protestant, and that this was your first step.   Do you not see that the Protestants only praise you ?   Do you not blush to be praised only by heretics ?   Without suspecting it, you are just entering a road which leads to your ruin.   You have publicly covered yourself with such ridicule that I fear your usefulness is at an end, not only in Beauport, but in all my diocese. I do not conceal it from you : my first thought, when an eye-witness told me yesterday what you had done, was to interdict you. I have been prevented from taking that step only by the hope that you will undo what you have done. I hope that you will yourself dissolve that anti-Catholic association, and promise to put an end to those novelties, which have too strong a smell of heresy to be tolerated by your bishop."

I answered : " My lord, your lordship has not forgotten that it was absolutely against my own will that I was appointed curate of Beauport ; and God knows that you have only to say a word, and, without a murmur, I will give you my resignation, that you may put a better priest at the head of that people, which I consider, and which is really, to-day the noblest and the most sober people of Canada.   But I will put a condition to the resignation of my position. It is, that I will be allowed to publish before the world that the Rev. Mr. Begin, my predecessor, has never been troubled by his bishop for having allowed his people, during twenty-three years, to swim in the mire of drunkenness ; and that I have been disgraced by my bishop, and turned out from that same parish, for having been the instrument, by the mercy of God, in making them the most sober people in Canada."

The poor bishop felt, at once, that he could not stand on the ground he had taken with me. He was a few moments without knowing what to say. He saw also that his threats had no influence over me, and that I was not ready to undo what I had done. After a painful silence of a minute or two, he said : " Do you not see that the solemn promises you have extorted from those poor drunkards are rash and unwise ; they will break them at the first opportunity ? Their future state of degradation, after such an excitement, will be worse than the first."

I answered : " I would partake of your fears if that change were my work ; but as it is the Lord's work, we have nothing to fear. The works of men are weak, and of short duration, but the works of God are solid and permanent. About the prophecy of the venerable Mr. Demars, that I have taken my first step towards Protestantism by turning a drunken into a sober people, I have only to say that if that prophecy be true, it would show that Protestantism is more apt than our holy religion to work for the glory of God and the good of the people. I hope that your lordship is not ready to accept that conclusion, and that you will not then trouble yourself with the premises. The venerable Grand Vicar, with many other priests, would do better to come and see what the Lord is doing in Beauport, than to slander me and turn false prophets against its curate and people. My only answer to the remarks of your lordship, that the Protestants alone praise me, when the Roman Catholic priests and people condemn me, proves only one thing, viz., that Protestants, on this question, understand the Word of God, and have more respect for it than we Roman Catholics. It would prove also that they understand the interests of humanity better than we do, and that they have more generosity than we have, to sacrifice their selfish propensities to the good of all. I take the liberty of saying to your lordship, that in this, as in many other things, it is high time that we should open our eyes to our false position.

" Instead of remaining at the lowest step of the ladder of one of the most Christian virtues, temperance, we must raise ourselves to the top, where Protestants are reaping so many precious fruits. Besides, would your lordship be kind enough to tell me why I am denounced and abused here, and by my fellow-priests and my bishop, for forming a temperance society in my parish, when Father Mathew, who wrote me lately to encourage and direct me in that work, is publicly praised by his bishops and blessed by the Pope for covering Ireland with temperance societies ? Is your lordship ready to prove to me that Samson was a heretic in the camp of Israel when he fulfilled the promise made by his parents that he would never drink any wine, or beer ; and John the Baptist, was he not a heretic and a Protestant as I am, when, to obey the voice of God, he did what I do to-day, with my dear people of Beauport ? "

At that very moment, the sub-secretary entered to tell the bishop that a gentleman wanted to see him immediately on pressing business, and the bishop abruptly dismissed me, to my great comfort ; and my impression was that he was as glad to get rid of me as I was to get rid of him.

With the exception of the Secretary, Mr. Cazeault, all the priests I met that day and the next month, either gave me the cold shoulder or overwhelmed me with their sarcasms. One of them who had friends in Beauport, was bold enough to try to go through the whole parish to turn me into ridicule by saying that I was half crazy, and the best thing the people could do was to drink moderately to my health when they went to town. But at the third house he met a woman, who, after listening to the bad advice he was giving to her husband, said to him : " I do not know if our pastor is a fool in making people sober, but I know you are a messenger of the devil, when you advise my husband to drink again. You know that he was one of the most desperate drunkards of Beauport. You personally know also what blows I have received from him when he was drunk ; how poor and miserable we were ; how many children had to run on. the streets, half naked, and beg in order not to starve with me ! Now that my husband has taken the pledge of temperance, we have every comfort ; my dear children are well fed and clothed, and I find myself as in a little paradise. If you do not go out of this house at once, I will turn you out with my broomstick." And she would have fulfilled her promise, had not the priest had the good sense to disappear at the " double quick."

The next four months after the foundation of the society in Beauport, my position when with the other priests was very painful and humiliating. I consequently avoided their company as much as possible. And, as for my bishop, I took the resolution never to go and see him, except he should order me into his presence. But my merciful God indemnified me by the unspeakable joy I had in seeing the marvellous change wrought by Him among my dear people. Their fidelity in keeping the pledge was really wonderful, and soon became the object of the admiration of the whole city of Quebec, and of the surrounding country. The change was sudden, so complete and so permanent, that the scoffing bishop and priests, with their friends, had, at last, to blush and be silent.

The public aspect of the parish was soon changed, the houses were repaired, the debts paid, the children well clad. But what spoke most eloquently about the marvellous reform was that the seven thriving saloons of Beauport were soon closed, and their owners forced to take other occupations. Peace, happiness, abundance, and industry, everywhere took the place of the riots, fighting, blasphemies and the squalid misery which prevailed before. The gratitude and respect of that noble people for their young curate knew no bounds ; as my love and admiration for them cannot be told by human words.

However, though the great majority of that good people had taken the pledge, and kept it honourably, there was a small minority, composed of the few who never had been drunkards, who had not yet enrolled themselves under our blessed banners. Though they were glad of the reform, it was very difficult to persuade them to give up their social glass! I thought it was my duty to show them in a tangible way, what I had so often proved with my words only, that the drinking of the social glass of wine, or of beer, is an act of folly, if not a crime. I asked my kind and learned friend, Dr. Douglas, to analyse, before the people, the very wine and beer used by them, to show that it was nothing else but a disgusting and deadly poison. He granted my favour. During four days that noble philanthropist extracted the alcohol, which is not only in the most common, but in the most costly and renowned wines, beer, brandy, and whisky. He gave that alcohol to several cats and dogs, which died in a few minutes in the presence of the whole people.

These learned and most interesting experiments, coupled with his eloquent and scientific remarks, made a most profound impression. It was the corner-stone of the holy edifice which our merciful God built with His own hands in Beauport. The few recalcitrants joined with the rest of their dear friends.

CHAPTER XXXV.

THE people of Beauport had scarcely been a year enrolled under the banners of temperance, when the seven thriving taverns of that parish were deserted and their owners forced to try some more honourable trade for a living. This fact, published by the whole press of Quebec, more than anything forced the opponents, especially among the clergy, to silence, without absolutely reconciling them to my views. However, it was becoming every day more and more evident to all that the good done in Beauport was incalculable, both in a material and moral point of view. Several of the best thinking people of the surrounding parishes began to say to one another : " Why should we not try to bring into our midst this temperance reformation which is doing so much good in Beauport ? " The wives of drunkards would say :

" Why does not our curate do here what the curate of Beauport has done there ? "

On a certain day, one of those unfortunate women who had received, with a good education, a rich inheritance, which her husband had spent in dissipation, came to tell me that she had gone to her curate to ask him to establish a temperance society in his parish, as we had done in Beauport; but he had told her " to mind her own business." She had then respectfully requested him to invite me to come and help to do for his parishioners what I had done for mine, but she had been sternly rebuked at the mention of my name. The poor woman was weeping when she said : " Is it possible that our priests are so indifferent to our sufferings, and that they will let the demon of drunkenness torture us as long as we live, when God gives us such an easy and honourable way to destroy his power for ever ? "

My heart was touched by the tears of that lady, and I said to her : " I know a way to put an end to the opposition of your curate, and force him to bring among you the reformation you so much desire; but it is a very delicate matter for me to mention to you. I must rely upon your most sacred promise of secrecy, before opening my mind to you on that subject."

" I take my God to witness," she answered, " that I will never reveal your secret." " Well, madam, if I can rely upon your discretion and secrecy, I will tell you an infallible way to force your priest to do what has been done here."

" Oh ! for God's sake," she said, " tell me what to do."

I replied : " The first time you go to confession, say to your priest that you have a new sin to confess which is very difficult to reveal to him. He will press you more to confess it. You will then say :

" ' Father, I confess I have lost confidence in you.' Being asked ' Why ? ' You will tell him : ' Father, you know the bad treatment I have received from my drunken husband, as well as hundreds of other wives in your parish, from theirs ; you know the tears we have shed on the ruin of our children, who are destroyed by the bad examples of their drunken fathers ; you know the daily crimes and unspeakable abominations caused by the use of intoxicating drinks ; you could dry our tears and make us happy wives and mothers, you could benefit our husbands and save our children by establishing the society of temperance here as it is in Beauport, and you refuse to do it. How, then, can I believe you are a good priest, and that there is any charity and compassion in you for us ? '

" Listen with a respectful silence to what he will tell you ; accept his penance, and when he asks you if you regret that sin, answer him that you cannot regret it till he has taken the providential means which God offers him to persuade the drunkards.

" Get as many other women whom you know are suffering as you do, as you can, to go and confess to him the same thing ; and you will see that his obstinacy will melt as the snow before the rays of the sun in May."

She was a very intelligent lady. She saw at once that she had in hand an irresistible power to face her priest out of his shameful and criminal indifference to the welfare of his people. A fortnight later she came to tell me that she had done what I had advised her and that more than fifty other respectable women had confessed to their curate that they had lost confidence in him, on account of his lack of zeal and charity for his people.

My conjectures were correct. The poor priest was beside himself, when forced every day to hear from the very lips of his most respectable female parishioners, that they were losing confidence in him. He feared lest he should lose his fine parish near Quebec, and be sent to some of the backwoods of Canada. Three weeks later he was knocking at my door, where he had not been since the establishment of the temperance society. He was very pale, and looked anxious. I could see in his countenance that I owed this visit to his fair penitents. However, I was happy to see him. He was considered a good priest, and had been one of my best friends before the formation of the temperance society. I invited him to dine with me, and made him feel at home as much as possible, for I knew by his embarrassed manner that he had a very difficult proposition to make. I was not mistaken. He at last said :

" Mr. Chiniquy, we had, at first, great prejudices against your temperance society ; but we see its blessed fruits in the great transformation of Beauport. Would you be kind enough to preach a retreat of temperance, during three days, to my people, as you have done here ? "

I answered : " Yes, sir ; with the greatest pleasure. But it is on condition that you will yourself be an example of the sacrifice, and the first to take the solemn pledge of temperance, in the presence of your people."

" Certainly," he answered ; " for the pastor must be an example to his people."

Three weeks later his parish had nobly followed the example of Beauport, and the good curate had no words to express his joy. Without losing a day, he went to the two other curates of what is called " La Cote de Beauprè," persuaded them to do what he had done, and six weeks after all the saloons from Beauport to St. Joachim were closed ; and it would have been difficult, if not impossible, to persuade anyone in that whole region to drink a glass of any intoxicating drink.

Little by little, the country priests were thus giving up their prejudices, and were bravely rallying around our glorious banners of temperance. But my bishop, though less severe, was still very cold toward me. At last the good providence of God forced him, through a great humiliation, to count our society among the greatest spiritual and temporal blessings of the age.

At the end of August, 1840, the public press informed us that the Count de Forbin Janson, Bishop de Nancy, in France, was just leaving New York for Montreal. That bishop, who was the cousin and minister to Charles the Tenth, had been sent into exile by the French people, after the king had lost his crown in the Revolution of 1830. Father Mathew had told me, in one of his letters, that this bishop had visited him, and blessed his work in Ireland, and had also persuaded the Pope to send him his apostolical benediction.

I saw at once the importance of gaining the approbation of this celebrated man, before he had been prejudiced by the bishop against our temperance societies. I asked and obtained leave of absence for a few days, and went to Montreal, which I reached just an hour after the French bishop. I went immediately to pay my homage to him, told him all about our temperance work, asking him, in the name of God, to throw bravely the weight of his great name and position in the scale in favour of our temperance societies. He promised he would, adding: " I am perfectly persuaded that drunkenness is not only the great and common sin of the people, but still more of the priests in America, as well as in Ireland. The social habit of drinking the detestable and poisonous wines, brandies, and beers used on this continent, and in the northern parts of Europe, where the vine cannot grow, is so general and strong, that it is almost impossible to save the people from becoming drunkards, except through an association in which the élite of society will work together to change the old and pernicious habits of common life. I have seen Father Mathew, who is doing an incalculable good in Ireland ; and, be sure of it, I shall do all in my power to strengthen your hands in that great and good work. But do not say to anybody that you have seen me."

Some days later, the Bishop of Nancy was in Quebec, the guest of the Seminary, and a grand dinner was given in his honour, to which more than one hundred priests were invited, with the Archbishop of Quebec, his coadjutor, N. G. Turgeon, and the Bishop of Montreal, M. Q. R. Bourget.

As one of the youngest curates, I had taken the last seat, which was just opposite the four bishops, from whom I was separated only by the breadth of the table. When the rich and rare viands had been well disposed of, and the most delicate fruits had replaced them, bottles of the choicest wines were brought on the table in incredible numbers.

Then the superior of the college, the Rev. Mr. Demars, knocked on the table to command silence, and rising on his feet, he said, at the top of his voice, " Please, my lord bishops, and all of you, reverend gentlemen, let us drink to the health of my Lord Count de Forbin Janson, Primate of Lorraine and Bishop of Nancy.

The bottles passing around were briskly emptied into the large glasses put before everyone of the guests. But when the wine was handed to me I passed it to my neighbour without taking a drop, and filled my glass with water. My hope was that nobody had paid any attention to what I had done ; but I was mistaken. The eyes of my bishop, my Lord Signaie, were upon me. With a stern voice, he said : " Mr. Chiniquy, what are you doing there ? Put wine in your glass, to drink with us the health of Mgr. de Nancy."

These unexpected words fell upon me as a thunderbolt, and really paralyzed me with terror. I felt the approach of the most terrible tempest I had ever experienced. My blood ran cold in my veins ; I could not utter a word. For what could I say there, without compromising myself for ever. To openly resist my bishop, in the presence of such an august assembly, seemed impossible ; but to obey him was also impossible ; for I had promised my God and my country never to drink any wine. I thought, at first, that I could disarm my superior by my modesty and my humble silence. However, I felt that all eyes were upon me. A real chill of terror and unspeakable anxiety was running through my whole frame. My heart began to beat so violently that I could not breathe. I wished then I had followed my first impression, which was not to come to that dinner. I think I would have suffocated had not a few tears rolled down from my eyes, and helped the circulation of my blood. The Rev. Mr. Lafrance, who was by me, nudged me, and said, " Do you not hear the order of my Lord Signaie ? Why do you not answer by doing what you are requested to do ? " I still remained mute, just as if nobody had spoken to me. My eyes were cast down ; I wished then I were dead. The silence of death reigning around the tables told me that everyone was waiting for my answer ; but my lips were sealed. After a minute of that silence, which seemed as long as a whole year, the bishop, with a loud and angry voice, which filled the large room, repeated : " Why do you not put wine in your glass, and drink to the health of my Lord Forbin Janson, as the rest of us are doing ? "

I felt I could not be silent any longer. " My lord," I said, with a subdued and trembling voice, " I have put in my glass what I want to drink. I have promised my God and my country that I would never drink any more wine."

The bishop, forgetting the respect he owed to himself and to those around him, answered me in the most insulting manner: "You are nothing but a fanatic, and you want to reform us."

These words struck me as the shock of a galvanic battery, and transformed me into a new man. It seemed as if they had added ten feet to my stature and a thousand pounds to my weight. I forgot that I was the subject of that bishop, and remembered that I was a man, in the presence of another man. I raised my head and opened my eyes, and as quick as lightning I rose to my feet, and addressing the Grand Vicar Demars, superior of the seminary, I said, with calmness, " Sir, was it that I might be insulted at your table that you have invited me here ? Is it not your duty to defend my honour when I am here, your guest ? But, as you seem to forget what you owe to your guests, I will make my own defence against my unjust aggressor." Then, turning towards the Bishop de Nancy, I said : " My Lord de Nancy, I appeal to your lordship from the unjust sentence of my own bishop. In the name of God, and of His Son, Jesus Christ, I request you to tell us here if a priest cannot, for His Saviour's sake, and for the good of his fellow-men, as well as for his own self-denial, give up for ever the use of wine and other intoxicating drinks, without being abused, slandered, and insulted, as I am here, in your pre-sence ? "

It was evident that my words had made a deep impression on the whole company. A solemn silence followed for a few seconds, which was interrupted by my bishop, who said to the Bishop de Nancy, " Yes, yes, my lord; give us your sentence."

No words can give an idea of the excitement of everyone in that multitude of priests, who, accustomed from their infancy abjectly to submit to their bishop, were, for the first time, in the presence of such a hand-to-hand conflict between a powerless, humble, unprotected, young curate, and his all-powerful, proud, and haughty archbishop.

The Bishop of Nancy at first refused to grant my request. He felt the difficulty of his position; but after Bishop Signaie had united his voice to mine, to press him to give his verdict, he rose and said :

" My Lord Archbishop of Quebec, and you, Mr. Chiniquy, please withdraw your request. Do not press me to give my views on such a new, but important subject. It is only a few days since I came in your midst. It will not do that I should so soon become your judge. The responsibility of a judgment in such a momentous matter is too great. I cannot accept it."

But when the same pressing request was repeated by nine-tenths of that vast assembly of priests, and that the archbishop pressed him more and more to pronounce his sentence, he raised his eyes and hands to heaven, and made a silent but ardent prayer to God. His counte-nance took an air of dignity, which I might call majesty, which gave him more the appearance of an old prophet than of a man of our day. Then casting his eyes upon his audience, he remained a considerable time meditating. All eyes were upon him, anxiously waiting for the sentence. There was an air of grandeur in him at that moment, which seemed to tell us that the purest blood of the great kings of France was flowing in his veins. At last, he opened his lips, but it was again pressingly to request me to settle the difficulty with the archbishop among ourselves, and to discharge him of that responsibility. But we both refused again to grant him his request, and pressed him to give his judgment. All this time I was standing, having publicly said that I would never sit again at that table unless that insult was wiped away.

Then he said with unspeakable dignity: "My Lord of Quebec! Here, before us, is our young priest, Mr. Chiniquy, who, once on his knees, in the presence of God and his angels, for the love of Jesus Christ, the good of his own soul and the good of his country, has promised never to drink! We are the witnesses that he is faithful to his promise, though he has been pressed to break it by your lordship. And because he keeps his pledge with such heroism, your lordship has called him a fanatic! Now, I am requested by everyone here to pronounce my verdict on that painful occurrence. Here it is. Mr. Chiniquy drinks no wine! But, if I look through the past ages, when God Himself was ruling His own people, through His prophets, I see Samson, who, by the special order of God, never drank wine or any other intoxicating drink. If from the Old Testament I pass to the New, I see John the Baptist, the precursor of our Saviour, Jesus Christ, who, to obey the command of God, never drank any wine! When I look at Mr. Chiniquy, and see Samson at his right hand to protect him, and John the Baptist at his left to bless him, I find his position so strong and impregnable, that I would not dare attack or condemn him!" These words were pronounced in the most eloquent and dignified manner, and were listened to with a most respectful and breathless attention.

Bishop de Nancy, keeping his gravity, sat down, emptied his wine glass into a tumbler, filled it with water and drank to my health.

The poor archbishop was so completely confounded and humiliated that everyone felt for him. The few minutes spent at the table, after this extraordinary act of justice, seemed oppressive to everyone. Scarcely anyone dared look at his neighbour, or speak, except in a low and subdued tone, as when a great calamity has just occurred. Nobody thought of drinking his wine; and the health of the Bishop de Nancy was left undrunk. But a good number of priests filled their glasses with water, and giving me a silent sign of approbation, drank to my health. The society of temperance had been dragged by her enemies to the battle-field, to be destroyed; but she bravely fought, and gained the victory. Now, she was called to begin her triumphant march through Canada.

CHAPTER XXXVI.

Has God given us ears to hear, eyes to see, and intelligence to understand? The Pope says, no! But the Son of God says, yes. One of the most severe rebukes of our Saviour to His disciples, was for their not paying sufficient attention to what their eyes had seen, their ears heard, and their intelligence perceived. "Perceive ye not yet, neither understand? Have ye your heart yet hardened? Having eyes, see ye not? and having ears, hear ye not? and do not ye remember?" (Mark viii. 17, 18).

This solemn appeal of our Saviour to our common sense, is the most complete demolition of the whole fabric of Rome. The day that a man ceases to believe that God would give us our senses and our intelligence to ruin and deceive us, but that they were given to guide us, he is lost to the Church of Rome. The Pope knows it; hence the innumerable encyclicals, laws, and regulations by which the Roman Catholics are warned not to trust the testimony of their ears, eyes, or intelligence.

"Shut your eyes," says the Pope to his priests and people; "I will keep mine opened, and I will see for you. Shut your ears, for it is most dangerous for you to hear what is said in the world. I will keep my ears opened, and will tell you what you must know. Remember that to trust your own intelligence, in the research of truth, and the knowledge of the Word of God, is sure perdition. If you want to know anything, come to me: I am the only sure infallible fountain of truth," saith the Pope. And this stupendous imposture is accepted by the people and the priests of Rome with a mysterious facility, and retained with a most desolating tenacity.

It is to them what the iron ring is to the nose of the ox, when a rope is once tied to it. The poor animal loses its self-control. Its natural strength and energies will avail it nothing; it must go left or right, at the will of the one who holds the end of the rope. Reader, please have no contempt for the unfortunate priests and people of Rome, but pity them, when you see them walking in the ways into which intelligent beings ought not to take a step. They cannot help it. The ring of the ox is at their nose, and the Pope holds the end of the rope. Had it not been for that ring, I would not have been long at the feet of the wafer god of the Pope. Let me tell you one of the shining rays of truth, which were evidently sent by our merciful God, with a mighty power, to open my eyes. But I could not follow it ; the iron ring was at my nose; and the Pope was holding the end of the rope.

This was after I had been put at the head of the magnificent parish of Beauport, in the spring of 1840. There was living at " La Jeune Lorette " an old retired priest, who was blind. He was born in France, where he had been condemned to death under the Reign of Terror. Escaped from the guillotine, he had fled to Canada, where the Bishop of Quebec had put him in the elevated post of chaplain of the Ursuline Nunnery. He had a fine voice, was a good musician, and had some pretensions to the title of poet. Having composed a good number of church hymns, he had been called " Père Cantique," but his real name was " Père Daule." His faith and piety were of the most exalted character among the Roman Catholics ; though these did not prevent him from being one of the most amiable and jovial men I ever saw. But his blue eyes, like the eyes of the dove; his fine yellow hair falling on his shoulders as a golden fleece ; his white rosy cheeks, and his constantly smiling lips, had been too much for the tender hearts of the good nuns. It was not a secret that " Pere Cantique," when young, had made several interesting conquests in the nunnery. There was no wonder at that. Indeed, how could that young and inexperienced butterfly escape damaging his golden wings, at the numberless burning lamps of the fair virgins ? But the mantle of charity had been put on the wounds which the old warrior had received on that formidable battlefield, from which even the Davids, Samsons, Solomons, and many others had escaped only after being mortally wounded.

To help the poor blind priest, the curates around Quebec used to keep him by turn in their parsonages, and give him the care and marks of respect due to his old age. After the Rev. Mr. Roy, curate of Charlesbourgh, had kept him five or six weeks, I had him taken to my parsonage. It was in the month of May—a month entirely consecrated to the worship of the Virgin Mary, to whom Father Daule was a most devoted priest. His zeal was really inexhaustible, when trying to prove to us how Mary was the surest foundation of the hope and salvation of sinners ; how she was constantly appeasing the just wrath of her son Jesus, who, were it not for His love and respect to her, would have long since crushed us down.

The Councils of Rome have forbidden the blind priests to say their mass ; but on account of high piety, he had got from the Pope the privilege of celebrating the short mass of the Virgin, which he knew perfectly by heart. One morning, when the old priest was at the altar, saying his mass, and I was in the vestry, hearing the confessions of the people, the young servant boy came to me in haste, and said, " Father Daule calls you ; please come quick."

Fearing something wrong had happened to my old friend, I lost no time, and ran to him. I found him nervously tapping the altar with his two hands, as in anxious search of some very precious thing. When very near to him, I said: "What do you want?" He answered with a shriek of distress : " The good god has disappeared from the altar. He is lost ! J'ai perdu le Bon Dieu. Il est disparu de dessus l'autel ! " Hoping that he was mistaken, and that he had only thrown away the good god, "Le Bon Dieu," on the floor, by some accident, I looked on the altar, at his feet, everywhere I could suspect that the *good god* might have been moved away by some mistake of the hand. But the most minute search was of no avail; the good god could not be found. I really felt stunned. At first, remembering the thousand miracles I had read of the disappearance, and marvellous changes of form of the wafer god, it came to my mind that we were in the presence of some great miracle ; and that my eyes were to see some of these great marvels of which the books of the Church of Rome are filled. But I had soon to change my mind, when a thought flashed through my memory which chilled the blood in my veins. The church of Beauport was inhabited by a multitude of the boldest and most insolent rats I have ever seen. Many times, when saying my mass, I had seen the ugly noses of several of them, who, undoubtedly attracted by the smell of the fresh wafer, wanted to make their breakfast with the body, blood, soul, and divinity of my Christ. But, as I was constantly in motion, or praying with a loud voice, the rats had invariably been frightened and fled away into their secret quarters. I felt terror-stricken by the thought that the good god (Le Bon Dieu) had been taken away and eaten by the rats.

Father Daule so sincerely believed what all the priests of Rome are bound to believe, that he had the power to turn the wafer into God, that, after he had pronounced the words by which the great marvel was wrought, he used to pass from five to fifteen minutes in silent adoration. He was then as motionless as a marble statue, and his feelings were so strong that often torrents of tears used to flow from his eyes on his cheeks. Leaning my head towards the distressed old priest, I asked him : " Have you not remained, as you are used, a long time motionless, in adoring the good god, after the consecration ?"

He quickly answered, " Yes ; but what has this to do with the loss of the good god ?"

I replied in a low voice, but with a real accent of distress and awe, " Some rats have dragged and eaten the good god !"

"What do you say?" replied Father Daule. "The good god carried away and eaten by rats!"

"Yes," I replied, "I have not the least doubt about it."

"My God! my God! what a dreadful calamity upon me!" rejoined the old man; and raising his hands and his eyes to heaven, he cried out again, "My God! my God! Why have you not taken away my life before such a misfortune could fall upon me!" He could not speak any longer; his voice was choked by his sobs.

At first I did not know what to say; a thousand thoughts, some very grave, some exceedingly ludicrous, crossed my mind more rapidly than I can say them. I stood there as nailed to the floor, by the old priest, who was weeping as a child, till he asked me, with a voice broken by his sobs, "What must I do now?" I answered him: "The Church has foreseen occurrences of that kind, and provided for them the remedy. The only thing you have to do is to get a new wafer, consecrate it, and continue your mass as if nothing strange had occurred. I will go and get you, just now, new bread." I went, without losing a moment, to the vestry, got and brought a new wafer, which he consecrated and turned into a new god, and finished his mass, as I had told him. After it was over, I took the disconsolate old priest by the hand to my parsonage for breakfast. But all along the way he rent the air with his cries of distress. He would hardly taste anything, for his soul was really drowned in a sea of distress. I vainly tried to calm his feelings, by telling him that it was no fault of his; that this strange and sad occurrence was not the first of that kind; and that it had been calmly foreseen by the Church, which had told us what to do in these circumstances; that there was no neglect, no fault, no offence against God or man on his part.

But as he would not pay the least attention to what I said, I felt the only thing I had to do was to remain silent, and respect his grief by telling him to unburden his heart by his lamentations and tears.

I had hoped that this good common sense would help him to overcome his feelings, but I was mistaken; his lamentations were as long as those of Jeremiah, and the expressions of his grief as bitter.

At last I lost patience, and said: "My dear Father Daule, allow me to tell you respectfully that it is quite time to stop these lamentations and tears. Our great and just God cannot like such an excess of sorrow and regret about a thing which was only, and entirely, under the control of His power and eternal wisdom."

"What do you say there?" replied the old priest, with a vivacity which resembled anger.

"I say that, as it was not in your power to foresee or to avoid that occurrence, you have not the least reason to act and speak as you do. Let us keep our regrets and our tears for our sins: we have both committed many; we cannot shed too many tears on them. But there is no sin here, and there must be some reasonable limits to our sorrow. If anybody had to weep and regret without measure what has happened, it would be Christ. For He alone could foresee that event, and He alone could prevent it. Had it been His will to oppose this sad and mysterious fact, it was in His, not in our power to prevent it. He alone has suffered from it, because it was His will to suffer it."

"Mr. Chiniquy," he replied, "you are quite a young man, and I see you have the want of attention and experience which are often seen among young priests. You do not pay sufficient attention to the awful calamity which has just occurred in your church. If you had more faith and piety you would weep with me, instead of laughing at my grief. How can you speak so lightly of a thing which makes the angels of God weep? Our dear Saviour dragged and eaten by rats! Oh! great God! does not this surpass the humiliation and horrors of Calvary?"

"My dear Father Daule," I replied, "allow me respectfully to tell you, that I understand, as well as you do, the nature of the deplorable event of this morning. I would have given my blood to prevent it. But let us look at that fact in its proper light. It is not a moral action for us; it did not depend on our will more than the spots of the sun. The only one who is accountable for that fact is our God! For, again I say, that He was the only one who could foresee and prevent it. And, to give you plainly my own mind, I tell you here that if I were God Almighty, and a miserable rat would come to eat me, I would strike him dead before he could touch me."

There is no need of confessing it here; every one who reads these pages, and pays attention to this conversation, will understand that my former so robust faith in my priestly power of changing the wafer into my God had melted away and evaporated from my mind, if not entirely, at least to a great extent.

Great and new lights had flashed through my soul in that hour; evidently my God wanted to open my eyes to the awful absurdities and impieties of a religion whose god could be dragged and eaten by rats. Had I been faithful to the saving lights which were in me then, I was saved in that very hour; and before the end of that day I would have broken the shameful chains by which the Pope had tied my neck to his idol of bread. In that hour it seemed to me evident that the dogma of transubstantiation was a most monstrous imposture, and my priesthood an insult to God and man.

My intelligence said to me with a thundering voice: "Do not remain any longer the priest of a god whom you make every day, and whom the rats can eat."

Though blind, Father Daule understood very well, by the stern accents of my voice, that my faith in the god whom he had created that morning, and whom the rats had eaten, had been seriously modified, if not entirely crumbled down. He remained silent for some time, after which he invited me to sit by him; and he spoke to me with a pathos and an authority which my youth and his old age alone could justify. He gave me the most awful rebuke I ever had; he really opened on my poor wavering intelligence, soul and heart, all the cataracts of heaven. He overwhelmed me with a deluge of Holy Fathers, Councils, and infallible Popes who had believed and preached before the whole world, in all ages, the dogma of transubstantiation.

If I had paid attention to the voice of my intelligence, and accepted the lights which my merciful God was giving me, I could easily have smashed the arguments of the old priest of Rome. But what has the intelligence to do in the Church of Rome? What could my intelligence say? I was forbidden to hear it. What was the weight of my poor, isolated intelligence, when put in the balance against so many learned, holy, infallible intelligences?

Alas! I was not aware then that the weight of the intelligence of God, the Father, Son, and Holy Ghost, was on my side; and that, weighted against the intelligence of the Popes, they were greater than all the worlds against a grain of sand.

One hour after, shedding tears of regret, I was at the feet of Father Daule, in the confessional box, confessing the great sin I had committed by doubting, for a moment, of the power of the priest to change a wafer into God.

The old priest, whose voice had been like a lion's voice when speaking to the unbelieving curate of Beauport, had become sweet as the voice of a lamb when he had me at his feet, confessing my unbelief. He gave me my pardon. For my penance he forbade me ever to say a word on the sad end of the god he had created that morning; for, said he, "This would destroy the faith of the most sincere Roman Catholics." For the other part of the penance I had to go on my knees every day, during nine days, before the fourteen images of the way of the cross, and say a penitential psalm before every picture, which I did. But the sixth day the skin of my knees was pierced, and the blood was flowing freely. I suffered real torture every time I knelt down, and at every step I made. But it seemed to me that these terrible tortures were nothing compared to my great iniquity!

I had refused, for a moment, to believe that a man can create his god with a wafer! and I had thought that a church which adores a god eaten by rats, must be an idolatrous church!

CHAPTER XXXVII.

A FEW days before the arrival of Bishop de Forbin Janson, I was alone in my study, considering my false position towards my ecclesiastical superiors, on account of my establishing the temperance society against their formal protest. My heart was sad. My partial success had not blinded me to the reality of my deplorable isolation from the great mass of the clergy. With very few exceptions, they were speaking of me as a dangerous man. They had even given me the nickname of " *Le reformateur au petit pied* " (small-sized reformer) and were losing no opportunity of showing me their supreme contempt and indignation, for what they called my obstinacy.

In that sad hour, there were many clouds around my horizon, and my mind was filled with anxiety; when, suddenly, a stranger knocked at my door. He was a good-sized man; his smiling lips and honest face were beaming with the utmost kindness. His large and noble forehead told me, at once, that my visitor was a man of superior intellect. His whole mien was that of a true gentleman.

He pressed my hand with the cordiality of an old friend and, giving me his name, he told me at once the object of his visit, in these words :

" I do not come here only in my name ; but it is in the name of many, if not of all, the English-speaking people of Quebec and Canada ; I want to tell you our admiration for the great reform you have accomplished in Beauport. We know the stern opposition of your superiors and fellow-priests to your efforts, and we admire you more for that.

" Go on, sir, you have on your side the great God of heaven, who has said to us all : ' Look not thou upon the wine when it is red, when it giveth its colour in the cup, when it moveth itself aright. At the last, it biteth like a serpent, and stingeth like an adder.' " (Prov. xxiii. 31, 32.) " Take courage, sir," he added ; " you have, on your side, the Saviour of the world, Jesus Christ Himself. Fear not man, sir, when God the Father, and His Son, Jesus Christ, are on your side. If you find any opposition from some quarter ; and if deluded men turn you into ridicule when you are doing such a Christian work, bless the Lord. For Jesus Christ has said : ' Blessed are they who do hunger and thirst after righteousness, for they shall be filled. Blessed are ye when men shall revile you and persecute you, and shall say all manner of evil against you, falsely, for My sake.' (Matt. v. 6, 11.) I come also to tell you, sir, that if there are men to oppose you, there are many more who are praying for you day and night, asking our heavenly Father to pour upon you His most abundant blessings. In-

toxicating drinks are the curse of this young country. It is the most
deadly foe of every father and mother, the most implacable enemy of
every child in Canada. It is the ruin of our rich families, as well as
the destruction of the poor. The use of intoxicating drinks, under
any form, or pretext, is an act of supreme folly; for alcohol kills the
body and damns the soul of its blind victims. You have, for the first
time, raised the glorious banners of temperance among the French
Canadian people; though you are alone, to-day, to lift it up, be not discouraged. For, before long, you will see your intelligent countrymen
rallying around it, to help you to fight and conquer. No doubt, the
seed you sow to-day is often watered with your tears. But, before
long, you will reap the richest crop; and your heart will be filled with
joy, when your grateful country will bless your name."

After a few other sentences of the same elevated sentiments, he
hardly gave me time enough to express my feelings of gratitude, and
said: "I know you are very busy, I do not want to trespass upon
your time. Good-bye, sir. May the Lord bless you, and be your
keeper in all your ways."

He pressed my hand, and soon disappeared. I would try, in vain,
to express what I felt when alone with my God, after that strange and
providential visit. My first thought was to fall on my knees and
thank that merciful God for having sent me such a messenger to cheer
me in one of the darkest hours of my life; for every word from his
lips had fallen on my wounded soul as the oil of the Good Samaritan
on the bleeding wounds of the traveller to Jericho. There had been
such an elevation of thought, such a ring of true, simple, but sublime
faith and piety; such love of man and fear of God in all that he had
said. It was the first time that I had heard words so conformable to
my personal views and profound convictions on that subject. That
stranger, whose visit had passed as quickly as the visit of an angel
from God, had filled my heart with such joy and surprise at the unexpected news that all the English-speaking people of Canada were
praying for me!

However, I did not fall on my knees to thank God; for my sentiments of gratitude to God were suddenly chilled by the unspeakable
humiliation I felt when I considered that that stranger was a Protestant! The comparison I was forced to make between the noble sentiments, the high philosophy, the Christian principles of that Protestant
layman, with the low expressions of contempt, the absolute want of
generous and Christian thoughts of my bishop and my fellow-priests
when they were turning into ridicule that temperance society which
God was so visibly presenting to us as the best, if not the only way, to
save the thousands of drunkards who were perishing around us, paralyzed my lips, bewildered my mind, and made it impossible for me to

utter a word of prayer. My first sentiments of joy and of gratitude to God soon gave way to sentiments of unspeakable shame and distress.

I was forced to acknowledge that these Protestants, whom my Church had taught me, through all her councils, to anathematize and curse as the slaves and followers of Satan, were, in their principles of morality, higher above us than the heavens are above the earth! I had to confess to myself that those heretics, whom my church had taught me to consider as rebels against Christ and His Church, knew the laws of God and followed them much more closely than ourselves. They had raised themselves to the highest degree of Christian temperance, when my bishops, with their priests, were swimming in the deadly waters of drunkenness!

A voice seemed crying to me, "Where is the superiority of holiness of your proud Church of Rome over those so-called heretics, who follow more closely the counsels and precepts of the gospel of Christ?" I tried to stifle that voice, but I could not. Louder and louder it was heard asking me, "Who is nearer God? The bishop who so obstinately opposes a reform which is so evidently according to the Divine Word, or those earnest followers of the gospel who make the sacrifice of their old and most cherished usages with such pleasure, when they see it is for the good of their fellow-men and the glory of God?" I wished them to be a hundred feet below the ground, in order not to hear those questions answered within my soul. But there was no help; I had to hear them, and to blush at the reality before my eyes. Pride! yes, diabolical pride! is the vice, *par excellence*, of every priest of Rome. Just as he is taught to believe and say that his church is far above every other church, so he is taught to believe and say that, as a priest, he is above all the kings, emperors, governors, and presidents of this world. *That* pride is the daily bread of the Pope, the bishop, the priests, and even the lowest layman in the Church of Rome. It is also the great secret of their power and strength. It is this diabolical pride which nerves them with an iron will, to bring down everything to their feet, subject every human being to their will, and tie every neck to the wheels of their chariot. It is this fearful pride which so often gives them that stoical patience and indomitable courage in the midst of the most cruel pain, or in the face of the most appalling death, which so many deluded Protestants take for Christian courage and heroism. The priest of Rome believes that he is called by God Almighty to rule, subdue, and govern the world; with all those prerogatives that he fancies granted him by heaven he builds up a high pyramid, on the top of which he sets himself, and from that elevation looks down with the utmost contempt on the rest of the world.

17

If anyone suspects that I exaggerate in thus speaking of the pride of the priest, let him read the following haughty words which Cardinal Manning puts in the lips of the Pope in one of his lectures:

"I acknowledge no civil power; I am the subject of no prince. I am more than this. I claim to be the supreme judge and director of the conscience of men : of the peasant who tills his field, and of the prince who sits upon the throne; of the household that lives in the shade of privacy, and the legislator that makes laws for the kingdom. I am the sole, last, supreme judge of what is right or wrong."

Is it not evident that the Holy Ghost speaks of this pride of the priests and of the Pope, the high priest of Rome, when He says: "That man of sin," that "son of perdition, who opposeth and exalteth himself above all that is called God, or that is worshipped; so that he, as God, sitteth in the temple of God, shewing himself that he is God" (2 Thess. ii. 3, 4).

That caste pride which was in me, though I did not see it then, as it is in every priest of Rome, though he does not suspect it, had received a rude check, indeed, from that Protestant visitor. Yes, I must confess it, he had inflicted a deadly wound on my priestly pride; he had thrown a barbed arrow into my priestly soul which I tried many times, but always in vain, to take away. The more I attempted to get rid of this arrow, the deeper it went through my very bones and marrow. That strange visitor, who caused me to pass so many hours and days of humiliation, when forcing me to blush at the inferiority of the Christian principles of my church compared with those of the Protestants, is well known in Canada, the United States, and Great Britain as the founder and first editor of two of the best religious papers of America, the *Montreal Witness* and the *New York Witness.* His name is John Dougall. As he is still living, I am happy to have this opportunity of thanking and blessing him again for the visit he paid to the young curate of Beauport forty-five years ago. I was not aware then that the wounds inflicted by that unknown but friendly hand was one of the great favours bestowed upon me by my merciful God; but I understand it now. Many rays of light have since come from the wounds which my priestly pride received that day. Those rays of light helped much to expel the darkness which surrounded me by leading me to see, in spite of myself, that the vaunted holiness of the Church of Rome is a fraud.

CHAPTER XXXVIII.

THE battle fought and gained at the grand dinner of the Quebec Seminary by the society of temperance had been decisive. The triumph was as complete as it was glorious. Hereafter her march to the conquest of Canada was to be a triumph. Her banners were soon to be planted over all the cities, towns, and villages of my dear country. To commemorate the expression of their joy and gratitude to God to the remotest generations, the people of Beauport erected the beautiful Column of Temperance, which is still seen half-way between Quebec and the Montmorency Falls. The Bishop de Nancy, my Lord Forbin Janson, blessed that first monument of Temperance, September 7th, 1841, in the midst of an immense multitude of people. The parishes of St. Peter, St. John, St. Famille (Orleans Island), with St. Michel were the first, after Lange Gardien, Chateau Richer, St. Anne and St. Joachin, to request me to preach on Temperance. Soon after, the whole population of St. Roch, Quebec, took the pledge with a wonderful unanimity, and kept it long with marvellous fidelity. In order to show to the whole country their feelings of gratitude, they presented me with a fine picture of the Column of Temperance and a complimentary address, written and delivered by one of the most promising young men of Quebec, Mr. John Cauchon, who was raised some years later to the dignity of a Cabinet Minister, and who has been the worthy Lieutenant-Governor of Manitoba.

That address was soon followed by another from the citizens of Quebec and Beauport, presented along with my portrait, by Mr. Joseph Parent, then editor of the *Canadien*, and afterwards Provincial Secretary of Canada.

What a strange being man is! How fickle are his judgments! In 1842, they had no words sufficiently flattering to praise the very man in the face of whom they were spitting in 1838, for doing the very same thing. Was I better for establishing the society of temperance in 1842, than I was in establishing it in 1838? No! And was I worse when, in 1838, bishops, priests, and people, were abusing, slandering, and giving me bad names for raising the banners of temperance over my country, than I was in continuing to lift it up in 1842? No! The sudden and complete judgments of men in such a short period of time had the good and providential effect of filling my mind with the most supreme indifference, not to say contempt, for what men thought or said of me. Yes! this sudden passage from condemnation to that of praise, when I was doing the very same work, had the good effect to cure me of that natural pride which one is apt to feel when publicly applauded by men.

It is to that knowledge, acquired when young, that I owe the preservation of my dignity as a man and priest, when all my bishops and their priests were arrayed against me at the dining table of the Seminary of Quebec. It is that knowledge, also, that taught me not to forget that I was nothing but a worm of the dust and an unprofitable servant of God, when the same men overwhelmed me with their unmerited praises. Let not my readers think, however, that I was absolutely indifferent to this change of public feeling. For no words can tell the joy I felt at the assurance which these public manifestations afforded me that the cause of temperance was to triumph everywhere in my country. Let me tell here a fact too honourable to the people of Beauport to be omitted. As soon as the demon of intemperance was driven from my parish, I felt that my first duty was to give my attention to education, which had been so shamefully neglected by my predecessors that there was not a single school in the parish worthy of that name. I proposed my plan to the people, asked their co-operation, and set to work without delay.

I began by erecting the fine stone school-house near the church, on the site of the old parsonage; the old walls were pulled down, and on the old foundation a good structure was soon erected with the free collections raised in the village. But the work was hardly half-finished when I found myself without a cent to carry it on. I saw at once that, having no idea of the value of education, the people would murmur at my asking any more money. I therefore sold my horse—a fine animal given me by a rich uncle—and with the money finished the building.

My people felt humiliated and pained at seeing their pastor obliged to walk when going to Quebec or visiting the sick. They said to each other: "Is it not a burning shame for us to have forced our young curate to sell his fine horse to build our school-houses, when it would have been so easy to do that work ourselves? Let us repair our faults."

On my return from establishing the society of temperance in St. John, two weeks later, my servant man said to me:

"Please, Mr. le Cure, come to the stable and see a very curious thing."

"What curious thing can there be?" I answered.

"Well, sir, please come, and you will see."

What was both my surprise and pleasure to find one of the most splendid Canadian horses there as mine! For my servant said to me, "During your absence the people have raised five hundred dollars, and bought this fine horse for you. They say they do not want any longer to see their curate walking in the mud. When they drove the horse here, that I might present him to you as a surprise on your arrival, I heard them saying that with the temperance society you have saved them more than five hundred dollars every week in money, time, and health, and that it was only an act of justice to give you the savings of a week."

The on'y way of expressing my gratitude to my noble people, was to redouble my exertions in securing the benefits of a good education to their children. I soon proposed to the people to build another school-house two miles distant from the first.

But I was not long without seeing that this new enterprise was to be still more uphill work than the first one among the people, of whom hardly one in fifty could sign his name.

"Have not our fathers done well without those costly schools?" said many. "What is the use of spending so much money for a thing that does not add a day to our existence, nor an atom to our comfort?"

I soon felt confronted by such a deadly indifference, not to say opposition, on the part of my best farmers, that I feared for a few days lest I had really gone too far. The last cent of my own revenues was not only given, but a little personal debt created to meet the payments, and a round sum of five hundred dollars had to be found to finish the work. I visited the richest man of Beauport to ask him to come to my rescue. Forty years before he had come to Beauport bare-footed, without a cent to work. He had employed his first earned dollars in purchasing some rum, with which he had doubled his money in two hours; and had continued to double his money, at that rate, in the same way, till he was worth nearly two hundred thousand dollars.

He then stopped selling rum, to invest his money in city properties. He answered me: "My dear curate, I would have no objections to give you the five hundred dollars you want, if I had not met the Grand Vicar Demars yesterday, who warned me, as an old friend, against what he calls your dangerous and exaggerated views in reference to the education of the people. He advised me, for your own good, and the good of the people, to do all in my power to induce you to desist from your plan of covering our parishes with schools."

"Will you allow me," I answered, "to mention our conversation to Mr. Demars, and tell him what you have just said about his advising you to oppose me in my efforts to promote the interests of education?"

"Yes, sir, by all means," answered Mr. Des Roussell. "I allow you to repeat to the venerable superior of the Seminary of Quebec, what he said to me yesterday; it was not a secret, for there were several other farmers of Beauport to whom he said the very same thing. If you ignore that the priests of Quebec are opposed to your plans of educating our children, you must be the only one who does not know it, for it is a public fact. Your difficulties in raising the funds you want, come only from the opposition of the rest of the clergy to you in this matter; we have plenty of money in Beauport to day, and we would feel happy to help you. But you understand that our good will be somewhat cooled by the opposition of men whom we are accustomed to respect."

I replied : " Do you not remember, my dear Mr. Des Roussell, that those very same priests opposed me in the same way, in my very first efforts to establish the temperance society in your midst ? "

" Yes, sir," he answered, with a smile, " we remember it well, but you have converted them to your views now."

" Well, my dear sir, I hope we shall convert them also in this question of education."

The very next morning, I was knocking at the door of the Rev. Grand Vicar Demars, after I had tied my splendid horse in the court-yard of the Seminary of Quebec. I was received with the utmost marks of courtesy. Without losing any time, I repeated to the old Superior what Mr. Des Roussell had told me of his opposition to my educational plans, and respectfully asked him if it were true.

The poor Grand Vicar seemed as if thunderstruck by my abrupt, though polite question. He tried, at first, to explain what he had said, by taking a long circuit, but I mercilessly brought him to the point at issue, and forced him to say, " Yes, I said it."

I then rejoined and said, " Mr. Grand Vicar, I am only a child before you, when comparing my age with yours ; however, I have the honour to be the curate of Beauport, it is in that capacity that I respectfully ask you by what right you oppose my plans for educating our children ! "

" I hope, Mr. Chiniquy," he answered, " that you do not mean to say that I am the enemy of education ; for I would answer you that this is the first house of education on this continent, and that I was at its head before you were born. I hope that I have the right to believe and say that the old Superior of the Seminary of Quebec understands, as well as the young curate of Beauport, the advantage of a good education. But I will repeat to you what I said to Mr. Des Roussell, that it is a great mistake to introduce such a general system of education as you want to do in Beauport. Let every parish have its well-educated notary, doctor, merchants, and a few others to do the public business ; that is enough. Our parishes of Canada are models of peace and harmony under the direction of their good curates, but they will become unmanageable the very day your system of education spreads abroad ; for then all the bad propensities of the heart will be developed with an irresistible force. Besides, you know that since the conquest of Canada by Protestant England, the Protestants are wait-ing for their opportunity to spread the Bible among our people. The only barrier we can oppose to that danger is to have, in future, as in the past, only a very limited number of our people who can read or write. For as soon as the common people are able to read, they will, like Adam and Eve, taste the forbidden fruit; they will read the Bible, turn Protestant, and be lost for time and eternity."

In my answer, among other things, I said : " Go into the country, look at the farm which is well-cultivated, ploughed with attention and skill, richly manured, and sown with good seed; is it not infinitely more pleasant and beautiful to live on such a farm, than on one which is neglected, unskilfully managed and covered with noxious weeds ? Well, the difference between a well educated and an uneducated people is still greater in my mind.

" I know that the priests of Canada, in general, have your views, and it is for that reason that the parish of Beauport with its immense revenues has been left without a school worthy the name, from its foundation to my going there. But my views are absolutely different. And as for your fear of the Bible, I confess we are antipodes to each other. I consider that one of the greatest blessings God has bestowed upon me, is that I have read the Bible, when I was on my mother's knees. I do not even conceal from you, that one of my objects in giving a good education to every boy and girl of Beauport, is to put the Gospel of Christ in their hands, as soon as they are able to read it."

At the end of our conversation, which was very excited on both sides, though kept in the bounds of politeness during nearly two hours, I said : " Mr. Grand Vicar, I did not come here to convert you to my views, this would have been impertinence on my part; nor can you convert me to yours, if you are trying it, for you know I have the bad reputation of being a hard case; I came to ask you, as a favour, to let me work according to my conscience in a parish which is mine and not yours. Do not interfere any more in my affairs between me and my parishoners, than you would like me to interfere in the management of your Seminary. As you would not like me to criticise you before your pupils and turn you into ridicule, please cease adding to my difficulties among my people, by continuing in the future what you have done in the past.

" You know, Mr. Grand Vicar, that I have always respected you as my father ; you have many times been my adviser, my confessor, and my friend ; I hope you will grant me the favour I ask from you in the name of our common Saviour. It is for the spiritual and temporal good of the people and pastor of Beauport that I make this prayer."

That old priest was a kind-hearted man ; these last words melted his heart. He promised what I wanted, and we parted from each other on better terms than I had expected at first.

When crossing the courtyard of the Seminary, I saw the Archbishop Signaie, who, coming from taking a ride, had stopped to look at my horse and admire it. When near him, I said : " My lord, this is a bishop's horse, and ought to be in your hands."

" It is what I was saying to my secretary," replied the bishop. " How long is it since you got it ? "

" Only a few days ago, my lord."

" Have you any intention of selling it ? "

" I would, if it would please my bishop," I replied.

" What is the price ? " asked the bishop.

" Those who gave it to me paid five hundred dollars for it," I replied.

" Oh! oh! that is too dear," rejoined the bishop, " with five hundred dollars, we can get five good horses. Two hundred would be enough."

" Your lordship is joking. Were I as rich as I am poor, one thousand dollars would not take that noble animal from my hands, except to have it put in the carosse of my bishop."

" Go and write a cheque of two hundred dollars to the order of Mr. Chiniquy," said the bishop to his sub-secretary, Mr. Belisle.

When the secretary had gone to write the cheque, the bishop being alone with me, took from his portfeuille three bank bills of one hundred dollars each, and put them into my hands, saying : " This will make up your five hundred dollars, when my secretary gives you the cheque. But, please, say nothing to anybody, not even to my secretary. I do not like to have my private affairs talked of around the corners of the streets. That horse is the most splendid I ever saw, and I am much obliged to you for having sold it to me."

I was also very glad to have five hundred dollars in hand. For with three hundred dollars I could finish my schoolhouse, and there was two hundred dollars more to begin another, three miles distant.

Just two weeks later, when I was dressing myself at sunrise, my servant man came to my room and said : " There are twenty men on horseback who want to speak to you."

" Twenty men on horseback who want to speak to me ! " I answered. " Are you dreaming ? "

" I do not dream," answered my young man ; " there they are at the door, on horseback, waiting for you."

I was soon dressed, and in the presence of twenty of my best farmers, on horseback, who had formed themselves in a half-circle to receive me.

" What do you want, my friends ? " I asked them.

One of them, who had studied a few years in the Seminary ot Quebec, answered :

" Dear pastor, we come in the name of the whole people of Beauport, to ask your pardon for having saddened your heart by not coming as we ought to your help in the superhuman efforts you make to give good schools to our children. This is the result of our ignorance. Having never gone to school ourselves, the greater part of us have never known the value of education. But the heroic sacrifices you have made lately have opened our eyes. They ought to have been opened at the sale of your first horse. But we were in need of another lesson to understand our meanness. However, the selling of the second horse has done more than anything else to awaken us from our shameful lethargy. The fear of receiving a new rebuke from us, if you made another appeal to our generosity, has forced you to make that new sacrifice. The first news came to us as a thunderbolt. But there is always some light in a thunderbolt; through that light we have seen our profound degradation, in shutting our ears to your earnest and paternal appeals in favour of our own dear children. Be sure, dear pastor, that we are ashamed of our conduct. From this day, not only our hearts, but our purses are yours, in all you want to do to secure a good education for our families. However, our principal object in coming here to-day is not to say vain words, but to do an act of reparation and justice. Our first thought, when we heard that you had sold the horse we had given you, was to present you with another. We have been prevented from doing this by the certainty that you would sell it again, either to help some poor people or to build another schoolhouse. As we cannot bear to see our pastor walking in the mud when going to the city, or visiting us, we have determined to put another horse into your hands, but in such a way that you will not have the right to sell it. We ask you, then, as a favour, to select the best horse here among these twenty which are before you, and to keep it as long as you remain in our midst, which we hope will be very long. It will be returned to its present possessor if you leave us; and be sure, dear pastor, that the one of us who leaves his horse in your hands will be the most happy and proudest of all."

When speaking thus, that noble hearted man had several times been unable to conceal the tears which were rolling down his cheeks, and more than once his trembling voice had been choked by his emotion.

I tried in vain at first to speak. My feelings of gratitude and admiration could be expressed only with my tears. It took some time before I could utter a single word. At last I said: "My dear friends, this is too much for your poor pastor. I feel overwhelmed by this grand act of kindness. I do not say that I thank you—the word thank is too small—too short and insignificant to tell you what your poor unworthy pastor feels at what his eyes see and his ears hear just now. The great and merciful God, who has put those sentiments into your hearts, alone can repay you for the joy with which you fill my soul. I would hurt your feelings, I know, by not accepting your offering : I accept it. But to punish your speaker, Mr. Parent, for his complimentary address, I will take his horse, for the time I am curate of Beauport, which, I hope, will be till I die." And I laid my hand on the bridle of the splendid animal.

There was then a struggle which I had not expected. Every one of the nineteen whom I left with their horses began to cry : " Oh ! do not take that horse ; it is not worth a penny ; mine is much stronger," said one. " Mine is much faster," cried out another. " Mine is a safe rider," said a third. Every one wanted me to take his horse, and tried to persuade me that it was the best of all; they really felt sorry that they were not able to change my mind. Has anyone ever felt more happy than I was in the midst of these generous friends ? The memory of that happy hour will never pass away from my mind.

CHAPTER XXXIX.

ON the morning of the 25th August, 1842, we blessed and opened the seventh school of Beauport. From that day all the children were to receive as good an education as could be given in any country place of Canada. Those schools had been raised on the ruins of the seven taverns which had so long spread ruin, shame, desolation, and death over that splendid parish. My heart was filled with an unspeakable joy at the sight of the marvellous things which, by the hand of God, had been wrought in such a short time.

At about two p.m. of that never-to-be-forgotten day, after I had said my vespers, and was alone, pacing the alleys of my garden, under the shade of the old maple trees bordering the northern part of that beautiful spot, I was reviewing the struggles and the victories of these last four years : it seemed that everything around me, not only the giant trees which were protecting me from the burning sun, but even the humblest grasses and flowers of my garden, had a voice to tell me, " Bless the Lord for His mercies."

At my feet the majestic St. Lawrence was rolling its deep waters ; beyond, the old capital of Canada, Quebec, with its massive citadel, its proud towers, its bristling cannons, its numerous houses and steeples, with their tin roofs reflecting the light of the sun in myriads of rays, formed such a spectacle of fairy beauty as no pen can describe. The fresh breeze from the river, mingled with the perfume of the thousand flowers of my parterre, bathed me in an atmosphere of fragrance. Never yet had I enjoyed life as at that hour. All the sanguine desires of my heart and the holy aspirations of my soul had been more than realized. Peace, harmony, industry, abundance, happiness, religion, and education had come on the heels of temperance, to gladden and cheer the families which God had entrusted to me. The former hard feelings of my ecclesiastical superiors had been changed into sentiments and acts of kindness, much above my merits. With the most sincere feelings of gratitude to God, I said with the old prophet, "Bless the Lord, O my soul."

By the great mercy of God that parish of Beauport, which at first had appeared to me as a bottomless abyss in which I was to perish, had been changed for me into an earthly paradise. There was only one desire in my heart. It was that I never should be removed from it. Like Peter on Mount Tabor, I wanted to pitch my tent in Beauport to the end of my life. But the rebuke which had shamed Peter came as quickly as lightning to show me the folly and vanity of my dreams.

Suddenly the carosse of the Bishop of Quebec came in sight, and rolled down to the door of the parsonage. The sub-secretary, the Rev. Mr. Belisle, alighting from it, directed his steps towards the garden, where he had seen me, and handed me the following letter from the Right Rev. Turgeon, Coadjutor of Quebec:

MY DEAR MONS. CHINIQUY:

His lordship Bishop Signaie and I wish to confer with you on a most important matter. We have sent our carriage to bring you to Quebec. Please come without the least delay.

Truly yours,

✠ FLAV. TURGEON.

One hour after, I was with the two bishops. My Lord Signaie said:

"Monseigneur Turgeon will tell you why we have sent for you in such haste."

"Mons. Chiniquy," said Bishop Turgeon, "is not Kamouraska your birthplace?"

"Yes, my lord."

"Do you like that place, and do you interest yourself much in its welfare?"

"Of course, my lord, I like Kamouraska; not only because it is my birthplace, and the most happy hours of my youth were spent in it, but also because, in my humble opinion, the beauties of its scenery, the purity of its atmosphere, the fine manners and proverbial intelligence of its people, make it the very gem of Canada."

"You know," rejoined the bishop, "that Rev. Mons. Varin has been too infirm, these last years, to superintend the spiritual interest of that important place, it is impossible to continue putting a young vicar at the head of such a parish, where hundreds of the best families of our aristocracy of Quebec and Montreal resort every summer. We have, too long, tried that experiment of young priests in the midst of such a people. It has been a failure. Drunkenness, luxury, and immoralities of the most degrading kind are eating up the very life of Kamouraska to-day. Not less than thirty illegitimate births are known and registered in different places from Kamouraska these last twelve months. It is quite time to stop that state of affairs, and you are the only one, Mons. Chiniquy, on whom we can rely for that great and difficult work."

These words passed through my soul as a two-edged sword. My lips quivered, I felt as if I were choking, and my tongue, with difficulty muttered : "My lord, I hope it is not your intention to remove me from my dear parish of Beauport."

"No, Mons. Chiniquy, we will not make use of our authority to break the sacred and sweet ties which unite you to the parish of Beauport. But we will put before your conscience the reasons we have to wish you at the head of the great and important parish of Kamouraska."

For more than an hour the two bishops made strong appeals to my charity for the multitudes who were sunk into the abyss of drunkenness and every vice, and had no one to save them.

"See how God and men are blessing you to-day," added the Archbishop Signaie, "for what you have done in Beauport! Will they not bless you still more, if you save that great and splendid parish of Kamouraska, as you have saved Beauport? Will not a double crown be put upon your forehead by your bishops, your country, and your God, if you consent to be the instrument of the mercies of God towards the people of your own birthplace, and the surrounding country, as you have just been for Beauport and its surrounding parishes? Can you rest and live in peace now in Beauport, when you hear day and night the voice of the multitudes, who cry : ' Come to our help, we are perishing ' ? What will you answer to God, at the last day, when He will show you the thousands of precious souls lost at Kamouraska, because you refused to go to their rescue ? As Monseigneur Turgeon has said, we will not make use of our authority to force you to leave your present position ; we hope that the prayers of your bishops will be enough for you. We know what a great sacrifice it will be for you to leave Beauport to-day ; but do not forget that the greater the sacrifice, the more precious will the crown be."

My bishops had spoken to me with such kindness! Their paternal and friendly appeals had surely more power over me than orders. Not without many tears, but with a true good will, I consented to give up the prospects of peace and comfort which were in store for me in

Beauport, to plunge myself again into a future of endless troubles and warfare, by going to Kamouraska.

There is no need of saying that the people of Beauport did all in their power to induce the bishops to let me remain among them some time longer. But the sacrifice had to be made. I gave my farewell address on the second Sabbath of September, in the midst of indescribable cries, sobs, and tears; and on the 17th of the same month, I was on my way to Kamouraska. I had left everything behind me at Beauport, even to my books, in order to be freer in that formidable conflict which seemed to be in store for me in my new parish.

When I took leave of the Bishop of Quebec, they showed me a letter just received by them from Mons. Varin, filled with the most bitter expressions of indignation on account of the choice of such a fanatic and firebrand as Chiniquy, for a place as well known for its peaceful habits and harmony among all classes. The last words of the letter were as follows :

" The clergy and people of Kamouraska and vicinity consider the appointment of Mons. Chiniquy to this parish as an insult, and we hope and pray that your lordship may change your mind on the subject."

In showing me the letter, my lords Signaie and Turgeon said : " We fear that you will have more trouble than we expected with the old curate and his partisans, but we commend you to the grace of God and the protection of the Virgin Mary, remembering that our Saviour has said : ' Be of good cheer; I have overcome the world ' " (John xvi. 33).

I arrived at Kamouraska the 21st of September, 1842, on one of the finest days of the year. But my heart was filled with an unspeakable desolation, for all along the way the curates had told me that the people, with their old pastor, were unanimous in their opposition to my going there. It was even rumoured that the doors of the church would be shut against me the next Sunday. To this bad news were added two very strange facts. My brother Achilles, who was living at St. Michel, was to drive me from that place to St. Roch des Aulnets, whence my other brother Louis, would take me to Kamouraska. But we had not travelled more than five or six miles, when the wheel of the newly-finished and beautifully painted buggy, having struck a stone, the seat was broken into fragments, and we both fell to the ground.

By chance, as my brother was blessing the man who had sold him that rig for a new and first-class conveyance, a traveller going the same way passed by. I asked him for a place in his calêche, bade adieu to my brother, and consoled him by saying: " As you have lost your fine buggy in my service, I will give you a better one."

Two days after, my second brother was driving me to my destination, and when about three or four miles from Kamouraska, his
fine horse stepped on a long nail which was on the road, fell down and
died in the awful convulsions of tetanus. I took leave of him, and
consoled him also by promising to give him another horse.

Another carriage took me safely to the end of my journey. However, having to pass by the church, which was about two hundred
yards from the parsonage, I dismissed my driver at the door of the
sacred edifice, and took my satchel in hand, which was my only bag-
gage, entered the church, and spent more than an hour in fervent
prayers, or rather in cries and tears. I felt so heart-sick that I needed
that hour of rest and prayer. The tears I shed there relieved my
burdened spirit.

A few steps from me, in the cemetery, lay the sacred remains of
my beloved mother, whose angelic face and memory were constantly
before me. Facing me was the altar where I had made my first
communion ; at my left was the pulpit which was to be the battlefield
where I had to fight the enemies of my people and of my God, who,
I had been repeatedly told, were cursing and grinding their teeth at
me. But the vision of that old curate I had soon to confront, and
who had written such an impudent letter against me to the bishops,
and the public opposition of the surrounding priests to my coming
into their midst, were the most discouraging aspects of my new position. I felt as if my soul had been crushed. My very existence
seemed an unbearable burden.

My new responsibilities came so vividly before my mind in that
distressing hour, that my courage for a moment failed me. I reproached myself for the act of folly in yielding to the request of the
bishops. It seemed evident that I had accepted a burden too heavy
for me to bear. But I prayed with all the fervour of my soul to God
and to the Virgin Mary, and wept to my heart's content.

There is a marvellous power in the prayers and tears which come
from the heart. I felt as a new man. I seemed to hear the trumpet
of God calling me to the battlefield. My only business then was to
go and fight, relying on Him alone for victory. I took my travelling
bag, went out of the church and walked slowly towards the parsonage,
which has been burnt since. It was a splendid two-storey building,
eighty feet in length, with capacious cellars. It had been built shortly
after the conquest of Canada, as a store for contraband goods ; but
after a few years of failure became the parsonage of the parish.

The Rev. Mons. Varin, though infirm and sick, had watched me
from his window, and felt bewildered at my entering the church and
remaining so long.

I knocked at the first door, but as nobody answered, I opened it, and crossed the first large room to knock at the second door; but, here also, no answer came except from two furious little dogs. I entered the room, fighting the dogs, which bit me several times. I knocked at the third and fourth doors with the same result—no one to receive me.

I knew that the next was the old curate's sleeping room. At my knocking, an angry voice called out : " Walk in."

I entered, made a step toward the old and infirm curate, who was sitting in his large arm-chair. As I was about to salute him, he angrily said : " The people of Beauport have made great efforts to keep you in their midst, but the people of Kamouraska will make as great efforts to turn you out of this place."

" Mons. le Cure," I answered calmly, " God knoweth that I never desired to leave Beauport for this place. But I think it is that great and merciful God who has brought me here by the hand ; and I hope He will help me to overcome all opposition, from whatever quarter it may come."

He replied angrily : " Is it to insult me that you call me ' Mons. le Cure ? ' I am no more the curate of Kamouraska. You are the curate now, Mr. Chiniquy."

" I beg your pardon, my dear Mr. Varin ; you are still, I hope you will remain all your life, the honoured and beloved curate of Kamouraska. The respect and gratitude I owe you have caused me to refuse the titles and honours which our bishop wanted to give me."

" But, then, if I am the curate, what are you ? " replied the old priest, with more calmness.

" I am nothing but a simple soldier of Christ, and a sower of the good seed of the Gospel ! " I answered. " When I fight the common enemy in the plain, as Joshua did, you, like Moses, will stand on the top of the mountain, lift up your hands to heaven, send your prayers to the mercy seat, and we will gain the day. Then both will bless the God of our salvation for the victory."

" Well! well! this is beautiful, grand, and sublime," said the old priest, with a voice filled with friendly emotions. " But where is your household furniture, your library ? "

" My household furniture," I answered, " is in this little bag, which I hold in my hand. I do not want any of my books as long as I have the pleasure and honour to be with the good Mons. Varin, who will allow me, I am sure of it, to ransack his splendid library, and study his rare and learned books."

" But what rooms do you wish to occupy ? " rejoined the good old curate.

" As the parsonage is yours and not mine," I answered, " please tell me where you want me to sleep and rest. I will accept, with gratitude, any room you will offer me, even if it were in your cellar or granary. I do not want to bother you in any way. When I was young, a poor orphan in your parish, some twenty years ago, were you not a father to me? Please continue to look upon me as your own child, for I have always loved and considered you as a father, and I still do the same. Were you not my guide and adviser in my first steps in the ways of God? Please continue to be my guide and adviser to the end of your life. My only ambition is to be your right-hand man, and to learn from your old experience and your sincere piety, how to live and work as a good priest of Jesus Christ."

I had not finished the last sentence when the old man burst into tears, threw himself into my arms, pressed me to his heart, bathed me with his tears, and said, with a voice half-suffocated by his sobs: "Dear Mr. Chiniquy, forgive me the evil things I have written and said about you. You are welcome in my parsonage, and I bless God to have sent me such a young friend, who will help me to carry the burden of my old age."

I then handed him the bishop's letter, which had confirmed all I had said about my mission of peace towards him.

From that day to his death, which occurred six months after, I never had a more sincere friend than Mr. Varin.

I thanked God, who had enabled me at once, not only to disarm the chief of my opponents, but to transform him into my most sincere and devoted friend. My hope was that the people would soon follow their chief and be reconciled to me, but I did not expect that this would be so soon and from such an unforeseen and unexpected cause.

The principal reason the people had to oppose my coming to Kamouraska was that I was the nephew of the Hon. Amable Dionne, who had made a colossal fortune at their expense. The Rev. Mr. Varin, who was always in his debt, was also forced by the circumstances, to buy everything, both for himself and the church, from him, and had to pay without murmur the most exorbitant prices for everything.

In that way, the church and the curate, though they had very large revenues, had never enough to clear their accounts. When the people heard that the nephew of Mons. Dionne was their curate, they said to each other: "Now our poor church is for ever ruined, for the nephew will, still more than the curate, favour his uncle, and the uncle will be less scrupulous than ever in asking more unreasonable prices for his merchandise." They felt they had more than fallen from Charybdis into Scylla.

The very next day after my arrival, the beadle told me that the church needed a few yards of cotton for some repairs, and asked me if he would not go, as usual, to Mr. Dionne's store. I told him to go there first, ask the price of that article, and then go to the other stores, ordering him to buy at the cheapest one. Thirty cents was asked at Mr. Dionne's, and only fifteen cents at Mr. St. Pierre's; of course, we bought at the latter's store.

The day was not over, before this apparently insignificant fact was known all over the parish, and was taking the most extraordinary and unforeseen proportions. Farmers would meet with their neighbours and congratulate themselves that, at last, the yoke imposed upon them by the old curate and Mr. Dionne, was broken; that the taxes they had to pay the store were at an end, with the monopoly which had cost them so much money. Many came to Mr. St. Pierre to hear from his own lips that their new curate had, at once, freed them from what they considered the long and ignominious bondage, against which they had so often but so vainly protested. For the rest of this week this was the only subject of conversation. They congratulated themselves that they had, at last, a priest with such an independent and honest mind, that he would not do them any injustice even to please a relative in whose house he had spent the years of his childhood. This simple act of fair play towards that people won over their affection. Only one little dark spot remained in their minds against me. They had been told that the only subject on which I could preach was: Rum, whiskey, and drunkenness. And it seemed to them exceedingly tedious to hear nothing else from the curate, particularly when they were more than ever determined to continue drinking their social glasses of brandy, rum, and wine.

There was an immense crowd at church, the next Sunday. My text was: "As the Father has loved Me, so have I loved you" (John xv. 9). Showing them how Jesus had proved that He was their friend. But their sentiments of piety and pleasure at what they had heard were nothing compared to their surprise when they saw that I preached nearly an hour without saying a word on whiskey, rum or beer. People are often compared to the waters of the sea, in the Holy Scriptures. When you see the roaring waves dashing on that rock to-day, as if they wanted to demolish it, do not fear that this fury will last long. The very next day, if the wind has changed, the same waters will leave that rock alone, to spend their fury on the opposite rock. So it was in Kamouraska. They were full of indignation and wrath when I set my feet in their midst; but a few days later, those very men would have given the last drop of their blood to protect me. The dear Saviour had evidently seen the threatening storm which was to destroy His poor unprofitable servant. He had heard the roaring waves which were dashing against me. So He came down and bid the storm " be still " and the waves be calm.

CHAPTER XL.

Two days after my arrival at Kamouraska, I received a letter from the surrounding priests, at the head of whom was the Grand Vicar Mailloux, expressing the hope that I would not try to form any temperance society in my new parish, as I had done in Beauport; for the good reasons they said, that drunkenness was not prevailing in that part of Canada, as it was in the city of Quebec. I answered them, politely, that so long as I should be at the head of this new parish, I would try, as I had ever done, to mind my own business, and I hoped that my neighbouring friends would do the same. Not long after, I saw that the curates felt ashamed of their vain attempt to intimidate me. The next Sabbath, the crowd was greater than at the first. Having heard that the merchants were to start the next day, with their schooners, to buy their winter provisions of rum, I said, in a very solemn way, before my sermon:

"My friends, I know that, to-morrow, the merchants leave for Quebec to purchase their rum. Let me advise them, as their best friend, not to buy any; and as the ambassador of Christ, I forbid them to bring a single drop of those poisonous drinks here. It will surely be their ruin, if they pay no attention to this friendly advice; for they will not sell a single drop of it, after next Sabbath. That day, I will show to the intelligent people of this parish, that rum and all the other drugs, sold here, under the name of brandy, wine and beer, are nothing else than disgusting, deadly, and cursed poisons."

I then preached on the words of our Saviour: "Be ye also ready; for in such an hour as ye think not, the Son of Man of cometh" (Matt. xxiv. 44). Though the people seemed much pleased and impressed by that second sermon, they felt exceedingly irritated at my few warning words to the merchants. When the service was over, they all rallied around the merchants to tell them not to mind what they had heard.

"If our young curate," said they, "thinks he will lead us by the nose, as he has done with the drunkards of Beauport, he will soon see his mistake. Instead of one hundred tons, as you brought last fall, bring us two hundred, this year; we will drink them to his health. We have a good crop and we want to spend a jolly winter."

It is probable that the church of Kamouraska had never seen within its walls such a crowd as on the second Sabbath of October, 1842. It was literally crammed. Curiosity had attracted the people who, not less eager to hear my first sermon against rum, than to see the failure they expected, and wished, of my first efforts to form a temperance society. Long before the public service, at the door of the church, as well as during the whole preceding week, the people had pledged themselves never to give up their strong drink, and never to join the temperance society. But what are the resolutions of man against God ? Is He not their master ? The half of that first sermon on temperance was not heard, when that whole multitude had forgotten their public promises. The hearts were not only touched—they were melted and changed by God, who wanted to show, once more, that His works of mercy were above all the works of His hands.

From the very day of my arrival in Kamouraska, I had made a serious and exact inquiry about the untold miseries brought upon the people by intoxicating drinks. I had found that, during the last twenty years, twelve men had been drowned and eight had been frozen to death, who had left twenty widows and sixty orphans in the most distressing poverty. Sixty farmers had lost their lands and had been obliged to emigrate to other places, where they were suffering all the pangs of poverty from the drunkenness of their parents ; several other families had their properties mortgaged for their whole value to the rum merchants, and were expected, every day, to be turned out from their inheritances, to pay their rum bills. Seven mothers had died in delirium tremens, one had hung herself, another drowned herself when drunk. One hundred thousand dollars had been paid to the rum merchants during the last fifteen years. Two hundred thousand more were due to the storekeeper ; three-fourths of which were for strong drink. Four men had been murdered, among whom was their landlord, Achilles Tache, through their drunken habits !

When I had recapitulated all these facts, which were public and undeniable, and depicted the desolation of the ruined families, composed of their own brothers, sisters, and dear children ; when I brought before their minds, the tears of the widows, the cries of the starving and naked children, the shame of the families, the red hand of the murderers and the mangled bodies of their victims ; the eternal cries of the lost from drunkenness, the broken-hearted fathers and mothers whose children had been destroyed by strong drink ; when I proved to them that there was not a single one in their midst who had not suffered, either in his own person, or in that of his father or mother, brothers, sisters or children—yes, when I had given them the simple and awful story of the crimes committed in their midst ; the ruin and deaths, the misery of thousands of precious souls for whom Christ died in vain, the church was filled with such sobs and cries that I often could not be heard. Many times my voice was drowned by the indescribable confusion and lamentation of that whole multitude. Unable to contain myself, several times I stopped and mingled my sobs and cries with those of my people.

When the sermon, which lasted two hours, was finished, I asked all those who were determined to help me in stopping the ravages of intoxicating drinks, in drying the tears which they caused to flow, and saving the precious souls they were destroying, to come forward and take the public pledge of temperance by kissing a crucifix which I held in my hand. Thirteen hundred and ten came. Not fifty of the people had refused to enrol themselves under the blessed and glorious banners of temperance! and these few recalcitrants came forward, with a very few exceptions, the next time I spoke cn the subject.

The very same day, the wives of the merchants sent despatches to their husbands in Quebec, to tell them what had been done, and not a single barrel of intoxicating drinks was brought by them. The generous example of the admirable people of Kamouraska spoke with an irresistible eloquence to the other parishes of that district, and before long, the banners of temperance floated over all the populations of St. Pascal, St. Andrew, Isle Verte, Cacouna, Riviere du Loup, Rimouski, Matane, St. Anne, St. Roch, Madawaska, St. Benoit, St. Luce, etc., on the south side of the St. Lawrence, and the Eboulements, La Malbaye, and the other parishes on the north side of the river; and the people kept their pledge with such fidelity that the trade in rum was literally killed in that part of Canada, as it had been in Beauport and its vicinity.

The blessed fruits of this reform were soon felt and seen everywhere, in the public prosperity and the spread of education. Kamouraska, which was owing two hundred thousand dollars to the merchants in 1842, had not only paid its interest, but had reduced its debt to only one hundred thousand dollars, when I left it to go to Montreal in 1846. God only knows my joy at these admirable manifestations of His mercies towards my country. However, the joys of man are never without their mixture of sadness.

In the good providence of God, being invited by all the curates to establish temperance societies among their people, I had the sad opportunity, as no priest ever had in Canada, to know the secret and public scandals of each parish. When I went to the Eboulements, on the north side of the river, invited by the Rev. Noel Toussignant, I learned from the very lips of that young priest, and the ex-priest Tetreau, the history of the most shameful scandals.

In 1830, a young priest of Quebec, called Derome, had fallen in love with one of his young female penitents of Vercheres, where he had preached a few days, and he had persuaded her to follow him to the parsonage of Quebec. The better to conceal their iniquity from the public, he persuaded his victim to dress herself as a young man, and throw her dress into the river, to make her parents and the whole parish believe that she was drowned. I had seen her many times at the parsonage of Quebec, under the name of Joseph, and had much admired her refined manners, though more than once I was very much inclined to think that the smart Joseph was no one else than a lost girl. But the respect I had for the curate of Quebec (who was the coadjutor of the bishop) and his young vicars, caused me to reject those suspicions as unfounded. However, many even among the first citizens of the city had the same suspicions, and they pressed me to go to the coadjutor and warn him; but I refused, and told those gentlemen to do that delicate work themselves, and they did it.

The position of that high dignitary and his vicar was not then a very agreeable one. Their bark had evidently drifted into dangerous waters. To keep Joseph among themselves was impossible, after the friendly advice from such high quarters, and to dismiss him was not less dangerous. He knew too well how the curate of Quebec, with his vicars, were keeping their vows of celibacy, to dismiss him without danger to themselves; a single word from his lips would destroy them. Happily for them, Mr. Clement, then curate of the Eboulements, was in search of such a servant, and took him to his parsonage, after persuading the bishop-coadjutor to give Joseph a large sum of money to seal his lips.

Things went on pretty smoothly between Joseph and the priest for several years, till some suspicions arose in the minds of the sharp-sighted people of the parish, who told the curate that it would be safer and more honourable for him to get rid of his servant. In order to put an end to those suspicions, and to retain him in the parsonage, the curate persuaded him to marry the daughter of a poor neighbour.

The banns were published three times, and the two girls were duly married by the curate, who continued his criminal intimacies, in the hope that no one would trouble him any more on that subject. But not long after he was removed to La Petite Riviere, and in 1838 the Rev. M. Tetreau was appointed curate of the Eboulements. This new priest, knowing nothing of the abominations which his predecessor had practised, continued to employ Joseph. One day, when Joseph was working at the gate of the parsonage, in the presence of several people, a stranger came and asked him if Mr. Tetreau was at home.

"Yes, sir, Mr. Curate is at home," answered Joseph; "but as you seem a stranger to the place, would you allow me to ask you from what parish you come?"

"I am not ashamed of my parish," answered the stranger. "I come from Vercheres."

At the word "Vercheres," Joseph turned so pale that the stranger was puzzled. He looked carefully at him, and exclaimed:

"Oh! my God! What do I see here? Genevieve! Genevieve!

over whom we have mourned so long as drowned! Here you are disguised as a man!"

"Dear uncle" (it was her uncle); "for God's sake, not a word more here!"

But it was too late; the people who were there had heard the uncle and the niece. Their long and secret suspicions were well-founded. One of their former priests had kept a girl, under the disguise of a man, in his house; and to blind his people more thoroughly, he had married that girl to another, in order to have them both in his house when he pleased, without awakening any suspicion!

The news went, almost as quickly as lightning, from one end to the other of the parish, and spread all over the country, on both sides of the St. Lawrence. I had heard of that horror, but could not believe it. However, I had to believe it, when, on the spot, I heard from the lips of the ex-curate, M. Tetreau, and the new curate, M. Noel Toussignant, and from the lips of the landlord, the Honourable Laterriere, the following details, which had come to light only a short time before.

The justice of the peace had investigated the matter, in the name of public morality. Joseph was brought before the magistrates, who decided that a physician should be charged to make, not a *post-mortem*, but an *ante-mortem* inquest. The Honourable Laterriere, who made the inquest, declared that Joseph was a girl, and the bonds of marriage were legally dissolved.

At the same time, the curate M. Tetreau, had sent a dispatch to the Right Rev. Bishop-coadjutor of Quebec, informing him that the young man whom he had kept in his house, several years, was legally proved a girl; a fact which, I need hardly state, was well-known by the bishop and his vicars! They immediately sent a trustworthy man with £500, to induce the girl to leave the country without delay, lest she should be prosecuted and sent to the penitentiary. She accepted the offer, and crossed the lines to the United States with her two thousand dollars, where she was soon married, and where she still lives.

I wished that this story had never been told me, or at least, that I might be allowed to doubt some of its circumstances; but there was no help. I was forced to acknowledge that in my Church of Rome, there was such corruption from head to foot, which could scarcely be surpassed in Sodom. I remember what the Rev. Mr. Perras had told me of the tears and desolation of Bishop Plessis, when he had discovered that all the priests of Canada, with the exception of three, were atheists.

I should not be honest, did I not confess that the personal knowledge of that fact, which I learned in all its scandalous details from the very lips of unimpeachable witnesses, saddened me, and for a time, shook my faith in my religion, to its foundation. I felt secretly ashamed to belong to a body of men so completely lost to every sense of honesty, as the priests and bishops of Canada. I had heard of many scandals before. The infamies of the Grand Vicar Manceau and Quiblier of Montreal, Cadieux at Three Rivers, and Viau at Riviere Ouelle; the public acts of depravity of the priests Lelievre, Tabeau, Pouliot, Belisle, Brunet, Quevillon, Huot, Lajuste, Rabby, Crevier, Bellecourt, Valle, Mignault, Noel, Pinet, Duguez, Davely and many others, were known by me, as well as by the whole clergy. But the abominations of which Joseph was the victim seemed to overstep the conceivable limits of infamy. For the first time, I sincerely regretted that I was a priest. The priesthood of Rome seemed then, to me, the very fulfilment of the prophecy of Revelation, about the great prostitute who made the nations drunk with the wine of her prostitutions (Rev. xvii. 1—5).

Auricular confession, which I knew to be the first, if not the only cause, of these abominations, appeared to me, what it really is, a school of perdition for the priest and his female penitents. The priest's oath of celibacy was, to my eyes, in those hours of distress, but a shameful mask to conceal a corruption which was unknown in the most depraved days of old paganism. New and bright lights came, then, before my mind which, had I followed them, would have guided me to the truth of the gospel. But I was blind! The Good Master had not yet touched my eyes with His divine and life-giving hand. I had no idea that there could be any other church than the Church of Rome, in which I could be saved. I was, however, often saying to myself: "How can I hope to conquer on a battlefield where so many, as strong and even much stronger than I am, have perished?"

I felt no longer at peace. My soul was filled with trouble and anxiety. I not only distrusted myself, but I lost confidence in the rest of the priests and bishops. In fact, I could not see any one in whom I could trust. Though my beautiful and dear parish of Kamouraska was, more than ever, overwhelming me with tokens of its affection, gratitude, and respect, it had lost its attraction for me. To whatever side I turned my eyes, I saw nothing but the most seducing examples of perversion. It seemed as if I were surrounded by numberless snares, from which it was impossible to escape. I wished to depart from this deceitful and lost world.

When my soul was as drowned under the waves of a bitter sea, the Rev. Mr. Guignes, Superior of the Monastery of the Fathers of Oblates of Mary Immaculate, at Longueil, near Montreal, came to pass a few days with me, for the benefit of his health. I spoke to him of that shameful scandal, and did not conceal from him that my courage failed me, when I looked at the torrent of iniquity which was sweeping everything, under our eyes, with an irresistible force. " We are here alone, in the presence of God," I said to him. " I confess that I feel an unspeakable horror at the moral ruin which I see everywhere in our church. My priesthood, of which I was so proud till lately, seems to me, to-day, the most ignominious yoke, when I see it dragged in the mud of the most infamous vices, not only by the immense majority of the priests, but even by our bishops. How can I hope to save myself, when I see so many, stronger than I am, perishing all around me ?"

The Reverend Superior, with the kindness of a father and becoming gravity, answered me : " I understand your fears, perfectly. They are legitimate and too well-founded. Like you, I am a priest ; and like you, if not more than you, I know the numberless and formidable dangers which surround the priest. It is because I know them too well, that I have not dared to be a secular priest a single day. I knew the humiliating and disgraceful history of Joseph and the coadjutor Bishop of Quebec. Nay ! I know many things still more horrible and unspeakable which I have learned when preaching and hearing confessions in France and in Canada. My fear is that, to-day, there are not many more undefiled souls among the priests than in Sodom, in the days of Lot. The fact is, that it is morally impossible for a secular priest to keep his vows of celibacy, except by a miracle of the grace of God. Our holy church would be a modern Sodom long ago, had not our merciful God granted her the grace that many of her priests have always enrolled themselves among the armies of the regular priests in the different religious orders which are, to the church, what the ark was to Noah and his children in the days of the deluge. Only the priests whom God calls, in His mercy, to become members of any of those orders, are safe. For they are under the paternal care and surveillance of superiors whose zeal and charity are like a shield to protect them. Their holy and strict laws are like strong walls and high towers which the enemy cannot storm."

He then spoke to me, with an irresistible eloquence, of the peace of soul which a regu'ar priest enjoys within the walls of his monastery. He represented, in the most attractive colours, the spiritual and constant joys of the heart which one feels when living, day and night, under the eyes of a superior to whom he has vowed a perfect submission. He added, " Your providential work is finished in the diocese of Quebec. The temperance societies are established almost everywhere. We are in need of your long experience and your profound studies on that subject in the diocese of Montreal. It is true that the good Bishop de Nancy has done what he could to

support that holy cause, but, though he is working with the utmost
zeal, he has not studied that subject enough to make a lasting
impression on the people. Come with us. We are more than thirty
priests, Oblates of Mary Immaculate, who will be too happy to second
your efforts in that noble work, which is too much for one man alone.
Moreover, you cannot do justice to your great parish of Kamouraska
and to the temperance cause together. You must give up one, to
consecrate yourself to the other. Take courage, my young friend!
Offer to God the sacrifice of your dear Kamouraska, as you made the
sacrifice of your beautiful Beauport, some years ago, for the good of
Canada and in the interest of the Church, which calls you to its help."

It seemed to me that I could oppose no reasonable argument to
these considerations. I fell on my knees, and made the sacrifice of my
beautiful and precious Kamouraska. The last Sabbath of September
I gave my farewell address to the dear and intelligent people of
Kamouraska, to go to Longueil and become a novice of the Oblates of
Mary Immaculate.

CHAPTER XLI.

The year 1843 will be long remembered in the Church of Rome for the
submission of Dr. Newman to her authority. This was considered by
many Roman Catholics as one of the greatest triumphs ever gained by
their church against Protestantism. But some of us, more acquainted
with the daily contradictions and tergiversations of the Oxford divine,
could not associate ourselves in the public rejoicings of our church.

From almost the very beginning of his public life, Dr. Newman as
well as Dr. Pusey appeared to many of us as cowards and traitors in
the Protestant camp, whose object was to betray the church which was
feeding them, and which they were sworn to defend. They both
seemed to us to be skilful but dishonest conspirators.

Dr. Newman, caught in the very act of that conspiracy, has boldly
denied it. Brought before the tribunal of public opinion as a traitor
who, though enrolled under the banners of the Church of England,
was giving help and comfort to its foe, the Church of Rome, he has
published a remarkable book under the title of "Apologia pro vita
sua," to exculpate himself. I hold in my hands the New York edition
of 1865. Few men will read that book from beginning to end; and
still fewer will understand it at its first reading. The art of throwing
dust in the eyes of the public is brought to perfection in that work. I
have read many books in my long life, but I have never met with
anything like the Jesuit ability shown by Dr. Newman in giving a
colour of truth to the most palpable errors and falsehoods. I have
had to read it at least four times, with the utmost attention, before
being sure of having unlocked all its dark corners and sophistries.

That we may be perfectly fair towards Dr. Newman, let us forget what his adversaries have written against him, and let us hear only what he says in his own defence. Here it is. I dare say that his most bitter enemies could never have been able to write a book so damaging against him as this one, which he has given us for his apology.

Let me tell the reader at once that I, with many other priests of Rome, felt at first an unspeakable joy at the reading of many of the "Tracts for the Times." It is true that we keenly felt the blows Dr. Newman was giving us now and then; but we were soon consoled by the more deadly blows which he was striking at his own Church—the Church of England. Besides that, it soon became evident that the more he was advancing in his controversial work, the nearer he was coming to us. We were not long without saying to each other : "Dr. Newman is evidently, though secretly, for us; he is a Roman Catholic at heart, and will soon join us. It is only from want of moral courage and honesty that he remains a Protestant."

But from the very beginning there was a cloud in my mind, and in the minds of many other of my co-priests, about him. His contradictions were so numerous, his sudden transitions from one side to the other extreme, when speaking of Romanism and Anglicanism; his eulogiums of our Church to-day, and his abuses of it the very next day; his expressions of love and respect for his own Church in one tract, so suddenly followed by the condemnation of her dearest doctrines and practices in the next, caused many others, as well as myself, to suspect that he had no settled principles, or faith in any religion.

What was my surprise, when reading this strange book, I found that my suspicions were too well founded; that Dr. Newman was nothing else than one of those free-thinkers who had no real faith in any of the secret dogmas he was preaching, and on which he was writing so eloquently! What was my astonishment when, in 1865, I read in his own book the confession made by that unfortunate man that he was nothing else but a giant weathercock, when the whole people of England were looking upon him as one of the most sincere and learned ministers of the Gospel. Here is his own confession, pages 111, 112. Speaking of the years he had spent in the Episcopal Church as a minister, he says : "Alas! It was my portion, for whole years, to remain without any satisfactory basis for my religious profession; in a state of moral sickness, neither able to acquiesce in Anglicanism, nor able to go to Rome!" This is Cardinal Newman, painted by himself! He tells us how *miserable* he was when an Episcopalian minister, by feeling that his religion had no basis—no foundation!

What is a preacher of religion who feels that he has no basis, no foundation, no reason to believe in that religion? Is he not that blind man of whom Christ speaks, "who leads other blind men into the ditch?"

Note it is not Rev. Charles Kingsley; it is not any of the able Protestant controversialists; it is not even the old Chiniquy who says that Dr. Newman was nothing else but an unbeliever, when the Protestant people were looking upon him as one of their most pious and sincere Christian theologians. It is Dr. Newman himself who, without suspecting it, is forced by the marvellous providence of God to reveal that deplorable fact in his "Apologia pro vita sua."

Now, what was the opinion entertained by him of the high and low sections of his church? Here are his very words, p. 91: "As to the High Church and the Low Church, I thought that the one had not much more of a logical basis than the other; while I had a thorough contempt for the Evangelical!" But please observe that, when this minister of the Church of England had found, with the help of Dr. Pusey, that this church had no logical basis, and that he had a "thorough contempt for the Evangelical," he kept a firm and continuous hold upon the living which he was enjoying from day to day. Nay, it is when paid by his church to preach her doctrines and fight her battles, that he set at work to raise another church! Of course, the new church was to have a firm basis on logic, history, and the Gospel: the new church was to be worthy of the British people —it was to be the modern ark to save the perishing world!

The reader will, perhaps, think I am joking, and that I am caricaturing Dr. Newman. No! the hour in which we live is too solemn to be spent in jokes—it is rather with tears and sobs that we must approach the subject. Here are the very words of Dr. Newman about the new church he wished to build after demolishing the Church of England as established by law. He says (page 116): "I have said enough on what I consider to have been the general objects of the various works which I wrote, edited, or prompted in the years which I am reviewing. *I wanted to bring out in a substantive form a living Church of England, in a position proper to herself and founded on distinct principles; as far as paper could do it,* and as earnestly preaching it and influencing others towards it could tend to make it a fact; a living church, made of flesh and blood, with voice, complexion, motion, and action, and a will of its own." (The italics are mine.) If I had not said that these words were written by Dr. Newman, would the reader have suspected it?

What is to be the name of the new church? Dr. Newman himself has called it "Via Media." As the phrase indicates, it was to stand between the rival Churches of England and Rome, and it was to be built with the materials taken, as much as possible, from the ruins of both.

The first thing to be done was, then, to demolish that huge, illogical, unscriptural, unchristian church restored by the English Reformers. Dr. Newman bravely set to work, under the eye and direction of Dr. Pusey. His merciless hammer was heard almost day and night, from 1833 to 1843, striking alternately with hard blows, now against the church of the Pope, whom he called Antichrist, and then against his own church, which he was, very soon, to find still more corrupted and defiled than its anti-christian rival. For as he was proceeding in his work of demolition, he tells us that he found more clearly, every day, that the materials and the foundations of the Church of Rome were exceedingly better than those of his own. He then determined to give a *coup de grace* to the Church of England, and strike such a blow that her walls would be for ever pulverised. His perfidious Tract XC. aims at this object.

Nothing can surpass the ability and the pious cunning with which Dr. Newman tries to conceal his shameful conspiracy in his " Apologia."

Hear the un-British and unmanly excuses which he gives for having deceived his readers, when he was looked upon as the most reliable theologian of the day, in defence of the doctrines of the Church of England. In pages 236—7 he says : " How could I ever hope to make them believe in a second theology, when I had cheated them in the first ? With what face could I publish a new edition of a dogmatic creed, and ask them to receive it as gospel ? Would it not be plain to them that no certainty was to be found anywhere ? Well, in my defence I could but make a lame apology; however, it was the true one, viz., that I had not read the Fathers critically enough ; that in such nice points as those which determine the angle of divergence between the two churches, I had made considerable miscalculations ; and how came this about ? Why, the fact was, unpleasant as it was to avow, that I had leaned too much upon the assertions of Usher, Jeremy Taylor, or Barrow, and had been deceived by them."

Here is a specimen of the learning and honesty of the great Oxford divine ! Dr. Newman confesses that when he was telling his people, " St. Augustine says this, St. Jerome says that "—when he assured them that St. Gregory supported this doctrine, and Origen that, it was all false. Those holy fathers had never taught such doctrines. It was Usher, Taylor, and Barrow who were citing them, and they had deceived him !

Is it not a strange thing that such a shrewd man as Dr. Newman should have so completely destroyed his own good name in the very

book he wrote, with so much care and ingenuity, to defend himself?
One remains confounded—he can hardly believe his own eyes at such
want of honesty in such a man. It is evident that his mind was
troubled at the souvenir of such a course of procedure. But he wanted
to excuse himself by saying it was the fault of Usher, Taylor, and
Barrow!

Are we not forcibly brought to the solemn and terrible drama in
the Garden of Eden? Adam hoped to be excused by saying, "The
woman whom Thou gavest to be with me, she gave me the fruit of the
tree, and I did eat." The woman said, "The serpent beguiled me,
and I did eat." But what was the result of those excuses? We read:
"Therefore the Lord God sent him forth from the Garden of Eden."
Dr. Newman has lost the precious inheritance God had given him.
He has lost the lamp he had received to guide his steps, and he is now
in the dark dungeon of Popery, worshipping, as a poor slave, the wafer
god of Rome.

But what has become of that new church, or religion, the *Via
Media* which had just come out from the sickly brain of the Oxford
professor? Let us hear its sad and premature end from Dr. Newman
himself. Let me, however, premise, that when Dr. Newman began
his attack against his church, he at first so skilfully mixed the most
eloquent eulogiums with his criticisms, that, though many sincere
Christians were grieved, few dared to complain. The names of Pusey
and Newman commanded such respect that few raised their voice
against the conspiracy. This emboldened them. Month after month
they become unguarded in their denunciations of the Church of
England, and more explicit in their support of Romanism. In the
meantime the Church of Rome was reaping a rich harvest of perverts;
for many Protestants were unsettled in their faith, and were going the
whole length of the road to Rome so cunningly indicated by the conspirators. At last, the 90th Tract appeared in 1843. It fell as a
thunderbolt on the church. A loud cry of indignation was raised all
over England against those who had so mercilessly struck at the heart
of that church which they had sworn to defend. The bishops almost
unanimously denounced Dr. Newman and his Romish tendencies, and
showed the absurdity of his *Via Media*.

Now, let us hear him telling himself this episode of his life. For I
want to be perfectly fair to Dr. Newman. It is only from his own
words and public acts that I want the reader to judge him.

Here is what he says of himself, after being publicly condemned:
"I saw indeed clearly that my place in the movement was lost. Public
confidence was at an end. My occupation was gone. It was simply
an impossibility that I could say anything henceforth to good effect,
when I had been posted up by the Marshal on the buttery hatch of

every college of my University after the manner of discommoned pastry-cooks, and when, in every part of the country, and every class of society, through every organ and occasion of opinion, in news- papers, in periodicals, at meetings, in pulpits, at dinner tables, in coffee-rooms, in railway carriages, I was denounced as a traitor who had laid his train, and was detected in the very act of firing it against the time-honoured establishment." . . . . "Confidence in me was lost. But I had already lost full confidence in myself" (p. 132).

Let the reader hear these words from the very lips of Dr. Newman —" *Confidence in me was lost ! But I had already lost full confidence in myself*" (p. 132). Are these words the indications of a brave, innocent man ? Or are they not the cry of despair of a cowardly and guilty conscience ?

Was it not when Wishart heard that the Pope and his millions of slaves had condemned him to death, that he raised his head as a giant, and showed that he was more above his accusers and his judges than the heavens are above the earth ? Had he lost his confidence in him- self and in his God when he said, " I am happy to suffer and die for the cause of Truth ? " Did Luther lose confidence in himself and in his God when condemned by the Pope and all his Bishops, and ordered to go before the Emperor to be condemned to death, if he would not retract ? No ! it is in those hours of trial that he made the world to re-echo the sublime words of David : " God is our refuge and our strength, a present help in trouble. Therefore we will not fear, though the earth be removed, and though the mountains be carried into the midst of the sea. Though the waters thereof roar and be troubled, though the mountains shake with the swelling thereof." But Luther had a good cause. He knew, he felt that the God of Heaven was on his side, when Dr. Newman knew well that he was deceiving the world, after having deceived himself. Luther was strong and fearless ; for the voice of Jesus had come through the fifteen centuries to tell him : " Fear not, I am with thee." Dr. Newman was weak, trembling before the storm, for his conscience was reproaching him for his treachery and his unbelief.

Did Latimer falter and lose his confidence in himself and in his God, when condemned by his judges and tied to the stake to be burnt ? No ! It is then that he uttered those immortal and sublime words : " Master Ridley : Be of good comfort and play the man ; we shall, this day, light a candle, by God's grace, in England, as I trust shall never be put out ! "

This is the language of men who are fighting for Christ and His Gospel. Dr. Newman could not use such noble language when he was betraying Christ and His Gospel.

Now, let us hear from himself when, after having lost the confidence of his Church and his country, and had also lost his own confidence in himself, he saw a ghost and found that the Church of Rome was right. At page 157, he says: "My friend, an anxiously religious man, pointed out the palmary words of St. Augustine which were contained in one of the extracts made in the (Dublin) *Review,* and which had escaped my observation, 'Securus judicat orbis terrarum.' He repeated these words again and again; and when he was gone, they kept ringing in my ears. . . . The words of St. Augustine struck me with a power which I never had felt from any words before. To take a familiar instance, they were like the 'Turn again, Whittington.' of the chime; or to take a more serious one, they were like the 'tolle lege' of the child which converted St. Augustine himself. 'Securus judicat orbis terrarum!' By those great words of the ancient father, the theory of the *Via Media* was absolutely pulverised. I became excited at the view thus opened upon me. . . . I had seen the shadow of a hand upon the wall. . . . He who has seen a ghost cannot be as if he had never seen it. The heaven had opened and closed again. The thought, for the moment, had been: 'The Church of Rome will be found right, after all'" (158).

It would be amusing, indeed, if it were not so humiliating, to see the *naivete* with which Dr. Newman confesses his own aberrations, want of judgment and honesty in reference to the pet scheme of his whole theological existence at Oxford. "By these words," he says, "the *Via Media* was absolutely pulverised!"

We all know the history of the mountain in travail, which gave birth to a mouse. Dr. Newman tells us frankly that, after ten years of hard and painful travail, he produced something less than a mouse. His *Via Media* was pulverised; it turned to be only a handful of dust.

Remember the high sounding of his trumpet about his plan of a new church, that New Jerusalem on earth, the church of the future, which was to take the place of his rotten Church of England. Let me repeat to you his very words about that new ark of salvation with which the professor of Oxford was to save the world. (Page 116): "I wanted to bring out, in a substantive form, a living Church of England, in a position proper to herself and founded on distinct principles, as far as paper could do it, and as earnestly preaching it and influencing others towards it could tend to make it a fact; a living church, made of flesh and blood, with voice, complexion, and motion, and action, and a will of its own."

Now, what was the end of that masterpiece of theological architecture of Dr. Newman? Here is its history, given by the great architect himself: "I read the palmary words of St. Augustine, '*Securus judicat orbis terrarum!*' By those great words of the ancient father, the theory of the *Via Media* was pulverised! I become excited at the view thus opened before me. I had seen the shadow of a hand on the wall. He who has seen a ghost can never be as if he had not seen it; the heavens had opened and closed again. The thought, for a moment, was 'The Church of Rome will be found right, after all'" (158). Have we ever seen a man destroying himself more completely at the very moment that he tries to defend himself? Here he does ingeniously confess what everyone knew before, that his whole work, for the last ten years, was not only a self-deception, but a supreme effort to deceive the world—his *Via Media* was a perfect string of infidelity, sophism, and folly. The whole fabric had fallen to the ground at the sight of a ghost! To build a grand structure, in the place of his Church which he wanted to demolish, he had thought it was sufficient to throw a great deal of glittering sand, with some blue, white, and red dust, in the air! He tells us that one sad hour came when he heard five Latin words from St. Augustine, saw a ghost—and his great structure fell to the ground!!

What does this all mean? It simply means that God Almighty has dealt with Dr. Newman as He did with the impious Pharaoh in the Red Sea, when he was marching at the head of his army against the church of old, His chosen people, to destroy them.

Dr. Newman was not only marching with Dr. Pusey at the head of an army of theologians to destroy the Church of God, but he was employing all the resources of his intellect, all his false and delusive science, to raise an idolatrous church in its place; and when Pharaoh and Dr. Newman thought themselves sure of success, the God of heaven confounded them both. The first went down with his army to the bottom of the sea as a piece of lead. The second lost, not his life, but something infinitely more precious—he lost his reputation for intelligence, science, and integrity; he lost the light of the Gospel, and became perfectly blind, after having lost his place in the kingdom of Christ!

I have never judged a man by the hearsay of any one, and I would prefer to have my tongue cut out than to repeat a word of what the adversaries of Dr. Newman have said against him. But we have the right, and I think it is our duty, to hear and consider what he says of himself, and to judge him on his own confession.

At page 174 we read these words from his own pen to a friend: "I cannot disguise from myself that my preaching is not calculated to defend that system of religion which has been received for three hundred years, and of which the Heads of Houses are the legitimate maintainers in this place. . . . . I fear I must allow that, whether I will or no, I am disposing them (the young men) towards Rome." Here Dr. Newman declares, in plain English, that he was disposing his hearers and students at Oxford to join the Church of Rome! I ask it : what can we think of a man who is paid and sworn to do a thing, who not only does it not, but who does the very contrary? Who would hesitate to call such a man dishonest? Who would hesitate to say that such a one has no respect for those who employ him, and no respect for himself?

Dr. Newman writes this whole book to refute the public accusation that he was a traitor, that he was preparing the people to leave the Church of England and to submit to the Pope. But, strange to say, it is in that very book we find the irrefutable proof of his shameful and ignominious treachery! In a letter to Dr. Russell, President of the Roman Catholic College of Maynooth, he wrote, page 227 : "Roman Catholics will find this to be the state of things in time to come, whatever promise they may fancy there is of a large secession to their church. This man or that may leave us, but there will be no general movement. There is, indeed, an incipient movement of our church towards yours, and this your leading men are doing all they can to frustrate by their unwearied efforts, at all risks, to carry off individuals. When will they know their position, and embrace a larger and wiser policy?" Is it not evident here that God was blinding Dr. Newman, and that He was making him confess his treachery in the very moment that he was trying to conceal it? Do we not see clearly that he was complaining of the unwise policy of the leaders of the Church of Rome who were retarding *that incipient movement* of his church towards Romanism, for which he was working day and night with Dr. Pusey?

But had not Dr. Newman confessed his own treachery, we have, to-day, its undeniable proof in the letter of Dr. Pusey to the English Church Union, written in 1879. Speaking of Dr. Newman and the other Tractarians, he says : " An acute man, Dr. Hawkins, Provost of Oriel, said of the 'Tracts,' on their first appearance, 'I know they have a forced circulation.' We put the leaven into the meal, and waited to see what would come of it. Our object was to Catholicise England."

And this confession of Dr. Pusey, that he wanted to Catholicise England, is fully confirmed by Dr. Newman (pages 108, 109) where he says : "I suspect it was Dr. Pusey's influence and example which set me and made me set others on the larger and more careful works in defence of the principles of the movement which followed " (towards Rome) " in a course of years."

Nothing is more curious than to hear from Dr. Newman himself with what skill he was trying to conceal his perfidious efforts in preparing that movement towards Rome. He says on that subject, page 124 : " I was embarrassed in consequence of my wish to go as far as was possible in interpreting the articles in the direction of Roman dogma, without disclosing what I was doing to

19

the parties whose doubts I was meeting, who might be, thereby, encouraged to go still further than, at present, they found in themselves any call to do."

A straw fallen on the water indicates the way the tide goes. Here we have the straw, taken by Dr. Newman himself, and thrown by him on the water. A thousand volumes written by the ex-Professor of Oxford to deny that he was a conspirator at work to lead his people to Rome, when in the service of the Church of England, could not destroy the evident proof of his guilt given by himself in this strange book.

If we want to have a proof of the supreme contempt Dr. Newman had for his readers, and his daily habit of deceiving them by sophistries and incorrect assertions, we have it in the remarkable lines which I find at page 123 of his *Apologia*. Speaking of his " Doctrinal Development," he says: "I wanted to ascertain what was the limit of that elasticity in the direction of Roman dogma. But, next, I had a way of inquiry of my own which I state without defending. I instanced it afterward in my essay on 'Doctrinal Development.' That work, I believe, I have not read since I published it, and I doubt not at all that I have made many mistakes in it, partly from my ignorance of the details of doctrine as the Church of Rome holds them, but partly from my impatience to clear as large a range for the *Principles* of doctrinal development (waiving the question of historical *fact*) as was consistent with the strict apostolicity and identity of the Catholic creed. In like manner, as regards the Thirty Nine Articles, my method of inquiry was to leap *in medias res* " (123-124).

Dr. Newman is the author of two new systems of theology; and, from his own confession, the two systems are a compendium of error, absurdities, and folly. His *Via Media* was "pulverised" by the vision of a ghost, when he heard the four words of St. Augustine: "*Securus judicat orbis terrarum.*" The second, known under the name of " Doctrinal Development," is, from his own confession, full of errors on account of his ignorance of the subject on which he was writing, and his own impatience to support his sophisms.

Dr. Newman is really unfortunate in his paternity. He is the father of two literary children. The first-born was called *Via Media;* but as it had neither head nor feet, it was suffocated on the day of its birth by a " ghost." The second, called " Doctrinal Development," was not *viable*. The father is so shocked with the sight of the monster, that he publicly confesses its deformities and cries out, " Mistake! mistake! mistake! " (pages 123, 124 " *Apologia pro vita sua.*")

The troubled conscience of Dr. Newman has forced him to confess (page 111) that he was miserable, from his want of faith, when a minister of the Church of England and a Professor of Theology of Oxford: "Alas! it was my portion for whole years to remain without any satisfactory basis for my religious profession!" At pages 174 and 175 he tells us how miserable and anxious he was when the voice of his conscience reproached him in the position he held in the Church of England, while leading her people to Rome. At page 158 he confesses his unspeakable confusion when he saw his supreme folly in building up the *Via Media*, and heard its crash at the appearance of a ghost. At page 123 he acknowledges how he deceived his readers, and deceived himself, in his "Doctrinal Development." At page 132 he tells us how he had not only completely lost the confidence of his country, but lost confidence in himself. And it is after this humiliating and shameful course of life that he finds out "that the Church of Rome is right!"

Must we not thank God for having forced Dr. Newman to tell us through what dark and tortuous ways a Protestant, a disciple of the Gospel, a minister of Christ, a Professor of Oxford, fell into that sea of Sodom called Romanism or Papism! A great lesson is given us here. We see the fulfilment of Christ's words about those who have received great talents and have not used them for the " Good Master's honour and glory."

Dr. Newman, without suspecting it, tells us that it was his course of action towards that branch of the Church of Christ of which he was a minister, that caused him to lose the confidence of his country, and troubled him so much that it caused him to lose that self-confidence which is founded on our faith and our union with Christ, who is our rock, our only strength in the hour of trial. Having lost her sails, her anchor, and her helm, the poor ship was evidently doomed to become a wreck. Nothing could prevent her from drifting into the engulfing abyss of Popery.

Dr. Newman confesses that it is only when his guilty conscience was uniting its thundering voice with that of his whole country to condemn him that he said, "After all, the Church of Rome is right!"

These are the arguments, the motives, the lights which have led Dr. Newman to Rome! And it is from himself that we have it! It is a just, an avenging God who forces His adversary to glorify Him and say the truth in spite of himself in this "*Apologia pro vita sua.*"

No one can read that book, written almost with a superhuman skill, ability, and fineness, without a feeling of unspeakable sadness at the sight of such bright talents, such eloquence, such extensive studies, employed by the author to deceive himself and deceive his readers; for it is evident, on every page, that Dr. Newman has deceived himself before deceiving his readers. But no one can read that book without feeling a sense of terror also. For he will hear, at every page, the thundering voice of the God of the Gospel, "Because they received not the love of the truth that they might be saved, God shall send them strong delusions, that they should believe a lie " (2 Thess. ii. 10—11).

What, at first, most painfully puzzles the mind of the Christian reader of this book is the horror which Dr. Newman has for the Holy Scriptures. The unfortunate man who is perishing from hydrophobia does not keep himself more at a distance from water than he does from the Word of God. It seems incredible, but it is the fact, that from the first page of the history of his "Religious Opinions" to page 261, where he joins the Church of Rome, we have not a single line to tell us that he has gone to the Word of God for light and comfort in his search after truth. We see Dr. Newman at the feet of Daniel Wilson, Scott, Milner, Whately, Hawkins, Blanco White, William James, Butler, Keble, Froude, Pusey, etc., asking them what to believe, what to do to be saved; but you do not see him a single minute, no, not a single minute, at the feet of the Saviour, asking him, "Master, what must I do to have 'Eternal Life'?" The sublime words of Peter to Christ, which are filling all the echoes of heaven and earth, these eighteen hundred years, "Lord! to whom shall we go? Thou hast the words of eternal life!" have never reached his ears! In the long and gloomy hours, when his soul was chilled and trembling in the dark night of infidelity; when his uncertain feet were tired by vainly going here and there, to find the true way, he has never heard Christ telling him: "Come unto Me. I am the Way; I am the Door; I am the Life!" In those terrible hours of distress of which he speaks so eloquently, when he cries (page 111) "Alas, I was without any basis for my religious profession, in a state of moral sickness: neither able to acquiesce in Anglicanism, nor able to go to Rome:" when his lips were parched with thirst after truth, he never, no never, went to the fountain from which flow the waters of eternal life!

One day he goes to the Holy Fathers. But what will he find there? Will he see how St. Cyprian sternly rebuked the impudence of Stephen, Bishop of Rome, who pretended to have some jurisdiction over the See of Carthage? Will he find how Gregory positively says that the Bishop who will pretend to be the "Universal Bishop" is the forerunner of Antichrist? Will he hear St. Augustine declaring that when Christ said to Peter, "Thou art Peter, and upon this rock I will build my Church," He was speaking of Himself as the rock upon which the Church would stand? No. The only thing which Dr. Newman brings us from the Holy Fathers is so ridiculous and so unbecoming that I am ashamed to have to repeat it. He tells us (page 78), "I have an idea. The mass of the Fathers (Justin, Athenagoras, Irenæus, Clement, Tertullian, Origen, Ambrose) hold that, though Satan fell from the beginning, the angels fell before the deluge, falling in love with the daughters of men. This has lately come across me as a remarkable solution of a notion I cannot help holding."

Allow me here to remind the reader that, though the Fathers have written many beautiful evangelical pages, some of them have written the greatest nonsense and the most absurd things which human folly can imagine. Many of them were born and educated as pagans. They had learned and believed the history and immorality of their demi-gods; they had brought those notions with them into the Church; and they had attributed to the angels of God, the passions and love for women which was one of the most conspicuous characters of Jupiter, Mars, Cupid, Bacchus, etc. And Dr. Newman, whose want of accuracy and judgment is so often revealed and confessed by him in this book, has not been able to see that those sayings of the Fathers were nothing but human aberrations. He has accepted that as Gospel truth, and he has been silly enough to boast of it.

The bees go to the flowers to make their precious honey; they wisely choose what is more perfect, pure and wholesome in the flowers to feed themselves. Dr. Newman does the very contrary; he goes to those flowers of past ages, the Holy Fathers, and takes from them what is impure for his food. After this, is it a wonder that he has so easily put his lips to the cup of the great enchantress who is poisoning the world with the wine of her prostitution?

When the reader has followed with attention the history of the religious opinions of Dr. Newman in his " *Apologia pro vita sua*," and he sees him approaching, day after day, the bottomless abyss of folly, corruption, slavery, and idolatry of Rome, into which he suddenly falls (page 261), he is forcibly reminded of the strange spectacle recorded in the eloquent pages of Chateaubriand, about the Niagara Falls.

More than once, travellers standing at the foot of that marvel of the marvels of the works of God, looking up towards heaven, have been struck by the sight of a small, dark spot moving in large circles, at a great distance above the fall. Gazing at that strange object, they soon remarked, that in its circular march in the sky, the small dark spot was rapidly growing larger, as it was coming down towards the thundering fall. They soon discovered the majestic form of one of the giant eagles of America! And the eagle, balancing himself in the air, seemed to looked down on the marvellous fall as if absolutely taken with admiration at its grandeur and magnificence! For some time, the giant of the air remained above the majestic cataract describing his large circles. But when coming down nearer and nearer the terrific abyss, he was suddenly dragged as by an irresistible power into the bottomless abyss to disappear. Some time later the body, bruised and lifeless, is seen floating on th rapid and dark waters, to be for ever lost in the bitter waters of the sea, at a long distance below.

Rome is a fall. It is the name which God Himself has given her: "There come a falling away" (2 Thess. ii. 3). As the giant eagle of America, when imprudently coming too near the mighty Fall of Niagara, is often caught in the irresistible vortex which attracts it from a long distance, so that eagle of Oxford, Dr. Newman, whom God had created for better things, has imprudently come too near the terrific papal fall. He has been enchanted by its beauty, its thousand bright rainbows : he has taken for real suns the fantastic jets of light which encircle its misty head, and conceal its dark and bottomless abyss. Bewildered by the bewitching voice of the enchantress, he has been unable to save himself from her perfidious and almost irresistible attractions. The eagle of Oxford has been caught in the whirlpool of the engulfing powers of Rome, and you see him to-day, bruised, lifeless, dragged on the dark waters of Popery towards the shore of a still darker eternity.

Dr. Newman could not make his submission to Rome without perjuring himself. He swore that he would never interpret the Holy Scriptures except according to the unanimous consent of the Holy Fathers. Well, I challenge him here, to meet me and show me that the Holy Fathers are unanimous on the supremacy of the power of the Pope over the other bishops ; that he is infallible ; that the priest has the power to make his God with a wafer ; that the Virgin Mary is the only hope of sinners. I challenge him to show us that auricular confession is an ordinance of Christ. Dr. Newman knows well that those things are impostures. He has never believed, he never will believe them.

The fact is that Dr. Newman confesses that he never had any faith when he was a minister of the Church of England ; and it is clear that he is the same since he became a Roman Catholic. In page 282 we read this strange exposition of his faith : " We are called upon not to profess anything, but to submit and be silent," which is just the faith of the mute animal which obeys the motion of the bridle, without any resistance or thought of its own. This is—I cannot deny it—the true, the only faith in the Church of Rome ; it is the faith which leads directly to Atheism or idiotism. But Christ gave us a very different idea of the faith He asks from His disciples when He said : " The hour cometh, and now is, when the true worshippers shall worship the Father in spirit and in truth " (John iv. 23).

That degrading and brutal religion of Dr. Newman surely was not the religion of Paul, when he wrote, " I speak as to wise men ; judge ye what I say " (1 Cor. x. 15). Dr. Newman honestly tells us (page 228), when speaking of the worship of the Virgin Mary :

" Such devotional manifestations in honour of our Lady had been my great *Crux* as regards Catholicism. I say frankly I do not fully enter into them now . . . they are suitable for Italy, but are not suitable for England." He has only changed his appearance—his heart is what it was formerly, when a minister of the Church of England. He wanted then another creed, another Church for England. So now, he finds that this and that practice of Rome may do for the Italians, but not for the English people !

Was he pleased with the promulgation of Papal infallibility ? No. It is a public fact that one of his most solemn actions, a few years since his connection with the Church of Rome, was to protest against the promulgation of that dogma. More than that, be expressed his doubts about the wisdom and the right of the Council to proclaim it.

Let us read his interesting letter to Bishop Ullathorne—" Rome ought to be a name to lighten the heart at all times; and a council's proper office is, when some great heresy or other evil impends, to inspire hope and confidence in the faithful. But now we have the greatest meeting which ever has been, and that at Rome, infusing into us by the accredited organs of Rome and of its partisans (such as the *Civilta*, the *Armonia*, the *Univers*, and the *Tablet*) little else than fear and dismay ! When we are all at rest and have no doubts, and—at least practically, not to say doctrinally—hold the Holy Father to be infallible, suddenly there is thunder in the clear sky, and we are told to prepare for something, we know not what, to try our faith, we know not how—no impending danger is to be averted, but a great difficulty is to be created. Is this the proper work of an Œcumenical Council ? As to myself personally, please God, I do not expect any trial at all : but I cannot help suffering with the many souls who are suffering, and I look with anxiety at the prospect of having to defend decisions which may not be difficult to my own private judgment, but may be most difficult to maintain logically in the face of historical facts.

" What have we done to be treated as the faithful never were treated before ? When has a definition *de fide* been a luxury of devotion, and not a stern, painful necessity ? Why should an aggressive, insolent faction be allowed to ' make the heart of the just sad, whom the Lord hath not made sorrowful ? ' Why cannot we be let alone, when we have pursued peace, and thought no evil !

" I assure you, my Lord, some of the truest minds are driven one way and another, and do not know where to rest their feet—one day determining ' to give up all theology as a bad job,' and recklessly to believe henceforth almost that the Pope is impeccable : at another, tempted to ' believe all the worst which a book like *Janus* says :' others doubting about ' the capacity possessed by bishops drawn from corners of the earth, to judge what is fitting for European society'; and then, again, angry with the Holy See for listening to 'the flattery of a clique of Jesuits, redemptorists, and converts.'

"Then, again, think of the store of Pontifical scandals in the history of eighteen centuries, which have partly been poured forth and partly are still to come. What Murphy inflicted upon us in one way, M. Veuillot is indirectly bringing on us in another. And then, again, the blight which is falling upon the multitude of Anglican Ritualists, etc., who, themselves, perhaps—at least, their leaders—may never become Catholics, but who are leavening the various English denominations and parties (far beyond their own range), with principles and sentiments tending towards their ultimate absorption into the Catholic Church.

"With these thoughts ever before me, I am continually asking myself whether I ought not to make my feelings public: but all I do is to pray those early doctors of the Church whose intercession would decide the matter (Augustine, Ambrose, and Jerome, Athanasius, Chrysostom, and Basil) to avert this great calamity.

"If it is God's will that the Pope's infallibility be defined, then is it God's will to throw back 'the times and movements' of that triumph which He has destined for His kingdom, and I shall feel I have but to bow my head to His adorable, inscrutable providence.

"You have not touched upon the subject yourself, but I think you will allow me to express to you feelings, which, for the most part, I keep to myself."*

These eloquent complaints of the new convert exceedingly irritated Pius IX. and the Jesuits at Rome: they entirely destroyed their confidence in him. They were too shrewd to ignore that he had never been anything else but a kind of free-thinker, whose Christian faith was without any basis, as he has himself confessed. They had received him, of course, with pleasure, for he was the very best man in England to unsettle the minds of the young ministers of the Church, but they had left him alone in his oratory of Birmingham, where they seemed to ignore him.

However, when the protest of the new so-called convert showed that his submission was but a sham, and that he was more Protestant than ever, they lashed him without mercy. But before we hear the stern answers of the Roman Catholics to their new recruit, let us remember the fact that when that letter appeared, Dr. Newman had lost the memory of it; he boldly denied its paternity at first; it was only when the proofs were publicly given that he had written it,

---

* "The Pope, the Kings, and the People " (Mullan & Son, Paternoster Square), pp. 269-70.   Also see (London) *Standard*, 7th April, 1870.

that he acknowledged it, saying for his excuse that he had forgotten his writing it!!

Now let us hear the answer of the *Civilta*, the organ of the Pope, to Dr. Newman: "Do you not see that it is only temptation that makes you see everything black? If the holy doctors whom you invoke, Ambrose, Jerome, etc., do not decide the controversy in your way, it is not, as the Protestant *Pall Mall Gazette* fancies, because they will not or cannot interpose, but because they agree with St. Peter and with the petition of the majority. Would you have us make procession in sackcloth and ashes to avert this scourge of the definition of a verity?" (*Ibid.*, p. 271).

The clergy of France, through their organ *L'Univers* (Vol. II., pp. 31—34), were still more severe and sarcastic. They had just collected £4,000 to help Dr. Newman to pay the enormous expenses of the suit for his slanders against Father Achilli, which he had lost.

Dr. Newman, as it appears by the article from the pen of the celebrated editor of the *Univers*, had not even had the courtesy to acknowledge the gift, nor the exertions of those who had collected that large sum of money. Now let us see what they thought and said in France about the ex-professor of Oxford whom they called the "Respectable convict." Speaking of the £4,000 sent from France, Veuillot says: "The respectable convict received it, and was pleased; but he gave no thanks and showed no courtesy. Father Newman ought to be more careful in what he says: everything that is comely demands it of him. But, at any rate, if his Liberal passion carries him away, till he forgets what he owes to us and to himself, what answer must one give him, but that he had better go on as he set out, silently ungrateful." (*L'Univers*, Vol. II., pp. 32—34; *Ibid.*, p. 272).

These public rebukes, addressed from Paris and Rome by the two most popular organs of the Church of Rome, tell us the old story; the services of traitors may be accepted, but they are never trusted. Father Newman had not the confidence of the Roman Catholics.

But some will say: "Has not the dignity of Cardinal, to which he has lately been raised, proved that the present Pope has the greatest confidence in Dr. Newman?"

Had I not been twenty-five years a priest of Rome, I would say "Yes!" But I know too much of their tactics for that. The dignity of Cardinal has been given to Drs. Manning and Newman as the baits which the fishermen of Prince Edward Island throw into the sea to attract the mackerels. The Pope, with those long scarlet robes thrown over the shoulders of the two renegades from the Church of England, hopes to catch more English mackerel.

Besides that, we all know the remarkable words of St. Paul:

"And those members of the body which we think to be less honourable, upon these we bestow more abundant honour, and our uncomely parts have more abundant comeliness" (1 Cor. xii. 23).

It is on that principle that the Pope has acted. He knew well that Dr. Newman had played the act of a traitor at Oxford, that he had been caught in the very act of conspiracy by his Bishops, that he had entirely lost the confidence of the English people. These public facts paralysed the usefulness of the new convert. He was really a member of the Church of Rome, but he was one of the most uncomely ones; so much so that the last Pope, Pius IX., had left him alone, in a dark corner, for nearly eighteen years. Leo XIII. was more shrewd. He felt that Newman might become one of the most powerful agents of Romanism in England, if he were only covering his uncomeliness with the rich red Cardinal robe.

But will the scarlet colours which now clothe Dr. Newman make us forget that, to-day, he belongs to the most absurd, immoral, abject, and degrading form of idolatry the world has ever seen? Will we forget that Romanism, these last six centuries, is nothing else but old paganism in its most degrading forms, coming back under a Christian name? What is the divinity which is adored in those splendid temples of modern Rome? Is it anything else but the old Jupiter Tonans! Yes, the Pope has stolen the old gods of paganism, and he has sacrilegiously written the adorable name of Jesus in their faces, that the deluded modern nations may have less objection to accept the worship of their pagan ancestors. They adore a Christ in the Church of Rome: they sing beautiful hymns to His honour: they build Him magnificent temples; they are exceedingly devoted to Him—they make daily enormous sacrifices to extend His power and glory all over the world. But what is that Christ? It is simply an idol of bread, baked every day by the servant-girl of the priest, or the neighbouring nuns.

I have been twenty-five years one of the most sincere and zealous priests of that Christ. I have made Him with mine own hands, and the help of my servants, for a quarter of a century; I have a right to say that I know Him perfectly well. It is that I may tell what I know of that Christ that the God of the Gospel has taken me by the hand, and granted me to give my testimony before the world. Hundreds of times I have said to my servant-girl what Dr. Newman and all the priests of Rome say, every day, to their own servants or their nuns: "Please make me some wafers, that I may say mass and give the communion to those who want to receive it." And the dutiful girl took some wheat flour, mixed it with water, and put the dough between these two well-polished and engraven irons, which she had well heated before. In less time than I can write it, the dough was baked into wafers. Handing them to me, I brought them to the altar, and performed a ceremony which is called "the mass." In the very midst of that mass, I pronounced on that wafer five magic words, "*Hoc est enim corpus meum,*" and had to believe, what Dr. Newman and all the priests of Rome profess to believe, that there were no more wafers, no more bread before me, but that what were wafers, had been turned into the great Eternal God who had created the world. I had to prostrate myself, and ask my people to prostrate themselves before the god I had just made with five words from my lips; and the people, on their knees, bowing their heads, and bringing their faces to the dust, adored god whom I had just made, with the help of these heated irons and my servant-girl.

Now, is this not a form of idolatry more degrading, more insulting to the infinite majesty of God than the worship of the gold calf? Where is the difference between the idolatry of Aaron and the Israelites adoring the gold calf in the wilderness and the idolatry of Dr. Newman adoring the wafer in his temple? The only difference is, that Aaron worshipped a god infinitely more respectable and powerful, in melted gold, than Dr. Newman worshipping his baked dough.

The idolatry of Dr. Newman is more degrading than the idolatry of the worshippers of the sun.

When the Persians adore the sun, they give their homage to the greatest, the most glorious being which is before us. That magnificent fiery orb, millions of miles in circumference, which rises as a giant, every morning, from behind the horizon, to march over the world and pour everywhere its floods of heat, light and life, cannot be contemplated without feelings of respect, admiration, and awe. Man must raise his eyes up to see that glorious sun—he must take the eagle's wings to follow his giant strides throughout the myriads of worlds which are there, to speak to us of the wisdom, the power, and love of our God. It is easy to understand that poor, fallen, blind men may take that great being for their god. Would not every one perish and die, if the sun would forget to come every day, that we may bathe and swim in his ocean of light and life?

Then, when I see the Persian priests of the sun, in their magnificent temple, with censers in their hands, waiting for the appearance of its first rays, to intone their melodious hymns and sing their sublime canticles, I know their error and I understand it; I was about to say, I almost excuse it. I feel an immense compassion for these deluded idolaters. However, I feel they are raised above the dust of the earth : their intelligence, their souls cannot but receive some sparks of light and life from the contemplation of that inexhaustible focus of light and life. But is not Dr. Newman with his Roman Catholic people a thousand times more worthy of our compassion and our tears, when they are abjectly prostrated before this ignoble wafer—to adore it as their Saviour, their Creator, their God? Is it possible to imagine a spectacle more humiliating, blasphemous, and sacrilegious, than a multitude of men and women prostrating their faces to the dust to adore a god whom the rats and mice have, thousands of times, dragged and eaten in their dark holes? Where are the rays of light and life coming from that wafer? Instead of being enlarged and elevated at the approach of this ridiculous modern divinity, is not the human intelligence contracted, diminished, paralysed, chilled, and struck with idiocy and death at its feet?

Can we be surprised that the Roman Catholic nations are so fast falling into the abyss of infidelity and atheism, when they hear their priests telling them that more than 200,000 times, every day, this contemptible wafer is changed by them into the great God who has created heaven and earth at the beginning, and who has saved this perishing world by sacrificing the body and the blood which He has taken as His tabernacle to show us His eternal love!

Come with me and see those multitudes of people with their faces prostrated in the dust, adoring their white elephant of Siam.

Oh! what ignorance and superstition! what blindness and folly! you will exclaim. To adore a white elephant as God!

But there is a spectacle more humiliating and more deplorable: there is a superstition, an idolatry below that of the Siamese. It is the idolatry practised by Dr. Newman and his millions of co-religionists to-day. Yes! The elephant god of the Asiatic people is infinitely more respectable than the wafer god of Dr. Newman. That elephant may be taken as the symbol of strength, magnanimity, patience, etc. There is life, motion in that noble animal—he sees with his eyes, he walks with his feet. Let some one attack him, he will protect himself—with his mighty trunk he will throw his enemy high in the air—he will crush him under his feet.

But look at this modern divinity of Rome. It has eyes, but does not see; feet, but does not move; a mouth, but does not speak. There is neither life nor strength in the wafer god of Rome.

But if the fall of Dr. Newman into the bottomless abyss of the idolatry of Rome is a deplorable fact, there is another fact still more deplorable.

How many fervent Christians, how many venerable ministers of Christ everywhere, are, just now, prostrated at the dear Saviour's feet, telling Him with tears: "Didst Thou not sow the good Gospel seed all over our dear country, through the hands of our heroic and martyred fathers? From whence, then, hath it these Popish and idolatrous tares?" And the "Good Master" answers, to-day, what He answered eighteen hundred years ago: "While men slept, the enemy came during the night; he has sowed those tares among the wheat, and he went away" (Matthew xiii. 25).

And if you want to know the name of the enemy who has sowed tares, in the night, amongst the wheat, and went away, you have only to read this "*Apologia pro vita sua.*" You will find this confession of Dr. Newman at page 174 : —

"I cannot disguise from myself that my preaching is not calculated to defend that system of religion which has been received for three hundred years, and of which the Heads of Houses are the legitimate maintainers in this place. . . . I must allow that I was disposing 'the minds of young men' towards Rome!"

Now, having obtained from the very enemy's lips how he has sowed tares during the night (secretly), read page 262, and you will see how he went away and prostrated himself at the feet of the most implacable enemy of all the rights and liberties of men, to call him "Most Holy Father." Read how he fell at the knees of the very power which prepared and blessed the Armada destined to cover his native land, England, with desolation, ruins, tears and blood, and enchain those of her people who would not have been slaughtered on the battle-field! See how the enemy, after having sown the tares, went away to the feet of a Sergius III., the public lover of Marozia— and to the feet of his bastard, John XI., who was still more debauched than his father—and to the feet of Leo VI., killed by an outraged citizen of Rome, in the act of such an infamous crime that I cannot name it here—to the feet of an Alexander, who seduced his own daughter, and surpassed in cruelty and debauchery Nero and Caligula. Let us see Dr. Newman falling at the feet of all these monsters of depravity, to call them, "Most Holy Fathers," "Most Holy Heads of the Church," "Most Holy and Infallible Vicars of Jesus Christ!"

At the sight of such a fall, what can we do, but say with Isaiah :

"The Lord has broken the staff of the wicked, and the sceptre of the ruler. . . . How art thou fallen, O Lucifer, Son of the morning! how art thou cut down to the ground?" (Is. xiv.)

CHAPTER XLII.

On the first Sabbath of November, 1846, after a retreat of eight days, I fell on my knees, and asked as a favour, to be received as a novice of the religious order of the Oblates of Mary Immaculate of Longueuil, whose object is to preach retreats (revivals) among the people. No child of the Church of Rome ever enrolled himself with more earnest-ness and sincerity under the mysterious banners of her monastic armies than I did, that day. It is impossible to entertain more exalted views of the beauty and holiness of the monastic life, than I had. To live among the holy men who had made the solemn vows of poverty, obedience, and chastity, seemed to me the greatest and the most blessed privilege which my God could grant on earth.

Within the walls of the peaceful monastery of Longueuil, among those holy men who had, long since, put an impassable barrier between themselves and that corrupted world, from the snares of which I was just escaping, my conviction was that I should see nothing but actions of the most exalted piety; and that the deadly weapons of the enemy could not pierce those walls protected by the Immaculate Mother of God!

The frightful storms which had covered with wrecks the roaring sea, where I had so often nearly perished, could not trouble the calm waters of the port where my bark had just entered. Every one of the members of the community was to be like an angel of charity, humility, modesty, whose example was to guide my steps in the ways of God. My superior appeared to be less a superior than a father, whose protecting care, by day and night, would be a shield over me. Noah, in the ark, safe from the raging waves which were destroying the world, did not feel more grateful to God than I was, when once in this holy solitude. The vow of perfect poverty was to save me for ever from the cares of the world. Having, hereafter, no right to possess a cent, the world would become to me a paradise, where food, clothing, and lodging would come without anxiety or care. My father superior would supply all these things, without any other condition on my part, than to love and obey a man of God whose whole life was to be spent in guiding my steps in the ways of the most exalted evangelical virtues. Had not that father himself made a solemn vow to renounce not only all the honours and dignities of the church, that his whole mind and heart might be devoted to my holiness on earth, and my salvation in heaven?

How easy to secure that salvation now! I had only to look to that father on earth, and obey him as my Father in Heaven. Yes! The will of that father was to be, for me, the will of my God. Though I might err in obeying him, my errors would not be laid to my charge. To save my soul, I should have only to be like a corpse, or a stick in the hands of my father superior. Without any anxiety or any responsibility whatever of my own, I was to be led to heaven as the new-born child in the arms of his loving mother, without any fear, thoughts, or anxiety of his own.

With the Christian poet I could have sung:

> " Rocks and storms I fear no more,
> When on that eternal shore,
> Drop the anchor !   Furl the sail !
> I am safe within the vail."

But how short were to be these fine dreams of my poor deluded mind !   When on my knees, Father Guigues handed me, with great solemnity, the Latin books of the rules of that monastic order, which is their real gospel, warning me that it was a *secret book*, that there were things in it I ought not to reveal to anyone ; and he made me solemnly promise that I would never show it to any one outside of the order.

When alone, the next morning, in my cell, I thanked God and the Virgin Mary for the favours of the last day, and the thought came involuntarily to my mind : " Have you not, a thousand times, heard and said that the Holy Church of Rome absolutely condemns and anathematizes secret societies.   And do you not belong, to-day, to a secret society ?   How can you reconcile the solemn promise of secrecy you made last night, with the anathemas hurled by all your popes against secret societies ? "   After having, in vain, tried, in my mind, to reconcile these two things, I happily remembered that I was a corpse, that I had for ever given up my private judgment—that my only business now was to obey.   " Does a corpse argue against those who turn it from side to side ?   Is it not in perfect peace, whatever may be the usage to which it is exposed, or to whatever place it is dragged.   Shall I lose the rich crown which is before me, at my first step in the ways of perfection ? "

I bade my rebellious intelligence to be still, my private judgment to be mute, and, to distract my mind from this first temptation, I read that book of rules with the utmost attention.   I had not gone through it all before I understood why it was kept from the eyes of the curates and the other secular priests.   To my unspeakable amazement, I found that, from the beginning to the end, it speaks with the most profound contempt for them all.   I said to myself: " What would be the indignation of the curates, if they should suspect that these strangers from France have such a bad opinion of them all !   Would the good curates receive them as angels from heaven, and raise them so high in the esteem of the people, if they knew that the first thing an Oblate has to learn, is that the secular priest is, to-day, steeped in immorality, ignorance, worldliness, laziness, gluttony, etc. ; that he is the disgrace of the church, which would speedily be destroyed, was she not providentially sustained, and kept in the ways of God, by the holy monastic men whom she nurses as her only hope !   Clear as the light of the sun on a bright day, the whole fabric of the order of the Oblates presented itself to my mind, as the most perfect system of Pharisaism the world had ever seen."

The Oblate, who studies his book of rules, his only gospel, must have his mind filled with the idea of his superior holiness, not only over the poor sinful, secular priest, but over every one else. The Oblate alone is Christian, holy, and sacred; the rest of the world is lost! The Oblate alone is the salt of the earth, the light of the world! I said to myself: "Is it to attain to this pharisaical perfec. tion that I have left my beautiful and dear parish of Kamouraska, and given up the honourable position which my God had given me in my country!"

However, after some time spent in these sad and despondent reflections, I again felt angry with myself. I quickly directed my mind to the frightful, unsuspected, and numberless scandals I had known in almost every parish I had visited. I remembered the drunkenness of that curate, the impurities of this, the ignorance of another, the worldliness, and absolute want of faith of others, and concluded that, after all, the Oblates were not far from the truth in their bad opinion of the secular clergy. I ended my sad afflictions by saying to myself: "After all, if the Oblates live a life of holiness, as I expect to find here, is it a crime that they should see, feel, and express among themselves, the difference which exists between a regular and a secular clergy? Am I come here to judge and condemn these holy men? No! I came here to save myself by the practice of the most heroic Christian virtues, the first of which, is that I should absolutely and for ever, give up my *private judgment*—consider myself as a corpse in the hand of my superior."

With all the fervour of my soul, I prayed to God and to the Virgin Mary, day and night, that week, that I might attain that supreme state of perfection, when I would have no will, no judgment of my own. The days of that first week passed very quickly, spent in prayer, reading and meditation of the Scriptures, study of ecclesiastical history and ascetical books, from half-past five in the morning till half-past nine at night. The meals were taken at the regular hours of seven, twelve, and six o'clock, during which, with rare exceptions, silence was kept, and pious books were read. The quality of the food was good; but, at first, before they got a female cook to preside over the kitchen, everything was so unclean, that I had to shut my eyes at meals, not to see what I was eating. I should have complained, had not my lips been sealed by that strange monastic view of perfection that every religious man is a corpse! What does a corpse care about the cleanliness or uncleanliness of what is put into its mouth? The third day, having drank at breakfast a glass of milk which was literally mixed with the dung of the cow, my stomach rebelled; a circumstance which I regretted exceedingly, attributing it to my want of monastic perfection. I envied the high state of holiness of the other fathers who had so perfectly attained to the sublime perfection of submission that they could drink that impure milk just as if it had been clean.

Everything went on well the first week, with the exception of a dreadful scare I had at the dinner of the first Friday. Just after eating soup, when listening with the greatest attention to the reading of the life of a saint, I suddenly felt as if the devil had taken hold of my feet; I threw down my knife and fork, and I cried at the top of my voice, "My God! my God! what is there?" and as quick as lightning I jumped on my chair to save myself from Satan's grasp. My cries were soon followed by an inexpressible burst of convulsive laughter from everyone.

"But what does that mean? Who has taken hold of my feet?" I asked. Father Guigues tried to explain the matter to me, but it took him a considerable time. When he began to speak, an irrepressible burst of laughter prevented his saying a word. The fits of laughter became still more uncontrollable, on account of the seriousness with which I was repeatedly asking them who could have taken hold of my feet! At last some one said, "It is Father Lagier who wanted to kiss your feet!" At the same time, Lagier walking on his hands and knees, his face covered with sweat, dust, and dirt, was crawling out from under the table; literally rolling on the floor, in such an uncontrollable fit of laughter that he was unable to stand on his feet. Of course, when I understood that no devil had tried to drag me by the feet, but that it was simply one of the father Oblates, who, to go through one of the common practices of humility in that monastery, had crawled under the table, to take hold of the feet of every one and kiss them, I joined with the rest of the community, and laughed to my heart's content.

Not many days after this, we were going, after tea, from the dining-room to the chapel, to pass five or ten minutes in adoration of the wafer god; we had two doors to cross, and it was pretty dark. Being the last who had entered the monastery, I had to walk first, the other monks following me. We were reciting, with a loud voice, the Latin Psalm: "*Miserere mei Deus.*" We were all marching pretty fast, when, suddenly, my feet met a large, though unseen object, and down I fell, and rolled on the floor; my next companion did the same, and rolled over me, and so did five or six others, who, in the dark, had also struck their feet on that object. In a moment, we were five or six "Holy Fathers" rolling on each other on the floor, unable to raise up, splitting our sides with convulsive laughter. Father Brunette, in one of his fits of humility, had left the table a little before the rest, with the permission of the Superior, to lay himself flat on the floor, across the door. Not suspecting it, and unable to see anything, from the want of sufficient light, I had entangled my

20

feet on that living corpse, as also the rest of those who were walking too close behind me, to stop before tumbling over one another.

No words can describe my feelings of shame when I saw, almost every day, some performance of this kind going on, under the name of Christian humility. In vain I tried to silence the voice of my intelligence, which was crying to me, day and night, that this was a mere diabolical caricature of the humility of Christ. Striving to silence my untamed reason, by telling it that it had no right to speak, and argue, and criticise, within the holy walls of a monastery, it, nevertheless, spoke louder, day after day, telling me that such acts of humility were a mockery. In vain, I said to myself, " Chiniquy, thou art not come here to philosophize on this and that, but to sanctify thyself by becoming like a corpse, which has no preconceived ideas, no acquired store of knowledge, no rule of common sense to guide it! Poor, wretched, sinful Chiniquy, thou art here to save thyself by admiring every iota of the holy rules of your superiors, and to obey every word of their lips! "

I felt angry against myself, and unspeakably sad when, after whole weeks and months of efforts, not only to silence the voice of my reason, but to kill it, it had more life than ever, and was more and more loudly protesting against the unmanly, unchristian, and ridiculous daily usages and rules of the monastery. I envied the humble piety of the other good Fathers, who were apparently so happy, having conquered themselves so completely, as to destroy that haughty reason, which was constantly rebelling in me.

Twice, every week, I went to reveal to my guide and confessor, Father Allard, the master of novices, my interior struggles; my constant, though vain efforts, to subdue my rebellious reason. He always gladdened me with the promise that, sooner or later, I should have that interior perfect peace which is promised to the humble monk when he has attained the supreme monastic perfection of considering himself as a corpse, as regards the rules and will of his superiors. My sincere and constant efforts to reconcile myself to the rules of the monastery were, however, soon to receive a new and rude check. I had read in the book of rules, that a true monk must closely watch those who live with him, and secretly report to his superior the defects and sins which he detects in them. The first time I read that strange rule, my mind was so taken up by other things, that I did not pay much attention to it. But the second time I studied that clause, the blush came to my face, and in spite of myself, I said : "Is it possible that we are a band of spies?" I was not long in seeing the disastrous effects of this most degrading and immoral rule. One of the fathers, for whom I had a particular affection for his many good qualities, and who had many times given me the sincere proof of his friendship, said to me one day : "For God's sake, my dear Father Chiniquy, tell me if it is you who denounced me to the Superior for having said that the conduct of Father Guigues towards me was uncharitable?"

"No! my dear friend," I answered, "I never said such a thing against you, for two reasons : The first is, that you have never said a word in my presence which could give me the idea that you had such an opinion of our good Father Superior ; the second reason is, that though you might have told me anything of that kind, I would prefer to have my tongue cut, and eaten by dogs, than to be a spy, and denounce you!"

"I am glad to know that," he rejoined, "for I was told by some of the fathers that you were the one who had reported me to the Superior as guilty, though I am innocent of that offence, but I could not believe it." He added with tears, "I regret having left my parish to be an Oblate, on account of that abominable law which we are sworn to fulfil. That law makes a real hell of this monastery, and, I suppose, of all the monastic orders, for I think it is a general law with all the religious houses. When you have passed more time here, you will see that that law of detection puts an insurmountable wall between us all ; it destroys every spring of Christian and social happiness."

"I understand, perfectly well, what you say," I answered him ; "the last time I was alone with Father Superior, he asked me why I had said that the present Pope was an old fool ; he persisted in telling me that I must have said it, 'for,' he added, 'one of our most reliable fathers has assured me you said it.' 'Well, my dear Father Superior,' I answered him, 'that reliable father has told you a big lie ; I never said such a thing, for the good reason that I sincerely think that our present Pope is one of the wisest that ever ruled the church.' I added, 'Now I understand why there is so much unpleasantness in our mutual intercourse, during the hours we are allowed to talk. I see that nobody dares to speak his mind on any grave subject. The conversations are colourless and without life.'"

"That is just the reason," answered my friend. When some of the fathers, like you and me, would prefer to be hung rather than become spies, the great majority of them, particularly among the French priests recently imported from France, will not hear ten words from your lips on any subject, without finding an opportunity of reporting eight of them as unbecoming and unchristian, to the superiors. I do not say that it is always through malice that they give such false reports ; it is more through want of judgment. They are very narrow minded ; they do not understand the half of what they hear in its true sense ; and they give their false impressions to the superiors, who, unfortunately, encourage that system of spying, as the best way of transforming every one of us into corpses. As we are never confronted with our false accusers, we can never know them, and we lose confidence in each other; thus it is that the sweetest and holiest springs of true Christian love are for ever dried up.   It is on this spying system which is the curse and the hell of our monastic houses, that a celebrated French writer, who had been a monk himself, wrote of all the monks :

" Ils rentrent dans leurs monastères sans se connaître; ils y vivent, sans s'aimer: et ils se separent sans se regretter" (Monks enter a monastery without knowing each other; they live there, without loving each other; and they depart from each other without any regret.)

However, though I sincerely deplored that there was such a law of espionage among us, I tried to persuade myself that it was like the dark spots of the sun, which do not diminish its beauty, its grandeur and its innumerable blessings.   The Society of the Oblates was still to me the blessed ark where I should find a sure shelter against the storms which were desolating the rest of the world.

Not long after my reception as a novice, the providence of God put before our eyes one of those terrible wrecks which would make the strongest of us tremble.   Suddenly, at the hour of breakfast, the superior of the Seminary of St. Sulpice, and grand vicar of the Diocese of Montreal, the Rev. Mr. Quiblier, knocked at our door, to rest an hour, and breakfast with us, when on his way to France.

This unfortunate priest, who was among the best orators and the best looking men Montreal had ever seen, had lived such a profligate life with his penitent nuns and ladies of Montreal, that a cry of indignation from the whole people had forced Bishop Bourget to send him back to France.   Our father superior took the opportunity of the fall of that talented priest, to make us bless God for having gathered us behind the walls of our monastery, where the efforts of the enemy were powerless.   But, alas! we were soon to know, at our own expense, that the heart of man is weak and deceitful everywhere.

It was not long after the public fall of the grand vicar of Montreal, when a fine-looking widow was engaged to preside over our kitchen. She was more than forty years old, and had very good manners. Unfortunately, she had not been four months in the monastery, when she fell in love with her father confessor, one of the most pious of the French father Oblates.   The modern Adam was not stronger than the old one against the charms of the new Eve.   Both were found, in an evil hour, forgetting one of the holy laws of God.   The guilty priest was punished and the weak woman dismissed.   But an unspeakable shame remained upon us all!   I would have preferred to have my sentence of death, than the news of such a fall inside the walls of that house where I had so foolishly believed that Satan could not lay his snares. From that day, it was the will of God that the strange and beautiful illusions which had brought me to that monastery, should fade away one after the other, like the white mist which conceals the bright rays of the morning sun. The Oblates began to appear to me pretty much like other men. Till then, I had looked at them with my eyes shut, and I had seen nothing but the glittering colours with which my imagination was painting them. From that day, I studied them with my eyes opened, and I saw them just as they were.

In the spring of 1847, having a severe indisposition, the doctor ordered me to go to the Hotel Dieu of Montreal, which was, then, near the splendid St. Mary's Church. I made there, for the first time, the acquaintance of a venerable old nun, who was very talkative. She was one of the superiors of the house ; her family name was Urtubise. Her mind was still full of indignation at the bad conduct of two father Oblates, who, under the pretext of sickness, had lately come to her monastery to seduce the young nuns who were serving them. She told me how she had turned them out ignominiously, forbidding them ever to come again, under any pretext, into the hospital. She was young, when Bishop Lartigue, being driven away from the Sulpician Seminary of Montreal, in 1824, had taken refuge, with his secretary, the Rev. Ignace Bourget, into the modest walls of that nunnery. She told me how the nuns had soon to repent having received that bishop with his secretary and other priests.

"It was nearly the ruin of our community. The intercourse of the priests with a certain number of nuns," she said, " was the cause of so much disorder and scandal, that I was deputed with some other nuns, to the bishop to respectfully request him not to prolong his stay in our nunnery. I told him, in my name, and in the name of many others, that if he would not comply with our legitimate request, we should instantly leave the house, go back to our families and get married, that it was better to be honestly married than to continue to live as the priests, even our father confessors, wanted us to do."

After she had given me several other spicy stories of those interesting distant days, I asked her if she had known Maria Monk, when she was in their house, and what she thought of her book, " Awful Disclosures?" "I have known her well," she said. "She spent six months with us. I have read her book, which was given me, that I might refute it. But after reading it, I refused to have anything to do with that deplorable *exposure*. There are surely some inventions and suppositions in that book. But there is a sufficient amount of truth to cause all our nunneries to be pulled down by the people, if only the half of them were known to the public!"

She then said to me : " For God's sake, do not reveal these things to the world, till the last one of us is dead, if God spares you." She then covered her face with her hands, burst into tears, and left the room.

I remained horrified. Her words fell upon me as a thunderbolt. I regretted having heard them, though I was determined to respect her request not to reveal the terrible secret she had entrusted to me. My God knows that I never repeated a word of it till now. But I think it is my duty to reveal to my country and the whole world the truth on that grave subject, as it was given me by a most respectable and unimpeachable eye-witness.

The terrible secrets which Sister Urtubise had revealed to me rendered my stay in the Hotel Dieu as unpleasant as it had been agreeable at first. Though not quite recovered I left, the same day, for Longueuil, where I entered the monastery with a heavy heart. The day before, two of the fathers had come back from a two or three months' evangelical excursion among the lumber men, who were cutting wood in the forests along the Ottawa River and its tributaries, from one to two hundred miles north-west of Montreal. I was glad to hear of their arrival. I hoped that the interesting history of their evangelical excursions, narrow escapes from the bears and the wolves of the forests; their hearty receptions by the honest and sturdy lumber men, which the superior had requested me, some weeks before, to write, would cause a happy diversion from the deplorable things I had recently learned. But only one of those fathers could be seen, and his conversation was anything but interesting and pleasant. There was evidently a dark cloud around him. And the other Oblate, his companion, where was he? The very day of his arrival, he had been ordered to keep his room, and make a retreat of ten days, during which time he was forbidden to speak to anyone.

I inquired from a devoted friend among the old Oblates the reason of such a strange thing. After promising never to reveal to the superiors the sad secret he trusted me with, he said : " Poor Father D—— has seduced one of his fair penitents, on the way. She was a married woman, the lady of the house where our missionaries used to receive the most cordial hospitality. The husband having discovered the infidelity of his wife, came very near killing her; he ignominiously turned out the two fathers, and wrote a terrible letter to the superior. The companion of the guilty father denounced him, and confessed everything to the superior, who has seen that the letter of the enraged husband was only giving too true and correct a version of the whole unfortunate and shameful occurrence. Now, the poor, weak father for his penance, is condemned to ten days of seclusion from the rest of the community. He must pass that whole time in prayer, fasting, and acts of humiliation, dictated by the superior."

"Do these deplorable facts occur very often among the father Oblates?" I asked.

My friend raised his eyes, filled with tears, to heaven, and with a deep sigh, he answered: "Dear Father Chiniquy, would to God that I might be able to tell you that it is the first crime of that nature committed by an Oblate. But alas! you know, by what has occurred with our female cook not long ago, that it is not the first time that some of our fathers have brought disgrace upon us all. And you know also the abominable life of Father Telmont with the two nuns at Ottawa!"

"If it be so," I replied, "where is the spiritual advantage of the regular clergy over the secular?"

"The only advantage I see," answered my friend, "is that the regular clergy gives himself with more impunity to every kind of debauch and licentiousness than the secular. The monks being concealed from the eyes of the public, inside the walls of their monastery, where nobody, or at least very few people, have any access, are more easily conquered by the devil, and more firmly kept in his chains, than the secular priests. The sharp eyes of the public, and the daily intercourse the secular priests have with their relations and parishioners, form a powerful and salutary restraint upon the bad inclinations of our depraved nature. In the monastery, there is no restraint except the childish and ridiculous punishments of retreats, kissing of the floor, or of the feet, prostration upon the ground, as Father Brunette did, a few days after your coming among us.

"There is surely more hypocrisy and selfishness among the regular than the secular clergy. That great social organization which forms the human family is a divine work. Yes! those great social organizations which are called the city, the township, the country, the parish, and the household, where every one is called to work in the light of day, is a divine organization, and makes society as strong, pure, and holy as it can be.

"I confess that there are also terrible temptations, and deplorable falls there, but the temptations are not so unconquerable, and the falls not so irreparable, as in these dark recesses and unhealthy prisons raised by Satan only for the birds of night, called monasteries or nunneries.

"The priest and the woman who falls in the midst of a well-organized Christian society, break the hearts of the beloved mother, covers with shame a venerable father, cause the tears of cherished sisters and brothers to flow, pierce, with a barbed arrow, the hearts of thousands of friends; they for ever lose their honour and good name. These considerations are so many providential, I dare say Divine, shields, to protect the sons and daughters of Eve against

their own frailty. The secular priest and the woman shrink before
throwing themselves into such a bottomless abyss of shame, misery,
and regret. But behind the thick and dark walls of the monastery,
or the nunnery, what has the fallen monk or nun to fear? Nobody
will hear of it, no bad consequences worth mentioning will follow,
except a few days of retreat, some insignificant, childish, ridiculous
penances, which the most devoted in the monastery are practising
almost every day.

"As you ask me in earnest what are the advantages of a monastic
life over a secular, in a moral and social point of view, I will answer
you. In the monastery, man, as the image of God, forgets his divine
origin, loses his dignity; and as a Christian, he loses the most holy
weapons Christ has given to His disciples to fight the battle of life.
He, at once and for ever, loses that law of self-respect, and respect for
others, which is one of the most powerful and legitimate barriers
against vice. Yes! That great and divine law of self-respect, which
God Himself has implanted in the heart of every man and woman
who live in a Christian society, is completely destroyed in the monastery and nunnery. The foundation of perfection in the monk and the
nun is that they must consider themselves as corpses. Do you not
see that this principle strikes at the root of all that God has made
good, grand, and holy in man? Does it not sweep away every idea
of holiness, purity, greatness! every principle of life which the Gospel
of Christ had for its mission to reveal to the fallen children of
Adam?

"What self-respect can we expect from a corpse? and what respect
can a corpse feel for the other corpses which surround it? Thus it is
that the very idea of monastic perfection carries with it the destruction of all that is good, pure, holy, and spiritual in the religion of the
Gospel. It destroys the very idea of life to put death into its place.

"It is for that reason that if you study the true history, *not the
lying history*, of monachism, you will find the details of a corruption
impossible, anywhere else, not even among the lowest houses of
prostitution. Read the Memoirs of Scipio de Ricci, one of the most
pious and intelligent bishops our Church has ever had, and you will see
that the monks and the nuns of Italy live the very life of the brutes in
the fields. Yes! read the terrible revelations of what is going on
among those unfortunate men and women, whom the iron hand of
monachism keeps tied in their dark dungeons, you will hear from the
very lips of the nuns that the monks are more free with them than
the husbands are with their legitimate wives; you will see that every
one of those monastic institutions is a new Sodom!

"The monastic axiom, that the highest point of perfection is
attained only when you consider yourself a corpse in the hand of your

superior, is anti-social and Antichristian : it is simply diabolical. It transforms into a vile machine that man whom God had created in His likeness, and made for ever free.　It degrades below the brute that man whom Christ, by His death, has raised to the dignity of a child of God, and an inheritor of an eternal kingdom in Heaven.　Everything is mechanical, material, false, in the life of a monk and a nun.　Even the best virtues are deceptions and lies.　The monks and the nuns being perfect only when they have renounced their own free-will and intelligence to become corpses, can have neither virtues nor vices.

" Their best actions are mechanical.　Their acts of humility are to crawl under the table and kiss the feet of each other, or to make a cross on a dirty floor with the tongue, or lie down in the dust to let the rest of the monks or the nuns pass over them !　Have you not remarked how those so-called monks speak with the utmost contempt of the rest of the world ?　One must have opportunities as I have had of seeing the profound hatred which exists among all monastic orders against each other.　How the Dominicans have always hated the Franciscans, and how they both hate the Jesuits, who pay them back in the same coin !　What a strong and nameless hatred divides the Oblates, to whom we belong, from the Jesuits !　The Jesuits never lose an opportunity of showing us their supreme contempt !　You are aware that, on account of those bad feelings, it is absolutely forbidden to an Oblate to confess to a Jesuit, as we know it is forbidden to the Jesuits to confess to an Oblate, or to any other priest.

" I need not tell you, for you know, that their vow of poverty is a mask to help them to become rich with more rapidity than the rest of the world.　Is it not under the mask of that vow that the monks of England, Scotland, and France became the masters of the richest lands of those countries, which the nations were forced, by bloody revolutions, to wrench from their grasp ?

" Is it not still under the mask of extreme poverty that the monks of Italy are among the richest proprietors in that unfortunate country ?

" I have seen much more of the world than you.　When a young priest, I was the chaplain, confessor, and intimate friend of the Duchess de Berry, the mother of Henry V., now the only legitimate king of France.　When, in the midst of those great and rich princes and nobles of France, I never saw such a love of money, of honour, of vainglory, as I have seen among the monks since I have become one of them.　When the Duchess de Berry finished her providential work in France, after making the false step which ruined her, I threw myself into the religious order of the Chartreux.　I have lived several years in their palatial monastery of Rome ; have cultivated and enjoyed their sweet fruits in their magnificent gardens ; but I was not there long without seeing the fatal error I had committed in becoming a monk.

During the many years I resided in that splendid mansion, where laziness, stupidity, filthiness, gluttony, superstition, tediousness, ignorance, pride, and unmentionable immoralities, with very few exceptional cases, reigned supreme, I had every opportunity to know what was going on in their midst. Life soon became an unbearable burden, but for the hope I had of breaking my fetters. At last I found out that the best, if not the only way of doing this, was to declare to the Pope that I wanted to go and preach the gospel to the savages of America, which was, and is still true.

" I made my declaration, and by the Pope's permission the doors of my gaol were opened, with the condition that I should join the order of the Oblates Immaculate, in connection with which I should evangelize the savages of the Rocky Mountains.

" I have found among the monks of Canada the very same things I have seen among those of France and Italy. With very few exceptions they are all corpses, absolutely dead to every sentiment of true honesty and real Christianity ; they are putrid carcases, which have lost the dignity of manhood.

" My dear Father Chiniquy," he added, " I trust you as I trust myself, when I tell you for your own good a secret which is known to God alone. When I am on the Rocky Mountains, I will raise myself up, as the eagles of those vast countries, and I shall go up to the regions of liberty, light, and life; I will cease being a corpse, to become what my God has made me—a free and intelligent man : I will cease to be a corpse, in order to become one of the redeemed of Christ, who serve God in spirit and in truth.

" Christ is the light of the world; monachism is its night! Christ is the strength, the glory, the life of man; monachism is its decay, shame, and death ! Christ died to make us free; the monastery is built up to make slaves of us ! Christ died that we might be raised to the dignity of children of God; monachism is established to bring us down much below the living brutes, for it transforms us into corpses ! Christ is the highest conception of humanity; monachism is its lowest.

" Yes, yes, I hope my God will soon give me the favour I have asked so long ! When I shall be on the top of the Rocky Mountains, I will, for ever, break my fetters. I will rise from my tomb; I will come out from among the dead, to sit at the table of the redeemed, and eat the bread of the living children of God !"

I do regret that the remarkable monk, whose abridged views on monachism I have here given, should have requested me never to give his name, when he allows me to tell some of his adventures, which will make a most interesting romance. Faithful to his promise, he went, as an Oblate, to preach to the savages of the Rocky Mountains, and there, without noise, he slipped out of their hands; broke his chains to live the life of a freedman of Christ, in the holy bonds of a Christian marriage with a respectable American lady.

Weak and timid soldier that I was once; frightened by the ruins spread everywhere on the battle-field, I looked around to find a shelter against the impending danger; I thought that the monastery of the Oblates of Mary Immaculate was one of those strong towers, built by my God, where the arrows of the enemy could not reach me, and I threw myself into it.

But, hardly beginning to hope that I was out of danger, behind those dark and high walls, when I saw them shaking like a drunken man; and the voice of God passed like a hurricane over me.

Suddenly, the high towers and walls around me fell to the ground, and were turned into dust. Not one stone remained on another.

And I heard a voice saying to me: "Soldier! come out and get in the light of the sun; trust no more in the walls built by the hand of man; they are nothing but dust. Come and fight in the open day, under the eyes of God, protected only by the gospel banner of Christ! Come out from behind those walls—they are a diabolical deception, a snare, a fraud!"

I listened to the voice, and I bade adieu to the inmates of the monastery of the Oblates of Mary Immaculate.

When, on the 1st of November, 1847, I pressed them on my heart for the last time, I felt the burning tears of many of them falling on my cheeks, and my tears moistened their faces: for they loved me, and I loved them. I had met there several noble hearts and precious souls worthy of a better fate. Oh! if I could have, at the price of my life, given them the light and liberty which my merciful God had given me!

But they were in the dark; and there was no power in me to change their darkness into light. The hand of God brought me back to my dear Canada, that I might again offer it the sweat and the labours, the love and life of the least of its sons.

CHAPTER XLIII.

The eleven months spent in the monastery of the Oblates of Mary Immaculate, were among the greatest favours God has granted me. What I had read of the monastic orders, and what my honest, though deluded imagination, had painted of the holiness, purity, and happiness of the monastic life, could not be blotted out of my mind, except by a kind of miraculous interposition. No testimony whatever could have convinced me that the monastic institutions were not one of the most blessed of the Gospel. Their existence, in the bosom of the Church of Rome, was, for me, an infallible token of her divine institution, and miraculous preservation; and their absence among Protestants, one of the strongest proofs that these heretics were entirely separated from Christ. Without religious orders the Protestant denominations were to me, as dead and decayed branches cut from the true vine, which are doomed to perish.

But, just as the eyes of Thomas were opened, and his intelligence was convinced of the divinity of Christ, only after he had seen the wounds in his hands and side, so I could never have believed that the monastic institutions were of heathen and diabolical origin, if my God had not forced me to see with my own eyes, and to touch with my fingers, their unspeakable corruptions.

Though I remained, for some time longer, a sincere Catholic priest, I dare say that God Himself had just broken the strongest tie of my affections and respect for that Church.

It is true that several pillars remained, on which my robust faith in the holiness and apostolicity of the Church rested for a few years longer, but I must here confess to the glory of God, that the most solid of these pillars had for ever crumbled to pieces, when in the monastery of Longueuil.

Long before my leaving the Oblates, many influential priests of the district of Montreal had told me that my only chance of success, if I wanted to continue my crusade against the demon of drunkenness, was to work alone. "Those monks are pretty good speakers on temperance," they unanimously said, "but they are nothing else than a band of comedians. After delivering their eloquent tirades against the use of intoxicating drinks, to the people, the first thing they do is to ask for a bottle of wine, which soon disappears! What fruit can we expect from the preaching of men who do not believe a word of what they say, and who are the first, among themselves, to turn their own arguments into ridicule? It is very different with you; you believe what you say; you are consistent with yourself; your hearers feel it; your profound, scientific, and Christian convictions pass into them with an irresistible power. God visibly blesses your work with a marvellous success! Come to us," said the curates, "not as sent by the superior of the Oblates, but as sent, by God Himself, to regenerate Canada. Present yourself as a French Canadian priest; a child of the people. That people will hear you with more pleasure, and follow your advice with more perseverance. Let them know and feel that Canadian blood runs in your veins; that a Canadian heart beats in your breast; continue to be, in the future, what you have been in the past. Let the sentiments of the true patriot be united with those of a Catholic priest; and when you address the people of Canada, the citadels of Satan will crumble everywhere before you in the district of Montreal, as they have done in that of Quebec."

At the head of the French Canadian curates, who thus spoke, was my venerable personal friend and benefactor, the Rev. Mr. Brassard, curate of Longueuil. He had not only been one of my most devoted friends and teachers, when I was studying in the college of Nicolet, but had helped me, with his own money, to go through the last four years of my studies, when I was too poor to meet my collegiate expenses. No one had thought more highly than he of the Oblates of Mary Immaculate, when they first settled in Canada. But their monastery was too near his parsonage for their own benefit. His sharp eyes, high intelligence, and integrity of character, soon detected that there was more false varnish than pure gold, on their glittering escutcheon. Several love scrapes between some of the Oblates and the pretty young ladies of his parish, and the long hours of night spent by Father Allard with the nuns, established in his village, under the pretext of teaching them grammar and arithmetic, had filled him with disgust. But what had absolutely destroyed his confidence, was the discovery of a long-suspected iniquity, which at first seemed incredible to him. Father Guigues, the superior, after his nomination, but before his installation to the Bishopric of Ottawa, had been closely watched, and at last discovered when opening the letters of Mr. Brassard, which, many times, had passed from the post office, through his hands. That criminal action had come very near to being brought before the legal courts by Mr. Brassard; this was avoided only by Father Guigues acknowledging his guilt, asking pardon in the most humiliating way, before me and several other witnesses.

Long before I left the Oblates, Mr. Brassard had said to me : " The Oblates are not the men you think them to be. I have been sorely disappointed in them, and your disappointment will be no less than mine, when your eyes are opened. I know that you will not remain long in their midst. I offer you, in advance, the hospitality of my parsonage, when your conscience calls you out of their monastery !"

I availed myself of this kind invitation on the evening of the 1st of November, 1847.

The next week was spent in preparing the memoir which I intended to present to my Lord Bourget, Bishop of Montreal, as an explanation of my leaving the Oblates. I knew that he was disappointed and displeased with the step I had taken.

The curate of Chambly, Rev. Mr. Mignault, having gone to the bishop, to express his joy that I had left the monks, in order to serve again the church, in the ranks of the secular clergy, had been very badly received. The bishop had answered him : " Mr. Chiniquy may leave the Oblates if he likes ; but he will be disappointed if he expects to work in my diocese. I do not want his services."

This did not surprise me. I knew that those monks had been

imported by him, from France, and that they were pets of his. When I entered their monastery, just eleven months before, he was just starting for Rome, and expressed to me the pleasure he felt that I was to join them. My reasons, however, were so good, and the memoir I was preparing was so full of undoubted facts and unanswerable arguments, that I was pretty sure, not only to appease the wrath of my bishop, but to gain his esteem more firmly than before. I was not disappointed in my expectation.

A few days later I called upon his lordship, and was received very coldly. He said: "I cannot conceal from you my surprise and pain at the rash step you have just taken. What a shame, for all your friends to see your want of consistency and perseverance! Had you remained among those good monks, your moral strength could have been increased more than tenfold. But you have stultified yourself in the eyes of the people, as well as in mine; you have lost the confidence of your best friends, by leaving, without good reasons, the company of such holy men. Some bad rumours are already afloat against you, which give us to understand that you are an unmanageable man, a selfish priest, whom the superiors have been forced to turn out as a black sheep, whose presence could not be any longer tolerated inside the peaceful walls of that holy monastery."

Those words were uttered with an expression of bad feeling which told me that I had not heard the tenth part of what he had in his heart. However, as I came into his presence prepared to hear all kinds of bad reports, angry reproaches, and humiliating insinuations, I remained perfectly calm. I had, in advance, resolved to hear all his unfriendly, insulting remarks, just as if they were addressed to another person, a perfect stranger to me. The last three days had been spent in prayers to obtain that favour. My God had evidently heard me; for the storm passed over me without exciting the least unpleasant feelings in my soul.

I answered: "My lord, allow me to tell you that, in taking the solemn step of leaving the monastery of Longueuil, I was not afraid of what the world would say, or think of me. My only desire is to save my soul, and give the rest of my life to my country and my God, in a more efficacious way than I have yet done. The rumours which seem to trouble your lordship about my supposed expulsion from the Oblates do not affect me in the least, for they are without the least foundation. From the first to the last day of my stay in that monastery, all the inmates, from the superior to the last one, have overwhelmed me with the most sincere marks of kindness, and even of respect. If you had seen the tears which were shed by the brothers, when I bade them adieu, you would have understood that I never had more devoted and sincere friends than the members of that religious community. Please read this important document, and you will see that I have kept my good name during my stay in that monastery." I handed him the following testimonial letter which the superior had given me when I left :

"I, the undersigned, Superior of the Noviciate of the Oblates of Mary Immaculate at Longueuil, do certify that the conduct of Mr. Chiniquy, when in our monastery, has been worthy of the sacred character which he possesses, and after this year of solitude, he does not less deserve the confidence of his brethren in the holy ministry than before. We wish, moreover, to give our testimony of his persevering zeal in the cause of temperance. We think that nothing was more of a nature to give a character of stability to that admirable reform, and to secure its perfect success, than the profound reflections and studies of Mr. Chiniquy, when in the solitude of Longueuil, on the importance of that work.

"T. F. ALLARD,
" *Superior of the Noviciate O. M. I.*"

It was really most pleasant for me to see that every line of that document read by the bishop was blotting out some of the stern and unfriendly lines which were on his face, when speaking to me. Nothing was more amiable than his manners, when he handed it back to me, saying : " I thank God to see that you are still as worthy of my esteem and confidence, as when you entered that monastery. But would you be kind enough to give me the real reasons why you have so abruptly separated from the Oblates ? "

" Yes, my lord, I will give them to you; but your lordship knows that there are things of such a delicate nature, that the lips of man shiver and rebel when required to utter them. Such are some of the deplorable things which I have to mention to your lordship. I have put those reasons in these pages, which I respectfully request your lordship to read," and I handed him the *Memoir*, about thirty pages long, which I had prepared. The bishop read, very carefully five or six pages, and said : " Are you positive as to the exactness of what you write here ? "

" Yes, my lord ! They are as true and real as I am here."

The bishop turned pale and remained a few minutes silent, biting his lips, and after a deep sigh, said : " Is it your intention to reveal those sad mysteries to the world, or can we hope that you will keep that secret ? "

" My lord," I answered, " if your lordship and the Oblates deal with me, as I hope they will do, as with an honourable Catholic priest; if I am kept in the position which an honest priest has a right to fill in the church, I consider myself bound, in conscience and honour, to keep those things secret. But, if from any abuse, persecutions emanating from the Oblates, or any other party, I am obliged to give to the world the true reasons of my leaving that monastic order, your lordship understands that, in self-defence, I will be forced to make these revelations ! "

"But the Oblates cannot say a word, or do anything wrong against you," promptly answered the bishop, "after the honourable testimony they have given you."

"It is true, my lord, that I have no reason to fear anything from the Oblates!" I answered; "but those religious men are not the only ones who might force me to defend myself. You know another who has my future destinies in his hands. You know that my future course will be shaped by his own toward me."

With an amiable smile the bishop answered:

"I understand you. But I pledge myself that you have nothing to fear from that quarter. Though I frankly tell you that I would have preferred seeing you work as a member of that monastic institution, it may be that it is more according to the will of God, that you should go among the people, as sent by God, rather than by a superior, who might be your inferior in the eyes of many, in that glorious temperance, of which you are evidently the blessed apostle in Canada. I am glad to tell you that I have spoken of you to his holiness, and he requested me to give you a precious medal, which bears his most perfect features, with a splendid crucifix. His holiness has graciously attached three hundred days' for indulgences to every one who will take the pledge of temperance in kissing the feet of that crucifix. Wait a moment," added the bishop, "I will go and get them and present them to you."

When the bishop returned, holding in his hands those two infallible tokens of the kind sentiments of the Pope towards me, I fell on my knees to receive them and press them both to my lips with the utmost respect. My feelings of joy and gratitude in that happy hour cannot be expressed. I remained mute, for some time, with surprise and admiration, when holding those precious things which were coming to me, as I then sincerely believed, from the very successor of Peter, and the true Vicar of Christ Himself. When handing me those sacred gifts, the bishop addressed me the kindest words which a bishop can utter to his priest, or a father to his beloved son. He granted me the power to preach and hear confessions all over his diocese, and he dismissed me only after having put his hand on my head and asked God to pour upon me His most abundant benedictions everywhere I should go to work in the holy cause of temperance in Canada.

CHAPTER XLIV.

Our adorable Saviour said : "What king, going to make war against another king, sitteth not down first, and consulteth whether he be able, with ten thousand, to meet him that cometh against him with twenty thousand?" (Luke xiv. 31). To follow that advice, how often had I fallen on my knees before my God, to implore the necessary strength and wisdom to meet that terrible enemy which was marching against me and my brethren! Often I was so discouraged by the sense of my personal incapacity, that I came near fainting and flying away at the sight of the power and resources of the foe! But the dear Saviour's voice had as many times strengthened me, saying! "Fear not, I am with thee!" He seemed at every hour to whisper in my ears, "Be of good cheer, I have overcome the world!" (John xvi. 33). Trusting, then, in my God, alone, for victory, I nevertheless understood that my duty was to arm myself with the weapons which the learned and the wise men of the past ages had prepared. I again studied the best works written on the subject of wine, from the learned naturalist, Pliny, to the celebrated Sir Astley Cooper. I not only compiled a multitude of scientific notes, arguments, and facts from these books, but prepared a "Manual of Temperance," which obtained so great a success, for such a small country as Canada, that it went through four editions of twenty-five thousand copies in less than four years. But my best source of information and wisdom was from letters received from Father Mathew, and my personal interviews with him, when he visited the United States.

The first time I met him, in Boston, he told me how he regretted his having, at first, too much relied on the excitement and enthusiasm of the multitudes. "Those fits," he said, "pass away as quickly as the clouds of the storm; and they, too often, leave no more traces of their passage. Persevere in the resolution you have taken in the beginning, never to give the pledge, except when you give a complete course of lectures on the damning effects of intoxicating drinks. How can we expect that the people will for ever give up beverages which they honestly, though ignorantly, believe to be beneficial and necessary to their body? The first thing we do we must demonstrate to them that these alcoholic drinks are absolutely destructive of their temporal, as well as of their eternal life. So long as the priest and the people believe, as they do to-day, that rum, brandy, wine, beer, and cider give strength to help man to keep up his health in the midst of his hard labours; that they warm his blood in winter and cool it in the summer; all our efforts, and even our successes, will be like the burning bundle of straw, which makes a bright light, attracts the attention for a moment, and leaves nothing but smoke and cinders.

"Hundreds of times I have seen my Irish countrymen honestly taking the pledge for life; but before a week had elapsed, they had obtained a release from their priests, under the impression that they were unable to earn their own living and support their families, without drinking those detestable drugs. Very few priests in Ireland have

21

taken the pledge, and still fewer have kept it. In New York, only two Irish priests have given up their intoxicating glass, and the very next week I met both of them drunk! Archbishop Hughes turned my humble efforts into ridicule, before his priests, in my own presence, and drank a glass of brandy to my health with them at his own table to mock me. And here in Boston the drinking habits of the bishop and his priests are such, that I have been forced, through self-respect, to quietly withdraw from his palace and come to this hotel. This bad conduct paralyses and kills me."

In saying these last words, that good and noble man burst into a fit of convulsive sobs and tears ; his breast was heaving under his vain efforts to suppress his sighs. He concealed his face in his hands, and for nearly ten minutes he could not utter a word.

The spectacle of the desolation of a man whom God had raised so high, and so much blessed, and the tears of one who had himself dried up so many tears, and brought so much joy, peace, and comfort, to so many desolate homes, has been one of the most solemn lessons my God ever gave me. I then learned more clearly than ever, that all the glory of the world is *Vanity*, and that one of the greatest acts of folly is to rely, for happiness, on the praises of men and the success of our own labours. For who had received more merited praises, and who had seen his own labours more blessed by God and man, than Father Mathew, whom all ages will call " The Apostle of Temperance of Ireland ? "

My gratitude to Mr. Brassard caused me to choose his parish, near Montreal, for the first grand battlefield of the impending struggle against the enemy of my God and my country ; and the first week of Advent determined upon for the opening of the campaign. But the nearer the day chosen to draw the sword against the modern Goliath, the more I felt the solemnity of my position, and the more I needed the help of Him on whom alone we can trust for light and strength.

I had determined never to lecture on temperance in any place, without having previously inquired, from the most reliable sources, about :—(1) The number of deaths and accidents caused by drunkenness the last fifteen or twenty years. (2) The number of orphans and widows made by drunkenness. (3) The number of rich families ruined, and the number of poor families made poorer by the same cause. (4) The approximate sum of money expended by the people during the last twenty years.

As the result of my enquiries, I learned that during that short period, that 32 men had lost their lives when drunk ; and through their drunkenness 25 widows and 73 orphans had been left in the lowest degree of poverty ! 72 rich families had been entirely ruined and turned out of their once happy homes by the demon of intemperance, and 90 kept poor. More than three hundred thousand dollars (300,000 dollars) had been paid in cash, without counting the loss of time, for the intoxicating beverages drank by the people of Longueuil during the last twenty years.

For three days, I spoke twice a day to crowded houses. My first text was: "Look not thou upon the wine when it is red, when it giveth his colour in the cup : when it moveth itself aright. At the last it biteth like a serpent, and stingeth like an adder " (Prov. xxiii. 31, 32).

The first day I showed how alcoholic beverages were biting like a serpent and stinging like an adder, by destroying the lungs, the brains, and the liver, the nerves and the muscles, the blood and the very life of man. The second day I proved that intoxicating drinks were the most implacable and cruel enemies of the fathers, the mothers, the children; of the young and the old; of the rich and the poor; of the farmers, the merchants, and the mechanics ; the parish and the country. The third day I proved, clearly, that those intoxicating liquors were the enemy of the intelligence, and the soul of man ; the gospel of Christ and of His holy Church ; the enemy of all the rights of man and the laws of God. My conclusion was, that we were all bound to raise our hands against that gigantic and implacable foe, whose arm was raised against every one of us. I presented the thrilling tableau of our friends, near and dear relations, and neighbours, fallen and destroyed around us ; the thousands of orphans and widows, whose fathers and husbands had been slaughtered by strong drink. I brought before their minds the true picture of the starving children, the destitute widows and mothers, whose life had to be spent in tears, ignominy, desolation and unspeakable miseries, from the daily use of strong drink. I was not half through my address when tears flowed from every eye. The cries and sobs so much drowned my voice, that I had several times to stop speaking for a few minutes.

Then holding the crucifix, blessed and given to me by the Pope, I showed what Christ had suffered on the cross for sins engendered by the use of intoxicating drinks. And I requested them to listen to the voices of the thousands of desolate orphans, widows, wives and mothers, coming from every corner of the land ; the voices of their priests and their church ; the voices of the angels, the Virgin Mary and the saints in heaven; the voice of Jesus Christ their Saviour, calling them to put an end to the deluge of evils and unspeakable iniquities caused by the use of those cursed drinks; " for," said I, " those liquors are cursed by millions of mothers and children, widows and orphans, who owe to them a life of shame, tears, and untold desolation. They are cursed by the Virgin Mary and the angels who are the daily witnesses of the iniquities with which they deluge the world. They are cursed by the millions of souls which they have plunged into eternal misery. They are cursed by Jesus Christ, from whose hands they have wrenched untold millions of souls, for whom He died on Calvary."

Every one of those truths, incontrovertible for Roman Catholics, were falling with irresistible power on that multitude of people. The distress and consternation were so profound and universal, that they reacted, at last, on the poor speaker, who several times could not express what he himself felt except with his tears and his sobs.

When I hoped that, by the great mercy of God, all resistances were subdued, the obstacles removed, the intelligence enlightened, the wills conquered, I closed the address, which had lasted more than two hours, by an ardent prayer to God to grant us the grace to give up for ever the use of those terrible poisons, and I requested everyone to repeat with me, in their hearts, the solemn pledge of temperance in the following words:

"Adorable and dear Saviour, Jesus Christ, who died on the cross to take away my sins and save my guilty soul, for Thy glory, the good of my brethren and of my country, as well as for my own good, I promise, with Thy help, never to drink, nor to give to anybody any intoxicating beverages, except when ordered by an honest physician."

Our merciful God had visibly blessed the work and His unprofitable servant. The success was above our sanguine expectations. Two thousand three hundred citizens of Longueuil enrolled under the banners of temperance. Instead of inviting them to sign any written pledge, I asked them to come to the foot of the altar and kiss the crucifix I was holding, as the public and solemn pledge of their engagement.

The first thing done by the majority of the intelligent farmers of Longueuil, on the return from the church, was to break their decanters and their barrels, and spill the last drop of the accursed drink on the ground. Seven days later, there were eighty requests in my hands to go and show the ravages of alcoholic liquors to many other parishes. Boucherville, Chambly, Varennes, St. Hyacinthe, etc., Three Rivers, the great city of Montreal, with all the priests of St. Sulpice, the parishes along the Chambly River, Laprairie, Lachine. In a word, the vast diocese of Montreal, Three Rivers, and St. Hyacinthe, one after the other, raised the war cry against the usages of intoxicating drinks, with a unanimity and determination which seemed to be more miraculous than natural. During the four years, I gave 1,800 public addresses, in 200 parishes, with the same fruits, and enrolled more than 200,000 people under the banners of temperance. Everywhere, the taverns, the distilleries and breweries were shut, and their owners forced to take other trades to make a living; not on account of any stringent law, but by the simple fact that the whole people had ceased drinking their beverages, after having been fully persuaded that they were injurious to their bodies, opposed to their happiness, and ruinous to their souls.

The convictions were so unanimous and strong on that subject, that, in many places, the last evening I spent in their midst, the merchants used to take all their barrels of rum, beer, wine and brandy to the public squares, make a pyramid of them, to which I was invited to set fire. The whole population, attracted by the novelty and sublimity of that spectacle, would then fill the air with their cries and shouts of joy. When the husbands and wives, the parents and children of the re- deemed drunkards rent the air with their cries of joy at the destruction of their enemy, and the fire was in full blaze, one of the merchants would give me an axe to stave in the last barrel of rum. After the last drop was emptied, I usually stood on it to address some parting words to the people.

Such a spectacle baffles any description. The brilliant light of the pine and cedar trees, mixed with all kinds of inflammable materials which everyone had been invited to bring, changed the darkest hour of that night into the brightest of days. The flames, fed by the fiery liquid, shot forth their tongues of fire towards heaven, as if to praise their great God, whose merciful hand had brought the marvellous reformation we were celebrating. The thousand faces, illuminated by the blaze, beamed with joy. The noise of the cracking barrels, mixed with that of a raging fire; the cries and shouts of that multitude, with the singing of the Te Deum, formed a harmony which filled every soul with sentiments of unspeakable happiness. But where shall I find words to express my feelings, when I had finished speaking! The mothers and wives to whom our blessed temperance had given back a loving husband and some dear children, were crowding around me with their families and redeemed ones, to thank me, press my hands to their lips, and water them with their grateful tears.

The only thing which marred that joy were the exaggerated honours and unmerited praises with which I was really overwhelmed. I was, at first, forced to receive an ovation from the curates and people of Longueuil and the surrounding parishes, when they presented to me my portrait, painted by the artist Hamel, which filled me with confusion, for I felt so keenly that I did not deserve such honours. But it was still worse at the end of May, 1849. Judge Mondelet was deputed by the bishop and the priests and the city of Montreal, accompanied by 15,000 people, to present me with a gold medal, and a gift of four hundred dollars.

But the greatest surprise my God had in store for me, was kept for the end of June, 1850. At that time, I was deputed by 40,000 teetotalers, to present a petition to the Parliament of Toronto, in order to make the rum sellers responsible for the ravages caused to the families of the poor drunkards to whom they had sold their poisonous drugs. The House of Commons having kindly appointed a committee of ten members to help me to frame that bill, it was an easy matter to have it pass through the three branches. I was present when they discussed and accepted that bill. Napoleon was not more happy after he had won the battle of Austerlitz, than I was when I heard that my pet bill had become law, and that hereafter, the innocent victims of the drunken father or husband would receive an indemnity from the landsharks who were fattening on their poverty and unspeakable miseries.

But what was my surprise and consternation, when, immediately after the passing of that bill, the Hon. Dewitt rose and proposed that a public expression of gratitude should be given me by Parliament, under the form of a large pecuniary gift! His speech seemed to me filled with such exaggerated eulogiums, that I would have been tempted to think it was mockery, had I not known that the Protestant gentleman was one of my most sincere friends. He was followed by the Honourables Baldwin and Lafontaine, Ministers at the time, and half a dozen other members, who went still further into what I so justly consider the regions of exaggeration. It seemed to me bordering on blasphemy to attribute to Chiniquy a reformation which was so clearly the work of my merciful God. The speeches on that subject lasted two hours, and were followed by a unanimous vote to present me with £500, as a public testimony of the gratitude of the people for my labours in the temperance reform of Canada. Previous to that, the Bishops of Quebec and Montreal had given me tokens of their esteem which, though unmerited, had been better appreciated by me.

When in May, 1850, Archbishop Turgeon, of Quebec, sent the Rev. Charles Baillargeon, curate of Quebec, to Rome, to become his successor, he advised him to come to Longueuil, and get a letter from me, which he might present to the Pope, with a volume of my "Temperance Manual." I complied with his request, and wrote to the Pope. Some months later, I received the following lines:

ROME, *Aug.* 10*th*, 1850.

REV. MR. CHINIQUY :

SIR AND DEAR FRIEND ;—Monday, the 12th was the first opportunity given me to have a private audience with the Sovereign Pontiff. I presented him your book, with your letter, which he received, I will not say with that goodness which is so eminently characteristic of him, but with all special marks of satisfaction and approbation, while charging me to state to you that he accords his apostolic benediction to you and to the holy work of temperance you preach. I consider myself happy to have had to offer on your behalf, to the Vicar of Jesus Christ, a book which, after it had done so much good to my countrymen, had been able to draw from his venerable lips, such solemn words of approbation of the temperance society and of blessings on those who are its apostles ; and it is also, for my heart, a very sweet pleasure to transmit them to you.

Your Friend,
CHARLES BAILLARGEON,
Priest.

A short time before I received that letter from Rome, Bishop Bourget, of Montreal, had officially given me the title of " Apostle of Temperance ;" in the following document, which, on account of its importance, the readers will probably like to have in its original Latin :—

"IGNATIUS BOURGET, Miseratione Divina et Stæ. Sedis Apostolicæ Gratia, Episcopus Marianopolitanensis, etc., etc., etc."

"Universis præsentes litteras inspecturis, notum facimus et attestamur Venerabilem Carolum Chiniquy, Temperantiæ Apostolum, Nostræ Diocœcis Sacerdotem, Nobis optime notum esse, exploratumque habere illum vitam laudabilem et professione Ecclesiastica consonam agere, nullisque ecclesiasticis censuris, saltem quæ ad nostram devenerunt Notitiam innodatum ; qua propter, per viscera Misericordiæ Dei Nostri, obsecramus omnes et Singulos Archiepiscopos, Episcopos, cœterasque Ecclesiæ dignitates ad quos ipsum declinare contingerit, ut eum, pro Christi Amore, benigne tractare dignentur, et quando cumque ab eo fuerint requisiti, Sacrum Missæ Sacrificium ipsi celebrare, nec non alia munia Ecclesiastica, et pietatis opera exercere permittant, paratos nos ad similia et majora exhibentes : In quorum fidem, præsentes litteras signo sigilloque nostris, ac Secretarii Episcopatus nostri subscriptione communitas expediri mandavimus Marianopoli, in Œdibus Nostris Beati Jacobi, anno millesimo quinquagesimo. Die vero mensis Junii Sexta.

" ✠ IG. EPIS. MARIANOPOLITANENSIS.

"J. O. Pare, Can. Secrius."

TRANSLATION.

"IGNATIUS BOURGET, by the Divine Mercy and Grace of the Holy Apostolic See, Bishop of Montreal.

" To all who inspect the present letters, we make known and certify that the venerable Charles Chiniquy, 'Apostle of Temperance,' Priest of our Diocese, is very well known to us, and we regard him as proved, to lead a praiseworthy life, and one agreeable to his ecclesiastical profession. Through the tender mercies of our God, he is under no ecclesiastical censures, at least, which have come to our knowledge.

" We entreat each and all, Archbishop, Bishop, and other dignitaries of the Church, to whom it may happen that he may go, that they, for the love of Christ, entertain him kindly and courteously, and as often as they may be asked by him, permit him to celebrate the holy sacrifice of the mass, and exercise other ecclesiastical privileges of piety, being ourselves ready to grant him these and other greater privileges. In proof of this we have ordered the present letters to be prepared under our sign and seal, and with subscription of our secretary, in our palace of the blessed James, in the year one thousand eight hundred and fifty, on the sixth day of the month of June.

"✠ IGNATIUS, BISHOP OF MARIANOPOLIS.

"By order of the most illustrious and most Reverend Bishop of Marianopolis, D.D.

"J. O. PARE, Canon, Secretary."

No words from my pen can give an idea of the distress and shame I felt when these unmerited praises and public honours began to flow upon me. For, when the siren voice of my natural pride was near to deceive me, there was the noise of a sudden storm in my conscience, crying with a louder voice : " Chiniquy, thou art a sinner, unworthy of such praises and honours."

This conflict made me very miserable. I said to myself, " Are those great successes due to my merits, my virtues and my eloquence ? No ! Surely, No ! They are due to the great mercy of God for my dear country. Shall I not for ever be put to shame if I consent to these flattering voices which come to me from morning till night, to make me forget that to my God alone, and not to me, must be given the praise and glory of that marvellous reform ? "

These praises were coming every day, thicker and thicker, through the thousand trumpets of the press, as well as through the addresses daily presented me from the places which had been so thoroughly reformed. Those unmerited honours were bestowed on me by multitudes who came in carriages and on horseback, bearing flags, with bands of music, to receive me on the borders of their parishes, where the last parishes had just brought me with the same kind of ovations. Sometimes, the roads were lined on both sides, by thousands and thousands of maple, pine or spruce trees, which they had carried from distant forests, in spite of all my protests.

How many times the curates, who were sitting by me in the best carriages, drawn by the most splendid horses, asked me : " Why do you look so sad, when you see all these faces beaming with joy ? " I answered, " I am sad, because these unmerited honours these good people do me, seem to be the shortest way the devil has found to destroy me." " But the reform you have brought about is so admirable and so complete—the good which is done to the individuals, as well as to the whole country, is so great and universal, that the people want to show you their gratitude." " Do you know, my dear friends," I answered, " that that marvellous change is too great to be the work of man ? Is it not evidently the work of God ? To Him, and Him alone, then we ought to give the praise and the glory."

My constant habit, after these days of ovation, was to pass a part of the night in prayer to God, to the Virgin Mary, and to all the saints in heaven, to prevent me from being hurt by these worldly honours.   It was my custom then to read the passion of Jesus Christ, from His triumphant entry into Jerusalem to His death on the cross, in order to prevent this shining dust from adhering to my soul.   There was a verse of the Gospel which I used to repeat very often in the midst of those exhibitions of the vanities of this world : " What is a man profited, if he shall gain the whole world and lose his own soul ? " (Matt. xvi. 26).

Another source of serious anxiety for me was then coming from the large sums of money constantly flowing from the hands of my too kind and grateful reformed countrymen into mine.   It was very seldom that the public expression of gratitude presented me in their rhetorical addresses were not accompanied by a gift of from fifty dollars to two hundred dollars, according to the means and importance of the place. Those sums multiplied by the 365 days of the year would have soon made of me one of the richest men of Canada.   Had I been able to trust in my own strength against the dangers of riches, I should have been able, easily, to accumulate a sum of at least seventy thousand dollars, with which I might have done a great amount of good.

But I confess that, when in the presence of God, I went to the bottom of my heart, to see if it were strong enough to carry such a glittering weight, I found it, by far, too weak.   I knew so many who, though evidently stronger than I was, had fallen on the way and perished under too heavy burden of their treasures, that I feared for myself at the sight of such unexpected and immense fortune.   Besides, when only eighteen years old, my venerable and dear benefactor, the Rev. Mr. Leprohon, director of the College of Nicolet, had told me a thing I never had forgotten : " Chiniquy," he said, " I am sure you will be what we call a successful man in the world.   You will easily make your way among your contemporaries ; and, consequently, it is probable that you will have many opportunities of becoming rich.   But when the silver and gold flow into your hands, do not pile and keep it.   For, if you set your affections on it, you will be miserable in this world and damned in the next.   You must not do like the fattened hogs which give their grease only after their death. Give it while you are living.   Then you will not be blessed only by God and man, but you will be blessed by your own conscience.   You will live in peace and die in joy."

These solemn warnings from one of the wisest and best friends God had ever given me, when young, has never gone out of my mind.   I found them corroborated in every page of that Bible which I loved so much, and studied every day.   I found them also written, by God, in my heart.   I then, on my knees, took the resolution, without making an absolute vow of it, to keep only what I wanted for my daily support and give the rest to the poor, or some Christian or patriotic object. I kept my promise. The £500 given me by Parliament did not remain three weeks in my hands. I never put a cent in Canada in the vaults of any bank; and when I left for Illinois, in the fall of 1851, instead of taking with me 70,000 dollars, as it would have been very easy, had I been so minded, I had hardly 1,500 dollars in hand, the price of a part of my library, which was too heavy to be carried so far away.

CHAPTER XLV.

THE 15th of August, 1850, I preached in the Cathedral of Montreal, on the Blessed Virgin Mary's power in heaven, when interceding for sinners, I was sincerely devoted to the Virgin Mary. Nothing seemed to me more natural than to pray to her, and rely on her protection. The object of my sermon was to show that Jesus Christ cannot refuse any of the petitions presented to Him by His mother; that she has always obtained the favours she asked her Son, Jesus, to grant to her devotees. Of course, my address was more sentimental than scriptural, as it is the style among the priests of Rome. But I was honest; and I sincerely believed what I said.

"Who among you, my dear brethren," I said to the people, "will refuse any of the reasonable demands of a beloved mother? Who will break and sadden her loving heart when, with supplicating voice and tears, she presents to you a petition which it is in your power, nay, to your interest, to grant? For my own part, were my beloved mother still living, I would prefer to have my right hand crushed and burned into cinders, to have my tongue cut out, than to say, No! to my mother, asking me any favour which it was in my power to bestow. These are the sentiments which the God of Sinai wanted to engrave in the very hearts of humanity, when giving His laws to Moses, in the midst of lightning and thunders, and these are the sentiments which the God of the Gospel wanted to impress on our souls by the shedding of His blood on Calvary. The sentiments of filial respect and obedience to our mothers, Christ Jesus, the Son of God and Son of Mary, practised to perfection. Although God and man, He was still in perfect submission to the will of His mother, of which He makes a law to each of us. The Gospel says, in reference to His parents, Joseph and Mary, He ' was subject unto them ' (Luke ii. 51). What a grand and shining revelation we have in these few short words: Jesus was subject unto Mary! Is it not written, that Jesus is the same to-day, as He was yesterday, and will be for ever? (Heb. xiii. 8.) He has not changed. He is still the Son of Mary, as He was when only twelve years old. In His divine humanity, He is still subject unto Mary, as He was then. This is why our holy Church, which is the pillar and fountain of Truth, invites you and me, to-day, to put an unbounded confidence in her intercession. Remembering that Jesus has always granted the petitions presented to Him by His divine mother, let us put our petitions in her hands, if we want to receive the favours we are in need of.

"The second reason why we must all go to Mary, for the favours we want from heaven, is that we are sinners—rebels in the sight of God. Jesus ّChrist is our Saviour. Yes! but He is also our God, infinitely just, infinitely holy. He hates our sins with an infinite hatred. He abhors our rebellions with an infinite, a godly hatred. If we had loved and served Him faithfully we might go to Him, not only with the hope, but with the assurance of being welcomed. But we have forgotten and offended Him; we have trampled His blood under our feet; we have joined with those who nailed Him on the cross, pierced His heart with the lance, and shed His blood to the last drop. We belong to the crowd which mocked at His tortures, and insulted Him at His death. How can we dare to look at Him and meet His eyes? Must we not tremble in His presence? Must we not fear before that Lion of the tribe of Judah whom we have wounded and nailed to the cross? Where is the rebel who does not shiver, when he is dragged to the feet of the mighty Prince against whom he has drawn the sword? What will he do if he wants to obtain pardon? Will he go himself and speak to that offended Majesty? No! But he looks around the throne to see if he can find some of the great officers, and friends, or some powerful and influential person through whose intercession he can obtain pardon. If he finds any such, he goes immediately to him, puts his petitions into their hands, and they go to the foot of the throne to plead for the rebel, and the favour which would have been indignantly refused to the guilty subject, had he dared to speak himself, is granted, when it is asked by a faithful officer, a kind friend, a dear sister, or a beloved mother. This is why our holy church, speaking through her infallible supreme pontiff, the Vicar of Christ, Gregory XVI., has told us, in the most solemn manner, that ' Mary is the only hope of sinners.' "

Winding up my arguments, I added : " We are those insolent ungrateful rebels. Jesus is that King of kings against whom we have, a thousand times, risen in rebellion. He has a thousand good reasons to refuse our petitions, if we are impudent enough to speak to Him ourselves. But look at the right hand of the offended King, and behold His dear and divine mother. She is your mother also. For it is to every one of us, as well as to John, that Christ said on the cross, speaking of Mary, ' Behold thy mother ' (John xix. 27). Jesus has never refused any favour asked by that Queen of Heaven. He cannot rebuke His mother. Let us go to her ; let us ask her to be our advocate and plead our cause, and she will do it. Let us suppliantly request her to ask for our pardon, and she will get it."

I then sincerely took these glittering sophisms for the true religion of Christ, as all the priests and people of Rome are bound to take them to-day, and presented them with all the earnestness of an honest, though deluded mind.

My sermon had made a visible and deep impression. Bishop Prince, coadjutor of my Lord Bourget, who was among my hearers, thanked and congratulated me for the good effect it would have on the people, and I sincerely thought I had said what was true and right before God.

But when night came, before going to bed, I took my Bible as usual, knelt down before God, in the neat little room I occupied in the bishop's palace, and read the twelfth chapter of Matthew, with a praying heart and a sincere desire to understand it, and be benefited thereby. Strange to say! when I reached the 40th verse, I felt a mysterious awe, as if I had entered for the first time into a new and most holy land. Though I had read that verse and the following many times, they came to my mind with a freshness and newness as if I had never seen them before. There was a lull in my mind for some moments. Slowly, and with breathless attention, supreme veneration and respect, I read the history of that visit of Mary to the sacred spot where Jesus, my Saviour, was standing in the midst of the crowd feeding His happy hearers with the bread of life.

When I contemplated that blessed Mary, whom I loved, as so tenderly approaching the house where she was to meet her divine Son, who had been so long absent from her, my heart suddenly throbbed in sympathy with hers. I felt as if sharing her unspeakable joy at every step which brought her nearer to her adorable and beloved Son. What tears had she not shed when Jesus had left her alone, in her now, poor, and cheerless home, that He might preach the Gospel in the distant places, where His Father had sent Him! With Jesus in her humble home, was she not more happy then than the greatest queen on her throne! Did she not possess a treasure more precious than all the world! How sweet to her ears and heart were the words she had heard from His lips!

How lovely the face of the most beautiful among the sons of men! How happy she must have felt, when she heard that He was, now, near enough to allow her to go and see Him! How quick were her steps. How cheerful and interesting the meeting! How the beloved Saviour will repay by His respectful and divine love to His beloved mother, the trouble and the fatigue of her long journey! My heart beat with joy at the privilege of witnessing that interview, and of hearing the respectful words Jesus would address to His mother!

With heart and soul throbbing with these feelings, I slowly read—
"While He yet talked to the people, behold His mother and His brethren stood without, desiring to speak with Him. Then one said unto Him : Behold, Thy mother and Thy brethren stand without, desiring to speak with Thee. But He answered and said unto him that told Him : Who is My mother? and Who are My brethren? And He stretched forth His hands towards His disciples, and said : Behold My mother and My brethren! For whosoever shall do the will of My Father which is in Heaven, the same is My brother, and sister, and mother."

I had hardly finished reading the last verse, when big drops of sweat began to flow from my face, my heart beat with a tremendous speed, and I came near fainting; I sat in my large arm-chair, expecting every minute to fall on the floor. Those alone who have stood several hours at the falls of the marvellous Niagara, heard the thundering noise of its waters, and felt the shaking of the rocks under their feet, can have any idea of what I felt in that hour of agony.

A voice, the voice of my conscience, whose thunders were like the voice of a thousand Niagaras was telling me : "Do you not see that you have preached a sacrilegious lie this morning, when, from the pulpit, you said to your ignorant and deluded people, that Jesus always granted the petitions of His mother, Mary? Are you not ashamed to deceive yourself, and deceive your poor countrymen with such silly falsehoods?"

"Read, read again these words! and understand that, far from granting all the petitions of Mary, Jesus has always, except when a child, said No! to her requests. He has always rebuked her, when she asked Him anything in public! Here she comes to ask Him a favour before the whole people. It is the easiest, the most natural favour that a mother ever asked of her son. It is a favour that a son has never refused to a mother. He answers by a rebuke, a public and solemn rebuke! Is it through want of love and respect for Mary that He gave her that rebuke? No! Never a son loved and respected a mother as He did. But it was a solemn protest against the blasphemous worship of Mary as practised in the Church of Rome."

I felt at once so bewildered and confounded, by the voice which was shaking my very bones, that I thought it was the devil's voice; and, for a moment, I feared less I was possessed of a demon. "My God," I cried, "have mercy on me! Come to my help! Save me from my enemy's hands!" As quick as lightning the answer came : "It is not Satan's voice you hear. It is I, thy Saviour and thy God, who speaks to thee. Read what Mark, Luke, and John tell you about the way I received her petitions, from the very day I began to work, and speak publicly as the Son of God, and the Saviour of the world."

These cries of my awakening intelligence were sounding in my ears for more than one hour, before I consented to obey them. At last, with a trembling hand, and a distressed mind, I took my Bible and read in St. Mark : " There came then His brethren and his mother, and standing without, sent unto Him, calling Him. And the multitude sat about Him and they said unto Him, Behold, Thy mother and Thy brethren without, seek for Thee. And He answered them, saying, Who is My mother, or My brethren ? And He looked round about on them which sat about Him, and said, Behold My mother and My brethren. For whosoever shall do the will of God, the same is My brother, and My sister, and mother " (Mark iii. 31—35).

The reading of these words acted upon me as the shock of a sword going through and through the body of one who had already been mortally wounded. I felt absolutely confounded. The voice continued to sound in my ears : " Do you not see you have presented a blasphemous lie, every time you said that Jesus always granted the petitions of His mother ?"

I remained again, a considerable time, bewildered, not knowing how to fight down thoughts which were so mercilessly shaking my faith, and demolishing the respect I had kept, till then, for my Church. After more than half an hour of vain struggle to silence these thoughts, it came to my mind that St. Luke had narrated this interview of Mary and Jesus in a very different way. I opened the holy book again to read the eighth chapter. But how shall I find words to express my distress when I saw that the rebuke of Jesus Christ was expressed in a still sterner way by St. Luke than by the two other evangelists !

" Then came to Him His mother and His brethren, and could not come at Him for the press. And it was told Him by certain which said, Thy mother and Thy brethren stand without, desiring to see Thee. And He answered and said unto them, My mother and My brethren are these which hear the word of God, and do it " (Luke viii. 19—21).

It then seemed to me as if those three evangelists said to me : " How dare you preach with your apostate and lying Church, that Jesus has always granted all the petitions of Mary, when we were ordered by God to write and proclaim that all the public petitions she had presented to Him, when working as the Son of God, and the Saviour of the world, had been answered by a public rebuke ?"

What could I answer ? How could I stand the rebuke of these three evangelists ? Trembling from head to foot, I fell upon my knees, crying to the Virgin Mary to come to my help and pray that I might not succumb to this temptation, and lose my faith and confidence in her. But the more I prayed, the louder the voice seemed to say : " How dare you preach that Jesus has always granted the petitions of Mary, when we tell you the contrary by the order of God Himself ?"

My desolation became such, that a cold sweat covered my whole frame again ; my head was aching, and I think I would have fainted had I not been released by a torrent of tears. In my distress, I cried : " Oh ! my God ! my God ! look down upon me in Thy mercy ; strengthen my faith in Thy Holy Church ! Grant me to follow her voice and obey her commands with more and more fidelity ; she is Thy beloved Church. She cannot err. She cannot be an apostate Church." But in vain I wept and cried for help. My whole being was filled with dismay and terror from the voices of the three witnesses, who were crying louder and louder :

" How dare you preach that Christ has always granted the petitions of Mary, when the gospels, written under the inspiration of the Holy Ghost, tell you so clearly the contrary ? "

When I had, in vain, wept, prayed, cried, and struggled from ten at night till three in the morning, the miraculous change of water into wine, by Christ, at the request of his mother, suddenly came to my mind. I felt a momentary relief from my terrible distress, by the hope that I could prove to myself that in this case the Saviour had obeyed the demands of His holy mother. I eagerly opened my Bible again and read :

" And the third day there was a marriage in Cana of Galilee ; and the mother of Jesus was there. And both Jesus was called, and His disciples, to the marriage. And when they wanted wine, the mother of Jesus saith unto Him, They have no wine. Jesus saith unto her, Woman, what have I to do with thee ? Mine hour is not yet come. His mother saith unto the servants, Whatsoever He saith unto you, do it " (John ii. 1—5).

Till that hour I had always accepted that text in the sense given in the Church of Rome, as proving that the very first miracle of Jesus Christ was wrought at the request of His mother. And I was preparing myself to answer the three mysterious witnesses : " Here is the proof that you are three devils, and not three evangelists, when you tell me that Jesus has never granted the petitions of His mother, except when a child. Here is the glorious title of Mary to my confidence in her intercession ; here is the seal of her irresistible superhuman power over her divine Son ; here is the undeniable evidence that Jesus cannot refuse anything asked by His divine mother ! " But when, armed with these explanations of the church, I was preparing to meet what Matthew, St. Mark, and St. Luke had just told me, a sudden distressing thought came to my mind ; and this thought was as if I heard the three witnesses saying : " How can you be so blind as not to see that instead of being a favour granted to Mary, this first miracle is the first opportunity chosen by Christ to protest against her intercession. It is a solemn warning to Mary never to ask anything from Him, and to us, never to put any confidence in her requests. Here, Mary, evidently full of compassion for those poor people, who had not the means to provide the wine for the guests who had come with Jesus, wants her Son to give them the wine they wanted. How does Christ answer her requests? He answers it by a rebuke, a most solemn rebuke. Instead of saying: " Yes, mother, I will do as you wish," He says, "Woman, what have I to do with thee?" which clearly means, " Woman, thou hast nothing to do in this matter. I do not want you to speak to me of the bridegroom's distress. It was My desire to come to their help and show My divine power. I do not want you to put yourself between the wants of humanity and Me. I do not want the world to believe that you had any right, any power or influence over me, or more compassion on the miseries of man than I have. Is it not to Me and Me alone, the lost children of Adam must look to be saved? Woman, what have I to do with thee in My great work of saving this perishing world? Nothing, absolutely nothing. I know what I have to do to fulfil, not your will, but My Father's will!"

This is what Jesus meant by the solemn rebuke given to Mary. He wanted to banish all idea of her ever becoming an intercessor between man and Christ. He wanted to protest against the doctrine of the Church of Rome, that it is through Mary that He will bestow His favour to His disciples, and Mary understood it well when she said, "Whatsoever He saith unto you, do it." Never come to me, but go to Him. " For there is none other name under heaven given among men, whereby we must be saved " (Acts iv. 12).

Every one of these thoughts passed over my distressed soul like a hurricane. Every sentence was like a flash of lightning in a dark night. I was like the poor dismantled ship suddenly overtaken by the tempest in the midst of the ocean.

Till the dawn of day, I felt powerless against the efforts of God to pull down and demolish the huge fortress of sophisms, falsehoods, idolatries, which Rome had built around my soul. What a fearful thing it is to fight against the Lord!

During the long hours of that night, my God was contending with me, and I was struggling against Him. But though brought down to the dust, I was not conquered. My understanding was very nearly convinced. My rebellious and proud will was not yet ready to yield.

The chains by which I was tied to the feet of the idols of Rome, though rudely shaken, were not yet broken. However, to say the truth, my views about the worship of Mary had received a severe shock, and were much modified. That night had been sleepless; and in the morning my eyes were red, and my face swollen with my tears. When at breakfast, Bishop Prince, who was sitting by me, asked: "Are you sick? Your eyes are as if you had wept all night?" "Your lordship is not mistaken, I have wept the whole night!" I answered. "Wept all the night!" replied the bishop. "Might I know the cause of your sorrow?" "Yes, my lord. You can, you must know it. But please come to your room. What I have to say is of such a private and delicate nature, that I want to be alone with your lordship, when opening my mind to the cause of my tears."

Bishop Prince, then coadjutor of Bishop Bourget and late bishop of St. Hyacinthe, where he became insane in 1858 and died in 1860, had been my personal friend from the time I entered the college at Nicolet, where he was professor of Rhetoric. He very often came to confession to me, and had taken a lively interest in my labours on temperance.

When alone with him, I said: "My lord, I thank you for your kindness in allowing me to unburden my heart to you. I have passed the most horrible night of my life. Temptations against our holy religion such as I never had before, have assailed me all night. Your lordship remembers the kind words you addressed to me yesterday about the sermon I preached. But, last night, very different things came to my mind, which have changed the joys of yesterday into the most unspeakable desolation. You congratulated me yesterday on the manner I had proved that Jesus had always granted the requests of His mother, and that He cannot refuse any of her petitions. The whole night it has been told me that this was a blasphemous lie, and from the Holy Scriptures themselves, I have been nearly convinced that you and I, nay, that our holy church, are preaching a blasphemous falsehood every time we proclaim the doctrines of the worship of Mary as the Gospel truth."

The poor bishop, thunderstruck by this simple and honest declaration, quickly answered: "I hope you have not yielded to these temptations, and that you will not become a Protestant as so many of your enemies whisper to each other."

"It is my hope, my lord, that our merciful God will keep me, to the end of my life, a dutiful and faithful priest of our holy church. However, I cannot conceal from your lordship that my faith was terribly shaken last night.

"As a bishop, your portion of light and wisdom must be greater than mine. I hope you will grant me some of the lights which still brightly shine before your eyes: I have never been so much in need of the counsels of your piety and the help of your scriptural know-

22

ledge as to-day. Please help me to come out from the intellectual slough in which I spent the night.

"Your lordship has congratulated me for having said that Jesus Christ has always granted the petitions of Mary. Please tell me how you reconcile that proposition with the text;" and I handed him the Gospel of Matthew, pointing to the last five verses of the twelfth chapter, I requested him to read them aloud.

He read them and said : "Now, what do you want from me?"

"My lord, I want respectfully to ask you how we can say that Jesus has always granted the requests of His mother, when this evangelist tells us that He never granted her petitions, when acting in His capacity of Saviour of the world.

"Must we not fear that we proclaim a blasphemous falsehood when we support a proposition directly opposed to the Gospel?"

The poor bishop seemed absolutely confounded by this simple and honest question. I also felt confused and sorry for his humiliation. Beginning a phrase, he would give it up ; trying arguments, he could not push to their conclusion. It seemed to me that he had never read that text, or if he had read it, he, like myself and the rest of the priests of Rome, had never noted that they entirely demolish the stupendous impostures of the church, in reference to the worship of Mary.

In order to help him out of the inextricable difficulties into which I had at once pushed him, I said : "My lord, will you allow me to put a few more questions to you?"

"With pleasure," he answered.

"Well! my lord, who came to this world to save you and me? Is it Jesus or Mary?"

"It is Jesus," answered the bishop.

"Who was called, and is, in reality, the sinner's best friend? Was it Jesus or Mary?"

The bishop answered, "It was Jesus."

"Now, please allow me a few more questions."

"When Jesus and Mary were on earth, whose heart was most devoted to sinners? Who loved them with a more efficacious and saving love; was it Jesus or Mary?"

"Jesus, being God, His love was evidently more efficacious and saving than Mary's," answered the bishop.

"In the days of Jesus and Mary, to whom did Jesus invite sinners to go for their salvation; was it to Himself or Mary?" I asked again.

The bishop answered: "Jesus has said to all sinners, ' Come unto Me.' He never said, come or go to Mary."

"Have we any examples, in the Scriptures, of sinners, who, fearing to be rebuked by Jesus, have gone to Mary and obtained access to Him through her, and been saved through her intercessions?"

"I do not remember of any such cases," replied the bishop.

I then asked: "To whom did the penitent thief on the cross address himself to be saved; was it to Jesus or Mary?"

"It was to Jesus," replied the bishop.

"Did that penitent thief do well to address himself to Jesus on the cross, rather than to Mary who was at his feet?" said I.

"Surely he did better," answered the bishop.

"Now, my lord, allow me only one question more. You told me that Jesus loved sinners, when on earth, infinitely more than Mary; that He was infinitely more their true friend than she was; that He infinitely took more interest in their salvation than Mary; that it was infinitely better for sinners to go to Jesus than to Mary, to be saved; will you please tell me if you think that Jesus has lost, in heaven, since He is sitting at the right hand of His Father, any of His divine and infinite superiority of love and mercy over Mary for sinners; and can you show me that what Jesus has lost has been gained by Mary?"

"I do not think that Christ has lost any of His love and power to save us now that He is in heaven," answered the bishop.

"Now, my lord, if Jesus is still my best friend, my most powerful, merciful, and loving friend, why should I not go directly to Him? Why should we, for a moment, go to any one who is infinitely inferior, in power, love, and mercy, for our salvation?"

The bishop was stunned by my questions.

He stammered some unintelligible answer, excused himself for not being able to remain any longer, on account of some pressing business; and extending his hand to me before leaving, he said: "You will find an answer to your questions and difficulties in the Holy Fathers."

"Can you lend me the Holy Fathers, my lord?"

He replied: "No, sir, I have them not."

This last answer, from my bishop, shook my faith to its foundation, and left my mind in a state of great distress. With the sincere hope of finding in the Holy Fathers some explanations which would dispel my painful doubts, I immediately went to Mr. Fabre, the great bookseller of Montreal, who got me, from France, the splendid edition of the Holy Fathers, by Migné. I studied, with the utmost attention, every page where I might find what they taught of the worship of Mary, and the doctrines that Jesus Christ had never refused any of her prayers.

What was my desolation, my shame, and my surprise to find that the Holy Fathers of the first six centuries had never advocated the worship of Mary, and that the many eloquent pages on the power of Mary in heaven, and her love for sinners, found in every page of my theologians, and other ascetic books I had read till then, were but impudent lies; additions interpolated in their works, a hundred years after their death. When discovering these forgeries, under the name of the Holy Fathers, of which my church was guilty, how many times, in the silence of my long nights of study and prayerful meditations, did I hear a voice telling me: " Come out of Babylon !"

But where could I go ? Out of the Church of Rome, where could I find that salvation which was to be found only within her walls ? I said to myself, "Surely there are some errors in my dear church ! The dust of ages may have fallen on the precious gold of her treasures, but will I not find still more damnable errors among those hundreds of Protestant churches, which, under the name of Episcopalians, Presbyterians, Baptists, Methodists, etc., etc., are divided and subdivided into scores of contemptible sects, anathematizing and denouncing each other before the world ?"

My ideas of the great family of evangelical churches, comprised under the broad name of Protestantism, were so exaggerated then, that it was absolutely impossible for me to find in them that unity, which I considered the essentials of the church of Christ. The hour was not yet come, but it was coming fast, when my dear Saviour would make me understand His sublime words : " I am the vine, and ye are the branches."

It was some time later, when under the beautiful vine I had planted in my own garden, and which I had cultivated with mine own hands, I saw that there was not a single branch like another in that prolific vine. Some branches were very big, some very thin, some very long, some very short, some going up, some going down, some straight as an arrow, some crooked as a flash of lightning, some turning to the west, some to the east, some to the north, and others to the south. But, although the branches were so different from each other in so many things, they all gave me excellent fruit, so long as they remained united to the vine.

CHAPTER XLVI.

THE most desolate work of a sincere Catholic priest is the study of the Holy Fathers. He does not make a step in the labyrinth of their discussions and controversies without seeing the dreams of his theological studies and religious views disappear as the thick morning mist, when the sun rises above the horizon. Bound as he is, by a solemn oath, to interpret the Holy Scriptures only according to the unanimous consent of the Holy Fathers, the first thing which puzzles and distresses him is their absolute want of unanimity on the greater part of the subjects which they discuss. The fact is, that more than two-thirds of what one Father has written is to prove that what some other Holy Father has written is wrong and heretical.

The student of the Fathers not only detects that they do not agree with one another, but finds that many of them do not even agree with themselves. Very often they confess that they were mistaken when they said this or that; that they have lately changed their minds; that they now hold for saving truth what they formerly condemned as a damning error!

What becomes of the solemn oath of every priest in presence of this undeniable fact? How can he make an act of faith when he feels that its foundation is nothing but falsehood?

No words can give an idea of the mental tortures I felt when I saw positively that I could not, any longer, preach on the eternity of the suffering of the damned, nor believe in the real presence of the body, soul, and divinity of Christ in the sacrament of communion; nor in the supremacy of the sovereign Pontiff of Rome, nor in any of the other dogmas of my church, without perjuring myself! For there was not one of those dogmas which had not been flatly and directly denied by some Holy Fathers.

It is true, that in my Roman Catholic theological books I had long extracts of Holy Fathers, very clearly supporting and confirming my faith in those dogmas. For instance, I had the apostolic liturgies of St. Peter, St. Mark, and St. James, to prove that the sacrifice of the mass, purgatory, prayers for the dead, transubstantiation, were believed and taught from the very days of the apostles. But what was my dismay when I discovered that those liturgies were nothing else than vile and audacious forgeries presented to the world, by my Popes and my church, as gospel truths. I could not find words to express my sense of shame and consternation, when I became sure that the same church which had invented those apostolical liturgies, had accepted and circulated the false decretals of Isidore, and forged innumerable additions and interpolations to the writings of the Holy Fathers, in order to make them say the very contrary of what they intended.

How many times, when alone, studying the history of the shameless fabrications, I said to myself: "Does the man whose treasury is filled with pure gold, forge false coins, or spurious pieces of money? No! How, then, is it possible that my church does possess the pure truth, when she has been at work during so many centuries, to forge such egregious lies, under the names of liturgies and decretals, about the holy mass, purgatory, the supremacy of the Pope, etc. If those dogmas could have been proved by the gospel and the true writings of the Fathers, where was the necessity of forging lying documents? Would the Popes and councils have treasuries with spurious bank bills, if they had had exhaustless mines of pure gold in hand? What right has my church to be called holy and infallible, when she is publicly guilty of such impostures."

From my infancy I had been taught, with all the Roman Catholics, that Mary is the mother of God, and many times, every day, when praying to her, I used to say, " Holy Mary, mother of God, pray for me." But what was my distress when I read in the " Treatise on Faith and Creed," by Augustine, Chapter iv. § 9, these very words: " When the Lord said, ' Woman, what have I to do with thee ? Mine hour is not yet come ' (John ii. 4), He rather admonishes us to understand that, in respect of His being God, there was no mother for Him."

This was so completely demolishing the teachings of my church, and telling me that it was blasphemy to call Mary mother of God, that I felt as if struck with a thunderbolt.

Several volumes might be written, if my plan were to give the story of my mental agonies, when reading the Holy Fathers. I found their furious battles against each other, and reviewed their fierce divisions on almost every subject. The horror of many of them, at the dogmas which my church had taught to make me believe from my infancy, as the most solemn and sacred revelations of God to man, such as transubstantiation, auricular confession, purgatory, the supremacy of Peter, the absolute supremacy of the Pope over the whole Church of Christ. Yes! what thrilling pages I would give to the world, were it my intention to pourtray, in their true colours, the dark clouds, the flashing lights and destructive storms which, during the long and silent hours of the many nights I spent in comparing the Fathers with the Word of God and the teachings of my church. Their fierce and constant conflicts; their unexpected, though undeniable oppositions to many of the articles of the faith I had to believe and preach, were coming to me, day after day, as the barbed darts thrown at the doomed whale when coming out of the dark regions of the deep to see the light and breathe the pure air.

Thus, as the unexpected contradictions of the Holy Fathers to the tenets of my church, and their furious and uncharitable divisions among themselves, were striking me, I plunged deeper and deeper in the deep waters of the Fathers and the Word of God, with the hope of getting rid of the deadly darts which were piercing my Roman Catholic conscience. But, it was in vain. The deeper I went, the more the deadly weapons would stick to the flesh and bone of my soul. How deep was the wound I received from Gregory the Great, one of the most learned Popes of Rome, against the supremacy and universality of the power of the Pope of Rome as taught to-day, the following extracts from his writings will show: " I say confidently, Whosoever calls himself Universal Priest, or desires so to be called, is in his pride the forerunner of Antichrist, because, in his pride, he sets himself before the rest."*

These words wounded me very painfully. I showed them to Mr. Brassard, saying: "Do you not see here the incontrovertible proof of what I have told you many times, that, during the first six centuries of Christianity, we do not find the least proof that there was anything like our dogma of the supreme power and authority of the Bishop of Rome, or any other bishop, over the rest of the Christian world? If there is anything which comes to the mind with an irresistible force, when reading the Fathers of the first centuries, it is that, not one of them had any idea that there was, in the church, any man chosen by God, to be, in fact or name, the universal and supreme Pontiff. With such an undeniable fact before us, how can we believe and say that the religion we profess and teach is the same which was preached from the beginning of Christianity?"

"My dear Chiniquy," answered Mr. Brassard, "did I not tell you, when you bought the Holy Fathers, that you were doing a foolish and dangerous thing? In every age, the man who singularises himself and walks out of the common tracks of life is subject to fall into ridicule. As you are the only priest in Canada who has the Holy Fathers, it is thought and said, in many quarters, that it is through pride you got them; that it is to raise yourself above the rest of the clergy, that you study them, not only at home, but that you carry some wherever you go. I see, with regret, that you are fast losing ground in the mind, not only of the bishop, but of the priests in general, on account of your indomitable perseverance in giving all your spare time to their study. You are also too free and imprudent in speaking of what you call the contradictions of the Holy Fathers, and their want of harmony with some of our religious views. Many say that this too great application to study, without a moment of relaxation, will upset your intelligence and trouble your mind. They even whisper that there is danger ahead for your faith, which you do not suspect, and that they would not be surprised if the reading of the Bible and the Holy Fathers would drive you into the abyss of Protestantism. I know that they are mistaken, and I do all in my power to defend you. But, I thought, as your most devoted friend, that it was my duty to tell you those things, and warn you before it is too late."

I replied: "Bishop Prince told me the very same things, and I will give you the answer he got from me; 'When you ordain a priest, do

* "Ego . . . fidenter dico . . . Quisquis se Universalem Sacerdotem vocat, vel vocari desiderat, in elatione suâ Antichristum præcurrit, quia superbiendo se cæteris præponit." (Gregor. Magni Papae I. Op. Par. 1705. Epist. Lib. vii. Indict. xv. Ad Mauric. August. Epist. xxxiii. tom. ii. col. 881.)

you not make him swear that he will never interpret the Holy Scriptures except according to the unanimous consent of the Holy Fathers? Ought you not, then, to know what they teach? For, how can we know their unanimous consent without studying them? Is it not more than strange that, not only the priests do not study the Holy Fathers, but the only one in Canada who is trying to study them, is turned into ridicule and suspected of heresy? Is it my fault if that precious stone, called ' unanimous consent of [the Holy Fathers,' which is the very foundation of our religious belief and teaching, is to be found nowhere in them? Is it my fault if Origen never believed in the eternal punishment of the damned; if St. Cyprian denied the supreme authority of the Bishop of Rome; if St. Augustine positively said that nobody was obliged to believe in purgatory; if St. John Chrysostom publicly denied the obligation of auricular confession, and the real presence of the body of Christ in the eucharist? Is it my fault if one of the most learned and holy Popes, Gregory the Great, has called by the name of Antichrist, all his successors, for taking the name of supreme Pontiff, and trying to persuade the world that they had, by divine authority, a supreme jurisdiction and power over the rest of the church? "

"And what did Bishop Prince answer you?" rejoined Mr. Brassard.

"Just as you did, by expressing his fears that my too great application to the study of the Bible and the Holy Fathers, would either send me to the lunatic asylum, or drive me into the bottomless abyss of Protestantism."

I answered him, in a jocose way : "That if the too great study of the Bible and the Holy Fathers were to open me the gates of the lunatic asylum, I feared I would be left alone there, for I know that they are keeping themselves at a respectable distance from those dangerous writings." I added seriously, " So long as God keeps my intelligence sound, I cannot join the Protestants, for the numberless and ridiculous sects of these heretics are a sure antidote against their poisonous errors. I will not remain a good Catholic on account of the unanimity of the Holy Fathers, which does not exist, but I will remain a Catholic on account of the grand and visible unanimity of the prophets, apostles, and the evangelists with Jesus Christ. My faith will not be founded upon the fallible, obscure, and wavering words of Origen, Tertullian, Chrysostom, Augustine, or Jerome; but on the infallible word of Jesus, the Son of God, and of His inspired writers : Matthew, Mark, Luke, John, Peter, James, and Paul. It is Jesus, and not Origen, who will now guide me; for the second was a sinner, like myself, and the first is for ever my Saviour and my God. I know enough of the Holy Fathers to assure your lordship that the

oath we take of accepting the Word of God according to their unanimous consent is a miserable blunder, if not a blasphemous perjury.
It is evident that Pius IV., who imposed the obligation of that oath
upon us all, never read a single volume of the Holy Fathers. He
would not have been guilty of such an incredible blunder, if he had
known that the Holy Fathers are unanimous in only one thing, which
is to differ from each other on almost everything; except, we suppose,
that, like the last Pope, he was too fond of good champagne, and that
he wrote that ordinance after a luxurious dinner."

I spoke this last sentence in a half-serious and half-joking way.

The bishop answered: "Who told you that about our last
Pope?"

"Your lordship," I answered, "told me that, when you com-
plimented me on the apostolical benediction which the present Pope
sent me through my Lord Baillargeon, 'that his predecessor would
not have given me his benediction for preaching temperance, because
he was too fond of wine!'"

"Oh yes! yes! I remember it now," answered the bishop. "But
it was a bad joke on my part, which I regret."

"Good or bad joke," I replied, "it is not the less a fact that our
last Pope was too fond of wine. There is not a single priest of Canada
who has gone to Rome without bringing that back as a public fact
from Italy."

"And what did my Lord Prince say to that," asked again Mr.
Brassard.

"Just as when he was cornered by me, on the subject of the
Virgin Mary, he abruptly put an end to the conversation by looking
at his watch, and saying that he had a call to make at that very
hour."

Not long after that painful conversation about the Holy Fathers, it
was the will of God, that a new arrow should be thrust into my
Roman Catholic conscience, which went through and through, in
spite of myself.

I had been invited to give a course of three sermons at Varennes.
The second day, at tea time, after preaching and hearing confessions
for the whole afternoon, I was coming from the church with the
curate, when, half-way to the parsonage, we were met by a poor man,
who looked more like one coming out of the grave, than a living man;
he was covered with rags, and his pale and trembling lips indicated
that he was reduced to the last degree of human misery. Taking off
his hat, through respect for us, he said to Rev. Primeau, with a trembling voice: "You know, Mr. le Cure, that my poor wife died, and
was buried ten days ago, but I was too poor to have a funeral service
sung the day she was buried, and I fear she is in purgatory, for almost

every night I see her, in my dreams, wrapped up in burning flames. She cries to me for help, and asks me to have a high mass sung for the rest of her soul. I come to ask you to be so kind as to sing that high mass for her."

"Of course," answered the curate, "your wife is in the flames of purgatory, and suffers there the most unspeakable tortures, which can be relieved only by the offering of the holy sacrifice of mass. Give me five dollars and I will sing that mass to-morrow morning."

"You know very well, Mr. le Cure," answered the poor man, in a most supplicating tone, "that my wife has been sick, as well as myself, a good part of the year. I am too poor to give you five dollars!"

"If you cannot pay, you cannot have any mass sung. You know it is the rule. It is not in my power to change it."

These words were said by the curate with a high and unfeeling tone, which were in absolute contrast with the solemnity and distress of the poor sick man. They made a very painful impression upon me, for I felt for him. I knew the curate was well-off, at the head of one of the richest parishes of Canada; that he had several thousand dollars in the bank. I hoped, at first, that he would kindly grant the petition presented to him without speaking of the pay, but I was disappointed. My first thought, after hearing this hard rebuke, was to put my hand in my pocket and take out one of the several five-dollar gold pieces I had, and give it to the poor man, that he might be relieved from his terrible anxiety about his wife. It came also to my mind to say to him: "I will sing your high mass for nothing to-morrow." But alas! I must confess, to my shame, I was too cowardly to do that noble deed. I had a sincere desire to do it, but was prevented by the fear of insulting that priest, who was older than myself, and for whom I had always entertained great respect. It was evident to me that he would have taken my action as a condemnation of his conduct.

When I was feeling ashamed of my own cowardice, and still more indignant against myself than against the curate, he said to the disconcerted poor man: "That woman is your wife; not mine. It is your business, and not mine, to see how to get her out of purgatory."

Turning to me, he said, in the most amiable way: "Please, sir, come to tea."

We hardly started, when the poor man, raising his voice, said, in in a most touching way: "I cannot leave my poor wife in the flames of purgatory; if you cannot sing a high mass, will you please say five low masses to rescue her soul from those burning flames?"

The priest turned towards him and said: "Yes, I can say five masses to take the soul of your wife out of purgatory, but give me five shillings; for you know the price of a low mass is one shilling."

The poor man answered: "I can no more give one dollar than I can five. I have not a cent; and my three poor little children are as naked and starving as myself."

"Well! well," answered the curate, "when I passed this morning before your house, I saw two beautiful sucking pigs. Give me one of them, and I will say your five low masses."

The poor man said: "These small pigs were given me by a charitable neighbour, that I might raise them to feed my poor children next winter. They will surely starve to death, if I give my pigs away."

But I could not listen any longer to that strange dialogue; every word of which fell upon my soul as a shower of burning coals. I was beside myself with shame and disgust. I abruptly left the merchant of souls finishing his bargains, went to my sleeping-room, locked the door, and fell upon my knees to weep to my heart's content.

A quarter of an hour later, the curate knocked at my door, and said: "Tea is ready; please come down!" I answered: "I am not well; I want some rest. Please excuse me if I do not take my tea to-night."

It would require a more eloquent pen than mine, to give the correct history of that sleepless night. The hours were dark and long.

"My God! my God!" I cried, a thousand times, "is it possible that, in my so dear Church of Rome, there can be such abominations as I have seen and heard to-day? Dear and adorable Saviour, if Thou wert still on earth, and should see the soul of a daughter of Israel fallen into a burning furnace, wouldst Thou ask a shilling to take it out? Wouldst Thou force the poor father, with his starving children, to give their last morsel of bread, to persuade Thee to extinguish the burning flames? Thou hast shed the last drop of Thy blood to save her. And how cruel, how merciless, we, Thy priests, are, for the same precious soul! But are we really Thy priests? Is it not blasphemous to call ourselves Thy priests, when not only we will not sacrifice anything to save that soul, but will starve the poor husband and his orphans? What right have we to extort such sums of money from Thy poor children to help them out of purgatory? Do not Thy apostles say that Thy blood alone can purify the soul?

"Is it possible that there is such a fiery prison for the sinners after death, and that neither Thyself nor any of Thy apostles has said a word about it? Several of the Fathers consider purgatory as of Pagan origin. Tertullian spoke of it only after he had joined the sect of the Montanists, and he confesses that it is not through the Holy Scriptures, but through the inspiration of the Paraclete of Montanus that he knows anything about purgatory. Augustine, the most learned and pious of the Holy Fathers, does not find purgatory in the Bible, and positively says that its existence is dubious; that every one may believe what he thinks proper about it. Is it possible that I am so mean as to have refused to extend a helping hand to that poor distressed man, for fear of offending the cruel priest?

"We priests believe, and say that we can help souls out of the burning furnace of purgatory, by our prayers and masses: but instead of rushing to their rescue, we turn to the parents, friends, the children of those departed souls, and say: 'Give me five dollars; give me a shilling, and I will put an end to those tortures; but if you refuse us that money, we will let your father, husband, wife, child, or friend endure those tortures, hundreds of years more! Would not the people throw us into the river, if they could once understand the extent of our meanness and avarice? Ought we not to be ashamed to ask a shilling to take out of the fire a human being who calls us to the rescue? Who, except a priest, can descend so low in the regions of depravity?"

It would take too long to give the thoughts which tortured me during that terrible night. I literally bathed my pillow with my tears. Before saying my mass next morning, I went to confess my criminal cowardice and want of charity towards that poor man, and also the terrible temptation against my faith which tortured my conscience during the long hours of that night! And I repaired my cowardice by giving five dollars to that poor man.

I spent the morning in hearing confessions till ten o'clock, when I delivered a very exciting sermon on the malice of sin, proved by the sufferings of Christ on the cross. This address gave a happy diversion to my mind, and made me forget the sad story of the sucking pig. After the sermon, the curate took me by the hand to his dining-room, where he gave me, in spite of myself, the place of honour.

He had the reputation of having one of the best cooks of Canada, in the widow of one of the governors of Nova Scotia, whom he had as his housekeeper. The dishes before our eyes did not diminish his good reputation. The first dish was a sucking pig, roasted with an art and perfection as I had never seen; it looked like a piece of pure gold, and its smell would have brought water to the lips of the most penitent anchorite.

I had not tasted anything for the last twenty-four hours; had preached two exciting sermons, and spent six hours in hearing confessions. I felt hungry; and the sucking pig was the most tempting thing to me. It was a real epicurean pleasure to look at it and smell its fragrance. Besides, that was a favourite dish with me. I cannot conceal that it was with real pleasure that I saw the curate, after sharpening his long, glittering knife on the file, cutting a beautiful slice from the shoulder, and offering it to me. I was too hungry to be over patient. My knife and fork had soon done their work. I was carrying to my mouth the tempting and succulent mouthful when, suddenly, the remembrance of the poor man's sucking pig came to my mind. I laid the piece on my plate, and with painful anxiety, looked at the curate and said: "Will you allow me to put you a question about this dish?"

"Oh! yes: ask me not only one, but two questions, and I will be happy to answer you to the best of my ability," answered he, with his fine manners.

"Is this the sucking pig of the poor man of yesterday?" I asked.

With a convulsive fit of laughter, he replied: "Yes; it is just it. If we cannot take away the soul of the poor woman out of the flames of purgatory, we will, at all events, eat a fine sucking pig!" The other thirteen priests filled the room with laughter, to show their appreciation of their host's wit.

However, their laughter was not of long duration. With a feeling of shame and uncontrollable indignation, I pushed away my plate with such force, that it crossed the table and nearly fell on the floor; saying, with a sentiment of disgust which no pen can describe: "I would rather starve to death than eat of that execrable dish; I see in it the tears of the poor man; I see the blood of his starving children; it is the price of a soul. No! no, gentlemen; do not touch it. You know, Mr. Curate, how 30,000 priests and monks were slaughtered in France, in the bloody days of 1792. It was for such iniquities as this that God Almighty visited the church in France. The same future awaits us here in Canada, the very day that people will awaken from their slumber and see that, instead of being ministers of Christ, we are the vile traders of souls, under the mask of religion."

The poor curate, stunned by the solemnity of my words, as well as by the consciousness of his guilt, lisped some excuse. The sucking pig remained untouched; and the rest of the dinner had more the appearance of a burial ceremony than of a convivial repast. By the mercy of God, I had redeemed my cowardice of the day before. But I had mortally wounded the feelings of that curate and his friends, and for ever lost their good-will.

It is in such ways that God was directing the steps of His unprofitable servant through ways unknown to him. Furious storms were constantly blowing around my fragile bark, and tearing my sails into fragments. But every storm was pushing me, in spite of myself, towards the shores of eternal life, where I was to land safely, a few years later.

CHAPTER XLVII.

ON the 15th of December, 1850, I received the following letter :

"CHICAGO, ILL., *December 1st*, 1850.

"REV. FATHER CHINIQUY:

"Apostle of Temperance of Canada.

"DEAR SIR :—When I was in Canada, last fall, I intended to confer with you on a very important subject. But you were then working in the diocese of Boston, and my limited time prevented me from going so far to meet you. You are aware that the lands of the State of Illinois and the whole valley of the Mississippi are among the richest and most fertile of the world. In a near future, those regions, which are now a comparative wilderness, will be the granary, not only of the United States, but of the whole world ; and those who will possess them will not only possess the very heart and arteries of this young and already so great republic, but will become its rulers.

"It is our intention, without noise, to take possession of those vast and magnificent regions of the west in the name and for the benefit of our holy Church. Our plan to attain that object, is as sure as easy. There is, every year, an increasing tide of emigration from the Roman Catholic regions of Europe and Canada towards the United States. Unfortunately, till now, our emigrants have blindly scattered themselves among the Protestant populations, which too often absorb them and destroy their faith.

"Why should we not direct their steps to the same spot ? Why should we not, for instance, induce them to come and take possession of these fertile states of Illinois, Missouri, Iowa, Kansas, etc. They can get those lands now, at a nominal price. If we succeed, as I hope we will, our holy Church will soon count her children here by ten and twenty millions, and through their numbers, their wealth and unity, they will have such a weight in the balance of power that they will rule everything.

"The Protestants, always divided among themselves, will never form any strong party without the help of the united vote of our Catholic people ; and that party alone, which will ask and get our help by yielding to our just demands, will rule the country. Then, in reality, though not in appearance, our holy Church will rule the United States, as she is called by our Saviour Himself to rule the whole world. There is, to-day, a wave of emigrants from Canada towards the United States, which, if not stopped or well directed, is threatening to throw the good French Canadian people into the mire of Protestantism. Your countrymen, when once mixed with the numberless sects which try to attract them, are soon shaken in their faith. Their children sent to Protestant schools, will be unable to defend themselves against the wily and united efforts made to pervert them.

"But put yourself at the head of the emigrants from Canada, France and Belgium ; prevent them from settling any longer among the Protestants, by inducing them to follow you to Illinois, and with them, you will soon see here, a Roman Catholic people, whose number, wealth and influence will amaze the world. God Almighty has wonderfully blessed your labours in Canada in that holy cause of temperance. But now the work is done, the same Great God presents to your Christian ambition a not less great and noble work for the rest of your life. Make use of your great influence over your countrymen to prevent them from scattering any longer among Protestants, by inducing them to come here, in Illinois. You will then lay the foundation of a Roman Catholic French people, whose piety, unity, wealth and number will soon renew and revive, on this continent, the past and fading glories of the Church of France.

"We have already, at Bourbonnais, a fine colony of French Canadians. They long to see and hear you. Come and help me to make that comparatively small, though thriving people, grow with the immigrants from the French-speaking countries of Europe and America, till it covers the whole territory of Illinois with its sturdy sons and pious daughters. I will ask the Pope to make you my coadjutor, and you will soon become my successor, for I already feel too weak and unhealthy to bear alone the burden of my too large diocese.

"Please consider what I propose to you before God, and answer me. But be kind enough to consider this overture as strictly confidential between you and me, till we have brought our plans into execution.

" Truly Yours,   ✠ OLIV VANDEVELD,
                              " *Bishop of Chicago.*"

I answered him that the Bishops of Boston, Buffalo and Detroit, had already advised me to put myself at the head of the French Canadian immigration, in order to direct its tide towards the vast and rich regions of the west. I wrote him that I felt as he did, that it was the best way to prevent my countrymen from falling into the snares laid before them by Protestants, among whom they were scattering themselves. I told him that I would consider it a great honour and privilege to spend the last part of my life in extending the power and influence of our holy Church over the United States, and that I would, in June next, pay my respects to him in Chicago, when on my way towards the colony of my countrymen at Bourbonnais Grove. I added that after I should have seen those territories of Illinois and the Mississippi valley, with my own eyes, it would be more easy to give him a definite answer. I ended my letter by saying: " But I respectfully request your lordship to give up the idea of selecting me for your coadjutor, or successor. I have already twice refused to become a bishop. That high dignity is too much above my merits and capacities to be ever accepted by me. I am happy and proud to fight the battles of our holy Church; but let my superiors allow me to continue to remain in her ranks as a simple soldier, to defend her honour and extend her power. I may, then, with the help of God, do some good. But I feel, and know that I would spoil everything, if raised to an elevated position, for which I am not fit."

Without speaking to anybody of the proposition of the Bishop of Chicago, I was preparing to go and see the new field where he wanted me to work, when, in the beginning of May, 1851, I received a very pressing invitation from my Lord Lefebre, Bishop of Detroit, to lecture on temperance to the French Canadians who were, then, forming the majority of the Roman Catholics of that city.

That bishop had taken the place of Bishop Rese, whose public scandals and infamies had covered the whole Catholic Church of America with shame. During the last years he had spent in his diocese, very few weeks had passed without his being picked up beastly drunk in the lowest taverns, and even in the streets of Detroit, and dragged, unconscious to his palace.

After long and vain efforts to reform him, the Pope and the bishops of America had happily succeeded in persuading him to go to Rome, and pay his respects to the so-called vicar of Jesus Christ. This was a snare too skilfully laid to be suspected by the drunken bishop. He had hardly set his feet in Rome when the inquisitors threw him into one of their dungeons, where he remained till the republicans set him at liberty, in 1848, after Pope Pius IX. had fled to Civita Vecchia.

In order to blot out from the face of his Church the black spots with which his predecessor had covered it, Bishop Lefebre made the greatest display of zeal for the cause of temperance. As soon as he was inducted, he invited his people to follow his example and enrol themselves under its banners, in a very powerful address on the evils caused by the use of intoxicating drinks. At the end of his eloquent sermon, laying his right hand on the altar, he made a solemn promise never to drink any alcoholic liquors.

His telling sermon on temperance, with his solemn and public promise, were published through almost all the papers of that time, and I read it many times to the people with good effect. When, on my way to Illinois, I reached the city of Detroit to give the course of lectures demanded by the bishop, in the first week of June. Though the bishop was absent, I immediately began to preach to an immense audience in the Cathedral. I had agreed to give five lectures, and it was only during the third one that Bishop Lefebre arrived. After paying me great compliments for my zeal and success in the temperance cause, he took me by the hand to his dining-room, and said: "Let us go and refresh ourselves."

I shall never forget my surprise and dismay when I perceived the long dining table, covered with bottles of brandy, wine, beer, etc., prepared for himself and his six or seven priests, who were already around it, joyfully emptying their glasses. My first thought was to express my surprise and indignation, and leave the room in disgust, but by a second and better thought I waited a little to see more of that unexpected spectacle. I accepted the seat offered me by the bishop at his right hand.

"Father Chiniquy," he said, "this is the sweetest claret you ever drank." And before I could utter a word, he had filled my large glass with the wine, and drank his own to my health.

Looking at the bishop in amazement, I said, "What does this mean, my lord?"

"It means that I want to drink with you the best claret you ever tasted."

"Do you take me for a comedian? and have you called me here to play such a strange comedy?" I replied, with lips trembling with indignation.

"I did not invite you to play a comedy," he answered. "I invited you to lecture on temperance to my people, and you have done it in a most admirable way, these last three days. Though you did not see me, I was present at this evening's address. I never heard anything so eloquent on that subject as what you said. But now that you have fulfilled your duty, I must do mine, which is to treat you as a gentleman, and drink that bottle of wine with you."

"But, my lord, allow me to tell you that I would not deserve to be called or treated as a gentleman, were I vile enough to drink wine after the address I gave this evening."

"I beg your pardon for differing from you," answered the bishop. "Those drunken people to whom you spoke so well against the evils oi intemperance, are in need of the stringent and bitter remedies you offer them in your teetotalism. But here we are sober men and gentlemen, we do not want such remedies. I never thought that the physicians were absolutely bound to take the pills they administer to their patients."

"I hope your lordship will not deny me the right you claim for yourself, to differ with me in this matter. I entirely differ from you, when you say that men who drink as you do with your priests, have a right to be called sober men."

"I fear, Mr. Chiniquy, that you forget where you are, and to whom you speak just now," replied the bishop.

"It may be that I have made a blunder, and that I am guilty of some grave error in coming here, and speaking to you as I am doing, my lord. In that case, I am ready to ask your pardon. But before I retract what I have said, please allow me to respectfully ask you a very simple question."

Then taking from my pocket-book his printed address, and his public and solemn promise never to drink, neither to offer any intoxicating drinks to others, I read it aloud, and said:

"Are you the same Bishop of Detroit, called Lefebre, who has made this solemn promise? If you are not the same man, I will retract and beg your pardon, but if you are the same, I have nothing to retract."

My answer fell upon the poor bishop as a thunderbolt.

He lisped some unintelligible and insignificant explanation, which, however, he ended by a *coup d'etat*, in saying:

23

" My dear Mr. Chiniquy, I did not invite you to preach to the bishop, but only to the people of Detroit."

" You are right, my lord, I was not called to preach to the bishop, but allow me to tell you that if I had known sooner, that when the Bishop of Detroit, with his priests, solemnly, publicly, and with their right hand on the altar, promised that they would never drink any intoxicating drinks, it means that they will drink and fill themselves with those detestable liquors, till their brains shiver with their poison-ous fumes, I would not have troubled you with my presence or my remarks here. However, allow me to tell your lordship to be kind enough to find another lecturer for your temperance meetings. For I am determined to take the train to-morrow morning for Chicago."

There is no need to say that, during that painful conversation, the priests (with only one exception) were as full of indignation against me as they were full of wine. I left the table and went to my sleeping apartment, overwhelmed with sadness and shame.

Half an hour later, the bishop was with me, conjuring me to con-tinue my lectures, on account of the fearful scandals which would result from my sudden and unexpected exit from Detroit, when the whole people had the assurance from me, that very night, that I would continue to lecture the two following evenings. I acknowledged that there would be a great scandal, but I told him that he was the only one responsible for it by his want of faith and consistency.

He, at first, tried to persuade me that he was ordered to drink, by his own physicians, for his health; but I showed him that this was a miserable illusion. He then said that he regretted what had occurred, and confessed that it would be better if the priests practised what they preached to the people. After which, he asked me, in the name of our Lord Jesus Christ, to forget the errors of the bishops and priests of Detroit, in order to think only of the good which the conversion of the numberless drunkards of that city would do to the people.

He spoke to me with such earnestness of the souls saved, the tears dried, the happiness restored to hundreds of families, by temperance, that he touched the most sensitive chords of my heart, and got from me the promise that I would deliver the other two expected lectures. He was so glad, that he pressed me on his bosom, and gave me, what we call in France, *Le baiser de paix* (kiss of peace), to show me his esteem and gratitude.

When alone, I tried to drown in a sound sleep the sad emotions of that evening; but it was impossible. That night was to be again a sleepless one to me. The intemperance of that high dignitary and his priests filled me with an unspeakable horror and disgust. Many times, during the dark hours of that night, I heard as if it were a voice saying to me, " Do you not see that the bishops and priests of your church do not believe a word of their religion? Their only object is to throw dust in the eyes of the people, and live a jolly life. Do you not see that you do not follow the Word of God, but only the vain and lying traditions of men in the Church of Rome? Come out of it. Break the heavy yoke which is upon you, and follow the simple, pure religion of Jesus Christ."

I tried to silence that voice by saying to myself: "These sins are not the sins of my holy church; they are the sins of individuals. It was not the fault of Christ if Judas was a thief! It is not more the fault of my holy church if this bishop and his priests are drunkards and worldly men. Where will I go if I leave my church? Will I not find drunkards and infidels everywhere I may go in search of a better religion?"

The dawn of the next day found me feverish, and unable to get any rest in my bed. Hoping that the first fresh air of the morning would do me good, I went to the beautiful garden, covered with fruit trees of all kinds, which was, then, around the episcopal residence. But what was my surprise to see the bishop leaning on a tree, with his handkerchief over his face, and bathed in tears. I approached him with the least noise possible. I saw that he did 'not perceive me. By the motion of his head and shoulders, it became evident to me that he was in anguish of soul. I said to him: "My dear bishop, what is the matter? Why do you weep and cry at such an early hour?"

Pressing my hand convulsively in his, he answered:

"Dear Father Chiniquy, you do not yet know the awful calamity which has befallen me this night?"

"What calamity?" I asked.

"Do you not remember," he answered, "that young priest who was sitting at your right hand last evening? Well! he went away, during the night, with the wife of a young man, whom he had seduced, and stole four thousand dollars from me before he left."

"I am not at all surprised at that, when I remember how that priest emptied his glasses of beer and wine last night," I answered. "When the blood of a man is heated by those fiery liquors, it is sheer absurdity to think that he will keep his vow of chastity."

"You are right! You are right! God Almighty has punished me for breaking the public pledge I had taken never to drink any intoxicating drinks. We want a reform in our midst, and we will have it," he answered. "But what horrible scandal! One of my young priests gone with that young wife, after stealing four thousand dollars from me! Great God! Must we not hide our face now, in this city?"

I could say nothing to alleviate the sorrow of the poor bishop, but to mingle my tears of shame and sorrow with his. I went back to my room, where I wept a part of the day, to my heart's content, on the unspeakable degradations of that priesthood of which I had been so proud, and about which I had such exalted views when I entered its ranks, before I had an inside view of its dark mysteries.

Of course, the next two days that I was the guest of Bishop Lefebre, not a single drop of intoxicating drink was seen on the table. But I know that not long after, that representative of the Pope forgot again his solemn vows, and continued with his priests, drinking, till he died a most miserable death in 1875.

CHAPTER XLVIII.

THE journey from Detroit to Chicago, in the month of June, 1851, was not so pleasant as it is to-day. The Michigan Central Railroad was completed, then, only to New Buffalo. We took the steamer there and crossed Lake Michigan to Chicago, where we arrived the next morning, after nearly perishing in a terrible storm. On the 15th of June, I first landed, with the greatest difficulty, on a badly wrecked wharf, at the mouth of the river. Some of the streets I had to cross in order to reach the bishop's palace were almost impassable. In many places loose planks had been thrown across them to prevent people from sinking in the mud and quicksands.

The first sight of Chicago, was then far from giving an idea of what that city has become in 1884. Though it had rapidly increased the last ten years, its population was then not much more than 30,000. The only line of railroad finished was from Chicago to Aurora, about forty miles. The whole population of the State of Illinois was then not much beyond 200,000. To-day, Chicago alone numbers more than 500,000 souls within her limits. Probably more grain, lumber, beef and pork, are now bought and sold in a single day in Chicago than were then in a whole year.

When I entered the miserable house called the "bishop's palace," I could hardly believe my eyes. The planks of the lower floor, in the dining-room, were floating, and it required a great deal of ingenuity to keep my feet dry while dining with him for the first time. But the Christian kindness and courtesy of the bishop, made me more happy in his poor house, than I felt, later, in the white marble palace built by his haughty successor, C. Regan.

There were, then, in Chicago about 200 French Canadian families, under the pastorate of the Rev. M. A. Lebel, who, like myself, was born in Kamouraska. The drunkenness and other immoralities of the clergy, pictured to me by that priest, surpassed all I had ever heard known.

After getting my promise that I would never reveal the fact before his death, he assured me that the last bishop had been poisoned by one of his grand vicars in the following way. He said, the grand vicar, being father confessor of the nuns of Loretto, had fallen in love with one of the so-called virgins, who died a few days after becoming the mother of a still-born child.

This fact having transpired, and threatening to give a great deal of scandal, the bishop thought it was his duty to make an inquest, and punish his priest, if he should be found guilty. But the grand vicar, seeing that his crime was to be easily detected, found that the shortest way to escape exposure was to put an end to the inquest by murdering the poor bishop. A poison very difficult to detect, was administered, and the death of the prelate soon followed, without exciting any surprise in the community.

Horrified by the long and minute details of that mystery of iniquity, I came very near returning to Canada, immediately, without going any further. But after more mature consideration, it seemed to me that these awful iniquities on the part of the priests of Illinois was just the reason why I should not shut my ears to the voice of God, if it were His will that I should come to take care of the precious souls He would trust to me. I spent a week in Chicago lecturing on temperance every evening, and listening during the days to the grand plans the bishop was maturing, in order to make our Church of Rome the mistress and ruler of the magnificent valley of the Mississippi, which included the States of Minnesota, Iowa, Missouri, Kansas, Mississippi, etc. He clearly demonstrated to me, that once mistress of the incalculable treasures of those rich lands, through the millions of her obedient children, our church would easily command the respect and the submission of the less favoured States of the east. My zeal for my church was so sincere that I would have given, with pleasure, every drop of my blood, in order to secure to her such a future of power and greatness. I felt really happy and thankful to God that He should have chosen me to help the Pope and the bishops realise such a noble and magnificent project.

Leaving Chicago, it took me nearly three days to cross the vast prairies, which were then a perfect wilderness, between Chicago and Bourbonnais, where I spent three weeks in preaching and exploring the country, extending from the Kankakee river to the south-west, towards the Mississippi. It was only then that I plainly understood the greatness of the plans of the bishop, and that I determined to sacrifice the exalted position God had given me in Canada to guide the steps of the Roman Catholic emigrants from France, Belgium and Canada, towards the regions of the west, in order to extend the power and influence of my church all over the United States. On my return to

Chicago, in the second week of July, all was arranged with the bishop for my coming back in the autumn, to help him to accomplish his gigantic plans. However, it was understood between us that my leaving Canada for the United States, would be kept a secret till the last hour, on account of the stern opposition I expected from my bishop. The last thing to be done, on my return to Canada, in order to prepare the emigrants to go to Illinois, rather than any other part of the United States, was to tell them through the press the unrivalled advantages which God had prepared for them in the west. I did so by a letter, which was published not only by the press of Canada, but also in many papers of France and Belgium. The importance of that letter is such, that I hope my readers will bear with me in reproducing the following extracts from it.

MONTREAL, CANADA EAST.

August 13th, 1851.

It is impossible to give our friends, by narration, an idea of what we feel, when we cross, for the first time, the immense prairies of Illinois. It is a spectacle which must be seen to be well understood. As you advance in the midst of these boundless deserts, where your eyes perceive nothing but lands of inexhaustible richness, remaining in the most desolating solitude, you feel something which you cannot express by any words. Is your soul filled with joy, or your heart broken by sadness? You cannot say; you lift up your eyes to heaven, and the voice of your soul is chanting a hymn of gratitude. Tears of joy are trickling down your cheeks, and you bless God, whose curse seems not to have fallen on the land where you stand : "Cursed is the ground for thy sake;" "thorns also and thistles shall it bring forth to thee" (Gen. iii. 17, 18).

You see around you the most luxuriant verdure ; flowers of every kind, and magnificent above description. But, if in the silence of meditation, you look with new attention on those prairies, so rich, so magnificent, you feel an inexpressible sentiment of sadness, and addressing yourself to the blessed land, you say, "Why art thou so solitary? Why is the wild game alone here to glorify my God?" And if you continue to advance through those immense prairies, which, like a boundless ocean, are spreading their rolling waves before you, and seem to long after the presence of man, to cover themselves with incalculable treasures, you remember your friends in Canada, and more particularly those among them who, crushed down by misery, are watering with the sweat of their brow a sterile and desolated soil, you say : "Ah ! if such and such of my friends were here, how soon they would see their hard and ungrateful labours changed into the most smiling and happy position.

Perhaps I will be accused then of trying to depopulate my country, and drive my countrymen from Canada to the United States. No ! no. I never had so perverse a design. Here is my mind about the subject of emigration, and I see no reason to be ashamed of it, or to conceal it. It is a fact that a great number (and much greater than generally believed) of French Canadians are yearly emigrating from Canada, and nobody regrets it more than I do; but as long as those who govern Canada will not pay more attention to that evil, it will be an incurable one, and every year Canada will lose thousands and thousands of its strongest arms and noblest hearts, to benefit our happy neighbours. With many others, I had the hope that the eloquent voice of the poor settlers of our eastern townships would be heard, and that the government would help them; but that hope is gone like a dream, and we have now every reason to fear that our unfortunate settlers of the east will be left to themselves. The greatest part of them, for the want of roads to the markets of Quebec and Montreal, and still more by the tyranny of their cruel landlords, will soon be obliged to bid an eternal adieu to their country, and with an enraged heart against their haughty oppressors, they will seek, in exile to a strange land, the protection they could not find in their own country. Yes! If our Canadian government continues a little longer to show the same incomprehensible and stupid apathy for the welfare of its own subjects, emigration will increase every year from Canada, to swell the ranks of the American people.

Since we cannot stop that emigration, is it not our first duty to direct it in such a way that it will be, to the poor emigrants, as beneficial as possible? Let us do everything to hinder them from going to the large cities of the United States. Drowned in the mixed population of American cities, our unfortunate emigrating countrymen would be too much exposed to losing their morality and their faith. Surely there is not another country under the heavens where space, bread, and liberty are so universally assured to every member of the community, as the United States. But it is not in the great cities of the United States that our poor countrymen will sooner find these three gifts. The French Canadian who will stop in the large cities, will not, with a very few exceptions, raise himself above the unenviable position of a poor journeyman. But those among them who will direct their steps toward the rich and extensive prairies of Bourbonnais, will certainly find a better lot. Many in Canada would believe that I am exaggerating, were I to publish how happy, prosperous, and respectable is the French Canadian population of Bourbonnais. The French Canadians of Bourbonnais have had the intelligence to follow the good example of the industrious American farmers, in the manner of cultivating the lands. On their farms as well as on those of their neighbours, you will find the best machinery to cut their crops, to thresh their grain. They enjoy the just reputation of having the best horses of the country, and very few can beat them for the number and quality of their cattle.

Now, what can be the prospect of a young man in Canada, if he has not more than two hundred dollars? A whole life of hard labour and continued privation is his too certain lot. But, let that young man go directly to Bourbonnais, and if he is industrious, sober, and religious, before a couple of years he will see nothing to envy in the most happy farmer of Canada.

As the land he will take in Illinois is entirely prepared for the plough, he has no trees to cut or eradicate, no stones to move, no ditch to dig; his only work is to fence and break his land and sow it, and the very first year the value of the crop will be sufficient to pay for his farm. Holy Providence has prepared everything for the benefit of the happy farmers of Illinois. That fertile country is well watered by a multitude of rivers and large creeks, whose borders are generally covered with the most rich and extensive groves of timber of the best quality, as black oak, maple, white oak, burr oak, ash, etc. The seeds of the beautiful acacia (locust), after five or six years, will give you a splendid tree. The greatest variety of fruits are growing naturally in almost every part of Illinois; coal mines have been discovered in the very heart of the country, more than sufficient for the wants of the people. Before long, a railroad from Chicago to Bourbonnais will bring our happy countrymen to the most extensive market, the Queen city of the west— Chicago.

I will then say to my young countrymen who intend emigrating from Canada: "My friend, exile is one of the greatest calamities that can befall a man. Young

Canadian, remain in the country, keep thy heart to love it, thy intelligence to adorn it, and thine arms to protect it. Young and dear countryman, remain in thy beautiful country; there is nothing more grand and sublime in the world than the waters of the St. Lawrence. It is on its deep and majestic waters that, before long, Europe and America will meet and bind themselves to each other by the blessed bonds of an eternal peace ; it is on its shores that they will exchange their incalculable treasures. Remain in the country of thy birth, my dear son. Let the sweat of thy brow continue to fertilize it, and let the perfume of thy virtues bring the blessing of God upon it. But, my dear son, if thou hast no more room in the valley of the St. Lawrence, and if, by the want of protection from the Government, thou canst not go to the forest without running the danger of losing thy life in a pond, or being crushed under the feet of an English or Scotch tyrant, I am not the man to invite thee to exhaust thy best days for the benefit of the insolent strangers, who are the lords of the eastern lands. I will sooner tell thee, 'go my child,' there are many extensive places still vacant on the earth, and God is everywhere. That great God calleth thee to another land, submit thyself to His Divine will. But, before thou bid a final adieu to thy country, engrave on thy heart and keep as a holy deposit, the love of thy holy religion, of thy beautiful language, and of the dear and unfortunate country of thy birth. On thy way to the land of exile, stop as little as possible in the great cities, for fear of the many snares thy eternal enemy has prepared for thy perdition. But go straight to Bourbonnais. There you will find many of thy brothers who have erected the cross of Christ ; join thyself to them, thou shalt be strong of their strength ; go and help them to conquer to the Gospel of Jesus those rich countries, which shall, very soon, weigh more than is generally believed, in the balance of the nations.

"Yes, go straight to Illinois. Thou shalt not be entirely in a strange and alien country. Holy Providence has chosen thy fathers to find that rich country, and to reveal to the world its admirable resources. More than once that land of Illinois has been sanctified by the blood of thy ancestors. In Illinois thou shalt not make a step without finding indestructible proof of the perseverance, genius, bravery, and piety of the French forefathers. Go to Illinois, and the many names of Bourbonnais, Joliet, Dubuque, La Salle, St. Charles, St. Mary, etc., that you will meet everywhere, will tell you more than my words, that that country is nothing but the rich inheritance which your fathers have found for the benefit of their grandchildren.

"C. CHINIQUY."

I would never have published this letter, if I had foreseen its effects on the farmers of Canada. In a few days after its appearance their farms fell to half their value. Every one, in some parishes, wanted to sell their lands and emigrate to the west. It was only for want of purchasers that we did not see an emigration which would have surely ruined Canada. I was frightened by its immediate effect on the public mind. However, while some were praising me to the skies for having published it, others were cursing me and calling me a traitor. The very day after its publication, I was in Quebec, where the Bishops of Canada were met in council. The first one I met was my Lord De Charbonel, Bishop of Toronto. After having blessed me, he pressed my hand in his, and said :

"I have just read your admirable letter. It is one of the most beautiful and eloquently written articles I ever read. The Spirit of God has surely inspired every one of its sentences. I have, just now, forwarded six copies of it to different journals of France and Belgium, where they will be republished, and do an incalculable amount of good, by directing the French-speaking Catholic emigrants towards a country where they will run no risk of losing their faith, with the assurance of securing a future of unbounded prosperity for their families. Your name will be put among the names of the greatest benefactors of humanity."

Though these compliments seemed to me much exaggerated and unmerited, I cannot deny that they pleased me, by adding to my hopes and convictions that great good would surely come from the plan I had of gathering all the Roman Catholic emigrants on the same spot, to form such large and strong congregations; that they would have nothing to fear from heretics. I thanked the bishop for his kind and friendly words, and left him to go and present my respectful salutations to Bishop Bourget, of Montreal, and give him a short sketch of my voyage to the far west. I found him alone in his room, in the very act of reading my letter. A lioness, who had just lost her whelps, would not have looked upon me with more angry and threatening eyes than that bishop did.

"Is it possible," he said, "Mr. Chiniquy, that your hand has written and signed such a perfidious document? How could you so cruelly pierce the bosom of your own country, after her dealing so nobly with you? Do you not see that your treasonable letter will give such an impetus to emigration that our most thriving parishes will soon be turned into solitude? Though you do not say it, we feel at every line of that letter that you also will leave your country, to give help and comfort to our natural enemies."

Surprised by this unexpected burst of bad feeling, I kept my *sang froid*, and answered: "My lord, your lordship has surely misunderstood me, if you have found in my letter any treasonable plan to ruin our country. Please read it again, and you will see that every line has been inspired by the purest motives of patriotism, and the highest views of religion. How is it possible that the worthy Bishop of Toronto should have told me that the Spirit of God Himself had dictated every line of that letter, when my good bishop's opinion is so completely opposite?" The abrupt answer the bishop gave to these remarks, clearly indicated that my absence would be more welcome than my presence. I left him, after asking his blessing, which he gave me in the coldest manner possible.

On the 25th of August, I was back at Longueuil, from my voyage to Quebec, which I had extended as far as Kamouraska, to see again the noble-hearted parishioners, whose unanimity in taking the pledge of temperance, and admirable fidelity in keeping it then, had filled my heart with such joy.

I related my last interview with Bishop Bourget to my faithful friend Mr. Brassard. He answered me : " The present bad feelings of the Bishop of Montreal against you are not a secret to me. Unfortunately the low-minded men who surround and counsel him are as unable as the bishop himself to understand your exalted views in directing the steps of the Roman Catholics towards the splendid valley of the Mississippi. They are besides themselves, because they see that you will easily succeed in forming a grand colony of French-speaking people in Illinois. Now, I am sure of what I say, though I am not free to tell you how it came to my knowledge, there is a plot somewhere to dishonour and destroy you at once. Those who are at the head of that plot hope that if they can succeed in destroying your popularity, nobody will be tempted to follow you to Illinois. For, though you have concealed it as well as you could, it is evident to everyone now, that you are the man selected by the bishops of the west to direct the uncertain steps of the poor emigrants towards those rich lands."

" Do you mean, my dear Mr. Brassard," I replied, " that there are priests around the Bishop of Montreal, cruel and vile enough to forge calumnies against me, and spread them before the country in such a way that I shall be unable to refute them ? "

" It is just what I mean," answered Mr. Brassard ; " mind what I tell you ; the bishop has made use of you to reform his diocese. He likes you for that work. But your popularity is too great to-day for your enemies ; they want to get rid of you, and no means will be too vile or criminal to accomplish your destruction, if they can attain their object."

" But, my dear Mr. Brassard, can you give me any details of the plots which are in store against me ? " I asked.

" No ! I cannot, for I know them not. But be on your guard ; for your few, but powerful enemies, are jubilant. They speak of the absolute impotency to which you will soon be reduced, if you accomplish what they so maliciously and falsely call your treacherous objects."

I answered : " Our Saviour has said to all His disciples : ' In the world ye shall have tribulation. But be of good cheer, I have overcome the world ' (John xvi. 33). I am more determined than ever to put my trust in God, and to fear no man."

Two hours after this conversation, I received the following from the Rev. M. Pare, secretary to the bishop :

To the Rev. Mr. Chiniquy,

Apostle of Temperance.

My dear Sir,—My lord Bishop of Montreal would like to see you upon some important business. Please come at your earliest convenience.

Yours truly,

JOS. PARE, *Secretary.*

The next morning I was alone with Monseigneur Bourget, who received me very kindly. He seemed at first to have entirely banished the bad feelings he had shown in our last interview at Quebec. After making some friendly remarks on my continual labours and success in the cause of temperance, he stopped for a moment, and seemed embarrassed how to resume the conversation. At last he said:

"Are you not the father confessor of Mrs. Chenier?"

"Yes, my lord. I have been her confessor since I lived in Longueuil."

"Very well, very well," he rejoined, "I suppose that you know that her only child is a nun, in the Congregation Convent?"

"Yes! my lord, I know it," I replied.

"Could you not induce Mrs. Chenier to become a nun also?" asked the bishop.

"I never thought of that, my lord," I answered, "and I do not see why I should advise her to exchange her beautiful cottage, washed by the fresh and pure waters of the St. Lawrence, where she looks so happy and cheerful, for the gloomy walls of the nunnery."

"But she is still young and beautiful; she may be deceived by temptations when she is there, in that beautiful house, surrounded by all the enjoyments of her fortune," replied the bishop.

"I understand your lordship. Yes, Mrs. Chenier has the reputation of being rich; though I know nothing of her fortune; she has kept well the charms and freshness of her youth. However, I think that the best remedy against the temptations you seem to dread so much for her, is to advise her to marry. A good Christian husband seems to me a much better remedy against the dangers to which your lordship alludes, than the cheerless walls of a nunnery."

"You speak just as a Protestant," rejoined the bishop, with an evident nervous irritation. "We remark that, though you hear the confessions of a great number of young ladies, there is not a single one of them who has ever become a nun. You seem to ignore that the vow of chastity is the shortest way to a life of holiness in this world and happiness in the next."

"I am sorry to differ from your lordship, in that matter," I replied. "But I cannot help it, the remedy you have found against sin is quite modern. The old remedy offered by our God Himself, is very different and much better, I think."

"'It is not good that the man should be alone; I will make an help meet for him' (Gen. ii. 18), said our Creator in the earthly paradise. 'Nevertheless, to avoid fornication, let every man have his own wife, and let every woman have her own husband' (1 Cor. vii. 2), said the same God, through His Apostle Paul."

"I know too well how the great majority of nuns keep their vows of chastity, to believe that the modern remedy against the temptations you mention, is an improvement on the old one found and given by our God!" I answered.

With an angry look, the bishop replied: "This is Protestantism, Mr. Chiniquy. This is sheer Protestantism."

"I respectfully ask your pardon for differing from your lordship. This is not Protestantism. It is simply and absolutely the 'pure Word of God.' But, my lord, God knows that it is my sincere desire, as it is my interest and my duty, to do all in my power to deserve your esteem. I do not want to vex nor disobey you. Please give me a good reason why I should advise Mrs. Chenier to enter a monastery, and I will comply with your request the very first time she comes to confess."

Resuming his most amiable manner, the bishop answered me, " My first reason is, the spiritual good which she would receive from her vows of perpetual chastity and poverty in a nunnery. The second reason is, that the lady is rich, and we are in need of money. We would soon possess her whole fortune; for her only child is already in the Congregation Convent."

" My dear bishop," I replied, "you already know what I think of your first reason. After having investigated that fact, not in the Protestant books, but from the lips of the nuns themselves, as well as from their father confessors, I am fully convinced that the real virtue of purity is much better kept in the homes of our Christian mothers, married sisters, and female friends than in the secret rooms, not to say prisons, where the poor nuns are enchained by the heavy fetters assumed by their vows, which the great majority curse when they cannot break them. And for the second reason, your lordship gives me to induce Mrs. Chenier becoming a nun, I am again sorry to say that I cannot conscientiously accept it. I have not consecrated myself to the priesthood to deprive respectable families of their legal inheritance in order to enrich myself, or anybody else. I know she has poor relations who need her fortune after her death."

" Do you pretend to say that your bishop is a thief?" angrily rejoined the bishop.

" No, my lord! By no means. No doubt, from your high standpoint of view, your lordship may see things in a very different aspect, from what I see them, in the low position I occupy in the church. But, as your lordship is bound to follow the dictates of his conscience in everything, I also feel obliged to give heed to the voice of mine."

This painful conversation had already lasted too long. I was anxious to see the end of it; for I could easily read in the face of my superior, that every word I uttered was sealing my doom. I rose up to take leave of him, and said: "My lord, I beg your pardon for disappointing your lordship."

He coldly answered me: "It is not the first time; though I would it were the last, that you show such a want of respect and submission to the will of your superiors. But, as I feel it is a conscientious affair on your part, I have no ill-will against you, and I am happy to tell you that I entertain for you all my past esteem. The only favour I ask from you just now is, that this conversation may be kept secret."

I answered: "It is still more to my interest than yours to keep this unfortunate affair a secret between us. I hope that neither your lordship nor the great God, who alone has heard us, will ever make it an imperious duty for me to mention it."

"What good news do you bring me from the bishop's palace?" asked my venerable friend, Mr. Brassard, when I returned, late in the afternoon.

"I would have very spicy, though unpalatable news to give you, had not the bishop asked me to keep what has been said between us a secret."

Mr. Brassard laughed outright at my answer, and replied: "A secret! a secret! Ah! but it is a gazette secret; for the bishop has bothered me, as well as many others, with that matter, frequently, since your return from Illinois. Several times he has asked us to persuade you to advise your devoted penitent, Mrs. Chenier, to become a nun. I knew he invited you to his palace yesterday for that object. The eyes and heart of our poor bishop," continued Mr. Brassard, "are too firmly fixed on the fortune of that lady. Hence, his zeal about the salvation of her soul through the monastic life. In vain I tried to dissuade the bishop from speaking to you on that subject, on account of your prejudices against our good nuns. He would not listen to me. No doubt you have realized my worst anticipations; you have, with your usual stubbornness, refused to yield to his demands. I fear you have added to his bad feelings, and consummated your disgrace."

"What a deceitful man that bishop is!" I answered, indignantly. "He has given me to understand that this was a most sacred secret between him and me, when I see, by what you say, that it is nothing else than a farcical secret, known by the hundreds who have heard of it. But, please, my dear Mr. Brassard, tell me, is it not a burning shame that our nunneries are changed into real traps, to steal, cheat, and ruin so many unsuspecting families? I have no words to express my disgust and indignation, when I see that all those great demonstrations and eloquent tirades about the perfection and holiness of the nuns, on the part of our spiritual rulers, are nothing else, in reality, than a veil to conceal their stealing operations. Do you not feel, that those poor nuns are the victims of the most stupendous system of swindling the world has ever seen? I know that there are are some honourable exceptions. For instance, the nunnery you have founded here is an exception. You have not built it to enrich yourself, as you have spent your last cent in its erection. But you and I are only simpletons, who have, till now, ignored the terrible secrets which put that machine of the nunneries and monkeries in motion. I am more than ever disgusted and terrified, not only by the unspeakable corruptions, but also by the stupendous system of swindling, which is their foundation stone. If the cities of Quebec and Montreal could know what I know of the incalculable sums of money secretly stolen through the confessional, to aid our bishops in building the famous cathedrals and splendid palaces; or to cover themselves with robes of silk, satin, silver, and gold: to live more luxurious than the Pashas of Turkey; they would set fire to all those palatial buildings; they would hang the confessors, who have thrown the poor nuns into these dungeons under the pretext of saving their souls, when the real motive was to lay hands on their inheritance, and raise their colossal fortunes. The bishop has opened before me a most deplorable and shameful page of the history of our church. It makes me understand many facts which were a mystery to me till to-day. Now I understand the terrible wrath of the English people in the days of old, and of the French people more recently, when they so violently wrenched from the hands of the clergy the enormous wealth they had accumulated during the dark ages. I have condemned those great nations till now. But, to-day, I absolve them. I am sure that those men, though blind and cruel in their vengeance, were the ministers of the justice of God. The God of Heaven could not, for ever, tolerate a sacrilegious system of swindling, as I know, now, to be in operation from one end to the other, not only of Canada, but of the whole world, under the mask of religion. I know that the bishop and his flatterers will hate and persecute me for my stern opposition to his rapacity. But I do feel happy and proud of his hatred. The God of truth and justice, the God of the gospel, will be on my side when they attack me. I do not fear them; let them come. That bishop surely did not know me, when he thought that I would consent to be the instrument of his hypocrisy, and that, under the false pretext of a delusive perfection, I would throw that lady into a dungeon for her life, that he might become rich with her inheritance."

Mr. Brassard answered me : " I cannot blame you for your disobeying the bishop, in this instance. I foretold him what has occurred; for I knew what you think of the nuns. Though I do not go so far as you in that, I cannot absolutely shut my eyes to the facts which stare us in the face. Those monkish communities have, in every age, been the principal cause of the calamities which have befallen the church. For their love of riches, their pride and laziness, with their other scandals, have always been the same. Had I been able to foresee what has occurred inside the walls of the nunnery I built up here, I never would have erected it. However, now that I have built it, it is as the child of my old age, I feel bound to support it to the end. This does not prevent me from being afflicted when I see the facility with which our poor nuns yield to the criminal desires of their too weak confessors. Who could have thought, for instance, that that lean and ugly superior of the Oblates, Father Allard, could have fallen in love with his young nuns, and that so many would have lost their hearts on his account. Have you heard how the young men of our village, indignant at his spending the greater part of the night with the nuns, have whipped him, when he was crossing the bridge, not long before his leaving Longueuil for Africa? It is evident that our bishop multiplies too fast those religious houses. My fear is that they will, sooner than we expect, bring upon our Church of Canada the same cataclysms which have so often desolated her in England, France, Germany, and even in Italy."

The clock struck twelve just when this last sentence fell from the lips of Mr. Brassard. It was quite time to take some rest. When leaving me for his sleeping room he said :

" My dear Chiniquy, gird your loins well, sharpen your sword for the impending conflict. My fear is that the bishop and his advisers will never forget your wrenching from their hands the booty they were coveting so long. They will never forgive the spirit of independence with which you have rebuked them. In fact, the conflict is already begun, may God protect you against the open blows, and the secret machinations they have in store for you."

I answered him : " I do not fear them. I put my trust in God. It is for His honour I am fighting and suffering. He will surely protect me from those sacrilegious traders in souls."

CHAPTER XLIX.

THE first week of September, 1851, I was hearing confessions in one of the churches of Montreal, when a fine-looking girl came to confess sins, whose depravity surpassed anything I had ever heard. Though I forbade her twice to do it, she gave me the names of several priests who were the accomplices of her orgies. The details of her iniquities were told with such cynical impudence, that the idea struck me at once, that she was sent by some one to ruin me. I abruptly stopped her disgusting stories by saying: "The way you confess your sins is a sure indication that you do not come here to reconcile yourself to God, but to ruin me. By the grace of God, you will fail. I forbid you to come any more to my confessional. If I see you again among my penitents, I will order the beadle to turn you out of the church."

I instantly shut the door of the small aperture through which she was speaking to me. She answered something which I could not understand. But the tone of her voice, the shaking of her hands and head, with her manner of walking, when she left the confessional, indicated that she was beside herself with rage, as she went to speak a few words to a carter who was in the church, preparing himself to confess.

The next evening, I said to Rev. Mr. Brassard that I suspected that a girl was sent to my confessional to ruin me.

He answered: "Did I not warn you, some time ago, that there was a plot to destroy you? I have not the least doubt but that that girl was hired to begin that diabolical work. You have no idea of my anxiety about you. For I know your enemies will not shrink from any iniquity to destroy your good name, and prevent you from directing the tide of emigration from Canada to the valley of the Mississippi."

I replied, "That I could not partake of his fears; that God knew my innocence and the purity of my motives; He would defend and protect me."

"My dear Chiniquy," replied Mr. Brassard, "I know your enemies. They are not numerous, but they are implacable, and their power for mischief knows no limits. Surely, God can save you from their hands; but I cannot share your security for the future. Your answer to the bishop, in reference to Mrs. Chenier, when you refused to send her to the nunnery, that he might inherit her fortune, has for ever alienated him from you. Bishop Bourget has the merited reputation of being the most revengeful man in Canada. He will avail himself of the least opportunity to strike you without mercy."

I answered, "Though there should be a thousand Bishops Bourget to plot against me, I will not fear them, so long as I am in the right, as I am to-day." As the clock struck twelve, I bade him good-night, and ten minutes later, I was sound asleep.

The following days, I went to deliver a course of lectures on temperance to several parishes south of Laprairie, till the 28th of September, after which I came back from St. Constant to rest for a few days, and prepare to start for Chicago. On my arrival, I found, on my table, a short letter from Bishop Bourget telling me, that, for a criminal action, which he did not want to mention, committed with a person he would not name, he had withdrawn all my priestly powers and interdicted me. I handed the letter to Mr. Brassard and said: "Is not this the fulfilment of your prophecies? What do you think of a bishop who interdicts a priest without giving him a single fact, and without even allowing him to know his accusers?"

"It is just what I expected from the implacable vengeance of the Bishop of Montreal. He will never give you the reasons of your interdict, for he knows well you are innocent, and he will never confront you with your accusers; for it would be too easy for you to confound them."

"But is not this against all the laws of God and man? Is it not against the laws of the church?" I replied.

"Of course it is," answered he, "but do you not know that, on this continent of America, the bishops have, long ago, thrown overboard all the laws of God and man, and all the laws of the church, to rule and enslave the priests?"

I replied: "If it be so, are not Protestants correct, when they say that our church has rejected the Word of God to follow the traditions of man? What can we answer them when they tell us that our church has no right to be called the church of God? Would the Son of God have given up His life on the cross to save men, that they might be the property of a few lawless tyrants, who should have the right to take away their honour and life?"

"I am not ready to answer those puzzling questions," he answered, "but this is the fact. Though it is absolutely against all the laws of the church to condemn a priest without showing him his guilt, and confronting him with his accusers, our modern bishops, every week, condemn some of their priests without specifying any fact, or even giving them the names of their accusers."

"Mind what I tell you," I replied. "I will not allow the bishop to deal with me in that way. If he dares to trample the laws of the Gospel under his feet, to accomplish my ruin, and satisfy his vengeance, I will teach him a lesson that he will never forget. Thanks be to God, it is not the gory cross of the bloody Inquisition, but the emblem of the British Lion, which I see there floating on the tower, to protect our honour and life, in Canada. I am innocent; God knows it. My

24

trust is in Him; He will not forsake me. I will go immediately to the bishop. If he never knew what power there is in an honest priest, he will learn it to-day."

Two hours later, I was knocking at the bishop's door. He received me with icy politeness. "My lord," I said, "you already know why I am in your presence. Here is a letter from you, accusing me of a crime which is not specified, under the testimony of accusers whom you refuse to name! And before hearing me, and confronting me with my accusers, you punish me as guilty! You not only take away my honour with that unjust sentence, but my life! I come in the name of God, and of His Son, Jesus Christ, to respectfully ask you to tell me the crime of which I am accused, that I may show you my innocence. I want to be confronted with my accusers, that I may confound them."

The bishop was, at first, evidently embarrassed by my presence; his lips were pale and trembling, but his eyes were dry and red, like the tiger's eyes, in the presence of his prey. He answered: "I cannot grant your request, sir."

Opening then my New Testament, I read: "Receive no accusation against a priest, except under two or three witnesses" (1st Tim. v. 19). I added: "It was after I had heard this voice of God, and of His holy church, that I consented to be a priest. I hope it is not the intention of your lordship to put aside this Word of God and of His church. It is not your intention to break that solemn covenant made by Christ with His priests, and sealed with His blood?"

With an air of contempt and tyrannical authority, which I had never suspected to be possible in a bishop, he answered: "I have no lesson of Scripture or canonical law to receive from you, sir, and no answer to give to your impertinent questions; you are interdicted! I have nothing to do with you."

These words, uttered by the man whom I was accustomed to consider as my superior, had a strange effect upon me. I felt as if awakening from a long and painful dream. For the first time, I understood the sad prophecies of the Rev. Mr. Brassard, and I realized the horror of my position. My ruin was accomplished. Though I knew that that high dignitary was a monster of hypocrisy, injustice and tyranny, he had, among the masses, the reputation of a saint. His unjust sentence would be considered as just and equitable by the multitude over whom he was reigning supremely; at a nod of his head the people would fall at his feet, and obey his commands to crush me. All ears would be shut, and all hearts hardened against me. In that fatal hour, for the first time in my life, my moral strength and courage failed me. I felt as if I had just fallen into a bottomless abyss, out of which it was impossible to escape. What would my innocence, known only to God, avail me, when the whole world would believe me guilty? No words can give an idea of the mental torture of that horrible hour.

For more than a quarter of an hour, not a word was exchanged between the bishop and me. He seemed very busy writing letters, while I was resting my head between my hands, and shedding torrents of tears. At last I fell on my knees, took the hands of the bishop in mine, and, with a voice half-choked with sighs, I said : "My lord, in the name of our Lord Jesus Christ, and in the presence of God, I swear that I have done nothing which could bring such a sentence against me. I again implore your lordship to confront me with my accusers, that I may show you my innocence."

With a savage insolence, the bishop withdrew his hands, as if I had contaminated them, and said, after rising from his chair : "You are guilty; go out of my presence."

A thousand times since I have thanked my God that I had no dagger with me, for I would have plunged it into his heart. But, strange to say, the diabolical malice and dishonesty of that depraved man suddenly brought back my former self-respect and courage. I, at once took the stern resolution to face the storm. I felt, in my soul, that giant strength which often God Himself implants in the breast of the oppressed, when he is in the presence of his merciless tyrants. It seemed that a flash of lightning had passed through my soul, after having written in letters of fire, on the walls of the palace : "Mystery of iniquity."

Relying entirely on the God of truth and justice, who knew my innocence and the great perversity of my oppressor, I left the room, without saying a word, and hastened back to Longueuil, to acquaint the Rev. Mr. Brassard with my firm resolution to fight the bishop to the end. He burst into tears when I told him what had occurred in the bishop's palace.

"Though innocent, you are condemned," he said. "The infallible proof of your innocence is the cruel refusal of allowing you to be confronted with your accusers. Were you guilty, they would be too glad to show it, by confounding you before those witnesses. But the perversity of your accusers is so well known, that they are ashamed of giving their names. The bishop prefers to crush you under the weight of his unmerited reputation for justice and holiness; for very few know him as we do. My fear is that he will succeed in destroying you. Though innocent, you are condemned and lost; you will never be able to contend against such a mighty adversary."

"My dear Mr. Brassard, you are mistaken," I replied. "I never was so sure of coming out victorious from a conflict as to-day. The monstrous iniquity of the bishop carries its antidote with itself. It was not a dream I saw when he so ignominiously turned me out of his room. A flash of lightning passed before my eyes, and wrote, as if on the walls of the palace : 'Mystery of iniquity!' When Canada, the whole of Christendom, shall know the infamous conduct of that dignitary; when they shall see the 'mystery of iniquity,' which I shall stamp upon his forehead, there will be only one cry of indignation against him! Oh! If I can only find out the names of my accusers! How I will force that mighty tyrant to withdraw that sentence, at double quick. I am determined to show, not only to Canada, but to the whole world, that this infamous plot is but the work of the vile male and female slaves by whom the bishop is surrounded. My first thought was to start immediately for Chicago, where Bishop Vandeveld expected me. But I am resolved not to go until I have forced my merciless oppressor to withdraw his unjust sentence. I will immediately go to the Jesuit College, where I purpose spending the next eight days in prayer and retreat. The Jesuits are the ablest men under heaven to detect the most hidden things. I hope they will help me to unearth that dark mystery of iniquity, and expose it to the world."

"I am glad to see that you do not fear the terrible storm which is upon you, and that your sails are so well trimmed," answered Mr. Brassard. "You do well in putting your trust in God first, and in the Jesuits afterwards. The fearless way in which you intend to meet the attacks of your merciless enemies, will give you an easy victory. My hope is that the Jesuits will help you to find out the names of your false accusers, and that you will make use of them to hurl back in the face of the bishop the shame and dishonour he had prepared for you."

At six p.m., in a modest, well-lighted and ventilated room of the Jesuit College, I was alone with the venerable Mr. Schneider, its director. I told him how the Bishop of Montreal, four years before, after giving up his prejudices against me when I had left the Oblates, had earnestly supported me in my labours. I acquainted him also with the sudden change of those good feelings into the most uncontrollable hatred, from the day I had refused to force Mrs. Chenier to become a nun, that he might secure her fortune. I told him also how those bad feelings had found new food in my plan of consecrating the rest of my life to direct the tide of the French Catholic emigration towards the Mississippi Valley. I exposed to him my suspicions about that miserable girl I had turned out from my confessional. "I have a double object in view," I added. "The first is to spend the last eight days of my residence in Canada in prayer. But my second is to ask the help of your charity, wisdom, and experience in forcing the bishop to withdraw his unjust sentence against me. I am determined, if he does not withdraw it, to denounce him before the whole country, and to challenge him, publicly, to confront me with my accusers."

"If you do that," answered Mr. Schneider, "I fear lest you not only do an irreparable damage to the Bishop of Montreal, but to our holy church also."

I replied: "Our holy church would indeed suffer an irreparable damage, if she sanctioned the infamous conduct of the bishop; but this is impossible."

"You are correct," rejoined the Jesuit. "Our holy church cannot sanction such criminal conduct. She has, hundreds of times, condemned those tyrannical and unjust actions in other bishops. Such want of common honesty and justice will be condemned everywhere, as soon as it is known. The first thing we have to do is to find out the names of your accusers. I have not the least doubt that they are the blind instruments of Machiavelist plots against you. But those plots have only to be brought to light, to vanish away. My impression is, that the miserable girl you have so abruptly and so wisely turned out of your confessional, knows more than the bishop wants us to find out, about the plots. It is a pity you did not ask her name and residence. At all events, you may rely on my efforts to persuade our bishop that his personal interest, as well as the interest of our holy religion, is, that he should speedily withdraw that sentence, which is a nullity by itself. It will not be difficult for me to show him that he is fallen into the very pit he has dug under your feet. He has taken a position against you which is absolutely untenable. Before your retreat is at an end, no doubt he will be too happy to make his peace with you. Only trust in God, and in the blessed Virgin Mary, and you have nothing to fear from the conflict. Our bishop has put himself above all the laws of man and God, to condemn the priest he had himself officially named 'the Apostle of Temperance of Canada.' There is not a single man in the Church, who will allow him to stand on that ground. The 200,000 soldiers you have enrolled under the holy banners of temperance, will force him to retract his too hasty and unjust sentence."

It would be too long to repeat here all the encouraging words which that wise Jesuit uttered. Father Schneider was a European priest, who was in Montreal only since 1849. He had won my confidence the very first time I met him, and I had chosen him, at once, for my confessor and adviser. The third day of my retreat, Father Schneider came to my room earlier than usual, and said:

"I have worked hard the last two days, to find out the name and residence of the carter to whom that miserable girl spoke in the church, after you had turned her out of your confessional, and I have it. If you have no objection I will send for him. He may know that girl and induce her to come here."

"By all means, dear father," I answered, "do it without losing a moment."

Two hours later, the carter was with me. I recognized him as one of those dear countrymen whom our society of temperance had transformed into a new man. I asked him if he remembered the name of the girl who, a few days before, had spoken to him in the church, after going out of my confessional.

"Yes sir! I know her well. She has a very bad name, though she belongs to a respectable family."

I added: "Do you think you can induce her to come here, by telling her that a priest, in the Jesuit College, wants to see her? But do not give her my name."

He answered: "Nothing is more easy. She will be here in a couple of hours, if I find her at home."

At three p.m., the carter was again knocking at my door, and said, with a low voice: "The girl you want is in the parlour; she has no idea you are here, for she told me that you were now preaching in St. Constant, she seems to be very angry against you, and bitterly complains against your want of courtesy, the very first time she went to confess to you."

"Is it possible that she told you that?" I replied.

"Yes sir! She told me that to explain her terrible excitement when coming out of your confessional, the other day; she then requested me to drive her home. She was really beside herself, and swore that she would make you pay for your harsh words and rude manners towards her. You will do well to be on your guard with her. She is one of the most depraved girls of Montreal, and has a most dangerous tongue, though to the shame of our holy religion, she is daily seen in the bishop's palace."

I immediately went to Father Schneider, and said: "My dear father, by the mercy of God, the girl we want to see is in the parlour. But what I have just heard from the carter who drove her, I have not the least doubt but that she is the one employed by the bishop to slander me, and get a pretext for what he has done. Please come with me to witness my innocence. But, take your Gospel, ink, paper and pen with you."

"All right," answered the wise Jesuit.

Two minutes later we were in her presence. It is impossible to describe her dismay when she saw me. She came near fainting. I feared she would not be able to utter a word. I spoke to her very kindly, and ran to get a glass of cold water, which did her good. When she recovered, I said to her, with a tone of mixed authority and kind firmness: "You are here in the presence of God and of two of His priests. That great God will hear every word which will fall from your lips. You must speak the truth. You have denounced me to the bishop as guilty of some great iniquity. You are the cause of my being interdicted. You, alone, can repair the injury you have done me. That injury is very great; but it can be easily repaired by you. In the presence of that venerable priest, say whether or not, I am guilty of the crime you have brought to my charge!"

At these words, the unfortunate girl burst into tears. She hid her face in her handkerchief, and with a voice half-suffocated with sighs, she said: "No sir! You are not guilty."

I added: "Confess another thing. Is it not a fact that you had come to my confessional more with the intention of tempting me to sin, than to reconcile yourself to God?"

"Yes sir!" she added, "this was my wicked intention."

"Continue to tell the truth, and our great and merciful God will forgive you. Is it not to revenge yourself for my rebuking you, that you have brought the false accusations to the bishop in order that he might interdict me?"

"Yes sir! that is the only reason I had for accusing you."

After Father Schneider had made four copies of those declarations, signed by him as witness, and after she had sworn on the Gospel, I forgave her the injury she had done me, I gave her some good advice and dismissed her.

"Is it not evident," I said to Father Schneider, "that our merciful God never forsakes those who trust in Him?"

"Yes, I never saw the interposition of God so marvellously manifested as in this perfect deliverance from the hands of your enemies. But, please, tell me why you requested me to make four copies of her sworn declaration of your innocence; was not one sufficient?" asked Mr. Schneider.

I answered: "One of those copies was for the bishop; another will remain in your hands, Mr. Brassard will have one, and I need one for myself. For the dishonesty of the bishop is so evident to me, now, that I think him able to destroy the copy I will send him, with the hope, after its destruction, of keeping me at his feet. If he does that new act of iniquity, I will confound him with the three other authentic copies which will remain. Besides, this unfortunate girl may die sooner than we expect. In that case, I would find myself again with the bishop's knife on my throat, if I had no other retractation to the perjured declaration which he has persuaded her to give him."

"You are right," replied Father Schneider; "now the only thing for you to do is to send that retractation to the bishop, with a firm and polite request to retract his unjust sentence against you. Let me do the rest with him. The battle is over. It has been fierce, but short. However, thanks be to God, you have a most complete victory over your unjust aggressors. The bishop will do all in his power, no doubt, to make you forget the darkest page of-his life."

The shrewd Jesuit was correct in his previsions. Never did any bishop receive me with so many marks, not only of kindness, but I dare say of respect, than Bishop Bourget, when, after my retreat, I went to take leave of him, before my departure from Canada for the United States.

"I trust, my lord," I said, "that, to-day, I can hope to possess the confidence and friendly feelings of your lordship?"

"Certainly, my dear Mr. Chiniquy, certainly; you possess my full confidence and friendship. I dare say more; you possess my most sincere gratitude, for what you have done in my diocese."

I answered: "I am much obliged to your lordship for this expression of your kind feelings. But, now, I have two new favours to ask from your lordship. The first, is a written document expressive of those kind feelings. The second, is a chalice from your hands to offer the holy sacrifice of mass the rest of my life."

"I will grant your request with the utmost pleasure," answered the bishop; and without losing a moment, he wrote the following letter, which I reproduce here, on account of its importance:

TRANSLATION.

MONTREAL, *Oct. 13th,* 1851.

SIR,—You request me to give you permission to leave my diocese, in order to go and offer your services to the Bishop of Chicago. As you still belong to the diocese of Quebec, I think you ought to address yourself to my lord of Quebec, to get the extract you want. As for me, I cannot but thank you for what you have done in our midst; and in my gratitude towards you, I wish you the most abundant blessing from heaven. Every day of my life I will remember you. You will always be in my heart, and I hope that on some future day the providence of God will give me some opportunity of showing you all the feelings of gratitude I feel towards you.

I remain, your most obedient servant,

✠ IGNACE,
Bishop of Montreal.

REV. C. CHINIQUY.

Though that letter was a most perfect recantation of all he had said and done against me, and was of immense value to me in such circumstances, the bishop added to its importance by the exceedingly kind manner in which he handed it to me.

As he was going into another room he said: "I will give you the silver chalice you want, to offer the holy sacrifice of mass the rest of your days." But he came back and said : " My secretary is absent, and has the key of the trunk which contains those vases."

"It makes no difference, my lord," I replied, "please order your secretary to put that chalice in the hands of Rev. Mr. Brassard, who will forward it, with a box of books which he has to send me to Chicago next week."

The bishop very kindly promised to do so ; and he fulfilled his promise. The next day, that precious gift was put in the hands of Mr. Brassard, in presence of several priests. It was sent, the following week, to Chicago, where I got it, and that fine silver chalice is still in my possession.

I then fell on my knees, and said : " My lord, I am just leaving Canada for the Far West, please give me your benediction." He blessed me and pressed me to his heart with the tenderness of a father, saying, " May God Almighty bless you, wherever you go and in everything you do, till the end of your life."

CHAPTER L.

THOUGH I had kept my departure from Canada as secret as possible, it had been suspected by many ; and Mr. Brassard, unable to resist the desire that his people should give me the expression of their kind feelings, had let the secret slip from his lips two days before I left. I was not a little surprised a few hours before my taking leave of him, to see his whole parish gathered at the door of his parsonage, to present me the following address :

TO THE REV. FATHER CHINIQUY.

VENERABLE SIR,—It is only three years since we presented you with your portrait, not only as an expression of our gratitude for your labours and success in the cause of temperance in our midst, but also as a memorial, which would tell our grandchildren the good you have done to our country. We were, then, far from thinking that we were so near the day when we would have the sorrow to see you separating yourself from us.

Your unforeseen exit from Canada fills us with a regret and sadness, which is increased by the fear we have, that the reform you have started, and so gloriously established everywhere, will suffer from your absence. May our merciful God grant that your faithful co-labourers may continue it, and walk in your footsteps.

While we submit to the decrees of Providence, we promise that we will never forget the great things you have done for the prosperity of our country. Your likeness, which is in every Canadian family, will tell to the future generations what Father Chiniquy has done for Canada.

We console ourselves by the assurance that, wherever you go, you will raise the glorious banners of temperance among those of our countrymen who are scattered in the land of exile. May these brethren put on your forehead the crown of immortality, which you have so well deserved for your noble work in our midst.   Signed,

L. M. BRASSARD, *Priest and Curate.*

H. HICKS, *Vicar*, and 300 others.

I answered :

GENTLEMEN,—I thank you for the honour you do me by your address. But allow me to tell you, that the more I look upon the incalculable good resulting from the Temperance Reform I have established, nearly from one end of Canada to the other, the more I would deceive myself, were I to attribute to myself the whole merit of that blessed work.

If our God has chosen me, His so feeble servant, as the instrument of His infinite mercies towards our dear country, it is because He wanted us to understand that He alone could make the marvellous change we see everywhere, and that we shall give all the glory to Him.

It is more to the fervent prayers, and to the good examples of our venerable bishops and curates, than to my feeble efforts, that we owe the triumph of temperance in Canada ; and it is my firm conviction that that holy cause will lose nothing by my absence.

Our merciful God has called me to another field. I have heard His voice. Though it is a great sacrifice for me to leave my own beloved country, I must go to work in the midst of a new people, in the distant lands of Illinois.

From many parts of Europe and Canada multitudes are rushing towards the western territories of the United States, to secure to their families the incalculable treasures which the good providence of God has scattered over those broad prairies.

Those emigrants are in need of priests. They are like those little ones of whom God speaks in His Word, who wanted bread and had nobody to give them any : "I have heard their cries, I have seen their wants." And in spite of the great sacrifice I am called upon to make, I must bless the Good Master who calls me to work in that vineyard, planted by His own hands in those distant lands.

If anything can diminish the sadness of my feelings, when I bid adieu to my countrymen, it is the assurance given me by the noble people of Longueuil, that I have in Canada many friends whose fervent prayers will constantly ascend to the throne of grace, to bring the benedictions of heaven upon me wherever I go.

C. CHINIQUY.

I arrived at Chicago on the 29th of October, 1851, and spent six days with Bishop Vandeveld, in maturing the plans of our Catholic colonization. He gave me the wisest advices, with the most extensive powers which a bishop can give a priest, and urged me to begin at once the work, by selecting the most suitable spot for such an important and vast prospect. My heart was filled with uncontrollable emotions when the hour came to leave my superior and go to the conquest of the magnificent State of Illinois, for the benefit of my church. I fell at his knees to ask his benediction, and requested him never to forget me in his prayers. He was not less affected than I was, and pressing me to his bosom, bathed my face with his tears, and blessed me.

It took me three days to cross the prairies from Chicago to Bour-bonnais. Those prairies were then a vast solitude, with almost impassable roads. At the invitation of their priest, Mr. Courjeault, several people had come long distances to receive and overwhelm me with the public expressions of their joy and respect.

After a few days of rest, in the midst of their interesting young colony, I explained to Mr. Courjeault that, having been sent by the bishop to found a settlement for Roman Catholic immigrants, on a sufficiently grand scale to rule the government of Illinois, it was my duty to go further south, in order to find the most suitable place for the first village I intended to raise. But to my unspeakable regret, I saw that my proposition filled the heart of that unfortunate priest with the most bitter feelings of jealousy and hatred. It had been just the same thing with Rev. Mr. Lebel, at Chicago.

The very moment I told him the object of my coming to Illinois, I felt the same spirit of jealousy had turned him into an implacable enemy. I had expected very different things from these two priests, for whom I had entertained, till then, most sincere sentiments of esteem. So long as they were under the impression that I had left Canada to help them increase their small congregations, by inducing the immigrants to settle among them, they loaded me, both in public and in private, with marks of their esteem. But the moment they saw that I was going to found, in the very heart of Illinois, settle-ments on such a large scale, they banded together to paralyze and ruin my efforts. Had I suspected such opposition from the very men on whose moral help I had relied for the success of my colonizing schemes, I would have never left Canada, for Illinois. But it was now too late to stop my onward march. Trusting in God alone for success, I felt that those two men were to be put among those unfore-seen obstacles which Heaven wanted me to overcome, if I could not avoid them. I persuaded six of the most respectable citizens of Bour-bonnais to accompany me, in three waggons, in search of the best site for the centre of my future colony. I had a compass, to guide me through those vast prairies, which were spread before me like a bound-less ocean. I wanted to select the highest point in Illinois for my first town, in order to secure the purest air and water for the new immi-grants.

I was fortunate enough, under the guidance of God, to succeed better than I expected, for the government surveyors have lately ac-knowledged that the village of St. Anne occupies the very highest point of that splendid state. To my great surprise, ten days after I had selected that spot, fifty families from Canada had planted their tents around mine, on the beautiful site which forms to-day the town of St. Anne. We were at the end of November, and though the weather was still mild, I felt I had not an hour to lose in order to secure shelters for every one of those families, before the cold winds and chilly rains of winter should spread sickness and death among them. The greater part were illiterate and poor people, without any idea of the dangers and incredible difficulties of establishing a new settlement, where everything had to be created. There were, at first, only two small houses, one 25 by 30, and the other 16 by 20 feet, to lodge us. With the rest of my dear immigrants, wrapped in buffalo robes, with my overcoat for my pillow, I slept soundly, many nights on the bare floor, during the three months which it took to get my first house erected.

Having taken the census of the people on the first of December, I found two hundred souls, one hundred of whom were adults. I said to them : " There are not three of you, if left alone, able to prepare a shelter for your families, this winter; but if, forgetting yourselves, you work for each other, as true friends and brethren, you will increase your strength tenfold, and in a few weeks, there will be a sufficient number of small, but solid buildings, to protect you against the storms and snow of the winter which is fast coming upon us. Let us go to the forest together and cut the wood, to-day ; and to-morrow we will draw that timber to one of the lots you have selected, and you will see with what marvellous speed the house will be raised, if your hands and hearts are perfectly united to work for each other, under the eyes and for the love of the merciful God who gives us this splendid country for our inheritance. But before going to the forest, let us kneel down to ask our Heavenly Father to bless the work of our hands, and grant us to be of one mind and one heart, and to protect us against the too common accidents of those forests and building works."

We all knelt on the grass, and, as much with our tears as with our lips, we sent to the mercy seat a prayer, which was surely heard by the One who said " Ask and it shall be given you " (Matt. vii. 7), and we started for the forest.

The readers would scarcely believe me, were I to tell them with what marvellous rapidity the first forty small, but neat houses were put up on our beautiful prairies. Whilst the men were cutting timber, and raising one another's houses, with a unity, a joy, a good-will and rapidity, which many times drew from me tears of admiration, the women would prepare the common meals. We obtained our flour and pork from Bourbonnais and Momence, at a very low price ; and, as I was a good shot, one or two friends and I used to kill, every day, enough prairie chickens, quails, ducks, wild geese, brants and deer, to feed more people than there were in our young colony.

Those delicious viands, which would have been welcomed on the table of the king, and which would have satisfied the most fastidious gourmand, caused many of my poor, dear immigrants to say: "Our daily and most common meals here are more sumptuous and delicate than the richest ones in Canada, and they cost almost nothing."

When I saw that a sufficient number of houses had been built to give shelter to every one of the first immigrants, I called a meeting, and said :

"My dear friends, by the great mercy of God, and in almost a miraculous way (thanks be to the unity and charity which have bound you to each other till now, as members of the same family) you are in your little, but happy homes, and you have nothing to fear from the winds and snow of the winter. I think that my duty now is to direct your attention to the necessity of building a two-story house. The upper part will be used as the schoolhouse for your children on week days, and for a chapel on Sundays, and the lower part will be my parsonage. I will furnish the money for the flooring, shingles, the nails, and the windows, and you will give your work gratis to cut and draw the timber and put it up. I will also pay the architect, without asking a cent from you. It is quite time to provide a school for your children ; for in this country, as in any other place, there is no possible prosperity or happiness for a people, if they neglect the education of their children. Now, we are too numerous to continue having our Sabbath worship in any private house, as we have done till now. What do you think of this ? "

They unanimously answered : "Yes! after you have worked so hard to give a home to every one of us, it is just that we should help you to make one for yourself. We are happy to hear that it is your intention to secure a good education for our children. Let us begin the work at once." This was the 16th of January, 1852. The sun was as warm as on a beautiful day of May in Canada. We again fell upon our knees to implore the help of God, and sang a beautiful French hymn.

The next day, we were seventy-two men in a neighbouring forest, felling the great oaks ; and on the 17th of April, only three months later, that fine two-story building, nearly forty feet square, was blessed by Bishop Vandeveld. It was surmounted by a nice steeple, thirty feet high, in which we had put a bell, weighing 250 pounds, whose solemn sound was to tell our joys and sorrows over the boundless prairies. On that day, instead of being only fifty families, as at the last census, we numbered more than one hundred, among whom more than five hundred persons were adults. The chapel which we thought at first would be too large, was filled to its utmost capacity on the day of its consecration to God.

Not a month later, we had to speak of making an addition of forty feet more, which, when finished, six months later, was found to be still insufficient for the accommodation of the constantly increasing flood of immigration, which came, not only from Canada, but from Belgium and France. It soon became necessary to make a new centre, and expand the limits of my first colony; which I did by planting a cross at l'Erable, about fifteen miles south-west of St. Anne, and another at a place we call St. Mary, twelve miles south-east, in the county of Iroquois. These settlements were soon filled; for that very spring more than one thousand new families came from Canada to join us.

No words can express the joy of my heart, when I saw with what rapidity my (then) so dear Church of Rome was taking possession of those magnificent lands, and how soon she would be unrivalled mistress, not only of the State of Illinois, but of the whole valley of the Mississippi. But the ways of men are not the ways of God. I had been called by the Bishops of Rome to Illinois, to extend the power of that church. But my God had called me there, that I might give to that church the most deadly blow she has ever received on this Continent.

My task is now to tell my readers, how the God of Truth, and Light, and Life, broke, one after another, all the charmed bonds by which I was kept a slave at the feet of the Pope; and how He opened my eyes, and those of my people, to the unsuspected and untold abominations of Romanism.

CHAPTER LI.

" PLEASE accompany me to Bourbonnais ; I have to confer with you and the Rev. Mr. Courjeault, on important matters," said the bishop, half an hour before leaving St. Anne, after having blessed the chapel.

"I intended, my lord, to ask your lordship to grant me that honour, before you offered it," I answered.

Two hours of good driving took us to the parsonage of the Rev. Mr. Courjeault, who had prepared a sumptuous dinner, to which several of the principal citizens of Bourbonnais had been invited.

When all the guests had departed, and the bishop, Mr. Courjeault, and I, were alone, he drew from his trunk a bundle of weekly papers of Montreal, Canada, in which several letters, very insulting and compromising for the bishop, were published, signed R. L. C. Showing them to me, he said :

"Mr. Chiniquy, can I know the reasons you had for writing such insulting things against your bishop ? "

" My lord," I answered, " I have no words to express my surprise and indignation, when I read those letters. But, thanks be to God, I am not the author of those infamous writings. I would rather have my right hand cut off, than allow it to pen such false and perfidious things against you or any one else."

"Do you assure me that you are not the writer of those letters ? Are you positive in that denial ; and do you know the contents of these lying communications ? " replied the bishop.

"Yes, my lord, I know the contents of these communications. I have read them, several times, with supreme disgust and indignation ; and I positively assert that I never wrote a single line of them."

"Then, can you tell me who did write them ? " said the bishop.

I answered: "Please, my lord, put that question to the Rev. Mr. Courjeault; he is more able than anyone to satisfy your lordship on that matter."

I looked at Mr. Courjeault with an indignant air, which told him that he could not any longer wear the mask behind which he had concealed himself for the last three or four months. The eyes of the bishop were also turned, and firmly fixed on the wretched priest.

No ! Never had I seen anything so strange as the countenance of that guilty man. His face, though usually ugly, suddenly took a cadaverous appearance ; his eyes were fixed on the floor, as if unable to move.

The only signs of life left in him were given by his knees, which were shaking convulsively; and by the big drops of sweat rolling down his unwashed face; for, I must say here, *en passant*, that, with very few exceptions, that priest was the dirtiest man I ever saw.

The bishop, with unutterable expressions of indignation, exclaimed : "Mr. Courjeault; you are the writer of those infamous and slanderous letters ! Three times you have written, and twice, you told me, verbally, that they were coming from Mr. Chiniquy ! I do not ask you if you are the author of these slanders against me, I see it written in your face. Your malice against Mr. Chiniquy is really diabolical. You wanted to ruin him in my estimation, as well as in that of his countrymen. And to succeed the better in that plot, you publish the most egregious falsehoods against me in the Canadian press, to induce me to denounce Mr. Chiniquy as an impostor. How is it possible that a priest can so completely give himself to the Devil ? "

Addressing me, the bishop said : "Mr. Chiniquy, I beg your pardon for having believed and repeated, that you were depraved enough to write those calumnies against your bishop : I was deceived by that deceitful man. I will immediately retract what I have written and said against you."

Then, addressing Mr. Courjeault he again said : "The least punishment I can give you is to turn you out of my diocese, and write to all the Bishops of America, that you are the vilest priest I ever saw, that they may never give you any position on this Continent."

These last words had hardly fallen from the lips of the bishop, when Mr. Courjeault fell on his knees before me, and bathing with his tears my hands, which he was convulsively pressing in his, said: "Dear Mr. Chiniquy, I see the greatness of my iniquity against you and against our common bishop. For the dear Saviour, Jesus' sake, forgive me. I take God to witness that you will never have a more devoted friend than I will be. And you, my lord, allow me to tell you, that I thank God that my malice and my great sin against both you and Mr. Chiniquy is known and punished at once. However, in the name of our crucified Saviour, I ask you to forgive me. God knows that, hereafter, you will not have a more obedient and devoted priest than I."

It was a most touching spectacle to see the tears, and hear the sobs of that repentant sinner. I could not contain myself, nor refrain my tears. They were mingled with those of the returning penitent. I answered: "Yes, Mr. Courjeault, I forgive you with all my heart, as I wish my merciful God to forgive me my sins. May the God who sees your repentance forgive you also!"

Bishop Vandeveld, who was gifted with a most sensitive and kind nature, was also shedding tears, when I lifted up Mr. Courjeault to press him to my heart, and to tell him again, with my voice choked by sobs, "I forgive you most sincerely, as I want to be forgiven."

He asked me: "What do you advise me to do? Must I forgive also? and can I continue to keep him at the head of this important mission?"

"Yes, my lord. Please forgive and forget the errors of that dear brother, he has already done so much good to my countrymen of Bourbonnais. I pledge myself that he will hereafter be one of your best priests."

And the bishop forgave him, after some very appropriate and paternal advice, admirably mixed with mercy and firmness.

It was then about three o'clock in the afternoon. We separated to say our vespers and matins (prayers which took nearly an hour). I had just finished reciting them in the garden, when I saw the Rev. Mr. Courjeault walking from the church towards me, but his steps were uncertain as one distracted or half-drunk. I was puzzled at the sight, for he was a strong teetotaler, and I knew he had no strong drink in the church. He advanced three or four steps, then retreated. At last he came very near, but his face had such an expression of terror and sadness, that he was hardly recognizable. He muttered something that I could not understand. "Please repeat your sentence," I said to him, "I did not understand you." He, then, put his hands on his face, and again muttered something; his voice was drowned in his tears and sobs. Supposing that he was coming to ask

me, again, to pardon his past malice and calumnies against me, I felt
an unspeakable compassion for him.   As there were a couple of seats
near by, I said to him : " My dear Mr. Courjeault, come and sit here
with me ; and do not think any more of the past.   I will never think
any more of your momentary errors, you may look upon me as your
most devoted friend."

   " Dear Mr. Chiniquy," he answered, " I have to reveal to you
another dark mystery of my miserable life.   Since more than a year,
I have lived with the beadle's daughter as if she were my wife !

   " She has just told me, that she is to become a mother in a few
days, and that I have to see to that, and give her five hundred dollars.
She threatens to denounce me publicly to the bishop and people, if I
do not support her and her offspring.   Would it not be better for me
to flee away, this night, and go back to France to live in my own
family, and conceal my shame ?   Sometimes, I am even tempted to
throw myself in the river, to put an end to my miserable and dishonoured existence.   Do you think that the bishop would forgive this
new crime, if I threw myself at his feet and asked pardon ?   Would
he give me some other place in his vast diocese, where my misfortunes
and my sins are not known ?   Please tell me what to do ? "

   I remained absolutely stupefied, and did not know what to answer.
Though I had compassion for the unfortunate man, I must confess
that this new development of his hypocrisy and rascality, filled me
with an unspeakable horror and disgust.   He had, till then, wrapped
himself in such a thick mantle of deception, that many of his people
looked upon him as an angel of purity.   His infamies were so well
concealed under an exterior of extreme moral rigidity, that several of
his parishioners looked upon him as a saint, whose relics could perform
miracles.   Not long before, two young couples, of the best families of
Bourbonnais, having danced in a respectable social gathering, had
been condemned by him, and compelled to ask pardon, publicly in the
church.   This pharisaical rigidity caused the secret vices of that
priest to be still more conspicuous and scandalous.   I felt that the
scandal which would follow the publication of this mystery of iniquity
would be awful ; that it would even cause many for ever to lose faith
in our church.   So many sad thoughts filled my mind, that I was confused and unable to give him any advice.   I answered :

   " Your misfortune is really great.   If the bishop were not here, I
might, perhaps, tell you my mind about the best thing to do, just
now.   But the bishop is here ; he is the only man to whom you have
to go to know how to come out of the bottomless abyss into which
you have fallen.   He is your proper counsellor; go and tell him,
frankly, everything, and follow his advice."

   With staggering step, and in such deep emotions that his sobs and cries could be heard for quite a distance, he went to the bishop. I remained alone, half-petrified at what I had heard.

Half an hour later, the bishop came to me. He was pale and his eyes reddened with his tears: he said to me:

"Mr. Chiniquy, what an awful scandal! What a new disgrace for our holy church! That Mr. Courjeault, whom I thought, till to-day, to be one of my best priests, is an incarnate devil; what shall I do with him? Please help me by your advice; tell me what you consider the best way of preventing the scandal, and protecting the faith of the good people against the destructive storm which is coming upon them."

"My dear bishop," I answered, "the more I consider these scandals here, the less I see how we can save the church from becoming a dreadful wreck. I feel too much the responsibility of my advice to give it. Let your lordship, guided by the Spirit of God, do what you consider best for the honour of the church and the salvation of so many souls, which are in danger of perishing when this scandal becomes known. For me, the only thing I can do, is to conceal my face with shame, go back to my young colony, to pray, and weep and work."

The bishop replied: "Here is what I intend to do: Mr. Courjeault tells me that there is not the least suspicion, among the people, of his sin, and that it is an easy thing to send that girl to the house provided in Canada for priests' offences, without awakening any suspicion. He seems so penitent, that I hope, hereafter, we have nothing to fear from him. He will now live the life of a good priest here, without giving any scandal. But if I remove him, then there will be some suspicions of his fall, and the awful scandal we want to avoid will come. Please lend me one hundred dollars, which I will give to Mr. Courjeault, to send that girl to Canada as soon as possible; and he will continue here, to work with wisdom, after this terrible trial. What do you think of that plan?"

"If your lordship is sure of the conversion of Mr. Courjeault, and that there is no danger of his great iniquity being known by the people, evidently, the wisest thing you can do is to send that girl to Canada, and keep Mr. Courjeault here. Though I see great dangers even in that way of dealing in this sad affair. But, unfortunately, I have not a cent in hand to-day, and I cannot lend you the one hundred dollars you want."

"Then," said the bishop, "I will give a draft on a bank of Chicago, but you must endorse it."

"I have no objection, my lord, to endorse any draft signed by your lordship," I replied.

Though it was late in the day, and that I had, at first, proposed to spend the night, I came back to my dear colony of St. Anne. Bourbonnais appeared to me like a burning house, in the cellar of which there was a barrel of powder, from which one could not keep himself too far away.

Five days later, four of the principal citizens of that interesting, but sorely tried place, knocked at my door. They were sent as a deputation from the whole village, to ask me what to do about their curate, Mr. Courjeault. They told me that several of them had, long since, suspected what was going on between that priest and the beadle's daughter, but they had kept that secret. However, yesterday, they said the eyes of the parish had been opened to the awful scandal.

The disgusting demonstrations and attention of the curate, when the victim of his lust took the diligence, left no doubt in the minds of any one, that she is to have a child in Montreal.

"Now, Mr. Chiniquy, we are sent here to ask your advice. Please tell us what to do?"

"My dear friends," I answered, "it is not from me, but from our common bishop, that you must ask what is to be done, in such deplorable affairs."

But they replied, "Would you not be kind enough to come to Bourbonnais with us, and go to our unfortunate priest to tell him that his criminal conduct is known by the whole people, and that we cannot decently keep him a day longer as our Christian teacher. He has rendered us great services in the past, which we will never forget. We do not want to abuse or insult him in any way. Though guilty, he is still a priest. The only favour we ask from him now, is, that he quits the place without noise and scandal, in the night, to avoid any disagreeable demonstrations which might come from his personal enemies, whom his pharisaical rigidity has made pretty numerous and bitter."

"I do not see any reason to refuse you that favour," I answered.

Three hours later, in the presence of those four gentlemen, I was delivering my sad message to the unfortunate curate. He received it as his death warrant. But he was humble and submitted to his fate.

After spending four hours with us in settling his affairs, he fell on his knees, with torrents of tears, he asked pardon for the scandal he had given, and requested us to ask pardon from the whole parish, and at twelve o'clock at night he left for Chicago. That hour was a sad one, indeed, for us all. But my God had a still sadder hour in store for me. The people of Bourbonnais had requested me to give them some religious evening services the next week, and I was just at the end of one of them, the 7th of May, when, suddenly, the Rev. Mr. Courjeault entered the church, walked through the crowd, saluting this one, smiling on that one, and pressing the hands of many. His face bore the marks of impudence and debauchery.

From one end of the church to the other, a whisper of amazement and indignation was heard.

"Mr. Courjeault! Mr. Courjeault!! Great God! what does this mean?"

I observed that he was advancing towards me, probably with the intention of shaking hands, before the people, but I did not give him time to do it, I left by the back door, and went to the parsonage, which was only a few steps distant. He then went back to the door to have a talk with the people, but very few gave him that chance. Though he affected to be exceedingly gay, jocose, and talkative, he could not get many people to stop and hear him. Every one, particularly the women, were filled with disgust at his impudence. Seeing himself nearly deserted at the church door, he turned his steps towards the parsonage, which he entered, whistling. When he beheld me, he laughed, and said:

"Oh oh! our dear little Father Chiniquy here? How do you do?"

"I am quite unwell," I answered, "since I see that you are so miserably destroying yourself."

"I do not want to destroy myself," he answered; "but it is you who want to turn me out of my beautiful parish of Bourbonnais, to take my place. With the four blockheads who accompanied you, the other day, you have frightened and persuaded me that my misfortune with Mary was known by all the people: but our good bishop has understood that this was a trick of yours, and that it was one of your lying stories; I came back to take possession of my parish, and turn you out."

"If the bishop has sent you back here to turn me out, that I may go back to my dear colony, he has just done what I asked him to do; for he knows better than any man, for what great purpose I came to this country, and that I cannot do my work as long as he asks me to take care of Bourbonnais. I go, at once, and leave you in full possession of your parsonage. But I pity you, when I see the dark cloud which is on your horizon. Good-bye!"

"You are the only dark cloud on my horizon," he answered. "When you are begone, I will be in as perfect peace as I was before you set your feet in Illinois. Good-bye; and, please, never come back here, except I invite you."

I left, and ordered my servant man to drive me back to St. Anne. But when crossing the village, I saw that there was a terrible excitement among the people. Several times they stopped me, and requested me to remain in their midst to advise them what to do.

But I refused, saying to them : "It would be an insult on my part to advise you anything, in a matter where your duty as men and Catholics is so clear. Consult the respect you owe to yourselves, to your families, and to your church, and you will know what to do."

It took me all night, which was very dark, to come back to St. Anne, where I arrived at dawn, the 9th of May, 1852. The next Sabbath day, I held a public service in my chapel, which was crowded, without making any allusion to that deplorable affair. On the Monday following, four citizens of Bourbonnais were deputed to tell me what they had done, and asked me not to desert them in that hour of trial, but to remember that I was their countryman, and that they had nobody else to whom they could look, to help to fulfil their religious duties. Here is the substance of their message :

"As soon as we saw that you had left our village, without telling us what to do, we called a public meeting, where we passed the following resolutions :

"1st. No personal insult shall be given to Mr. Courjeault.

"2d. We cannot consent to keep him a single hour as our pastor.

"3d. When, next Sabbath, he will begin his sermon, we will instantly leave the church, and go to the door, that he may remain absolutely alone, and understand our stern determination not to have him any more for our spiritual teacher.

"4th. We will send these resolutions to the bishop, and ask him to allow Mr. Chiniquy to divide his time and attention between his new colony and us, till we have a pastor able to instruct and edify us."

Strange to say, poor Mr. Courjeault shut up in his parsonage, during that night, knew nothing of that meeting. He had not found a single friend to warn him of what was to happen the next Sunday. That Sunday the weather was magnificent, and there never had been such a multitude of people at the church. The miserable priest, thinking by that unusual crowd, that everything was to be right with him that day, began his mass, and went to the pulpit to deliver his sermon. But he had hardly pronounced the first words, when, at a signal given by some one, the whole people, without a single exception, ran out of the church as if it had been on fire, and he remained alone. Of course, this fell upon him as a thunderbolt, and he came very nea fainting. However, recovering himself, he went to the door, and having, with his tears and sobs, as with his words, persuaded the people to listen to what he had to tell them, he said : "I see that the hand of God is upon me, and I deserve it. I have sinned, and made a mistake by coming back. You do not want me any more to be your pastor. I cannot complain of that; this is your right, you will be satisfied. I will leave the place for ever to-night. I only ask you to forgive my past errors and pray for me."

This short address was followed by the most deadly silence; not a voice was heard to insult him.   Many, on the contrary, were so much impressed with the sad solemnity of this occurrence that they could not refrain their tears.   The whole people went back to their homes with broken hearts.   Mr. Courjeault left Bourbonnais that very night, never to return again.   But the awful scandal he had given did not disappear with him.

Our Great and Merciful God, who, many times, has made the very sins and errors of His people to work for good, caused that public iniquity of the priest to remove the scales from many eyes, and prepare them to receive the light, which was already dawning at the horizon.   A voice from heaven was as if heard by many of us.   "Do you not see that in your Church of Rome, you do not follow the Word of God, but the lying traditions of men?   Is it not evident that your priests' celibacy is a snare and an institution of Satan?"

Many asked me to show them in the Gospel where Christ had established the law of celibacy.   "I will do better," I added, "I will put the Gospel in your hands, and you will look for yourselves in that holy book, what is said on that matter."   The very same day I ordered a merchant, from Montreal, to send me a large box filled with New Testaments, printed by the order of the Archbishop of Quebec; and on the 25th as many from New York.   Very soon it was known by every one of my immigrants that not only had Jesus never forbidden His apostles and priests to marry, but he had left them free to have their wives, and live with them, according to the very testimony of Paul.   "Have we not power to lead about a sister, a wife, as well as other apostles, and as the brethren of the Lord, and Cephas?   (1 Cor. ix. 5); they saw, by their Gospel, that the doctrine of celibacy of the priests was not brought from heaven by Christ, but had been forged in darkness, to add to the miseries of man.   They read and read over again these words of Christ: "If ye continue in My word, then are ye My disciples indeed.   And ye shall know the truth, and the truth shall make you free. . . .   If the Son, therefore, shall make you free, ye shall be free indeed" (John viii. 31, 32, 36).

And those promises of liberty, which Christ gave to those who read and followed His Word, made their hearts leap with joy.   They fell upon their minds as music from heaven.   They also soon found, by themselves, that every time the disciples of Christ had asked Him who would be the first ruler, or the Pope, in His church, He had always solemnly and positively said that, in His church, no body would ever become the first, the ruler or the Pope.   And they began, seriously, to suspect that the great powers of the Pope and his bishops were nothing but a sacrilegious usurpation.   I was not long without seeing that the reading of the Holy Scriptures by my dear countrymen was changing them into other men.   Their minds were evidently enlarged and raised to higher spheres of thought. They were beginning to suspect that the heavy chains which were wounding their shoulders were preventing them from making progress in wealth, intelligence, and liberty, as their more fortunate fellow-men, called Protestants.

This was not yet the bright light of the day, but it was the blessed dawn.

CHAPTER LII.

On the 20th of May, 1852, I received the following letter from Bishop Vandeveld :—

"REV. MR. CHINIQUY.

"MY DEAR MR. CHINIQUY,—The Rev. Mr. Courjeault is just returned from Bourbonnais, where he ought never to have gone back ; he has told me of his complete failure, and ignominious exit. I bitterly regret having allowed him to go there again. But he had so persuaded me that his criminal conduct with his servant girl was ignored by the people, that I had yielded to his request.

" I feel that this new attempt, on his part, to impose himself on that honest people, has added to the enormity of his first scandal. I advise him now to go back to France, where he can more easily conceal his shame than in America. But one of the darkest features of that disgusting affair is, that I am obliged to pay the five hundred dollars which the girl asked, in order to prevent Mr. Courjeault from being dragged before the civil tribunal, and sent to gaol.

" The malice of that priest against you has received its just reward. But my fear is that you have another implacable enemy here in Mr. Lebel, whose power to do evil is greater than Mr. Courjeault's.

" Before you began your great work of directing the flood of Roman Catholic immigration towards this country, to secure it to our holy church, he was in favour of that glorious scheme, but his jealousy against you has suddenly changed his mind.

" He has lately addressed a letter to the Canadian press, every word of which is an unmitigated falsehood. Of course, the Bishop of Montreal, who is more than ever opposed to our colonization plan, has published that lying letter in his journal ; more than that, he has reproduced the testimony of a perjured man, who swears that many of the people of Illinois are bitten and killed by the rattle-snakes, and those who escape are taxed six cents for each pane of glass of their windows.

" Will you be discouraged by this opposition ? I hope not. This opposition is the greatest evidence we could have that our scheme is from God, and that He will support you. I am tempted to interdict Mr. Lebel, and send him back to Canada, for writing things which he so well knows to be false. The want of a French-speaking priest for your countrymen of Chicago is the only thing which has prevented me from withdrawing his faculties. But I have warned him that, if he writes any more against the truth, I will punish him as he deserves.

" For you, my dear Sir, I will address to you the very words which God Himself addressed to His servant Joshua : ' Be strong, and of good courage ; for unto this people shalt thou divide, for an inheritance, the land which I swear unto their fathers to give them ' (Joshua i. 6).

"I agree with what you wrote me in your last letter, that the charge I have given you of Bourbonnais, pro tempore, will seriously interfere with your other numberless duties towards your dear immigrants. But there is no help; the only thing I can promise is to relieve you as soon as possible. I have no other priest to whom I can trust the interesting mission of Bourbonnais. For Father Huick is too old and infirm for such a work; it is evidently the will of God that you should extend your labours over the first limits you had fixed. Be faithful to the end, and the Lord will be with you, and support you throughout all your labours and tribulations.

"Truly yours,

✠ "OLIV VANDEVELD,

"Bishop of Chicago."

During the next six months, more than 500 families from France, Belgium, and Canada, came and gave to our colony a life, power, and prosperity, impossible for me to depict; the joy I felt at this unforeseen success was much diminished, however, by the sudden news that Mr. Courjeault had come back from France, where he spent only one month. Not daring to visit Bourbonnais again, he was lurking on the frontiers of Indiana, only a few miles distant, evidently with some sinister intention. Driven to a state of madness by his jealousy and hatred, that unfortunate man addressed to me, on the 23rd of January, 1853, the most abusive letter I ever received, and ended it by telling me that the fine (though unfinished) church of Bourbonnais, which he had built, was to be burned, and that my life would be in danger if I remained at the head of that mission.

I immediately sent that letter to the bishop, asking his advice. In his answer, he told me that he thought that Mr. Courjeault was wicked enough to fulfil his threats. He added: "Though I have not yet clear evidence of it, it is my fear that Mr. Lebel is united with Mr. Courjeault, in the diabolical plot of burning your church of Bourbonnais. Several people have reported to me that he says that your presence there will be the ruin of that people, and the destruction of their church. Oh! to what extremities bad priests can go, when once they have given themselves to their unbridled passions! The first thing I would advise you, my dear Mr. Chiniquy, in the presence of such a terrible calamity, is to insure that church without delay. I have tried to do it here, but they have refused, under the pretext that it is an unfinished, frame building, and that there are too many dangers of fire when people are still working at it. My impression is, that Mr. Lebel is on intimate terms with some insurance gentlemen, and has frightened them by speaking of that rumour of danger, of which he is probably the father, with that miserable Courjeault. Perhaps you may have a better chance, by addressing yourself to some insurance company which you might find at Joliet, or at Springfield."

After vain efforts to insure the church, I wrote to the bishop, " The only way to escape the impending danger, is to finish the church at once, and insure it after. I have just made a collection of four hundred dollars among the people of Bourbonnais, to which I added three hundred dollars from my own private resources ; and will go to work immediately if your lordship has no objections."

Having got the approbation of my superior, on the 1st of March, I began, to put the last hand to that building. We worked almost day and night, till the 1st of May, when it was all finished. I dare affirm, that for a country place, that church was unsurpassed in beauty. The inside frame-work was all made of the splendid black oak of Bourbonnais, polished and varnished by most skilful men, and they looked like a mirror. Very seldom have I seen anything more grand and beautiful than the altar, made also of that precious black oak. It was late as night, when, with my fellow-labourers, covered with dust and sweat, we could say with joy the solemn words, "It is finished!" Afterwards we sung the Te Deum. Had I had an opportunity, at that late hour, it was my thought and desire to insure it. But I was forced to postpone this till the next Monday.

The next day (the first Sabbath of May, 1853), the sun seemed to come out from the horizon and rise above our heads with more than usual magnificence. The air was calm and pure, and the numberless spring flowers of our gardens mingling their perfumes with the fragrant leaves of the splendid forest at the front of the village, the balmy atmosphere, the songs of the birds, seemed to tell us that this Sabbath day was to be the most happy one for me and my dear people of Bourbonnais. The church had never been so crowded. The hymns we sung had never been so melodious, and the words of gratitude which I addressed to my God, when I thanked Him for the church He had given us, in which to adore and bless Him, had never been so sincere and earnest ; never had our tears of joy flowed so profusely as on that splendid and never-to-be-forgotten Sabbath. Alas ! who would suspect that, six hours later, that same people, gathered around the smoking ruins of their church, would rend the air with their cries of desolation ! Such, however, was the case.

While taking my dinner, after the public service, two little boys, who had remained in the church to wait for the hour of the Catechism, ran to the parsonage, crying : " Fire ! Fire ! ! Fire ! ! ! " Bare headed, and half-paralyzed with the idea that my church was on fire, I went out to see the awful reality. A girdle of smoke and fire was already issuing from almost every part, between the top of the wooden walls and the roof. I had rushed to the church with a pail of water in my hand. But it was too late to make any use of it; the flames were already running and leaping with a fearful rapidity over the fresh varnish, like a long train of powder. In less than two hours all was finished again. No doubt could remain in our minds. This was the work of an incendiary, for there was no fire in the church after the service. Many strangers who had come from a distance had gone through the whole nave and the upper galleries, to have a better sight of the whole building, and two of them had been seen by the little boys, remaining ten or fifteen minutes alone; they had gone back to some of the houses of the village without being remarked by anybody, for it was dinner time, and there was nobody to watch them.

Though stunned by that awful calamity, the noble-hearted people of Bourbonnais did not lose their minds. Seeing that they were all gathered around the smoking ruins, at about six p.m. I addressed to them a few words to support their courage. I told them that it was only in the midst of great trials and difficulties that men could show their noblest qualities and their true manhood; that if we were true men, instead of losing our time in shedding tears and rending the air with our cries of desolation, we would immediately put our hands to the work, and begin the very next day, to raise up, not a frame building, which the flames could turn into ashes in a few minutes, and which the storm could blow down over our heads, but a stone church, which would stand before God and man as an imperishable monument of their faith, indomitable courage and liberality. We immediately started a subscription, to erect, without delay, a stone church. In less than one hour, four thousand dollars in money, and more than five thousand dollars in time, timber and stone and other material, were subscribed, every cent of which has been faithfully given for the erection of that fine stone church of Bourbonnais.

The next Thursday, Bishop Vandeveld came from Chicago to confer with me about what could be done to repair that terrible loss, and to inquire confidentially of me as to the author of the fire. All the facts we gathered pointed to the same direction. It was evident that the miserable Courjeault, with Lebel, the French-Canadian priest of Chicago, had done that evil work through their emissaries. No doubt of this remained in my mind when I learned that soon after, Mr. Courjeault had thrown himself into one of those dark dungeons called a monastery of La Trappe, which Satan has built on earth as a preparation for the dark hereafter of the wicked.

The unexpected visit of my bishop had at first rejoiced me by the hope that he would bring me words of encouragement. But what was my disappointment when he said to me: " Mr. dear Mr. Chiniquy, I must reveal to you a thing that I have not yet made known to anyone. It is confidential, and I request you not to say a word before it is accomplished. I cannot remain any longer Bishop of Illinois! No! I cannot any longer resume the responsibilities of such a high position, because it is beyond my power to fulfil my duties and do what the church requires of me. The conduct of the priests of this diocese is such, that, should I follow the regulations of the canon, I would be forced to interdict all my priests with the exception of you and two or three others. They are all either notorious drunkards, or given to public or secret concubinage ; several of them have children by their own nieces, and two by their own sisters. I do not think that ten of them believe in God. Religion is nothing to them but a well paying comedy. Where can I find a remedy to such a general evil ? Can I punish one of them and leave the others free in their abominable doings, when they are almost all equally guilty ? Would not the general interdiction of these priests be the death blow of our church in Illinois ? Besides, how can I punish them, when I know that many of them are ready to poison me the very moment I raise a finger against them. I suppose that you do not ignore the fact that my poor predecessor was poisoned, by one of those priests who had seduced several nuns, when he was in the very act of investigating the matter. I intend to go to Rome, as soon as I receive my permit from the Pope, to renounce at his feet the Bishopric of Chicago, which I will not keep on any consideration. If the Pope does not give me another diocese, with a better set of priests, I prefer to spend the rest of my life at the head of a small congregation, where I shall not have, on my shoulders, the awful responsibility which is killing me here. The last horrible deeds of Courjeault and Lebel, of which you are the victim to-day, has filled the bitter cup which God has put to my lips to drink. It is overflowing. I cannot any longer endure it."

When speaking so, the bishop's face was bathed with tears. It was very late; too late, indeed, to make the remonstrances which came to my mind, in order to change his resolutions.

I determined to wait till the next morning, when I should have plenty of time, I hoped, to expel his dark thoughts, and give him more courage. Besides, I was myself so discouraged by those awful disclosures, that I was in need of mental as well as bodily rest. But, alas! the next day was to be one of the darkest of my priestly life! When the hour for breakfast came the next morning, I went to awaken the bishop. What was my dismay when I found him drunk? Before going to bed, he had secretly asked my housekeeper to give him the bottle of wine which I used to celebrate mass. It was a large bottle, containing nearly a quart of wine,—which would last me, at least, six mouths—the whole of which he had drank during the night!

I had been told that Bishop Vandeveld was a drunkard, as well as the greater part of the bishops of the United States, but I had never believed it. He always drank very moderately before me, any time I sat at his table or he at mine. It appears that it was at night, when nobody could see him, that he gave himself up to that detestable habit. His room was filled with the odour of what he had vomited, after drinking such an enormous quantity of wine. He left the room, only at noon, after the fumes of the wine had almost entirely disappeared, and requested the housekeeper to cleanse it herself, without letting the servants know anything of the occurrence of the night. But words would fail to express my consternation, and the discouragement I felt. I had formed such a good and exalted opinion of that man! I had found in him such noble qualities! His intelligence was so bright, his learning so extensive, his heart so large, his plans so grand, his piety so sincere, his charity so worthy of a bishop of Christ! It was so pleasant for me to know, till then, that I was honoured with the full confidence of a bishop who, it seemed to me, had not a superior in our church!

The destruction of my dear church by the hands of incendiaries, was surely a great calamity for me; but the fall of my bishop, from the high position he had in my heart and mind, was still greater. I had the means, in hand, to rebuild that Church; but my confidence in my bishop was irremediably and for ever lost! Never had a son loved his father more sincerely than I had loved him; and never had any priest felt a more sincere respect for his bishop than I for him! Oh! what a terrible wound was made in my heart that day! what tortures I felt! But how many times since I have blessed my God for these wounds! Without them, I should never have known that instead of being in the bosom of the Immaculate Church of Christ, I was the slave of that great Babylon which poisons the nations with the wine of her abominations. My love and respect for Bishop Vandeveld were very strong chains, by which I was bound to the feet of the idols of Rome. I will eternally bless God for having Himself broken these chains, on that day of supreme desolation. The remaining part of the day, as well as the hour of the next morning which the bishop spent in my house, I remained almost mute in his presence. He was not less embarrassed when he asked me my views about his project of leaving the diocese. I answered him, in a few words, that I could not disapprove the purpose; for I would myself prefer to live in a dark forest, in the midst of wild animals, than among drunken, atheist priests and bishops.

Some months later I learned, without regret, that the Pope had accepted his resignation of the Bishopric of Chicago, and appointed him Bishop of Natchez, in Louisiana. His successor to the Bishopric of Chicago, was Rev. O'Regan. One of the very first things which this new bishop did, was to bring Bishop Vandeveld before the criminal tribunals as a thief, accusing him of having stolen one hundred thousand dollars from the Bishopric of Chicago, and carrying them away with him. There is no need to say that this action caused a terrible scandal. Not only in Illinois, but through all the United States, both priests and laymen had to blush and cast down their eyes before the world. The two bishops, employing the best lawyers to fight each other, came very near proving to the world that both of them were equally swindlers and thieves ; when the Pope forced them both to stop their contestation, and bring the affair before his tribunal at Rome. There it was decided that the one hundred thousand dollars which had really been taken from Chicago to the Natchez diocese, should be equally divided between the two bishops.

How many times did I feel my soul brought to the dust, in the midst of those horrible scandals! How many sleepless nights have I spent, when a voice, which I could not silence, seemed crying to me, louder than thunder: "What are you doing here, extending the power of a church which is a den of thieves, drunkards, and impure atheists ? A church, governed by men whom you know to be godless, swindlers, and vile comedians ? Do you not see that you do not follow the Word of God, but the lying traditions of men, when you consent to bow your knees before such men ? Is it not blasphemy to call such men the ambassadors, and the disciples of the humble, pure, holy, peaceful, and divine Jesus? Come out of that Church! Break the fetters, by which you are bound as a vile slave to the feet of such men! Take the Gospel for thine only guide and Christ for thine only Ruler !"

I was in desolation at finding that my faith in my Church was, in spite of myself, shaken by these scandals. With burning tears rolling down my cheeks, and with a broken and humiliated heart, I fell, one night, on my knees, and asked my God to have mercy upon me, by strengthening my faith and preserving it from ruin. But it seemed that neither my tears nor my cries were of any avail, and I remained the whole night, as a ship struck by a hurricane, drifting on an unknown sea, without a compass or a rudder.

I was not aware of it then, but I learned it after, that the divine and sure Pilot was directing my course towards the port of salvation! The next day, I had a happy diversion, in the arrival of fifty new immigrants, who knocked at my door, asking my advice about the best place to select for their future home. It seemed to me, though pretty long after that, that my duty was to go and pay my respects to my new bishop, and open to Him my heart as to my best friend, and the guide whom God Himself had chosen to heal the wounds of my soul, by pouring the oil and wine of charity into them.

I will never forget the day (the 11th of December, 1854), when I saw Bishop O'Regan, for the first time, nor the painful impressions I

received from that first interview. He was of medium stature, with a
repugnant face, and his head always in motion : all its motions seemed
the expression of insolence, contempt, tyranny, and pride; there was
absolutely nothing pleasant, either in his words or in his manners. I
fell on my knees to ask his benediction, when I had given him my
name and kissed his hand, which seemed as cold as that of a corpse.
" Ah! ah! you are Father Chiniquy," he said. "I am glad to see you,
though you have deferred your visit a long time ; please sit down. I
want some explanation from you about a certain very strange document, which I have just read to-day;" and he went, at the double
quick, to his room to get the document. There were two Irish priests
in the room, who came a few minutes before me. When we were
alone, one of them said: "We had hoped that we would gain by
changing Bishop Vandeveld for this one. But my fear is that we have
only passed from Charybdis into Scylla," and they laughed outright.
But I could not laugh. I was more inclined to weep. After less
than ten minutes of absence, the bishop returned, holding in his hand
a paper, which I understood, at once, to be the deed of the eleven acres
of land, which I had bought, and on which I had built my chapel of
St. Anne.

"Do you know this paper?" he asked me in an angry manner.

"Yes, my lord, I know it," I answered.

"But, then," he quickly replied, "you must know that that title is
a nullity—a fraud, which you ought never to have signed."

"Your venerable and worthy predecessor has accepted it," I
answered, "and what might have been incorrect has been made valid,
I hope, by his acceptation."

"I do not care a straw about what my predecessor has done," he
abruptly answered, "he is not here to defend himself; neither are we
here to discuss his merits or demerits. We have not to deal with my
lord Vandeveld, but with a document which is a nullity, a deception,
which must be thrown into the fire; you must give me another title
of that property !"

And saying this, he flung my deed on the floor. I calmly picked
it up and said: "I exceedingly regret, my lord, that my first interview with your lordship should be the occasion of such an unexpected
act. But I hope that this will not destroy the paternal sentiments
which God must have put into the heart of my bishop, for the last and
least of his priests. I see that your lordship is very busy; I do not
want to trespass on your valuable time; I take this rejected document with me, to make another one, which I hope will be more agreeable to your views;" and I then took my departure.

I leave the reader to imagine the sentiments which filled my mind
when coming back to my colony. I did not dare say a word to my

people about our bishop. When questioned by them, I gave the most
evasive answers I could. But I felt as the mariner feels when he
hears the rumbling thunder approaching. Though the sea is calm as the
oil of a lamp, he knows the storm is coming, he trims his sails, and
prepares for the impending hurricane. It seemed that my most pressing duty, after my first interview, was to bring my heart nearer to my
God than ever; to read and study my Bible with more attention, and to
get my people to take more than ever the Word of God as their daily
bread. I began, also, to speak more openly of our Christian rights,
as well as of our duties, as these are set forth in the Gospel of
Christ.

Some time, before this, feeling more than ever that I could not do
justice to my colony, by keeping any longer the charge of Bourbonnais, I had respectfully sent my resignation to the bishop, which had
been accepted. A priest had been called by him to take my place
there. But he too, was, ere long, guilty of a public scandal with his
servant girl. The principal citizens of Bourbonnais protested against
his presence in their midst, and soon forced the bishop to dismiss him.
His successor was the miserable priest, Lebel, who had been turned
out of Chicago for a criminal offence with his own niece, and was now
to be the curate of Bourbonnais. But his drunkenness and other
public vices caused him to be interdicted, and expelled from that place
in the month of September, 1855. About the same time, a priest who
had been expelled from Belgium for a great scandal, was sent to Kankakee, as the curate of the French Canadians of that interesting young
city. After his expulsion from Belgium he had come to Chicago,
where, under another name, he had made a fortune, and for five or six
years kept a house of prostitution. Becoming tired of that occupation, he offered five thousand dollars to the bishop, if he would accept
him as one of his priests, and give him a parish. Bishop O'Regan,
being in need of money, accepted the gift, and fulfilled the condition
by sending him as missionary to Kankakee.

As soon as he had taken possession of that interesting mission,
he came with Mr. Lebel to pay me a visit. I received them as politely
as possible, though they were both half drunk when they arrived.
After dinner, they went to shoot prairie chickens, and got so drunk
that one of them, Mr. Lebel, lost his boots in a slough, and came back
to my house barefooted, without noticing his loss. I had to help them
get their carriage, and the next day I wrote them, forbidding them to
ever set foot in my house again. But what was my surprise and sadness, not long before these two infamous priests were ignominiously
turned out by their people, to receive a letter from my bishop, which
ended in these words: "I am sorry to hear that you refuse to live on
good terms with your two neighbouring brother priests. This ought

not to be, and I hope to hear soon, that you have reconciled yourself with them, in a friendly way, as you ought to have done long ago."

I answered him : " It is my interest, as well as my duty, to obey my bishop. I know it. But as long as my bishop gives me for neighbours, priests, one of whom has lived publicly with his own niece, as his wife, and the other who has kept a house of prostitution in Chicago, I respectfully ask my bishop to be excused for not visiting them."

The bishop felt insulted by my letter, and was furious against me. It came to be a public fact that he had said before many people : " I would give anything to the one who would help me to get rid of that unmanageable Chiniquy." Among those who heard the bishop, was a land speculator, a real land-shark, against whom a bill for perjury had been found by the jury of Iroquois county, the 27th of April, 1854. That man was very angry against me for protecting my poor countrymen against his too sharp peculations. He said to the bishop, " If you pay the expense of the suit, I pledge myself to have Chiniquy put in gaol." The bishop had publicly answered him : " No sum of money will be too great to be delivered from a priest who alone gives me more trouble than the rest of my clergy." To comply with the desires of the bishop, this peculator dragged me before the criminal court of Kankakee, on the 16th day of May, 1855, but he lost his action, and was condemned to pay the cost.

It was my impression that the bishop, having so often expressed in public his bad feelings against me, would not visit my colony. But I was mistaken. On the 11th of June, taking the Rev. Mr. Lebel and Carthuval for his companions, he came to St. Anne to administer the sacrament of confirmation. As the infamous conduct of those two priests was known to every one of my people, I felt a supreme disgust at their arrival, and came very near forbidding them to sit at my table. Having, however, asked the bishop to give me half-an-hour of private interview, I respectfully, but energetically protested against the presence of these two degraded men in my house.

He coldly answered me : " Mr. Chiniquy, you forget that I am the Bishop of Illinois, and that you are a simple priest, whom I can interdict and remove from here when I like. I do not come here to receive your lessons, but to intimate to you my orders. You seem to forget that charity is above all others the virtue which must adorn the soul of a good priest. Your great zeal is nothing before God, and it is less than nothing before me, so long as you have not charity. It is my business, and not yours, to know what priests I must employ, or reject. Your business is to respect them, and forget their past errors, the very day I see fit to receive them among my priests."

"My lord," I answered "allow me respectfully to tell you, that though you are a bishop, and I am a simple priest, the Gospel of Christ, which we have to preach, tells us to avoid the company of publicly vicious and profligate men. My conscience tells me that through respect for myself and my people, and through respect for the Gospel I preach, I must avoid the company of men, one of whom has lived with his niece as his wife, and the other has, till very lately, been guilty of keeping a house of prostitution in Chicago. Your lordship may ignore these things, and, in consequence of that, may give your confidence to these men; but nothing is more apt to destroy the faith of our French Canadian people, than to see such men in your company when you come to administer the sacrament of confirmation. It is through respect for your lordship that I take the liberty of speaking thus."

He angrily answered me: "I see, now, the truthfulness of what people say about you. It is to the Gospel you constantly appeal on everything. The Gospel! The Gospel! is surely a holy book; but remember that it is the *Church* which must guide you. Christ has said, 'Hear My church.' I am here the interpreter, ambassador—the representative of the Church—when you disobey me, it is the Church you disobey."

"Now, my lord, that I have fulfilled what I consider a conscientious duty, I promise, that through respect for your lordship, and to keep myself in the bonds of peace with my bishop, I, to-day, will deal with these two priests, as if they were worthy of the honourable position you give them."

"All right! all right!" replied the bishop. "But it must be near the hour for dinner."

"Yes, my lord, I have just heard the bell calling us to the dining-room."

After the blessing of the table by the bishop, he looked at the Rev. Carthuval, who was sitting just before him, and said:

"What is the matter with you, Mr. Carthuval, you do not look well?"

"No, my lord," he answered, "I am not well; I want to go to bed."

He was correct, he was not well, for he was drunk.

During the public services, he had left the chapel to come down and ask for a bottle of the wine I kept to celebrate mass. The housekeeper, thinking he wanted the wine in the chapel, handed him the bottle, which he drank in her presence in less than five minutes. After which he went up the chapel to help the bishop in administering the confirmation to the 150 people whom I had prepared for the reception of that rite.

26

As soon as dinner was finished, the bishop requested me to go and take a walk with him. After giving me some compliments on the beauty of the site I had chosen for my first village and chapel, he saw at a short distance a stone building, which was raised only a little above the windows, and directing his steps towards it, he stopped only twenty or thirty feet distant, and asked me:

"Whose house is this?"

"It is mine, my lord."

"It is yours!" he replied; "and to whom does that fine garden belong?"

"It is mine also, my lord."

"Well! well!" he rejoined; "where did you get the money to purchase that fine piece of land and build that house?"

"I got the money where every honest man gets what he possesses, in my hard labour, and in the sweat of my brow," I replied.

"I want that house and that piece of land!" rejoined the bishop, with an imperative voice.

"So do I," I replied.

"You must give me that house, with the land on which it is built," said the bishop.

"I cannot give them as long as I am in need of them, my lord," I replied.

"I see that you are a bad priest, as I have often been told, since you disobey your bishop," he rejoined with an angry manner.

I replied: "I do not see why I am a bad priest, because I keep what my God has given me."

"Are you ignorant of the fact that you have no right to possess any property?" he answered.

"Yes! my lord, I am ignorant of any law in our holy church that deprives me of any such rights. If, however, your lordship can show me any such law, I will give you the title of that property just now."

"If there is not such a law," he replied, stamping on the ground with his feet, "I will get one passed."

"My lord," I replied, "you are a great bishop. You have great power in the church, but allow me to tell you that you are not great enough to have such a law passed in our holy church!"

"You are an insolent priest," he answered with an accent of terrible anger, "and I will make you repent for your insolence."

He then turned his face towards the chapel, without waiting for my answer, and ordered the horses to be put in the carriage, that he might leave in the shortest possible time. A quarter of an hour later he had left St. Anne, where he was never to come again. The visit of that mitred thief, with his two profligate priests, though very short, did much by the mercy of God, to prepare our minds to understand that Rome is the great harlot of the Bible, which seduces and intoxicates the nations with the wine of her prostitution. (Rev. xvii. 2.)

CHAPTER LIII.

The 8th December, 1854, Pope Pius IX. was sitting on his throne ; a triple crown of gold and diamonds was on his head; silk and damask —red and white vestments on his shoulders; five hundred mitred prelates were surrounding him ; and more than fifty thousand people were at his feet, in the incomparable St. Peter's Church of Rome. After a few minutes of most solemn silence, a cardinal, dressed with his purple robe, left his seat, and gravely walked towards the Pope, kneeled before him, and humbly prostrating himself at his feet, said :

" Holy Father, tell us if we can believe and teach that the Mother of God, the Holy Virgin Mary, was immaculate in her conception."

The Supreme Pontiff answered : "I do not know ; let us ask the light of the Holy Ghost."

The cardinal withdrew ; the Pope and the numberless multitude fell on their knees ; and the harmonious choir sang the " Veni Creator Spiritus."

The last note of the sacred hymn had hardly rolled under the vaults of the temple, when the same cardinal left his place, and again advanced towards the throne of the Pontiff, prostrated himself at his feet, and said :

" Holy Father, tell us if the Holy Mother of God, the blessed Virgin Mary, was immaculate in her conception."

The Pope again answered : " I do not know; let us ask the light of the Holy Ghost."

And again the " Veni Creator Spiritus " was sung.

The most solemn silence had a second time succeeded to the melodious sacred song, when again the eyes of the multitude were following the grave steps of the purple-robed cardinal, advancing, for the third time, to the throne of the successor of St. Peter, to ask again :

" Holy Father, tell us if we can believe that the blessed Virgin Mary, the Mother of God was immaculate."

The Pope, as if he had just received a direct communication from God, answered with a solemn voice :

" Yes ! we must believe that the Blessed Virgin Mary, the Mother of God, was immaculate in her conception. * * * There is no salvation to those who do not believe this dogma ! "

And, with a loud voice, the Pope intoned the Te Deum ; the bells of the three hundred churches of Rome rang; the cannons of the citadel were fired. The last act of the most ridiculous and sacrilegious comedy the world had ever seen, was over; the doors of heaven were for ever shut against those who would refuse to believe the anti-scriptural doctrine that there is a daughter of Eve who has not inherited the sinful nature of Adam, to whom the Lord said in His justice:

"Dust thou art, and unto dust shalt thou return!" (Gen. iii. 19), and of the children of whom the God of Truth has said, "There is none righteous; no, not one: for all have sinned!" (Rom. iii. 10, 23).

We look in vain to the first centuries of the Church to find any traces of that human aberration. The first dark clouds which Satan had brought to mar the Gospel truth, on that subject, appeared only between the eighth and ninth centuries. But, in the beginning, that error made very slow progress; those who propagated it, at first, were a few ignorant fanatics, whose names are lost in the night of the dark ages. It is only in the twelfth century that it began to be openly preached by some brainless monks. But then it was opposed by the most learned men of the time. We have a very remarkable letter of St. Bernard to refute some monks of Lyons who were preaching this new doctrine. A little later, Peter Lombard adopted the views of the monks of Lyons, and wrote a book to support that opinion; but he was refuted by St. Thomas Aquinas, who is justly considered by the Church of Rome, as the best theologian of that time. After that, the celebrated order of the Franciscans used all their influence to persuade the world that "Mary was immaculate in her conception;" but they were vigorously opposed and refuted by the not less celebrated order of the Dominicans. These two learned and powerful bodies, during more than a century, attacked each other without mercy on that subject, and filled the world with the noise of their angry disputes, both parties calling their adversaries heretics. They succeeded in driving the Roman Catholics of Europe into two camps of fierce enemies. The "Immaculate Conception" became the subject of burning discussions, not only between the learned universities, between the bishops and the priests and the nuns of those days; but it divided the families into two fiercely contending parties. It was discussed, attacked and defended, not only in the chairs of universities, and the pulpits of the cathedrals, but also in the fields, and in the very streets of the cities. And when the two parties had exhausted the reasons which their ingenuity, their learning, or their ignorant fanaticism could suggest to prove or deny the "Immaculate Conception," they often had recourse to the stick and to the sword to sustain their arguments.

It will appear almost incredible to-day, but it is a fact, the greatest number of the large cities of Europe, particularly in Spain, were then reddened with the blood of the supporters and opponents of that doctrine. In order to put an end to these contests, which were troubling the peace of their subjects, the Kings of Europe sent deputation after deputation to the Popes to know, from their infallible authority, what to believe on the subject. Philip III. and Philip IV. made what we may call supreme efforts to force the Popes, Paul V., Gregory XV., and Alexander VII. to stop the shedding of blood, and disarm the combatants, by raising the opinion in favour of the Immaculate Conception to the dignity of a Catholic dogma. But they failed. The only answer they could get from the infallible head of the Church of Rome was, that " that dogma was not revealed in the Holy Scriptures, had never been taught by the Apostles, nor by the Fathers, and had never been believed or preached by the Church of Rome as an article of faith ! "

The only thing the Popes could do to please the supplicant kings and bishops, and nations of Europe in those days, was to *forbid* both parties to call the other *heretics;* and to *forbid* to say that it was an article of faith which ought to be believed to be saved. At the Council of Trent, the Franciscans, and all the partisans of the "Immaculate Conception," gathered their strength to have a decree in favour of the new dogma; but the majority of the bishops were visibly against that sacrilegious innovation, and they failed. It was reserved to the unfortunate Pius IX. to drag the Church of Rome to that last limit of human folly. In the last century, a monk, called Father Leonard, had a dream, in which he heard the Virgin Mary telling him: "That there would be an end to the wars in the world, and to the heresies and schisms in the church, only after a Pope should have obliged, by a decree, all the faithful to believe that she was 'immaculate in her conception.'" That dream, under the name of a "celestial vision," had been extensively circulated by means of little tracts. Many believed it to be a genuine revelation from heaven; and, unfortunately, the good natured but weak-minded Pius IX. was among the number. When he was an exile in Gaeta, he had himself a dream, which he took for a vision, on the same subject. He saw the Virgin, who told him that he should come back to Rome, and get an eternal peace for the church, only after he should have promised to declare that the "Immaculate Conception" was a dogma, which every one had to believe to be saved. He awoke from his dream much impressed by it; and the first thing he did when up, was to make a vow to promulgate the new dogma as soon as he should be back to Rome, and the world has seen how he has fulfilled that vow.

But, by the promulgation of this new dogma, Pius IX., far from securing an eternal peace to his church, far from destroying what he is pleased to call the heresies which are attacking Rome on every side, has done more to shake the faith of the Roman Catholics than all their enemies.

By trying to force this new article of faith on the consciences of his people, in a time that so many can judge for themselves, and read the records of past generations, he has pulled down the strongest column which was supporting the whole fabric of his church; he for ever destroyed the best arguments which the priests had to offer to the ignorant, deluded multitudes which they keep so abjectly tied to their feet.

No words can sufficiently express the dignified and supreme contempt with which, before that epoch, the priests of Rome were speaking of the "new articles of faith, the novelties of the arch-heretics, Luther, Calvin, Knox, etc., etc!" How eloquent were the priests of Rome, before the 8th of December, 1854, when saying to their poor ignorant dupes: "In our holy Church of Rome there is no change, no innovations, no novelties, no new dogmas. We believe to-day just what our fathers believed, and what they have taught us; we belong to the apostolical church, which means we believe only what Apostles have believed and preached." And the ignorant multitudes were saying : "Amen !"

But, alas, for the poor priests of Rome to-day; those dignified nonsenses, those precious and dear illusions, are impossible! they have to confess that those high-sounding denunciations against what they call the *new* doctrines of the heretics, were nothing but big guns loaded to the mouth to destroy the Protestants, which are discharging their deadly missiles against the crumbling walls of their Church of Rome. They have to confess that their pretensions to an unchangeable creed is all mere humbug, shameful lies; they have to confess that the Church of Rome is FORGING NEW DOGMAS, NEW ARTICLES OF FAITH; they do not any longer dare to say to the disciples of the Gospel: "Where was your religion before the days of Luther and Calvin ? " for the secret voice of their conscience says to-day to the Roman Catholics : Where was your religion before the 8th of December, 1854 ? " and they cannot answer.

There is an inexorable and irresistible logic in the minds even of the most unlearned men, which defies, to-day, all the sophisms of the priests of Rome, if they dare to speak again on their pet subjects: " The novelties and new dogmas of the Protestants." There is a silent, but crushing voice, going to-day from the crowds to the priest, telling him : " Now, be quiet and silent on what you are used to call the novelties and new doctrines of the Protestants ! for, are you not preaching to us an awful novelty ? Are you not damning us to-day for disbelieving a thing which the church, during eighteen hundred years has, a hundred times, solemnly declared, by the mouth of the Popes, had never been revealed in the Holy Scriptures, had never been taught by the Fathers, had never been heard of by the church herself?"

I will never forget the sadness which overcame me when I received the order from Bishop O'Regan to proclaim that new dogma to my people (then all Roman Catholics). It was as if an earthquake had shaken and destroyed the ground on which my feet were resting. My most cherished illusions about the immutability and the infallibility of my church were crumbling down, in my intelligence, in spite of my efforts to keep them up. I have seen old priests, to whom I opened my mind on that subject, shed tears of sorrow on the injury this new dogma would do to their church.

The Archbishop of Paris, at the head of the most learned members of the clergy of France, had sent his protest to the Pope against this dogma before it was decreed; and he had eloquently foretold the deplorable consequences which would follow that innovation; but their warning voice failed to make any impression on the mind of the infatuated Pope.

And we, children of God, must we not acknowledge the hand of the Lord, in that blindness of "the man of sin" (2 Thess. ii. 3). The days are not far away that a cry of joy will be heard from one end of the world to the other: "Fear God, and give glory to Him! Babylon is fallen! Babylon is fallen! because she made all nations drink of the wine of the wrath of her fornication" (Rev. xiv. 7; xviii. 2, 3). For, when we see that "wicked one," "who exalteth himself above all that is called God" (2 Thess. ii. 4), destroying himself by the excess of his own folly and impurities, we must bless the Lord.

The proclamation of this new dogma is one of those great moral iniquities which carry their punishment and their remedy in their own hands. When the Pope, in the morning of the 8th of December, 1854, answered twice: "I do not know," to the question put to him, "Is the Virgin Mary Immaculate in her Conception?" and then, a minute after, to the same question, he answered: "Yes! I know it: the Holy Virgin Mary was Immaculate in her Conception," he proved to his most credulous dupes that he was nothing but a sacrilegious comedian. How would a jury of honest men deal with a witness who, being interrogated about what he knows of a certain fact, would answer, "I know nothing about it," and a moment after would acknowledge that "he knows everything about it?" Would not such a witness be justly punished as a perjurer?

Such is the sad and unenviable position which the Pope made to himself and to his church, on the 8th of December, 1854. Interrogated by the nations of Europe about what was to be believed on the "Conception of the Virgin Mary," the Church of Rome, during ten centuries, had answered : "I do not know." And let everyone remember that she wants to be believed INFALLIBLE when she says she "knows nothing about the Immaculate Conception." But, to-day, that same church assures us, through the infallible decree of Pius IX., that she knows, and that she has *always* known and believed the Virgin Mary was Immaculate ! Has the world ever seen such a want of self-respect, such an unblushing impudence ! What verdict will the Christian world give against that great mother of lies ? What punishment will the God of truth administer to that great culprit who swears "yes" and "no" on the same question ? It is a fact, that by the promulgation of this decree, Pius IX. has for ever destroyed his prestige in the minds of millions of his followers.

A few days after I had read to my congregation the decree of the Pope proclaiming the new dogma, and damning all those who would not believe it, one of my most intelligent and respectable farmers came to visit me, and put to me the following questions on the new articles of faith : "Mr. Chiniquy, please tell me, have I correctly understood the letter from the Pope you read us last Sabbath ? Does the Pope tell us in that letter that we can find this new dogma of the 'Immaculate Conception' in the Holy Scriptures, that it has been taught by the Fathers, and that the church has constantly believed it from the days of the Apostles ?"

I answered, "Yes, my friend, the Pope tells us all those things in his letter which I read in the church last Sabbath."

"But, sir, will you be so kind as to read me the verses of the Holy Scriptures which are in favour of the Immaculate Conception of the Holy Virgin Mary ?"

"My dear friend," I answered, "I am sorry to say that I have never found in the Holy Scriptures a single word to tell us that Mary is immaculate ; but I have found many words, and very clear words, which says the very contrary thing. For instance, the Holy Ghost, in the Epistle of St. Paul to the Romans, v. 18. 'By the *offence of one*, judgment came upon *all* men to condemnation.' This little, but inexhorable 'ALL,' includes the Virgin Mary in the condemnation and in the guilt. In the same Epistle to the Romans (ch. iii. 22, 23), the Holy Ghost, speaking of the children of Adam—Israelites and Gentiles—says there is no difference, they have ALL sinned and come short of the glory of God ! and in the 10th verse of the same chapter, the Holy Ghost, speaking of the Jews and Gentiles, says, 'There is none righteous—no, not one !' And the Lord has never repealed in any part that I know of the Holy Scriptures, this awful 'no—not one !'"

"Now, please tell me the name of the Holy Fathers who have preached that we must believe in the Immaculate Conception, or be for ever damned, if we do not believe in it ?"

I answered to my parishioner : " I would have preferred, my dear friend, that you should never come to put to me these questions ; but as you ask me the truth, I must tell you the truth. I have studied the Fathers with a pretty good attention, but I have not yet found a single one of them who was of that opinion in any way."

" I hope," added the good farmer, " you will excuse me if I put to you another question on this subject. Perhaps you do not know it, but there is a great deal of feeling and talking about this new article of faith among us since last Sabbath ; I want to know a little more about it. The Pope says in his letter that the Church of Rome has always believed and taught that dogma of Immaculate Conception. Is that correct ? "

" Yes, my friend, the Pope says that in his Encyclical ; but these last nine hundred years, more than one hundred Popes have declared that the church had never believed it. Even several Popes have forbidden to say ' that the Immaculate Conception was an article of faith ' — and they solemnly permitted us to believe and say what we please on that matter."

" If it be so with this new dogma, how can we know it is not so with the other dogmas of our church, as the confession, the purgatory, etc. ? " added the farmer.

" My dear friend, do not allow the devil to shake your faith. We are living in bad days indeed. Let us pray God to enlighten us and save us. I would have given much had you never put to me these questions ! "

My honest parishioner had left me ; but his awful questions (they were really awful, as they are still awful for a priest of Rome), and the answers I had been forced to give were sounding in my soul as thunder-claps. There was in my poor trembling heart, as the awful noise of an irresistible storm, which was to destroy all that I had so dearly cherished and respected in my then so dear and venerated Church of Rome. My head was aching. I fell on my knees ; but for a time I could not utter a word of prayer ; big tears were rolling on my burning cheeks ; new light was coming before the eyes of my soul ; but I took it for the deceitful temptation of Satan ; a voice was speaking to me ; it was the voice of my God, telling me, " Come out from Babylon ! " (Rev. xviii. 4). But I took that voice for the voice of Satan ; I was trying to silence it. The Lord was then drawing me away from my perishing ways ; but I did not know Him then ; I was struggling against Him to remain in the dark dungeons of error. But God was to be the stronger. In His infinite mercy He was to overpower His unfaithful servant. He was to conquer me, and with me many others.

CHAPTER LIV.

THERE are two women who ought to be constant objects of the compassion of the disciples of Christ, and for whom daily prayers ought to be offered at the mercy-seat—the Brahmin woman, who, deceived by her priests, burns herself on the corpse of her husband to appease the wrath of her wooden gods; and the Roman Catholic woman, who, not less deceived by her priests, suffers a torture far more cruel and ignominious in the confessional-box, to appease the wrath of her wafer-god.

For I do not exaggerate when I say, that for many noble-hearted, well-educated, high-minded women, to be forced to unveil their hearts before the eyes of a man, to open to him all the most secret recesses of their souls, all the most sacred mysteries of their single or married life, to allow him to put to them questions which the most depraved woman would never consent to hear from her vilest seducer, is often more horrible and intolerable than to be tied on burning coals.

More than once I have seen women fainting in the confessional-box, who told me afterwards that the necessity of speaking to an unmarried man on certain things, on which the most common laws of decency ought to have for ever sealed their lips, had almost killed them! Not hundreds, but thousands of times, I have heard from the lips of dying girls, as well as married women, the awful words: " I am for ever lost! All my past confessions and communions have been so many sacrileges! I have never dared to answer correctly the questions of my confessors! Shame has sealed my lips and damned my soul!"

How many times I remained as one petrified, by the side of a corpse, when these last words having hardly escaped the lips of one of my female penitents, who had been snatched out of my reach by the merciless hand of death, before I could give her pardon through the deceitful sacramental absolution? I then believed, as the dead sinner herself had believed, that she should not be forgiven except by that absolution.

For there are not only thousands, but millions of Roman Catholic girls and women, whose keen sense of modest and womanly dignity, are above all the sophisms and diabolical machinations of their priests. They can never be persuaded to answer " Yes " to certain questions of their confessors. They would prefer to be thrown into the flames, and burnt to ashes with the Brahmin widows, rather than allow the eyes of a man to pry into the sacred sanctuary of their souls. Though sometimes guilty before God, and under the impression that their sins will never be forgiven if not confessed, the laws of decency are stronger in their hearts than the laws of their perfidious Church. No consideration not even the fear of eternal damnation, can persuade them to declare to a sinful man, sins which God alone has the right to know, for He alone can blot them out with the blood of His Son, shed on the cross.

But what a wretched life must that be of those exceptional noble souls, which Rome keeps in the dark dungeons of her superstition? They read in all their books, and hear from all their pulpits, that if they conceal a single sin from their confessors, they are for ever lost! But, being absolutely unable to trample under their feet the laws of self-respect and decency, which God Himself has impressed in their souls, they live in constant dread of eternal damnation. No human words can tell their desolation and distress, when at the feet of their confessors they find themselves under the horrible necessity of speaking of things on which they would prefer to suffer the most cruel death rather than to open their lips, or to be for ever damned if they do not degrade themselves for ever in their own eyes, by speaking on matters which a respectable woman will never reveal to her own mother much less to a man!

I have known only too many of these noble-hearted women, who, when alone with God, in a real agony of desolation and with burning tears, had asked Him to grant them what they considered the greatest favour, which was to lose so much of their self-respect as to be enabled to speak of those unmentionable things just as their confessors wanted them to speak; and, hoping that their petition had been granted, they went again to the confessional-box, determined to unveil their shame before the eyes of that inexorable man. But when the moment had come for the self-immolation, their courage failed, their knees trembled, their lips became pale as death, cold sweat poured from all their pores! The voice of modesty and womanly self-respect was speaking louder than the voice of their false religion. They had to go out of the confessional-box unpardoned—nay, with the burden of a new sacrilege on their conscience.

Oh! how heavy is the yoke of Rome—how bitter is human life—how cheerless is the mystery of the cross to those deluded and perishing souls! How gladly they would rush into the blazing piles with the Brahmin women, if they could hope to see the end of their unspeakable miseries through the momentary tortures which would open to them a better life!

I do here publicly challenge the whole Roman Catholic priesthood to deny that the greater part of their female penitents remain a certain period of time—some longer, some shorter—under that most distressing state of mind.

Yes, by far the greater majority of women, at first, find it impossible to pull down the sacred barriers of self-respect, which God Himself has built around their hearts, intelligences, and souls, as the best safeguard against the snares of this polluted world.   Those laws of self-respect, by which they cannot consent to speak an impure word into the ears of a man, and which shut all the avenues of the heart against his unchaste questions, even when speaking in the name of God—those laws of self-respect are so clearly written in their con- science, and they are so well understood by them, to be a most Divine gift, that, as I have already said, many prefer to run the risk of being for ever lost by remaining silent.

It takes many years of the most ingenious (I do not hesitate to call it diabolical) efforts on the part of the priests to persuade the majority of their female penitents to speak on questions, which even pagan savages would blush to mention among themselves.   Some persist in remaining silent on those matters during the greater part of their lives, and many of them prefer to throw themselves into the hands of their merciful God, and die without submitting to the defiling ordeal, even after they have felt the poisonous stings of the enemy, rather than receive their pardon from a man, who, as they feel, would surely have been scandalized by the recital of their human frailties. All the priests of Rome are aware of this natural disposition of their female penitents.   There is not a single one—no, not a single one of their moral theologians, who does not warn the confessors against that stern and general determination of the girls and married women never to speak in the confessional on matters which may, more or less, deal with sins against the seventh commandment.   Dens, Liguori, Debreyne, Bailly, etc.,—in a word, all the theologians of Rome—own that this is one of the greatest difficulties which the confessors have to contend with in the confessional-box.

Not a single Roman Catholic priest will dare to deny what I say on this matter; for they know that it would be easy for me to over- whelm them with such a crowd of testimonials that their grand im- posture would for ever be unmasked.

I intend, at some future day, if God spares me and gives me time for it, to make known some of the innumerable things which the Roman Catholic theologians and moralists have written on this ques- tion.   It will form one of the most curious books ever written ; and it will give unanswerable evidence of the fact that, instinctively, with- out consulting each other, and with an unanimity which is almost marvellous, the Roman Catholic women, guided by the honest instincts which God has given them, shrink from the snares put before them in the confessional-box ; and that everywhere they struggle to nerve themselves with a superhuman courage, against the torturer who is sent by the Pope, to finish their ruin, and to make shipwrecks of their souls. Everywhere woman feels that there are things which ought never to be told, as there are things which ought never to be done, in the presence of the God of holiness. She understands that, to recite the history of certain sins, even of thought, is not less shameful and criminal than to do them; she hears the voice of God whispering into her ears, "Is it not enough that thou hast been guilty once, when alone in My presence, without adding to thine iniquity by allowing that man to know what should never have been revealed to him? Do you not feel that you make that man your accomplice, the very moment that you throw into his heart and soul the mire of your iniquities? He is as weak as you are; he is not less a sinner than yourself; what has tempted you will tempt him; what has made you weak will make him weak; what has polluted you will pollute him; what has thrown you down into the dust will throw him into the dust. Is it not enough that My eyes had to look upon your iniquities? must My ears, to-day, listen to your impure conversation with that man? Were that man as holy as My prophet David, may he not fall before the unchaste unveiling of a new Bathsheba? Were he as strong as Samson, may he not find in you his tempting Delilah? Were he as generous as Peter, may he not become a traitor at the maid-servant's voice?"

Perhaps the world has never seen a more terrible, desperate, solemn struggle than the one which is going on in the soul of a poor trembling young woman, who, at the feet of that man, has to decide whether or not she will open her lips on those things which the infallible voice of God, united to the no less infallible voice of her womanly honour and self-respect, tell her never to reveal to any man!

The history of that secret, fierce, desperate struggle has never yet, so far as I know, been fully given. It would draw the tears of admiration and compassion of the whole world, if it could be written with its simple, sublime, and terrible realities.

How many times have I wept as a child when some noble-hearted and intelligent young girl, or some respectable married woman, yielding to the sophisms with which I, or some other confessor, had persuaded them to give up their self-respect and their womanly dignity, to speak with me on matters on which a decent woman should never say a word with a man. They have told me of their invincible repugnance, their horror of such questions and answers, and they have asked me to have pity on them. Yes! I have often wept bitterly on my degradation, when a priest of Rome! I have realized all the strength, the grandeur, and the holiness of their motives for being silent on these defiling matters, and I could not but admire them. It seemed at times that they were speaking the language of angels of light; that I ought to fall at their feet, and ask their pardon for having spoken to them of questions, on which a man of honour ought never to converse with a woman whom he respects.

But alas ! I had soon to reproach myself, and regret those short instances of my wavering faith in the infallible voice of my Church ; I had soon to silence the voice of my conscience, which was telling me, " Is it not a shame that you, an unmarried man, dare to speak on these matters with a woman ?   Do you not blush to put such questions to a young girl ? Where is your self-respect ? Where is your fear of God? Do you not promote the ruin of that girl by forcing her to speak on these matters ? "

How many times my God has spoken to me as He speaks to all the priests of Rome, and said with a thundering voice : " What would that young man do, could he hear the questions you put to his wife ? Would he not blow out your brains ?   And that father, would he not thrust a dagger through your breast, if he could know what you ask from his poor trembling daughter ?   Would not the brother of that young girl put an end to your miserable life if he could hear the un-mentionable subjects on which you speak with her in the con-fessional ? "

I was compelled by all the Popes, the moral theologians, and the Councils of Rome, to believe that this warning voice of my merciful God was the voice of Satan ; I had to believe in spite of my own con-science and intelligence, that it was good, nay, necessary, to put those polluting, damning questions.   My infallible Church was mercilessly forcing me to oblige those poor, trembling, weeping, desolate girls and women, to swim with me and all her priests in those waters of Sodom and Gomorrah, under the pretext that their self-will would be broken down, their fear of sin and humility increased, and that they would be purified by our absolutions.

With what supreme distress, disgust, and surprise, we see, to-day, a great part of the noble Episcopal Church of England struck by a plague which seems incurable, under the name of Puseyism, or Ritualism, bringing again—more or less openly—in many places the diabolical and filthy auricular confession among the Protestants of England, Australia and America.   The Episcopal Church is doomed to perish in that dark and stinking pool of Popery—auricular confession, if she does not find a prompt remedy to stop the plague brought by the disguised Jesuits, who are at work everywhere, to poison and enslave her too unsuspecting daughters and sons.

In the beginning of my priesthood, when I was in Quebec, I was not a little surprised and embarrassed to see a very accomplished and beautiful young lady, whom I used to meet almost every week at her father's house, entering the box of my confessional.   She had been used to confess to another young priest of my acquaintance, and she was always looked upon as one of the most pious girls of the city. Though she had disguised herself as much as possible, in order that I might not know her, I felt sure that I was not mistaken—she was the amiable Mary * * *

Not being absolutely certain of the correctness of my impressions, I left her entirely under the hope that she was a perfect stranger to me. At the beginning she could hardly speak; her voice was suffocated by her sobs; and through the little apertures of the thin partition between her and me, I saw two streams of big tears trickling down her cheeks. After much effort, she said: " Dear Father, I hope you do not know me, and that you will never try to know me. I am a desperately great sinner. Oh! I fear that I am lost! But if there is still a hope for me to be saved, for God's sake do not rebuke me. Before I begin my confession, allow me to ask you not to pollute my ears by questions which our confessors are in the habit of putting to their female penitents; I have already been destroyed by those questions. Before I was seventeen years old, God knows that His angels are not more pure than I was; but the chaplain of the nunnery where my parents had sent me for my education, though approaching old age, put to me, in the confessional, a question which, at first, I did not understand, but, unfortunately, he had put the same questions to one of my young class-mates, who made fun of them in my presence, and explained them to me, for she understood them too well. This first unchaste conversation of my life plunged my thoughts into a sea of iniquity till then absolutely unknown to me; temptations of the most humiliating character assailed me for a week, day and night; after which, sins which I would blot out with my blood, if it were possible, overwhelmed my soul as with a deluge. But the joys of the sinner are short. Struck with terror at the thought of the judgments of God, after a few weeks of the most deplorable life, I determined to give up my sins and reconcile myself to God. Covered with shame, and trembling from head to foot, I went to confess to my old confessor, whom I respected as a saint and cherished as a father. It seems to me that, with sincere tears of repentance, I confessed to him the greatest part of my sins, though I concealed one of them, through shame and respect for my spiritual guide. But I did not conceal from him that the strange questions he had put to me at my last confession, were, with the natural corruption of my heart, the principal cause of my destruction.

" He spoke to me very kindly, encouraged me to fight against my bad inclinations, and at first gave me very kind and good advice. But when I thought he had finished speaking, and as I was preparing to leave the confessional-box, he put to me two new questions of such a polluting character that I fear neither the blood of Christ, nor all the fires of hell will ever be able to blot them out from my memory. Those questions have achieved my ruin; they have stuck to my mind like two deadly arrows; they are day and night before my imagination; they fill my very arteries and veins with a deadly poison.

"It is true that, at first, they filled me with horror and disgust; but alas! I soon got so accustomed to them that they seemed to be incorporated with me, and as if becoming a second nature. Those thoughts have become a new source of innumerable criminal thoughts, desires, and actions.

"A month later, we were obliged by the rules of our convent to go and confess; but by this time I was so completely lost that I no longer blushed at the idea of confessing my shameful sins to a man; it was the very contrary. I had a real, diabolical pleasure in the thought that I should have a long conversation with my confessor on those matters, and that he would ask me more of his strange questions. In fact, when I had told him everything without a blush, he began to interrogate me, and God knows what corrupting things fell from his lips into my poor criminal heart! Every one of his questions was thrilling my nerves and filling me with the most shameful sensations! After an hour of this criminal *tête-à-tête* with my old confessor (for it was nothing else but a criminal *tête-à-tête*), I perceived that he was as depraved as I was myself. With some half-covered words he made a criminal proposition, which I accepted with covered words also; and during more than a year we have lived together on the most sinful intimacy. Though he was much older than I, I loved him in the most foolish way. When the course of my convent instruction was finished, my parents called me back to their home. I was really glad of that change of residence, for I was beginning to be tired of my criminal life. My hope was that, under the direction of a better confessor, I should reconcile myself to God and begin a Christian life.

"Unfortunately for me, my new confessor, who was very young, began also his interrogations. He soon fell in love with me, and I loved him in a most criminal way. I have done with him things which I hope you will never request me to reveal to you, for they are too monstrous to be repeated, even in the confessional, by a woman to a man.

"I do not say these things to take away the responsibility of my iniquities with this young confessor from my shoulders, for I think I have been more criminal than he was. It is my firm conviction that he was a good and holy priest before he knew me; but the questions he put to me, and the answers I had to give him, melted his heart—I know it—just as boiling lead would melt the ice on which it flows.

"I know this is not such a detailed confession as our holy Church requires me to make, but I have thought it necessary for me to give

you this short history of the life of the greatest and most miserable
sinner who ever asked you to help her to come out from the tomb of
her iniquities. This is the way I have lived these last few years. But
last Sabbath, God, in His infinite mercy, looked down upon me. He
inspired you to give us the Prodigal Son as a model of true conversion,
and as the most marvellous proof of the infinite compassion of the
dear Saviour for the sinner. I have wept day and night since that
happy day, when I threw myself into the arms of my loving, merciful
Father. Even now I can hardly speak, because my regret for my past
iniquities, and my joy that I am allowed to bathe the feet of the
Saviour with tears, are so great that my voice is as choked.

"You understand that I have for ever given up my last confessor
I come to ask you to do me the favour to receive me among your
penitents. Oh! do not reject nor rebuke me, for the dear Saviour's
sake! Be not afraid to have at your side such a monster of iniquity!
But before going further, I have two favours to ask from you. The
first is, that you will never do anything to ascertain my name; the
second is, that you will never put to me any of those questions by
which so many penitents are lost and so many priests for ever
destroyed. Twice I have been lost by those questions. We come to
our confessors that they may throw upon our guilty souls the pure
waters which flow from heaven to purify us; but instead of that, with
their unmentionable questions they pour oil on the burning fires which
are already raging in our poor sinful hearts. Oh! dear father, let me
become your penitent, that you may help me to go and weep with
Magdalene at the Saviour's feet! Do respect me, as He respected
that true model of all the sinful, but repenting women! Did our
Saviour put to her any question? did He extort from her the history of
things which a sinful woman cannot say without forgetting the respect
she owes to herself and to God! No! you told us not long ago, that
the only thing our Saviour did was to look at her tears and her love.
Well, please do that, and you will save me!"

I was then a very young priest, and never had any words so
sublime come to my ears in the confessional-box. Her tears and her
sobs, mingled with the frank declaration of the most humiliating
actions, had made such a profound impression upon me that I was, for
some time, unable to speak. It had come to my mind also that I
might be mistaken about her identity, and that perhaps she was not
the young lady that I had imagined. I could, then, easily grant her
first request, which was to do nothing by which I could know her.
The second part of her prayer was more embarrassing; for the theologians are very positive in ordering the confessors to question their
penitents, particularly those of the female sex, in many circumstances.

FIFTY YEARS IN THE CHURCH OF ROME.

I encouraged her in the best way I could, to persevere in her good resolutions, by invoking the blessed Virgin Mary and St. Philomene, who was then *Sainte à la mode*, just as Marie Alacoque is to-day among the blind slaves of Rome. I told her that I would pray and think over the subject of her second request; and I asked her to come back in a week for my answer.

The very same day I went to my own confessor, the Rev. Mr. Baillargeon, then curate of Quebec, and afterwards Archbishop of Canada. I told him the singular and unusual request she had made, that I should never put to her any of those questions suggested by the theologians, to ensure the integrity of the confession. I did not conceal from him that I was much inclined to grant her that favour; for I repeated what I have already several times told him, that I was supremely disgusted with the infamous and polluting questions which the theologians forced us to put to our female penitents. I told him frankly that several old and young priests had already come to confess to me; and that, with the exception of two, they had told me that they could not put those questions and hear the answers they elicited without falling into the most damnable sins.

My confessor seemed to be much perplexed about what he should answer. He asked me to come the next day, that he might review some theological books in the interval. The next day I took down in writing his answer, which I find in my old manuscripts, and I give it here in all its sad crudity:—

"Such cases of the destruction of female virtue by the questions of the confessors is an unavoidable evil. It cannot be helped; for such questions are absolutely necessary in the greater part of the cases with which we have to deal. Men generally confess their sins with so much sincerity that there is seldom any need for questioning them, except when they are very ignorant. But St. Liguori, as well as our personal observation, tells us that the greatest part of girls and women, through a false and criminal shame, very seldom confess the sins they commit against purity. It requires the utmost charity in the confessors to prevent those unfortunate slaves of their secret passions from making sacrilegious confessions and communions. With the greatest prudence and zeal he must question them on those matters, beginning with the smallest sins, and going, little by little, as much as possible by imperceptible degrees, to the most criminal actions. As it seems evident that the penitent referred to in your questions of yesterday is unwilling to make a full and detailed confession of all her iniquities, you cannot promise to absolve her without assuring yourself by wise and prudent questions that she has confessed everything.

"You must not be discouraged when, through the confessional or any other way, you learn the fall of priests into the common frailties of human nature with their penitents. Our Saviour knew very well that the occasions and the temptations we have to encounter in the confessions of girls and women, are so numerous, and sometimes so irresistible, that many would fall. But He has given them the Holy Virgin Mary, who constantly asks and obtains their pardon; He has given them the sacrament of penance, where they can receive their pardon as often as they ask for it. The vow of perfect chastity is a great honour and privilege; but we cannot conceal from ourselves that it puts on our shoulders a burden which many cannot carry for ever. St. Liguori says that we must not rebuke the penitent priest who falls only once a month; and some other trustworthy theologians are still more charitable."

This answer was far from satisfying me. It seemed to me composed of soft soap principles. I went back with a heavy heart and an anxious mind; and God knows that I made many fervent prayers that this girl should never come again to give me her sad history. I was then hardly twenty-six years old, full of youth and life. It seemed to me that the stings of a thousand wasps to my ears could not do me so much harm as the words of that dear, beautiful, accomplished, but lost girl.

I do not mean to say that the revelations which she made had, in any way, diminished my esteem and my respect for her. It was just the contrary. Her tears and her sobs at my feet; her agonizing expressions of shame and regret; her noble words of protest against the disgusting and polluting interrogations of the confessors, had raised her very high in my mind. My sincere hope was that she would have a place in the kingdom of Christ with the Samaritan woman, Mary Magdalene, and all the sinners who have washed their robes in the blood of the Lamb.

At the appointed day, I was in my confessional listening to the confession of a young man, when I saw Miss Mary entering the vestry, and coming directly to my confessional-box, where she knelt by me. Though she had, still more than at the first time, disguised herself behind a long, thick, black veil, I could not be mistaken; she was the very same amiable young lady in whose father's house I used to pass such pleasant and happy hours. I had often listened with breathless attention to her melodious voice, when she was giving us, accompanied by her piano, some of our beautiful church hymns. Who could then see and hear her without almost worshipping her? The dignity of her steps, and her whole mien, when she advanced towards my confessional, entirely betrayed her and destroyed her incognito.

Oh! I would have given every drop of my blood in that solemn hour, that I might have been free to deal with her just as she had so eloquently requested me to do—to let her weep and cry at the feet of

Jesus to her heart's content.   Oh! if I had been free to take her by the hand and silently show her the dying Saviour, that she might have bathed His feet with her tears, and spread the oil of her love on His head, without my saying anything else but " Go in peace : thy sins are forgiven."

But, there, in that confessional-box, I was not the servant of Christ, to follow His Divine, saving words, and obey the dictates of my honest conscience.   I was the slave of the Pope!   I had to stifle the cry of my conscience, to ignore the inspirations of my God! There, my conscience had no right to speak ; my intelligence was a dead thing!   The theologians of the Pope alone had a right to be heard and obeyed!   I was not there to save, but to destroy ; for, under the pretext of purifying, the real mission of the confessor, often, if not always, in spite of himself, is to scandalize and damn the souls.

As soon as the young man who was making his confession at my left hand, had finished, I, without noise, turned myself towards her, and said, through the little aperture, " Are you ready to begin your confession ? "

But she did not answer me.   All that I could hear was : " Oh, my Jesus, have mercy upon me!   I come to wash my soul in Thy blood ; wilt Thou rebuke me ? "

During several minutes she raised her hands and eyes to heaven, and wept and prayed.   It was evident that she had not the least idea that I was observing her ; she thought the door of the little partition between her and me was shut.   But my eyes were fixed upon her ; my tears were flowing with her tears, and my ardent prayers were going to the feet of Jesus with her prayers.   I would not have interrupted her for any consideration, in this, her sublime communion with her merciful Saviour.

But after a pretty long time, I made a little noise with my hand, and putting my lips near the opening of the partition which was between us, I said in a low voice, " Dear sister, are you ready to begin your confession ? "

She turned her face a little towards me, and said, with trembling voice, " Yes, dear father, I am ready."

But she then stopped again to weep and pray, though I could not hear what she said.

After some time in silent prayer, I said, " My dear sister, if you are ready, please begin your confession."   She then said, " My dear father, do you remember the prayers which I made to you the other day ?   Can you allow me to confess my sins without forcing me to forget the respect that I owe to myself, to you, and to God, who hears us ?   And can you promise that you will not put to me any of those questions which have already done me such irreparable injury ? I frankly declare to you that there are sins in me that I cannot reveal to anyone, except to Christ, because He is my God, and that He already knows them all. Let me weep and cry at His feet: can you not forgive me without adding to my iniquities by forcing me to say things that the tongue of a Christian woman cannot reveal to a man ? "

" My dear sister," I answered, " were I free to follow the voice of my own feelings I would be only too happy to grant your request; but I am here only as the minister of our holy church, and bound to obey the laws. Through her most holy Popes and theologians she tells me that I cannot forgive your sins if you do not confess them all, just as you have committed them. The church tells me also that you must give the details, which may add to the malice or change the nature of your sins. I am sorry to tell you that our most holy theologians make it a duty of the confessor to question the penitent on the sins which he has good reason to suspect have been voluntarily omitted."

With a piercing cry she exclaimed, " Then, O my God, I am lost —for ever lost ! "

This cry fell upon me like a thunderbolt; but I was still more terror-stricken when, looking through the aperture, I saw she was fainting; I heard the noise of her body falling upon the floor, and of her head striking against the sides of the confessional-box.

Quick as lightning I ran to help her, took her in my arms, and called a couple of men, who were at a little distance, to assist me in laying her on a bench. I washed her face with some cold water and vinegar. She was as pale as death, but her lips were moving, and she was saying something which nobody but I could understand—

" I am lost—lost for ever ! "

We took her home to her disconsolate family, where, during a month, she lingered between life and death. Her two first confessors came to visit her ; but having asked every one to go out of the room, she politely, but absolutely, requested them to go away, and never come again. She asked me to visit her every day, " for," she said, " I have only a few more days to live. Help me to prepare myself for the solemn hour which will open to me the gates of eternity ! "

Every day I visited her, and I prayed and I wept with her.

Many times, when alone, with tears I requested her to finish her confession ; but, with a firmness which then seemed to be mysterious and inexplicable, she politely rebuked me.

One day, when alone with her, I was kneeling by the side of her bed to pray, I was unable to articulate a single word, because of the inexpressible anguish of my soul on her account, she asked me, " Dear father, why do you weep ? "

I answered, "How can you put such a question to your murderer! I weep because I have killed you, dear friend."

This answer seemed to trouble her exceedingly. She was very weak that day. After she had wept and prayed in silence, she said, "Do not weep for me, but weep for so many priests who destroy their penitents in the confessional. I believe in the holiness of the sacrament of penance, since our holy church has established it. But there is, somewhere, something exceedingly wrong in the confessional. Twice I have been destroyed, and I know many girls who have also been destroyed by the confessional. This is a secret, but will that secret be kept for ever? I pity the poor priests the day that our fathers will know what becomes of the purity of their daughters in the hands of their confessors. Father would surely kill my two last confessors, if he could only know they have destroyed his poor child."

I could not answer except by weeping.

We remained silent for a long time; then she said, "It is true that I was not prepared for the rebuke you have given me the other day in the confessional; but you acted conscientiously as a good and honest priest. I know you must be bound by certain laws."

She then pressed my hand with her cold hand and said, "Weep not, dear father, because that sudden storm has wrecked my too fragile bark. This storm was to take me out from the bottomless sea of my iniquities to the shore where Jesus was waiting to receive and pardon me. The night after you brought me, half dead, here to my father's house, I had a dream. Oh, no! it was not a dream, it was a reality. My Jesus came to me, He was bleeding; His crown of thorns was on His head, the heavy cross was bruising His shoulders. He said to me, with a voice so sweet that no human tongue can imitate it, 'I have seen thy tears, I have heard thy cries, and I know thy love for Me: thy sins are forgiven; take courage, in a few days thou shalt be with Me!'"

She had hardly finished her last word when she fainted, and I feared lest she should die just then, when I was alone with her.

I called the family, who rushed into the room. The doctor was sent for. He found her so weak that he thought proper to allow only one or two persons to remain in the room with me. He requested us not to speak at all, "For," said he, "the least emotion may kill her instantly; her disease is, in all probability, an aneurism of the aorta, the big vein which brings the blood to the heart : when it breaks, she will go as quick as lightning."

It was nearly ten at night when I left the house to go and take some rest. But it is not necessary to say that I passed a sleepless night. My dear Mary was there, pale, dying from the deadly blow which I had given her in the confessional. She was there, on her bed of death, her heart pierced with the dagger which my church had put into my hands! and instead of rebuking, and cursing me for my savage, merciless fanaticism, she was blessing me! She was dying from a broken heart! and I was not allowed by my church to give her a single word of consolation and hope, for had she not made her confession? I had mercilessly bruised that tender plant, and there was nothing in my hands to heal the wounds I had made!

It was very probable that she would die the next day, and I was forbidden to show her the crown of glory which Jesus has prepared in His kingdom for the repenting sinner?

My desolation was really unspeakable, and I think I would have been suffocated and have died that night, if the stream of tears which constantly flowed from my eyes had not been as a balm to my distressed heart.

How dark and long the hours of that night seemed to me!

Before the dawn of day, I arose to read my theologians again, and see if I could not find someone who would allow me to forgive the sins of that dear child, without forcing her to tell me anything she had done. But they seemed to me, more than ever, unanimously inexorable, and I put them back on the shelves of my library with a broken heart.

At nine a.m. the next day, I was by the bed of our dear sick Mary. I cannot sufficiently tell the joy I felt, when the doctor and whole family said to me, " She is much better; the rest of last night has wrought a marvellous change, indeed."

With a really angelic smile she extended her hand towards me, and said, " I thought, last evening, that the dear Saviour would take me to Him, but He wants me, dear father, to give you a little more trouble; however, be patient, it cannot be long before the solemn hour of the appeal will strike. Will you please read me the history of the suffering and death of the beloved Saviour, which you read me the other day? It does me so much good to see how He has loved me, such a miserable sinner."

There was a calm and solemnity in her words which struck me singularly, as well as all those who were there.

After I had finished reading, she exclaimed, "He has loved me so much that He died for my sins!" And she shut her eyes as if to meditate in silence, but there was a stream of big tears rolling down her cheeks.

I knelt down by her bed, with her family, to pray; but I could not utter a single word. The idea that this dear child was there, dying from the cruel fanaticism of my theologians and my own cowardice in obeying them, was as a millstone to my neck. It was killing me.

Oh! if by dying a thousand times, I could have added a single day to her life, with what pleasure I would have accepted those thousand deaths!

After we had silently prayed and wept by her bedside, she requested her mother to leave her alone with me.

When I saw myself alone, under the irresistible impression that this was her last day, I fell on my knees again, and with tears of the most sincere compassion for her soul, I requested her to shake off her shame and to obey our holy church, which requires every one to confess their sins if they want to be forgiven.

She calmly, but with an air of dignity which no human words can express. said, "Is it true that, after the sins of Adam and Eve, God Himself made coats and skins and clothed them, that they might not see each other's nakedness?"

"Yes," I said, "this is what the Holy Scriptures tell us."

"Well, then, how is it possible that our confessors dare to take away from us that holy, divine coat of modesty and self-respect? Has not Almighty God Himself made, with His own hands, that coat of womanly modesty and self-respect that we might not be to you and to ourselves a cause of shame and sin?"

I was really stunned by the beauty, simplicity, and sublimity of that comparison. I remained absolutely mute and confounded. Though it was demolishing all the traditions and doctrines of my church, and pulverising all my holy doctors and theologians, that noble answer found such an echo in my soul, that it seemed to me a sacrilege to try to touch it with my finger.

After a short time of silence, she continued, "Twice I have been destroyed by priests in the confessional. They took away from me that divine coat of modesty and self-respect which God gives to every human being who comes into this world, and twice I have become for those very priests a deep pit of perdition, into which they have fallen, and where I fear they are for ever lost! My merciful heavenly Father has given me back that coat of skins, that nuptial robe of modesty, self-respect, and holiness which had been taken away from me. He cannot allow you or any other man to tear again and spoil that vestment which is the work of His hands."

These words had exhausted her; it was evident to me that she wanted some rest. I left her alone, but I was absolutely beside myself. Filled with admiration for the sublime lessons which I had received from the lips of that regenerated daughter of Eve, who, it was evident, was soon to fly away from us, I felt a supreme disgust for myself, my theologians—shall I say it? yes, I felt in that solemn hour a supreme disgust for my church, which was cruelly defiling me and all her priests, in the confessional-box. I felt, in that hour, a supreme horror for that auricular confession, which is so often a pit of perdition and supreme misery for the confessor and penitent. I went out and walked two hours on the Plains of Abraham, to breathe the pure and refreshing air of the mountains· There, alone, I sat on a stone, on the very spot where Wolff and Montcalm fought aud died; and I wept to my heart's content on my irreparable degradation, and the degradation of so many priests through the confessional.

At four o'clock in the afternoon I went back again to the house of dear dying Mary. The mother took me apart, and very politely said, " My dear Mr. Chiniquy, do you not think it is time that our dear child should receive the last sacraments ? She seemed to be much better this morning, and we were full of hope; but she is now rapidly sinking. Please lose no time in giving her the holy viaticum and the extreme unction."

I said, " Yes, madam; let me pass a few minutes alone with our dear child, that I may prepare her for the last sacraments."

When alone with her, I again fell on my knees, and, amidst torrents of tears, I said, " Dear sister, it is my desire to give you the holy viaticum and the extreme unction : but tell me, how can I dare to do a thing so solemn against all the prohibitions of our holy church ? How can I give you the holy communion without first giving you absolution ? and how can I give you absolution when you earnestly persist in telling me that you have so many sins which you will never declare to me or any other confessor ?

" You know that I cherish and respect you as if you were an angel sent to me from heaven. You told me, the other day, that you blessed the day that you first saw and knew me. I say the same thing. I bless the day that I have known you ; I bless every hour that I have spent by your bed of suffering ; I bless every tear which I have shed with you on your sins and on my own ; I bless every hour we have passed together in looking to the wounds of our beloved, dying Saviour ; I bless you for having forgiven me your death ! for I know it, and I confess it in the presence of God, I have killed you, dear sister. But now I prefer a thousand times to die than to say to you a word which would pain you in any way, or trouble the peace of your soul. Please, my dear sister, tell me what I can and must do for you in this solemn hour."

Calmly, and with a smile of joy such as I had never seen before, nor seen since, she said, " I thank and bless you, dear father, for the parable of the Prodigal Son, on which you preached a month ago. You have brought me to the feet of the dear Saviour ; there I have found a peace and a joy surpassing anything that human heart can feel ; I have thrown myself into the arms of my Heavenly Father, and I know He has mercifully accepted and forgiven His poor prodigal child! Oh, I see the angels with their golden harps around the throne of the Lamb! Do you not hear the celestial harmony of their songs? I go—I go to join them in my Father's house. I SHALL NOT BE LOST!"

While she was thus speaking to me, my eyes were really turned into two fountains of tears; I was unable, as well as unwilling, to see anything, so entirely overcome was I by the sublime words which were flowing from the dying lips of that dear child, who was no more a sinner, but a real angel of Heaven to me. I was listening to her words; there was a celestial music in every one of them. But she had raised her voice in such a strange way, when she had begun to say, "I go to my Father's house," and she had made such a cry of joy when she had to let the last words, "not be lost," escape her lips, that I raised my head and opened my eyes to look at her. I suspected that something strange had occurred.

I got upon my feet, passed my handkerchief over my face to wipe away the tears which were preventing me from seeing with accuracy, and looked at her.

Her hands were crossed on her breast, and there was on her face the expression of a really superhuman joy; her beautiful eyes were fixed as if they were looking on some grand and sublime spectacle; it seemed to me, at first, that she was praying.

In that very instant the mother rushed into the room, crying, "My God! my God! what does that cry '*lost*' mean?" For her last words, "not be lost," particularly the last one, had been pronounced with such a powerful voice, that they had been heard almost everywhere in the house.

I made a sign with my hand to prevent the distressed mother from making any noise and troubling her dying child in her prayer, for I really thought that she had stopped speaking, as she used so often to do, when alone with me, in order to pray. But I was mistaken. The redeemed soul had gone, on the golden wings of love, to join the multitude of those who have washed their robes in the blood of the Lamb, to sing the eternal Alleluia.

The revelation of the unmentionable corruptions directly and unavoidably engendered by auricular confession, had come to me from the lips of that young lady, as the first rays of the sun which were to hurl back the dark clouds of night by which Rome had wrapped my intelligence on that subject.

So miserable by her fall and her sins, but so admirable by her conversion, that young lady was standing before me, for the rest of my priestly life, as the bright beacon raised on the solitary rock stands before the sailor whose ship is drifting through the shoals, in a dark and stormy night.

She was brought there by the merciful hand of God, to right my course.

Lost and degraded by auricular confession, only after having given it up, that precious soul was to find peace and life, when washed in the blood of the Lamb, as the only hope and refuge of sinners.

Her words, filled with a superhuman wisdom, and her burning tears, came to me, by the marvellous Providence of God, as the first beams of the Sun of Righteousness, to teach me that auricular confession was a Satanic invention.

Had this young person been the only one to tell me that, I might still have held some doubt about the diabolical origin of that institution. But thousands and thousands, before and after her, have been sent by my merciful God to tell me the same tale, till after twenty-five years of experience it became a certitude to me that that modern invention of Rome must, sooner or later, with very few exceptions, drag both the confessor and his female penitents into a common and irreparable ruin.*

CHAPTER LV.

On the first of August, 1855, I received the following letter :—

THE COLLEGE, *Chicago, July 24th,* 1855.

REV. MR. CHINIQUY,

You will have the goodness to attend a spiritual retreat to be given next month at the college, in Chicago, for the clergy of the diocese of Chicago and Quincy.

The spiritual exercises, which will be conducted by the Rt. Rev. the Bishop of Louisville, are to commence on Tuesday, the 28th of August, and will terminate on the following Sunday. This arrangement will necessitate your absence from your church on Sunday, the 14th, after Pentecost, which you will make known to your congregation. No clergyman is allowed to be absent from this retreat without the previous written consent of the bishop of the diocese, which consent will not be given except in cases which he will judge to be of urgent necessity.

By order of Rt. Rev. Bishop,

MATTHEW DILLON,

Pro Secretary.

Wishing to study the *personnel* of that Irish clergy of which Bishop Vandeveld had told such frightful things, I went to St. Mary's University, two hours ahead of time.

Never did I see such a band of jolly fellows. Their dissipation

---

* Those who would like to know all about the abominations of auricular confession should have my volume " The Priest, the Woman and the Confessional." It is probably the only book ever written on that subject which completely unveils the mask of Rome, by telling the whole truth.

and laughter. Their exchange of witty, and too often, unbecoming expressions, the tremendous noise they made in addressing each other, at a distance: Their "Hallo, Patrick!" "hallo, Murphy!" "hallo, O'Brien! how do you do? How is Bridget? Is Marguerite still with you?" The answers: "Yes! yes! She will not leave me;" or "No! no! the crazy girl is gone," were invariably followed by outbursts of laughter.

Though nine-tenths of them were evidently under the influence of intoxicating drinks, not one could be said to be drunk. But the strong odour of alcohol, mixed with the smoke of cigars, soon poisoned the air and made it suffocating.

I had withdrawn in a corner, alone, in order to observe everything.

What stranger, in entering that large hall, would have suspected that those men were about to begin one of the most solemn and sacred actions of a priest! With the exception of five or six, they looked more like a band of carousing raftsmen than priests.

About an hour before the opening of the exercises, I saw one of the priests with hat in hand, accompanied by two of the fattest and most florid of the band, going to every one, collecting money and with the utmost hilarity and pleasure, each one threw his bank bills into the hat. I supposed that this collection was intended to pay for our board, during the retreat, and I prepared the fifteen dollars I wanted to give. When they came near me—the big hat was literally filled with five and ten dollar bills. Before handing my money to them, I asked: "What is the object of that collection?"

"Ah! ah!" they answered with a hearty laugh. "Dear Father Chiniquy, is it possible that you do not know it yet? Don't you know that, when we are so crowded as we will be here, this week the rooms are apt to become too warm, and we get thirsty? Then a little drop to cool the throat and quench the thirst, is needed," and the collectors laughed outright.

I answered politely, but seriously: "Gentlemen, I came here to meditate and pray; and when I am thirsty, the fresh and pure water of Lake Michigan will quench my thirst. I have given up, long ago, the use of intoxicating drinks. Please excuse me, I am a teetotaler."

"So we are!" they answered, with a laugh; "we have all taken the pledge from Father Mathew; but this does not prevent us from taking a little drop to quench our thirst and keep up our health. Father Mathew is not so merciless as you are."

"I know Father Mathew well," I answered. "I have written to him and seen him many times. Allow me to tell you that we are of the same mind about the use of intoxicating drink."

"Is it possible! you know Father Mathew! and you are exchanging letters with him! What a holy man he is, and what good he has done in Ireland, and everywhere!" they answered.

"But the good he has done will not last long," I said, "if all his disciples keep their pledges as you do."

As we were talking, a good number of priests came around us to hear what was said; for it was evident to all that the bark of their collectors, not only had come to shallow waters, but had struck on a rock.

One of the priests said: "I thought we were to be preached to by Bishop Spaulding. I had no idea that it was Father Chiniquy who had that charge."

"Gentlemen," I answered, "I have as much right to preach to you in favour of temperance as you have to preach to me in favour of intemperance. You may do as you please about the use of strong drink, during the retreat; but I hope I also may have the right to think and do as I please in that matter."

"Of course," they all answered, "but you are the only one who will not give us a cent to get a little drop."

"So much the worse for you all, gentlemen, if I am the only one. But please excuse me, I cannot give you a cent for that object."

They then left me, saying something which I could not understand, but they were evidently disgusted with what they considered my stubbornness and want of good manners.

I must, however, say here, that two of them, Mr. Dunn, pastor of one of the best congregations of Chicago, and the other unknown to me, came to congratulate me on the stern rebuke I had given the collectors.

"I regret," said Mr. Dunn, "the five dollars I have thrown into the hat. If I had spoken to you before, and had known that you would be brave enough to rebuke them, I would have stood by you, and kept my money for better use. It is really a shame that we should be preparing ourselves for a retreat by wasting five hundred dollars for such a shameful object. They have just told me that they have raised that sum for the champagne, brandy, whisky and beer they will drink this week. Ah! what disgrace! What a cry of indignation would be raised against us, if such a shameful thing should be known! I am sorry about the unkind words those priests have spoken to you; but you must excuse them, they are already full of bad whisky.

"Do not think, however, that you are friendless, here, in our midst. You have more friends than you think among the Irish priests; and I am one of them, though you do not know me. Bishop Vandeveld has often spoken to me of your grand colonization work among the French."

Mr. Dunn, then, pressed my hand in his, and taking me a short

distance from the others, said: " Consider me, hereafter, as your
friend: you have won my confidence by the fearless way in which you
have just spoken, and the common sense of your arguments. You
have lost a true friend in Bishop Vandeveld. I fear that our present
bishop will not do you justice. Lebel and Carthuval have prejudiced
him against you. But I will stand by you, if you are ever unjustly
dealt with, as I fear you will, by the present administration of the
diocese. I fear we are on the eve of great evils. The scandalous suit
which Bishop O'Regan has brought against his predecessor is a
disgrace. If he has gained fifty thousand dollars by it, he has for ever
lost the respect and confidence of all his priests and diocesans.

"After the mild and paternal ruling of Bishop Vandeveld, neither
the priests nor the people of Illinois will long bear the iron chains
which the present bishop has in store for us all."

I thanked Mr. Dunn for his kind words, and told him that I had
already tasted the paternal love of my bishop by being twice dragged
by Spink before the criminal courts for having refused to live on good
terms with the two most demoralized priests I have ever known. He,
then, speaking with a more subdued voice, said: " I must tell you,
confidentially, that one of those priests, Lebel, will be turned out
ignominiously from the diocese during the retreat. Last week, a new
fact, which surpasses all his other abominations, has been revealed and
proved to the bishop, for which he will be interdicted."

At that moment, the bell called us to the chapel to hear the regulations of the bishop in reference to the retreat, after which we sang
the matins. At 8 p.m. we had our first sermon by Bishop Spaulding,
from Kentucky. He was a fine-looking man, a giant in stature, and a
good speaker. But the way in which he treated his subject, though
very clever, left, in my mind, the impression that he did not believe a
word of what he said. At certain times, there was much fire in his
elocution, but it was a fire of straw. He delivered two sermons each
day; and the Rev. Mr. Vanhulest, a Jesuit, gave us two meditations,
each of them lasting from forty to fifty minutes. The rest of the
time was spent in reading aloud the life of a saint, reciting the breviarum, examination of conscience, and going to confession. We had
half-an-hour for meals, followed by one hour of recreation. Thus were
the days spent. But the nights! the nights! what shall I say of them?
What pen can describe the orgies I witnessed during those dark
nights! and who can believe what I shall have to say about them!
though I will not and cannot say the half of what I have seen and
heard!

I got from the Rev. Mr. Dunn, then one of the bishop's counsellors,
and soon after Vicar General, the statement that the sum of five hundred dollars was expended in intoxicating drinks during the six days

of the retreat. I ought to say during the five nights. My pen refuses
to write what my eyes saw and my ears heard during the long hours
of those nights, which I cannot forget, though I should live a thousand
years.

The drinking used to begin about nine o'clock, as soon as the lights
were put out. Some were handing the bottles from bed to bed, while
others were carrying them to those at a distance, at first, with the least
noise possible ; but half-an-hour had not elapsed before the alcohol
was beginning to unloose the tongues, and upset the brain. Then the
bons mots, the witty stories, at first, were soon followed by the most
indecent and shameful recitals. Then the songs, followed by the
barking of dogs, the croaking of frogs, the howling of wolves. In a
word, the cries of all kinds of beasts, often mixed with the most
lascivious songs, the most infamous anecdotes flying from bed to bed,
from room to room, till one or two o'clock in the morning.

One night, three priests were taken with delirium tremens, almost
at the same time. One cried out that he had a dozen rattle-snakes at
his shirt ; the second was fighting against thousands of bats, which
were trying to tear his eyes from their sockets; and the third, with a
stick, was repulsing millions of spiders, which, he said, were as big as
wild turkeys, all at work to devour him. The cries and lamentations
of those three priests were really pitiful! To those cries add the
lamentations of some dozens of them whose overloaded stomachs were
ejecting in the beds and all around, the enormous quantity of drink
they had swallowed ! The third day, I was so disgusted and indignant,
that I determined to leave, without noise, under the pretext that I was
sick. It was not a false pretext ; for I was really sick. There was
no possibility of sleeping before two or three o'clock. Besides, the
stench in the dormitories was horrible.

There was, however, another thing which was still more overwhelming me. It was the terrible moral struggle in my soul from morning till night, and from night till morning, when the voice of my
conscience, which I had to take for the voice of Satan, was crying in
my ears : " Do you not clearly see that your church is the devil's
church—that those priests, instead of being the Lamb's priests, are the
successors of the old Bacchus priests ? Read your Bible a little more
attentively, and see if this is not the reign of the great harlot, which is
defiling the world with her abominations ? How can you remain in
such a church ? how long will you remain in this sea of Sodom ? Come
out ! come out of Babylon, if you do not want to perish with her ! Can
the tree which bears such fruits be the tree of life ? Can the priests
who surround you, be the priests, the ambassadors of the Saviour ?
Can the Son of God come down every morning in body, in soul, and
divinity, into the hands and stomach of such men ? Can the nations

be led into the ways of God by them? Are you not guilty of an un-pardonable crime when you are planting, with your own hands, over this magnificent country, a tree bearing such fruits? How dare you meet your God, after you have so deceived yourself and the people as to believe and say that these are the representatives, the leaders, the priests of the church out of which there is no salvation!"

Oh! what an awful thing it is to resist the voice of God! To take Him for the evil one, when, by His warnings, He seeks to save your soul! Although the horrible scandal I had seen distressed me more than human words can tell, those mental conflicts were still more dis-tressing. Fearing lest I should entirely lose my faith in my religion, and become an absolute infidel, by remaining any longer in the midst of such profligacy, I determined to leave; but before doing so, I wanted to consult the new friend whom the providence of God had given me in Mr. Dunn. It seemed the unbearable burden which was on my shoulders would become lighter, by sharing it with such a sympathetic brother priest.

I went to him, after dinner, and taking him apart, I told him all about the orgies of last night, and asked his advice on my determina-tion not to continue that retreat, which was evidently nothing else than a blind, and a sacrilegious comedy, to deceive the world.

He answered: "You teach me nothing, for I spent last night in the same dormitory where you were. One of the priests told me all about those orgies, yesterday; I could hardly believe what he said, and I determined to see and hear for myself what was going on. You do not exaggerate, you do not even mention half of the horrors of last night. It baffles any description. It is simply incredible for any one who has not himself witnessed them. However, I do not advise you to leave. It would for ever ruin you in the mind of the bishop, who is not already too well disposed in your favour. The best thing you can do is to go and say everything to Bishop Spaulding. I have done it this morning; but I felt that he did not believe the half of what I told him. When the same testimony comes from you, then he will believe it, and will probably take some measures, with our own bishop, to put an end to those horrors. I have something to tell you, confidentially, which surpasses, in a measure, anything you know of the abominations of these last three nights.

"A respectable policeman, who belongs to my congregation, came to me this morning, to tell me that the first night, six prostitutes, dressed as gentlemen, and last night twelve came to the University, after dark, entered the dormitory, and went, directed by signals, to those who had invited them, each being provided with the necessary key. I have just reported the thing to Bishop O'Regan; but instead of paying any attention to what I said, he became furious against me, and nearly turned me out of his room, saying, 'Do you think that I am going to come down from my dignity of bishop to hear the reports of degraded policemen, or of vile spies? Shall I become the spies of my priests? If they want to damn themselves, there is no help, let them go to hell! I am not more obliged or able than God Himself to stop them! Does God stop them? Does He punish them? No! Well! you cannot expect from me more zeal and power than in our common God!'

"With these fine words ringing in my ears," said good Mr. Dunn, "I had to leave his room at the double quick. It is of no use for us to speak to Bishop O'Regan on that matter. It will do no good. He wants to get a large subscription from those priests, at the end of the retreat, and he is rather inclined to pet than punish them, till he obtains the hundred thousand dollars he wants to build his white marble palace on the lake shore."

I replied: "Though you add to my desolation, instead of diminishing it, by what you say of the strange principles of our bishop, I will speak to my lord Spaulding as you advise me." Without a moment's delay, I went to his room. He received me very kindly, and did not at all seem surprised at what I said. It was as if he had been accustomed to see the same, or still worse abominations. However, when I told him the enormous quantity of liquor drank, and that the retreat would be only a ridiculous comedy, if no attempt at reform was tried, he agreed with me; "but it would be advisable to try it," he said. "Though this is not in our programme, we might give one or two sermons on the necessity of priests giving an example of temperance to their people. Will you please come with me to the room of my lord O'Regan, that we may confer on the matter, after you have told him what is going on?"

Although the Bishop of Chicago seemed puzzled at seeing me entering his room with my lord Spaulding, he was as polite as possible. He listened with more attention than I expected to the narrative I gave of what was going on among the priests. After telling him my sad story, Bishop Spaulding said: "My lord of Chicago, these facts are very grave, and there cannot be any doubt about the truth of what we have just heard. Two other gentlemen gave me the same testimony this morning."

"Yes!" said Bishop O'Regan, "it is very sad to see that our priests have so little self-respect, even during such solemn days as those of a public retreat. The Rev. Mr. Dunn has just told me the same sad story as Father Chiniquy. But what remedy can we find for such a state of things? Perhaps it might do well to give them a good sermon on temperance. Mr. Chiniquy, I am told that you are called 'the temperance apostle of Canada,' and that you are a powerful speaker on that subject; would you not like to give them one or two addresses on the injury they are doing to themselves and to our holy church, by their drunkenness? "

"If those priests could understand me in French," I replied, "I would accept the honour you offer me with pleasure ; but to be understood by them, I would have to speak in English; and I am not sufficiently free in that language to attempt it. My broken English would only bring ridicule upon the holy cause of temperance. But my lord Spaulding has already preached on that subject in Kentucky, and an address from his lordship would be listened to with more attention and benefit from him than from me."

It was then agreed that he should change his programme, and give two addresses on temperance, which he did. But though these addresses were really eloquent, they were pearls thrown before swine. The drunken priests slept, as usual; and even snored, almost through the whole length of the delivery. It is true that we could notice a little improvement, and less noise the following nights ; the change, however, was very little.

The fourth day of the retreat, the Rev. Mr. Lebel came to me with his bag in hand. He looked furious. He said : "Now, you must be satisfied, I am interdicted and turned out ignominiously from this diocese. It is your work ! But mind what I tell you : you will, also, soon be turned out from your colony by the mitred tyrant who has just struck me down. He told me, several times, that he would, at any cost, break your plans of French colonization, by sending you to the south-west of Illinois, along the Mississippi, to an old French settlement, opposite St. Louis. He is enraged against you, for your refusing to give him your fine property at St. Anne."

I answered him : "You are mistaken when you think that I am the author of your misfortunes. You have disgraced yourself by your own acts. God has given you talents and qualities which, if cultivated, would have exalted you in the church, but you have preferred to destroy those great gifts, in order to follow the evil inclinations of your poor degraded human nature ; you reap to-day what you have sown. Nobody is more sorry than I am for your misfortune, and my most sincere wish is that the past may be a lesson to guide your steps in the future. The desire of the bishop to turn me out of my colony does not trouble me. If it is the will of God to keep me at the head of that great work, the Bishop of Chicago will go down from his episcopal throne before I go down the beautiful hill of St. Anne. Adieu!" He soon disappeared. But how the fall of this priest, whom I had so sincerely loved, saddened me !

The next Sabbath was the last day of the retreat. All the priests went in procession to the cathedral, to receive the holy communion, and every one of them ate, what we had to believe was the true body, soul, and divinity of Jesus Christ. This, however, did not prevent thirteen of them from spending the greater part of the next night in calabooses, to which they had been taken by the police, from houses of ill-fame, where they were rioting and fighting. The next morning they were discharged from the hands of the police by paying pretty round sums of money for the trouble of the night!

The next day, I went to Mr. Dunn's parsonage to ask him if he could give me any explanation of the rumour which was afloat, and to which Mr. Lebel had made allusion, that it was the intention of the bishop to remove me from my colony to some distant part of his diocese.

"It is unfortunately too true," said he. "Bishop O'Regan thinks that he has a mission from heaven to undo all his predecessor has done, and as one of the best and grandest schemes of Bishop Vandeveld was to secure the possession of this magnificent State of Illinois to our church, by inducing all the Roman Catholic emigrants from France, Belgium and Canada, to settle here, our present bishop does not conceal that he will oppose that plan by removing you to such a distance, that your colonization plans will be at an end. He says that the French are, as a general thing, rebels and disobedient to their bishops. He prefers seeing the Irish coming, on account of their proverbial docility to their ecclesiastical superiors. I have, in vain, tried to change his mind. I told you before that he often asks my opinion on what I think the best thing to be done for the good of the diocese. But do not think that he intends to follow my advice; it is just the contrary. My impression now is, that he wants to know our views, only for the pleasure of acting diametrically in opposition to what we advise."

I must not omit to say that we had been requested to spend the forenoon of Monday in the University, for an important affair which the bishop had to propose to his clergy. We were all there, in the great hall, at the appointed hour. Even the thirteen priests who had spent the best part of the night at the police station, heard the voice of their bishop, and they were there, as docile lambs.

We knew beforehand the proposition which was to be put before us. It was to build a palace for our bishop, worthy of the great Illinois State, the cost of which would be about one hundred thousand dollars.

Though every one of us felt that this was most extravagant in such a young and poor diocese, nobody dared to raise his voice against that act of pride and supreme folly. Every one promised to do all in his power to raise that sum, and to show our good-will, we raised among ourselves, at once, seven thousand dollars, which we gave in cash or in promissory notes. After this act of liberality, we were blessed and dismissed by our bishop.

I was but a few steps from the University, when an Irish priest, unknown to me, ran after me to say, " My lord O'Regan wants to see you immediately." And, five minutes later, I was alone with my bishop, who, without any preface, told me, " Mr. Chiniquy, I hear very strange and damaging things about you, from every quarter. But the worst of all is that you are a secret Protestant emissary; that, instead of preaching the true doctrines of our holy church, about the immaculate conception, purgatory, the respect and obedience due to their superiors by the people, auricular confession, etc., etc., you spend a part of your time in distributing Bibles and New Testaments among your immigrants; I want to know from your own lips, if this be true or not."

I answered, " A part of what the people told you about the matter is not true, the other is true. It is not true that I neglect the preaching of the doctrines of our holy church, about purgatory, immaculate conception of Mary, auricular confession, or the respect due to our superiors. But it is true that I do distribute the Holy Bible and the Gospel of Christ, among my people."

" And instead of blushing at such unpriestly conduct, you seem to be proud of it," angrily replied the bishop.

" I do not understand, my lord, why a priest of Christ could blush for distributing the Word of God among his people; as I am bound to preach that Holy Word, it is not only my right but my duty to give it to them. I am fully persuaded that there is no preaching so efficacious and powerful as the preaching of our God Himself, when speaking to us in His Holy Book."

" This is sheer Protestantism, Mr. Chiniquy, this is sheer Protestantism," he answered me angrily.

" My dear bishop," I answered calmly, " if to give the Bible to the people and invite them to read and meditate on it is Protestantism, our holy Pope Pius VI. was a good Protestant, for in his letter to Martini, which is probably in the first pages of the beautiful Bible I see on your lordship's table, he not only blesses him for having translated that Holy Book into Italian, but invites the people to read it."

The bishop, assuming an air of supreme contempt, replied : " Your answer shows your complete ignorance on the subject on which you speak so boldly. If you were a little better informed on that grave subject, you would know that the translation by Martini, which the Pope advised the Italian people to read, formed a work of twenty-three big volumes in folio, which, of course, nobody, except very rich and idle people could read. Not one in ten thousand Italians have the means of purchasing such a voluminous work; and not one in twenty thousand have the time or the will to peruse such a mass of endless commentaries. The Pope would never have given such an advice to read a Bible, as the one you distribute so imprudently."

"Then, my lord, do you positively tell me that the Pope gave permission to read Martini's translation, because he knew that the people could never get it on account of its enormous size and price, and do you assure me that he would never have given such advice, had the same people been able to purchase and read that holy work."

"Yes, sir! It is what I mean," answered the bishop, with an air of triumph, "for I know positively that this is the fact."

I replied, calmly: "I hope your lordship is unwillingly mistaken; for if you were correct, the stern and unflinching principles of logic would force me to think and say that that Pope and all his followers were deceivers, and that encyclical a public fraud in his own hands; for we Catholic priests make use of it, all over the world, and reprint it at the head of our own Bibles, to make the people, both Protestants and Catholics believe that we approve of their reading our own versions of that Holy Book."

Had I thrown a spark of fire in a keg of powder, the explosion would not have been more prompt and terrible than the rage of that prelate. Pointing his finger to my face, he said: "Now, I see the truth of what I have been told, that you are a disguised Protestant, since the very day that you were ordained a priest. The Bible! The Bible is your motto! For you the Bible is everything, and the holy church, with her Popes and bishops nothing! what an insolent, I dare say, what a blasphemous word, I have just heard from you? You dare call an encyclical letter of one of our most holy Popes, a *fraud!*"

In vain, I tried to explain, he would not listen; and he silenced me by saying: "If our holy church has, in an unfortunate day, appointed you one of her priests in my diocese, it was to preach the doctrines, and not to distribute the Bible! If you forget that, I will make you remember it!" And with that threat on my head as a Damocles' sword, I had to take the door which he had opened, without any *au revoir*. Thanks be to God, this first persecution and these outrages I received for my dear Bible's sake, did not diminish my love, my respect for God's Holy Word, nor my confidence in it. On the contrary, on reaching home, I took it, fell on my knees, and pressing it to my heart, I asked my heavenly Father to grant me the favour to love it more sincerely, and follow its divine teachings with more fidelity till the end of my life.

CHAPTER LVI.

A MONTH had scarcely elapsed since the ecclesiastical retreat, when all the cities of Illinois were filled by the most strange and humiliating clamours against our bishop. From Chicago to Cairo, it would have been difficult to go to a single town without hearing, from the most respectable people, or reading in big letters, in some of the most influential papers, that Bishop O'Regan was a thief or a simoniac, a perjurer, or even something worse. The bitterest complaints were crossing each other over the breadth and length of Illinois, from almost every congregation: "He has stolen the beautiful and costly vestments we bought for our church," cried the French Canadians of Chicago. "He has swindled us out of a fine lot given us to build our church, sold it for 40,000 dollars, and pocketed the money, for his own private use, without giving us any notice," said the Germans. "His thirst for money is so great," said the whole Catholic people of Illinois, "that he is selling even the bones of the dead to fill his treasures!"

I had not forgotten the bold attempt of the bishop to wrench my little property from my hands, at his first visit to my colony. The highway thief, who puts his dagger at the breast of the traveller, threatening to take away his life if he does not give him his purse, does not appear more infamous to his victim than that bishop appeared to me that day. But my hope then was, that this act was an isolated and exceptional case in the life of my superior; and I did not whisper a word of it to anybody. I began to think differently, however, when I saw the numerous articles in the principal papers of the State, signed by the most respectable names, accusing him of theft, simony, and lies. My hope, at first, was that there were many exaggerations in those reports. But as they came thicker day after day, I thought my duty was to go to Chicago and see for myself to what extent those rumours were true. I went directly to the French Canadian church; and to my unspeakable dismay, I found that it was too true that the bishop had stolen the fine church vestments, which my countrymen had bought for their own priest for grand festivals, and he had transferred them to the cathedral of St. Mary for his own personal use. The indignation of my poor countrymen knew no bounds. It was really deplorable to hear with what supreme disgust and want of respect they were speaking of their bishop. Unfortunately, the Germans and Irish people were still ahead of them in their unguarded, disrespectful denunciations. Several spoke of prosecuting him before the civil courts, to force him to disgorge what he had stolen; and it was with the greatest difficulty that I succeeded in preventing some of them from mobbing and insulting him publicly in the streets, or even in his own palace. The only way I could find to appease them was to promise them that I would speak to his lordship, and tell him that it was the desire of my countrymen to have those vestments restored to them.

The second thing I did was to go to the cemetery, and see for myself to what extent it was true or not that our bishop was selling the very bones of his diocesans, in order to make money. On my way to the Roman Catholic graveyard, I met a great many cart loads of sand, which, I was told by the carters, had been taken from the cemetery; but I did not like to stop them till I was at the very door of the consecrated spot. There I found three carters, who were just leaving the grounds. I asked and obtained from them the permission to search the sand which they carried, to see if there were not some bones. I could not find any in the first cart; and my hope was that it would be the same in the two others. But, to my horror and shame, I found the lower jaw of a child in the second, and part of the bones of an arm, and almost the whole foot of a human being, in the third cart! I politely requested the carters to show me the very place where they had dug that sand, and they complied with my prayer. To my unspeakable regret and shame, I found that the bishop had told an unmitigated falsehood when, to appease the public indignation against his sacrilegious trade, he had published that he was selling only the sand which was outside of the fence, on the very border of the lake.

It is true that, to make his case good, he had ordered the old fence to be taken away, in order to make a new one, many feet inside the old one. But this miserable and shameful subterfuge rendered his crime still greater than it had at first appeared. What added to the gravity of that public iniquity, is that the Bishop of Chicago had received that piece of land from the city, for a burial ground, only after he had taken a solemn oath to use it only for burying the dead. Every load of that ground sold then, was not only an act of simony, but the breaking of a solemn oath! No words can express the shame I felt, after convincing myself of the correctness of what the press of Chicago, and of the whole State of Illinois had published against our bishop, about this sacrilegious traffic.

Slowly retracing my steps to the city from the cemetery, I went directly to the bishop, to fulfil the promise I had made to the French Canadians, to try to obtain the restoration of their fine vestments. But I was not long with him without seeing that I would gain nothing but his implacable enmity in pleading the cause of my poor countrymen. However, I thought my duty was to do all in my power to open the eyes of my bishop to the pit he was digging for himself and for all us Catholics, by his conduct. "My lord," I said, "I shall not

surprise your lordship, when I tell you that all the true Catholics of
Illinois are filled with sorrow by the articles they find, every day, in
the press, against their bishop."

"Yes! yes!" he abruptly replied, "the good Catholics must be
sad indeed to read such disgusting diatribes against their superior;
and I presume that you are one of those that are sorry. But, then,
why do you not prevent your insolent and infidel countrymen from
writing those things! I see that a great part of those libels are
signed by the French Canadians."

I answered, "It is to try, as much as it is in my power, to put an
end to those scandals that I am in Chicago, to-day, my lord."

"Very well, very well," he replied, "as you have the reputation of
having a great influence over your countrymen, make use of it to stop
them in their rebellious conduct against me, and I will, then, believe
that you are a good priest."

I answered, "I hope that I will succeed in what your lordship
wants me to do. But there are two things to be done, in order to
secure my success."

"What are they?" quickly asked the bishop.

"The *first* is, that your lordship give back the fine church vestments which you have taken from the French Canadian congregation
of Chicago.

"The *second* is, that your lordship abstain, absolutely, from this
day, to sell the sand of the burying ground, which covers the tombs
of the dead."

Without answering a word, the bishop struck his fist violently
upon the table, and crossed the room at a quick step, two or three
times; then turning towards me, and pointing his finger to my face,
he exclaimed in an indescribable accent of rage:

"Now, I see the truth of what Mr. Spink told me! you are not
only my bitterest enemy, but you are at the *head* of my enemies. You
take sides with them against me. You approve of their libellous
writings against me! I will never give back those church vestments.
They are mine, as the French Canadian church is mine! Do you not
know that the ground on which the churches are built, as well as the
churches themselves, and all that belongs to the church, belongs to
the bishop? Was it not a burning shame to use those fine vestments
in a poor miserable church of Chicago, when the bishop of that important city was covered with rags! It was in the interest of the episcopal dignity, that I ordered those rich and splendid vestments, which
were mine by law, to be transferred from that small and insignificant
congregation, to my cathedral of St. Mary, and if you had an ounce of
respect for your bishop, Mr. Chiniquy, you would immediately go to
your countrymen and put a stop to their murmurs and slanders

against me, by simply telling them that I have taken what was mine from that church, which is mine also, to the cathedral, which is altogether mine. Tell your countrymen to hold their tongues, and respect their bishop, when he is in the right, as I am to-day."

I had, many times, considered the infamy and injustice of the law which the bishops have had passed all over the United States, making every one of them a corporation, with the right of possessing personally all the church properties of the Roman Catholics. But I had never understood the infamy and tyranny of that law so clearly as in that hour. It is impossible to describe with ink and paper the air of pride and contempt with which the bishop really in substance, if not in words, told me: "All those things are mine. I do what I please with them, you must be mute and silent when I take them away from you. It is against God Himself that you rebel when you refuse me the right of dispossessing you of all those properties which you have purchased with your own money, and which have not cost me a cent!" In that moment I felt that the law which makes every bishop the only master and proprietor of all the religious goods, houses, churches, lands and money of their people as Catholics, is simply diabolical: and that the church which sanctions such a law, is antichristian. Though it was at the risk and peril of everything dear to me, that I should openly protest against that unjust law, there was no help; I felt constrained to do so with all the energy I possessed.

I answered: "My lord, I confess that this is the law in the United States; but this is a human law, directly opposed to the Gospel. I do not find a single word in the Gospel which gives this power to the bishop. Such a power is an abusive, not a divine power, which will sooner or later destroy our holy church in the United States, as it has already mortally wounded her in Great Britain, in France and in many other places. When Christ said, in the Holy Gospel, that He had not enough of ground whereon to lay His head, He condemned, in advance, the pretensions of the bishops who lay their hands on our church properties as their own. Such a claim is an usurpation and not a right, my lord. Our Saviour Jesus Christ protested against that usurpation, when asked by a young man to meddle in his temporal affairs with his brothers; He answered that 'He had not received such power.' The Gospel is a long protest against that usurpation, in every page, it tells us that the kingdom of Christ is not of this world. I have myself given fifty dollars to help my countrymen to buy those church vestments. They belong to them and not to you!"

My words, uttered with an expression of firmness which the bishop had never yet seen in any of his priests, fell upon him, at first, as a thunderbolt. They so puzzled him, that he looked at me, a moment, as if he wanted to see if it were a dream or a reality, that one of his priests had the audacity to use such language, in his presence. But! soon, recovering from his stupor, he interrupted me by striking his fist again on the table, and saying in anger: "You are half a Protestant! Your words smell of Protestantism! The Gospel! the Gospel! that is your great tower of strength against the laws and regulations of our holy church! If you think, Mr. Chiniquy, that you will frighten me with your big words of the Gospel, you will soon see your mistake, at your own expense. I will make you remember that it is *the Church* you must obey, and it is through your bishop that the church rules you!"

"My lord," I answered, "I want to obey the church. Yes! but it is a church founded on the Gospel; a church that respects and follows the Gospel, that I want to obey!"

These words threw him into a fit of rage, and he answered: "I am too busy to hear your impertinent babblings any longer. Please let me alone, and remember that you will soon hear from me again if you cannot teach your people to respect and obey their superiors!" The bishop kept his promise. I heard of him very soon after, when his agent, Peter Spink, dragged me, again a prisoner, before the Criminal Court of Kankakee, accusing me falsely of crimes which his malice alone could have invented. My lord O'Regan had determined to interdict me; but, not being able to find any cause in my private or public life as a priest to found such a sentence, he had pressed that land speculator, Spink, to prosecute me again; promising to base his interdict on the condemnation which, he had been told, would be passed against me by the Criminal Court of Kankakee. But the bishop and Peter Spink were again to be disappointed; for the verdict of the court, given on the 13th of November, 1855, was again in my favour.

My heart filled with joy at this new and great victory my God had given me against my merciless persecutors. I was blessing Him, when my two lawyers, Messrs. Osgood and Paddock, came to me and said: "Our victory, though great, is not so decisive as was expected; for Mr. Spink has just taken an oath that he has no confidence in this Kankakee Court, and he has appealed, by a change of venue, to the Court of Urbana, in Champaign County. We are sorry to have to tell you that you must remain a prisoner, under bail, in the hands of the sheriff, who is bound to deliver you to the sheriff of Urbana, the 19th of May, next spring."

I nearly fainted when I heard this. The ignominy of being again in the hands of the sheriff for so long a time; the enormous expenses, far beyond my means, to bring my fifteen to twenty witnesses such a long distance of nearly one hundred miles; the new ocean of insults, false accusations, and perjuries with which my enemies were to overwhelm me again; and the new risk of being condemned, though innocent, at that distant court; all those things crowded themselves in my mind to crush me. For a few minutes I was obliged to sit down; for I would surely have fallen down had I continued to stand on my feet. A kind friend had to bring me some cold water and bathe my forehead, to prevent me from fainting. It seemed that God had forsaken me for the time being, and that He was to let me fall powerless in the hand of my foes. But I was mistaken. That merciful God was near me, in that dark hour, to give me one of the marvellous proofs of His paternal and loving care.

The very moment I was leaving the court with a heavy heart, a gentleman, a stranger, came to me and said : " I have followed your suit from the beginning. It is more formidable than you suspect. Your prosecutor, Spink, is only an instrument in the hands of the bishop. The real prosecutor is the land shark who is at the head of the diocese, and who is destroying our holy religion by his private and public scandals. As you are the only one among his priests who dares to resist him, he is determined to get rid of you : he will spend all his treasures and use the almost irresistible influence of his position to crush you. The misfortune for you is that, when you fight a bishop, you fight all the bishops of the world. They will unite all their wealth and influence to Bishop O'Regan's to silence you, though they hate and despise him. There was no danger of any verdict against you in this part of Illinois, where you are too well known for the perjured witnesses they have brought to influence your judges. But when you are among strangers, mind what I tell you : the false oaths of your enemies may be accepted as gospel truths by the jury, and then, though innocent, you are lost. Though your two lawyers are expert men, you will want something better at Urbana. Try to secure the services of Abraham Lincoln, of Springfield. If that man defends you, you will surely come out victorious from that deadly conflict !"

I answered : " I am much obliged to you for your sympathetic words : but would you please allow me to ask your name ?"

" Be kind enough to let me keep my incognito here," he answered. " The only thing I can say is, that I am a Catholic like you, and one who, like you, cannot bear any longer the tyranny of our American bishops. With many others, I look to you as our deliverer, and for that reason I advise you to engage the services of Abraham Lincoln."

" But," I replied, " who is that Abraham Lincoln ? I never heard of that man before."

He replied: "Abraham Lincoln is the best lawyer and the most honest man we have in Illinois."

I went immediately, with that stranger, to my two lawyers, who were in consultation only a few steps from us, and asked them if they would have any objection that I should ask the services of Abraham Lincoln, to help them to defend me at Urbana.

They both answered: "Oh! if you can secure the services of Abraham Lincoln, by all means do it. We know him well; he is one of the best lawyers, and one of the most honest men we have in our State."

Without losing a minute, I went to the telegraph office with that stranger, and telegraphed to Abraham Lincoln to ask him if he would defend my honour and my life (though I was a stranger to him) at the next May term of the court at Urbana.

About twenty minutes later I received the answer:

"Yes, I will defend your honour and your life at the next May term at Urbana.   "ABRAHAM LINCOLN."

My unknown friend then paid the operator, pressed my hand, and said: "May God bless and help you, Father Chiniquy. Continue to fight fearlessly for truth and righteousness against our mitred tyrants; and God will help you to the end." He then took a train for the north, and soon disappeared, as a vision from heaven. I have not seen him since, though I have not let a day pass without asking my God to bless him. A few minutes later, Spink came to the office to telegraph to Lincoln, asking his services at the next May term of the Court, at Urbana. But it was too late.

Before being dragged to Urbana, I had to renew, at Easter, 1856, the oil which is used for the sick, in the ceremony which the Church of Rome calls the Sacrament of Extreme Unction, and in the Baptism of Children. I sent my little silver box to the bishop by a respectable young merchant of my colony, called Dorion. But he brought it back without a drop of oil, with a most abusive letter from the bishop, because I had not sent five dollars to pay for the oil. It was just what I expected. I knew that it was his habit to make his priests pay five dollars for that oil, which was not worth more than two or three cents.

This act of my bishop was one of the many evident cases of simony of which he was guilty every day. I took his letter, with my small silver box, to the Archbishop of St. Louis, my lord Kenrick, before whom I brought my complaints against the Bishop of Chicago, on the 9th April, 1856. That high dignitary told me that many priests of the diocese of Chicago had already brought the same complaints before him, and exposed the infamous conduct of their bishop. He agreed with me that the rapacity of Bishop O'Regan, his thefts, his lies, his acts of simony were public and intolerable, but that he had no remedy for them, and said: "The only thing I advise you to do is to write to the Pope directly. Prove your charges against that guilty bishop as clearly as possible. I will myself write to corroborate all you have told me; for I know it is true. My hope is that your complaints will attract the attention of the Pope. He will, probably, send some one from Rome to make an enquiry, and then that wicked man will be forced to offer his resignation. If you succeed, as I hope, in your praiseworthy efforts to put an end to such scandals, you will have well deserved the gratitude of the whole church. For that unprincipled dignitary is the cause that our holy religion is not only losing her prestige in the United States, but is becoming an object of contempt wherever those public crimes are known."

I was, however, forced to postpone my writing to the Pope. For, a few days after my return from St. Louis to my colony, I had to deliver myself again into the hands of the Sheriff of Kankakee, who was obliged by Spink to take me prisoner, and deliver me as a criminal into the hands of the Sheriff of Champaign County, on the 19th of May, 1856.

It was then that I met Mr. Abraham Lincoln for the first time. He was a giant in stature; but I found him still more a giant in the noble qualities of his mind and heart. It was impossible to converse five minutes with him without loving him. There was such an expression of kindness and honesty in that face, and such an attractive magnetism in the man, that after a few moments' conversation one felt as tied to him by all the noblest affections of the heart. When pressing my hand, he told me: "You were mistaken when you telegraphed that you were unknown to me. I know you, by reputation, as the stern opponent of the tyranny of your bishop, and the fearless protector of your countrymen in Illinois; I have heard much of you from two priests; and, last night, your lawyers, Messrs. Osgood and Paddock have acquainted me with the fact that your bishop is employing some of his tools to get rid of you. I hope it will be an easy thing to defeat his projects, and protect you against his machinations." He then asked me how I had been induced to desire his services. I answered by giving him the story of that unknown friend who had advised me to have Mr. Abraham Lincoln for one of my lawyers, for the reason that "he was the best lawyer and the most honest man in Illinois." He smiled at my answer with that inimitable and unique smile, which we may call the "Lincoln smile," and replied: "That unknown friend would surely have been more correct had he told you that Abraham Lincoln was the ugliest lawyer of the country!" and he laughed outright.

I spent six long days at Urbana as a criminal, in the hands of the sheriff, at the feet of my judges. During the greatest part of that time, all that human language can express of abuse and insult was heaped on my poor head. God only knows what I suffered in those days; but I was providentially surrounded, as by a strong wall. I had Abraham Lincoln for my defence—" the best lawyer and the most honest man of Illinois," and the learned and upright David Davis for my judge. The latter became Vice-president of the United States in 1882; and the former its most honoured President from 1861 to 1865.

I never heard anything like the eloquence of Abraham Lincoln when he demolished the testimonies of the two perjured priests, Lebel and Carthuval, who, with ten or twelve other false witnesses, had sworn against me. I would have surely been declared innocent after that eloquent address and the charge of the learned Judge Davis, had not my lawyers, by a sad blunder, left a Roman Catholic on the jury. Of course, that Irish Roman Catholic wanted to condemn me, when the eleven honest and intelligent Protestants were unanimous in voting " Not guilty." The court, having at last found that it was impossible to persuade the jury to give an unanimous verdict, discharged them. But Spink again forced the sheriff to keep me prisoner, by obtaining from the court the permission to begin the prosecution *de novo* at the term of the fall, the 19th of October, 1856. Humanly speaking, I would have been one of the most miserable of men, had I not had my dear Bible, which I was meditating and studying day and night in those dark days of trial. But, though I was then still in the desolate wilderness, far away yet from the Promised Land, my heavenly Father never forsook me. He many times let the sweet manna fall from heaven to feed my desponding soul, and cheer my fainting heart. More than once, when I was panting with spiritual thirst, He brought me near the Rock, from the side of which the living waters were gushing to refresh and renew my strength and courage.

Though the world did not suspect it, I knew from the beginning, that all my tribulations were coming from my unconquerable attachment and my unfaltering love and respect for the Bible, as the root and source of every truth given by God to man; and I felt assured that my God knew it also;—that assurance supported my courage in the conflict. Every day my Bible was becoming dearer to me. I was then constantly trying to walk in its marvellous light and divine teaching. I wanted to learn my duties and rights. I like to acknowledge that it was the Bible which gave me the power and wisdom I then so much needed, to face fearlessly so many foes. That power and wisdom I felt were not mine. On this very account my dear Bible enabled me to remain calm in the very lions' den; and it gave me, from the very beginning of that terrible conflict, the assurance of a final victory; for every time I bathed my soul in its Divine light, I heard my merciful heavenly Father's voice, saying, "Fear not, for I am with thee" (Isaiah xliii. 5).

CHAPTER LVII.

THE Holy Scriptures say that an abyss* calls for another abyss (*abyssus abyssum invocat*). That axiom had its accomplishment in the conduct of Bishop O'Regan. When once on the declivity of iniquity, he descended to its lowest depths with more rapidity than a stone thrown into the sea. Not satisfied with the shameful theft of the rich vestments of the French Canadian Church of Chicago, he planned iniquity which was to bring upon him, more than ever, the execration of the Roman Catholics of Illinois. It was nothing less than the complete destruction of the thriving congregations of my French Canadian countrymen of Chicago and St. Anne. The removal of the French-speaking priest of Chicago from his people, as well as my removal from my colony, were determined.

Our churches were at first to be closed, and after some time sold to the Irish people, or to the highest bidder, for their own use. It was in Chicago that this great iniquity was to begin. Not long after Easter, 1856, the Rev. Mons. Lemaire was turned out, interdicted, and ignominiously driven from the diocese of Chicago, without even giving the shadow of a reason, and the French Canadians suddenly found themselves without a pastor. A few days after, the parsonage they had built for their priest in Clark Street was sold for 1,200 dollars to an American. The beautiful little church which they had built on the lot next to the parsonage, at the cost of so many sacrifices, was removed five or six blocks south-west, and rented by the bishop to the Irish Catholics for about 2,000 dollars per annum, and the whole money was pocketed, without even a word of notice to my countrymen.

Though accustomed to his acts of perfidy, I could not believe at first the rumours which reached me of those transactions! They seemed to be beyond the limits of infamy, and to be impossible. I went to Chicago, hoping to find that the public rumour had exaggerated the evil. But alas! nothing had been exaggerated!

The wolf had dispersed the sheep and destroyed the flock. The once thriving French congregation of Chicago was no more! Wherever I went, I saw tears of distress among my dear countrymen, and

---

* Psalm xlii. 7, " Deep calleth unto deep."—A.V.

heard cries of indignation against the destroyer.   Young and old, rich
and poor among them, with one voice, denounced and cursed the
heartless mitred brigand, who had dared to commit publicly such a
series of iniquities, to satisfy his thirst for gold and his hatred of the
French Canadians.

They asked me what they should do : but what could I answer!
They requested me to go again to him and remonstrate.   But I showed
them that after my complete failure when I had tried to get back the
sacerdotal vestments, there was no hope that he would disgorge the
house and the church.   The only thing I could advise them was to
select five or six of the most influential members of their congregation to go and respectfully ask him by what right he had taken away,
not only their priest, but the parsonage and the church they had built,
and transferred them to another people.   They followed my advice.
Messrs. Franchere and Roffinot (who are still living) and six other
respectable French Canadians, were sent by the whole people to put
those questions to their bishop.   He answered them :

"French Canadians ! you do not know your religion !   Were you
a little better acquainted with it, you would know that I have the
right to sell your churches and church properties, pocket the money,
and go, eat and drink it where I please."   After that answer they
were ignominiously turned out from his presence into the street.
Posterity will scarcely believe those things, though they are true.

The very next day, Aug. 19th, 1856, the bishop having heard that
I was in Chicago, sent for me.   I met him after his dinner.   Though
not absolutely drunk, I found him full of wine, and terribly excited.

"Mr. Chiniquy," he said, " you had promised me to make use of
your influence to put an end to the rebellious conduct of your countrymen against me.   But I find that they are more insolent and unmanageable than ever ; and my firm belief is that it is your fault.   You,
and the handful of French Canadians of Chicago, give me more trouble
than all the rest of my priests and my people of Illinois.   You are too
near Chicago, sir, your influence is too much felt on your people here.   I
must remove you to a distant place, where you will have enough to do
without meddling in my administration.   I want your service to
Kahokia, in my diocese of Quincy; and if you are not there by the
15th of Sept. next, I will interdict and excommunicate you, and for
ever put an end to your intrigues."

These words fell upon me as a thunderbolt.   The tyranny of the
bishop of my church, and the absolute degradation of the priest whose
honour, position and life are entirely in his hands, had never been
revealed to me so vividly as in that hour.   What could I say or do to
appease that mitred despot ?   After some moments of silence, I tried
to make some respectful remonstrances by telling him that my posi-

tion was an exceptional one; that I had not come to Illinois as his other priests, to be at the head of any existing congregation, but that I had been invited by his predecessor to direct the tide of the emigration of the French-speaking people of Europe and America. That I had come to a wilderness which, by the blessing of God, I had changed into a thriving country, covered with an industrious and religious people. I further told him, that I had left the most honourable position which a priest had ever held in Canada, with the promise from his predecessor that, as long as I lived the life of a good priest, I should not be disturbed in my work. As I soon perceived that he was too much under the influence of liquor to understand me, and speak with intelligence, I only added:

" My lord, you speak of interdict and excommunication! Allow me to respectfully tell you that if you can show me that I have done anything to deserve to be interdicted or excommunicated, I will submit in silence to your sentence. But before you pass that sentence, I ask you, in the name of God, to make a public inquest about me, and have my accusers confront me. I warn your lordship, that if you interdict or excommunicate me without holding an inquest, I will make use of all the means which our holy church puts in the hands of her priests to defend my honour and prove my innocence; I will also appeal to the laws of our great Republic, which protects the character of all her citizens against any one who slanders them. It will, then, be at your risk and peril that you will pass such a sentence against me."

My calm answer greatly excited his rage. He violently struck the table with his fist, and said: "I do not care a straw about your threats. I repeat it, Mr. Chiniquy, if you are not at Kahokia by the 15th of next month, I will interdict and excommunicate you."

Feeling that it was a folly on my part to argue with a man who was beside himself by passion and excess of wine, I replied. " With the help of God, I will never bear the infamy of an interdict or excommunication. I will do all that religion and honour will allow me to prevent such a dark spot from defiling my name, and the man who does try it, will learn at his own expense that I am not only a priest of Christ, but also an American citizen. I respectfully tell your lordship that I neither smoke nor use intoxicating drinks. The time which your other priests give to those habits, I spend in the study of books, and especially of my Bible. I found in them, not only my duties, but my rights; and just as I am determined, with the help of God, to perform my duties, I will stand by my rights." I then immediately left the room to take the train to St. Anne.

Having spent a part of the night praying God to change the heart of my bishop, and keep me in the midst of my people, which were

29

becoming dearer and dearer to me, in proportion to the efforts of the enemy to drive me away from them, I addressed the following letter to the bishop:—

To the RT. REV. O'REGAN, Bishop of Chicago.

MY LORD.—The more I consider your design to turn me out of the colony which I have founded, and of which I am the pastor, the more I believe it a duty which I owe to myself, my friends, and to my countrymen, to protest before God and man against what you intend to do.

Not a single one of your priests stands higher than I do in the public mind, neither is more loved and respected by his people than I am. I defy my bitterest enemies to prove the contrary. And that character which is my most precious treasure, you intend to despoil me of by ignominiously sending me away from among my people! Certainly, I have enemies, and I am proud of it. The chief ones are well known in this country as the most depraved of men. The cordial reception they say they have received from you, has not taken away the stains they have on their foreheads.

By this letter, I again request you to make a public and most minute inquest into my conduct. My conscience tells me that nothing can be found against me. Such a public and fair dealing with me would confound my accusers. But I speak of accusers, when I do not really know if I have any. Where are they? What are their names? Of what sin do they accuse me? All these questions which I put to you, last Tuesday, were left unanswered! and would to God that you would answer them to-day, by giving me their names. I am ready to meet them before any tribunal. Before you strike the last blow on the victim of this most hellish plot, I request you, in the name of God, to give a moment's attention to the following consequences of my removal from this place at present.

You know I have a suit with Mr. Spink at the Urbana Court, for the beginning of October. My lawyers and witnesses are all in Kankakee and Iroquois counties; and in the very time I want most to be here to prove my innocence and guard my honour, you order me to go to a place more than three hundred miles distant! Did you ever realize that by that strange conduct, you help Spink against your own priest? When at Kahokia, I will have to bear the heavy expenses of travelling more than three hundred miles, many times. to consult my friends, or be deprived of their valuable help! Is it possible that you thus try to tie my hands and feet, and deliver me into the hands of my remorseless enemies? Since the beginning of that suit, Mr. Spink proclaims that you help him, and that, with the perjured priests, you have promised to do all in your power to crush me down! For the sake of the sacred character you bear, do not show so publicly that Mr. Spinks' boastings are true. For the sake of your high position in the church, do not so publicly lend a helping hand to the heartless land speculator of L'Erable. He has already betrayed his Protestant friends to get a wife; he will, ere long, betray you for less. Let me then live in peace here, till that suit is over.

By turning me away from my settlement, you destroy it. More than nine-tenths of the emigrants come here to live near me; by striking me you strike them all.

Where will you find a priest who will love that people so much as to give them, every year, from one to two thousand dollars, as I have invariably done? It is at the price of those sacrifices that, with the poorest class of emigrants from Canada, I have founded, here, in four years, a settlement which cannot be surpassed, or even equalled, in the United States, for its progress. And now that I have spent my last cent to form this colony, you turn me out of it. Our college, where one hundred and fifty boys are receiving such a good education, will be closed the very day I leave. For, you know very well the teachers I got from Montreal will leave as soon as I will.

Ah! if you are merciless towards the priest of St. Anne, have pity on these poor children. I would rather be condemned to death than to see them destroy their intelligence by running in the streets. Let me then finish my work here, and give me time to strengthen these young institutions which would fall to the ground with me.

If you turn me out or interdict me, as you say you will do, if I disobey your orders, my enemies will proclaim that you treat me with that rigour because you have found me guilty of some great iniquity; and this necessarily will prejudice my judges against me. They will consider me as a vile criminal. For who will suppose, in this free country, that there is a class of men who can judge a man and condemn him as our Bishop of Chicago is doing to-day, without giving him the names of his accusers, or telling him of what crimes he is accused?

In the name of God, I again ask you not to force me to leave my colony before I prove my innocence, and the iniquity of Spink, to the honest people of Urbana.

But, if you are deaf to my prayers, and if nothing can deter you from your resolution, I do not wish to be in the unenviable position of an interdicted priest among my countrymen; send me, by return mail, my letters of mission for the new places you intend trusting to my care. The sooner I get there the better for me and my people. I am ready! When on the road of exile, I will pray the God of Abraham to give me the fortitude and the faith He gave to Isaac, when laying his head on the altar, he willingly presented his throat to the sword. I will pray my Saviour, bearing His heavy cross to the top of Calvary, to direct and help my steps towards the land of exile you have prepared for your

Devoted Priest,

C. CHINIQUY.

This letter was not yet mailed when we heard that the drunkard priests around us were publishing that the bishop had interdicted me, and they had received orders from him to take charge of the colony of St. Anne. I immediately called a meeting of the whole people and told them : " The bishop has not interdicted me as the neighbouring priests publish ; he has only threatened to do so, if I do not leave this place for Kahokia, by the 15th of next month. But though he has not interdicted me, it may be that he does to-day, falsely publish that he has done it. We can expect anything from the destroyer of the fine congregation of the French Canadians of Chicago. He wants to destroy me and you as he has destroyed them. But before he immolates us, I hope that, with the help of God, we will fight as Christian soldiers, for our life, and we will use all the means which the laws of our church, the Holy word of God, and the glorious Constitution of the United States allow us to employ against our merciless tyrant.

" I ask you, as a favour, to send a deputation of four members of our colony, in whom you place the most implicit confidence, to carry this letter to the bishop. But before delivering it, they will put to him the following questions, the answers of which they will write down with great care in his presence, and deliver them to us faithfully. It is evident that we are now entering into a momentous struggle. We must act with prudence and firmness." Messrs. J. B. Lemoine, Leon Mailloux, Francis Bechard, and B. Allaire, having been unanimously chosen for that important mission, we gave them the following questions to put to the bishop:—

1st. " Have you interdicted Mr. Chiniquy ?

2nd. " Why have you interdicted him ? Is Mr. Chiniquy guilty of any crime to deserve to be interdicted ? Have those crimes been proved against him in a canonical way ?

3rd. " Why do you take Mr. Chiniquy away from us ?

[Our deputies came back from Chicago with the following report and answers, which they swore to, some time after before the Kankakee court.]

1st. " I have suspended Mr. Chiniquy on the 19th inst., on account of his stubbornness and want of submission to my orders, when I ordered him to Kahokia.

2nd. " If Mr. Chiniquy has said mass since, as you say, he is irregular, and the Pope alone can restore him in his ecclesiastical and sacerdotal functions.

3rd. " I take him away from St. Anne. despite his prayers and yours, because he has not been willing to live in peace and friendship with the Rev. Messrs. Lebel and Carthuval.

[The bishop, being asked if those two priests had not been interdicted by him for public scandals, was forced to say : " Yes !"]

4th. " My second reason for taking Mr. Chiniquy from St. Anne, and sending him to his new mission, is to stop the law-suit Mr. Spink has instituted against him.

[The bishop being asked if he would promise that the suit would be stopped by the removal of Mr. Chiniquy, answered: " I cannot promise that."]

5th. " Mr. Chiniquy is one of the best priests in my diocese, and I do not want to deprive myself of his services, no accusation against his morality has been proved before me.

6th. " Mr. Chiniquy has demanded an inquest to prove his innocence against certain accusations made against him ; he asked me the names of his accusers, to confound them ; I have refused to grant this request.

[After the bishop had made those declarations, the deputation presented him the letter of Mr. Chiniquy ; it evidently made a deep impression upon him. As soon as he read it, he said :]

7th. " Tell Mr. Chiniquy to come and meet me to prepare for his new mission, and I will give him the letters he wants, to go and labour there.

(Signed)
                                    FRANCIS BECHARD,
                                    J. B. LEMOINE,
                                    BASILIQUE ALLAIRE,
                                    LEON MAILLOUX."*

After the above had been read and delivered to the people, I showed them the evident falsehood and contradictions of the bishop when he said in his second answer: " If Mr. Chiniquy said mass since I interdicted him, he is irregular, and the Pope alone can restore him

* Those gentlemen, with the exception of Mr. Allaire, are still living, 1885.

in his ecclesiastical functions," and then in the seventh, "tell Mr Chiniquy to come and meet me to prepare for his new mission, and I will give him the letters he wants to go and labour there."

The last sentence, I said, proves that he knew he had not interdicted me as he said at first. For, had he done so, he could not give me letters to administer the sacraments and preach at Kahokia before my going before the Pope, who, alone, as he said himself, could give me such powers, after he (the bishop) knew that I had said mass since my return from Chicago. Now, my friends, here is the law of our holy church, not the saying, or the law of a publicly degraded man, as the Bishop of Chicago: "If a man had been unjustly condemned, let him pay no attention to the unjust sentence: let him even do nothing to have that unjust sentence removed." *

"If the bishop had interdicted me on the 19th, his sentence would be unjust, for, from his own lips, we have the confession, ' that no accusation has ever been proved before him ; that I am one of his best priests ; that he does not want to be deprived of my services.' Yes, such a sentence, if passed, would have been unjust, and our business, to-day, would be to treat it with the contempt it would deserve. But that unjust sentence has not even been pronounced, since, after saying mass every day since the 19th, the bishop himself wants to give me letters to go to Kahokia and work as one of his best priests ! It strikes me, to-day, for the first time, that it is more your destruction, as a people, than mine, which the bishop wants to accomplish. It is my desire to remain in your midst to defend your rights as Catholics. If you are true to me, as I will be to you, in the impending struggle, we have nothing to fear ; for our holy Catholic Church is for us ; all her laws and canons are in our favour ; the Gospel of Christ is for us. The God of the Gospel is for us. Even the Pope, to whom we will appeal, will be for us. For, I must tell you a thing, which, till to day I kept secret ; viz. : The Archbishop of St. Louis, to whom I brought my complaint, in April last, advised me to write to the Pope and tell him, not all, for it would make too large a volume, but something of the criminal deeds of the roaring lion who wants to devour us. He is, to-day, selling the bones of the dead which are resting in the Roman Catholic cemetery of Chicago ! But if you are true to yourselves as Catholics and Americans, that mitred tyrant will not sell the bones of our friends and relatives which rest here in our burying ground. He has sold the parsonage and the church which our dear countrymen had built in Chicago. Those properties are, to-day, in the hands of the Irish : but if you promise to stand by your rights as Christian men and American citizens, I will tell that avaricious bishop : " Come

* Canon of the Church, by Pope Gelasius.

and sell our parsonage and our church here, if you dare!' As I told you before, we have a glorious battle to fight. It is the battle of freedom against the most cruel tyranny the world has ever seen: it is the battle of truth against falsehood: It is the battle of the old Gospel of Christ against the new gospel of Bishop O'Regan. Let us be true to ourselves to the end, and our holy church, which that bishop dishonours, will bless us. Our Saviour Jesus Christ, whose Gospel is despised by that adventurer, will be for us, and give us a glorious victory. Have you not read in your Bibles that Jesus wanted His disciples to be free, when He said: 'If the Son therefore shall make you free, ye shall be free indeed' (John viii. 36). Does that mean that the Son of God wants us to be the slaves of Bishop O'Regan? 'No!' cried out the whole people. May God bless you for your understanding of your Christian rights. Let all those who want to be free, with me, raise their hands.

"Oh! blessed be the Lord," I said, "there are more than 3,000 hands raised towards heaven to say that you want to be free! Now, let those who do not want to defend their rights as Christians, and as American citizens, raise their hands. Thanks be to God," I again exclaimed, "there is not a traitor among us! You are all the true, brave and noble soldiers of liberty, truth and righteousness! May the Lord bless you all!"

It is impossible to describe the enthusiasm of the people. Before dismissing them, I said: "We will, no doubt, very soon, witness one of the most ludicrous comedies ever played on this continent: that comedy is generally called excommunication. Some drunkard priests, sent by the drunkard Bishop of Chicago, will come to excommunicate us. I expect their visit in a few days. That performance will be worth seeing; and I hope that you will see and hear the most amusing thing in your life."

I was not mistaken. The very next day, we heard that the 3rd of September had been chosen by the bishop to excommunicate us.

I said to the people: "When you see the flag of the free and the brave floating from the top of our steeple, come and rally around that emblem of liberty."

There were more than 3,000 people on our beautiful hill, when the priests made their appearance. A few moments before, I had said to that immense gathering:

"I bless God that you are so many to witness the last tyrannical act of Bishop O'Regan. But I have a favour to ask of you, it is, that no insult or opposition whatever will be made to the priests who come to play that comedy. Please do not say an angry word; do not move a finger against the performers. They are not responsible for what they will do, for two reasons. 1. They will probably be drunk.

2. They are bound to do that work, by their master and Lord Bishop O'Regan.

The priests arrived at about two o'clock p.m., and never such shouting and clapping of hands had been heard in our colony as on their appearance. Never had I seen my dear people so cheerful and good-humoured, as when one of the priests, trembling from head to foot with terror and drunkenness, tried to read the following sham act of excommunication; which he nailed on the door of the chapel :

The Reverend Monsieur Chiniquy, heretofore curate of St. Anne, Colonie of Beaver, in the Diocese of Chicago, has formally been interdicted by me for canonical causes.

The said Mr. Chiniquy, notwithstanding that interdict, has maliciously performed the functions of the holy ministry, in administering the holy sacraments and saying mass. This has caused him to be irregular, and in direct opposition to the authority of the church, consequently, he is a schismatic.

The said Mr. Chiniquy, thus named by my letters and verbal injunction, has absolutely persisted in violating the laws of the church, and disobeyed her authority, is by this present letter excommunicated.

I forbid any Catholic having any communication with him, in spiritual matters, under pain of excommunication. Every Catholic who goes against this suspense, is excommunicated.

(Signed)   ✠ ANTHONY,
Bishop of Chicago, and administrator of Quincy.

Sept. 3rd., 1856.

As soon as the priests, who had nailed this document to the door of our chapel, had gone away at full speed, I went to see it, and found, what I had expected, that it was not signed by the bishop, neither by his grand vicar, nor any known person, and, consequently it was a complete nullity, according to the laws of the church. Fearing I would prosecute him, as I threatened, he shrank from the responsibility of his own act, and had not signed it. He was probably ignorant of the fact that he was himself excommunicated, *ipso facto*, for not having signed the document himself, or by his known deputies. I learned afterwards, that he got a boy twelve years old to write and sign it. In this way, it was impossible for me to bring that document before any court, on account of its want of legal and necessary forms. That act was also a nullity, for being brought by three priests who were not *compos mentis*, from their actual state of drunkenness. And again, it was a nullity from the evident falsehood which was its base.

It alleged that the bishop had interdicted and suspended me on the 19th of August, for canonical causes. But he had declared to the four deputies we had sent him : "That Mr. Chiniquy was one of my best priests, that nothing had been proved against him," consequently, no canonical cause could exist for the allegation. The people under-

456	FIFTY YEARS IN THE CHURCH OF ROME.

stood very well that the whole affair was a miserable farce, designed to separate them from their pastor. It had just, by the good providence of God, the contrary effect. They had never shown me such sincere respect and devotedness as since that never-to-be-forgotten day.

The three priests, after leaving, entered the house of one of our farmers, called Bellanger, a short distance from the chapel, and asked permission to rest awhile. But after sitting and smoking a few minutes they all went out to the stables. The farmer thinking this very strange, went after them to see what they would do in his stables; to his great surprise and disgust, he found them drinking the last of their whiskey. He exclaimed, "Is it not a shame to see three priests in a stable drinking spirits?"

They made no answer, but went immediately to their carriage and drove away as quickly as possible, singing with all their might, a bacchanalian song! Such was the last act of that excommunication, which has done more than anything else to prepare my people and myself to understand that the Church of Rome is a den of thieves, a school of infidelity and the very antipodes of the Church of Christ.

CHAPTER LVIII.

THE Sabbath afternoon after the three drunken priests nailed their unsigned, unsealed, untestified, and consequently null sentence of excommunication, to the door of our chapel, the people had gathered from every part of our colony into the large hall of the court-house of Kankakee City to hear several addresses on their duties of the day, and they unanimously passed the following resolutions:

"*Resolved*,—That we, French Canadians of the County of Kankakee, do hereby decide to give our moral support to Rev. C. Chiniquy, in the persecution now exerted against him by the Bishop of Chicago, in violation of the laws of the church, expressed and sanctioned by the Councils."

After this resolution had been voted, Mr. Bechard, who is now one of the principal members of the Parliament of Canada, and who was then a merchant of Kankakee City, presented to me the following address, which had also been unanimously voted by the people:

"DEAR AND BELOVED PASTOR :—For several years we have been witnesses of the persecution of which you are the subject, on the part of the bad priests, your neighbours, and on the part of the unworthy Bishop of Chicago; but we also have been the witnesses of your sacerdotal virtues—of your forbearance of their calumnies—and our respect and affection for your person has but increased at the sight of all those trials.

"We know that you are persecuted, not only because you are a Canadian priest, and that you like us, but also because you do us good in making a sacrifice of your own private fortune to build school-houses, and to feed our teachers at your own table. We know that the Bishop of Chicago, who resembles more an angry wolf than a pastor of the church, having destroyed the prosperous congregation of Chicago by taking away from them their splendid church, which they had built at the cost of many sacrifices, and giving it to the Irish population, and having discouraged the worthy population of Bourbonnais Grove in forcing on them drunken and scandalous priests, wants to take you away from among us, to please Spink, the greatest enemy of the French population. They even say that the bishop, carrying iniquity to its extreme bounds, wanted to interdict you. But as our church cannot, and is not willing to sanction evil and calumny, we know that all those interdicts, based on falsehoods and spite, are null and void.

" We, therefore, solicit you not to give way in presence of the perfidious plots of your enemies, and not to leave us. Stay among us as our pastor and our father, and we solemnly promise to sustain you in all your hardships to the end, and to defend you against our enemies. Stay among us, to instruct us in our duties by your eloquent speeches, and to enlighten us by your pious examples. Stay among us, to guard us against the perfidious designs of the Bishop of Chicago, who wants to discourage and destroy our prosperous colony, as he has already discouraged and destroyed other congregations of the French Canadians, by leaving them without a pastor, or by forcing on them unworthy priests."

The stern and unanimous determination of my countrymen to stand by me in the impending struggle is one of the greatest blessings which God has ever given me. It filled me with a courage which nothing could hereafter shake. But the people of St. Anne did not think that it was enough to show to the bishop that nothing could ever shake the resolution they had taken to live and die free men. They gathered in a public and immense meeting on the Sabbath after the sham excommunication, to adopt the following address to the Bishop of Chicago, a copy of which was sent to every bishop of the United States and Canada, and to Pope Pius IX. :

"To HIS LORDSHIP, ANTHONY O'REGAN OF CHICAGO:—We, the undersigned, inhabitants of the parish of St. Anne, Beaver settlement, seeing with sorrow that you have discarded our humble request, which we have sent you by the four delegates, and have persisted in trying to drive away our honest and worthy priest, who has edified us in all circumstances by his public and religious conduct, and having, contrary to the rules of our holy church and common sense, struck our worthy pastor, Mr. Chiniquy, with excommunication, having caused him to be announced as a schismatic priest, and having forbidden us to communicate with him in religious matters, are hereby protesting against the unjust and iniquitous manner in which you have struck him, refusing him the privilege of justifying himself and proving his innocence.

"Consequently, we declare that we are ready at all times as good Catholics, to obey all your orders and ordinances that are in accordance with the laws of the Gospel and the Church, but that we are not willing to follow you in all your errors of judgments, in your injustices and covetous caprices. Telling you, as St. Jerome wrote to his bishop, that as long as you will treat us as your children, we will obey you as a father ; but as soon as you will treat us as our master, we shall cease to consider you as our father. Considering Mr. Chiniquy as a good and virtuous priest, worthy of the place he occupies, and possessing as yet all his sacerdotal powers, in spite of your null and ridiculous sentence, we have unani-

mously decided to keep him among us as our pastor ; therefore praying your lordship not to put yourself to the trouble of seeking another priest for us.   More
yet; we have unanmiously decided to sustain him and furnish him the means to
go as far as Rome, if he cannot have justice in America.

" We further declare that it has been dishonourable and shameful for our
bishop and for our holy religion to have seen, coming under the walls of our chapel,
bringing the orders of the prince of the church, a representative of Christ, three
men covered with their sacerdotal garments, having their tongues half paralyzed
by the effects of whiskey, and who, turning their backs to the church, went to the
house and the barn of one of our settlers and there emptied their bottles. And from
there, taking their seats in the buggies, went toward the settlement of L'Erable,
singing drunken songs and hallooing like wild Indians.   Will your lordship be
influenced by such a set of men, who seem to have for their mission to degrade the
sacerdos and Catholicism ?

" We conclude, in hoping that your lorship will not persist in your decision,
given in a moment of madness and spite ; that you will reconsider your acts, and
that you will retract your unjust, null and ridiculous excommunication, and by
these means avoid the scandal of which your precipitation is the cause.   We then
hope that, changing your determination, you will work to the welfare of our holy
religion, and not to its degradation, into which your intolerant conduct would lead
us, and that you will not persist in trying to drive our worthy pastor, Rev.
Charles Chiniquy, from the flourishing colony that he has founded at the cost of
the abandonment of his native land, of the sacrifice of the high position he had in
Canada ; that you will bring peace between you and us, that we shall have in the
Bishop of Chicago not a tyrant, but a father, and that you will have in us not
rebels, but faithful children, by our virtues and our good example.   Subscribing
ourselves the obedient children of the church.

" THEOPILE DORIEN,	J. B. LEMOINE, N. P.,
" DET. VANIER,	OLIVER SENECHALL,
" J. B. BELANGER,	BASILIQUE ALLAIR,
" CAMILE BETOURNEY,	MICHEL ALLAIR,
" STAN'LAS GAGNE,	JOSEPH GRISI,
" ANTOINE ALLAIN,	JOSEPH ALLARD,

" And five hundred others."

This address, signed by more than five hundred men, all heads of
families, and reproduced by almost the whole press in the United
States, fell as a thunderclap on the head of the heartless destroyer of
our people.   But it did not change his destructive plans.   It had just
the contrary effect.   As a tiger, mortally wounded by the sure shots
of the hunters, he filled the country with his roaring, hoping to
frighten us by his new denunciations.   He published the most lying
stories to explain his conduct, and to show the world that he had good
reasons for destroying the French cogregration of Chicago, and trying
the same experiment on St. Anne.

In order to refute his false statements, and show more clearly to
the whole world the reasons I had, as a Catholic priest, to resist him,
I addressed the following letter to his lordship :

"St. Anne, Kankakee County, Ill.,

"*Sept.* 25, 1856.

"Rt. Rev'd O'Regan:—You seem to be surprised that I have offered the holy sacrifice of mass since our last interview. Here are some of my reasons for so doing.

" 1st. You have not suspended me; far from it, you have given me fifteen days to consider what I should do, threatening only to interdict me after that time, if I would not obey your orders.

" 2nd. If you have been so ill-advised as to suspend me, for the crime of telling you that my intention was to live the life of a retired priest in my little colony, sooner than to be exiled at my age, your sentence is ridiculous and null ; and if you were as expert in the *jure Canonico* as in the art of pocketing our money, you would know that you are yourself suspended *ipso facto* for a year, and that I have nothing to fear or expect from you now.

" 3rd. When I bowed down before the altar of Jesus Christ, twenty-four years ago, to receive the priesthood, my intention was to be the minister of the Catholic Church, but not a slave of a lawless tyrant.

" 4th. Remember the famous words of Tertullian, ' *Nimia potestas, nulla potestas.*' For the sake of peace, I have, with many others, tolerated your despotism till now ; but my patience is at an end, and for the sake of our holy church, which you are destroying, I am determined with many to oppose an insurmountable wall to your tyranny.

" 5th. I did not come here, you know well, as an ordinary missionary ; but I got from your predecessor the permission to form a colony of my emigrating countrymen. I was not sent here in 1851 to take care of any congregation. It was a complete wilderness ; but I was sent to form a colony of Catholics. I planted my cross in a wilderness. In a great part, with my own money, I have built a chapel, a college and a female academy. I have called from everywhere my countrymen—nine-tenths of them came here only to live with me, and because I had the pledged word of my bishop to do that work. And as long as I live the life of a good priest I deny you the right to forbid me to remain in my colony which wants my help and my presence.

" 6th. You have never shown me your authority (but once) except in the most tyrannical way. But now, seeing that the more humble I am before you the more insolent you grow, I have taken the resolution to stand by my rights as a Catholic priest and as an American citizen.

" 7th. You remember, that in our second interview you forbade me to have the good preceptors we have now for our children, and you turned into ridicule the idea I had to call them from Canada. Was that the act of a bishop or of a mean despot ?

" 8th. A few days after you ordered me to live on good terms with R. R. Lebel and Carthuval, though you were well acquainted with their scandalous lives, and twice you threatened me with suspension for refusing to become a friend of those two rogues ! And you have so much made a fool of yourself before the four gentlemen I sent to you to be witnesses of your iniquity and my innocence, that you have acknowledged before them that one of your principal reasons for turning me out of my colony was, that I had not been able to keep peace with two priests whom you acknowledge to be depraved and unworthy priests ! Is not that surpassing wickedness and tyranny of anything recorded in the blackest pages of the most daring tyrants ? You want to punish by exile a gentleman and a good priest, because he cannot agree to become the friend of two public rogues! I thank you, Bishop O'Regan, to have made that public confession in the presence of unimpeachable witnesses. I do not want to advise you to be hereafter very prudent in what you intend to do against the reputation and character of the priest of St. Anne. If you continue to denounce me as you have done since a few weeks, and to tell the people what you think fit against me, I have awful things to publish of your injustice and tyranny.

"As Judas sold our Saviour to His enemies, so you have sold me to my enemy of L'Erable. But be certain that you shall not deliver up your victim as you like.

"For withdrawing a suit which you have instituted against my honour, and which you shall certainly lose, you drag me out from my home and order me to the land of exile, and you cover that iniquity with the appearance of zeal for the public peace, just as Pilate delivered his victim into the hands of their enemies to make peace with them.

"Shame on you, Bishop O'Regan! For the sake of God, do not oblige me to reveal to the world what I know against you. Do not oblige me, in self-defence, to strike you, my merciless persecutor. If you have no pity for me, have pity on yourself, and on the church which that coming struggle will so much injure.

"It is not enough for you to have so badly treated my poor countrymen of Chicago—your hatred against the French Canadians cannot be satisfied except when you have taken away from them the only consolation they have in this land of exile—to possess in their midst a priest of their own nation whom they love and respect as a father! My poor countrymen of Chicago, with many hard sacrifices, had built a fine church for themselves and a house for their priest. *You have taken their church from their hands and given it to the Irish;* you have sold the house of their priest, after turning him out; and what have you done with the one thousand five hundred dollars you got as its price? Public rumour says that you are employing that money to support the most unjust and infamous suit against one of their priests. Continue a little longer, and you may be sure that the cursing of my poor countrymen against you will be heard in heaven, and that the God of Justice will give them an avenger.

"You have, at three different times, threatened to interdict and excommunicate me if I would not give you my little personal properties; and as many times you have said in my teeth, that I was a bad priest, because I refused to act according to your rapacious tyranny!

"The impious Ahab, murdering Naboth to get his fields, is risen from the dead in your person. You cannot kill my body, *since I am protected by the glorious flag of the United States;* but you do worse, you try to destroy my honour and my character, which are dearer to me than my life. In a moral way you give my blood to be licked by your dogs. But remember the words of the prophet to Ahab, 'In this place where dogs licked the blood of Naboth shall dogs lick thy blood, even thine' (1 Kings xxi. 19). For every false witness you shall bring against me, I shall have a hundred unimpeachable ones against you. Thousands and thousands of religious Irish, and generous Germans, and liberty and fair-play-loving French Canadians, will help me in that struggle. I do not address you these words as a threat, but as a friendly warning.

"Keep quiet, my lord; do not let yourself be guided by your quick temper; do not be so free in the use of suspense and interdicts. These terrible arms are two-edged swords, which very often hurt more the imprudent who make use of them than those whom they intend to strike."

" I wish to live in peace with you. I take my God to witness, that to this day, I have done everything to keep peace with you. But the peace I want is the peace which St. Jerome speaks of when, writing to his bishop, he tells him :

" ' It is no use to speak of peace with the lips, if we destroy it with our works. It is a very different way to work for peace, from trying to submit every one to an abject slavery. We also want peace. Not only we desire it, but we implore you instantly to give it. However, the peace we want is the peace of Christ—a true peace, a peace without hatred, a peace which is not a masked war, a peace which is not to crush enemies, but a peace which unites friends. How can we call that peace which is nothing but tyranny ? Why should we not call everything by its proper name ? Let us call hatred—what is hatred ; and let us say that peace reigns only when a true love exists. We are not the authors of the troubles and divisions which exist in the church. A father must love his children. A bishop, as well as a father, must wish to be loved, but not feared. The old proverb says, *One hates whom he fears*, and we naturally wish for the death of the one we hate. If you do not try to crush the religious men under your power they will submit themselves to your authority. Offer them the kiss of love and peace and they will obey you. But liberty refuses to yield as soon as you try to crush it down. The best way to be obeyed by a free man is not to deal with him as with a slave. We know the laws of the church, and we do not ignore the rights which belong to every man. We have learned many things, not only from experience, but also from the study of books. The king who strikes his subjects with an iron rod, or who thinks that his fingers must be heavier than his father's hand, has soon destroyed the kingdom even of the peaceful and mild David. The people of Rome refused to bear the yoke of their proud king. We have left our country in order to live in peace. In this solitude our intention was to respect the authority of the pontiffs of Christ (we mean those who teach the true faith). We want to respect them not as our masters, but as our fathers. Our intention was to respect them as bishops, not as usurpers and tyrants who want to reduce us to slavery by the abuse of their power. We are not so vain as to ignore what is due to the priests of Christ, for to receive them is to receive the very one whose bishops they are. But let them be satisfied with the respect which is due to them. Let them remember that they are fathers, not masters of those who have given up everything in order to enjoy the privileges of a peaceful solitude. May Christ who is our mighty God grant that we should be united, not by a false peace, but by a true and loyal love, lest that by biting each other we destroy each other."

[Letter of St. Jerome to his bishop.]

" You have a great opinion of the episcopal power, and so have I. But St. Paul and all the Holy Fathers that I have read, have also told us many things of the dignity of the priest (alter Christus Sacerdos). I am your brother and equal in many things ; do not forget it. I know my dignity as a man and a priest, and I shall sooner lose my life than to surrender them to any man, even a bishop. If you think you can deal with me as a carter with his horse, drawing him where he likes, you will very soon see your error.

" I neither drink strong wines nor smoke, and the many hours *that others spent in emptying their bottles and smoking their pipes*, I read my dear books—I study the admirable laws of the church and the Gospel of Christ. I love my books and the holy laws of our church, because they teach me my rights as well as my duties. They tell me that many years ago a general council, which is something above you, has annulled your unjust sentence, and brought upon your head the very penalty you intended to impose upon me. They tell me that any sentence from you, coming (from your own profession) from bad and criminal motives, is null, and will fall powerless at my feet.

"But I tell you again, that I desire to live in peace with you. The false reports of Lebel and Carthuval have disturbed that peace; but it is still in your power to have it for yourself and give it to me. I am sure that the sentence you say you have preferred against me comes from a misunderstanding, and your wisdom and charity, if you can hear their voice, can very easily set everything as it was two months ago. It is still in your power to have a warm friend, or an immovable adversary in Kankakee County. It would both be equitable and honourable in you to extinguish the fires of discord which you have so unfortunately enkindled, by drawing back a sentence which you would never have preferred if you had not been deceived. You would be blessed by the Church of Illinois, and particularly by the 10,000 French Canadians who surround me, and are ready to support me at all hazards.

"Do not be angry from the seeming harsh words which you find in this letter. Nobody, but I, could tell you these sad truths, though every one of your priests, and particularly those who flatter you the most, repeat them every day. By kind and honest proceedings you can get everything from me, even the last drop of my blood; but you will find me an immovable rock if you approach me as you have always done (but once) with insult and tyrannical threats.

"You have not been ordained a bishop to rule over us according to your fancy, but you have the eternal laws of justice and equity to guide you. You have the laws of the church to obey as well as her humblest child, and as soon as you do anything against these imperishable laws you are powerless to obtain your object. It is not only lawful, but a duty to resist you. When you strike without a legitimate or a canonical cause; when you try to take away my character to please some of your friends; when you order me to exile to stop a suit which you are inciting against me; when you punish me for the crime of refusing to obey the orders you gave me to be the friend of two public rogues; when you threatened me with excommunication, because I do not give you my little personal properties, I have nothing to fear from your interdicts and excommunication.

"What a sad lot for me, and what a shame for you, if by your continual attacks at the doors of our churches or in the public press, you oblige me to expose your injustice. It is yet time for you to avoid that. Instead of striking me like an outcast, come and give me the paternal hand of charity, instead of continuing that fratricidal combat, come and heal the wounds you have made and already received. Instead of insulting me by driving me away from my colony to the land of exile, come and bless the great work I have begun here for the glory of God and the good of my people. Instead of destroying the college and the female academy, for the erection of which I have expended my last cent, and whose teachers are fed at my table, come and bless the three hundred little children who are daily attending our schools. Instead of sacrificing me to the hatred of my enemies, come and strengthen my heart against their fury.

"I tell you again, that no consideration whatever will induce me to surrender my right as a Catholic priest *and as an American citizen*. By the first title you cannot interdict me, as long as I am a good priest, for the crime of wishing to live in my colony and among my people. *By the second title, you cannot turn me out from my home.*

"C. CHINIQUY."

It was the first time that a Roman Catholic priest, with his whole people, had dared to speak such language to a bishop of Rome on this continent. Never yet had the unbearable tyranny of those haughty men received such a public rebuke. Our fearless words fell as a bombshell in the camp of the Roman Catholic hierarchy of America.

With very few exceptions, the press of the State of Illinois, whose columns had so often echoed the cries of indignation raised everywhere against the tyranny of Bishop O'Regan, took sides with me. Hundreds of priests, not only from Illinois, but from every corner of the United States, addressed their warmest thanks to me for the stand I had taken, and asked me, in the name of God and for the honour of the church, not to yield an inch of my rights. Many promised to support us at the court of Rome, by writing themselves to the Pope, to denounce not only the Bishop of Illinois, but several others, who, though not so openly bad, were yet trampling under their feet the most sacred rights of the priests and the people. Unfortunately those priests gave me a saddening knowledge of their cowardice by putting in their letters " *absolutely confidential.*" They all promised to help me when I was storming the strong fortress of the enemy, provided I would go alone in the gap, and that they would keep themselves behind thick walls, far from shot and shell.

However, this did not disturb me, for my God knows it, my trust was not in my own strength, but in His protection. I was sure that I was in the right, that the Gospel of Christ was on my side, that all the canons and laws of the councils were in my favour.

My library was filled with the best books on the canons and laws passed in the great councils of my church. It was written in big letters in the celebrated work, "*Histoire du Droit Canonique.*" There is no arbitrary power in the Church of Christ.*

The Council of Augsburg, held in 1548 (Can. 24), had declared that, " no sentence of excommunication will be passed, except for great crimes."

The Pope St. Gregory had said : " That censures are null when not inflicted for great sins or for faults which have not been clearly proved."

" An unjust excommunication does not bind before God those against whom it has been hurled. But it injures only the one who has proffered it." †

" If an unjust sentence is pronounced against any one, he must not pay any attention to it ; for, before God and His Church, an unjust sentence cannot injure anybody. Let, then, that person do nothing to get such an unjust sentence repealed, for it cannot injure him." ‡

The canonists conclude, from all the laws of the church on that matter, " That if a priest is unjustly interdicted or excommunicated he may continue to officiate without any fear of becoming irregular." §

* Vol. iii., page 139.   † Eccl. Laws, by Hericourt, c. xxii., No. 50.
‡ Pope Gelasius.   § Eccl. Laws, by Hericourt, c. xxii., No. 51.

Protected by these laws, and hundreds of others too long to enumerate, which my church had passed in every age, strengthened by the voice of my conscience, which assured me that I had done nothing to deserve to be interdicted or excommunicated; sure, besides, of the testimony brought by our four delegates that the bishop himself had declared that I was one of his best priests, that he wanted to give to me my letters to go and perform the functions of my ministry in Kahokia: above all, knowing the unanimous will of my people that I should remain with them and continue the great and good work so providentially entrusted to me in my colony, and regarding this as an indication of the Divine will, I determined to remain, in spite of the Bishop of Chicago. All the councils of my church were telling me that he had no power to injure me, and that all his official acts were null.

But if he were spiritually powerless against me, it was not so in temporal matters. His power and his desire to injure us had increased with his hatred, since he had read our letters and seen them in all the papers of Chicago. The first thing he did was to reconcile himself to the priest Lebel, whom he had turned out ignominiously from his diocese some time before. The priest had since that obtained a fine situation in the diocese of Michigan. He invited him to his palace, and petted him several days. I felt that the reconciliation of those two men meant nothing good for me. But my hope was, more than ever, that the merciful God who had protected me so many times against them, would save me again from their machinations. The air was, however, filled with the strangest rumours against me. It was said everywhere that Mr. Lebel was to bring such charges against my character that I would be sent to the penitentiary.

What were the new iniquities to be laid to my charge? No one could tell. But the few partisans and friends of the bishop, Messrs. Lebel and Spink, were jubilant and sure that I was to be for ever destroyed.

At last the time arrived when the Sheriff of Kankakee had to drag me again as a criminal and a prisoner to Urbana, and deliver me into the hands of the sheriff of that city. I arrived there on the 20th of October, with my lawyers, Messrs. Osgood and Paddock, and a dozen witnesses. Mr. Abraham Lincoln had preceded me only by a few minutes from Springfield. He was in the company of Judge David Davis, since Vice-President of the United States, when I met him.

The jury having been selected and sworn, the Rev. Mr. Lebel was the first witness called to testify and say what he knew against my character.

Mr. Lincoln objected to that kind of testimony, and tried to prove that Mr. Spink had no right to bring his new suit against me by attacking my character. But Judge Davis ruled that the prosecution had that right in the case that was before him. Mr. Lebel had, then, full liberty to say anything he wanted, and he availed himself of his privilege. His testimony lasted nearly an hour, and was too long to be given here. I will only say that he began by declaring that "Chiniquy was one of the vilest men of the day—that every kind of bad rumours were constantly circulating against him." He gave a good number of those rumours, though he could not positively swear if they were founded on truth or not, for he had not investigated them. But he said there was one of which he was sure, for he had authenticated it thoroughly. He expressed a great deal of apparent regret that he was forced to reveal to the world such things which were not only against the honour of Chiniquy, but, to some extent, involved the good name of a dear sister, Madame Bossey. But as he was to speak the truth before God, he could not help it—the sad truth was to be told. "*Mr. Chiniquy,*" he said, "*had attempted to do the most infamous things with my own sister, Madame Bossey.* She herself has told me the whole story under oath, and she would be here to unmask the wicked man to-day before the whole world, if she were not forced to silence at home from a severe illness."

Though every word of that story was a perjury, there was such a colour of truth and sincerity in my accuser, that his testimony fell upon me and my lawyers and all my friends as a thunderbolt. A man who has never heard such a calumny brought against him before a jury in a court-house packed with people, composed of friends and foes, will never understand what I felt in this the darkest hour of my life. My God only knows the weight and the bitterness of the waves of desolation which then passed over my soul.

After that testimony was given, there was a lull, and a most profound silence in the court-room. All the eyes were turned upon me, and I heard many voices speaking of me, whispering, " The villain ! " Those voices passed through my soul as poisoned arrows. Though innocent, I wished that the ground would open under my feet and bring me down to the darkest abysses, to conceal me from the eyes of my friends and the whole world.

However, Mr. Lincoln soon interrupted the silence by addressing to Lebel such cross-questions that his testimony, in the minds of many, soon lost much of its power. And he did still more destroy the effect of his (Lebel's) false oath, when he brought my twelve witnesses, who were among the most respectable citizens of Bourbonnais, formerly the parishioners of Mr. Lebel. Those twelve gentlemen swore that Mr. Lebel was such a drunkard and vicious man, that he was so publicly my enemy on account of the many rebukes I

30

had given to his private and public vices, that they would not believe a word of what he said, even upon his oath.

At ten p.m. the court was adjourned, to meet again the next morning, and I went to the room of Mr. Lincoln, with my two other lawyers, to confer about the morning's work. My mind was unspeakably sad. Life had never been such a burden to me as in that hour. I was tempted, like Job, to curse the hour when I was born. I could see in the face of my lawyers, though they tried to conceal it, that they were also full of anxiety.

"My dear Mr. Chiniquy," said Mr. Lincoln, "though I hope, to-morrow, to destroy the testimony of Mr. Lebel against you, I must concede that I see great dangers ahead. There is not the least doubt in my mind that every word he has said is a sworn lie; but my fear is that the jury thinks differently. I am a pretty good judge in these matters. I feel that our jurymen think that you are guilty. There is only one way to perfectly destroy the power of a false witness—it is by another direct testimony against what he has said, or by showing from his very lips that he has perjured himself. I failed to do that last night, though I have diminished, to a great extent, the force of his testimony. Can you not prove an *alibi*, or can you not bring witnesses who were there in the same house that day, who would flatly and directly contradict what your remorseless enemy has said against you?"

I answered him: "How can I try to do such a thing when they have been shrewd enough not to fix the very date of the alleged crime against me?"

"You are correct, you are perfectly correct, Mr. Chiniquy," answered Mr. Lincoln, "as they have refused to precise the date, we cannot try that. I have never seen two such skilful rogues as those two priests. There is really a diabolical skill in the plan they have concocted for your destruction. It is evident that the bishop is at the bottom of the plot. You remember how I have forced Lebel to confess that he was now on the most friendly terms with the Bishop of Chicago, since he has become the chief of your accusers. Though I do not give up the hope of rescuing you from the hands of your enemies, I do not like to conceal from you that I have several reasons to fear that you will be declared guilty, and condemned to a heavy penalty, or to the penitentiary, though I am sure you are perfectly innocent. It is very probable that we will have to confront that sister of Lebel to-morrow. Her sickness is probably a feint, in order not to appear here except after the brother will have prepared the public mind in her favour. At all events, if she does not come, they will send some justice of the peace to get her sworn testimony, which will be more difficult to rebut than her own verbal declarations. That woman is evidently in the hands of the bishop and her brother priest,

ready to swear anything they order her, and I know nothing so difficult as to refute such female testimonies, particularly when they are
absent from the court. The only way to be sure of a favourable
verdict to-morrow is, that God Almighty would take our part and
show your innocence! Go to Him and pray, for He alone can save
you." Mr. Lincoln was exceedingly solemn when he addressed those
words to me, and they went very deep into my soul.

I have often been asked if Abraham Lincoln had any religion?
But I never had any doubt about his profound confidence in God,
since I heard those words falling from his lips in that hour of anxiety.
I had not been able to conceal my deep distress. Burning tears were
rolling on my cheeks when he was speaking, and there was on his face
the expression of friendly sympathy which I shall never forget.
Without being able to say a word, I left him to go to my little room.
It was nearly eleven o'clock. I locked the door and fell on my knees
to pray, but I was unable to say a single word. The horrible sworn
calumnies thrown at my face by a priest of my own church were
ringing in my ears! my honour and my good name so cruelly and for
ever destroyed! all my friends and my dear people covered with an
eternal confusion! and more than that, the sentence of condemnation
which was probably to be hurled against me the next day in the
presence of the whole country, whose eyes were upon me! All those
things were before me, not only as horrible phantoms, but as heavy
mountains, under the burdens of which I could not breathe. At last
the fountains of tears were opened, and it relieved me to weep; I could
then speak and cry: "Oh, my God! have mercy upon me! Thou
knowest my innocence! hast Thou not promised that those who trust
in Thee cannot perish! Oh! do not let me perish, when Thou art
the only One in whom I trust! Come to my help! Save me!"

From eleven p.m. to three in the morning I cried to God, and
raised my supplicating hands to His throne of mercy. But I confess,
to my confusion, it seemed to me in certain moments, that it was useless to pray and cry, for though innocent, I was doomed to perish. I
was in the hands of my enemies. My God had forsaken me!

What an awful night I spent! I hope none of my readers will ever
know by their own experience the agony of spirit I endured. I had no
other expectation than to be for ever dishonoured, and sent to the penitentiary next morning! But God had not forsaken me! He had again
heard my cries, and was once more to show me His infinite mercy!

At three o'clock a.m. I heard three knocks at my door, and I
quickly went to open it. "Who was there?" Abraham Lincoln,
with a face beaming with joy! I could hardly believe my eyes. But
I was not mistaken. It was my noble-hearted friend, the most honest
lawyer of Illinois!—one of the noblest men Heaven had ever given to

earth!—it was Abraham Lincoln. On seeing me bathed with tears, he exclaimed, " Cheer up, Mr. Chiniquy, I have the perjured priests in my hands. Their diabolical plot is all known, and if they do not fly away before the dawn of day, they will surely be lynched. Bless the Lord, you are saved !"

The sudden passage of extreme desolation to an extreme joy came near killing me. I felt as if suffocated, and unable to utter a single word. I took his hand, pressed it to my lips, and bathed it with tears of joy. I said: " May God for ever bless you, dear Mr. Lincoln. But please tell me how you can bring me such glorious news !"

Here is the simple but marvellous story, as told me by that great and good man, whom God had made the messenger of His mercies towards me: " As soon as Lebel had given his perjured testimony against you yesterday," said Mr. Lincoln, " one of the agents of the Chicago press telegraphed to some of the principal papers of Chicago: 'It is probable that Mr. Chiniquy will be condemned; for the testimony of the Rev. Mr. Lebel seems to leave no doubt that he is guilty.' And the little Irish boys, to sell their papers, filled the streets with the cries: 'Chiniquy will be hung! Chiniquy will be hung!' The Roman Catholics were so glad to hear that, that ten thousand extra copies have been sold. Among those who bought those papers was a friend of yours, called Terrien, who went to his wife and told her that you were to be condemned, and when the woman heard that, she said, 'It is too bad, for I know Mr. Chiniquy is not guilty.'

" ' How do you know that ?' said the husband. She answered : ' I was there when the priest Lebel made the plot, and promised to give his sister two eighties of good land if she would swear a false oath—and accuse him of a crime which that woman said he had not even thought of with her.'

" ' If it be so,' said Terrien, ' we cannot allow Mr. Chiniquy to be condemned. Come with me to Urbana.'

" But that woman being quite unwell, said to her husband, ' You know well I cannot go; but Miss Philomene Moffat was with me then. She knows every particular of that wicked plot as well as I do. She is well: go and take her to Urbana. There is no doubt that her testimony will prevent the condemnation of Mr. Chiniquy. Narcisse Terrien started immediately : and when you were praying God to come to your help, He was sending your deliverer at the full speed of the railroad cars. Miss Moffat has just given me the details of that diabolical plot. I have advised her not to show herself before the Court is opened. I will, then, send for her, and when she will have given, under oath, before the Court, the details she has just given me, I pity Spink with his perjured priests. As I told you, I would not be surprised if they were lynched: for there is a terrible excitement in town among many people, who from the beginning suspect that the priests have perjured themselves to destroy you. Now your suit is gained, and, to-morrow, you will have the greatest triumph a man ever got over his confounded foes. But you are in need of rest as well as myself. Good bye." After thanking God for that marvellous deliverance, I went to bed and took the needed rest.

But what was the priest Lebel doing in that very moment? Unable to sleep after the awful perjury he had just made, he had watched the arrival of the trains from Chicago with an anxious mind; for he was aware, through the confessions he had heard, that there were two persons in that city who knew his plot and his false oath; and though he had the promises from them that they would never reveal it to anybody, he was not without some fearful apprehension that I might, by some way or other, become acquainted with his abominable conspiracy. Not long after the arrival of the trains from Chicago, he came down from his room to see in the book where travellers register their names, if there were any new comers from Chicago, and what was his dismay when he saw the first name entered was "*Philomene Moffat!*" That very name, Philomene Moffat, who some time before, had gone to confess to him that she had heard the whole plot from his own lips, when he had promised 160 acres of land to persuade his sister to perjure herself in order to destroy me. A deadly presentiment chilled the blood in his veins! "Would it be possible that this girl is here to reveal and prove my perjury before the world?"

He immediately sent for her, when she was just coming from meeting Mr. Lincoln.

"Miss Philomene Moffat here!" he exclaimed, when he saw her. "What are you coming here for this night?" he said.

"You will know it, sir, to-morrow morning," she answered.

"Ah! wretched girl! you come to destroy me?" he exclaimed.

She replied: "I do not come to destroy you, for you are already destroyed. Mr. Lincoln knows everything."

"Oh! my God! my God!" he exclaimed, striking his forehead with his hands. Then taking a big bundle of bank-notes from his pocket-book, he said: "Here are one hundred dollars for you if you take the morning train and go back to Chicago."

"If you would offer me as much gold as this house could contain, I would not go," she replied.

He then left her abruptly, ran to the sleeping-room of Spink, and told him: "Withdraw your suit against Chiniquy; we are lost; he knows all." Without losing a moment, he went to the sleeping-room of his co-priest, and told him: "Make haste—dress yourself and let us take the train; we have no business here: Chiniquy knows all our secrets."

When the hour of opening the court came, there was an immense crowd, not only inside, but outside its walls. Mr. Spink, pale as a man condemned to death, rose before the Judge and said : "Please the court, allow me to withdraw my prosecution against Mr. Chiniquy. I am now persuaded that he is not guilty of the faults brought against him before this tribunal."

Abraham Lincoln, having accepted that reparation in my name, made a short, but one of the most admirable speeches I have ever heard, on the cruel injustices I had suffered from my merciless persecutors, and denounced the rascality of the priests who had perjured themselves with such terrible colours, that it had been very wise on their part to fly away and disappear before the opening of the court, for the whole city was ransacked for them by hundreds, who blamed me for forgiving them and refusing to have my revenge for the wrong they had done me. But I really thought that my enemies were sufficiently punished by the awful public disclosures of their infernal plot. It seemed that the dear Saviour, who had so visibly protected me, was to be obeyed, when He was whispering in my soul, "Forgive them and love them as thyself."

Was not Spink sufficiently punished by the complete ruin which was brought upon him by the loss of the suit? For having gone to Bishop O'Regan to be indemnified for the enormous expenses of such a long prosecution, at such a distance, the bishop coldly answered him : "I had promised to indemnify if you would put Chiniquy down, as you promised me. But as it is Chiniquy who has put you down, I have not a cent to give you."

Abraham Lincoln had not only defended me with the zeal and talent of the ablest lawyer I have ever known, but as the most devoted and noblest friend I ever had. After giving more than a year of his precious time to my defence, when he had pleaded, during two long sessions of the Court of Urbana, without receiving a cent from me, I considered that I was owing him a great sum of money. My two other lawyers, who had not done the half of his work, asked me a thousand dollars each, and I had not thought that too much. After thanking him for the inappreciable services he had rendered me, I requested him to show me his bill, assuring him that, though I would not be able to pay the whole cash, I would pay him to the last cent, if he had the kindness to wait a little for the balance.

He answered me with a smile and an air of inimitable kindness, which was peculiar to him : "My dear Mr. Chiniquy, I feel proud and honoured to have been called to defend you. But I have done it less as a lawyer than as a friend. The money I should receive from you would take away the pleasure I feel at having fought your battle. Your case is unique in my whole practice. I have never met a man so cruelly persecuted as you have been, and who deserves it so little.

Your enemies are devils incarnate. The plot they had concocted against you is the most hellish one I ever knew. But the way you have been saved from their hands, the appearance of that young and intelligent Miss Moffat, who was really sent by God in the very hour of need, when, I confess it again, I thought everything was nearly lost, is one of the most extraordinary occurrences I ever saw. It makes me remember what I have too often forgotten, and what my mother often told me when young—that our God is a prayer-hearing God. This good thought, sown into my young heart by that dear mother's hand, was just in my mind when I told you, ' Go and pray, God alone can save you.' But I confess to you that I had not faith enough to believe that your prayer would be so quickly and so marvellously answered by the sudden appearance of that interesting young lady, last night. Now let us speak of what you owe me. Well!—Well!— how much do you owe me? You owe me nothing! for I suppose you are quite ruined. The expenses of such a suit, I know, must be enormous. Your enemies want to ruin you. Will I help them to finish your ruin, when I hope I have the right to be put among the most sincere and devoted of your friends ? "

"You are right," I answered him; "you are the most devoted and noblest friend God ever gave me, and I am nearly ruined by my enemies. But you are the father of a pretty large family; you must support them. Your travelling expenses in coming twice here for me from Springfield; your hotel bills during the two terms you have defended me, must be very considerable. It is not just that you should receive nothing in return for such work and expenses."

"Well! well!" he answered, "I will give you a promissory note which you will sign." Taking then a small piece of paper, he wrote:

Urbana, May 23—1857

Dear A Lincoln

fifty dollars,

for value received—

C Chiniquy

He handed me the note, saying, " Can you sign that ? "

After reading it, I said, " Dear Mr. Lincoln, this is a joke. It is not possible that you ask only fifty dollars for services which are worth at least two thousand dollars."

He then tapped me with the right hand on the shoulders and said : " Sign that; it is enough. I will pinch some rich men for that, and make them pay the rest of the bill," and he laughed outright.

When Abraham Lincoln was writing the due-bill, the relaxation of the great strain upon my mind, and the great kindness of my bene-factor and defender in charging me so little for such a service, and the terrible presentiment that he would pay with his life what he had done for me caused me to break into sobs and tears.

As Mr. Lincoln had finished writing the due-bill, he turned round to me, and said, " Father Chiniquy, what are you crying for ? Ought you not to be the most happy man alive ? you have beaten your enemies and gained the most glorious victory, and you will come out of all your troubles in triumph."

" Dear Mr. Lincoln," I answered, " allow me to tell you that the joy I should naturally feel for such a victory is destroyed in my mind by the fear of what it may cost you. There were then in the crowd not less than ten or twelve Jesuits from Chicago and St. Louis, who came to hear my sentence of condemnation to the penitentiary. But it was on their heads that you have brought the thunders of heaven and earth ! nothing can be compared to the expression of their rage against you, when you not only wrenched me from their cruel hands, but you were making the walls of the court-house tremble under the awful and superhumanly eloquent denunciation of their infamy, diabolical malice, and total want of Christian and human principle, in the plot they had formed for my destruction. What troubles my soul just now and draws my tears, is that it seems to me that I have read your sentence of death in their fiendish eyes. How many other noble victims have already fallen at their feet !

He tried to divert my mind, at first, with a joke, " Sign this," said he, " it will be my warrant of death."

But after I had signed, he became more solemn, and said, " I know that Jesuits never forget nor forsake. But man must not care how and where he dies, provided he dies at the post of honour and duty," and he left me.

Here is the sworn declaration of Miss Philomene Moffat, now Mrs. Philomene Schwartz.

" STATE OF ILLINOIS,   } ss.
      Cook County,   }

" Philomene Schwartz, being first duly sworn, deposes and says : That she is of the age of forty-three years, and resides at 484, Milwaukee Avenue, Chicago ; that her maiden name was Philomene Moffat; that she knew Father Lebel, the Roman Catholic priest of the French Catholics of Chicago during his lifetime, and knows Rev. Father Chiniquy; that about the month of May, A.D. 1854, in company with Miss Eugenia Bossey, the housekeeper of her uncle, the Rev. Mr. Lebel, who was then living at the parsonage on Clark Street, Chicago, while we were sitting in the room of Miss Bossey, the Rev. Mr. Lebel was talking with his sister, Mrs. Bossey, in the adjoining room, not suspecting that we were there hearing his conversation, through the door, which was partly opened; though we could neither see him nor his sister, we heard every word of what they said together, the substance of which is as follows—Rev. Mr. Lebel said in substance, to Mrs. Bossey, his sister:

"'You know that Mr. Chiniquy is a dangerous man, and he is my enemy, having already persuaded several of my congregation to settle in his colony. You must help me to put him down, by accusing him of having tried to do a criminal action with you.'

"Madame Bossey answered: 'I cannot say such a thing against Mr. Chiniquy, when I know it is absolutely false.'

"Rev. Mr. Lebel replied: 'If you refuse to comply with my request, I will not give you the one hundred and sixty acres of land I intended to give you; you will live and die poor.'

"Madame Bossey answered: 'I prefer never to have that land, and I like better to live and die poor, than to perjure myself to please you.'

"The Rev. Mr. Lebel, several times, urged his sister, Mrs. Bossey, to comply with his desires, but she refused. At last, weeping and crying, she said: 'I prefer never to have an inch of land than to damn my soul for swearing to a falsehood.'

"The Rev. Mr. Lebel then said:

"'Mr. Chiniquy will destroy our holy religion and our people if we do not destroy him. If you think the swearing I ask you to do is a sin, you will come to confess to me, and I will pardon it in the absolution I will give you.'

"'Have you the power to forgive a false oath?' replied Mrs. Bossey to her brother, the priest.

"'Yes,' he answered, 'I have that power; for Christ has said to all His priests, "What you shall bind on earth shall be bound in heaven, and what you shall loose on earth shall be loosed in heaven."'

"Mrs. Bossey then said: 'If you promise that you will forgive that false oath, and if you give me the one hundred and sixty acres of land you promised, I will do what you want.'

"The Rev. Mr. Lebel then said: 'All right!' I could not hear any more of that conversation, for in that instant Miss Eugenia Bossey, who had kept still and silent with us, made some noise and shut the door.

"Affiant further states: That, some time later, I went to confess to Rev. Mr. Lebel, and I told him that I had lost confidence in him. He asked me why? I answered: 'I lost my confidence in you since I heard your conversation with your sister, when you tried to persuade her to perjure herself in order to destroy Father Chiniquy.

"Affiant further says: That in the month of October, A.D. 1856, the Rev. Mr. Chiniquy had to defend himself, before the civil and criminal court of Urbana, Illinois, in an action brought against him by Peter Spink; some one wrote from Urbana to a paper of Chicago, that Father Chiniquy was probably to be condemned. The paper which published that letter was much read by the Roman Catholics, who were glad to hear that that priest was to be punished. Among those who read that paper was Narcisse Terrien. He had lately been married to Miss Sara Chaussey, who told him that Father Chiniquy was innocent; that she was present with me when Rev. Lebel prepared the plot with his sister, Mrs. Bossey, had promised her a large piece of land if she would swear falsely against Father Chiniquy. Mr. Narcisse Terrien wanted to go with his wife to the help of Father Chiniquy, but she was unwel and could not go. He came to ask me if I remembered well the conversation of Rev. Mr. Lebel, and if I would consent to go to Urbana to expose the whole plot before the court, and I consented.

"We started that same evening for Urbana, where we arrived late at night. I immediately met Mr. Abraham Lincoln, one of the lawyers of Father Chiniquy, and told him all that I knew about the plot.

"That very same night the Rev. Mr. Lebel, having seen my name on the hotel register, came to me much excited and troubled, and said, ' Philomene, what are you here for ?'

"I answered him : ' I cannot exactly tell you that ; but you will probably know it to-morrow at the court-house ?'

" ' Oh, wretched girl !' he exclaimed, ' you have come to destroy me.'

" ' I do not come to destroy you,' I replied, ' for you are already destroyed !'

"Then drawing from his porte-monnaie-book a big bundle of bank-notes, which he said was worth one hundred dollars, he said : ' I will give you all this money if you will leave by the morning train and go back to Chicago.'

"I answered him ; ' Though you would offer me as much gold as this room can contain, I cannot do what you ask.'

"He then seemed exceedingly distressed, and he disappeared. The next morning Peter Spink requested the court to allow him to withdraw his accusations against Father Chiniquy, and stop his prosecutions, having, he said, found out that he, Father Chiniquy, was innocent of the things brought against him, and his request was granted. Then the innocence and honesty of Father Chiniquy was acknowledged by the court after it had been proclaimed by Abraham Lincoln, who was afterwards elected President of the United States.

" (Signed)   PHILOMENE SCHWARTZ.

"I, Stephen R. Moore, a Notary Public in the County of Kankakee, in the State of Illinois, and duly authorized by law to administer oaths, do hereby certify that, on this 21st day of October, A.D. 1881, Philomene Schwartz personally appeared before me, and made oath that the above affidavit by her subscribed is true, as therein stated. In witness whereto, I have hereunto set my hand and notarial seal.

"STEPHEN R. MOORE,
"Notary Public."

CHAPTER LIX.

WHEN it became evident, in 1851, that my plan of forming a grand colony of Roman Catholic French-speaking people on the prairies of Illinois was to be a success, D'Arcy McGee, then editor of *The Freeman's Journal*, official Journal of the Bishop of New York, wrote me to know my views, and immediately determined to put himself at the head of a similar enterprise in behalf of the Irish Roman Catholics. He published several able articles to show that the Irish people, with very few exceptions, were demoralized, degraded and kept poor, around their groggeries, and showed how they would thrive, become respectable and rich, if they could be induced to exchange their grog shops for the fertile lands of the west. Through his influence, a large assembly, principally composed of priests, to which I was invited, met at Buffalo, in the spring of 1852. But what was his disappointment, when he saw that the greatest part of those priests were sent by the Bishops of the United States to oppose and defeat his plans!

He vainly spoke with a burning eloquence for his pet scheme. The majority coldly answered him: "We are determined, like you, to take possession of the United States and rule them; but we cannot do that without acting secretly and with the utmost wisdom. If our plans are known, they will surely be defeated. What does a skilful general do when he wants to conquer a country? Does he scatter his soldiers over the farm lands, and spend their energy and power in ploughing the fields and sowing grain? No! he keeps them well united around his banners, and marches at their head, to the conquest of the strongholds, the rich and powerful cities. The farming countries then submit and become the price of his victory without moving a finger to subdue them. So it is with us. Silently and patiently, we must mass our Roman Catholics in the great cities of the United States, remembering that the vote of a poor journeyman, though he be covered with rags, has as much weight in the scale of power as the millionaire Astor, and that if we have two votes against his one, he will become as powerless as an oyster. Let us then multiply our votes; let us call our poor but faithful Irish Catholics from every corner of the world, and gather them into the very hearts of those proud citadels which the Yankees are so rapidly building under the names of Washington, New York, Boston, Chicago, Buffalo, Albany, Troy, Cincinnati, etc. Under the shadows of those great cities, the Americans consider themselves a giant and unconquerable race. They look upon the poor Irish Catholic people with supreme contempt, as only fit to dig their canals, sweep their streets and work in their kitchens. Let no one awake those sleeping lions, to-day. Let us pray God that they may sleep and dream their sweet dreams, a few years more. How sad will their awakening be, when with our out-numbering votes, we will turn them for ever, from every position of honour, power and profit! What will those hypocritical and godless sons and daughters of the fanatical Pilgrim Fathers say, when not a single judge, not a single teacher, not a single policeman, will be elected if he be not a devoted Irish Roman Catholic? What will those so-called giants think of their matchless shrewdness and ability, when not a single Senator or member of Congress will be chosen, if he be not submitted to our holy father the Pope! What a sad figure those Protestant Yankees will cut when we will not only elect the President, but fill and command the armies, man the navies and hold the keys of the public treasury? It will then be time for our faithful

Irish people to give up their grog shops, in order to become the judges and governors of the land. Then, our poor and humble mechanics will leave their damp ditches and muddy streets, to rule the cities in all their departments, from the stately mansion of Mayor to the more humble, though not less noble position of teacher.

"Then, yes! then, we will rule the United States, and lay them at the feet of the Vicar of Jesus Christ, that he may put an end to their godless system of education, and impious laws of liberty of conscience which are an insult to God and man!"

D'Arcy McGee was left almost alone when the votes were taken. From that, the Catholic priests, with the most admirable ability and success, have gathered their Irish legions into the great cities of the United States, and the American people must be very blind indeed, if they do not see that if they do nothing to prevent it, the day is very near when the Jesuits will rule their country, from the magnificent White House at Washington to the humblest civil and military department of this vast Republic. They are already the masters of New York, Baltimore, Chicago, St. Paul, New Orleans, Mobile, Savannah, Cincinnati, Albany, Troy, Milwaukee, St. Louis, San Francisco, etc. Yes! San Francisco, the rich, the great queen of the Pacific, is in the hands of the Jesuits!

From the very first days of the discovery of the gold mines of California, the Jesuits had the hopes of becoming masters of those inexhaustible treasures, and they secretly laid their plans, with the most profound ability and success. They saw, at once, that the great majority of the lucky miners, of every creed and nation, were going back home as soon as they had enough to secure an honourable competence to their families. It became then evident, that of those multitudes which the thirst of gold had brought from every corner of the world, not one out of fifty would fix their homes in San Francisco. The Jesuits saw at a glance that if they could persuade the Irish Catholics to settle and remain there, they would soon be the masters and rulers of that golden city whose future is so bright and so great! And that scheme, worked day and night, with the utmost perseverance, has been crowned with perfect success.

The consequence is, that while you find only a few Americans, Germans, Scotch, and English millionaires in San Francisco, you find more than fifty Catholic Irish millionaires in that city. Its richest bank (Nevada Bank) is in their hands, and so are all the street railways. The principal offices of the city are filled with Irish Roman Catholics. Almost all the police are composed of the same class, as well as the volunteer military associations. Their compact unity, in the hands of the Jesuits, with their enormous wealth, make them almost supreme masters of the mines of California and Nevada.

When one knows the absolute, abject submission of the Irish Roman Catholics, rich or poor, to their priests, how the mind, the soul, the will, the conscience, are firmly and irrevocably tied to the feet of their priests, he can easily understand that the Jesuits of the United States form one of the richest and most powerful corporations the world ever saw.   It is well known that those fifty Catholic millionaires, with their myriads of employés are, through their wives, and by themselves, continually at the feet of the Jesuits, who swim in a golden sea.   No one, if he be not a Roman Catholic, or one of those so-called Protestants who give their daughters to the nuns, and their sons to the Jesuits to be educated, has much hopes, where the Jesuits rule, of having a lucrative office in the United States to-day.

The Americans, with few exceptions, do not pay any attention to the dark cloud which is rising at their horizon, from Rome.   Though that cloud is filled with rivers of tears and blood, they let it grow and rise without even caring how they will escape from the impending hurricane.

It is to San Francisco that you must go to have an idea of the number of secret and powerful organizations with which the Church of Rome prepares herself for the impending conflict, through which she hopes to destroy the schools, and every vestige of human rights and liberties in the United States.

In order to more easily drill the Roman Catholics and prepare them for the irrepressible struggle, the Jesuits have organized them into a great number of secret societies, the principal of which are: Ancient Order of Hibernians, Irish American Society, Knights of St. Patrick, St. Patrick's Cadets, St. Patrick Mutual Alliance, Apostles of Liberty, Benevolent Sons of the Émerald Isle, Knights of St. Peter, Knights of the Red Branch, Knights of the Columskill, The Secret Heart, etc., etc.

Almost all these secret associations are military ones.   They have their headquarters at San Francisco, but their rank and file are scattered all over the United States.   They number seven hundred thousand soldiers, who, under the name of U.S. Volunteer Militia, are officered by some of the most skilful generals and officers of this Republic.

Another fact, to which the American Protestants do not sufficiently pay attention, is that the Jesuits have been shrewd enough to have a vast majority of Roman Catholic generals and officers to command the army and man the navy of the United States.

Rome is in constant conspiracy against the rights and liberties of man all over the world ; but she is particularly so in the United States.

Long before I was ordained a priest, I knew that my church was the most implacable enemy of this Republic. My professors of philosophy, history, and theology had been unanimous in telling me that the principles and laws of the Church of Rome were absolutely antagonistic to the laws and principles which are the foundation-stones of the Constitution of the United States.

1st. The most sacred principle of the United States Constitution is the equality of every citizen before the law. But the fundamental principle of the Church of Rome is the denial of that equality.

2nd. Liberty of conscience is proclaimed by the United States, a most sacred principle which every citizen must uphold, even at the price of his blood. But liberty of conscience is declared by all the Popes and Councils of Rome, a most godless, unholy, and diabolical thing, which every good Catholic must abhor and destroy at any cost.

3rd. The American Constitution assures the absolute independence of the civil from the ecclesiastical or church power ; but the Church of Rome declares, through all her Pontiffs and Councils, that such independence is an impiety and a revolt against God.

4th. The American Constitution leaves every man free to serve God according to the dictates of his conscience ; but the Church of Rome declares that no man has ever had such a right, and that the Pope alone can know and say what man must believe and do.

5th. The Constitution of the United States denies the right in any body to punish any other for differing from him in religion. But the Church of Rome says that she has a right to punish with the confiscation of their goods, or the penalty of death, those who differ in faith from the Pope.

6th. The United States have established schools all over their immense territories, where they invite the people to send their children, that they may cultivate their intelligence and become good and useful citizens. But the Church of Rome has publicly cursed all those schools, and forbidden their children to attend them, under pain of excommunication in this world and damnation in the next.

7th. The Constitution of the United States is based on the principle that the people are the primary source of all civil power. But hundreds of times, the Church of Rome has proclaimed that this principle is impious and heretical. She says that "all government must rest upon the foundation of the Catholic faith ; with the Pope alone as the legitimate and infallible source and interpreter of the law."

I could cite many other things, proving that the Church of Rome is an absolute and irreconcilable enemy of the United States ; but it would be too long. These are sufficient to show to the American people that Rome is a viper, which they feed and press upon their bosom. Sooner or later that viper will bite to death and kill this Republic. This was foretold by Lafayette, and is now promulgated by the greatest thinkers of our time.

The greatest inventor, or rather the immortal father of electric telegraphy, Samuel Morse, found it out when in Rome, and published it in 1834, in his remarkable work, "Conspiracies against the Liberties of the United States." The learned Dr. S. Ireneus Prime, in his life of Professor Morse, says, "When Mr. Morse was in Italy, he became acquainted with several ecclesiastics of the Church of Rome, and he was led to believe, from what he learned from them, that a political conspiracy, under the cloak of a religious mission, was formed against the United States. When he came to Paris and enjoyed the confidence and friendship of Lafayette, he stated his convictions to the General, who fully concurred with him in the reality of such a conspiracy."

That great statesman and patriot, the late Richard W. Thompson, Secretary of the Navy, in his admirable work, " The Papacy and the Civil Power," says, " Nothing is plainer than that, if the principles of the Church of Rome prevail here, our constitution would necessarily fall. The two cannot exist together. They are in open and direct antagonism with the fundamental theory of our government and of all popular government everywhere."

The eloquent Spanish orator, Castelar, speaking of his own Church of Rome, said, in 1869 : " There is not a single progressive principle that has not been cursed by the Catholic Church. This is true of England and Germany, as well as all Catholic countries. The Church cursed the French Revolution, the Belgian Constitution, and the Italian Independence. Not a constitution has been born, not a step of progress made, not a solitary reform effected, which has not been under the terrific anathemas of the Church."

But why ask the testimony of Protestants or Liberals to warn the American people against that conspiracy, when we have the public testimony of all the bishops and priests to prove it? With the most daring impudence, the Church of Rome, through her leading men, is boasting of her stern determination to destroy all the rights and privileges which have cost so much blood to this American people. Let the Americans, who have eyes to see and intelligence to understand, read the following unimpeachable documents, and judge for themselves of what will become of this country, if Rome is allowed to grow strong enough to execute her threats.

" The church is of necessity intolerant. Heresy, she endures when and where she must, but she hates it, and directs all her energies to destroy it."

" If Catholics ever gain a sufficient numerical majority in this country, religious freedom is at an end. So our enemies say, so we believe."*

"No man has a right to choose his religion. Catholicism is the most intolerant of creeds. It is intolerance itself. We might as rationally maintain that two and two does not make four as the theory of Religious Liberty. Its impiety is only equalled by its absurdity." †

"The church is instituted, as every Catholic who understands his religion believes, to guard and defend the right of God against any and every enemy, at all times, in all places. She, therefore, does not, and cannot accept, or in any degree favour, liberty in the Protestant sense of liberty." ‡

"The Catholic Church is the medium and channel through which the will of God is expressed. While the State has rights, she has them only in virtue and by permission of the Superior Authority, and that authority can be expressed only through the Church."§

"Protestantism has not, and never can have, any right where Catholicity has triumphed. Therefore we lose the breath we expend in declaiming against bigotry and intolerance and in favour of Religious Liberty, or the right of any man to be of any religion as best pleases him."‖

"Religious Liberty is merely endured until the opposite can be carried into effect without peril to the Catholic Church."—Rt. Rev. O'Connor, Bishop of Pittsburgh.

"The Catholic Church numbers one-third the American population ; and if its membership shall increase for the next thirty years as it has the thirty years past, in 1900 Rome will have a majority, and be bound to take this country and keep it. There is, ere long, to be a state religion in this country, and that state religion is to be the Roman Catholic.

"1st. The Roman Catholic is to wield his vote for the purpose of securing Catholic ascendency in this country.

"2nd. All legislation must be governed by the will of God, unerringly indicated by the Pope.

"3rd. Education must be controlled by Catholic authorities, and under education the opinions of the individual and the utterances of the press are included, and many opinions are to be forbidden by the secular arm, under the authority of the Church, even to war and bloodshed."¶

---

* *The Shepherd of the Valley*, official journal of the Bishop of St. Louis, Nov. 23, 1851.

† *New York Freeman*, official journal of Bishop Hughes, Jan. 26, 1852.

‡ *Catholic World*, April, 1870.   § *Catholic World*, July 1870.

‖ *Catholic Review*, June, 1865.   ¶ Father Hecker, *Catholic World*, July, 1870.

" It was proposed that all religious persuasions should be free and their worship publicly exercised. But we have rejected this article as contrary to the canons and councils of the Catholic Church."*

Every one knows that one of the first and most solemn acts of the present Pope, Leo XIII., was to order that the theology of St. Thomas Aquinas should be taught in all the colleges, seminaries, and universities of the Church of Rome throughout the whole world, as the most accurate teaching of the doctrines of his church. Well, on the 30th December, 1880, I forced the Rt. Rev. Foley, Bishop of Chicago, to translate from Latin into English, before the court of Kankakee, and to swear that the following law was among those promulgated by St. Thomas as one of the present and unchangeable laws of the Church of Rome :

" Though heretics must not be tolerated because they deserve it, we must bear with them, till, by a second admonition, they may be brought back to the faith of the church. But those who, after a second admonition, remain obstinate in their errors, must not only be excommunicated, but they must be delivered to the secular power to be exterminated."†

After the bishop had sworn that this was the true doctrine of the Church of Rome expressed by St. Thomas, and taught in all the colleges, seminaries, and universities of the Church of Rome, I forced him to declare, under oath, that he, and every priest of Rome, once a year, under pain of eternal damnation, is obliged to say, in the presence of God, in his Breviarum (his official prayer-book), that that doctrine was so good and holy, that every word of it has been inspired by the Holy Ghost to St. Thomas.

The same Bishop Foley was again forced by me, before the same court of Kankakee, to translate from Latin into English, the following decree of the Council of Lateran, and to acknowledge, under oath, that it was as much the law of the Church of Rome to-day as on the day it was passed in the year 1215.

" We excommunicate and anathematize every heresy that exalts itself against the holy orthodox and Catholic faith, condemning all heretics, by whatever name they may be known, for though their faces differ, they are tied together by their tails. Such as are condemned are to be delivered over to the existing secular powers to receive due punishment. If laymen, their goods must be confiscated. If priests, they shall be degraded from their respective orders, and their property applied to the church in which they officiated. Secular powers of all ranks and degrees are to be warned, induced, and, if necessary, compelled by ecclesiastical censure, to swear that they will exert them-

* Pope Pius VII., *Encyclical*, 1808.
† St. Thomas Aquinas, *Summa Theologia*, Vol. iv. p. 90.

selves to the utmost in the defence of the faith, and extirpate all heretics denounced by the church, who shall be found in their territories. And whenever any person shall assume government, whether it be spiritual or temporal, he shall be bound to abide by this decree.

"If any temporal lord, after having been admonished and required by the church, shall neglect to clear his territory of heretical depravity, the Metropolitan and Bishop of the Province, shall unite in excommunicating him. Should he remain contumacious a whole year, the fact shall be signified to the Supreme Pontiff, who will declare his vassals released from their allegiance from that time, and will bestow his territory on Catholics, to be occupied by them, on condition of exterminating the heretics and preserving the said territory in the faith.*

"Catholics who shall assume the cross for the extermination of heretics, shall enjoy the same indulgence, and be protected by the same privileges as are granted to those who go to the help of the Holy Land. We decree further that all those who have dealings with heretics, and especially such as receive, defend and encourage them, shall be excommunicated. He shall not be eligible to any public officer. He shall not be admitted as a witness. He shall neither have the power to bequeath his property by will, nor succeed to an inheritance. He shall not bring any action against any person, but any one can bring action against him. Should he be a judge, his decision shall have no force, nor shall any cause be brought before him. Should he be an advocate, he shall not be allowed to plead. Should he be a lawyer, no instruments made by him shall be held valid, but shall be condemned with their authors."

Cardinal Manning, speaking in the name of the Pope, said: "I acknowledge no civil power; I am the subject of no prince; and I claim more than this. I claim to be the supreme judge and director of the consciences of men—of the peasants that till the fields, and of the prince that sits upon the throne; of the household that lives in the shade of privacy, and the legislator that makes laws for kingdoms —I am sole, last, supreme judge of what is right and wrong. Moreover, we declare, affirm, define, and pronounce it to be necessary to salvation to every human creature, to be subject to the Roman Pontiff!!"†

---

* "Et si necesse fuerit, per censuram ecclesiasticam compellantur sæculares potestates, quibuscumque fungantur officiis—quod de terris suæ juridictioni subjectis universos hæreticos et Ecclesia denotatos bona fide pro viribus exterminare studebunt. . . . Et si satisfacere contempserit infra annum, significetur hoc Summo Pontifici; ut ex tunc ipse vasallos ab ejus fidelitate denunciet absolutos, et terram exponat Catholicis occupandam, qui eam, exterminatis hæreticis, sine ulla contradictione possideant, et in fidei puritate conservent."—(Concil. Labb., tom. xi. col. 148; Concil. Later. IV. can. iii., De Hæreticis. Fol. Paris, 1671.)

† Tablet, Oct. 9, 1864.

" Undoubtedly it is the intention of the Pope to possess this country. In this intention he is aided by the Jesuits, and all the Catholic prelates and priests."*

" For our own part, we take this opportunity to express our hearty delight at the suppression of the Protestant chapel in Rome. This may be thought intolerant; but when, we ask, did we profess to be tolerant of Protestantism, or to favour the question that Protestantism ought to be tolerated. On the contrary, we hate Protestantism. We detest it with our whole heart and soul, and we pray our aversion for it may never decrease."†

" No good government can exist without religion, and there can be no religion without an Inquisition, which is wisely designed for the promotion and protection of the true faith." ‡

" The Pope has the right to pronounce sentence of deposition against any sovereign when required by the good of the Spiritual Order." §

" The power of the church exercised over sovereigns in the middle ages was not a usurpation, was not derived from the concessions of princes or the consent of the people, but was and is held by divine right, and whoso resists it rebels against the King of kings and Lord of lords." ‖

The Council of Constance, held in 1414, declared, " That any person who has promised security to heretics shall not be obliged to keep his promise, by whatever he may be engaged."

It is, in consequence of that principle that *no faith must be kept with heretics*, that John Huss was publicly burned on the scaffold, the 6th July, 1415, in the city of Constance, though he had a safe passport from the Emperor.

" Negroes have no rights which the white man is bound to respect." ¶

" If the liberties of the American people are ever destroyed, they will fall by the hands of the Catholic clergy."—*Lafayette.*

" If your son or daughter is attending a State School, you are violating your duty as a Catholic parent, and conducing to the ever-lasting anguish and despair of your child. Take him away. Take him away if you do not wish your deathbed to be tormented with the spectre of a soul which God has given you as a secret trust, surren-dered to the great enemy of mankind. Take him away, rather than incur the wrath of his God, and the loss of his soul." **

---

* *Brownson's Review,* May, 1864.
† *Pittsburg Catholic Visitor,* July, 1848, official journal of the Bishop.
‡ *Boston Pilot,* official journal of the Bishop.
§ *Brownson's Review,* 1849.   ‖ *Brownson's Review,* June 1851.
¶ *Roman Catholic Chief-Justice Tany,* in his Dred Scot Decision.
** *Western Tablet,* official paper of the Bishop of Chicago.

All the echoes of the United States, are still repeating the same denunciations against our public schools made by Mgr. Capel, a prelate attached to the household of the Pope. That Roman Catholic dignitary has not only passed again the sentence of death against the schools of the United States, but he has warned the Americans that the time is not far away when the Roman Catholics, at the order of the Pope, will refuse to pay their school tax, and will send bullets to the breasts of the government agents, rather than pay it. "The order can come any day from Rome," said the prelate. "It will come as quickly as the click of the trigger, and it will be obeyed, of course, as coming from God Almighty Himself!"

The *Catholic Columbian*, edited under the immediate supervision of the Right Rev. Bishop of Columbus, Ohio, says : " Secular (government) schools, are unfit for Catholic children. Catholic parents cannot be allowed the sacraments, who choose to send their children to them, when they could make use of the Catholic schools."

" The absurd and erroneous doctrines, or ravings, in defence of liberty of conscience, are a most pestilential error, a pest of all others, to be dreaded in the State." *

" You should do all in your power to carry out the intentions of his holiness the Pope. Where you have the electoral franchise, give your votes to none but those who assist you in so holy a struggle."†

" Catholic votes should be cast solidly for the democracy at the next election. It is the only possible hope to break down the school system." ‡

" It is of faith that the Pope has the right of deposing heretical and rebel kings. Monarchs so deposed by the Pope are converted into notorious tyrants, and may be killed by the first who can reach them.

" If the public cause cannot meet with its defence in the death of a tyrant, it is lawful for the first who arrives, to assassinate him." §

" See, sir, from this chamber, I govern, not only to Paris, but to China ; not only to China, but to all the world, without anyone knowing how I do it." ‖

" A man who has been excommunicated by the Pope may be killed anywhere, as Escobar and Deaux teach, because the Pope has an indirect jurisdiction over the whole world, even in temporal things, as all the Catholics maintain, and as Suarez proves against the King of England." ¶

The Roman Catholic historian of the Jesuits, Crétineau Joly, in his

---

* *Encyclical Letters of Pope Pius IX.*, August 15, 1854.
† *Daniel O'Connell.*   ‡ *Toledo Catholic Review.*
§ Suarez, *Defensio Fidei ;* Book VI. c. 4, Nos. 13, 14.
‖ *Tamburini ;* General of the Jesuits.
¶ Busembaum.—Lacroix, *Theologia Moralis*, 1757.

Vol. II., page 435, approvingly says : " Father Guivard, writing about Henry IV., King of France, says : 'If he cannot be deposed, let us make war; and if we cannot make war, let him be killed.' "

The great Roman Catholic theologian, Dens, puts to himself the question : " Are heretics justly punished with death ? "   He answers, " St. Thomas says : Yes ! 2.2. Question 11, Art. 3.   Because forgers of money, or other disturbers of the State, are justly punished with death; therefore, all heretics who are forgers of faith and, as experience testifies, grievously disturb the State.   This is confirmed, because God, in the Old Testament, ordered the false prophets to be slain, and in Deuteronomy it is decreed that if any one will act proudly, and will not obey the commands of the priests, let him be put to death.   The same is proved from the condemnation of the 14th Article of John Huss in the Council of Constance." *

" That we may in all things attain the truth.   That we may not err in anything, we ought ever to hold, as a fixed principle, that what I see white, I believe to be black, if the superior authorities of the church define it to be so." †

" As for holy obedience, this virtue must be perfect in every point, in execution, in will, in intellect, doing which is enjoined with all celerity, spiritual joy, and perseverance ; persuading ourselves that everything is just, suppressing every repugnant thought and judgment of one's own, in a certain obedience, should be moved and directed under Divine Providence, by his superior, just as if he were a corpse (*Perinde acsi cadaver esset*) which allows itself to be moved and led in every direction." ‡

" If the Holy Church so requires, let us sacrifice our own opinions, our knowledge, our intelligence, the splendid dreams of our imagination and the sublime attainments of human understanding." §

" No more cunning plot was ever devised against the intelligence, the freedom, the happiness and virtue of mankind than Romanism." ||

The principle and most efficacious means of practising obedience due to superiors, and of rendering it meritorious before God, is to consider that, in obeying them, we obey God Himself, and that by

---

* " An hæretici recte puniuntur morte ?   II. Respondet S. Thomas 2. 2. quæst 11. art. 3, in ' Corp.' affirmative : quid falsarii pecuniæ, vel alii Rempublicam turbantes, juste morte puniuntur : ergo etiam hæretici, qui sunt falsarii fidei, et, experientiâ teste, Rempublicam graviter perturbant.   Confirmatur ex eo quod Deus in veteri Lege jusserit occidi falsos Prophetas, et Deut. cap. 17, v. 12 statuatur, ut, ' qui superbierit, nolens obedire Sacerdotis imperio' . . . . . moriatur.   Vide etiam cap. 18.   Idem probatur ex condemnatione 14 Joan Hus. in Concilio Constantiensi."   (Dens, *Theologia Moralis*, tom. ii. n. 56 de pœnis criminis hæresis, p. 89.   Dublinii [R. Coyne] 1832.)

† *Spiritual Exercise*, by Ignatius Loyola, founder of the Jesuits.
‡ Ignatius Loyola, *Spiritual Exercise.*
§ Pope Gregory XVI., *Encyclical*, August 15th, 1832.
|| Gladstone, *Letter to Lord Aberdeen.*

despising their commands, we despise the authority of the Divine Master.

"When, thus, a Religious receives a precept from her prelate, superior, or confessor, she should immediately execute it, not only to please them, but principally to please God, whose will is known by their command.

"If, then, you receive a command from one who holds the place of God, you should observe it as if it came from God Himself. It may be added that there is more certainty of doing the will of God by obedience to our superiors than by obedience to Jesus Christ, should He appear in person and give His command.

"St. Philip used to say that the Religious shall be most certain of not having to render an account of the actions performed through obedience, for these, the superiors only, who command them, shall be accountable." *

"In the name and by the authority of Jesus Christ, the plentitude of which resides in His Vicar, the Pope, we declare that the earth is not the centre of the world, and that it moves with a diurnal motion, is absurd, philosophically false, and erroneous in faith." †

In consequence of that infallible decree of the infallible Pope, Galileo, in order to escape death, was obliged to fall on his knees and perjure himself, by signing the following declaration on the 22nd of June, 1663:

"I abjure, curse and detest the error and heresy of the motion of the earth around the sun."

In obedience to that decree, the two learned Jesuit astronomers, Lesueur and Jacquier, in Rome, only a few years ago, made the following declaration: "Newton assumes in his third book, the hypothesis of the earth moving round the sun. The proposition of that author could not be explained, except through the same hypothesis; we have, therefore, been forced to act a character not our own. But we declare our entire submission to the decrees of the supreme Pontiff of Rome against the motion of the earth." ‡

"A Catholic should never attach himself to any political party composed of heretics. No one who is truly, at heart, a thorough and complete Catholic, can give his entire adhesion to a Protestant leader; for in so doing, he divides his allegiance, which he owes entirely to the church." §

"Would he (the priest) be warranted in withholding any sacra-

---

* Saint Liguori, *The Nun Sanctified.*

† Decree of Pope Urban XIII. (signed) by Cardinals Felia, Guido, Desiderio, Antonio, Belligero, and Fabricius.

‡ *Newton's Principia*, by Fathers Lesueur and Jacquier, vol. iii., p. 450.

§ *Univers*, the official Catholic paper of the Bishops of France, March 28th, 1868.

ment of the church from a man by reason of his preferring one candidate to the other! Absolutely speaking, he would; because a priest is not only warranted, but bound to withhold, the scraments from a man who is disposed to commit a mortal sin!!"*

"Our business is to contrive:

"1st. That the Catholics be imbued with hatred for the heretics, whoever they may be, and that this hatred shall constantly increase, and bind them closely to each other.

"2nd. That it be, nevertheless, *dissembled,* so as not to transpire until the day when *it shall be appointed to break forth.*

"3rd. That this secret hate be combined with great activity in endeavouring to detach the faithful from every government inimical to us, and employ them, when they shall form a detached body, to strike deadly blows at heresy."†

Henry IV., King of France, after being wounded by an assassin sent by the Jesuits, said: "I am compelled to do one of these two things: Either recall the Jesuits, free them from the infamy and disgrace with which they are covered, or to expel them in a more absolute manner, and prevent them from approaching either my person or my kingdom.

"But, then, we will drive them to despair and to the resolution of attempting my life again, which would render it so miserable to me, being always under the apprehension of being murdered or poisoned. For these people have correspondence everywhere, and are so very skilful in disposing the minds of men to whatever they wish, that I think it would be better that I should be already dead."‡

"Let us bring all our skill to bear upon this part of our plan. Our chief concern must be to mould the people to our purposes. Doubtless, the first generation will not be wholly ours; but the second will nearly belong to us; and the third entirely."§

"The state, is, therefore, only an inferior court, bound to receive the law from the superior court (the church) and liable to have its decrees reversed on appeal."||

"The Jesuits are a *military organization,* not a religious order. Their chief is a general of an army, not the mere father abbot of a monastery. And the aim of this organization is: POWER. Power in its most despotic exercise. Absolute power, universal power, power to control the world by the volition of a single man. Jesuitism is the

---

* Bishop Vaughan's address to the Catholic Club at Salford, England, January 2nd, 1873.

† *Secret Plans of the Jesuits, revealed by Abbate Leon,* p. 127.

‡ *Sully's Memoirs,* tom. ii. chap. iii.   § *The Secret Plan,* pp. 127-128

|| *Brownson's Essays,* pp. 282-284.

most absolute of despotisms; and at the same time the greatest and the most enormous of abuses."*

"The general of the Jesuits insists on being master, sovereign, over the sovereign. Wherever the Jesuits are admitted they will be masters, cost what it may. Their society is by nature dictatorial, and therefore it is the irreconcilable enemy of all constituted authority. Every act, every crime, however atrocious, is a meritorious work, if committed for the interest of the Society of the Jesuits, or by the order of its general."†

In the allocution of September, 1851, Pope Pius IX. said:

"That he had taken that principle for basis: That the Catholic religion, with all its votes, ought to be exclusively dominant in such sort that every other worship shall be banished and interdicted!

"You ask if the Pope were lord of this land and you were in a minority, what he would do to you? That, we say, would entirely depend on circumstances. If it would benefit the cause of Catholicism, he would tolerate you; if expedient, he would imprison, banish you, probably he might even hang you. But be assured of one thing, he would never tolerate you for the sake of your glorious principles of civil and religious liberty."‡

Lord Acton, one of the Roman Catholic peers of England, reproaching her bloody and anti-social laws to his own church, wrote: "Pope Gregory VII. decided it was no murder to kill excommunicated persons. This rule was incorporated in the canon law. During the revision of the code, which took place in the 16th century, and which produced a whole volume of corrections, the passage was allowed to stand. It appears in every reprint of the *Corpus Juris*. It has been for 700 years, and continues to be, part of the ecclesiastical law. Far from being a dead letter, it obtained a new application in the days of the Inquisition; and one of the later Popes has declared that the murder of a Protestant is so good a deed that it atones, and more than atones, for the murder of a Catholic."§

In the last council of the Vatican, has the Church of Rome expressed any regret for having promulgated and executed such bloody laws? No! On the contrary, she has anathematized all those who think or say that she was wrong when she deluged the world with the blood of the millions she ordered to be slaughtered to quench her thirst for blood; she positively said that she had the right to punish those heretics by tortures and death.

* *Memorial of the Captivity of Napoleon at St. Helena*, by General Montholon, vol. ii. p. 62.
† *Memorial of the Captivity of Napoleon at St. Helena*, vol. ii. p. 174.
‡ *Rambler*, one of the most prominent Catholic papers of England, September, 1851.
§ *The London Times*, July 20th, 1872.

Those bloody and anti-social laws, were written on the banners of the Roman Catholics, when slaughtering 100,000 Waldenses in the mountains of Piedmont, and more than 50,000 defenceless men, women and children in the city of Bezières. It is under the inspiration of those diabolical laws of Rome, that 75,000 Protestants were massacred, the night and following week of St. Bartholomew.

It was to obey those bloody laws that Louis XIV. revoked the Edict of Nantes, caused the death of half a million of men, women and children, who perished in all the highways of France, and caused twice that number to die in the land of exile, where they had found a refuge.

Those anti-social laws, to-day, are written on her banners with the blood of ten millions of martyrs. It is under those bloody banners that 6,000 Roman Catholic priests, Jesuits and bishops, in the United States, are marching to the conquest of this Republic, backed by their seven millions of blind and obedient slaves.

Those laws, which are still the ruling laws of Rome, were the main cause of the last rebellion of the Southern States.

Yes! without Romanism, the last awful civil war would have been impossible. Jeff Davis would never have dared to attack the North, had he not had assurance from the Pope, that the Jesuits, the bishops, the priests and the whole people of the Church of Rome, under the name and mask of *Democracy*, would help him.

These diabolical and anti-social laws of Rome caused a Roman Catholic (Beauregard) to be the man chosen to fire the first gun at Fort Sumter, against the flag of Liberty, on the 12th of April, 1861. Those anti-christian and anti-social laws caused the Pope of Rome to be the only crowned prince in the whole world, so depraved as to publicly shake hands with Jeff Davis, and proclaim him President of a legitimate government.

These are the laws which led the assassins of Abraham Lincoln to the house of a rabid Roman Catholic woman, Mary Surratt, which was not only the rendezvous of the priests of Washington, but the very dwelling-house of some of them.

That woman, gifted by God to be an angel of peace and mercy on earth, was changed by those laws into a bloodthirsty tigress; for she had smelt the blood which everywhere comes from the robe, the hands, and the lips of the priest of Rome.

Those bloody and infernal laws of Rome nerved the arm of the Roman Catholic, Booth, when he slaughtered one of the noblest men God has ever given to the world.

Those bloody and anti-social laws of Rome, after having covered Europe with ruins, tears, and blood for ten centuries, have crossed the oceans to continue their work of slavery and desolation, blood, and tears, ignorance and demoralization, on this continent. Under the mask and name of Democracy they have raised the standard of rebellion of the South against the North, and caused more than half a million of the most heroic sons of America to fall on the fields of carnage.

In a very near future, if God does not miraculously prevent it, those laws of dark deeds and blood will cause the prosperity, the rights, the education, and the liberties of this too confident nation to be buried under a mountain of smoking and bloody ruins. On the top of that mountain, Rome will raise her throne and plant her victorious banners.

Then she will sing her Te Deums and shout her shouts of joy, as she did when she heard the lamentations and cries of desolation of the millions of martyrs burning in the five thousand auto-da-fés she had raised in all the capitals and great cities of Europe.

CHAPTER LX.

EQUALITY AND FRATERNITY OF MEN PROCLAIMED BY CHRIST.

" Be ye not called Rabbi. For one is your Master, even Christ ; and all ye are brethren " (Matt. xxiii. 8).

" God is no respecter of persons ; but in every nation, he that feareth Him and worketh righteousness is accepted with Him " (Acts x. 34, 35).

" Jesus called them unto Him and said, Ye know that the princes of the Gentiles exercise dominion over them, and they that are great exercise authority upon them.

" But it shall not be so among you : but whosoever will be great among you, let him be your minister; and whosoever will be chief among you, let him be your servant.

" Even as the Son of Man came not to be ministered unto, but to minister, and give His life as a ransom for many " (Matt. xx. 25, 28).

PRINCIPLES OF LIBERTY PROCLAIMED BY CHRIST.

" If ye continue in My word, then are ye My disciples indeed, and ye shall know the truth, and the truth shall make you free. . . . If the Son shall make you free, ye shall be free indeed " (John viii. 31, 32, 36).

" The spirit of the Lord is upon me, because He hath anointed me to preach the Gospel to the poor ; He hath sent Me to heal the broken-hearted, to preach deliverance to the captives, and recovering of sight to the blind, to set at liberty them that are bruised " (Luke iv. 18).

" Where the Spirit of the Lord is, there is liberty " (2 Cor. iii. 17).

TOLERANCE AND LIBERTY OF CONSCIENCE PROCLAIMED BY CHRIST.

" And they did not receive Him (Christ), because His face was as though He would go to Jerusalem. And when His disciples, James and John, saw this, they said, Lord, wilt Thou that we command fire to come down from heaven and consume them, even as Elias did?

"But He turned and rebuked them, and said, Ye know not what manner of spirit ye are of:

"For the Son of Man is not come to destroy men's lives, but to save them" (Luke ix. 53, 56).

"Then Simon Peter, having a sword, drew it, and smote the high priest's servant, and cut off his right ear. The servant's name was Malchus.

"Then said Jesus unto Peter, Put up thy sword into the sheath; the cup which my Father hath given Me, shall I not drink it? For all they that take the sword, shall perish with the sword" (John xviii. 10, 11; Matt. xxvi. 51, 52).

It is no wonder that the people of Judea, filled with admiration at these sublime doctrines of equality, fraternity, liberty and tolerance, should exclaim, "Never man spake like this man!"

Is it on those admirable principles that the Church of Rome is founded? No! for she has, thousands of times, proclaimed that her mission was to destroy them all, even if she had to wade in the blood of those who support them.

But just as the Romish Church is not only the very antipodes and the most implacable enemy of those admirable doctrines and principles, so the constitution of the United States is the ripe fruit of this divine seed, sown by the Son of God Himself in the bosom of humanity, eighteen hundred years ago.

Yes, in reference to those principles of fraternity, equality, liberty, and tolerance, the constitution of the United States is to the Gospel of Christ what the fruit is to the tree which has given it. And this is the verdict given by the whole world, the Church of Rome excepted.

Why is it that the poor, the bruised, the wounded, and the oppressed from every land turn their eyes, their hearts, and their steps towards this country? It is because all the echoes of heaven and earth have told them that the United States Republic is, *par excellence*, the land of fraternity, fair play, equality, and liberty.

The Pope of Rome and his Jesuits know this better than any one. Hence their constant and supreme efforts to destroy this Republic. Believing and preaching that it is their duty to exterminate the individuals who differ from them in religion, they assume that it is their duty to destroy the governments and the nations who refuse to submit to their yoke, when they can do it safely.

The mission of Rome being to teach that the inferior, the people, must obey his superior, just as the corpse obeys the hand which moves it, or as the stick obeys the arm which directs it, she knows well that she cannot fulfil her mission and attain her object so long as this government of a free, sovereign people, stands; she is, then, bound to oppose, paralyse, and destroy that government when she finds her opportunity.

With lynx eye, she watched that opportunity : and with anxiety and rage she spied from her cradle the onward march of this young giant Republic. She knew that it was in the bosom of every true citizen of the United States to propagate those accursed (by her) principles of equality, fraternity, and liberty all over the world. She saw that the irresistible influence of those principles were felt on the most distant nations, as well as on the poor, miserable Irish people, she was keeping under her heavy and ignominious yoke; she understood that there was a real danger for her very existence, if those principles would continue to spread ; that her slavery star would go down as the liberty star would rise on the horizon. In a word, Rome saw at once that the very existence of the United States was a formidable menace to her own life. Already she had seen the chains of two millions of her Irish slaves melted at the simple touch of the warm rays of liberty which had fallen from the stars and stripes banners. From the very beginning she perfidiously sowed the germs of division and hatred between the two great sections of this country, and she felt an unspeakable joy when she saw that she had succeeded in dividing its South from the North, on the burning question of slavery. She looked upon that division as her golden opportunity. To crush one party by the other, and reign over the bloody ruins of both, has invariably been her policy. She hoped that the hour of her supreme triumph over this continent was come. She ordered her elder son, the Emperor of France, to keep himself ready to help her to crush the North, by having an army in Mexico ready to support the South, and she bade all the Roman Catholic bishops, priests, and people to enrol themselves under the banners of slavery, by joining themselves to the party of the Democracy. And everybody knows how the Roman Catholic bishops and priests, almost to a man, obeyed that order. Only one bishop dared to disobey. Above everything, it was ordered to oppose the election of Lincoln at any cost. For, from the very first day that his eloquent voice had been heard, a thrill of terror had gone through the hearts of the partisans of slavery. The Democratic press, which was then, as it is still now, almost entirely under the control of the Roman Catholics, and the devoted tool of the Jesuits, deluged the country with the most fearful denunciations against him. They called him an ape, a stupid brute, a most dangerous lunatic, a bloody monster, a merciless tyrant, etc., etc. In a word, Rome exhausted all her resources of language, she ransacked the English dictionary to find the most suitable expressions to fill the people with contempt, hatred, and horror against him. But it was written in the decrees of God that honest Abraham Lincoln should be proclaimed President of the United States, the 4th of March, 1861.

At the end of August, having known from a Roman Catholic

priest, whom, by the mercy of God, I had persuaded to leave the errors of Popery, that there was a plot among them to assassinate the President, I thought it was my duty to go and tell him what I knew, at the same time giving him a new assurance of gratitude for what he had done for me.

Knowing that I was among those who were waiting in the ante-chamber, he sent immediately for me, and received me with greater cordiality and marks of kindness than I could expect.

"I am so glad to meet you again," he said: "you see that your friends, the Jesuits, have not yet killed me. But they would have surely done it when I passed through their most devoted city, Baltimore, had I not defeated their plans, by passing incognito a few hours before they expected me. We have the proof that the company which had been selected and organized to murder me was led by a rabid Roman Catholic, called Byrne; it was almost entirely composed of Roman Catholics; more than that, there were two disguised priests among them, to lead and encourage them. I am sorry to have so little time to see you: but I will not let you go before telling you that, a few days ago, I saw Mr. Morse, the learned inventor of electric telegraphy: he told me that when he was in Rome, not long ago, he found out the proofs of a most formidable conspiracy against this country and all its institutions. It is evident that it is to the intrigues and emissaries of the Pope that we owe, in great part, the horrible civil war which is threatening to cover the country with blood and ruins.

"I am sorry that Professor Morse had to leave Rome before he could know more about the secret plans of the Jesuits against the liberties and the very existence of this country. But do you know that I want you to take his place and continue that investigation? My plan is to attach you to my ambassador of France, as one of the secretaries. In that honourable position you would go from Paris to Rome, where you might find, through the directions of Mr. Morse, an opportunity of re-uniting the broken threads of his researches. 'It takes a Greek to fight a Greek.' As you have been twenty-five years a priest of Rome, I do not know any man in the United States so well acquainted as you are with the tricks of the Jesuits, and on the devotedness of whom I could better rely. And when, once on the staff of my ambassador, even as one of the secretaries, might you not soon yourself become the ambassador? I am in need of Christian men in every department of the public service, but more in those high positions. What do you think of that?"

"My dear President," I answered, "I feel overwhelmed by your kindness. Surely nothing could be more pleasant to me than to grant your request. The honour you want to confer upon me is much above my merit: but my conscience tells me that I cannot give up the preaching of the Gospel to my poor French Canadian countrymen, who are still in the errors of Popery. For I am about the only one who, by the Providence of God, has any real influence over them. I am, surely, the only one the bishops and priests seem to fear in that work. The many attempts they have made to take away my life are a proof of it. Besides that, though I consider the present President of the United States much above the Emperors of France, Russia, and Austria, much above the greatest kings of the world, I feel that I am the servant, the ambassador of One who is as much above even the good and great President of the United States as the heavens are above the earth. I appeal to your own Christian and honourable feelings to know if I can forsake the one for the other."

The President became very solemn, and replied: "You are right! you are right! There is nothing so great under heaven as to be the ambassador of Christ."

But then, coming back to himself, with one of his fine jokes, which he had always ready, he added: "Yes! yes! You are the ambassador of a greater Prince than I am: but He does not pay you with so good cash as I would do." He then added: "I am exceedingly pleased to see you. However, I am so pressed just now, by most important affairs, that you must excuse me if I ask you to give your place to one of my generals who is there, waiting for me. Please come again to-morrow at ten o'clock; I have a very important question to ask you on a matter which has been constantly before my mind these last few weeks."

The next day I was, at the appointed hour, with my noble friend, who said: "I could not give you more than ten minutes yesterday, but I will give you twenty to-day. I want your views about a thing which is exceedingly puzzling to me, and you are the only one to whom I like to speak on that subject. A great number of Democratic papers have been sent to me lately, evidently written by Roman Catholics, publishing that I was born a Roman Catholic, and baptized by a priest. They call me a renegade, an apostate, on account of that; and they heap upon my head mountains of abuses. At first I laughed at that, for it is a lie. Thanks be to God, I have never been a Roman Catholic. No priest of Rome has ever laid his hand on my head. But the persistency of the Romish press to present this falsehood to their readers as a gospel truth, must have a meaning. Please tell me, as briefly as possible, what you think about that."

"My dear President," I answered, "it was just this strange story published about you, which brought me here yesterday. I wanted to say a word about it; but you were too busy. Let me tell you that I wept as a child when I read that story for the first time. For, not only my impression is that it is your sentence of death; but I have from the lips of a converted priest, that it is in order to excite the fanaticism of the Roman Catholic murderers, whom they hope to find sooner or later, to strike you down; they have invented that false story of your being born in the Church of Rome, and of your being baptized by a priest. They want, by that, to brand your face with the ignominious mark of apostasy. Do not forget that, in the Church of Rome, an apostate is an outcast, who has no place in society, and who has no right to live.

"The Jesuits want the Roman Catholics to believe that you are a monster, an open enemy of God and of His Church, that you are an excommunicated man. For every apostate is, *ipso facto* (by that very fact) excommunicated. I have brought to you the theology of one of the most learned and approved of the Jesuits of his time, Busembaum, who, with many others, say that the man who will kill you will do a good and holy work. More than that, here is a copy of a decree of Gregory VII., proclaiming that the killing of an apostate, or an heretic and an excommunicated man, as you are declared to be, is not murder; nay, that it is a good, a Christian action. That decree is incorporated in the canon law, which every priest must study, and which every good Catholic must follow.

"My dear President, I must repeat to you here what I said when at Urbana in 1856. My fear is that you will fall under the blows of a Jesuit assassin if you do not pay more attention than you have done, till now, to protect yourself. Remember that because Coligny was an heretic, as you are, he was brutally murdered in the St. Bartholomew night; that Henry IV. was stabbed by the Jesuit assassin, Revaillac, the 14th of May, 1610, for having given liberty of conscience to his people; and that William the Taciturn was shot dead by another Jesuit murderer, called Girard, for having broken the yoke of the Pope. The Church of Rome is absolutely the same to-day as she was then; she does believe and teach to-day, as then, that she has the right and that it is her duty to punish by death any heretic who is in her way as an obstacle to her designs. The unanimity with which the Catholic hierarchy of the United States is on the side of the rebels is an incontrovertible evidence that Rome wants to destroy this republic, and as you are, by your personal virtues, your popularity, your love for liberty, your position, the greatest obstacle to their diabolical schemes, their hatred is concentrated upon you; you are the daily object of their maledictions; it is at your breast they will direct their blows. My blood chills in my veins when I contemplate the day which may come, sooner or later, when Rome will add to all her other iniquities the murder of Abraham Lincoln."

When saying these things to the President, I was exceedingly moved, my voice was as choked, and I could hardly retain my tears. But the President was perfectly calm. When I had finished speaking, he took the volume of Busembaum from my hand, read the lines which I had marked with red ink, and I helped him to translate them into English. He then gave me back the book, and said :

"I will repeat to you what I said at Urbana, when for the first time you told me your fears lest I would be assassinated by the Jesuits: 'Man must not care where and when he will die, provided he dies at the post of honour and duty.' But I may add, to-day, that I have a presentiment that God will call me to Him through the hand of an assassin. Let His will, and, not mine be done !" He then looked at his watch and said, "I am sorry, that the twenty minutes I had consecrated to our interview have almost passed away ; I will be for ever grateful for the warning words you have addressed to me about the dangers ahead to my life, from Rome. I know that they are not imaginary dangers. If I were fighting against a Protestant South, as a nation, there would be no danger of assassination. The nations who read the Bible, fight bravely on the battle-fields, but they do not assassinate their enemies. The Pope and the Jesuits, with their infernal Inquisition, are the only organized powers in the world which have recourse to the dagger of the assassin to murder those whom they cannot convince with their arguments or conquer with the sword.

"Unfortunately, I feel more and more, every day, that it is not against the Americans of the South, alone, I am fighting, it is more against the Pope of Rome, his perfidious Jesuits and their blind and blood-thirsty slaves, than against the real American Protestants, that we have to defend ourselves. Here is the real danger of our position. So long as they will hope to conquer the North, they will spare me ; but the day we will rout their armies (and that day will surely come, with the help of God), take their cities, and force them to submit, then, it is my impression that the Jesuits, who are the principal rulers of the South, will do what they have almost invariably done in the past. The dagger, or the pistol of one of their adepts, will do what the strong hands of the warriors could not achieve. This civil war seems to be nothing but a political affair to those who do not see, as I do, the secret springs of that terrible drama. But it is more a religious than a civil war. It is Rome who wants to rule and degrade the North, as she has ruled and degraded the South, from the very day of its discovery. There are only very few of the Southern leaders who are not more or less under the influence of the Jesuits, through their wives, family relations, and their friends. Several members of the family of Jeff Davis belong to the Church of Rome. Even the Protestant ministers are under the influence of the Jesuits without suspecting it. To keep her ascendancy in the North, as she does in the South, Rome is doing here what she has done in Mexico, and in all the South American Republics ; she is paralyzing, by a civil war, the arms of the soldiers of Liberty.   She divides our nation, in order to weaken, subdue and rule it.

"Surely we have some brave and reliable Roman Catholic officers and soldiers in our armies, but they form an insignificant minority when compared with the Roman Catholic traitors against whom we have to guard ourselves, day and night.   The fact is, that the immense majority of Roman Catholic bishops, priests and laymen, are rebels in heart, when they cannot be in fact; with very few exceptions, they are publicly in favour of slavery.   I understand, now, why the patriots of France, who determined to see the colours of Liberty floating over their great and beautiful country, were forced to hang or shoot almost all the priests and the monks as the irreconcilable enemies of Liberty. For it is a fact, which is now evident to me, that, with very few exceptions, every priest and every true Roman Catholic is a determined enemy of Liberty.   Their extermination in France, was one of those terrible necessities which no human wisdom could avoid ; it looks to me now as an order from heaven to save France.   May God grant that the same terrible necessity be never felt in the United States !   But there is a thing which is very certain; it is, that if the American people could learn what I know of the fierce hatred of the generality of the priests of Rome against our institutions, our schools, our most sacred rights, and our so dearly bought liberties, they would drive them away, to-morrow, from among us, or they would shoot them as traitors. But I keep those sad secrets in my heart; you are the only one to whom I reveal them, for I know that you learned them before me.   The history of these last thousand years tells us that wherever the Church of Rome is not a dagger to pierce the bosom of a free nation, she is a stone to her neck, and a ball to her feet, to paralyze her, and prevent her advance in the ways of civilization, science, intelligence, happiness and liberty.   But I forget that my twenty minutes are gone long ago.

"Please accept my sincere thanks for the new lights you have given me on the dangers of my position, and come again.   I will always see you with a new pleasure."

My second visit to Abraham Lincoln was at the beginning of June, 1862.   The grand victory of the "Monitor" over the "Merrimac," and the conquest of New Orleans, by the brave and Christian Farragut had filled every heart with joy ; I wanted to unite my feeble voice to that of the whole country to tell him how I blessed God for that glorious success.   But I found him so busy that I could only shake hands with him.

The third and last time I went to pay my respects to the doomed

President, and warn him against the impending dangers which I knew were threatening him, was on the morning of June 8th, 1864, when he was absolutely besieged by people who wanted to see him. After a kind and warm shaking of hands, he said:

"I am much pleased to see you again. But it is impossible, to-day, to say anything more than this: To-morrow afternoon, I will receive the delegation of the deputies of all the loyal states, sent to officially announce the desire of the country that I should remain the President four years more. I invite you to be present with them at that interesting meeting. You will see some of the most prominent men of our Republic, and I will be glad to introduce you to them. You will not present yourself as a delegate of the people, but only as the guest of the President; and that there may be no trouble, I will give you this card, with a permit to enter with the delegation. But do not leave Washington before I see you again; I have some important matters on which I want to know your mind."

The next day, it was my privilege to have the greatest honour ever received by me. The good President wanted me to stand at his right hand, when he received the delegation, and hear the address presented by Governor Dennison, the President of the Convention, to which he replied in his own admirable simplicity and eloquence; finishing by one of his most witty anecdotes. "I am reminded in this convention of a story of an old Dutch farmer, who remarked to a companion, wisely, 'That it was not best to swap horses when crossing a stream.'"

The next day, he kindly took me with him in his carriage, when visiting the thirty thousand wounded soldiers picked up on the battle-fields of the seven days' battle of the Wilderness, and the thirty days' battle around Richmond, where Grant was just breaking the backbone of the rebellion. On the way to and from the hospitals, I could not talk much. The noise of the carriage rapidly drawn on the pavement was too great. Besides that, my soul was so much distressed, and my heart so much broken by the sight of the horrors of that fratricidal war, that my voice was as stifled. The only thought which seemed to occupy the mind of the President was the part which Rome had in that horrible struggle. Many times he repeated:

"This war would never have been possible without the sinister influence of the Jesuits. We owe it to Popery that we now see our land reddened with the blood of her noblest sons. Though there were great differences of opinion between the South and the North, on the question of slavery, neither Jeff Davis nor any one of the leading men of the Confederacy would have dared to attack the North, had they not relied on the promises of the Jesuits, that, under the mask of Democracy, the money and the arms of the Roman Catholic, even the arms of France, were at their disposal, if they would attack us. I pity the priests, the bishops and the monks of Rome in the United States, when the people realize that they are, in great part, responsible for the tears and the blood shed in this war; the later the more terrible will the retribution be. I conceal what I know, on that subject, from the knowledge of the nation; for if the people knew the whole truth, this war would turn into a religious war, and it would, at once, take a tenfold more savage and bloody character, It would become merciless as all religious wars are. It would become a war of extermination on both sides. The Protestants of both the North and the South would surely unite to exterminate the priests and the Jesuits, if they could hear what Professor Morse has said to me of the plots made in the very city of Rome to destroy this Republic, and if they could learn how the priests, the nuns, and the monks, which daily land on our shores, under the pretext of preaching their religion, instructing the people in their schools, taking care of the sick in the hospitals, are nothing else but the emissaries of the Pope, of Napoleon, and the other despots of Europe, to undermine our institutions, alienate the hearts of our people from our constitution, and our laws, destroy our schools, and prepare a reign of anarchy here as they have done in Ireland, in Mexico, in Spain, and wherever there are any people who want to be free, etc."

When the President was speaking thus, we arrived at the door of his mansion. He invited me to go with him to his study, and said:

"Though I am very busy, I must rest an hour with you. I am in need of that rest. My head is aching, I feel as crushed under the burden or affairs which are on my shoulders. There are many important things about the plots of the Jesuits that I can learn only from you. Please wait just a moment, I have just received some despatches from General Grant, to which I must give an answer. My secretary is waiting for me. I go to him. Please amuse yourself with those books, during my short absence."

Twenty-five minutes later, the President had returned, with his face flushed with joy. " Glorious news ! General Grant has again beaten Lee, and forced him to retreat towards Richmond, where he will have to surrender before long. Grant is a real hero. But let us come to the question I want to put to you. Have you read the letter of the Pope to Jeff Davis, and what do you think of it ? "

"My dear President," I answered, "it is just that letter which brought me to your presence again, the day before yesterday. I wanted to come and see you, from the very day I read it. But I knew you were so overwhelmed with the affairs of your government, that I would not be able to see you. However, the anxieties of my mind were so, that I determined to go over every barrier to warn you again against the new dangers and plots which I knew would come out from that perfidious letter, against your life.

"That letter is a poisoned arrow thrown by the Pope, at you personally; and it will be more than a miracle if it be not your irrevocable warrant of death. Before reading it, it is true that every Catholic could see by the unanimity of the bishops siding with the rebel cause, that their church as a whole, was against this free Republican government. However, a good number of liberty-loving Irish, German and French Catholics, following more the instincts of their noble nature, than the degrading principles of their church, enrolled themselves under the banners of Liberty, and they have fought like heroes. To detach these men from the rank and file of the Northern armies, and force them to help the cause of the rebellion, became the object of the intrigues of the Jesuits. Secret and pressing letters were addressed from Rome to the bishops, ordering them to weaken your armies by detaching those men from you. The bishops answered, that they could not do that without exposing themselves to be shot. But they advised the Pope to acknowledge, at once, the legitimacy of the Southern Republic, and to take Jeff Davis under his supreme protection, by a letter, which would be read everywhere.

"That letter, then, tells logically the Roman Catholics that you are a blood-thirsty tyrant! a most execrable being when fighting against a government which the infallible and holy Pope of Rome recognizes as legitimate. The Pope, by this letter, tells his blind slaves that you are an infamous usurper, when considering yourself the President of the Southern States; that you are outraging the God of heaven and earth, by continuing such a sanguinary war to subdue a nation over whom God Almighty has declared, through His infallible pontiff, the Pope, that you have not the least right: that letter means that you will give an account to God and man for the blood and tears you cause to flow in order to satisfy your ambition.

"By this letter of the Pope to Jeff Davis you are not only an apostate, as you were thought before, whom every man had the right to kill, according to the canonical laws of Rome; but you are more vile, criminal and cruel than the horse thief, the public banditti, and the lawless brigand, robber and murderer, whom it is a duty to stop and kill, when we take them in their acts of blood, and that there is no other way to put an end to their plunders and murders.

"And, my dear President, the meaning I give you of this perfidious letter of the Pope to Jeff Davis, is not a fancy imagination on my part, it is the unanimous explanation given me by a great number of the priests of Rome, with whom I have had occasion to speak on that subject. In the name of God, and in the name of our dear country, which is in so much need of your services, I conjure you to pay more attention to protect your precious life, and not continue to expose it as you have done till now."

The President listened to my words with breathless attention. He replied:

"You confirm me in the views I had taken of the letter of the Pope. Professor Morse is of the same mind with you. It is, indeed, the most perfidious act which could occur under present circumstances. You are perfectly correct when you say that it was to detach the Roman Catholics who had enrolled themselves in our armies. Since the publication of that letter, a great number of them have deserted their banners and turned traitors; very few, comparatively, have remained true to their oath of fidelity. It is, however, very lucky that one of those few, Sheridan, is worth a whole army by his ability, his patriotism and his heroic courage. It is true, also, that Meade has remained with us, and gained the bloody battle of Gettysburgh. But how could he lose it, when he was surrounded by such heroes as Howard, Reynolds, Buford, Wadsworth, Cutler, Slocum, Sickles, Hancock, Barnes, etc. But it is evident that his Romanism superseded his patriotism after the battle. He let the army of Lee escape, when it was so easy to cut his retreat and force him to surrender, after having lost nearly the half of his soldiers in the last three days' carnage.

"When Meade was to order the pursuit, after the battle, a stranger came, in haste, to the headquarters, and that stranger was a disguised Jesuit. After a ten minutes' conversation with him, Meade made such arrangements for the pursuit of the enemy, that he escaped almost untouched, with the loss of only two guns!

"You are right," continued the President, "when you say that this letter of the Pope has entirely changed the nature and the ground of the war. Before they read it, the Roman Catholics could see that I was fighting against Jeff Davis and his Southern Confederacy. But now, they must believe that it is against Christ and His holy vicar, the Pope, that I am raising my sacrilegious hands; we have the daily proofs that their indignation, their hatred, their malice, against me, are a hundredfold intensified.] New projects of assassination are detected almost every day, accompanied with such savage circum stances, that they bring to my memory the massacre of the St. Bartholomew and the Gunpowder Plot. We feel, at their investigation, that they come from the same masters in the art of murder, the Jesuits.

"The New York riots were evidently a Romish plot from beginning to end. We have the proofs in hand that they were the work of Bishop Hughes and his emissaries. No doubt can remain in the minds of the most incredulous about the bloody attempts of Rome to destroy

New York, when we know the easy way it was stopped. I wrote to Bishop Hughes, telling him that the whole country would hold him responsible for it if he would not stop it at once. He then gathered the rioters around his palace, called them his 'dear friends,' invited them to go back home peacefully, and all was finished! so Jupiter of old used to raise a storm and stop it with a nod of his head!

"From the beginning of our civil war, there has been, not a secret, but a public alliance, between the Pope of Rome and Jeff Davis, and that alliance has followed the common laws of this world affairs. The greater has led the smaller, the stronger has guided the weaker. The Pope and his Jesuits have advised, supported, and directed Jeff Davis on the land, from the first gun shot at Fort Sumter, by the rabid Roman Catholic Beauregard. They are helping him on the sea by guiding and supporting the other rabid Roman Catholic pirate, Semmes, on the ocean. And they will help the rebellion when firing their last gun to shed the blood of the last soldier of Liberty, who will fall in this fratricidal war. In my interview with Bishop Hughes, I told him 'that every stranger who had sworn allegiance to our government by becoming a United States citizen, as himself, was liable to be shot or hung as a perjured traitor and an armed spy, as the sentence of the court-martial may direct. And he will be so shot and hanged accordingly, as there will be no exchange of such prisoners.' After I had put this flea in the ears of the Romish bishop, I requested him to go and report my words to the Pope. Seeing the dangerous position of his bishops and priests when siding with the rebels, my hope was that he would advise them, for their own interests, to become loyal and true to their allegiance and help us through the remaining part of the war. But the result has been the very contrary. The Pope has thrown away the mask, and shown himself the public partisan and the protector of the rebellion, by taking Jeff Davis by the hand, and impudently recognizing the Southern States as a legitimate government. Now, I have the proof in hand that that very Bishop Hughes, whom I had sent to Rome that he might induce the Pope to urge the Roman Catholics of the North at least, to be true to their oath of allegiance, and whom I thanked publicly, when, under the impression that he had acted honestly, according to the promise he had given me, is the very man who advised the Pope to recognize the legitimacy of the Southern Republic, and put the whole weight of his tiara in the balance against us in favour of our enemies! Such is the perfidy of those Jesuits. Two cankers are biting the very entrails of the United States to-day: the Romish and the Mormon priests. Both are equally at work to form a people of the most abject, ignorant and fanatical slaves, who will recognize no other authority but their supreme pontiffs. Both are aiming at the destruction of our schools, to raise themselves upon our ruins. Both shelter themselves under our grand and holy principles of liberty of conscience, to destroy that very liberty of conscience, and bind the world before their heavy and ignominious yoke. The Mormon and the Jesuit priests are equally the uncompromising enemies of our constitution and our laws; but the more dangerous of the two is the Jesuit—the Romish priest, for he knows better how to conceal his hatred under the mask of friendship and public good: he is better trained to commit the most cruel and diabolical deeds for the glory of God.

"Till lately, I was in favour of the unlimited liberty of conscience as our constitution gives it to the Roman Catholics. But now, it seems to me that, sooner or later, the people will be forced to put a restriction to that clause towards the Papists. Is it not an act of folly to give absolute liberty of conscience to a set of men who are publicly sworn to cut our throats the very day they have their opportunity for doing it? It is right to give the privilege of citizenship to men who are the sworn and public enemies of our constitution, our laws, our liberties, and our lives?

"The very moment that Popery assumed the right of life and death on a citizen of France, Spain, Germany, England, or the United States, it assumed to be the power, the government of France, Spain, England, Germany, and the United States. Those States then committed a suicidal act by allowing Popery to put a foot on their territory with the privilege of citizenship. The power of life and death is the *supreme power*, and two *supreme powers* cannot exist on the same territory without *anarchy*, riots, bloodshed, and civil wars without end. When Popery will give up the power of life and death which it proclaims on its own divine power, in all its theological books and canon laws, then, and then alone, it can be tolerated and can receive the privileges of citizenship in a free country.

"Is it not an absurdity to give to a man a thing which he is sworn to hate, curse, and destroy? And does not the Church of Rome hate, curse, and destroy liberty of conscience whenever she can do it safely? I am for liberty of conscience in its noblest, broadest, highest sense. But I cannot give liberty of conscience to the Pope and to his followers, the Papists, so long as they tell me, through all their councils, theologians, and canon laws, that their conscience orders them to burn my wife, strangle my children, and cut my throat when they find their opportunity! This does not seem to be understood by the people to-day. But sooner or later, the light of common sense will make it clear to every one that no liberty of conscience can be granted to men who are sworn to obey a Pope, who pretends to have the right to put to death those who differ from him in religion.

"You are not the first to warn me against the dangers of assassination. My ambassadors in Italy, France, and England, as well as Professor Morse, have many times warned me against the plots of the murderers which they have detected in those different countries. But I see no other safeguard against those murderers but to be always ready to die, as Christ advises it. As we must all die sooner or later, it makes very little difference to me whether I die from a dagger plunged through the heart or from an inflammation of the lungs. Let me tell you that I have lately read a passage in the Old Testament which has made a profound, and, I hope, a salutary impression on me. Here is that passage."

The President took his Bible, opened it at the third chapter of Deuteronomy, and read from the 22nd to the 28th verse :—

"Ye shall not fear them : for the Lord your God He shall fight for you. And I besought the Lord at that time, saying, O Lord God, Thou hast begun to shew Thy servant Thy greatness and Thy mighty hand ; for what God is there, in heaven or in earth, that can do according to Thy works, and according to Thy might ! I pray Thee, let me go over, and see the good land that is beyond Jordan, that goodly mountain, and Lebanon. But the Lord was wroth with me for your sakes, and would not hear me : and the Lord said unto me, Let it suffice thee : speak no more unto Me of this matter. Get thee up into the top of Pisgah, and lift up thine eyes westward, and northward, and southward, and eastward, and behold it with thine eyes : for thou shalt not go over this Jordan."

After the President had read these words with great solemnity, he added : "My dear Father Chiniquy, let me tell you that I have read these strange and beautiful verses several times these last five or six weeks. The more I read them, the more it seems to me that God has written them for me as well as for Moses. Has He not taken me from my poor log cabin by the hand, as He did of Moses in the reeds of the Nile, to put me at the head of the greatest and the most blessed of modern nations, just as He put that prophet at the head of the most blessed nation of ancient times ? Has not God granted me a privilege which was not granted to any living man, when I broke the fetters of 4,000,000 of men and made them free ? Has not our God given me the most glorious victories over our enemies ? Are not the armies of the Confederacy so reduced to a handful of men when compared to what they were two years ago, that the day is fast approaching when they will have to surrender ?

"Now, I see the end of this terrible conflict, with the same joy of Moses, when, at the end of his trying forty years in the wilderness ; and I pray my God to grant me to see the days of peace, and untold prosperity, which will follow this cruel war, as Moses asked God to see the other side of Jordan and enter the Promised Land. But do you know that I hear in my soul, as the voice of God, giving me the rebuke which was given to Moses ?

"Yes! every time that my soul goes to God to ask the favour of seeing the other side of Jordan, and eating the fruits of that peace, after which I am longing with such an unspeakable desire, do you know that there is a still, but solemn voice, which tells me that I will see those things, only from a long distance, and that I will be among the dead, when the nation which God granted me to lead through those awful trials, will cross the Jordan, and dwell in that Land of Promise, where peace, industry, happiness, and liberty, will make every one happy ; and why so ? Because He has already given me favours which He never gave, I dare say, to any man, in these latter days.

"Why did God Almighty refuse to Moses the favour of crossing the Jordan, and entering the Promised Land ? It was on account of his own nation's sins ! That law of divine retribution and justice, by which one must suffer for another. is surely a terrible mystery. But it is a fact which no man who has any intelligence and knowledge can deny. Moses, who knew that law, though he probably did not understand it better than we do, calmly says to his people, ' God was wroth with me for your sakes.'

"But though we do not understand that mysterious and terrible law, we find it written in letters of tears and blood wherever we go. We do not read a single page of history, without finding undeniable traces of its existence.

"Where is the mother who has not shed tears and suffered real tortures, for her children's sake ?

"Who is the good king, the worthy emperor, the gifted chieftain, who have not suffered unspeakable mental agonies, or even death, for their people's sake ?

"Is not our Christian religion the highest expression of the wisdom, mercy, and love of God ! But what is Christianity if not the very incarnation of that eternal law of divine justice in our humanity ?

"When I look on Moses, alone, silently dying on the Mount Pisgah, I see that law, in one of its most sublime human manifestations, and I am filled with admiration and awe.

"But when I consider that law of justice, and expiation in the death of the Just, the divine Son of Mary, on the mountain of Calvary. I remain mute in my adoration. The spectacle of that crucified one which is before my eyes, is more than sublime, it is divine ! Moses died for his people's sake, but Christ died for the whole world's sake ! Both died to fulfil the same eternal law of the divine justice, though in a different measure.

"Now would it not be the greatest of honours and privileges bestowed upon me, if God, in His infinite love, mercy and wisdom, would put me between His faithful servant, Moses, and His eternal Son, Jesus, that I might die as they did, for my nation's sake!

"My God alone knows what I have already suffered for my dear country's sake. But my fear is that the justice of God is not yet paid. When I look upon the rivers of tears and blood drawn by the lashes of the merciless masters from the veins of the very heart of those millions of defenceless slaves, these two hundred years. When I remember the agonies, the cries, the unspeakable tortures of those unfortunate people, at which I have, to some extent, connived with so many others, a part of my life, I feel that we are still far from the complete expiation. For the judgments of God are true and righteous.

"It seems to me that the Lord wants, to-day, as He wanted in the days of Moses, another victim—a victim which he has himself chosen, anointed and prepared for the sacrifice, by raising it above the rest of His people. I cannot conceal from you that my impression is that I am that victim. So many plots have already been made against my life, that it is a real miracle that they have all failed, when we consider that the great majority of them were in the hands of skilful Roman Catholic murderers, evidently trained by Jesuits. But can we expect that God will make a perpetual miracle to save my life? I believe not. The Jesuits are so expert in those deeds of blood, that Henry IV. said that it was impossible to escape them, and he became their victim, though he did all that could be done to protect himself. My escape from their hands, since the letter of the Pope to Jeff Davis has sharpened a million of daggers to pierce my breast, would be more than a miracle.

"But just as the Lord heard no murmur from the lips of Moses when He told him that he had to die, before crossing the Jordan, for the sins of his people; so I hope and pray that He will hear no murmur from me when I fall for my nation's sake.

"The only two favours I ask of the Lord are, first, that I may die for the sacred cause in which I am engaged, and when I am the standard bearer of the rights and liberties of my country.

"The second favour I ask of God is, that my dear son, Robert, when I am gone, will be one of those who lift us that flag of Liberty which will cover my tomb, and carry it with honour and fidelity, to the end of his life, as his father did, surrounded by the millions who will be called with him to fight and die for the defence and honour of our country."

Never had I heard such sublime words : Never had I seen a human face so solemn and so prophet-like as the face of the President, when uttering these things. Every sentence had come to me as a hymn from heaven, reverberated by the echoes of the mountains of Pisgah and Calvary. I was beside myself. Bathed in tears, I tried to say something, but I could not utter a word.

I knew the hour to leave had come, I asked from the President permission to fall on my knees, and pray with him that his life might be spared : and he knelt with me. But I prayed more with my tears and sobs, than with my words.

Then I pressed his hand on my lips and bathed it with my tears, and with a heart filled with an unspeakable desolation, I bade him Adieu! It was for the last time!

For the hour was fast approaching when he was to fall by the hands of Jesuit assassin, for his nation's sake.

CHAPTER LXI.

EVERY time I met President Lincoln I wondered how such elevation of thought and such childish simplicity could be found in the same man. After my interviews with him many times, I said to myself: "How can this rail-splitter have so easily raised himself to the highest range of human thought and philosophy?"

The secret of this was, that Lincoln had spent a great part of his life at the school of Christ, and that he meditated his sublime teachings to an extent unsuspected by the world. I found in him the most perfect type of Christianity I ever met. Professedly, he was neither a strict Presbyterian, nor a Baptist, nor a Methodist; but he was the embodiment of all which is more perfect and Christian in them. His religion was the very essence of what God wants in man. It was from Christ Himself he had learned to love God and his neighbour, as it was from Christ he had learned the dignity and the value of man. "Ye are all brethren, the children of God," was his great motto.

It was from the Gospel that he had learned his principles of equality, fraternity, and liberty, as it was from the Gospel he had learned that sublime, childish simplicity which, alone, and for ever, won the admiration and affection of all those who approached him. I could cite many facts to illustrate this, but I will give only one, not to be too long: it is taken from the Memoirs of Mr. Bateman, Superintendent of Public Instruction for the State of Illinois.

"Mr. Lincoln paused: for long minutes, his features surcharged with emotion. Then he rose and walked up and down the reception room, in the effort to retain or regain his self-possession. Stopping at last, he said, with a trembling voice and his cheeks wet with tears: I know there is a God, and that He hates injustice and slavery. I see the storm coming, and I know that His hand is in it. If He has a place and work for me, and I think He has, I believe I am ready! I am nothing, but truth is everything! I know I am right, because I know that liberty is right: for Christ teaches it, and Christ is God. I have told them that a house divided against itself cannot stand, and Christ and reason say the same thing, and they will find it so. Douglas does not care whether slavery is voted up or down. But God cares, and humanity cares, and I care. And with God's help, I will not fail. I may not see the end, but it will come, and I shall be vindicated; and those men will see that they have not read their Bible right! Does it not appear strange that men can ignore the *moral aspect* of this contest? A revelation could not make it plainer to me that slavery, or the Government, must be destroyed. The future would be something awful, as I look at it, but for this ROCK on which I stand (alluding to the Gospel book he still held in his hand). It seems as if God had borne with slavery until the very teachers of religion had come to defend it from the Bible, and to claim for it a Divine character and sanction. And now the cup of iniquity is full, and the vials of wrath will be poured out.' "

Mr. Bateman adds: "After this, the conversation was continued for a long time. Everything he said was of a very deep, tender, and religious tone, and all was tinged with a touching melancholy. He repeatedly referred to his conviction 'that the day of wrath was at hand,' and that he was to be an actor in the struggle which would end in the overthrow of slavery, though he might not live to see the end. After further reference to a belief in Divine Providence, and the fact of God, in history, the conversation turned upon prayer. He freely stated his belief in the duty, privilege, and efficacy of prayer; and he intimated, in no unmistakable terms, that he had sought, in that way, the divine guidance and favour."

The effect of this conversation upon the mind of Mr. Bateman, a Christian gentleman whom Mr. Lincoln profoundly respected, was to convince him that Mr. Lincoln had, in his quiet way, found a path to the Christian standpoint, that he had found God, and rested on the eternal truth of God. As the two men were about to separate, Mr. Bateman remarked: "I had not supposed that you were accustomed to think so much upon this class of subjects; certainly your friends generally are ignorant of the sentiments you have expressed to me."

He quickly replied: "I know they are, but I think more on these subjects than upon all others, and I have done so for years; and I am willing you should know it."*

More than once I felt as if I were in the presence of an old

* *The Inner Life of Lincoln.* By Carpenter. Pp. 193—195.

prophet, when listening to his views about the future destinies of the United States. In one of my last interviews with him, I was filled with an admiration which it would be difficult to express, when I heard the following views and predictions:

"It is with the Southern leaders of this civil war as with the big and small wheels of our railroad cars. Those who ignore the laws of mechanics are apt to think that the large, strong, and noisy wheels they see are the motive power, but they are mistaken. The real motive power is not seen; it is noiseless and well concealed in the dark, behind its iron walls. The motive power are the few well-concealed pails of water heated into steam, which is itself directed by the noiseless, small, but unerring engineer's finger.

"The common people see and hear the big, noisy wheels of the Southern Confederacy's cars; they call them Jeff Davis, Lee, Toombs, Beauregard, Semmes, etc., and they honestly think that they are the motive power, the first cause of our troubles. But this is a mistake. The true motive power is secreted behind the thick walls of the Vatican, the colleges and schools of the Jesuits, the convents of the nuns, and the confessional boxes of Rome.

"There is a fact which is too much ignored by the American people, and with which I am acquainted only since I became President; it is that the best, the leading families of the South have received their education in great part, if not in whole, from the Jesuits and the nuns. Hence those degrading principles of slavery, pride, cruelty, which are as a second nature among so many of those people. Hence that strange want of fair play, humanity; that implacable hatred against the ideas of equality and liberty as we find them in the Gospel of Christ. You do not ignore that the first settlers of Louisiana, Florida, New Mexico, Texas, South California and Missouri were Roman Catholics, and that their first teachers were Jesuits. It is true that those states have been conquered or bought by us since. But Rome had put the deadly virus of her anti-social and anti-christian maxims into the veins of the people before they became American citizens. Unfortunately, the Jesuits and the nuns have in great part remained the teachers of those people since. They have continued in a silent, but most efficacious way, to spread their hatred against our institutions, our laws, our schools, our rights and our liberties in such a way that this terrible conflict became unavoidable between the North and the South. As I told you before, it is to Popery that we owe this terrible civil war.

"I would have laughed at the man who would have told me that before I became the President. But Professor Morse has opened my eyes on that subject. And now I see that mystery; I understand that engineering of hell which, though not seen nor even suspected by the country, is putting in motion the large, heavy, and noisy wheels of the state cars of the Southern Confederacy. Our people is not yet ready to learn and believe those things, and perhaps it is not the proper time to initiate them to those dark mysteries of hell; it would throw oil on a fire which is already sufficiently destructive.

"You are almost the only one with whom I speak freely on that subject. But sooner or later the nation will know the real origin of those rivers of blood and tears, which are spreading desolation and death everywhere. And then those who have caused those desolations and disasters will be called to give an account of them.

"I do not pretend to be a prophet. But though not a prophet, I see a very dark cloud on our horizon. And that dark cloud is coming from Rome. It is filled with tears of blood. It will rise and increase till its flanks will be torn by a flash of lightning, followed by a fearful peal of thunder. Then a cyclone, such as the world has never seen, will pass over this country, spreading ruin and desolation from north to south. After it is over, there will be long days of peace and prosperity: for Popery, with its Jesuits and merciless Inquisition, will have been for ever swept away from our country. Neither I nor you, but our children, will see those things."

Many of those who approached Abraham Lincoln felt that there was a prophetic spirit in him, and that he was continually walking and acting with the thought of God in his mind, and only in view to do His will and work for His glory. Speaking of the slaves, he said one day before the members of his cabinet:

"I have not decided against a proclamation of liberty to the slaves, but I hold the matter under advisement. And I can assure you that the subject is on my mind, by day and by night, more than any other. Whatever shall appear to be God's will, I will do." *

A few days before that proclamation, he said, before several of his counsellors: "I made a solemn vow before God that if General Lee was driven back from Pennsylvania, I would crown the result by the declaration of freedom to the slaves." †

But I would have volumes to write, instead of a short chapter, were I to give all the facts I have collected of the sincere and profound piety of Abraham Lincoln.

I cannot, however, omit his admirable and solemn act of faith in the eternal justice of God, as expressed in the closing words of his last inaugural address of the 4th of March, 1865.

"Fondly do we hope, fervently do we pray, that this mighty scourge of war may speedily pass away. Yet, if God wills that it continue until all the wealth piled by the bondsman's 250 years of unrequited toil shall be sunk, and until every drop of blood drawn by

---

* *Six Months in the White House.* By Carpenter. P. 86.   † Ibid.

the lash shall be paid by another drawn by the sword, as was said 3,000 years ago, so still it must be said: The judgments of the Lord are true and righteous altogether."

These sublime words, falling from the lips of the greatest Christian whom God ever put at the head of a nation, only a few days before his martyrdom, sent a thrill of wonder through the whole world. The God-fearing people and the upright of every nation listened to them as if they had just come from the golden harp of David. Even the infidels remain mute with admiration and awe. It seemed to all that the echoes of heaven and earth were repeating that last hymn, falling from the heart of the noblest and truest Gospel man of our days: "The judgments of the Lord are true and righteous altogether" (Psalm xix. 9).

The 6th of April, 1865, President Lincoln was invited by General Grant to enter Richmond, the capital of the rebel states, which he had just captured. The ninth, the beaten army of Lee, surrounded by the victorious legions of the soldiers of Liberty, were forced to lay down their arms and their banners at the feet of the generals of Lincoln. The tenth, the victorious President addressed an immense multitude of the citizens of Washington, to invite them to thank God and the armies for the glorious victories of the last few days, and for the blessed peace which was to follow these five years of slaughter.

But he was on the top of the mountain of Pisgah, and though he had fervently prayed that he might cross the Jordan and enter with his people into the Land of Promise, after which he had so often sighed, he was not to see his request granted. The answer had come from heaven, "You will not cross the Jordan, and you will not enter that Promised Land, which is there, so near. You must die for your nation's sake!" The lips, the heart, and the soul of the New Moses were still repeating the sublime words, "The judgments of the Lord are true and righteous altogether," when the Jesuit assassin, Booth, murdered him, the 14th of April, 1865, at ten o'clock p.m.

Let us hear the eloquent historian, Abbot, on that sad event:

"In the midst of unparalleled success, and while all the bells of the land were ringing with joy, a calamity fell upon us which overwhelmed the country in consternation and awe. On Friday evening, April 14th, President Lincoln attended Ford's Theatre, in Washington. He was sitting quietly in his box, listening to the drama, when a man entered the door of the lobby leading to the box, closing the door behind him. Drawing near to the President, he drew from his pocket a small pistol, and shot him in the back of the head. As the President fell, senseless and mortally wounded, and the shriek of his wife, who was seated at his side, pierced every ear, the assassin leaped from the box, a perpendicular height of nine feet, and as he rushed across the stage, bare-headed, brandished a dagger, exclaiming, ' Sic semper tyrannis ! ' and disappeared behind the side scenes. There was a moment of silent consternation. Then ensued a scene of confusion which it is in vain to attempt to describe.

"The dying President was taken into a house near by ,and placed upon a bed. What a scene did that room present ! The chief of a mighty nation lay there, senseless, drenched in blood, his brains oozing from his wound ! Sumner, Farwell, and Colfax and Stanton, and many others were there, filled with grief and consternation.

"The surgeon, General Barnes, solemnly examined the wound. There was silence as of the grave, the life and death of the nation seemed dependent on the result. General Barnes looked up sadly and said, ' The wound is mortal ! '

"'Oh ! No ! General, no ! no ! ' cried out Secretary Stanton, and sinking into a chair, he covered his face and wept like a child. Senator Sumner tenderly held the head of the unconscious martyr.

"Though all unused to weep, he sobs as though his great heart would break. In his anguish, his head falls upon the blood-stained pillow, and his black locks blend with those of the dying victim, which care and toil has rendered grey, and which blood has crimsoned. What a scene ! Sumner, who had lingered through months of agony, having himself been stricken down by the bludgeon of slavery, now sobbing and fainting in anguish over the prostrate form of his friend, whom slavery had slain ! This vile rebellion, after deluging the land in blood, has culminated in a crime which appals all nations.

"Noble Abraham, true descendant of the father of the faithful ; honest in every trust, humble as a child, tender-hearted as a woman, who could not bear to injure even his most envenomed foes : who, in the hour of triumph, was saddened lest the feelings of his adversaries should be wounded by their defeat, with ' charity for all, malice towards none,' endowed with ' common sense,' intelligence never surpassed, and with power of intellect which enabled him to grapple with the most gigantic opponents in debates, developing abilities as a statesman, which won the gratitude of his country and the admiration of the world, and with graces and amiability which drew to him all generous hearts ; dies by the bullet of the assassin ! " *

But who was that assassin ? Booth was nothing but the tool of the Jesuits. It was Rome who directed his arm, after corrupting his heart and damning his soul.

After I had mixed my tears with those of the grand country of my adoption, I fell on my knees and asked my God to grant me to show to the world what I knew to be the truth, viz., that that horrible crime was the work of popery. And, after twenty years of constant and most difficult researches, I come fearlessly to-day before the American people, to say and prove that the President, Abraham Lincoln, was assassinated by the priests and the Jesuits of Rome.

In the book of the testimonies given in the prosecution of the assassin of Lincoln, published by Ben Pitman, and in the two volumes of the trial of John Surratt, in 1867, we have the legal and irrefutable proof that the plot of the assassins of Lincoln was matured, if not started, in the house of Mary Surratt, No. 561, H. Street, Washington City, D. C. But who were living in that house, and who were visiting that family ? The legal answer says : " The most devoted Catholics in the city ! " The sworn testimonies show more than that. They

* *History of the Civil War.* By Abbot. Vol. ii., p. 594.

show that it was the common rendezvous of the priests of Washington. Several priests swear that they were going there "sometimes," and when pressed to answer what they meant by "sometimes," they were not sure if it was not once a week or once a month. One of them, less on his guard, swore that he seldom passed before that house without entering ; and he said he never passed less than once a week. The devoted Roman Catholic (an apostate from Protestantism) called L. J. Weichman, who was himself living in that house, swears that Father Wiget was *very often* in that house, and Father Lahiman swears that he was living with Mrs. Surratt in the same house !   *   *   *

What does the presence of so many priests in that house reveal to the world ? No man of common sense, who knows anything about the priests of Rome, can entertain any doubt that, not only they knew all that was going on inside those walls, but that they were the advisers, the counsellors, the very soul of that infernal plot. Why did Rome keep one of her priests, under that roof, from morning till night and from night till morning ? Why did she send many others, almost every day of the week, into that dark nest of plotters against the very existence of the great republic, and against the life of her President, her principal generals and leading men, if it were not to be the advisers, the rulers, the secret motive power of the infernal plot.

No one, if he is not an idiot, will think and say that those priests, who were the personal friends and the father confessors of Booth, John Surratt, Mrs. and Misses Surratt, could be constantly there without knowing what was going on, particularly when we know that every one of those priests was a rabid rebel in heart. Every one of those priests, knowing that his infallible Pope had called Jeff Davis his dear son, and had taken the Southern Confederacy under his protection, was bound to believe that the most holy thing a man could do, was to fight for the Southern cause, by destroying those who were its enemies.

Read the history of the assassination of Admiral Coligny, Henry III. and Henry IV., and William the Taciturn, by the hired assassins of the Jesuits ; compare them with the assassination of Abraham Lincoln, and you will find that one resembles the other as one drop of water resembles another. You will understand that they all come from the same source, Rome !

In all those murders, you will find that the murderers, selected and trained by the Jesuits, were of the most exalted Roman Catholic piety, living in the company of priests, going to confess very often, receiving the communion the day before, if not the very day of the murder. You will see in all those horrible deeds of hell, prepared behind the dark walls of the holy inquisition, that the assassins were considering themselves as the chosen instruments of God, to save the

33

nations by striking its tyrant; that they firmly believed that there was no sin in killing the enemy of the people of the holy church, and of the infallible Pope!

Compare the last hours of the Jesuit Ravaillac, the assassin of Henry IV., who absolutely refuses to repent, though suffering the most horrible torture on the rack, with Booth, who suffering also the most horrible tortures from his broken leg, writes in his daily memorandum, the very day before his death: "I can never repent, though we hated to kill. Our country owed all her troubles to him (Lincoln), and God simply made me the instrument of his punishment."*

Yes! Compare the bloody deeds of those two assassins, and you will see that they had been trained in the same school; they had been taught by the same teachers. Evidently the Jesuit Ravaillac, calling all the saints of heaven to his help, at his last hour; and Booth pressing the medal of the Virgin Mary on his breast, when falling mortally wounded,† are both coming out from the same Jesuit mould.

Who has lost his common sense enough to suppose that it was Jeff Davis who had filled the mind and the heart of Booth with that religious and so exalted fanaticism! Surely Jeff Davis had promised the money to reward the assassins and nerve their arms, by the hope of becoming rich. The testimonies on that account say that he had promised one million dollars.‡

That arch-rebel could give the money; but the Jesuits alone could select the assassins, train them, and show them a crown of glory in heaven, if they would kill the author of the bloodshed, the famous renegade and apostate—the enemy of the Pope and of the Church—Lincoln.

Who does not see the lessons given by the Jesuits to Booth, in their daily intercourse in Mary Surratt's house, when he reads those lines written by Booth a few hours before his death: "I can never repent; God made me the instrument of His punishment!" Compare these words with the doctrines and principles taught by the councils, the decrees of the Pope, and the laws of holy inquisition, as you find them in Chapter LIX. of this volume, and you will find that the sentiments and belief of Booth flow from those principles, as the river flows from its source.

And that pious Miss Surratt who, the very next day after the murder of Lincoln, said, without being rebuked, in the presence of several other witnesses: "The death of Abraham Lincoln is no more than the death of any nigger in the army"—where did she get that

---

* *Trial of Surratt,* vol. i. p. 310.   † Ibid. p. 310.
‡ *Assassination of Abraham Lincoln,* pp. 51, 52.

maxim, if not from her church? Had not that church recently pro-claimed, through her highest legal and civil authority, the devoted Roman Catholic Judge Taney, in his Dred Scot decision, the negroes have no right, which the white is bound to respect! By bringing the President on a level with the lowest nigger, Rome was saying that he had no right even to his life; for this was the maxim of the rebel priests, who, everywhere, had made themselves the echoes of the sentence of their distinguished co-religionist—Taney.

It was from the very lips of the priests, who were constantly coming in and going out of their house, that those young ladies had learned those anti-social and anti-christian doctrines. Read in the testimony concerning Mrs. Mary E. Surratt (pp. 122, 123), how the Jesuits had perfectly drilled her in the art of perjuring herself. In the very moment when the government officer orders her to prepare herself, with her daughter, to follow him as prisoners, at about ten p.m., Payne, the would-be murderer of Seward, knocks at the door and wants to see Mrs. Surratt. But instead of having Mrs. Surratt to open the door, he finds himself confronted, face to face, with the government detective, Major Smith, who swears :

" I questioned him in regard to his occupation, and what business he had at the house at this late hour of the night. He stated that he was a labourer, and had come to dig a gutter at the request of Mrs. Surratt.

" I went to the parlour door, and said, 'Mrs. Surratt, will you step here a minute?' She came out, and I asked her, ' Do you know this man, and did you hire him to come and dig a gutter for you?' She answered, raising her right hand, 'Before God, sir, I do not know this man ; I have never seen him, and I did not hire him to dig a gutter for me.' "*

But it was proved after, by several unimpeachable witnesses, that she knew very well that Payne was a personal friend of her son, who, many times, had come to her house, in company of his friend and pet, Booth. She had received the communion just two or three days before that public perjury. Just a moment after making it, the officer ordered her to step out into the carriage. But before doing it, she asked permission to kneel down and pray ; which was granted.†

I ask it from any man of common sense, could Jeff Davis have imparted such a religious calm and self-possession to that woman when her hands were just reddened with the blood of the President, and she was on her way to trial !

No ! such *sang froid*, such calm in that soul, in such a terrible and solemn hour, could come only from the teachings of those Jesuits who,

* *Assassination of Lincoln*, p. 122.   † Ibid. p. 123.

for more than six months, were in her house, showing her a crown of eternal glory if she could help to kill the monster, apostate—Lincoln —the only cause of that horrible civil war! There is not the least doubt that the priests had perfectly succeeded in persuading Mary Surratt and Booth that the killing of Lincoln was a most holy and deserving work, for which God had an eternal reward in store.

There is a fact to which the American people have not yet given a sufficient attention. It is that, without a single exception, the conspirators were Roman Catholics. The learned and great patriot, General Baker, in his admirable report, struck and bewildered by that strange, mysterious and portentous fact, said :

"I mention, as an exceptional and remarkable fact, that every conspirator, in custody, is by education a Catholic."

But those words which, if well undertood by the United States, would have thrown so much light on the true causes of their untold and unspeakable disasters, fell as if on the ears of deaf men. Very few, if any, paid attention to them. As General Baker says, all the conspirators were attending Catholic Church services and were educated Roman Catholics. It is true that some of them, as Atzeroth, Payne and Harold, asked for Protestant ministers, when they were to be hung. But they had been considered, till then, as converts to Romanism. At page 437 of *The Trial of John Surratt*, Louis Weichman tells us that he was going to St. Aloysin's Church with Atzeroth, and that it was there that he introduced him to Mr. Brothy (another Roman Catholic).

It is a well authenticated fact, that Booth and Weichman, who were themselves Protestant perverts to Romanism, had proselytized a good number of semi-Protestants and infidels who, either from conviction, or from hope of the fortunes promised to the successful murderers, were themselves very zealous for the Church of Rome. Payne, Atzeroth and Harold, were among those proselytes. But when those murderers were to appear before the country, and receive the just punishment of their crime, the Jesuits were too shrewd to ignore that if they were all coming on the scaffold as Roman Catholics, and accompanied by their father confessors, it would, at once, open the eyes of the American people, and clearly show that this was a Roman Catholic plot. They persuaded three of their proselytes to avail themselves of the theological principles of the Church of Rome, that a man is allowed to conceal his religion, nay, that he may say that he is a heretic, a Protestant, though he is a Roman Catholic, when it is for his own interest or the best interests of his church to conceal the truth and deceive the people. Here is the doctrine of Rome on that subject.

" It is often more to the glory of God and the good of our neighbour to cover the faith than to confess it; for example, if concealed among heretics, you may accomplish a greater amount of good; or if, by declaring our religion more of evil would follow—for example, great trouble, death, the hostility of a tyrant."*

It is evident that the Jesuits had never had better reasons to suspect that the declaration of their religion would damage them and excite the wrath of their tyrant, viz., the American people. Lloyds, in whose house Mrs. Surratt concealed the carbine which Booth wanted for protection, when just after the murder he was to flee towards the Southern States, was a firm Roman Catholic. Dr. Nudd, at whose place Booth stopped, to have his broken leg dressed, was a Roman Catholic, and so was Garrett, in whose barn Booth was caught and killed. Why so? Because, as Jeff Davis was the only man to pay one million dollars to those who would kill Abraham Lincoln, the Jesuits were the only men to select the murderers and prepare everything to protect them after their diabolical deed, and such murderers could not be found except among their blind and fanatical slaves.

The great, the fatal mistake of the American Government in the prosecution of the assassins of Abraham Lincoln was to constantly keep out of sight the religious element of that terrible drama. Nothing would have been more easy, then, than to find out the complicity of the priests, who were not only coming every week and every day, but who were even living in that den of murderers. But this was carefully avoided from the beginning to the end of the trial. When, not long after the execution of the murderers, I went, incognito, to Washington to begin my investigation about its true and real authors, I was not a little surprised to see that not a single one of the Government men to whom I addressed myself, would consent to have any talk with me on that matter, except after I had given my word of honour that I would never mention their names in connection with the result of my investigation. I saw, with a profound distress, that the influence of Rome was almost supreme in Washington. I could not find a single statesman who would dare to face that nefarious influence and fight it down.

Several of the government men in whom I had more confidence, told me: "We had not the least doubt that the Jesuits were at the bottom of that great iniquity; we even feared, sometimes, that this would come out so clearly before the military tribunal, that there would be no possibility of keeping it out of the public sight. This

* "Cum non rogaris de fide, non solum licet sed saepe melius est ad Dei honorem, et utilitatem proximi, tegere fidem quam fateri; ut si latens inter hereticos plus boni facias; vel si ex confessione plus mali sequeretur, verbi gratia turbatio, neces, exacerbatio tyranni." (*Liguori, Theologia Moralis*, t. ii. n. 14, p. 117. Mechlin, 1845.)

was not through cowardice, as you think, but through a wisdom which you ought to approve, if you cannot admire it. Had we been in days of peace, we know that with a little more pressure on the witnesses, many priests would have been compromised ; for Mrs. Surratt's house was their common rendezvous ; it is more than probable that several of them might have been hung. But the civil war was hardly over. The Confederacy, though broken down, was still living in millions of hearts ; murderers and formidable elements of discord were still seen everywhere, to which the hanging or exiling of those priests would have given a new life. Riots after riots would have accompanied and followed their execution. We thought we had had enough of blood, fires, devastations and bad feelings. We were all longing after days of peace : the country was in need of them. We concluded that the best interests of humanity was to punish only those who were publicly and visibly guilty ; that the verdict might receive the approbation of all, without creating any new bad feelings. Allow us also tell you that this policy was that of our late President. For you know it well, there was nothing which that good and great man feared so much as to arm the Protestants against the Catholics, and the Catholics against the Protestants."

But if any one has still any doubts of the complicity of the Jesuits in the murder of Abraham Lincoln, let them give a moment of attention to the following facts, and their doubts will be for ever removed. It is only from the very Jesuit accomplices' lips that I take my sworn testimonies.

It is evident that a very elaborate plan of escape had been prepared by the priests of Rome to save the lives of the assassins and the conspirators. It would be too long to follow all the murderers when, Cain-like, they were fleeing in every direction, to escape the vengeance of God and man. Let us fix our eyes on John Surratt, who was in Washington the 14th of April, helping Booth in the perpetration of the assassination. Who will take care of him ? Who will protect and conceal him ? Who will press him on their bosom, put their mantles on his shoulders to conceal him from the just vengeance of the human and divine laws ? The priest, Charles Boucher,* swears that only a few days after the murder, John Surratt was sent to him by Father Lapierre, of Montreal; that he kept him concealed in his parsonage of St. Liboire from the end of April to the end of July, then he took him back, secretly, to Father Lapierre, who kept him secreted in his own father's house, under the very shadow of the Montreal bishop's palace. He swears† that Father Lapierre visited him (Surratt) often, when secreted at St. Liboire, and that he (Father

---

* *Trial of John Surratt*, vol. ii. pp. 904—912.   † Ibid. pp. 905—914.

Boucher) visited him, at least, twice a week, from the end of July to September, when concealed in Father Lapierre's house in Montreal.

That same father, Charles Boucher, swears that he accompanied John Surratt in a carriage, in the company of Father Lapierre, to the steamer " Montreal," when starting for Quebec : that Father Lapierre kept him (John Surratt) under lock during the voyage from Montreal to Quebec, and that he accompanied him, disguised from the Montreal steamer to the ocean steamer, " Peruvian."*

The doctor of the steamer "Peruvian," L. I. A. McMillan, swears† that Father Lapierre introduced him to John Surratt under the false name of McCarthy, whom he was keeping locked in his state room, and whom he conducted disguised to the ocean steamer "Peruvian," and with whom he remained till she left Quebec for Europe, the 15th September, 1865.

But who is that Father Lapierre who takes such a tender, I dare say a paternal care of Surratt ? It is not less a personage than the canon of Bishop Bourget, of Montreal. He is the confidential man of the bishop ; he lives with the bishop, eats at his table, assists him with his counsel, and has to receive his advice in every step of life. According to the laws of Rome, the canons are to the bishop what the arms are to the body.

Now, I ask : Is it not evident that the bishops and the priests of Washington have trusted this murderer to the care of the bishops and priests of Montreal, that they might conceal, feed, and protect him for nearly six months, under the very shadow of the bishop's palace ? Would they have done that if they were not his accomplices ? Why did they so continually remain with him day and night, if they were not in fear that he might compromise them by an indiscreet word ? Why do we see those priests (I ought to say, those two ambassadors and anointed representatives of the Pope), alone in the carriage which takes that great culprit from his house of concealment to the steamer ? Why do they keep him there, under lock, till they transfer him, under a disguised name, to the ocean steamer, the "Peruvian," on the 15th July, 1865 ? Why such tender sympathies for that stranger ? Why going through such trouble and expense for that young American among the bishops and priests of Canada ? There is only one answer. He was one of their tools, one of their selected men to strike the great Republic of Equality and Liberty to the heart. For more than six months before the murder, the priests had lodged, eaten, conversed, slept with him under the same roof in Washington. They had trained him to his deed of blood, by promising him protection on earth, and a crown of glory in heaven,

---

* *Trial of John Surratt*, p. 910.   † Ibid. vol. i. p. 460.

if he would only be true to their designs to the end. And he had been true to the end.

Now the great crime is accomplished! Lincoln is murdered! Jeff Davis, the dear son of the Pope, is avenged! The great Republic has been struck to the heart! The soldiers of Liberty all over the world are weeping over the dead form of the one who had led them to victory: a cry of desolation goes from earth to heaven.

It seems as if we heard the death-knell of the cause of freedom, equality and fraternity among men. It was many centuries since the implacable enemies of the rights and liberties of men had struck such a giant foe: their joy was as great as their victory complete.

But do you see that man fleeing from Washington towards the north? He has the mark of Cain on his forehead, his hands are reddened with blood, he is pale and trembling, for he knows it; a whole outraged nation is after him for her just vengeance; he hears the thundering voice of God: "Where is thy brother?" Where will he find a refuge? Where, outside of hell, will he meet friends to shelter and save him from the just vengeance of God and men?

Oh! He has sure refuge in the arms of that church who, for more than a thousand years, is crying: "Death to all the heretics! death to all the soldiers of Liberty!" He has devoted friends among the very men who, after having prepared the massacre of Admiral Coligny, and his 75,000 Protestant countrymen, rang the bells of Rome to express their joy when they heard that, at last, the King of France had slaughtered them all.

But where will those bishops and priests of Canada send John Surratt when they find it impossible to conceal him any longer from the thousands of detectives of the United States, who are ransacking Canada to find out his retreat? Who will conceal, feed, lodge, and protect him after the priests of Canada pressed his hand for the last time on board of the "Peruvian," the 15th of September, 1865?

Who can have any doubt about that? Who can suppose that any one but the Pope himself and his Jesuits will protect the murderer of Abraham Lincoln in Europe?

If you want to see him after he has crossed the ocean, go to Vitry, at the door of Rome, and there you will find him enrolled under the banners of the Pope, in the 9th company of his Zouaves, under the false name of Watson. Of course, the Pope was forced to withdraw his protection over him, after the Government of the United States had found him there, and he was brought back to Washington to be tried.

But on his arrival as a prisoner in the United States, his Jesuit father confessor whispered in his ear: "Fear not, you will not be condemned! Through the influence of a high Roman Catholic lady, two or three of the jurymen will be Roman Catholics, and you will be safe."

Those who have read the two volumes of the trial of John Surratt know that never more evident proofs of guilt were brought against a murderer than in that case. But the Roman Catholic jurymen had read the theology of St. Thomas, a book which the Pope has ordered to be taught in every college, academy, and university of Rome, they had learned that it is the duty of the Roman Catholics to exterminate all the heretics.*

They had read the decree of the Councils of Constance, that no faith was to be kept with heretics. They had read in the Council of Lateran that the Catholics who arm themselves for the extermination of heretics, have all their sins forgiven, and receive the same blessings as those who go and fight for the rescue of the Holy Land.

Those jurymen were told by their father confessors that the most holy father, the Pope, Gregory VII., had solemnly and infallibly declared that " the killing of an heretic was no murder."—*Jure Canonico.*

After such teachings, how could the Roman Catholic jurymen find John Surratt guilty of murder for killing the heretic Lincoln? The jury having disagreed, no verdict could be given. The Government was forced to let the murderer go unpunished.

But when the irreconcilable enemies of all the rights and liberties of men were congratulating themselves on their successful efforts to save the life of John Surratt, the God of heaven was stamping again on their faces the mark of murder, in such a way that all eyes will see it.

" Murder will out," is a truth repeated by all nations from the beginning of the world. It is the knowledge of that truth which has sustained me in my long and difficult researches of the true authors of the assassination of Lincoln, and which enables me to-day to present to the world a fact, which seems almost miraculous, to show the complicity of the priests of Rome in the murder of the martyred President.

Some time ago, I providentially met the Rev. Mr. F. A. Conwell, at Chicago. Having known that I was in search of facts about the assassination of Abraham Lincoln, he told me he knew one of those facts which might perhaps throw some light on the subject of my researches.

" The very day of the murder," he said, "he was in the Roman Catholic village of St. Joseph, Minnesota State, when, at about six o'clock in the afternoon, he was told by a Roman Catholic of the place, who was a purveyor for a great number of priests who lived in that town, where they have a monastery, that the State Secretary Seward and President Lincoln had just been killed. This was told me," he said, "in the presence of a most respectable gentleman, called

* *St. Thomas' Theology,* vol. iv. p. 90.

Bennett, who was not less puzzled than me. As there were no rail-road lines nearer than forty miles, nor telegraph offices nearer than eighty miles from that place, we could not see how such news was spread in that town. The next day, the 15th of April, I was at St. Cloud, a town about twelve miles distant, where there were neither railroad nor telegraph ; I said to several people that I had been told in the priestly village of St. Joseph, by a Roman Catholic, that Abraham Lincoln and the Secretary Seward had been assassinated. They answered me that they had heard nothing about it. But the next Sabbath, the 16th of April, when going to the church of St. Cloud, to preach, a friend gave me a copy of a telegram sent to him on the Saturday, reporting that Abraham Lincoln and Secretary Seward had been assassinated the very day before, which was Friday, the 14th, at 10 p.m. But how could the Roman Catholic purveyor of the priests of St. Joseph have told me the same thing, before several witnesses, just four hours before its occurrence ? I spoke of that strange thing to many that same day, and, the very next day, I wrote to the St. Paul ' Press ' under the heading of ' a strange coincidence.' Some time later, the editor of the St. Paul ' Pioneer,' having denied what I had written on that subject, I addressed him the following note, which he had printed, and which I have kept. Here it is, you may keep it as an infallible proof of my veracity.

"TO THE EDITOR OF THE ST. PAUL ' PIONEER.' "

" You assume the non-truth of a short paragraph furnished by me to the St. Paul ' Press,' viz :

"A STRANGE COINCIDENCE !

"At 6.30 p.m., Friday last, April 14th, I was told as an item of news, eight miles west of this place, that Lincoln and Seward had been assassinated. This was three hours after I had heard the news."

"ST. CLOUD, 17th of April, 1865.

" The integrity of history requires that the above coincidence be established. And if anyone calls it in question, then proofs more ample than reared their sanguinary shadows to comfort a traitor can now be given.

" Respectfully,
" F. A. CONWELL."

I asked that gentleman if he would be kind enough to give me the fact under oath, that I might make use of it in the report I intended to publish about the assassination of Lincoln. And he kindly granted my request in the following form :—

State of Illinois, } s.s.
Cook County.

Rev. F. A. Conwell being sworn, deposes and says that he is seventy-one years old, that he is a resident of North Evanston, in Cook County, State of Illinois, that he has been in the ministry for fifty-six years, and is now one of the chaplains of the "Seamen's Bethel Home," in Chicago; that he was chaplain of the 1st Minnesota Regiment, in the war of the rebellion. That, on the 14th day of April, A.D. 1865, he was in St. Joseph, Minnesota, and reached there so early as six o'clock in the evening, in company with Mr. Bennett, who, then and now, is a resident of St. Cloud, Minnesota. That on that date, there was no telegraph nearer than Minneapolis, about eighty miles from St. Joseph; and there was no railroad communication nearer than Avoka, Minnesota, about forty miles distant. That when he reached St. Joseph, on the 14th day of April, 1865, one Mr. Linneman, who then kept the hotel of St. Joseph, told affiant that President Lincoln and Secretary Seward were assassinated, that it was not later than half-past six o'clock, on Friday, April 14th, 1865, when Mr. Linneman told me this. Shortly thereafter, Mr. Bennett came in the hotel, and I told him that Mr. Linneman said the President Lincoln and Secretary Seward were assassinated; and then, the same Mr. Linneman reported the same conversation to Mr. Bennett in my presence. That during that time, Mr. Linneman told me that he had the charge of the friary or college for young men, under the priests, who were studying for the priesthood of St. Joseph. That there was a large multitude of this kind at St. Joseph, at this time. Affiant says that, on Saturday morning, April 15th, 1865, he went to St. Cloud, a distance of about ten miles, and reached there about eight o'clock in the morning. That there was no railroad or telegraph communication to St. Cloud. When he arrived at St. Cloud, he told Mr. Haworth, the hotel keeper, that he had been told that President Lincoln and Secretary Seward had been assassinated, and asked if it was true. He further told Henry Clay, Wait, Charles Gilman, who was afterwards Lieutenant Governor of Minnesota, and Rev. Mr. Tice, the same thing, and inquired of them if they had any such news; and they replied that they had not heard anything of the kind.

Affiant says that, on Sunday morning, April 16th, 1865, he preached in St. Cloud, and on the way to the church, a copy of telegram was handed him, stating that the President and Secretary were assassinated Friday evening at about nine o'clock. This telegram had been brought to St. Cloud by Mr. Gorton, who had reached St. Cloud by stage; and this was the first intelligence that had reached St. Cloud of the event.

Affiant says further that on Monday morning, April 17th, 1865, he furnished the "Press," a paper of St. Paul, a statement that three hours before the event took place, he had been informed at St. Joseph, Minnesota, that the President had been assassinated, and this was published in the "Press."

FRANCIS ASBURY CONWELL.

Subscribed and sworn to by Francis A. Conwell, before me, a Notary Public of Kankakee County, Illinois, at Chicago, Cook County, this 6th day of September, 1883.

STEPHEN R. MOORE, Notary Public.

Though this document was very important and precious to me, I felt that it would be much more valuable if it could be corroborated by the testimonies of Messrs. Bennett and Linneman, themselves, and I immediately sent a magistrate to find out if they were still living, and if they remembered the facts of the sworn declaration of Rev. Mr. Conwell. By the good providence of God, both of these gentlemen were found living, and both gave the following testimonies:

State of Minnesota, }
Sterns County, City }
of St. Cloud. }

Horace P. Bennett, being sworn, deposes and says that he is aged sixty-four years; that he is a resident of St. Cloud, Minnesota, and has resided in this county since 1856; that he is acquainted with the Rev. F. A. Conwell, who was chaplain of the 1st Minnesota Regiment in the war of the rebellion; that on the 14th of April, 1865, he was in St. Joseph, Minnesota, in company with Mr. Francis A. Conwell; that they reached St. Joseph about sundown of said April 14th; that there was no railroad or telegraph communication with St. Joseph, at that time, nor nearer than Avoka, about forty miles distant. That affiant, on reaching the hotel kept by Mr. Linneman, went to the barn while Rev. F. A. Conwell entered the hotel; and shortly afterwards, affiant had returned to the hotel, Mr. Conwell told him that Mr. Linneman had reported to him the assassination of President Lincoln; that Linneman was present and substantiated the statement.

That on Saturday morning, April 15th, affiant and Rev. Conwell came to St. Cloud and reported that they had been told at St. Joseph about the assassination of President Lincoln, that no one at St. Cloud had heard of the event at this time, that the first news of the event which reached St. Cloud was on Sunday morning, April 16th, when the news was brought by Leander Gorton, who had just come up from Avoka, Minnesota; that they spoke to several persons of St. Cloud, concerning the matter, when they reached there, on Sunday morning, but affiant does not now remember who those different persons were, and further affiant says not.

HORACE P. BENNETT.

Sworn before me, and subscribed in my presence, this 18th of October, A.D. 1883.

ANDREW C. ROBERTSON, Notary Public.

Mr. Linneman having refused to swear on his written declaration, which I have in my possession, I take only from it what refers to the principal fact, viz., that three or four hours before Lincoln was assassinated at Washington, the 14th of April, 1865, the fact was told as already accomplished, in the priestly village of St. Joseph, Minnesota.

"He (Linneman) remembers the time that Messrs. Conwell and Bennett came to this place (St. Joseph, Minnesota) on Friday evening, before the President was killed, and he asked them, if they had heard he was dead, and they replied they had not. He heard this rumour in his store from people who came in and out. But he cannot remember from whom.

"J. H. LINNEMAN.

"October 20th, 1883."

I present here to the world a fact of the greatest gravity, and that fact is so well authenticated that it cannot allow even the possibility of a doubt.

Three or four hours before Lincoln was murdered in Washington, the 14th of April, 1865, that murder was not only known by some one, but it was circulated and talked of in the streets, and in the houses of the priestly and Romish town of St. Joseph, Minnesota. The fact is undeniable; the testimonies are unchallengeable: and there were no railroad nor any telegraph communications nearer than forty or eighty miles from the nearest station to St. Joseph.

Naturally every one asked: "How could such news spread? Where is the source of such a rumour?" Mr. Linneman, who is a Roman Catholic, tells us that though he heard this from many in his store, and in the streets, he does not remember the name of a single one who told him that. And when we hear this from him, we understand why he did not dare to swear upon it, and shrank from the idea of perjuring himself. For every one feels that his memory cannot be so poor as that, when he remembers so well the names of the two strangers, Messrs. Conwell and Bennett, to whom he had announced the assassination of Lincoln, just seventeen years before. But if the memory of Mr. Linneman is so deficient on that subject, we can help him, and tell him with mathematical accuracy:

"You got the news from your priests of St. Joseph! The conspiracy which cost the life of the martyred President was prepared by the priests of Washington, in the house of Mary Surratt, No. 541, H. Street. The priests of St. Joseph were often visiting Washington, and boarding, probably, at Mrs. Surratt's, as the priests of Washington were often visiting their brother priests at St. Joseph. Those priests of Washington were in daily communication with their co-rebel priests of St. Joseph; they were their intimate friends. There were no secrets among them, as there are no secrets among priests. They are the members of the same body, the branches of the same tree. The details of the murder, as the day selected for its commission, were as well known among the priests of St. Joseph, as they were among those of Washington. The death of Lincoln was such a glorious event for those priests! That infamous apostate, Lincoln, who, baptized in the Holy Church, had rebelled against her, broken his oath of allegiance to the Pope, taken the very day of his baptism, and lived the life of an apostate! That infamous Lincoln, who had dared to fight against the Confederacy of the South after the Vicar of Christ had solemnly declared that their cause was just, legitimate and holy! That bloody tyrant, that godless and infamous man, was to receive, at last, the just chastisement of his crimes, the 14th of April! What glorious news!"

How could the priests conceal such a joyful event from their bosom friend, Mr. Linneman? He was their confidential man: he was their purveyor: he was their right hand man among the faithful of St. Joseph. They thought that they would be guilty of a want of confidence in their bosom friend, if they did not tell him all about the glorious event of that great day. But, of course, they requested him not to mention their names, if he would spread the joyful news among the devoted Roman Catholics who, almost exclusively, formed the people of St. Joseph. Mr. Linneman has honourably and faithfully kept his promise never to reveal their names, and to-day, we have in our hand, the authentic testimonies signed by him that, though some body, the 14th of April, told him that President Lincoln was assassinated, he does not know who told him that!

But there is not a man of sound judgment who will have any doubt about that fact, The 14th of April, 1865, the priests of Rome knew and circulated the death of Lincoln four hours before its occurrence in their Roman Catholic town of St. Joseph, Minnesota. But they could not circulate it without knowing it, and they could not know it, without belonging to the band of conspirators who assassinated President Lincoln.

CHAPTER LXII.

WHEN alone, on my knees, in the presence of God, on the 1st of January, 1855, I took the resolution of opposing the acts of simony and tyranny of Bishop O'Regan, I was far from understanding the logical consequences of my struggle with that high dignitary. My only object was to force him to be honest, just and Christian towards my people. That people, with me, had left their country and had bid an eternal adieu to all that was dear to them in Canada, in order to live in peace in Illinois, under what we then considered the holy authority of the Church of Christ. But we were absolutely unwilling to be slaves of any man in the land of Liberty.

If any one, at that hour, could have shown me that this struggle would lead to a complete separation from the Church of Rome, I would have shrank from the task. My only ambition was to purify my church from the abuses which, one after the other, had crept everywhere about her, as noxious weeds. I felt that those abuses were destroying the precious truths which Jesus Christ and His apostles had revealed to us. It seemed to me that was a duty imposed upon every priest to do all in our power to blot from the face of our church the scandals which were the fruits of the iniquities and tyranny of the bishops. I had most sincerely offered myself to God for this work.

From the beginning, however, I had a presentiment that the power of the bishops would be too much for me, and that, sooner or later, they would crush me. But my hope was that when I should have fallen, others would have taken my place and fight the battles of the Lord, till a final victory would bring the church back to the blessed days when she was the spotless spouse of the Lamb.

The great and providential victory I had gained at Urbana, had strengthened my conviction that God was on my side, and that He would protect me, so long as my only motives were in the interests of truth and righteousness. It seemed, in a word, that I could not fail so long as I should fight against the official lies, tyrannies, superstitions and deceits which the bishops had everywhere in the United States and Canada, substituted in the place of the Gospel, the primitive laws of the church, and the teachings of the holy fathers.

In the autumn of 1856, our struggle against the Bishop of Chicago had taken proportions which could not have been anticipated either by me or by the Roman Catholic hierarchy of America. The whole press of the United States and Canada, both political and religious, were discussing the causes and the probable results of the contest.

At first, the bishops were indignant at the conduct of my lord O'Regan. They had seen with pleasure, that a priest from his own diocese would probably force him to be more cautious and less scandalous in his public and private dealings with the clergy and the people. But they also hoped that I should be paralyzed by the sentence of excommunication, and that the people, frightened by those fulminations, would withdraw the support they had, at first, given me. They were assured by Spink, that I would lose my suit at Urbana, and should, when lodged in the penitentiary, become powerless to do any mischief in the church.

But their confidence was soon changed into dismay when they saw that the people laughed at the excommunication; that I had gained my suit, and that I was triumphing on that very battle-field from which no priest, since Luther and Knox, had come out unscathed. Everywhere, the sound of alarm was heard, and I was denounced as a rebel and schismatic. The whole body of the bishops prepared to hurl their most terrible fulminations at my devoted head. But before taking their last measure to crush me, a supreme effort was made to show us what they considered our errors. The Rev. Messrs. Brassard, curate of Longueuil, and Rev. Isaac Desaulnier, President of St. Hyacinthe College, were sent by the people and bishops of Canada to show me what they called the scandal of my proceedings, and press me to submit to the will of the bishop, by respecting the so-called sentence of excommunication.

The choice of those two priests was very wise. They were certainly the most influential that could be sent. Mr. Brassard had not only been my teacher at the college of Nicolet, but my benefactor, as I have already said. When the want of means, in 1825, had forced me to leave the college and bid adieu to my mother and my young brothers, in order to get to a very distant land, in search of a position, he stopped me on the road to exile and brought me back to the college; and along with the Rev. Mr. Leprohon, he paid all my

expenses to the end of my studies. He had loved me since, as his own
child, and I cherished and respected him as my own father. The other,
Rev. I. Desaulnier, had been my classmate in the college from 1822
to 1829, and we had been united during the whole of that period, as
well as since, by the bonds of the sincerest esteem and friendship.
They arrived at St. Anne on November 24th, 1856.

I heard of their coming only a few minutes before their arrival;
and nothing can express the joy I felt at the news. The confidence I
had in their honesty and friendship, gave me, at once, the hope that
they would soon see the justice and holiness of our cause, and they
would bravely take our side against our aggressor. But they had very
different sentiments. Sincerely believing that I was an unmanageable
schismatic, who was creating an awful scandal in the church, they had
not only been forbidden by the bishops to sleep in my house, but also
to have any friendly and Christian communication with me. With no
hatred against me, they were yet filled with horror at the thought that
I should be so scandalous a priest, and so daring, as to trouble the
peace, and destroy the unity of the church.

On their way from Canada to St. Anne, they had often been told
that I was not the same man as they knew me formerly to be, and that
I had become sour and gloomy, abusive, insolent, and haughty; that
also I would insult them, and perhaps advise the people to turn them
away from my premises, as men who had no business to meddle in our
affairs. They were pleasantly disappointed, however, when they saw
me running to meet them, as far as I could see them, to press them
to my heart, with the most sincere marks of affection and joy. I told
them that all the treasures of California brought to my house would
not make me half so happy as I was made by their presence.

I at once expressed my hope that they were the messengers sent
by God to bring us peace and put an end to the deplorable state of
things which was the cause of their long journey. Remarking that
they were covered with mud, I invited them to go to their sleeping
rooms, to wash and refresh themselves.

"Sleeping rooms! sleeping rooms!!" said Mr. Desaulnier, "but
our written instructions from the bishops who sent us, forbid us to
sleep here on account of your excommunication."

Mr. Brassard answered, "I must tell you, my dear Mr. Desaulnier,
a thing which I have kept secret till now. After reading that prohibition of sleeping here, I said to the bishop that if he would put
such a restraint upon me, he might choose another one to come here.
I requested him to let us both act according to our conscience and
common sense when we should be with Chiniquy, and to-day my conscience and common sense tell me that we cannot begin our mission
of peace by insulting a man who gives us such a friendly and Christian

reception. The people of Canada have chosen us as their deputies, because we are the most sincere friends of Chiniquy. It is by keeping that character that we will best fulfil our sacred and solemn duties. I accept, with pleasure, the sleeping room offered me."

Mr. Desaulnier rejoined: "I accept it also, for I did not come here to insult my best friend, but to save him."

These kind words of my guests added to the joy I experienced at their coming. I told them: "If you are here to obey the voice of your conscience and the dictates of your common sense, there is a glorious task before you. You will soon find that the people and priest of St. Anne have also done nothing but listened to the voice of their honest conscience, and followed the laws of common sense in their conduct towards the bishop. But," I added, "this is not the time to explain my position, but the time to wash your dusty faces and refresh yourselves. Here are your rooms, make yourselves at home."

After supper, which had been spent in the most pleasant way, and without any allusion to our troubles, they handed me the letters addressed to me by the bishops of Montreal, London, and Toronto, to induce me to submit to my superior, and offer me the assurance of their most sincere friendship and devotedness if I would obey.

Mr. Desaulnier then said: "Now, my dear Chiniquy, we have been sent here by the people and bishops of Canada to take you away from the bottomless abyss into which you have fallen with your people. We have only one day and two nights to spend here, we must lose no time, but begin at once to fulfil our solemn mission."

I answered: "If I have fallen into a bottomless abyss as you say, and that you will draw me out of it, not only God and men will bless you, but I will also for ever bless you for your charity. The first thing, however, you have to do here, is to see if I am really fallen, with my people, into that bottomless abyss of which you speak."

"But are you not excommunicated," quickly rejoined Mr. Desaulnier, "and, notwithstanding that excommunication, have you not continued to say your mass, preach, and hear the confessions of your people? Are you not then fallen into that state of irregularity and schism which separate you entirely from the church, and to which the Pope alone can restore you?"

"No, my dear Desaulnier," I answered, "I am not more excommunicated than you are. For the simple reason that an act of excommunication which is not signed and certified, is a public nullity; unworthy of any attention. Here is the act of the so-called excommunication, which makes so much noise in the world! Examine it yourself; look if it is signed by the bishop, or any one else you know; consider with attention if it is certified by anybody." And I handed him the document.

34

After he had examined it, and turned it every way for more than half an hour, with Mr. Brassard, without saying a word, he at last broke his silence, and said: " If I had not seen it with my own eyes, I could never have believed that a bishop can play such a sacrilegious comedy in the face of the world. You have several times published it in the press, but I confess that your best friends, and I among the rest, did not believe you. It could not enter our minds that a bishop should be so devoid, I do not say of every principle of religion, but of the most common honesty, as to have proclaimed before the whole world that you were excommunicated, when he had to offer us only that ridiculous piece of rag to support his assertion. But, in the name of common sense, why is it that he has not signed his sentence of excommunication, or get it signed and countersigned by some authorized people, when it is so evident that he wanted to excommunicate you ? "

" His reason for not putting his name, nor the name of any known person at the bottom of that so-called excommunication is very clear," I answered; "though our bishop is one of the most accomplished rogues of Illinois, he is still more a coward than a rogue. I had threatened to bring him before the civil court of the country if he dared to destroy my character by a sentence of interdict or excommunication; and he found that the only way to save himself in the same time that he was outraging me, was not to sign that paper; he thereby took away from me the power of prosecuting him. For, the first thing I would have to do in a prosecution in that case, would be to prove the signature of the bishop. Where could I find a witness who would swear that this is his signature? Would you swear it yourself, my dear Desaulnier ? "

" Oh ! no, for surely it is not his signature, nor that of his grand vicar or secretary. But without going any further," added he, " we must confess to you that we have talked to the bishop, when passing through Chicago, asking him if he had made any public or private inquest against you, and if he had found you guilty of any crime. As he felt embarrassed by our questions, we told him that it was in our public character as deputies of the bishops and people of Canada towards you that we were putting to him those questions. That it was necessary for us to know all about your public and private character, when we were coming to press you to reconcile yourself to your bishop. He answered that he had never made any inquest about you, though you had requested him several times to do it, for the simple reason that he was persuaded that you were one of his best priests. Your only defect, he said, was a spirit of stubbornness and want of respect and obedience to your superior, and your meddling with his dealings with his diocesans, with which you had no business. He told us also

that you refused to go to Kahokia. But his face became so red, and his
tongue was so strangely lisping when he said that, that I suspected it
was a falsehood; and we have now, before our eyes, that document,
signed by four unimpeachable witnesses, that it was more than a
falsehood—it was a lie. He proffered another lie also, we see it now,
when he said that he had signed himself the act of excommunication;
for surely this is not his handwriting. Such conduct from a bishop is
very strange. If you would appeal to the Pope, and go to Rome with
such documents in hand against that bishop, you would have an
easy victory over him. For, the canons of the church are clear and
unanimous on that subject. A bishop who pronounces such grave
sentences against a priest, and makes use of false signatures to certify
his sentences, is himself suspended and excommunicated, *ipso facto*,
for a whole year."

Mr. Brassard added: " Cannot we confess to Chiniquy that the
opinion of the bishops of Canada is, that Bishop O'Regan is a perfect
rogue, and that if he (Chiniquy) would submit at once, under protest,
to those unjust sentences, and appeal to the Pope, he would gain his
cause, and soon be reinstated by a public decree of his Holiness."

Our discussion about the troubles I had had, and the best way to
put an end to them, having kept us up till three o'clock in the morning
without being able to come to any satisfactory issue, we adjourned to
the next day, and went to take some rest after a short prayer.

The 25th of November, at 10 a.m., after breakfast and a short walk
in our public square, to breathe the pure air and enjoy the fine scenery
of our beautiful hill of St. Anne, we shut ourselves up in my study,
and resumed the discussion of the best plans of putting an end to the
existing difficulties.

To show them my sincere desire of stopping those noisy and
scandalous struggles without compromising the sacred principles
which had guided me from the beginning of our troubles, I consented
to sacrifice my position as pastor of St. Anne, provided Mr. Brassard
would be installed in my place. It was decided, however, that I
should remain with him, as his vicar and help, in the management of
the spiritual and temporal affairs of the colony. The promise was
given me that on that condition the bishop would withdraw his
so-called sentence, give back to the French Canadians of Chicago the
church he had taken away from them, put a French-speaking priest at
the head of the congregation, and forgive and forget what he might
consider our irregular conduct towards him, after we should have
signed the following document:

To his Lordship O'Regan, Bishop of Chicago.

My Lord :—As my actions and writing in opposition to your orders have, since a few months, given some scandals, and caused some people to think that I would rather prefer to be separated from our holy church than to submit to your authority, I hasten to express the regret I feel for such acts and writings. And to show to the world and to you, my bishop, my firm desire to live and die a Catholic, I hasten to write to your lordship that I submit to your sentence, and that I promise hereafter to exercise the holy ministry only with your permission. In consequence, I respectfully request your lordship to withdraw the censures and interdicts you have pronounced against me and those who have had any spiritual communication with me. I am, my lord, your devoted son in Christ,

C. CHINIQUY.

It was eleven o'clock at night when I consented to sign this document, which was to be handed to the bishop and have any value, only on the above conditions. The two deputies were beside themselves with joy at the success of their mission, and at my readiness to sacrifice myself for the sake of peace. Mons. Desaulnier said :

"Now we see, evidently, that Chiniquy has been right with his people from the beginning, that he never meant to create a schism and to put himself at the head of a rebellious party, to defy the authority of the church. If the bishop does not want to live in peace with the people and pastor of St. Anne after such a sacrifice, we will tell him that it is not Chiniquy, but Bishop O'Regan, who wants a schism—we will appeal to the Pope—I will go with Chiniquy, and we will easily get there the removal of that bishop from the diocese of Chicago."

Mr. Brassard confirmed that sentence, and added that he also would accompany me to Rome to be the witness of my innocence, and the bad conduct of the bishop. He added that it would not take him a week to raise twice the amount of money in Montreal we would require to go to Rome.

After thanking them for what they had done and said, I asked Mr. Desaulnier if he would be brave enough to repeat before my whole people what he had just said before me and Mr. Brassard in the presence of God.

"Surely, I would be most happy to repeat before your whole people that it is impossible to find fault with you in what you have done till now. But, you know very well, I will never have such an opportunity, for it is now eleven o'clock at night, your people are soundly sleeping, and I must start to-morrow morning, at six o'clock, to take the Chicago train at Kankakee at 8 a.m.

I answered : "All right!"

We knelt together to make a short prayer, and I led them to their rooms, wishing them refreshing sleep, after the hard work of the day.

Ten minutes later I was in the village, knocking at the door of six of my most respectable parishioners, and telling them :

" Please do not lose a moment; go with your fastest horse to such and such a part of the colony; knock at every door and tell the people to be at the church at five o'clock in the morning, to hear with their own ears what the deputies from Canada have to say about past struggles with the Bishop of Chicago. Tell them to be punctual at five o'clock in their pews, where the deputies will address them words which they must hear at any cost."

A little before five the next morning Mr. Desaulnier, full of surprise and anxiety, knocked at my door and said:

" Chiniquy, do you not hear the strange noise of buggies and carriages which seem to be coming from every quarter of the globe. What does it mean? Have your people become crazy to come to church at this dark hour, so long before the dawn of day?"

" What! what!" I answered, "I was sleeping so soundly that I have heard nothing yet. What do you mean by this noise of carriages and buggies around the chapel? Are you dreaming?"

" No, I am not dreaming," he answered; " not only do I hear the noise of a great many carriages, waggons, and buggies; but, though it is pretty dark, I see several hundred of them around the chapel. I hear the voices of a great multitude of men, women, and even children, putting questions to each other, and giving answers which I cannot understand. They make such a noise by their laughing and jokes! Can you tell me what this means? I have never been so puzzled in my life."

I answered him: " Do you not see that you are dreaming. Let me dress myself that I may go and see something of that strange and awful dream!"

Mr. Brassard, though a little more calm than Desaulnier, was not, himself, without some anxiety at the strange noise of that multitude of carriages, horses, and people around my house and chapel at such an hour. Knocking at my door, he said: " Please, Chiniquy, explain that strange mystery. Do that people come to play us some bad trick, and punish us for our intruding in their affairs?"

" Be quiet," I answered, "my dear friends. You have nothing to fear from that good and intelligent people. Do you not remember that, last night, a few minutes before eleven o'clock, Desaulnier said that he would be honest and brave enough to repeat before my whole people what he had said before you and me, and in the presence of God. I suppose that some of the angels of heaven have heard those words, and have carried them this night to every family, inviting them to be here at the chapel, that they might hear from your own lips what you think of the grand and glorious battle they are fighting in this distant land for the principles of truth and justice, as the gospel secures them to every disciple of Christ."

" Well ! well !" said Desaulnier, "there is only one Chiniquy in the world to take me in such a trap, and there is only one people under heaven to do what this people is doing here. I would never have given you that answer had I not been morally sure that I would never have had the opportunity to fulfil it. Who would think you would play me such a trick ? But," he added, " though I know that this will terribly compromise me before certain parties, it is too late to retract, and I will fulfil my promise."

It is impossible to express my own joy and the joy of that noble people when they heard from the very lips of those deputies that, after spending a whole day and two nights in examining all that had been done by their pastor and by them in that solemn and fearful contest, they declared that they had not broken any law of God, nor of His holy church; and that they had kept themselves in the very way prescribed by the canons.

Tears of joy were rolling down every cheek when they heard Mr. Desaulnier telling them, which Mr. Brassard confirmed after, that the bishop had no possible right to interdict their pastor, since he had told them that he was one of his best priests ; and that they had done well not to pay any attention to an act of excommunication which was a sham and sacrilegious comedy, not having been signed nor certified by any known person. Both deputies said :

"Mr. Brassard will be your pastor, and Mr. Chiniquy, as his vicar, will remain in your midst. He has signed an act of submission, which we have found sufficient, on the condition that the bishop will let you live in peace, and withdraw the sentence he says he has fulminated against you. If he does not accept those conditions we will tell him, it is not Mr. Chiniquy, but he, who wants a schism, and we will go with Mr. Chiniquy to Rome, to plead his cause and prove his innocence before his Holiness."

After this, we all knelt to thank and bless God ; and never people went back to their homes with more cheerful hearts than the people of St. Anne on that morning of the 25th of November, 1856.

At six o'clock a.m., Mr. Desaulnier was on his way back to Chicago, to present my conditional act of submission to the bishop, and press him, in the name of the bishops of Canada, and in the name of all the most sacred interests of the church, to accept the sacrifice and the submission of the people of St. Anne, and to give them the peace they wanted and were purchasing at such a price. The Rev. Mr. Brassard had remained with me, waiting for a letter from the bishop to accompany me and put the last seal to our reconciliation.

The next day he received the following note from Mr. Desaulnier :

"BISHOPRIC OF CHICAGO, Nov. 26th, 1856.

"The REV. MR. BRASSARD,

"MONSIEUR,—It is advisable and indispensable that you should come here, with Mr. Chiniquy, as soon as possible. In consequence, I expect you both day after to-morrow, in order to settle that matter definitely.

"Respectfully yours,   "ISAAC DESAULNIER."

After reading that letter with Mr. Brassard, I said:

" Do you not feel that these cold words mean nothing good ? I regret that you have not gone with Desaulnier to the bishop. You know the levity and weakness of his character, always bold with his words, but soft as wax at the least pressure which he feels. My fear is that the bulldog tenacity of my lord O'Regan has frightened him, and all his courage and bravados have melted away before the fierce temper of the Bishop of Chicago. But let us go. Be sure, however, my dear Mr. Brassard, that if the bishop does not accept you to remain at the head of this colony, to protect and guide it, no consideration whatever will induce me to betray my people and let them become the prey of the wolves which want to devour them."

We arrived at the Illinois Central depot of Chicago, the 28th, at about ten a.m. Mr. Desaulnier was there, waiting for us. He was pale as a dead man. The marks of Cain and Judas were on his face. Having taken him at a short distance from the crowd, I asked him :

" What news ? "

He answered : " The news is, that you and Mr. Brassard have nothing to do but to take your bags and go away from St. Anne, to Canada. The bishop is unwilling to make any arrangements with you. He wants me to be the pastor of St. Anne, *pro tempore*, and he wants you, with Mr. Brassard, to go back quietly to Canada, and tell the bishops to mind their own business."

" And what has become of the promise you have given me and to my people, to go with me and Mr. Brassard to Rome, if the bishop refused the proposed arrangements you had fixed yourselves ? "

" Tat! tat! tat!" answered he. " The bishop does not care a straw about your going, or not going to Rome. He has put me as his grand vicar at the head of the colony of St. Anne, from which you must go in the shortest time possible."

" Now, Desaulnier," I answered, " you are a traitor, and a Judas, and if you want to have the pay of Judas, I advise you to go to St. Anne. There, you will receive what you deserve. The beauty and importance of that great colony have tempted you, and you have sold me to the bishop, in order to become a grand vicar and eat the fruits of the vine I have planted there. But, you will soon see your mistake. If you have any pity for yourself, I advise you never to put your feet into that place any more."

Desaulnier answered : " The bishop will not make any arrangements with you unless you retract publicly what you have written against him, on account of his taking possession of the church of the French Canadians of Chicago, and you must publish, in the press, that he was right and honest in what he did in that circumstance."

"My dear Mr. Brassard," I said, " can I make such a declaration conscientiously and honourably?" That venerable man answered me :

"You cannot consent to do such a thing."

"Desaulnier," I said, " do you hear? Mr. Brassard and your conscience, if you have any, tell you the same thing. If you take sides against me with a man whom you have yourself declared, yesterday, to be a sacrilegious thief, you are not better than he is. Go and work with him. As for me, I go back into the midst of my dear and noble people of St. Anne."

"What will you do there," answered Mr. Desaulnier, " when the bishop has forbidden you to remain? "

"What will I do? " I answered. " I will teach those true disciples of Jesus Christ to despise and shun the tyrants and the traitors, even though wearing a mitre, or a square bonnet (un bonnet carré). Go, traitor! and finish your Judas work! Adieu!"

I then threw myself into the arms of Mr. Brassard, who was almost speechless, suffocated in his sobs and tears. I pressed him to my heart and said! "Adieu! my dear Mr. Brassard. Go back to Canada and tell my friends, how the cowardice and ambition of that traitor has ruined the hope we had of putting an end to this deplorable state of affairs. I go back among my brethren of St. Anne, with more determination than ever to protect them against the tyranny and impiety of our despotic rulers. It will be more easy than ever to show them that the Son of God has not redeemed us, on the cross, that we might be slaves of those heartless traders in souls. I will more earnestly than ever teach my people to shun the modern gospel of the bishops, in order to follow the old Gospel of Jesus Christ, as the only hope and life of our poor fallen humanity."

Mr. Brassard wanted to say something ; but his voice was suffocated by his sobs. The only words he could utter, when pressing me to his heart, were : " Adieu, dear friend, adieu ! "

CHAPTER LXIII.

It was evident that the betrayal of Mr. Desaulnier would be followed by new efforts on the part of the bishop to crush us. Two new priests were sent from Canada, Mr. Mailloux, a vicar general, and Mr. Campo, to strengthen his hands, and press the people to submit. Mr. Brassard wrote me from Canada in December :

" All the bishops are preparing to hurl their thunders against you, and your people, on account of your heroic resistance to the tyranny of the Bishop of Chicago. I have told them the truth, but they don't want to know it. My lord Bourget told me positively that you must be forced, at any cost, to yield to the authority of your bishop ; and he has threatened to excommunicate me if I tell the people what I know of the shameful conduct of Desaulnier. If I were alone I would not mind his excommunication, and would speak the truth, but such a sentence against me would kill my poor old mother. I hope you will not find fault with me if I remain absolutely mute. I pray you to consider this letter confidential. You know very well the trouble you would put me into by its publication."

The French Canadians of Chicago saw, at once, that their bishop, strengthened by the support of Desaulnier, would be more than ever obstinate in his determination to crush them. They thought that the best way to force him to do them justice, was to publish a manifesto of their grievances against him, and make a public appeal to all the bishops of the United States, and even to the Pope.

On the 22nd of January, 1857, *The Chicago Tribune* was requested by them to publish the following document :

At a public meeting of the French and Canadian Catholics of Chicago, held in the hall of Mr. Bodicar, on the 22nd January, 1857, Mr. Rofinot being called to preside, and Mr. Franchere,* acting as a secretary, the following addresses and resolutions being read, have been unanimously approved :

"EDITORS OF THE 'TRIBUNE.'—Will you allow a thousand voices from the dead to speak to the public through your valuable paper ?

"Everybody in Chicago knows that, a few years ago, there was a flourishing congregation of French people coming from France and Canada in this city. They had their priest, their church, their religious meeting. All that is now dispersed and destroyed. The present Bishop of Chicago has breathed his deadly breath upon us. Instead of coming to us as a father, he came as a savage enemy ; instead of helping us as a friend, he has put us down as a revengeful foe. He has done the very contrary to which was commanded him by the Gospel. ' The bruised reed He shall not break, and the smoking flax He shall not quench.' Instead of guiding us with the cross of the meek Jesus, he has ruled over us with an iron rod.

"Every Sunday, the warm-hearted and generous Irish goes to his church to hear

---

* These two gentlemen are still living in Chicago, 1885.

the voice of his priest in his English language. The intelligent Germans have their pastors to address them in their mother tongue.

"The French people are the only ones now who have no priest and no church. They are the only ones whose beautiful language is prohibited, and which is not heard from any pulpit in Chicago. And is it from lack of zeal and liberality? Ah! no, we take the whole city of Chicago as a witness of what we have done. There was not in Chicago a better looking little church than the French Canadian church called St. Louis. But, alas! we have been turned out of it by our very bishop. As he is now publishing many stories to contradict that fact, we owe to ourselves and to our children to raise from the tomb, where Bishop O'Regan has buried us, a voice to tell the truth.

"As soon as Bishop O'Regan came to Chicago, he was told that the French priest was too popular, that his church was attended not only by his French Canadian people, but that many Irish and Germans were going daily to him for their religious duties. It was whispered in the ears of his Rt. Reverence that, on account of this, many dollars and cents were going to the French priest which would be better stored in his Rt. Reverence's purse.

"Till that time the bishop was not, in appearance, taking much trouble about us. But as soon as he saw that there were dollars and cents at stake, we had the honour to occupy his thoughts day and night. Here are the facts, the undeniable public facts. He (the bishop) began by sending for our priest, and telling him that he had to prepare himself to be removed from Chicago to some other place. As soon as we knew that determination, a deputation was sent to his Rt. Reverence to get the promise that we would get another French priest, and we received from him the assurance that our just request would be granted. But the next Sunday an Irish priest having been sent to officiate instead of a French one, we sent a deputation to ask him where the French priest was that he had promised us? He answered, 'That we ought to take any priest we could get, and be satisfied.' This short and sharp answer raised our French blood, and we began speaking more boldly to his Reverence, who got up and walked through the room in a rage, saying some half a dozen times, 'You insult me!' But seeing that we were a fearless people, and determined to have no other priest but one whom we could understand, he at last promised again a French priest, if we were ready to pay the debt of our church and priest house. We said we would pay them, but our verbal promise was nothing to his Reverence. He immediately wrote an agreement, though it was Sunday, and we signed it. But to attain, sooner or later, his object, he imposed upon that unfortunate priest a condition that he knew no Christian could obey.

"This condition was that he should not receive in his church any one but the French. This was utterly impossible, as many Irish, Germans, and American Catholics had been in the habit, for years past, of coming to our church: it was impossible to turn them out at once.

"We did everything in our power to help our priest in the matter, by taking all the seats in the church, against the will of the respectable people of the different nations who had occupied them for years. Finding themselves turned out of the church, and unable to conceive the reason of so gross an insult from a fellow-Christian people, they said to us, 'Have we not paid for our seats in your church till this day? Double the rent if you like; we are ready to pay for it; but, for God's sake, permit us to come and pray with you at the foot of the same altars.'

"We explained to them the tyrannical orders of the bishop, and they, too, commenced cursing the bishop and the ship that brought him over.

"They continued, however, to come to our church, though they had no seat. They attended divine service in the aisles of the church, and we did not like to disturb them ; but our feelings were too Christian for the bishop. He kept a watch over our priest, and, of course, found out that he was receiving many who were forbidden by him to attend our religious meetings.

"The bishop, then, thought once more of his dear French priest, so he came in person to his house, and asked him if he had kept his orders. The priest answered that it was quite impossible to obey such orders, and remain a Christian. He acknowledged that, in many instances, he had been obliged, by the laws of charity, to give religious help to some who were not French people.

"'Well then,' answered the bishop, 'from this very moment, I silence you, and I forbid you the functions of priest in my diocese.'

"The poor trembling priest, thunderstruck, could not say a word.

"He went to some friends to relate what had just happened him; and he was advised by them to go back to the bishop immediately to beg the privilege of remaining at the head of his congregation till Lent was over. The bishop said:

"'I will consent to your request, if your pay me one hundred dollars.'

"'I will give you the sum as soon as I can collect it, and will give you my note for thirty days,' answered the priest.

"'I want the money, cash down,' said the bishop; 'go to some of your friends, you can easily collect that amount.'

"This poor priest went away in search of the almighty dollars; but he could not find them as soon as he wished, and did not return to his lordship that day. The bishop started that night for St. Louis, but he did not forget his dear French people in his long journey. As soon as he arrived in St. Louis, he wrote to his grand vicar, Rev. Mr. Dunn, that the French priest pay him one hundred dollars or remain suspended.

"This goodwill of the bishop for our spiritual welfare, and his paternal love for our purses, did not fail to strike us. Our priest made a new effort that very day; he went to see an old friend who had been absent from town for some time, and related to him his sad position. This old friend (P. F. Rofinot), seeing that he could redeem a priest for so little a sum (for the priest had collected part of it himself), immediately proceeded with the priest to the house of very Reverend Dunn, with the money in hand, to satisfy the bishop.

"But, alas! that bargain did not last very long; for as soon as the bishop returned, the watch that he had left behind him performed his duty well, and told him that the French priest was going on as before. So the poor priest had to go again to the bishop to explain his conduct. But this time he could not bear the idea of officiating any longer under such a tyrant. He left us to fight the hardest battles ourselves against the bishop.

"As the church and the house of our priest were on leased grounds, the lease had to be renewed or the buildings removed. We went to the bishop, who advised us to buy a lot and remove the church on it, and sell the house to help pay for the lot. Suspecting nothing wrong in that advice, we followed it. We bargained for a lot, agreed to sell the house, and went to report our progress.

"But we were going too fast. The bishop must stop us, or he would be frustrated in his calculations, for he had a lot himself to put the church on: he opposed our removing our church, by telling us that there was another lot adjoining the one we had bargained for; and that we must buy it also. We went immediately and bought the lot on ninety days' time. But he objected to this again, saying that he would not allow us to touch the church, unless we had the whole lot paid for, and put the deed in his hands, and that the deed should be made to himself personally.

"This had the effect desired by the bishop. We had collected all the money that could be collected then, in our small congregation; it was impossible for us to do any more, so we concluded to give up the battle. The bishop then went on, took the money we had sold the house for (one thousand two hundred dollars). A Catholic lady, whose husband had bought the house, had subscribed one hundred dollars for removing the church, providing the bishop would promise that it would remain in the hands of the French, and attended by a French priest. The bishop proffered again to that lady the lie, which he so often uttered to us, everywhere, even from the altar, that upon his word of bishop, it should remain a French church, and that they should have a French priest. (This we shall call lie number one.) He then moved the church to another lot of his own, sent an Irish priest to officiate in it, put the money in his pocket, and made the congregation, which is now Irish, pay for the lot, the moving and repairing of the church, and he takes quarterly the revenues, which are no less than two thousand dollars a year.

"This is the way we have been swindled out of our church, of the house of our priest, and of our all, by the tyrant, Bishop O'Regan ; and when a French priest visits our city, he forbids him to address us in our mother tongue. This is the way we French Catholics, as a society, have been blotted out of the book of the living !

"And when Rev. Father Chiniquy has publicly accused Bishop O'Regan to have deprived us most unjustly of our church, he has proffered a truth which has as many witnesses as there are Catholic and Protestants in Chicago.

"We know well that Bishop O'Regan is proclaiming that he has not deprived us of our church, that if it is in the hands of the Irish, it is because the Irish and not the French built it. 'This is lie number two, which can be proved by more than a thousand witnesses.'

"We would like to know if he has forgotten the agreement (mentioned above) which he made us sign in bargaining for a French priest. He has the receipts for every cent that was due up to the time he took possession of our church. He then proffered these words with the French gentlemen who brought him the receipts : "It takes the French to collect money quick these hard times,' (being in the winter).

"We must also add that we, French people, have paid for the very vestments that the bishop uses in his cathedral, which he has taken from our church. But he uses them only on some high feasts, thinking too much of stolen property, to use them on a common day.

"Will it be out of my place here, to say that the cathedral of Chicago was built by the French, and that the lot which it is built on was given by a Frenchman ? It is very reluctantly that we expose all these facts before the eyes of the public; but having waited patiently, during two long years, and having used all the influence we could command in France and Canada, to no purpose, we must resort to the sympathy of the public for justice, through the free press of the United States.

"RESOLUTIONS.

"Resolved, 1st. That the Right Rev. O'Regan, Bishop of Chicago, has entirely lost the confidence of the French and Canadian population of Chicago since he has taken away from us our church.

"Resolved, 2nd. That the Right Rev. O'Regan has published a base slander against the French and Canadian population of Chicago, when he said he took our church from our hands on the pretence that we could not pay for it.

"Resolved, 3rd. That the Right Rev. O'Regan, having said to our deputies, who went to inquire from him by what right he was taking our church from us to give it to another congregation : 'I have the right to do what I like with your church, and your church properties; I can sell them and put the money in my pocket, and go where I please with it,' has assumed a power too tyrannical to be obeyed by a Christian and a free people.

"*Resolved*, 4th. That the nature of the different suits which the Right Rev. O'Regan has had before the civil courts of this state, and which he has almost in-variably lost, have proved to the whole people of Illinois that he is quite unworthy of the position he holds in the Catholic Church.

"*Resolved*, 5th. That the Right Rev. O'Regan is here publicly accused of being guilty of simony for having extorted one hundred dollars from a priest to give him permission to officiate and administer the sacraments among us.

"*Resolved*, 6th. That the Right Rev. O'Regan, in forbidding the Irish and German Catholics to communicate with the French Catholic Church, and allowing the French and Canadians to communicate with the Irish and German Churches, has acted with a view to deprive the French Church of religious fees and other donations, which acts we consider unjust and against the spirit of the church, and more resembling a mercantile transaction than a Christian work.

"*Resolved*, 7th. That the French and Canadian people of Illinois have seen with feelings of grief and surprise that the Rev. Mr. Desaulnier has made himself the humble valet of the merciless and shameless persecutor of his countrymen.

"*Resolved*, 8th. That the Rev. Mr. Chiniquy, pastor of St. Anne, deserves the gratitude of every Catholic of Illinois, for having, the first, put a stop to the rapacious tyranny of the Bishop of Chicago.

"*Resolved*, 9th. That the French Catholics of Chicago are determined to give all support in their power to the Rev. Mr. Chiniquy, in his struggle against the Bishop of Chicago.

"*Resolved*, 10th. That a printed copy of these resolutions be sent to every bishop and archbishop of the United States and Canadas, that they may see the necessity of giving to the church of Illinois a bishop more worthy of that high position.

"*Resolved*, 11th. That a copy of these resolutions be sent to His Holiness Pius IX., that he may be incited to make inquiries about the humiliated position of the church in Illinois, since the present bishop is among us.

"*Resolved*, 12th. That the independent and liberty-loving press of the United States be requested to publish the above address and resolutions all over the country.

"P. F. ROFINOT, President,

"DAVID FRANCHERE, Secretary."

That cry of more than two thousand Roman Catholics of Chicago, which was reproduced by almost the whole press of Illinois, and the United States, fell as a thunderbolt upon the head of my lord O'Regan and Desaulnier; they wrote to all the bishops of America, to hasten to their rescue, and for several months the pulpits of the Roman Catholic Churches had no other mission than to repeat the echoes of the Episcopal fulminations hurled against my devoted head. Many bishop's letters and mandements were published denouncing me and my people as infamous schismatics, whose pride and obstinacy were troubling the peace of the church. But the most bitter of all these was a letter from my lord Bourget, Bishop of Montreal, who thought the best, if not the only way to force the people to desert me, was by for ever destroying my honour. But he had the misfortune to fall into the pit he had dug for me in 1851.

The miserable girl he had associated with himself, to satisfy his implacable hatred, was dead. But, he had still in hand the lying accusations obtained from her against me. Having probably destroyed her sworn recantation written by the Jesuit Father Schneider, and not having the least idea that I had kept three other sworn copies of her recantations—he thought he could safely publish that I was a degraded man, who had been driven from Canada by him, after being convicted of some enormous crime, and interdicted.

This declaration was brought before the public, for the first time, by him, with an hypocritical air of compassion and mercy for me, which added much to the deadly effect he expected to produce by it. Here are his own words, addressed to the people of Bourbonnais, and through them, to the whole world:

" I must tell you that on the 27th of September, 1851, I withdrew all his powers, and interdicted him, for reasons which I gave him in my letter addressed to him; a letter which he has probably kept. Let him publish that letter, if he finds that I have persecuted him unjustly."

I could hardly believe my eyes when I read this ignominious act of perfidy on the part of that high dignitary: it seemed incredible, and surpassed anything I had ever seen, even in Bishop O'Regan. I cannot say, however, that it took me entirely by surprise, for I had anticipated it. When Father Schneider asked me why I had taken four sworn copies of the recantation of the unfortunate girl whose tears of regret were flowing before us, I told him that I knew so much of the meanness and perfidy of Bishop Bourget, that I thought he might destroy the copy we were sending him, in order to pierce me again with his poisonous arrows, whilst, if I kept three other copies, one for him, one for Mr. Brassard, and one for myself, I would have nothing to fear. I am convinced that my merciful God knew the malice of that bishop against me, and gave me that wisdom to save me.

I immediately sent him, through the press, the following answer:

To Monsignor Bourget:

St. Anne, *April 18th*, 1857.

My Lord :—In your letter of the 19th of March, you assure the public that you have interdicted me, a few days before my leaving Canada for the United States, and you invite me to give the reasons of that sentence. I will satisfy you. On the 28th of September, 1851, I found a letter on my table from you, telling me that you had suspended me from my ecclesiastical offices, on account of a great crime that I had committed, and of which I was accused. But the name of the accuser was not given, nor the nature of the crime. I immediately went to see you, and protesting my innocence, I requested you to give me the name of my accusers, and allow me to be confronted by them, promising that I would prove my innocence. You refused to grant my request.

Then I fell on my knees, and with tears, in the name of God, I requested you again to allow me to meet my accusers and prove my innocence. You remained deaf to my prayer and unmoved by my tears ; you repulsed me with a malice and air of tyranny which I had thought impossible in you.

During the twenty-four hours after this, sentiments of an inexpressible wrath crossed my mind. I tell it to you frankly, in that terrible hour I would have preferred to be at the feet of a heathen priest, whose knife would have slaughtered me on his altars, to appease his infernal gods, rather than be at the feet of a man who, in the name of Jesus Christ, and under the mask of the gospel, should dare to commit such a cruel act. You had taken away my honour—you had destroyed me with the most infamous calumny—and you had refused me every means of justification! You had taken under your protection the cowards who were stabbing me in the dark !

Though it is hard to repeat it, I must tell it here publicly, I cursed you on that horrible day.

With a broken heart I went to the Jesuit college, and I showed the wounds of my bleeding soul to the noble friend who was generally my confessor, the Rev. Father Schneider, the director of the college.

After three days, having providentially got some reasons to suspect who was the author of my destruction, I sent some one to ask her to come to the college, without mentioning my name.

When she was in the parlour, I said to Father Schneider :

"You know the horrible iniquity of the bishop against me ; with the lying words of a prostitute, he has tried to destroy me ; but please come and be the witness of my innocence."

When in the presence of that unfortunate female, I told her :

"You are in the presence of God Almighty, and two of His priests. They will be the witnesses of what you say ! Speak the truth. Say in the presence of God and this venerable priest, if I have ever been guilty of what you have accused me to the bishop."

At these words, the unfortunate female burst into tears; she concealed her face in her hands, and with a voice half suffocated with her sobs, she answered :

"No, sir; you are not guilty of that sin ! "

"Confess here another truth," I said to her : "Is it not true that you came to confess to me more with the desire to tempt me than to reconcile yourself to God ? "

She said, "Yes, sir, that is the truth." Then I said again, "Continue to say the truth, and I will forgive you, and God also will forgive your iniquity. Is it not through revenge for having failed in your criminal designs, that you have tried to destroy me by that false accusation to the bishop ? "

"Yes, sir, it was the only reason which has induced me to accuse you falsely."

And all I say here, at least in substance, has been heard, written, and signed by the Right Rev. Schneider, one of your priests, and the present director of the Jesuit College. That venerable priest is still living in Montreal; let the people of Canada go and interrogate him. Let the people of Canada also go to the Rev. Mr. Brassard, who has in his hands an authentic copy of that declaration.

Your lordship gives the public to understand that I was disgraced by that sentence, some days before I left Canada for Illinois. Allow me to give you my reasons for differing from you in this matter.

There is a canon law of the church which says :

"If a censure is unjust and unfounded, let the man against whom the sentence has been passed pay no attention to it. For, before God and His church, no unjust sentence can bring any injury against any one. Let the one against whom such unfounded and unjust judgment has been pronounced even take no step to annul it, for it is a nullity by itself."

You know very well that the sentence you had passed against me was null and void for many good reasons; that it was founded on a false testimony. Father Schneider is there, ready to prove it to you, if you have any doubt.

The second reason I have to believe that you had yourself considered your sentence a nullity, and that I was not suspended by it from my ecclesiastical dignity and honour, is founded on a good testimony, I hope—the testimony of your lordship.

A few hours before my leaving Canada for the United States, I went to ask your benediction, which you gave me with every mark of kindness. I then asked your lordship to tell me frankly if I had to leave with the impression that I was disgraced in his mind? You gave me the assurance of the contrary.

Then I told you that I wanted to have a public and irrefutable testimony of your esteem, written with your own hand, and you gave me the following letter :

"MONTREAL, CANADA, October 13, 1851.

"SIR,—You ask me permission to leave my diocese to go and offer your services to the Bishop of Chicago. As you belong to the diocese of Quebec, I think it belongs to my lord the archbishop to give you the exeat you wish. As for me, I can not but thank you for your labours among us, and I wish you in return the most abundant blessings from heaven. You shall ever be in my remembrance and in my heart, and I hope that Divine Providence will permit me, at a future time, to testify all the gratitude I owe you.

"Meanwhile, I remain your very humble and obedient servant,

✠ "IGNATIUS, Bishop of Montreal.

"MR. CHINIQUY, Priest."

I then asked you to give me some other tangible token of your esteem, which I might show everywhere I should go.

You answered that you would be happy to give me one, and you said : " What do you wish ? "

" I wish," I said, " to have a chalice from your hands to offer the holy sacrifice of the mass the rest of my life."

You answered: " I will do that with pleasure ; " and you gave an order to one of your priests to bring you a chalice that you might give it to me. But that priest had not the key of the box containing the sacred vases ; that key was in the hands of another priest, who was absent for a few hours.

I had not the time to wait ; the hour of the departure of the trains had come ; I told you : " Please, my lord, send that chalice to the Rev. Mr. Brassard, of Longueuil, who will forward it to me in a few days to Chicago." And the next day one of your secretaries went to the Rev. Mr. Brassard, gave him the chalice you had promised me, which is still in my hands. And the Rev. Mr. Brassard is there still living, to be the witness of what I say, and to bring that fact to your memory if you have forgotten it.

Well, my lord, I do believe that a bishop will never give a chalice to a priest to say mass, when he knows that that priest is interdicted. And the best proof that you know very well that I was not interdicted by your rash and unjust sentence, is that you gave me that chalice as a token of your esteem, and of my honesty, etc.

Respectfully,

C. CHINIQUY.

Ten thousand copies of this exposure of the depravity of the bishop were published in Montreal. I asked the whole people of Canada to go to the Rev. Mr. Schneider and to the Rev. Mr. Brassard to know the truth, and many went. The bishop remained confounded.

It was proved that he had committed against me a most outrageous act of tyranny and perfidy ; and that I was perfectly innocent and honest, and that he knew it, in the very hour that he tried to destroy my character. Probably the Bishop of Montreal had destroyed the copy of the declaration of the poor girl he had employed, and thinking that this was the only copy of her declaration of my innocence and honesty, he thought he could speak of the so-called interdict after I was a Protestant. But in that he was cruelly mistaken, for as I have already said, by the great mercy of God, three other authenticated copies had been kept : one by the Rev. Mr. Schneider himself, another by the Rev. Mr. Brassard, another by one whom it is not necessary to mention, and then he had no suspicion that the revelation of his unchristian conduct, and of his determination to destroy me with the false oath of a prostitute, were in the hands of too many people to be denied.

The Bishop of Chicago, whom I met a few days after, told me what I was well aware of before. "That such a sentence was a perfect nullity in every way, and it was a disgrace only for those who were blind enough to trample under their feet the laws of God and men to satisfy their bad passions."

A few days after the publication of that letter in Canada, Mr. Brassard wrote me : "Your last letter has completely unmasked our poor bishop, and revealed to the world his malice, injustice and hypocrisy. He felt so confounded by it, that he has been three days without being able to eat or drink anything, and three nights without sleeping. Everyone says that the chastisement you have given him is a terrible one, when it is in the face of the whole world; but he deserved it."

When I received that last friendly letter from Mr. Brassard on the 1st of April, 1857, I was far from suspecting that on the 15th of the same month, I should read in the press of Canada, the following lines from him :

St. Roch de l'Achigan, le 9 avril, 1857.

Messieurs :—I request you to insert the following lines in your journal. As some people suspect that I am favouring the schism of Mr. Chiniquy, I think it is my duty to say that I have never encouraged him by my words or writings in that schism. I must say that, last November, when I went to St. Anne, accompanied by Mr. Desaulnier, Superior of St. Hyacinthe College, my only object was to persuade that old friend to leave the bad ways in which he was walking. And in Chicago I pressed him to put himself in a canonical way.

I, more than anyone else, deplore the fall of a man whom, I confess, I loved much, but for the sake of whom I will not sacrifice the sacred ties of Catholic unity. I hope that all the Canadians who were attached to Mr. Chiniquy when he was united to the church, will withdraw from him in horror of his schism. For before anything else, we must be truly and faithfully Catholic.

However, we have a duty to perform towards the man who has fulfilled such a holy

35

mission in our midst, by establishing the society of temperance. It is to call back, with our prayers, that stray sheep who has left the true Pastor's fold.

I request all journals to reproduce this declaration.

Truly yours,

MOSES BRASSARD, Pastor.

MM., the Editors of the *Courier du Canada.*

I felt that there was not a line, not a sentiment of Mr. Brassard in that letter. It smelt Bishop Bourget's hand, from the beginning to the end. I thought, however, that it was my duty to address him the following answer :

ST. ANNE, KANKAKEE COUNTY, ILLINOIS, April 23, 1857.

MY DEAR MR. BRASSARD :—I have just received your letter of the 9th inst., but no! I will not call it a letter, it will be better named a bitter tear, and a sad wail of a heart as good as it is noble and generous.

You have been a witness how the people and missionary of St. Anne have been betrayed by Mr. Desaulnier. You were at my side as a friend and father, when this traitor said to me, as well as to my brethren, " Sign this act of submission to the Bishop of Chicago ; this act alone is enough to make him withdraw the sentence which fills your Canadian friends with anxiety. If the bishop does not give you the place you want, and if he does not withdraw the excommunication after having been presented with this act, I will tell him, ' It is neither the pastor nor the people of St. Anne who wish a schism, they have done that which religion and honour commanded, to prove it ; it is you who wishes it.' " Your tears were mingled with mine, and the incense of your prayer ascended with those of my brethren, when on the 26th of November Mr. Desaulnier said to the people of St. Anne, " You cannot be blamed for what you have done since the beginning of your difficulties with your bishop." You were a witness that our first condition to the signing of the act which you and Mr. Desaulnier presented to us, was that you should be the pastor of St. Anne, and that I should remain with you as long as you would find it to the interest of my colony. You know that he gave me his word of honour, in presence of all the people, that if the bishop would not give us peace after the signing of the act, he (Mr. Desaulnier) would go with us to St. Louis and even to Rome, to plead my cause and show the iniquity and unbearable tyranny of the Bishop of Chicago. Did he not assure us that, in case the Bishop should refuse to accept the act of submission we had signed, your mission to St. Anne was finished, and that you both would return to Canada, after your voyage to St. Louis ? Is it not true that when in Chicago, in reply to our question, " What news ? " Mr. Desaulnier said, " You have only to take your bags and both return to Canada at once." Mr. Desaulnier denies all those facts, with an impudence of which he alone is capable. You are my only witness before our Canada, which wishes and has a right to know the truth in this matter.

I took you as my witness, and you replied in many of your letters, that you could not say the truth without compromising yourself. Is not this an acknowledgment that we, priests of Jesus Christ, are groaning under the weight of the most frightful tyranny ; and that we are in the power of men who threaten our honour and life, if we dare speak the truth in favour of an oppressed brother ? And this is the system which proclaims itself as the divine and ineffable news which the Messiah brought to the world !! And this abominable oppression, this system of deceit, is the religion which the Son of the God of truth, justice, and mercy, has established to save the world ? This is the foundation stone of the church of Christ !!! No! You do not believe that, my dear Mr. Brassard. Neither do I. I never did, and never will believe it.

They tell us it is for the greater good of the church that they act thus; that it is to preserve the respect which is due to the Holy Catholic Hierarchy, that they take those extreme measures against the people of St. Anne!

But I have carefully studied the laws of the church upon these great questions, and I see they say precisely the contrary. I see that the Catholic church said to us, 1. "In the church there is no arbitrary power." 2. "The censures are null when they have been pronounced against sins which have not been committed. 3. Never receive any accusation against a priest, which has not been proven by two or three witnesses. 4. If a sentence is visibly unjust, the condemned must not pay any attention to it; for before God and His Church, no unjust sentence can injure anyone. 5. The unjust excommunication is not binding neither before God nor the people, when that people know its injustice, because the Holy Ghost cannot abandon those who have not deserved it."

You wish me to act according to the canons of the church. I have already told you that if I had been interdicted on the 19th of August, I would have been able to appeal from that sentence, but I had not. I had fifteen days to consider. How could I have appealed from a sentence which had not been pronounced? What witness could I bring against a fact which, I knew, had never taken place? But you will say: "The excommunication? Should it not give you some anxiety?" "Not the least." St. Thomas said positively that an excommunication of which the injustice is known by the people, ought not to prevent a priest from exercising his ministry among them. They will perhaps say, "But where did the people get the right to judge in such things?" St. Thomas must have believed that the people had that right, since he said it. St. Thomas was neither a heretic nor schismatic for believing these things.

Why, then, should I be one for having thought, spoken, and acted, according to the doctrine of *him* whom the church has named the angel of the school? Besides that, you know that the excommunication was a nullity from want of being signed.

The reason of this surprise about the right which the people has to exercise its judgment upon this question, is that, lately, the bishops have not only stripped the priests, but also the people, of the holy and just rights which Jesus Christ had given them. Those who have carefully studied the history of the church in the first centuries know this as well as I do. But be it known, there are rights against which time does not prescribe. There are rights which the priests and people have never renounced, and which the Church of Christ will always like to see them enjoy. I do not say that the bishops are not ordained to govern the Christian people, but I say that the bishops are not appointed by the church to govern the flock according to their caprices, but according to the unchangeable rules of justice, equity, and truth of the gospel. In the primitive church, every time that a bishop forgets this, other bishops reminded him of it.

Do we not see in the gospel, that the first Christians complained bitterly to the apostles themselves of the manner in which they had administered the goods entrusted to them? Were they excommunicated for that? Did they receive in answer the insolent reply that the people receive to-day? viz.: "You are but the laity, that does not concern you?" No! The apostles listened to the complaints of the people; they found them just, and the people were allowed to choose the administrators of their goods. The people, then, were looked upon as something worthy of attention and respect, and were not tied, as to-day, to the feet of a dignitary, and obliged to go right and left at the good pleasure of their pretended master. The people were not, then, bridled; were not mere machines to pay tithes, build palaces, raise proud cathedrals; nor were they degraded, demoralized, as to-day; obliged to believe they had minds, but had no right to make use of them; they were not, then, as now, poor beasts of burthen, whose only duty is to obey their master. But their wants and wishes were consulted, their voice was heard. They had not yet the idea that the Holy Ghost was to enlighten only a certain class of men, and that the rest of humanity were given up to ignorance, only to walk in the light of a few privileged luminaries.

But the spirit of wisdom, charity, and tolerance, this respect for the will and wishes of the people, where do you find them to-day ? On the contrary, we find tyranny on the one side, and stern and necessary resistance on the other; resistances which are but the expression of the law of God. Let the tolerant conduct of the apostles, who listened with so much humility to the complaints of the first Christians, be compared to that of Bishop O'Regan when questioned by the French people of Chicago upon the right he had to deprive them of their church, to give it to another congregation, put them out of doors saying, " You do not know your religion ; I have the right to sell your churches, and the grounds attached to them, put the money in my pocket, and eat and drink where I like."

This is what Bishop O'Regan has said and done ; and this is what the Bishop of Canada approves and sanctions in the name of the gospel ! They try to make you believe that it is the doctrine of Jesus Christ which these high dignitaries preach and practise. Let the poor people of Canada believe this if they wish ; as for us in St. Anne, we do not, and never will believe it. Are not these men who cry the loudest to make us respect the canons of the church the very men who publicly trample the most holy laws of the people and of the church under their feet ? How easy it would be to put to those powerful personages questions which they would call impertinent, but which would shed great light in the midst of the profound darkness in which a certain corner of the world is kept to-day ? You who overwhelm us with curses and send us to hell if we are not ready to say amen to all you say, what have you done with the canon of the holy Council of Nice, which forbids you to change a priest's charge without his permission ? Where is the canon of a general council which allows the bishops to add the words " *usque ad revocationem* " in the powers given to the priests ! While one of the canons of the church says : " It is the authority of the canons and the examination of the conduct of the priests which ought to give or take away the ecclesiastical dignities, and not the *will of the prelates.*"

History has preserved the names of certain tyrants who forced the trembling hand of a father to set fire to the pile which consumed his own child. Ah ! why do these bishops of Canada remind us of that lamentable page of past centuries in commanding you to throw burning coals on the pile to which they have led me. You are more than a friend to me. I have the right to call you " Father." When still very young, domestic misfortunes forced me to leave for a strange country in search of a living ; you stretched out to me a helping hand. Although poor yourself, you shared your bread with the poor orphan. You opened to me the doors of the college where I studied. And ever since, when a tempest threatened my fragile bark with shipwreck, in your arms I found a sure port. Every time I received a wound in the struggles of life, in your affection I found a remedy. When heaven chose your poor friend to change the face of our dear country, it was beneath your hospitable roof that I found rest. Your hand was the last one which pressed mine, when in 1851 I left Canada to consecrate myself to the service of the emigrants ; and lastly, when the thunders of three deluded prelates fell upon my head, I said to myself : I have in Canada a friend, a father. I am so sure of his heart that I do not even need to call him to aid ; there is a voice in his soul which cries to him : " Go, go to the aid of thy friend, of thy child !" I was not mistaken. On the 24th of November you pressed me to your heart ; your words of peace and charity cheered my broken heart. For the love of God and for your sake also, my dear Mr. Brassard, I have consented to do all you required of me. Ah ! why did you not come alone ? How easily everything would have been safely settled ! But without knowing it, you had with you a traitor, who came to give the people and pastor of St. Anne the kiss of Judas before delivering them into the hands of their enemies. To-day you are commanded to add your efforts to those of this traitor, to strike me. They want you to add a new thorn to that crown of shame which the bishops have placed on my forehead. But how can I be guilty for having called you as a witness of the iniquities of my enemies? Have you forgotten with what sincerity and promptitude I signed, as well as my brethren of St. Anne, the act of submission to the Bishop O'Regan? Have you forgotten the desolation of your heart and mine when (on the conditions you well know) I declared to my people that I would no longer be their pastor?

Since the bishops of Canada command you to speak, in the name of the God of truth and justice, I also ask you to speak. Yes, state to the people of Canada how shamefully Mr. Desaulnier has deceived the generous people who surround me here. Yes! tell your surprise, your just indignation, your bitter sorrow when Mr. Desaulnier refused, in Chicago, to fulfil the sacred promise he had made! Tell the nature of the new document which he wanted me to sign at Chicago. Declare honestly that you said to me: "My poor friend, you cannot sign that act without lying and dishonouring yourself for ever."

Since the bishops of Canada command you to speak, raise your voice to say to the Canadian people what you wrote to Dr. Letourneaux and to myself: They do not wish to know the truth in Canada more than at Chicago about the shameful conduct of Mr. Desaulnier in this affair! Yes, speak! Give to my dear Canada the reply which the Bishop of Chicago made when you asked: "Have you any accusation in hand against the character of Mr. Chiniquy?" I need your testimony upon this question for the Bishop of Chicago, forgetting what he confessed to you is circulating, through my enemies, a thousand calumnies against me, which are reproduced to-day by the Bishop of Montreal. Say to Canada that the Bishop of Chicago assured you that he had interdicted me *only* because I disobeyed him in refusing to leave St. Anne, whilst, at the very time he held a letter brought by four witnesses, saying that I was ready to obey, and that I would prefer going to the end of the world rather than be interdicted.

If, having said all these things, you are still commanded to strike me, do so, dear friend. Though your blows go more directly to my heart than all the thunders of Bishop O'Regan, they will never shake my constancy, nor make me betray my brethren; they will neither make me change my convictions, nor force me any longer to bend the knee before men who wish us to submit to their caprices and impious commands rather than to the laws of the God of justice, truth and mercy, whose priest I have the honour to be. I have sworn at the foot of the altar to preach truth and justice, nothing will make me break my oath. Do you remember with what dignity you refused one day to bow before one of those modern divinities, who believe that everything is allowed them on earth. Do you not recollect that the Bishop of Ottawa had the audacity to take one of your letters out of the post office and read it, hoping the shameful act would never be known? I shall never forget the noble independence with which you protested against that abuse of power, and with what indignation you threatened to drag that haughty bishop before the courts of justice if he did not ask pardon for that outrage! Were you revolting against the church of Christ then? No! for you knew that her principles of truth and justice could not sanction such brigandage. So I did not revolt against the church of Christ when I resisted the insolence and outrages of the Bishop of Chicago.

Like St. Jerome, I know the rights of the bishops. I respect their authority. The Catholic Hierarchy is to me a holy and venerable institution. But when men, sheltering themselves behind those holy institutions, trample under their feet the principles of justice, truth, and holiness which the Gospel of Christ inculcates, I will fight to the end, with my poor emigrants, for the preservation of their Christian rights. You say that before all, we must be frankly and sincerely " Catholics." I answer, yes. But when one is wrongfully deprived of this glorious name before men because he opposes, as I have done, the brigandage of a bishop who believes all is allowed him, he can remain in peace, and be like St. Paul, who did not care what men said or thought of him. To be anathematized, because I have devoted myself to the welfare of my brethren, is not such a sad destiny as some people think. St. Paul said : " I could wish that myself were accursed from Christ for my brethren, my kinsmen according to the flesh." The favour after which the apostle of the Gentiles sighed has been accorded me. I cannot complain of it. Besides, does not Christ Himself say to those who labour to scatter seeds of justice and truth upon the earth, that they ought not expect to be treated better than He?

From every part of Canada and the United States men of distinction cease not to cry, Courage ! It is true that several curse us, but it is because they are forced to do it. Many keep silent for fear of their masters, but their prayers and sympathies are for us. The bishops will see, sooner or later, that in order to retain their power on earth that power must be founded, as in heaven, upon justice and truth.

When the priests of Canada, to please the bishops, contrary to their convictions, have degraded their own sacerdotal character in my person ; when they have burned the effigy of the proscribed, having no more the glorious privilege of burning his body ; when the father whom, by the grace of God, I have snatched from an abyss, cursed me ; when this dear young man who has, so many times blessed me, because I have shown him the Gospel, the way of honour and virtue, by removing the stumbling block of intemperance offered to his weakness, has been forced to curse me ; when that poor woman who, by the grace of God, owes me the bread she eats, and the few days of holy felicity she has enjoyed upon earth, has cursed me ; when this fine little child, who has so many times blessed my name, because God made use of me to give him back a father, has cursed me, there will be a silence of sorrow in Canada around my proscribed name. Then a reaction will take place. A great prestige will be destroyed. A great power, holy and benevolent in its origin, but fallen by its excesses, will be destroyed. God grant that, in the midst of those ruins, there may be no tears, no blood. This is not prophecy, it is history. Yes, let the Canadian clergy open the records of the past, and they will find where their blind and demoralizing obedience to the bishops leads them and their good and generous people, if not to infidelity and atheism.

You advise me, dear Mr. Brassard, to put myself in the canonical ways ; but have I not already done so ? Have not the bishops of Canada told you that the letter signed by me had already placed me in that position ? Has not Mr. Desaulnier said, in your presence, to my people and myself at St. Anne : " Sign this act, and if the bishop does not take away his sentence of excommunication, I will say to him : ' It is not Mr. Chiniquy, neither his people, who wish a schism ; they have done what religion and honour commanded them ; it is the Bishop of Chicago who makes the schism.'" What have we gained by taking that public step ? Nothing, but to be cruelly and shamefully betrayed. Was not Jesus Christ betrayed only once by Judas ? Do not, then, expect that we will be stronger than the Son of God. The bishops of Canada, by their emissary, have already betrayed us, of which you have been witness. The people and missionary of St. Anne do not feel strong enough to present their cheek again to the smiter. In spite of the clamours which rise around us, we are convinced that we may be good Catholics without submitting to that degradation twice.

The bishops of Canada want you to speak. Very well ! my dear Mr. Brassard, I also implore you to speak. In the name of the friendship which has united us for forty years, I implore you to tell the truth. Did you not, after reading the document

which the Bishop of Chicago commanded me to sign as the only condition of peace,
say to me :

"My dear friend, you cannot sign such a writing without lying and dishonouring
yourself for ever?" And behold! to-day you cry to my brethren to destroy and
abandon me, when you know that the position in which I stand is but the result of
my refusal to sign a most infamous, lying, and degrading document.

These things, and many others which you know, would serve wonderfully to open
the eyes of the people upon the awful abuse of power, which certain bishops are,
every day, guilty. This would aid to unmask certain modern divinities who pretend
that we cannot go to heaven without their permission ; who preach that it is not the
blood of Jesus Christ, but a certain passport, of which they hold the patent, which
assures us a place among the elect of God. A sentence founded upon a public lie,
and which was resisted, cannot constitute a schism. Christian men who, like the
Catholics of Chicago, Kankakee, and St. Anne, resist iniquity, may be condemned by
men, but not by God.

I was not suspended on the 19th of August, and so I could exercise the holy functions of my ministry the following morning and after. It is the church which assures
me of this, through her greatest theologians. As it is not enough to say, "My God !
My God !" to be saved ; so, it is not enough to cry, "You are lost ! you are lost !" for
one to be lost. The Son of God, who gave His life to save man, gave us a thousand
proofs that the salvation of our soul has a foundation more certain than the capricious
will of a sinful being. He has given to no one the power to save or condemn according to his pleasure. If some bishops and priests believe this, it is not the faith of the
people of Chicago, Kankakee, and St. Anne.

I will tell you again, my dear Mr. Brassard, that if, in order to obey the Bishop of
Montreal, you should strip me of the little honour which surrounds my name in
Canada, I shall still never forget the good you have done me. Yes! command my
friends to betray me, to trample me under their feet, to turn away from me in horror.
Never will you be able to weaken my sentiments of respect and gratitude for you !

I will still love and bless you; for I know the hand which forced yours to do so.
I will always know that your own heart was first struck and wounded by the blows
they commanded you to give to your friend and son in Jesus Christ,

C. CHINIQUY.

The effect of that letter upon Mr. Brassard was still more powerful than I had expected. It forced him to blush at his own cowardice,
and to ask my pardon for the unjust sentence he had passed upon
me to obey the bishop. Here are the parts of the letter bearing on
that subject :—

St. Roch, 29 *Mai*, 1857.

Mon cher Chiniquy,—Je suis plus convaincu que jamais que tu n'as jamais été
interdit legalement, depuis que j'ai appris par Monseigneur de Montreal, que l'évêque
de Chicago t'a interdit de vive voix, dans sa chambre ; ce que Ligoury dit être nul et
de nul effet."

I am more than ever convinced that you have never been legally interdicted, since
Bishop Bourget told me that Bishop O'Regan had interdicted you privately, *viva voce*
in his private room. Ligouri says that it is a nullity, and that it can have no effect. I
beg your pardon for what I wrote against you. I have been forced to do it. Because
I had not yet sufficiently condemned you, and that my name, which you were citing
in your writings, was giving you too much power, and a too clear condemnation of

Bishop O'Regan, the Bishop of Montreal, abusing his authority over me, forced me to sign that document against you. I would not do it to-day if it were to be done again. Keep silence on what I tell you in this letter. It is all confidential. You understand it.

Your devoted friend,

L. M. BRASSARD.

No priest in Canada had more deservedly enjoyed the reputation of a man of honour than Mr. Brassard. Not one ever stood so high in my esteem and respect. His sudden and unexpected fall filled my heart with an unspeakable sadness. I may say that it snapped the last thread which held me to the Church of Rome. Till then, it was not only my hope, but my firm conviction, that there were many honest, upright priests in that church, and Mr. Brassard was, to me, the very personification of honesty. How can I describe the shock I felt when I saw him there, in the mud, a monument of the unspeakable corruption of my church! The perfidious Delilah had seduced and destroyed this modern Samson, enchained, as a trembling slave, at the feet of the new implacable Moloch, "The authority of the bishop!" He had not only lost the fear of God, and the respect he owed to himself, by publicly declaring that I was guilty, when he knew that I was innocent, but he had so completely lost every sentiment of honesty, that he wanted me to keep secret his declaration of my innocence, at the very moment he was inviting my whole country, through the press, to abhor and condemn me as a criminal!

I read again and again the strange letter. Every word of it was destroying the last illusions which had concealed from my mind the absolute and incurable perversity of the Church of Rome. I had no hard feelings against this last friend whom she had poisoned with the wine of her prostitutions. I felt only a profound compassion for him. I pitied and forgave him from the bottom of my heart. But every word of his letter sounded in my ears as the warning voice of the angel sent to save Lot from the doomed city of Sodom: "Escape for thy life. Look not behind thee; neither stay thou in all the plain. Escape to the mountain lest thou be consumed" (Gen. xix. 17).

CHAPTER LXIV.

I HAD not forgotten the advice given me by Archbishop Kenrick, of St. Louis, April 9th, 1856, to address my complaints to the Pope himself. But the terrible difficulties and trials which had constantly followed each other, had made it impossible to follow that advice. The betrayal of Mons. Desaulnier and the defection of Mons. Brassard, however, had so strangely complicated my position, that I felt the only way to escape the wreck which threatened myself and my colony, and to save the holy cause God had entrusted to me, was to strike such a blow to our haughty persecutor that he could not survive it. I determined to send to the Pope all the public accusations which had been legally proved and published against the bishop, with a copy of the numerous and infamous suits which he had sustained before the civil courts, and had almost invariably lost, with the sentences of the judges who had condemned him. This took me nearly two months of the hardest labours of my life. I had gathered all those documents, which covered more than two hundred pages of foolscap. I mailed them to Pope Pius IX., accompanied by only the following words : "Holy Father, for the sake of your precious lambs which are slaughtered and devoured in this vast diocese by a ravening wolf, Bishop O'Regan, and in the name of our Saviour Jesus Christ, I implore your Holiness to see if what is contained in these documents is correct or not. If everything is found correct, for the sake of the blood shed on Calvary, to save our immortal souls, please take away from our midst the unworthy bishop whose daily scandals cannot longer be tolerated by a Christian people."

In order to prevent the Pope's servants from throwing my letter with those documents into their waste-paper baskets, I sent a copy of them all to Napoleon III., Emperor of France, respectfully requesting him to see, through his ambassador at Washington, and his consul at Chicago, whether these papers contained the truth or not. I told him how his countrymen were trampled under the feet of Bishop O'Regan, and how they were ruined and spoiled to the benefit of the Irish people ; how the churches built by the money of the French were openly stolen, and transferred to the emigrants from Ireland. Napoleon had just sent an army to punish the Emperor of China on account of some injustice done to a Frenchman. I told him "the injustice done to that Frenchman in the Chinese Empire is nothing to what is done here every day, not against one, but hundreds of your majesty's countrymen. A word from the Emperor of France to His Holiness will do here what your armies have done in China : force the unjust and merciless oppressor of the French of Illinois to do them justice."

I ended my letter by saying : " My grandfather, though born in Spain, married a French lady, and became, by choice and adoption, a French citizen. He became a captain in the French navy, and for gallant service, was awarded lands in Canada, which by the fate of war fell into the hands of Great Britain. Upon retiring from the service of France he settled upon his estates in Canada, where my father and myself were born. I am thus, with other Canadians who have come to this country, a British subject by birth, an American citizen by adoption, but French still in blood and Roman Catholic in religion. I, therefore, on the part of a noble French people, humbly ask your majesty to aid us by interceding with his Holiness, Pope Pius IX., to have these outrages and wrongs righted."

The success of this bold step was more prompt and complete than I had expected. The Emperor was, then, all powerful at Rome. He had not only brought the Pope from Civita Vecchia to Rome, after taking that city from the hands of the Italian Republicans, a few years before, but he was still the very guardian and protector of the Pope.

A few months later, when in Chicago, the Grand Vicar Dunn showed me a letter from Bishop O'Regan, who had been ordered to go to Rome and give an account of his administration, in which he had said: " One of the strangest things which has occurred to me in Rome, is that the influence of the Emperor Napoleon is against me here. I cannot understand what right he has to meddle in the affairs of my diocese."

I had learned since, that it was really through the advice of Napoleon that Cardinal Bidini, who had been previously sent to the United States to inquire about the scandal given by Bishop O'Regan, gave his opinion in our favour. The cardinals, having consulted the bishops of the United States, who unanimously denounced O'Regan as unfit and unworthy of such a high position, immediately ordered him to go to Rome, where the Pope unceremoniously transferred him from the bishopric of Chicago to a diocese extinct more than 1,200 years ago, called " Dora." This was as good as a bishopric in the moon. He consoled himself in his misfortune by drawing the hundreds of thousands of dollars of stolen money he had sent at different times, to be deposited in the banks of Paris, and went to Ireland, where he established a bank, and died in 1865.

On the 11th of March, 1858, at about ten o'clock p.m., I was not a little pleased and surprised to hear the voice of my devoted friend, Rev. M. Dunn, grand vicar of Chicago, asking my hospitality for the night. His first words were: " My visit here must be absolutely incognito. In ordering me to come and see you, the Bishop of Dubuque, who is just named administrator of Chicago, advised me to come as secretly as possible." He said : " Your triumph at Rome is perfect. You have gained the greatest victory a priest ever won over his unjust bishop; but you must thank the Emperor Napoleon for it. It is to his advice, which, under the present circumstances, is equal to an order, that you owe the protection of the Cardinal Bidini. His report to the Pope is, that all the documents you sent to Rome were correct. The inquiry of the cardinal has brought facts to the knowledge of the Pope, still more compromising than what you have written against him. Several bishops of the United States have unanimously denounced Bishop O'Regan as a most depraved man, entirely unworthy of his position, and have advised the Pope to take him away and choose another bishop for Chicago. It is acknowledged, at Rome, that all the sentences pronounced by that bishop against you, are unjust and null. Our good administrator has been advised to put an end, at once, to all the troubles of your colony, by treating you as a good and faithful priest.

"I come here, not only to congratulate you on your victory, but also to thank you, in my name, and in the name of the church, for having saved our diocese from such a plague; for Bishop O'Regan was a real plague. A few more years of such administration would have destroyed our holy religion in Illinois. However, as you handled the poor bishop pretty roughly, it is suspected, at a distance, that you and your people are more Protestants than Catholics. We know better here; for, from the beginning, it was evident that the act of excommunication, posted at the door of your chapel by three priests too drunk to know what they were about, is a nullity, having never been signed by the bishop. It was a shameful and sacrilegious comedy. But, in many distant places, that excommunication was accepted as valid, and you are considered by many as a real schismatic. Bishop Smith has thought it advisable to ask you to give him a written and canonical act of submission, which he will publish to show the world that you are still a good Roman Catholic priest."

I thanked the grand vicar for his kind words, and the good news he was giving me, and I asked him to help me to thank God for having so visibly protected and guided me through all these terrible difficulties. We both knelt and repeated the sublime words of gratitude and joy of the old prophet: "Bless the Lord, oh! my soul, and all that is within me, bless His holy name," etc. (Ps. ciii.) I then said I had no objection to give the renewed act of my faith and submission to the church, that it might be published. I took a piece of paper, and with emotion of joy and gratitude to God, which it would be impossible to express, I slowly prepared to write. But as I was considering what form I should give to that document, a sudden, strange thought struck my mind: "Is this not the golden opportunity to put an end to the terrible temptations which have shaken my faith and distressed me for so many years." I said to myself:

"Is not this a providential opportunity to silence those mysterious voices which are troubling me almost every hour, that, in the church of Rome, we do not follow the Word of God, but the lying traditions of men?"

I determined then to frame my act of submission in such a way that I would silence those voices, and be, more than ever, sure that my faith, the faith of my dear church, which had just given me such a glorious victory at Rome, was based upon the Holy Word of God, on the divine doctrines of the Gospel. I then wrote down, in my own name, and in the name of my people:

"My lord Bishop Smith, Bishop of Dubuque and administrator of the diocese of Chicago:—We want to live and die in the holy Catholic, apostolic and Roman church, out of which there is no salvation, and to prove this to your lordship, we promise to obey the authority of the church according to the word and commandments of God as we find them expressed in the Gospel of Christ.

"C. CHINIQUY."

I handed this writing to Mr. Dunn, and said:

"What do you think of this act of submission?" He quickly read it, and answered:

"It is just what we want from you."

"All right," I rejoined. "But I fear the bishop will not accept it. Do you not see that I have put a condition to our submission? I say that we will submit ourselves to the bishop's authority, but only according to the Word of God and the Gospel of Christ."

"Is not that good?" quickly replied Mr. Dunn.

"Yes, my dear Mr. Dunn, this is good, very good indeed," I answered, "but my fear is that it is too good for the bishop and the Pope!"

"What do you mean?" he replied.

"I mean that though this act of submission is very good, I fear lest the Pope and the bishop reject it."

"Please explain yourself more clearly," answered the grand vicar. "I do not understand the reason for such a fear."

"My dear Mr. Dunn," I continued, "I must confess to you here a thing which is known only to God. I must show you a bleeding wound which is in my soul for many years. A wound which has never been healed by any of the remedies I have applied to it. It is a wound which I never dared to show to any man, except to my confessor, though it has often made me suffer almost the tortures of hell. You know well that there is not a living priest who has studied the Holy Scriptures and the Holy Fathers, with more attention and earnestness, these last few years than I have. It was not only to strengthen my own faith, but also the faith of our people, and to be able to fight the battles of our church against her enemies, that I spent so many hours of my days and nights in those studies. But, though I am confounded and ashamed to confess it to you, I must do it. The more I have studied and compared the Holy Scriptures and the Holy Fathers with the teachings of our church, the more my faith has been shaken, and the more I have been tempted to think, in spite of myself, that our church has, long ago, given up the Word of God and the Holy Fathers, in order to walk in the muddy and crooked ways of human and false traditions. Yes! the more I study, the more I am troubled by the strange and mysterious voices which haunt me day and night, saying : ' Do you not see that in your Church of Rome, you do not follow the Word of God, but only the lying traditions of men ? ' What is more strange and painful is, that the more I pray to God to silence these voices, the louder they repeat the same distressing things. It is to put an end to those awful temptations that I have written this conditional submission. I want to prove to myself that I will obey the Word of God and the Gospel of Christ in our church, and I shall be happy all the rest of my life, if the bishops accept this submission. But I fear it will be rejected."

Mr. Dunn promptly replied :

"You are mistaken, my dear Mr. Chiniquy. I am sure that our bishop will accept this document as canonical, and sufficient to show your orthodoxy to the world."

"If it be so," I replied, "I will be a most happy man." It was agreed that on the 25th of March I would go with him to Dubuque, to present my act of submission to the administrator of the diocese, after the people had signed it. Accordingly, at seven p.m. on that day, we both took the train at Chicago for Dubuque, where we arrived next morning. At eleven a.m. I went to the palace of the bishop, who received me with marks of the utmost cordiality and affection. presented him our written act of submission with a trembling hand, fearing he would reject it. He read it twice, and throwing his arms around me, he pressed me to his heart. I felt his tears of joy mixed with mine, rolling down my cheeks, as he said : "How happy I am to see that submission! How happy the Pope and all the bishops of the United States will be to hear of it, for I will not conceal it from you ; we feared that both you and your people would separate from the church, by refusing to submit to her authority." I answered that I was not less happy to see the end of those painful difficulties, and I promised him that, with the help of God, our holy church would not have a more faithful priest than myself.

While engaged in that pleasant conversation, the dinner hour came. He gave me the place of honour on his right, before the two grand vicars, and nothing could be more pleasant than the time we spent around the table, which was served with a good and well prepared, though frugal meal. I was happy to see that the bishop, with his priests, were teetotalers. No wine nor beer to tempt the weak. Before the dinner was over, the bishop said to Mr. Dunn : " You will accompany Mr. Chiniquy to St. Anne in order to announce, in my name, to the people, the restoration of peace, next Sabbath. No doubt it will be joyful news to the colony of Father Chiniquy. After so many years of hard fighting, the pastor and the people of St. Anne will enjoy the days of peace and rest which are now secured to them."

Then, addressing himself to me, the bishop said : " The only condition of that peace is that you will spend fifteen days in retreat and meditation in one of the religious houses you will choose yourself. I think that, after so much noise and exciting controversies, it will do you good to pass those days in meditation and prayer, in some of our beautiful and peaceful solitudes." I answered him : "If your lordship had not offered me the favour of those days of perfect and Christian rest, I would have asked you to grant it. I consider it as a crowning of all your acts of kindness to offer me those few days of calm and meditation, after the terrible storms of those last three years. If your lordship has no objection to my choice, I will go to the beautiful solitude where M. Saurin has built the celebrated Monastery, College, and University of St. Joseph, Indiana. I hope that nothing will prevent my being there next Monday, after going next Sabbath in the company of Grand Vicar Dunn, to proclaim the restoration of the blessed peace to my people of St. Anne." " You cannot make a better choice," answered the bishop. "But, my lord," I rejoined, " I hope your lordship will have no objection to give me a written assurance of the perfect restoration of that long-sought peace. There are people who, I know, will not believe me, when I tell them how quickly and nobly your lordship has put an end to all those deplorable difficulties. I want to show them that I stand to-day in the same relation with my superiors and the church in which I stood previous to these unfortunate strifes." " Certainly," said the bishop, "you are in need of such a document from your bishop, and you shall have it. I will write it at once."

But he had not yet written two lines, when Mr. Dunn looked at his watch and said : "We have not a minute to lose, if we want to be in time for the Chicago train." I then said to the bishop : "Please, my lord, address me that important document to Chicago, where I will get it at the post-office, on my way to the University of St. Joseph, next Monday; your lordship will have plenty of time to write it, this afternoon." The bishop having consented, I hastily took leave of him, with Mr. Dunn, after having received his benediction.

On our way back to St. Anne, the next day, we stopped at Bourbonnais to see the Grand Vicar Mailloux, one of the priests who had been sent by the Bishops of Canada to help my lord O'Regan to crush me. We found him as he was going to his dining-room to take his dinner. He was visibly humiliated by the complete defeat of Bishop O'Regan, at Rome.

After Mr. Dunn had told him that he was sent to proclaim peace to the people of St. Anne, he coldly asked the written proof of that strange news. Mr. Dunn answered him : " Do you think, sir, that I would be mean enough to tell you a lie ? "

" I do not say that you are telling me a lie," replied Mr. Malloux, " I believe what you say. But, I want to know the condition of that unexpected peace. Has Mr. Chiniquy made his submission to the church ? "

" Yes, sir," I replied, " here is a copy of my act of submission."

He read it, and coldly said : " This is not an act of submission to the church, but only to the authority of the Gospel, which is a very different thing. This document can be presented by a Protestant; but it cannot be offered by a Catholic priest to his bishop. I cannot understand how our bishop did not see that at once."

Mr. Dunn answered him : " My dear Grand Vicar Mailloux, I have always been told that it does not do to be more loyal than the king. My hope was that you would rejoice with us at the news of the peace. I am sorry to see that I was mistaken. However, I must tell you that if you want to fight, you will have nobody to fight against; for Father Chiniquy was yesterday accepted as a regular priest of our holy church by the administrator. This ought to satisfy you."

I listened to the unpleasant conversation of those two grand vicars, with painful feelings, without saying a word. For, I was troubled by those mysterious voices which were reiterating in my mind the cry : " Do you not see that in the Church of Rome, you do not follow the Word of God, but only the lying traditions of men ? "

I felt much relieved, when I left the house of that so badly disposed confrère, to come to St. Anne, where the people had gathered on the public square, to receive us, and rend the air with their cries of joy at the happy news of peace.

The next day, 27th of March, was Palm Sunday, one of the grand festivites of the Church of Rome ; there was an immense concourse of people, attracted not only by the religious solemnity of the feast ; but also by the desire to see and hear the deputy sent by their bishop to proclaim peace. He did it in a most elegant English address, which I translated into French. He presented me with a blessed palm, and I offered him another loaded with beautiful flowers, in the presence of the people, as a public sign of the concord which was restored between my colony and the authorities of the church.

That my Christian readers may understand my blindness, and the mercies of God towards me, I must confess here, to my shame, that I was glad to have made my peace with those sinful men, which was not peace with my God. But, that great God had looked down upon me in mercy. He was soon to break that peace with the great apostate church, which is poisoning the world with the wine of her enchantments, that I might walk in the light of the Gospel and possess that peace and joy which passeth all understanding.

CHAPTER LXV.

BISHOP SMITH had fulfilled his promise in addressing to me a testimonial letter, which would show to both friends and foes that the most honourable and lasting peace between us was to succeed the deplorable years of strife through which we had just passed. I read it with Grand Vicar Dunn, who was not less pleased than I with the kind expressions of esteem towards my people and myself with which it was filled. I had never had a document in which my private and public character were so kindly appreciated. I put it in my portfolio as the most precious treasure I had ever possessed, and my gratitude to the bishop who had written such friendly lines, was boundless. I, at once, addressed a short letter to thank and bless him: and I requested him to pray for me during the happy days of retreat I was to spend at the monastery of St. Joseph.

The venerable Grand Vicar Saurin, and his assistant, Rev. M. Granger, received me as two Christian gentlemen receive a brother priest, and I may say that, during my stay in the monastery, they constantly overwhelmed me with the most sincere marks of kindness. I found in them both the very best types of priests of Rome. A volume, and not a chapter, would be required, were I to tell what I saw there of the zeal, devotedness, ability and marvellous success of their labours. Suffice it to say, that Grand Vicar Saurin is justly considered one of the greatest and highest intellects Rome has ever given to the United States. There is not, perhaps, a man who has done so much for the advancement of that church in this country as that highly gifted priest. My esteem, respect, I venture to say, my veneration for him, increased every time I had the privilege of conversing with him. The only things which pained me were:

1st. When some of his inferior monks came to speak to him, they had to kneel and prostrate themselves as if he had been a god, and they had to remain in that humble and degrading posture, till, with a sign of his hand or a word from his lips, he told them to rise.

2nd. Though he promised to the numerous Protestant parents, who entrusted their boys and girls to his care for their education, never to interfere with their religion, he was, nevertheless, incessantly proselytizing them. Several of his Protestant pupils were received in the Church of Rome, and renounced the religion of their fathers, in my presence, on the eve of Easter of that year.

While, as a priest, I rejoiced in the numerous conquests of my church over her enemies, in all her colleges and nunneries, I objected to the breach of promise, always connected with those conversions. I, however, then thought, as I think to-day, that a Protestant who takes his children to a Roman Catholic priest or a nun for their education, had no religion. It is simply an absurdity to promise that we will respect the religion of a man who has none. How can we respect that which does not exist ?

As a general thing, there are too few people who understand the profound meaning of our Saviour's words to His disciples : " Come ye yourselves apart into a desert place and rest awhile." These words, uttered after the apostles had gathered themselves together unto Jesus, and told Him all things both what they had done and taught, ought to receive more attention, on the part of those whom the Son of God has chosen to continue the great work of preaching His Gospel to the world. I had never before so well realized how good it was to be alone with Christ, and tell Him all I had done, said, and taught. Those few days of rest and communion with my Saviour were one of the greatest favours my merciful God had ever given me.

My principal occupation was to read and meditate on the Gospel. That divine book had never been so precious to me as since God had directed me to put it as the fundamental stone of my faith in the act of submission I had just given to my bishop: and my church had never been so dear to me as since she had accepted that conditional submission. I felt a holy pride and joy at having finally silenced the voice of the enemy which, so often, troubled my faith by crying to my soul: "Do you not see that in your Church of Rome, you do not follow the Word of God, but only the lying traditions of men." My church, through her bishop, had just given me what I considered an infallible assurance of the contrary, by accepting the document signed by me and by my people, where we had clearly said that we would never obey any authority or any superior, except when " their orders or doctrines would be based upon the Gospel of Christ." My soul was rejoicing in those thoughts, when on the 5th of April (Monday after Easter) Grand Vicar Saurin handed me a letter from Mr. Dunn, telling me that a new storm, brought by the Jesuits, and more formidable than the past ones, was about to break on me; that I had to prepare for new and more serious conflicts than I had ever experienced.

The next morning, Mr. Saurin handed me another letter from the Bishop of Dubuque, and with a sympathy which I will never forget, he said: "I am sorry to see that you are not at the end of your troubles, as you expected. Bishop Smith orders you back to Dubuque with words which are far from being friendly." But, strange to say, this bad news, which would have saddened and discouraged me in other circumstances, left me perfectly calm and cheerful on that day. In my dear Gospel, which had been my daily bread, the last eight days, I had found the helmet for my head, the breastplate and the shield to protect me, and the unconquerable sword with which to fight. From every page, I heard my Saviour's voice: "Fear not, I am with thee " (Isaiah xliii. 5).

When on my way back to Dubuque, I stopped at Chicago to know from my faithful friend, Mr. Dunn, the cause of the new storm. He said:

" You remember how Grand Vicar Mailloux was displeased with the conditional submission you had given to the bishop. As soon as we had left him, he sent the young priest who is with him to the Jesuits of Chicago to tell them that the authority of the church and of the bishop would be for ever lost if Chiniquy were allowed to submit on such a condition. He wanted them to notice that it was not to the authority of the bishops and the church you had submitted; but only to the authority of the Bible. The Jesuits were of the same mind. They immediately sent to Dubuque, and said to the bishop: 'Do you not see that Chiniquy is a disguised Protestant; that he has deceived you by presenting you such an act of submission. Does not your lordship see that Chiniquy has not submitted himself to your authority, but to the authority of his Bible alone? Do you not fear that the whole body of the bishops and the Pope himself will condemn you for having fallen into the trap prepared by that disguised Protestant?' Our administrator, though a good man when left to himself, is weak, and like soft wax, can be manipulated in every way. The Jesuits, who want to rule the priests and the church with an iron rod, and who are aiming to change the Pope and the bishops into the most heartless tyrants, have advised the administrator to force you to give an unconditional act of submission. It is not the Word of God which must rule us now. It is the old Jupiter who is coming back to rule us under the name of a modern divinity, called 'the authority of the bishops.' The administrator and the Jesuits themselves have telegraphed your submission to several bishops, who have unanimously answered that it must be rejected, and another, without condition, requested from you. You were evidently too correct when you told me, the other day, that your act of submission was too good for the bishops and the Pope. What will you do?"

I replied: "I do not know what I will do, but be sure of this, my dear Mr. Dunn, I will do what our great and merciful God will tell me."

" Very well, very well," he answered ; " may God help you ! " *
After warmly shaking hands with me, I left to take the train for
Dubuque, where I arrived next morning. I went immediately to
the bishop's palace. I found him in the company of a Jesuit, and
I felt myself as a poor helpless ship between two threatening ice-
bergs.

" Your lordship wants to see me again," I said.

" Yes, sir, I want to see you again," he answered.

" What do you want from me, my lord ? " I replied.

" Have you the testimonial letter I addressed to you at Chicago
last week ?"

" Yes, my lord, I have it with me."

" Will you please show it to me ?" he replied.

" With pleasure—here it is;" and I handed him the precious
document.

As soon as he had assured himself that it was the very letter
in question, he ran to the stove and threw it into the fire. I felt so
puzzled at the action of my bishop that I remained almost paralyzed ;
but soon coming to myself, I ran to save from the flames that
document which was more valuable and precious to me than all
the gold of California, but it was too late. It was in ashes. I turned
to the bishop and said : " How can you take from me a document
which is my property, and destroy it without my permission ?"

He answered me with an impudence that cannot be expressed
on paper : " I am your superior, and have no account to give you."

I replied : " Yes, my lord, you are my superior indeed ! You are a
great bishop in our church, and I am nothing but a poor miserable
priest. But there is an Almighty God in heaven, who is as much
above you as He is above me. That great God has granted me
rights which I will never give up to please any man. In the presence
of that God I protest against your iniquity."

" Have you come here to lecture me ? " replied the bishop.

" No, my lord, I did not come to lecture you; I come at your
command, but I want to know if it was to insult me as you have just
done that you requested me to come here again."

" I ordered you to come here again because you deceived me the
last time you were here," he answered : " you gave me an act of submission which you know very well is not an act of submission. I
accepted it then, but I was mistaken ; I reject it to-day."

I answered : " How can you say that I deceived you ? The
document I presented you is written in good, plain English. It
is there, on your table, I see it : you read it twice, and understood

* That same Mr. Dunn was also excommunicated not long after by his bishop, and
died after publicly refusing to be relieved from that sentence.

it well. If you were deceived by its contents, you deceived yourself. You are, then, a self-deceiver, and you cannot accuse me of having deceived you."

He then took the document, read it slowly; and when at the words, "we submit ourselves to your authority, according to the Word of God as we find it in the Gospel of Christ," he stopped and said : "What do you mean by this?"

I answered, "I mean what you see there. I mean that neither I nor my people will ever submit ourselves to anybody, except according to the eternal laws of truth, justice, and holiness of God, as we find them expressed in the Bible."

He angrily answered, "Such language on your part is sheer Protestantism. I cannot accept such a conditional submission from any priest."

Then again I seemed to hear the mysterious voice, "Do you not see that in your Church of Rome you do not follow the Word of God, but the lying traditions of men ?"

Thanks be to God, I did not silence the voice in that solemn hour. An ardent, though silent prayer, went from the bottom of my heart to the mercy seat. With all the fervour of my soul I said : "Oh my God ! speak, speak again to Thy poor servant, and grant me the grace to follow Thy holy Word !" I then said to the bishop :—

"You distress me by rejecting this act of submission, and asking another. Please explain yourself more clearly, and tell me the nature of the new one you require from me and my people."

Taking then a more subdued and polite tone, the bishop said :

"I hope, Mr. Chiniquy, that, as a good priest, you do not want to rebel against your bishop, and that you will give me the act of submission I ask from you. Take away these 'Words of God,' 'Gospel of Christ,' and 'Bible' from your present document, and I will be satisfied."

"But, my lord, with my people I have put these words because we want to obey only the bishops who follow the Word of God. We want to submit only to the church which respects and follows the Gospel of Christ."

In an irritated manner he quickly answered : "Take away from your act of submission those 'Words of God,' and 'Gospel of Christ,' and 'Bible!' or I will punish you as a rebel."

"My lord," I replied, "those expressions are there to show us and to the whole world that the Word of God, the Gospel of Christ, and the Bible are the fundamental stones of our holy church. If we reject those precious stones, on what foundations will our church and our faith rest ?"

He answered angrily : "Mr. Chiniquy, I am your superior, I do not want to argue with you. You are my inferior: your business is to obey me. Give me at once an act of submission, in which you will simply say that you and your people will submit yourselves to my authority, and promise to do anything I will bid you."

I calmly answered: "What you ask me is not an act of submission, it is an act of adoration. I do absolutely refuse to give it."

"If it be so, sir," he answered, "you can no longer be a Roman Catholic priest."

I raised my hands to heaven, and cried with a loud voice : "May God Almighty be for ever blessed."

I took my hat, and left to go to my hotel. When alone in my room I locked the door and fell on my knees, to consider, in the presence of God, what I had just done. There the awful, undeniable truth stared me in the face. My church could not be the church of Christ! That sad truth had not been revealed to me by any Protestant, nor any other enemy of the church. It was from her own lips I had got it! It had been told me by one of her most learned and devoted bishops! My church was the deadly, the irreconcilable enemy of the Word of God, as I had so often suspected! I was not allowed to remain a single day longer in that church without positively and publicly giving up the Gospel of Christ! It was evident to me that the Gospel was only a blind, a mockery to conceal her iniquities, tyrannies, superstitions, and idolatries. The only use of the Gospel in my church was to throw dust in the eyes of the priests and people! It had no authority. The only rule and guide were the will, the passions, and the dictates of sinful men!

There, on my knees, and alone with God, it was evident to me that the voice which had so often troubled and shaken my faith, was the voice of my merciful God. It was the voice of my dear Saviour, who was bringing me out of the ways of perdition in which I had been walking. And I had tried so often to silence that voice!

"My God! my God!" I cried, "The Church of Rome is not Thy church. To obey the voice of my conscience, which is Thine, I gave it up. When I had the choice between giving up that church or the Bible, I did not hesitate. I could not give up Thy Holy Word. I have given up Rome! But, oh Lord, where is Thy church? Oh! speak!! where must I go to be saved?"

For more than one hour I cried to God in vain; no answer came. In vain I cried for a ray of light to guide me. The more I prayed and wept, the greater was the darkness which surrounded me! I then felt as if God had forsaken me, and an unspeakable distress was the result of that horrible thought. To add to that distress, the thought flashed across my mind that by giving up the Church of

Rome, I had given up the church of my dear father and mother, of my brother, my friends, and my country—in fact, all that was near and dear to me!

I hope that none of my readers will ever experience what it is to give up friends, relatives, parents, honour, country—everything! I did not regret the sacrifice, but I felt as if I could not survive it. With tears, I cried to God for more strength and faith to bear the cross which was laid on my too weak shoulders, but all in vain.

Then I felt that an implacable war was to be declared against me, which would end only with my life. The Pope, the bishops, and priests, all over the world, would denounce and curse me. They would attack and destroy my character, my name and my honour, in their press, from their pulpit, and in their confessionals, where the man they strike can never know whence the blow is coming! Almost in despair, I tried to think of some one who would come to my help in that formidable conflict, but could find none. Every one of the millions of Roman Catholics were bound to curse me. My best friends—my own people—even my own brothers, were bound to look upon me with horror as an apostate, a vile outcast! Could I hope for help or protection from Protestants? No! for my priestly life had been spent in writing and preaching against them. In vain would I try to give an idea of the desolation I felt when that thought struck my mind.

Forsaken by God and man, what would become of me? Where would I go when out of that room? Expelled with contempt by my former Roman Catholic friends; repulsed with still more contempt by Protestants: where could I go to hide my shame and drag on my miserable existence? How could I go again into that world where there was no more room for me; where there was no hand to press mine; none to smile upon me! Life suddenly became to me an unbearable burden. My brain seemed to be filled with burning coals. I was losing my mind. Yea, death, an instant death, seemed to me the greatest blessing in that awful hour! and, will I say it? Yes! I took my knife to cut my throat, and put an end to my miserable existence! But my merciful God, who wanted only to humble me, by showing me my own helplessness, stopped my hand, and the knife fell on the floor.

Though I felt the pangs of that desolation for more than two hours, I constantly cried to God for a ray of His saving light, for a word telling me what to do, where to go to be saved. At last, drops of cold sweat began to cover again my face and my whole body. The pulsations of my heart began to be very slow and weak: I felt so feeble that I expected to faint at any moment, or fall dead! At first, I thought that death would be a great relief, but then, I said to myself, "If I die, where will I go, when there is no faith, nor a ray

of light to illumine my poor perishing soul! Oh, my dear Saviour,"
I cried, "come to my help! Lift up the light of Thy reconciled countenance upon me."

In that very instant, I remembered that I had my dear New Testament with me, which I used then, as now, to carry everywhere. The
thought flashed across my mind that I would find in that Divine book
the answer to my prayer, and light to guide me through that dark
night, to that house of refuge and salvation, after which my soul was
ardently longing. With a trembling hand and a praying heart, I
opened the book at random—but, no! not I, my God himself opened
it for me. My eyes fell on these words : "YE ARE BOUGHT
WITH A PRICE. BE NOT YE THE SERVANTS OF MEN"
(1 Cor. vii. 23).

Strange to say! Those words came to my mind, more as a light
than an articulated sound. They suddenly but most beautifully and
powerfully gave me, as much as a man can know it, the knowledge
of the great mystery of a perfect salvation through Christ alone.
They at once brought a great and delightful calm to my soul. I said
to myself : " Jesus has bought me, then I am His; for when I have
bought a thing it is mine, absolutely mine! Jesus has bought me!
I, then, belong to Him! He alone has a right over me. I do not
belong to the bishops, to the popes, not even to the church, as I have
been told till now. I belong to Jesus and to Him alone! His Word
must be my guide, and my light by day and by night. Jesus has
bought me," I said again to myself; " then He has saved me! and if so,
I am saved, perfectly saved, for ever saved! for Jesus cannot save me
by half. Jesus is my God ; the works of God are perfect. My salvation must, then, be a perfect salvation. But how has He saved me ?
What price has He paid for my poor guilty soul ? " The answer came as
quickly as lightning : " He bought you with His blood shed on the
cross ! He saved you by dying on Calvary ! "

I then said to myself again : " If Jesus has perfectly saved me by
shedding His blood on the cross, I am not saved, as I have thought
and preached till now, by my penances, my prayers to Mary and the
saints, my confessions and indulgences, not even by the flames of
purgatory ! "

In that instant, all things which, as a Roman Catholic, I had to
believe to be saved—all the mummeries by which the poor Roman
Catholics are so cruelly deceived, the chaplets, indulgences, scapularies, auricular confession, invocation of the virgin, holy water,
masses, purgatory, etc., given as means of salvation, vanished from
my mind as a huge tower, when struck at the foundation, crumbles to
the ground. Jesus alone remained in my mind as the Saviour of my
soul !

Oh! what a joy I felt at this simple, but sublime truth! But it was the will of God that this joy should be short. It suddenly went away with the beautiful light which had caused it; and my poor soul was again wrapped in the most awful darkness. However profound that darkness was, a still darker object presented itself before my mind. It was as a very high mountain, but not composed of sand or stones, it was the mountain of my sins. I saw them all standing before me. And still more horrified was I when I saw it moving towards me as if, with a mighty hand, to crush me. I tried to escape, but in vain. I felt tied to the floor, and the next moment it had rolled over me. I felt as crushed under its weight; for it was as heavy as granite. I could scarcely breathe! My only hope was to cry to God for help. With a loud voice, heard by many in the hotel, I cried: "O my God! have mercy upon me! My sins are destroying me! I am lost, save me!" But, it seemed God could not hear me. The mountain was between, to prevent my cries from reaching Him, and to hide my tears. I suddenly thought that God would have nothing to do with such a sinner, but to open the gates of hell to throw me into that burning furnace prepared for his enemies, and which I had so richly deserved!

I was mistaken. After eight or ten minutes of unspeakable agony, the rays of a new and beautiful light began to pierce through the dark cloud which hung over me. In that light, I clearly saw my Saviour. There He was, bent under the weight of His heavy cross. His face was covered with blood, the crown of thorns was on His head, and the nails in His hands. He was looking to me with an expression of compassion, of love, which no tongue can describe. Coming to me, He said: "I have heard thy cries, I have seen thy tears, I have given Myself for thee. My blood and My bruised body have paid thy debts; wilt thou give Me thy heart? Wilt thou take My Word for the only lamp of thy feet, and the only light of thy path? I bring thee eternal life as a gift!"

I answered: "Dear Jesus, how sweet are Thy words to my soul! Speak, oh! speak again! Yes, beloved Saviour, I want to love Thee; but dost Thou not see that mountain which is crushing me? Oh! remove it! Take away my sins!"

I had not done speaking when I saw His mighty hand stretched out. He touched the mountain, and it rolled into the deep and disappeared. At the same time, I felt as if a shower of the blood of the Lamb were falling upon me to purify my soul. And, suddenly, my humble room was transformed into a real paradise. The angels of God could not be more happy than I was in that most mysterious and blessed hour of my life. With an unspeakable joy, I said to my Saviour: "Dear Jesus, the gift of God! Thou hast brought me the pardon of my sins as a gift. Thou hast brought me eternal life as a gift! Thou hast redeemed and saved me, beloved Saviour; I know, I feel it. But this is not enough. I do not want to be saved alone. Save my people also. Save my whole country! I feel rich and happy in that gift; grant me to show its beauty, and preciousness, to my people, that they may rejoice in its possession."

This sudden revelation of that marvellous truth of salvation as a gift, had so completely transformed me, that I felt quite a new man. The unutterable distress of my soul had been changed into an unspeakable joy. My fears had gone away, to be replaced by a courage and a strength such as I had never experienced. The Popes, with their bishops and priests, and millions of abject slaves might now attack me, I felt that I was a match for them all. My great ambition was to go back to my people and tell them what the Lord had done for my soul. I washed my tears away, paid my bill, and took the train which brought me back into the midst of my dear countrymen. At that very same hour they were very anxious and excited, for they had just received, at Kankakee City, a telegram from the Bishop of Dubuque, telling them: "Turn away your priest, for he has refused to give me an unconditional act of submission."

They had gathered in great numbers to hear the reading of that strange message. But they unanimously said: "If Mr. Chiniquy has refused to give an unconditional act of submission, he has done right, we will stand by him to the end." However, I knew nothing of that admirable resolution. I arrived at St. Anne on a Sabbath day at the hour of the morning service. There was an immense crowd at the door of the chapel. They rushed to me, and said: "You are just coming from the bishop; what good news have you to bring us?"

I answered: "No news here, my good friends; come to the chapel and I will tell you what the Lord has done for my soul."

When they had filled the large building, I told them:

"Our Saviour, the day before His death, said to His disciples: 'I will be a scandal * to you, this night.' I must tell you the same thing. I will be, to-day, I fear, the cause of a great scandal to every one of you. But, as the scandal which Christ gave to His disciples has saved the world, I hope that, by the great mercy of God, the scandal I will give you will save you. I was your pastor till yesterday! But I have no more that honour to-day, for I have broken the ties by which I was bound as a slave at the feet of the bishops and of the Pope."

This sentence was scarcely finished, when a universal cry of sur-

* Σκανδαλισθήσεσθε, "All ye shall be offended because of Me this night" (Matt. xxvi. 31, Mark xiv. 27).

prise and sadness filled the church: "Oh! what does that mean!" exclaimed the congregation.

"My dear countrymen," I added, "I have not come to tell you to follow me! I did not die to save your immortal souls; I have not shed my blood to buy you a place in heaven; but Christ has done it. Then follow Christ and Him alone! Now, I must tell you why I have broken the ignominious and unbearable yoke of men, to follow Christ. You remember that, on the 21st of March last, you signed, with me, an act of submission to the authority of the Bishop of the Church of Rome, with the conditional clause that we would obey him only in matters which were according to the teachings of the Word of God as found in the Gospel of Christ. In that act of submission we did not want to be slaves of any man, but the servants of God, the followers of the Gospel. It was our hope then, that our church would accept such a submission. And your joy was great when you heard that Grand Vicar Dunn was here on the 28th of March to tell you that Bishop Smith had accepted the submission. But that acceptation was revoked. Yesterday, I was told, in the presence of God, by the same bishop, that he ought not to have accepted an act of submission from any priest or people based on the Gospel of Christ! Yes! yesterday Bishop Smith rejected, with the utmost contempt, the act of submission we had given him, and which he had accepted only two weeks ago, because 'the Word of God' was mentioned in it! When I respectfully requested him to tell me the nature of the new act of submission he wanted from us, he ordered me to take away from it 'the Word of God, the Gospel of Christ, and the Bible,' if we wanted to be accepted as good Catholics! We had thought, till then, that the sacred Word of God and the Holy Gospel of Christ were the fundamental and precious stones of the Church of Rome. We loved her on that account, we wanted to remain in her bosom, even when we were forced to fight as honest men, against that tyrant, O'Regan. Believing that the Church of Rome was the child of the Word of God, that it was the most precious fruit of the Divine tree planted on the earth, under the name of the Gospel, we would have given the last drop of our blood to defend her!

"But, yesterday, I have learned from the very lips of a Bishop of Rome, that we were a band of simpletons in believing those things. I have learned that the Church of Rome has nothing to do with the Word of God, except to throw it overboard, to trample it under their feet, and to forbid us even to name it even in the solemn act of submission we had given. I have been told that we could no longer be Roman Catholics, if we persisted in putting the Word of God and the Gospel of Christ as the foundation of our religion, our faith and our submission. When I was told by the bishop that I had either to renounce the Word of God as the base of my submission, or the title of the priest of Rome, I did not hesitate. Nothing could induce me to give up the Gospel of Christ; and so I gave up the title and position of priest in the Roman Catholic Church. I would rather suffer a thousand deaths than renounce the Gospel of Christ. I am no longer a priest of Rome; but I am more than ever a disciple of Christ, a follower of the Gospel. That Gospel is for me, what it was for Paul, 'The power of God unto salvation' (Rom. i. 16). It is the bread of my soul. In it we can satisfy our thirst with the waters of eternal life! No! no!! I could not buy the honour of being any longer a slave to the bishops and popes of Rome, by giving up the Gospel of Christ!

"When I requested the bishop to give me the precise form of submission he wanted from us, he answered: "Give me an act of submission, without any condition, and promise that you will do anything I bid you.' I replied:

"'This is not an act of submission, it is an act of adoration! I will never give it to you!'

"'If so,' said he, 'you can no longer be a Roman Catholic priest.'

"I raised my hands to heaven, and with a loud and cheerful voice, I said: 'May God Almighty be for ever blessed!'"

I then told them something of my desolation, when alone, in my room; of the granite mountain which had been rolled over my shoulders, of my tears, and of my despair. I told them also how my bleeding, dying, crucified Saviour had brought me the forgiveness of my sins; how He had given me eternal salvation, as a gift, and how rich, happy, and strong I felt in that gift. I then spoke to them about their own souls.

My address lasted more than two hours, and God blessed it in a marvellous way. Its effects were profound and lasting, but it is too long to be described here. In substance, I said: "I respect you too much to impose myself upon your honest consciences, or to dictate what you ought to do on this most solemn occasion. I feel that the hour has come for me to make a great sacrifice; I must leave you! but, no! I will not go away before you tell me to do so. You wil yourselves break the ties so dear which have united us. Please, pay attention to these, my parting words: If you think it is better for you to follow the Pope than to follow Christ; that it is better to trust in the works of your hands, and in your own merits, than in the blood of the Lamb, shed on the cross, to be saved; if you think it is better for you to follow the traditions of men than the Gospel; and if you believe that it is better for you to have a priest of Rome, who will keep you tied as slaves to the feet of the bishops, and who will preach to you the ordinances of men, rather than have me preach to you nothing but the pure Word of God, as we find it in the Gospel of Christ, tell it to me by rising up, and I will go!" But, to my great surprise, nobody moved. The chapel was filled with sobs; tears were flowing from every eye; but not one moved to tell me to leave them! I was puzzled. For though I had hoped that many, enlightened by the copies of the New Testament that I had given them, tired of the tyranny of the bishops, and disgusted with the superstitions of Rome, would be glad to break the yoke with me, to follow Christ, I was afraid that the greatest number would not dare to break their allegiance to the church, and publicly give up her authority. After a few minutes of silence, during which I mixed my tears and my sobs with those of my people, I told them: " Why do you not at once rise up and tell me to go? You see that I can no longer remain your pastor after renouncing the tyranny of the bishops and the traditions of men to follow the Gospel of Christ as my only rule. Why do you not bravely tell me to go away?"

But this new appeal was still without any answer. I was filled with astonishment. However, it was evident to me that a great and mysterious change was wrought in that multitude. Their countenances, their manners, were completely changed. They were speaking to me with their eyes filled with tears, and their manly faces beaming with joy. Their sobs, in some way, told me that they were filled with new light; that they were full of new strength, and ready to make the most heroic sacrifices, and break their fetters to follow Christ, and Him alone. There was something in those brave, honest and happy faces which was telling me more effectually than the most eloquent speech: " We believe in the gift, we want to be rich, happy, free, and saved in the gift: we do not want anything else: remain among us and teach us to love both the gift and the giver !"

A thought suddenly flashed across my mind, and with an inexpressible sentiment of hope and joy, I told them: "My dear countrymen! The Mighty God, who gave me His saving light, yesterday, can grant you the same favour to-day. He can, as well, save a thousand souls as one. I see, in your noble and Christian faces, that you do not want any more to be slaves of men. You want to be the free children of God, intelligent followers of the Gospel! The light is shining, and you like it. The gift of God has been given to you! With me, you will break the fetters of a captivity, worse than that of Egypt, to follow the Gospel of Christ, and take possession of the Promised Land : let all those who think it is better to follow Jesus Christ than the Pope, better to follow the Word of God than the traditions of men : let all those of you who want me to remain here and preach to you nothing but the Word of God, as we find it in

the Gospel of Christ, tell it to me, by rising up. I am your man!
Rise up !"

Without a single exception, that multitude arose! More than a
thousand of my countrymen had, for ever, broken their fetters. They
had crossed the Red Sea and exchanged the servitude of Egypt for
the blessings of the Promised Land !

CHAPTER LXVI.

WHERE shall I find words to express the sentiments of surprise,
admiration and joy I felt when, after divine service, alone in my
humble study, I considered, in the presence of God, what His mighty
hand had just wrought under my eyes. The people who surrounded
the Saviour when He cried to Lazarus to come forth, were not more
amazed at seeing the dead coming out of his grave than I was when I
had seen, not one, but more than a thousand, of my countrymen so
suddenly and unexpectedly coming out from the grave of the degrading slavery in which they were born and brought up. No, the heart
of Moses was not filled with more joy than mine, when on the shores
of the Red Sea, he sang his sublime hymn :

"I will sing unto the Lord: for He hath triumphed gloriously :
the horse and his rider hath He thrown into the sea. The Lord is my
strength and song, and He is become my salvation : He is my God,
and I will prepare Him an habitation : my fathers' God, and I will
exalt Him " (Ex. xv. 2).

My joy was, however, suddenly changed into confusion, when I
considered the unworthiness of the instrument which God had chosen
to do that work. I felt this was only the beginning of the most
remarkable religious reform which had ever occurred on this continent
of America, and I was dismayed at the thought of such a task ! I
saw, at a glance, that I was called to guide my people into regions
entirely new and unexplored. The terrible difficulties which Luther,
Calvin and Knox had met, at almost every step, were to meet me.
Though giants, they had, at many times, been brought low and almost
discouraged in their new positions. What would become of me, seeing
that I was so deficient in knowledge, wisdom and experience !

Many times, during the first night after the deliverance of my
people from the bondage of the Pope, I said to my God in tears :
" Why hast not Thou chosen a more worthy instrument of Thy mercies
towards my brethren ?" I would have shrank before the task, had not
God said to me in His Word : "For ye see your calling, brethren, how
that not many wise men after the flesh, not many mighty, not many

noble, are called ; but God hath chosen the foolish things of the world to confound the wise. And God hath chosen the weak things of the world to confound the things which are mighty, and base things of the world and things which are despised, hath God chosen; yea, the things which are not, to bring to naught the things that are, that no flesh should glory in His presence " (1 Cor. i. 26—29).

These words calmed my fears and gave me new courage. Next morning, I said to myself : " Is it not God alone who has done the great things of yesterday? Why should I not rely upon Him for the things which remain to be done ? I am weak, it is true, but He is strong and mighty. I am unwise, but He is the God of light and wisdom : I am sinful, but He is the God of holiness : He wants the world to know that He is the worker."

It would make the most interesting book, were I to tell all the marvellous episodes of the new battle my dear countrymen and I had to fight against Rome, in those stormy but blessed days. Let me ask my readers to come with me to that Roman Catholic family, and see the surprise and desolation of the wife and children when the father returned from public service and said : " My dear wife and children, I have, for ever, left the Church of Rome, and hope that you will do the same. The ignominious chains by which we were tied, as the slaves of the bishops and of the Pope, are broken. Christ Jesus alone will reign over us now. His Holy Word alone will rule and guide us. Salvation is a gift : I am happy in its possession."

In another house, the husband had not been able to come to church, but the wife and children had. It was now the wife who announced to her husband that she had, for ever, renounced the usurped authority of the bishops and the Pope : and that it was her firm resolution to obey no other master than Christ, and accept no other religion than the one taught in the Gospel.

At first, this was considered only as a joke ; but as soon as it was realized to be a fact, there were, in many places, confusion, tears, angry words and bitter discussions. But the God of truth, light and salvation was there ; and as it was His work, the storms were soon calmed, the tears dried, and peace restored.

A week had scarcely passed, when the Gospel cause had achieved one of the most glorious victories over its implacable enemy, the Pope. In a few days, 405 out of 500 families which were around me in St. Anne, had not only accepted the Gospel of Christ, as their only authority in religion ; but had publicly given up the name of Roman Catholics, to call themselves Christian Catholics.

A few months later, a Romish priest, legally questioned on the subject, by the Judge of Kankakee, had to swear that only fifteen families had remained Roman Catholics in St. Anne.

A most admirable feature of this religious movement, was the strong determination of those who had never been taught to read, to lose no time in acquiring the privilege of reading for themselves the Divine Gospel which had made them free from the bondage of man. Half of the people had never been taught to read while in Canada; but as their children were attending the schools we had established in different parts of the colony, every house, as well as our chapel, on Sabbath days, was soon turned into a school-house, where our schoolboys and girls were the teachers, and the fathers and mothers, the pupils. In a short time, there were but few, except those who refused to leave Rome, who could not read for themselves the Holy Word of God.

But, however great the victory we had gained over the Pope, it was not yet complete. It was true that the enemy had received a deadly wound. The beast, with the seven heads, had its principal one severed. The usurped authority of the bishops had been destroyed, and the people had determined to accept none but the authority of Christ. But many false notions, drank with the milk of their mothers, had been retained. Many errors and superstitions still remained in their minds, as a mist after the rising of the sun, to prevent them from seeing clearly the saving light of the Gospel, it was my duty to destroy those superstitions, and root out these noxious weeds. But, I knew the formidable difficulties the reformers of the fifteenth century had met, the deplorable divisions which had spread among them, and the scandals which had so seriously retarded and compromised the reformation.

I cried to God for wisdom and strength. Never had I understood so clearly, as I did in that most solemn and difficult epoch of my life, the truth that prayer is to the troubled mind what oil is to the raging waves of the sea. My people and I, as are all Roman Catholics, were much given to the worship of images and statues. There were fourteen beautiful pictures hung on the walls of our chapel called: "The Way of the Cross," on which the circumstances of the passion of Jesus Christ were represented, each surmounted with a cross. One of our favourite devotional exercises, was to kneel, three or four times a week, before them, prostrate ourselves and say, with a loud voice: "Oh! holy cross, we adore thee." We used to address our most fervent prayers to them, as if they could hear us, asking them to change our hearts and purify our souls! Our blind devotions were so sincere that we used to bow our heads to the ground before them. I may say the same of a beautiful statue, or rather idol, of the Virgin Mary, represented as a child learning to read at the feet of her mother, St. Anne.

The group was a masterpiece of art, sent to me by some rich

friends from Montreal, not long after I had left that city to form the colony of St. Anne, in 1852. We had frequently addressed our most fervent prayers to those statues, but after the blessed pentecost on which we had broken the yoke of the Pope, I never entered my church without blushing at the sight of those idols on the altar.

I would have given much to have the pictures, crosses and images removed, but dare not lay hands suddenly on them, I was afraid, lest I should do harm to some of my people who, it seemed to me, were yet too weak in their religious views to bear it. I was just then reading how Knox and Calvin had made bonfires of all those relics of old Paganism, and I wished I could do the same; but I felt like Jacob, who could not follow the rapid march of his brother, Esau, towards the land of Seir. "The children are tender and the flocks and herds with young are with me. If men should overdrive them one day, all the flock will die" (Gen. xxxiii. 13).

Our merciful God saw the perplexity in which I was, and taught me how to get rid of those idols without harming the weak.

One Sabbath, on which I preached on the Second Commandment: "Thou shalt not make to thyself any graven image," etc. (Exod. xx. 4), I remained in the chapel to pray after the people had left. I looked up to the group of statues on the altar, and said to them: "My good ladies, you must come down from that high position: God Almighty alone is worshipped here now : if you could walk out of this place I would politely invite you to do it. But you are nothing but mute, deaf, blind and motionless idols : you have eyes, but you cannot see : ears, but you cannot hear: feet, but you cannot walk. What will I do with you now ? Your reign has come to an end."

It suddenly came to my mind that when I had put these statues on their high pedestal, I had tied them with a very slender, but strong silk cord, to prevent them from falling. I said to myself: "If I were to cut that string, the idols would surely fall, the first day the people would shake the floor when entering or going out." Their fall and destruction would then scandalize no one. I took my knife and scaled the altar, cut the string, and said: "Now, my good ladies, take care of yourselves, especially when the chapel is shaken by the wind, or the coming in of the people."

I never witnessed a more hearty laugh than at the beginning of the religious services, on the next Sabbath. The chapel, being shaken by the action of the whole people who fell on their knees to pray, the two idols, deprived of their silk support, after a couple of jerks which, in former days, we might have taken for a friendly greeting, fell down with a loud crash, and broke into fragments. Old and young, strong and weak, and even babes in the faith, after laughing to their hearts' content at the sad end of their idols, said to each other : "How foolish and blind were we, to put our trust in, and pray to these idols, that they might protect us, when they cannot take care of themselves ! " The last vestige of idol worship among our dear converts, disappeared for ever with the dust and broken fragments of those poor help-less statues. The very next day, the people themselves took away all the images before which they had so often abjectly prostrated them-selves, and destroyed them.

From the beginning of this movement, it had been my plan to let the people draw their own conclusions as much as possible from their own study of the Holy Scriptures. I used to direct their steps, in such a way, that they might understand that I was myself led with them by the mighty and merciful arm of God, in our new ways. It was also evident to me that, from the beginning, the great majority, after searching the Scriptures with prayerful attention, had found out that Purgatory was a diabolical invention used by the priests of Rome, to enrich themselves, at the expense of their poor blind slaves. But I was also convinced that quite a number were not altogether free from that imposture. I did not know how to attack and destroy that error without wounding and injuring some of the weak children of the Gospel. After much praying, I thought that the best way to clear the clouds which were still hovering around the feeblest intelligences, was to have recourse to the following device :

The All Souls Day (1st Nov.) had come, when it was the usage to take up collections for the sake of having prayers and masses said for the souls in purgatory. I then said to the people, from the pulpit : " You have been used, from your infancy, to collect money, to-day, in order to have prayers said for the souls in purgatory. Since we have left the Church of Rome for the Church of Christ, we have spent many pleasant hours together in reading and meditating upon the Gospel. You know that we have not found in it a single word about purgatory. From the beginning to the end of that divine book, we have learned that it was only through the blood of the Lamb, shed on the Cross, that our guilty souls could be purified from their sins. I know, however, that a few of you have retained something of the views taught to you, when in the Church of Rome, concerning purgatory. I do not want to trouble them by useless discussions on the subject, or by refusing the money they want to give for the souls of their dear departed parents and friends. The only thing I want to do is this : You used to have a small box passed to you to receive that money. To-day, instead of one box, two boxes will be passed, one white, the other black. Those who, like myself, do not believe in purgatory, will put their donations in the white box, and the money will be given to the poor widows and orphans of the parish, to help them to get food and clothing for next winter. Those of you who still believe in pur-

37

gatory, will put their money into the black box, for the benefit of the dead. The only favour I ask of them is that they should tell me how to convey their donations to their departed friends. I tell you frankly that the money you give to the priests, never goes to the benefit of the souls of purgatory. The priests, everywhere, keep that money for their own bread and butter."

My remarks were followed by a general smile. Thirty-five dollars were put in the white box for the orphans and widows, and not a cent fell into the box for the souls of purgatory.

From that day, by the great mercy of God, our dear converts were perfectly rid of the ridiculous and sacrilegious belief in purgatory. That is the way I have dealt with all the errors and idolatries of Rome. We had two public meetings every week, when our chapel was as well filled as on Sabbath. After the religious exercises, every one had the liberty to question me and argue on the various subjects announced at the last meeting.

The doctrines of auricular confession, prayers in an unknown language, the mass, holy water and indulgences, were calmly examined, discussed, and thrown overboard, one after the other, in a very short time. The good done in those public discussions was incalculable. Our dear converts not only learned the great truths of Christianity, but they learned also how to defend and preach them to their relations, friends and neighbours. Many would come from long distances to see for themselves that strange religious movement which was making so much noise all over the country. It is needless to say that few of them went back without having received some rays of the saving light which the Sun of Righteousness was so abundantly pouring upon me and my dear brethren of St. Anne.

Three months after our exit from the land of bondage, we were not less than six thousand French Canadians marching towards the Promised Land.

How can I express the joy of my soul, when, under cover of the darkness of night, I was silently pacing the streets of our town, I heard, from almost every house, sounds of reading the Holy Scriptures, or the melodies of our delightful French hymns! How many times did I then, uniting my feeble voice with that old prophet, say in the rapture of my joy: "Bless the Lord, O my soul: and all that is within me, bless His holy name" (Ps. ciii. 1).

But it was necessary that such a great and blessed work should be tried. Gold cannot be purified without going through the fire.

On the 27th of July, a devoted priest, through my friend, Mr. Dunn, of Chicago, sent me the following copy of a letter, written by the Roman Catholic Bishop of Illinois (Duggan) to several of his co-bishops: "The schism of the apostate, Chiniquy, is spreading with an incredible and most irresistible velocity. I am told that he has not less than ten thousand followers from his countrymen. Though I hope that this number is an exaggeration, it shows that the evil is great ; and that we must not lose any time in trying to open the eyes of the deluded people he is leading to perdition. I intend (D.V.) to visit the very citadel of that deplorable schism, next Tuesday, the 3rd of August. As I speak French almost as well as English, I will address the deluded people of St. Anne in their own language. My intention is to unmask Chiniquy, and show what kind of a man he is. Then I will show the people the folly of believing that they can read and interpret the Scriptures, by their own private judgment. After which, I will easily show them that out of the Church of Rome there is no salvation. Pray to the blessed Virgin Mary that she may help me reclaim that poor deceived people."

Having read that letter to the people on the first Sabbath of August, I said : " We know a man only after he has been tried. So we know the faith of a Christian only after it has been through the fire of tribulations. I thank God that next Tuesday will be the day chosen by Him to show the world that you are worthy of being in the front rank of the great army Jesus Christ is gathering to fight His implacable enemy, the Pope, on this continent. Let every one of you come and hear what the bishop has to say. Not only those who are in good health must come, but even the sick must be brought to hear and judge for themselves. If the bishop fulfils his promise to show you that I am a depraved and wicked man, you must turn me out. You must give up or burn your Bibles, at his bidding, if he proves that you have neither the right to read, nor the intelligence to understand them ; and if he shows you that, out of the Church of Rome, there is no salvation, you must, without an hour's delay, return to that church and submit yourselves to the Pope's bishops. But if he fails (as he will surely do) you know what you have to do. Next Tuesday will be a most glorious day for us all. A great and decisive battle will be fought here, such as this continent has never witnessed, between the great principles of Christian truth and liberty, and the principles of lies and tyranny of the Pope. I have only one word more to say : From this moment to the solemn hour of the conflict, let us humbly, but fervently ask our great God, through His beloved and eternal Son, to look down upon us in His mercy, enlighten and strengthen us, that we may be true to Him, to ourselves, and to His Gospel, and then, the angels of heaven will unite with all the elect of God on earth to bless you for the great and glorious victory you will win."

Never had the sun shone more brightly on our beautiful hill than on the 3rd of August, 1858. The hearts had never felt so happy, and the faces had never been so perfectly the mirrors of joyful minds, as on that day, among the multitudes which began to gather from every corner of the colony, a little after twelve o'clock, noon.

Seeing that our chapel, though very large, would not be able to contain half the audience, we had raised a large and solid platform, ten feet high, in the middle of the public square, in front of the chapel. We covered it with carpets, and put a sofa, with a good number of chairs, for the bishop, his long suite of priests, and one for myself, and a large table for the different books of references I wanted to have at hand, to answer the bishop.

At about two o'clock p.m., we perceived his carriage, followed by several others filled with priests. He was dressed in his white surplice, and his official "bonnet carré" on his head, evidently to more surely command the respect and awe of the multidude.

I had requested the people to keep silence and show him all the respect and courtesy due a gentleman who was visiting them, for the first time.

As soon as his carriage was near the chapel, I gave a signal, and up went the American flag to the top of a mast put on the sacred edifice. It was to warn the ambassador of the Pope that he was not treading the land of the holy inquisition and slavery, but the land of Freedom and Liberty. The bishop understood it. For, raising his head to see that splendid flag of stripes and stars, waving to the breeze, he became pale as death. And his uneasiness did not abate, when the thousands round him rent the air with the cry : " Hurrah for the flag of the free and the brave ! " The bishop and his priests thought this was the signal I had given to slaughter them; for they had been told several times, that I and my people were so depraved and wicked that their lives were in great danger among us. Several priests who had not much relish for the crown of martyrdom, jumped from their carriages and ran away, to the great amusement of the crowd. Perceiving the marks of the most extreme terror on the face of the bishop, I ran to tell him that there was not the least danger, and assured him of the pleasure we had to see him in our midst.

I offered my hand to help him down from his carriage, but he refused it. After some minutes of trembling and hesitation, he whispered a few words in the ear of his Grand Vicar Mailloux, who was well known by my people, and of whom I have already spoken. I knew that it was by his advice that the bishop was among us, and it was by his instigation that Bishop Smith had refused the submission we had given him.

Rising slowly, he said with a loud voice: "My dear French Canadian countrymen, here is your holy bishop. Kneel down, and he will give you his benediction."

But, to the great disgust of the poor grand vicar, this so well laid plan for beginning the battle failed entirely. Not a single one of that immense multitude cared for the benediction. Nobody knelt.

Thinking that he had not spoken loud enough, he raised his voice to the highest pitch and cried:

"My dear fellow countrymen: This is your holy bishop. He comes to visit you. Kneel down, and he will give you his benediction."

But nobody knelt, and, what was worse, a voice from the crowd answered:

"Do you not know, sir, that here we no longer bend the knee before any man? It is only before God we kneel."

The whole people cried "Amen!" to that noble answer. I could not refrain a tear of joy from falling down my cheeks, when I saw how this first effort of the ambassador of the Pope to entrap my people had signally failed. But though I thanked God from the bottom of my heart for this first success He had given to His soldiers, I knew the battle was far from being over.

I implored Him to bide with us, to be our wisdom and our strength to the end. I looked at the bishop, and seeing his countenance as distressed as before, I offered him my hand again, but he refused it the second time with supreme disdain, but accepted the invitation I gave him to come to the platform.

When half way up the stairs he turned, and seeing me following him, he put forth his hand to prevent me from ascending any further, and said: "I do not want you on this platform; go down, and let my priests alone accompany me."

I answered him: "It may be that you do not want me there, but I want to be at your side to answer you. Remember that you are not on your own ground here, but on mine!"

He then, silently and slowly, walked up. When on the platform, I offered him a good arm-chair, which he refused, and sat on one of his own choice, with his priests around him. I then addressed him as follows:

"My lord, the people and pastor of St. Anne are exceedingly pleased to see you in their midst. We promise to listen attentively to what you have to say, on condition that we have the privilege of answering you."

He answered angrily: "I do not want you to say a word here."

Then stepping to the front, he began his address in French, with a trembling voice. But it was a miserable failure from beginning to end. In vain did he try to prove that out of the Church of Rome, there is no salvation. He failed still more miserably to prove that the people have neither the right to read the Scriptures, nor the intelligence to understand them. He said such ridiculous things on that point, that the people went into fits of laughter, and some said: "This is not true. You do not know what you are talking about. The Bible says the very contrary."

But I stopped them by reminding them of the promise they had made of not interrupting him.

A little before closing his address, he turned to me and said: "You are a wicked, rebel priest against your holy church. Go from here into a monastery to do penance for your sins. You say that you have never been excommunicated in a legal way! Well, you will not say that any longer, for I excommunicate you now before this whole people."

I interrupted him and said: "You forget that you have no right to excommunicate a man who has publicly left your church long ago."

He seemed to realize that he had made a fool of himself in uttering such a sentence, and stopped speaking for a moment. Then, recalling his lost courage, he took a new and impressive manner of speaking. He told the people how their friends, their relatives, their very dear mothers and fathers in Canada were weeping over their apostasy. He spoke for a time with great earnestness of the desolation of all those who loved them, at the news of their defection from their holy mother church. Then, resuming, he said: "My dear friends: Please tell me what will be your guide in the ways of God after you have left the holy church of your fathers, the church of your country; who will lead you in the ways of God?"

Those words, which had been uttered with great emphasis and earnestness, were followed by a most complete and solemn silence. Was that silence the result of a profound impression made on the crowd, or was it the silence which always precedes the storm? I could not say. But I must confess that, though I had not lost confidence in God, I was not without anxiety. Though silent and ardent prayers were going to the mercy-seat from my heart, I felt that that poor heart was troubled and anxious, as it had never been before. I could have easily answered the bishop and confounded him in a few words; but I thought that it was much better to let the answer and rebuke come from the people.

The bishop, hoping that the long and strange silence was a proof that he had successfully touched the sensitive cords of the hearts, and that he was to win the day, exclaimed a second time with still more power and earnestness: "My dear French Canadian friends: I ask you, in the name of Jesus Christ, your Saviour and mine, in the name of your desolated mothers, fathers, and friends who are weeping along the banks of your beautiful St. Lawrence River—I ask it in the name of your beloved Canada! Answer me! now that you refuse to obey the holy Church of Rome, who will guide you in the ways of salvation?"

Another solemn silence followed that impassionate and earnest appeal. But this silence was not to be long. When I had invited the people to come and hear the bishop, I requested them to bring their Bibles. Suddenly we heard the voice of an old farmer, who, raising his Bible over his head with his two hands, said: "This Bible is all we want to guide us in the ways of God. We do not want anything but the pure Word of God to teach us what we must do to be saved. As for you, sir, you had better go away and never come here any more."

And more than five thousand voices said "Amen!" to that simple and yet sublime answer. The whole crowd filled the air with cries: "The Bible! the Holy Bible, the holy Word of God is our only guide in the ways of eternal life! Go away, sir, and never come again!"

These words, again and again repeated by the thousands of people who surrounded the platform, fell upon the poor bishop's ears as formidable claps of thunder. They were ringing as his death-knell in his ears. The battle was over, and he had lost it.

Bathed in his tears, suffocated by his sobs, he sat or, to speak more correctly, he fell into the arm-chair, and I feared at first lest he should faint. When I saw that he was recovering and strong enough to hear what I had to say, I stepped to the front of the platform. But I had scarcely said two words when I felt as if the claws of a tiger were on my shoulders. I turned and found that it was the clenched fingers of the bishop, who was shaking me while he was saying with a furious voice: "No! no! not a word from you."

As I was about to show him that I had a right to refute what he had said, my eyes fell on a scene which baffles all description. Those only who have seen the raging waves of the sea suddenly raised by the hurricane can have an idea of it. The people had seen the violent hand of the bishop raised against me; they had heard his insolent and furious words forbidding me to say a single word in answer: and a universal cry of indignation was heard: "The infamous wretch! Down with him! He wants to enslave us again! he denies us the right of free speech! he refuses to hear what our pastor has to reply! Down with him!" At the same time a rush was made by many toward the platform to scale it, and others were at work to tear it down. That whole multitude, absolutely blinded by their uncontrollable rage, were as a drunken man who does not know what he does. I had *read* that such things had occurred before, but I hope I shall never see it again. I rushed to the head of the stairs, and with great difficulty repulsed those who were trying to lay their hands on the bishop. In vain I raised my voice to calm them, and make them realize the crime they wanted to commit. No voice could be heard in the midst of such terrible confusion. It was very providential that we had built the scaffold with strong materials, so that it could resist the first attempt to break it.

Happily, we had in our midst a very intelligent young man called Bechard, who was held in great esteem and respect. His influence, I venture to say, was irresistible over the people. I called him to the platform, and requested him, in the name of God, to appease the blind fury of that multitude. Strange to say, his presence and a sign from his hand acted like magic.

"Let us hear what Bechard has to say," whispered every one to his neighbour, and suddenly the most profound calm succeeded the most awful noise and confusion I had ever witnessed. In a few appropriate and eloquent words, that young gentleman showed the people that, far from being angry, they ought to be glad at the exhibition of the tyranny and cowardice of the bishop. Had he not confessed the weakness of his address when he refused to hear the answer? Had he not confessed that he was the vilest and the most impudent of tyrants when he had come into their very midst to deny them the sacred right of speech and reply? Had he not proved, before God and man, that they had done well to reject, for ever, the authority of the Bishop of Rome, when he was giving them such an unanswerable proof that that authority meant the most unbounded tyranny on his part, and the most degraded and ignominious moral degradation on the part of his blind slaves?

Seeing that they were anxious to hear me, I then told them:

"Instead of being angry, you ought to bless God for what you have heard and seen from the Bishop of Chicago. You have heard, and you are witnesses that he has not given us a single argument to show that we were wrong when we gave up the words of the Pope to follow the words of Christ. Was he not right when he told you that there was no need, on my part, to answer him? Do you not all agree that there was nothing to answer, nothing to refute in his long address? Has not our merciful God brought that bishop into your midst to-day to show you the truthfulness of what I have so often told you, that there was nothing manly, nothing honest, or true in him? Have you heard from his lips a single word which could have come from the lips of Christ? A word which could have come from that great God who so loved His people that He sent His eternal Son to save them? Was there a single sentence in all you have heard which would remind you that salvation through Christ was a gift?-- that eternal life was a *free* gift? Have you heard anything from him to make you regret that you are no longer his obedient and abject slaves?"

"No! no!" they replied.

"Then, instead of being angry with that man, you ought to thank him and let him go in peace," I added.

"Yes! yes!" replied the people, "but on condition that he shall never come again."

Then Mons. Bechard stepped to the front, raised his hat, and cried with his powerful voice; "People of St. Anne! you have just gained the most glorious victory which has ever been won by a people against their tyrants. Hurrah for St. Anne, the grave of the tyranny of the Bishops of Rome in America!"

That whole multitude, filled with joy, rent the air with the cry: "Hurrah for St. Anne, the grave of the tyranny of the Bishops of Rome in America!"

I then turned towards the poor bishop and his priests, whose distress and fear were beyond description, and told them: "You see that the people forgive you the indignity of your conduct, by not allowing them to answer you; but I advise you not to repeat that insult here. Please take the advice they gave you; go away as quickly as possible. I will go with you to your carriage, through the crowd, and I pledge myself that you will be safe, provided you do not insult them again."

Opening their ranks, the crowd made a passage, through which I led the bishop and his long suite of priests to their carriages. This was done in the most profound silence, only a few women whispering to the prelate as he was hurrying by: "Away with you, and never come here again. Henceforward we follow nothing but Christ."

Crushed by waves of humiliation, such as no bishop had ever met with on this continent, the weight of the ignominy which he had reaped in our midst completely overpowered his mind, and ruined him. He left us to wander every day nearer the regions of lunacy. That bishop, whose beginning had been so brilliant, after his shameful defeat at St. Anne, on the 3rd of August, 1858, was soon to end his broken career in the lunatic asylum of St. Louis, where he is still confined to-day.

CHAPTER LXVII.

THE marvellous power of the Gospel to raise a man above himself and give him a supernatural strength and wisdom in the presence of the most formidable difficulties has seldom been more gloriously manifested than on the 3rd of August, 1858, on the hill of St. Anne, Illinois.

Surely the continent of América had never seen a more admirable transformation of a whole people than was then and there accomplished. With no other help than the reading of the Gospel, that people had suddenly exchanged the chains of the most abject slavery for Christian Liberty.

By the strength of their faith they had pulverised the gigantic power of Rome, put to flight the haughty representative of the Pope, and had raised the banners of Christian Liberty on the very spot marked by the bishop as the future citadel of the empire of Popery in the United States. Such work was so much above my capacity, so much above the calculation of my intelligence, that I felt that I was more its witness than its instrument. The merciful and mighty hand of God was too visible to let any other idea creep into my mind; and the only sentiments which filled my soul were those of an unspeakable joy, and of gratitude to God. But I felt that the greater the favours bestowed upon us from heaven, the greater were the responsibilities of my new position.

The news of that sudden religious reformation spread with lightning speed all over the continents of America and Europe, and an incredible number of inquiring letters reached me from every corner. Episcopalians, Methodists, Congregationalists, Baptists and Presbyterians, of every rank and colour, kindly pressed me to give them some details. Of course, those letters were often accompanied by books considered the most apt to induce me to join their particular denominations.

Feeling too young and inexpert in the ways of God to give a correct appreciation of the Lord's doings among us, I generally answered those kind inquirers by writing them : " Please come and see with your own eyes the marvellous things our merciful God is doing in the midst of us, and you will help us to bless Him."

In less than six months, more than one hundred venerable ministers of Christ, and prominent Christian laymen of different denominations, visited us. Among those who first honoured us with their presence was the Right Rev. Bishop Helmuth, of London, Canada; then, the learned Dean of Quebec, so well known and venerated all over Great Britain and Canada. He visited us twice, and was one of the most blessed instruments of the mercies of God towards us.

I am happy to say that those eminent Christians, without any exception, after having spent from one to twenty days in studying for themselves this new religious movement, declared that it was the most remarkable and solid evangelical reformation among Roman Catholics they had ever seen. The Christians of the cities of Chicago, Baltimore, Washington, Philadelphia, New York, Boston, etc., having expressed the desire to hear from me of the doings of the Lord among us, I addressed them in their principal churches, and was received with such marks of kindness and interest, for which I shall never be able sufficiently to thank God.

I have previously said that we had, at first, adopted the beautiful name of Christian Catholics, but we soon perceived that unless we joined one of the Christian denominations of the day, we were in danger of forming a new sect.

After many serious and prayerful considerations, it seemed that the wisest thing we could do was to connect ourselves with that branch of the vine which was the nearest to, if not identical with, that of the French Protestants, which gave so many martyrs to the Church of Christ. Accordingly, it was our privilege to be admitted in the Presbyterian Church of the United States. The Presbytery of Chicago had the courtesy to adjourn their meeting from that city to our humble town, on the 15th of April, 1860, when I presented them with the names of nearly two thousand converts, who, with myself, were received into full communion with the Church of Christ.

This solemn action was soon followed by the establishment of missions and congregations in the cities and towns of Chicago, Aurora, Kankakee, Middleport, Watseka, Momence, Sterling, Manteno, etc., where the light of the Gospel had been received by large numbers of our French Canadian emigrants, whom I had previously visited.

The census of the converts taken then gave us about six thousand five hundred precious souls already wrenched from the iron grasp of Popery. It was a result much beyond my most sanguine hopes, and it would be difficult to express the joy it gave me. But my joy was not without a mixture of anxiety. It was impossible for me, if left alone, to distribute the bread of life to such multitudes, scattered over a territory of several hundred miles. I determined, with the help of God, to raise a college, where the children of our converts would be prepared to preach the Gospel.

Thirty-two of our young men, having offered themselves, I added, at once to my other labours, the daily task of teaching them the preparatory course of study for their future evangelical work.

That year (1860) had been chosen by Scotland to celebrate the tercentenary anniversary of her Reformation. The committee of management, composed of Dr. Guthrie, Professor Cunningham, and Dr. Begg, invited me to attend their general meetings in Edinburgh. On the 16th of August, it was my privilege to be presented by those venerable men to one of the grandest and noblest assemblies which the Church of Christ has ever seen. After the close of that great council, which I addressed twice, I was invited, during the next six months, to lecture in Great Britain, France, and Switzerland, and to raise the funds necessary for our college. It was during that tour that I had the privilege of addressing, at St. Etienne, the Synod of the Free Protestant Church of France, lately established through the indomitable energy and ardent piety of the Rev. Felix Monod.

Those six months' efforts were crowned with the most complete success, and more than 15,000 dollars were handed me for our college by the disciples of Christ.

But it was the will of God that I should pass through the purifying fires of the greatest tribulations. On my return from Europe into my colony, in the beginning of 1861, I found everything in confusion. The ambition of the young man I had invited to preach in my place, and in whom I had so imprudently put too much confidence, encouraged by the very man I had chosen for my representative and my attorney during my absence, came very near ruining that great evangelical work, by sowing the seeds of division and hatred among our dear converts. Through the dishonest and false reports of those two men, the money I had collected and left in England (in the hands of a gentleman who was bound to send it at my order) was retained nearly two years, and lost in the failure of the Gelpeck New York Bank, through which it was sent. The only way we found to save ourselves from ruin, was to throw ourselves into the hands of our Christian brothers of Canada.

A committee of the Presbyterian Church, composed of Revs. Dr. Kemp, Dr. Cavan, and Mr. Scott, was sent to investigate the causes of our troubles, and they soon found them. Dr. Kemp published a critical resumé of their investigation, which clearly showed where the trouble lay. Our integrity and innocence were publicly acknowledged, and we were solemnly and officially received as members of the Presbyterian Church of Canada, on the 11th of June, 1863. We may properly acknowledge here that the Christian devotedness, the admirable ability and zeal of the late Dr. Kemp in performance of that work, has secured him our lasting gratitude.

In 1874, I was again invited to Great Britain by the committee appointed to prepare the congratulatory address of the English people to the Emperor of Germany and Bismark, for their noble resistance to the encroachments of Popery. I addressed the meetings held for that purpose in Exeter Hall, under the presidency of Lord John Russell, on the 27th of January, 1874. The next day several Gospel ministers pressed me to publish my twenty-five years' experience of auricular confession, as an antidote to the criminal and too successful efforts of Dr. Pusey, who wanted to restore that infamous practice among the Protestants of England.

After much hesitation and many prayers, I wrote the book entitled: "The Priest, the Woman, and the Confessional," which God has so much blessed to the conversion of many, that twenty-seven editions have already been published.

I spent the next six months in lecturing on Romanism in the principal cities of England, Scotland and Ireland.

On my return, pressed by the Canadian Church to leave my colony of Illinois, for a time at least, to preach in Canada, I went to Montreal, where, in the short space of four years, we had the unspeakable joy to see seven thousand of French Canadian Roman Catholics and emigrants from France, publicly renouncing the errors of Popery to follow the Gospel of Christ.

In 1878, exhausted by the previous years of incessant labours, I was advised, by my physicians, to breathe the bracing air of the Pacific Ocean. I crossed the Rocky Mountains and spent two months lecturing in San Francisco, Portland, Oregon, and in Washington Territory, where I found a great many of my French countrymen, many of whom received the light of the Gospel with joy.

After this, I visited the Sandwich Islands, where I preached on my return, crossed the Pacific and went to the Antipodes, lecturing two years in Australia, Tasmania, and New Zealand. It would require a large volume to tell the great mercies of God towards me during that long, perilous, but interesting voyage. During those two years, I gave 610 public lectures, and came back to my colony of St. Anne with such perfectly restored health, that I could say with the Psalmist: "Bless the Lord, O my soul." "Thy youth is renewed like the eagle's" (Ps. ciii. 1, 5).

But the reader has the right to know something of the dangers through which it has pleased God to make me pass.

Rome is the same to-day as she was when she burned John Huss and Wishart, and when she caused 70,000 Protestants to be slaughtered in France, and 100,000 to be exterminated in Piedmont in Italy.

On the 31st of December, 1869, I forced the Rt. Rev. Bishop Foley, of Chicago, to swear before the civil court, at Kankakee, that the following sentence was an exact translation of the doctrine of the Church of Rome as taught to-day in all the Roman Catholic seminaries, colleges, and universities, through the "Summa Theologica" of Thomas Aquinas (vol. iv. p. 90). "Though heretics must not be tolerated because they deserve it, we must bear with them till, by a second admonition, they may be brought back to the faith of the church. But those who, after a second admonition, remain obstinate to their errors, must not only be excommunicated, but they must be delivered to the secular power to be exterminated."

It is on account of this law of the Church of Rome, which is to-day in full force, as it was promulgated for the first time, that not less than thirty public attempts have been made to kill me since my conversion.

The first time I visited Quebec, in the spring of 1859, fifty men were sent by the Bishop of Quebec (Baillargeon) to force me to swear that I would never preach the Bible, or to kill me in case of my refusal.

At 4 o'clock a.m., sticks were raised above my head, a dagger stuck in my breast, and the cries of the furious mob were ringing in my ears : " Infamous apostate ! Now you are in our hands, you are a dead man if you do not swear that you will never preach your accursed Bible."

Never had I seen such furious men around me. Their eyes were more like the eyes of tigers than of men. I expected every moment to receive the deadly blow, and I asked my Saviour to come and receive my soul. But the would-be murderers, with more horrible imprecations, cried again : " Infamous renegade ! Swear that you will never preach any more your accursed Bible, or you are a dead man ! "

I raised my eyes and hands towards heaven and said : " Oh ! my God ! hear and bless the last words of Thy poor servant : I solemnly swear, that so long as my tongue can speak, I will preach Thy Word, as I find it in the Holy Bible ! " Then opening my vest and presenting my naked breast, I said : " Now ! Strike ! "

But my God was there to protect me : they did not strike. I went through their ranks into the streets, where I found a carter, who drove me to Mr. Hall, the mayor of the city, for that day. I showed him my bleeding breast, and said : " I just escaped, almost miraculously, from the hands of men sworn to kill me if I preach again the Gospel of Christ. I am, however, determined to preach again to-day at noon, even if I have to die in the attempt." I put myself under the protection of the British flag.

Soon after, more than 1,000 British soldiers were around me, with fixed bayonets. They formed themselves into two lines along the streets through which the Mayor took me, in his own sleigh, to the lecture room. I could then deliver my address on " The Bible," to at least 10,000 people who were crowded inside and outside the walls of the large building. After this, I had the joy of distributing between five and six hundred Bibles to that multitude, who received them as thirsty and hungry people receive fresh water and pure bread, after many days of starvation.

I have been stoned twenty times. The principal places in Canada where I was struck and wounded, and almost miraculously escaped, were : Quebec, Montreal, Ottawa, Charlotte Town, Halifax, Antigonish, etc. In the last mentioned, on the 10th of July, 1873, the pastor, the Rev. P. Goodfellow, standing by me when going out of his church, was also struck several times by stones which missed me. At last, his head was so badly cut, that he fell on the ground bathed in blood. I took him up in my arms, though wounded and bleeding myself. We would surely have been slaughtered there, had not a noble Scotchman, named Cameron, opened the door of his house, at the peril of his own life, to give us shelter against the assassins of the Pope. The mob, furious that we had escaped, broke the windows and besieged the house from 10 a.m. till 3 next morning. Many times they threatened to set fire to Mr. Cameron's house, if he did not deliver me into their hands to be hung. They were prevented from doing so only from fear of burning the whole town, composed in part of their own dwellings. Several times they put long ladders against the walls, with the hope of reaching the upper rooms, where they could find and kill their victim. All this was done under the very eyes of five or six priests, who were only at a distance of a few rods.

At Montreal, in the winter of 1870, one evening, coming out of Cote Street Church, where I had preached, accompanied by Principal MacVicar, we fell into a kind of ambuscade, and received a volley of stones, which would have seriously, if not fatally, injured the doctor had he not been protected from head to foot by a thick fur cap and overcoat, worn in the cold days of winter in Canada.

After a lecture given at Paramenta, near Sidney, Australia, I was again attacked with stones by the Roman Catholics. One struck my left leg with such force that I thought it was broken, and I was lame for several days.

In New South Wales, Australia, I was beaten with whips and sticks, which left marks upon my shoulders.

At Marsham, in the same province, on the 1st of April, 1879, the Romanists took possession of the church where I was speaking, rushed towards me with daggers and pistols, crying : " Kill him ! Kill him ! "

In the tumult, I providentially escaped through a secret door. But I had to crawl on hands and knees a pretty long distance in a ditch filled with mud, not to be seen and escape death. When I reached the hospitable house of Mr. Cameron, the windows were broken with stones, much of the furniture destroyed, and it was a wonder I escaped with my life.

At Ballarat, in the same province, three times the houses where I lodged were attacked and broken. Rev. Mr. Inglis, one of the most eloquent ministers of the city, was one of the many who were wounded by my side. The wife of the Rev. Mr. Quick came also nearly being killed while I was under their hospitable roof.

In the same city, as I was waiting for the train at the station, a well-dressed lady came as near as possible and spat in my face. I was blinded, and my face covered with filth. She immediately fled, but was soon brought back by my secretary and a policeman, who said : " Here is the miserable woman who has just insulted you : what shall we do with her ? " I was then almost done cleaning my face with my handkerchief and some water, brought by some sympathizing friends. I answered : " Let her go home in peace. She has not done it of her own accord : she was sent by her confessor ; she thinks she has done a good action. When they spat in our Saviour's face, He did not punish those who insulted Him. We must follow His example." And she was set at liberty, to the great regret of the crowd.

The very next day (21st of April) at Castlemain, I was again fiercely attacked and wounded on the head as I came from addressing the people. One of the ministers who was standing by me was seriously wounded and lost much blood. At Geelong, I had again a very narrow escape from stones thrown at me in the streets. In 1879, while lecturing in Melbourne, the splendid capital of Victoria, Australia, I received a letter from Tasmania, signed by twelve ministers of the Gospel, saying :

" We are much in need of you here, for though the Protestants are in the majority, they leave the administration of the country almost entirely in the hands of Roman Catholics, who rule us with an iron rod. The governor is a Roman Catholic, etc. We wish to have you among us, though we do not dare to invite you to come. For we know that your life will be in danger day and night while in Tasmania. The Roman Catholics have sworn to kill you, and we have too many reasons to fear that they will fulfil their promises. But, though we do not dare ask you to come, we assure you that there is a great work for you here, and that we will stand by you with our people. If you fall, you will not fall alone."

I answered : " Are we not soldiers of Christ, and must we not be ready and willing to die for Him, as He did for us ? I will go."

On the 24th of June, as I was delivering my first lecture in Hobart Town, the Roman Catholics, with the approbation of their bishop, broke the door of the hall, and rushed towards me, crying, " Kill him ! kill him ! " The mob was only a few feet from me, brandishing their daggers and pistols, when the Protestants threw themselves between them and me, and a furious hand-to-hand fight occurred, during which many wounds were received and given. The soldiers of the Pope were overpowered, but the governor had to put the city under martial law for four days, and call the whole militia to save my life from the assassins drilled by the priests.

In a dark night, as I was leaving the steamer to take the train, on the Ottawa River, Canada, twice the bullets of the murderers whistled at no more than two or three inches from my ears. Several times in Montreal and Halifax the churches where I was preaching were attacked and the windows broken by the mobs sent by the priests, and several of my friends were wounded (two of whom, I believe, died from the effects of their wounds) whilst defending me.

The 17th of June, 1884, after I had preached in Quebec, on the text: "What would I do to have eternal life," a mob of more than 1,500 Roman Catholics, led by two priests, broke the windows of the church and attacked me with stones, with the evident object to kill me. More than one hundred stones struck me, and I would surely have been killed there had I not had, providentially, two heavy overcoats, which I put, one around my head, and the other around my shoulders. Notwithstanding that protection, I was so much bruised and wounded from head to feet, that I had to spend the three following weeks on a bed of suffering, between life and death. A young friend, Zotique Lefevore, who had heroically put himself between my would-be-assassins and me, escaped only after receiving six severe wounds in the face. The same year, 1884, in the month of November, I was attacked with stones and struck several times, when preaching or coming out from the church in the city of Montreal. Numbers of policemen and other friends who came to my rescue were wounded, my life was saved only by an organization of a thousand young men, who, under the name of Protestant Guard, wrenched me from the hands of the would-be murderers.

When the bishops and priests saw that it was so difficult to put me out of the way with stones, sticks, and daggers, they determined to destroy my character by calumnies, spread everywhere, and sworn before civil tribunals as Gospel truths. During eighteen years they kept me in the hands of the sheriffs a prisoner, under bail, as a criminal. Thirty-two times my name has been called before the civil and criminal courts of Kankakee, Joliet, Chicago, Urbana, and Montreal, among the names of the vilest and most criminal of men. I have been accused by Grand Vicar Mailloux of having killed a man and thrown his body into a river to conceal my crime. I have been accused of having set fire to the church of Bourbonnais and destroyed it. Not less than seventy-two false witnesses have been brought by the priests of Rome to support this last accusation. But, thanks be to God, at every time, from the very lips of the perjured witnesses, we got the proof that they were swearing falsely, at the instigation of their father confessors. And my innocence was proven by the very men who had been paid to destroy me. In this last suit, I thought it was my duty, as a Christian and citizen, to have one of those priests punished for having so cruelly and publicly trampled under his feet

38

the most sacred laws of society and religion. Without any vengeance on my part, God knows it, I asked the protection of my country against these incessant plots. Father Brunet, found guilty of having invented those calumnies and supported them by false witnesses, was condemned to pay 2,500 dollars or go to gaol for fourteen years. He preferred the last punishment, having the promise from his Roman Catholic friends that they would break the doors of the prison and let him go free to some remote place. He was incarcerated at Kankakee; but on a dark and stormy night, six months later, he was rescued, and fled to Montreal (distant about 900 miles). There he made the Roman Catholics believe that the blessed Virgin Mary, dressed in a beautiful white robe, had come in person to open for him the gates of the prison.

I do not mention these facts here, to create bad feelings against the poor blind slaves of the Pope. It is only to show to the world that the Church of Rome of to-day is absolutely the same as when she reddened Europe with the blood of millions of martyrs. My motive in speaking of those murderous attacks, is to induce the readers to help me to bless God, who has so mercifully saved me from the hands of the enemy. More than any living man, I can say with the old prophet: " The Lord is my Shepherd, I shall not want " (Ps. xxiii. 1). With Paul, I could often say : " We are troubled on every side, yet not distressed : we are perplexed, but not in despair : persecuted, but not forsaken : cast down, but not destroyed : always bearing about in the body the dying of the Lord Jesus, that the life also of Jesus might be manifest in our body " (2 Cor. iv. 8—10).

Those constant persecutions, far from hindering the onward march of the evangelical movement to which I have consecrated my life, seem to have given it a new impulse and a fresher life. I have even remarked that the very day after I had been bruised and wounded, the number of converts had invariably increased. I will never forget the day, after the terrible night when more than a thousand Roman Catholics had come to stone me, and on which I received a severe wound, more than one hundred of my countrymen asked me to enrol their names under the banner of the Gospel, and publicly sent their recantation of the errors of Rome to the bishop. To-day, the Gospel of Christ is advancing with an irresistible power among the French Canadians from the Atlantic to the Pacific Oceans. We find numbers of converts in almost every town and city from New York to San Francisco. Rallied around the banners of Christ, they form a large army of fearless soldiers of the Cross. Among those converts, we count now twenty-five priests and more than fifty young zealous ministers born in the Church of Rome.

In hundreds of places, the Church of Rome has lost her past

prestige, and the priests are looked upon with indifference, if not contempt, even by those who have not yet accepted the light.

A very remarkable religious movement has also been lately inaugurated among the Irish Roman Catholics, under the leadership of Revs. McNamara, O'Connor, and Quinn, which promises to keep pace with, if not exceed the progress of the Gospel among the French.

To-day, more than ever, we hear the good Master's voice: "Lift up your eyes and look on the fields, for they are white already to harvest" (John iv. 35).

Oh! may the day soon come when all my dear countrymen will hear the voice of the Lamb and come to wash their robes in His blood! Will I see the blessed hour when the dark night in which Rome keeps my dear Canada will be exchanged for the bright and saving light of the Gospel?

At all events, I cannot but bless God for what mine eyes have seen, and mine ears have heard of His mercies towards me and my countrymen. From my infancy, He has taken me into His arms, and led me most mercifully, through ways I did not know, from the darkest regions of superstition, to the blessed regions of light, truth and life!

From the day He granted me to read His divine word on my dear mother's knee, to the hour He came to me as "the Gift of God," He has not let a single day pass without speaking to me some of His warning and saving words. I have not always paid sufficient attention to His sweet voice, I confess it to my shame. My mind was so filled with the glittering sophisms of Rome, that many times, I refused to yield to the still voice which was almost night and day heard in my soul. But my God was not repelled by my infidelities, as the reader will find in this book. When driven away in the morning, He came back in the silent hours of the night. For more than twenty-five years, He forced me to see, as a priest, the abominations which exist inside the walls of the modern Babylon. I may say, He took me by the lock of mine head, as He did with the prophet of old, and said:

"Son of man, lift up thine eyes now the way towards the north. So I lifted up mine eyes the way towards the north, and behold, northward at the gate of the altar, this image of jealousy in the entry. He said furthermore unto me: 'Son of man, seest thou what they do, even the great abominations that the house of Israel committeth here, that I should go far off from my sanctuary? But turn thee yet again, and thou shalt see greater abominations.' And he brought me to the door of the court; and when I looked, behold a hole in the wall. Then said he unto me, 'Son of man, dig now in the wall;' and when I had digged in the wall, behold, a door. And he said, 'Go in and see the wicked abominations that they do here.' So I went in and saw; and behold every form of creeping things and abominable beasts, and all the idols of the house of Israel, pourtrayed upon the wall round about. And there stood before them seventy men of the ancients of the house of Israel, and in the midst of them stood Jaazaniah, the son of Shaphan, with every man his censer in his hand; and a thick cloud of incense went up. Then said he unto me: 'Son of man, hast thou seen what the ancients of the house of Israel do in the dark, every man in the chambers of his imagery?' for they say, 'The Lord seeth us not; the Lord hath forsaken the earth.' He said also unto me: 'Turn thee yet again, and thou shalt see greater abominations that they do.' Then he brought me to the door of the gate of the Lord's house, which was toward the north; and, behold, there sat women weeping for Tammuz. Then said he unto me: 'Hast thou seen this, O son of man? Turn thee yet again, and thou shalt see greater abominations than these.' And he brought me into the inner court of the Lord's house; and, behold, at the temple of the Lord, between the porch and the altar, were about five and twenty men, with their backs towards the temple of the Lord, and their faces towards the east; and they worshipped the sun towards the east. Then he said unto me: 'Hast thou seen this, O son of man? Is it a light thing to the house of Judah that they commit the abomi· nations which they commit here? for they have filled the land with violence and have returned to provoke me into anger; and lo! they put the branch to their nose. Therefore, will I also deal in fury; mine eye shall not spare, neither will I have pity; and they cry in mine ears, with a loud voice, yet will I not hear them" (Ezek. viii. 5—18).

I can say with John:

"And there came one of the seven angels which had the seven vials, and talked with me, saying unto me: 'Come hither: I will show unto thee the judgment of the great whore that sitteth upon many waters; with whom the kings of the earth have committed fornication, and the inhabitants of the earth have been made drunk with the wine of her fornication.' So he carried me away in the Spirit into the wilderness; and I saw a woman sit upon a scarlet coloured beast, full of names of blasphemy, having seven heads and ten horns. And the woman was arrayed in purple and scarlet colour, and decked with gold and precious stones and pearls, having a golden cup in her hand full of abominations and filthiness of her fornication: and upon her forehead was a name written: 'MYSTERY, BABYLON THE GREAT, THE MOTHER OF HARLOTS AND ABOMINATIONS OF THE EARTH.' And I saw the woman drunken with the blood of the saints, and with the blood of the martyrs of Jesus; and when I saw her, I wondered with great admiration" (Rev. xvii. 1—6).

And after the Lord had shown me all these abominations, He took me out as the eagle takes his own young ones on his wings. He brought me into His beautiful and beloved Zion, and He set my feet on the rock of my salvation. There, He quenched my thirst with the pure waters which flow from the fountains of eternal life, and He gave me to eat the true bread which comes from heaven.

Oh! that I might go all over the world, through this book, and say with the Psalmist: "Come, all ye that fear God, and I will declare what He hath done for my soul."

Let all the children of God who will read this book lend me their tongues to praise the Lord. Let them lend me their hearts, to love Him. For, alone, I cannot praise Him, I cannot love Him as He deserves. When I look upon the seventy-six years which have passed over me, my heart leaps for joy, for I find myself at the end of trials. I have nearly crossed the desert.

Only the narrow stream of Jordan is between me and the new Jerusalem. I already hear the great voice out of heaven saying: " Behold, the tabernacle of God is with men, and He will dwell with them, and they shall be His people, and God Himself shall be with them, and be their God, and God shall wipe away all tears from their eyes; and there shall be no more death, neither sorrow, nor crying, neither shall there be any more pain; for the former things have passed away......He that overcometh shall inherit all things " (Rev. xxi. 3, 4, 7).

Rich with the unspeakable gift which has been given me, and pressing my dear Bible to my heart, as the richest treasure, I hasten my steps with an unspeakable joy toward the Land of Promise. I already hear the angel's voice telling me: " Come: the Master calls thee."

A few days more and the bridegroom will say to my soul: "Surely I come quickly." And I will answer: "Even so, come Lord Jesus." AMEN.